TELEVISION
AND
SOCIAL BEHAVIOR

REPORTS AND PAPERS, VOLUME I:
MEDIA CONTENT AND CONTROL

A TECHNICAL REPORT TO THE
SURGEON GENERAL'S SCIENTIFIC ADVISORY COMMITTEE
ON TELEVISION AND SOCIAL BEHAVIOR

Edited By
George A. Comstock and Eli A. Rubinstein
Editorial Coordination: Susan Lloyd-Jones

U.S. DEPARTMENT OF HEALTH, EDUCATION, AND WELFARE
Health Services and Mental Health Administration

National Institute of Mental Health
5600 Fishers Lane
Rockville, Maryland

Staff Members

Eli A. Rubinstein   Vice Chairman, Surgeon General's
    Scientific Advisory Committee

George A. Comstock   Senior Research Coordinator

John P. Murray   Research Coordinator

Michael Adler   Staff Assistant

Eileen Marchak   Research Assistant

Susan S. Lloyd-Jones   Editor

Joseph D. Reckley   Administrative Officer

Margaret D. Salladay   Secretary

Laura A. De Lisi   Secretary

Former Staff Members

Douglas A. Fuchs   Senior Research Coordinator (through 6/70)

John P. Robinson   Research Coordinator (through 9/70)

Harold Leigh   Administrative Officer (through 10/70)

Thomas Brubeck   Information Officer (through 5/71)

Deborah Cutler   Research Assistant (through 8/70)

Jan W. Lipkin   Secretary (through 4/70)

Advisory Committee Members

Ira H. Cisin

Thomas E. Coffin

Irving L. Janis

Joseph T. Klapper

Harold Mendelsohn

Eveline Omwake

Charles A. Pinderhughes

Ithiel de Sola Pool

Alberta E. Siegel

Anthony F. C. Wallace

Andrew S. Watson

Gerhart D. Wiebe

PREFACE

This document is one of five volumes of technical reports resulting from a broad scientific inquiry about television and its impact on the viewer. In the spring of 1969, by Congressional request, the DHEW initiated a special program under the general auspices of a Surgeon General's Scientific Advisory Committee on Television and Social Behavior. The major emphasis was to be on an examination of the relationship between televised violence and the attitudes and behavior of children. During the ensuing two years, more than fifty scientists participated directly in this program of research and produced over forty scientific reports.

The reports which are included in these five volumes are the independent work of the participating researchers. These results have all been made available to the Scientific Advisory Committee as evidence from which the Committee could then evaluate those findings and draw its own conclusions in the preparation of its own report. However, this work is of significance in its own right and is being published independently as source material for other researchers and for such interest as the general public may have in these technical reports.

In any broad scientific undertaking of this nature, where many individuals are involved, a careful balance between collaboration and independence of responsibility must be established. During the two and half years that this program of research was active, a constant effort was made to protect the scientific independence of the individual investigators and, at the same time: 1) to foster both cooperation and exchange among the researchers, 2) to develop as much of a total program structure as possible, and 3) to permit maximum communication and feedback among the researchers, the full-time staff responsible for planning and implementing the total research program, and the Scientific Advisory Committee responsible for the final assessment and evaluation of the research.

This is not the place to describe in detail how that balance of collaboration and independence was established and maintained. I believe, however, that these five volumes of technical reports provide an accurate and meaningful indication of our success in achieving the goal. The reports themselves are the products of the respective authors. They have been edited only to insure some comparability of format and to delete any excessive redundancies in review of the literature or introductory material. In some instances, where a report seemed initially too long the author was requested to reduce the report without deleting any critical material. All editing done by staff was submitted for the author's approval. We believe the result has made each of these five volumes a more readable and integrated totality than would otherwise be expected from a collection of research reports produced under the time constraints of this program.

In each instance, the integration of the five volumes was further established by the inclusion of an overview paper which attempts to summarize and relate the papers in that volume. These overview papers are also the independent work of the respective authors.

It would be difficult to convey to the reader the extraordinary efforts required by all participants in this research program to bring the endeavor to its published conclusion within the time allotted. Despite that time pressure, these volumes demonstrate an unusually high level of both productivity and quality for an area of research which has had more than its share of complexity and controversy.

In addition to the work of all persons directly engaged in this program, a very large number of individuals at one time or another provided advice and guidance to the researchers, to the staff, and to the Scientific Advisory Committee. It would be impossible to provide a complete list of these additional consultants. The total count is in the hundreds. While their names are not visible in these products, their counsel was often a very significant factor in the course of an individual piece of research or in a decision on the direction of the research program. To all those individuals, this program owes a special debt of gratitude for the collective wisdom made available to us.

And finally, on behalf both of the members of the Scientific Advisory Committee and of the staff who served the program, I wish especially to express much appreciation to the participating researchers who did the work and wrote the reports that contributed the new knowledge contained in these volumes.

Eli A. Rubinstein
Vice-Chairman, Surgeon General's
Scientific Advisory Committee on
Television and Social Behavior

Contents

New Research on Media Content and Control (Overview)

George A. Comstock

The new research on television content and control sponsored by the Television and Social Behavior program has focused on three topics central to an understanding of the place of violence in television entertainment:

1) The amount and character of the violence portrayed on television.

2) The circumstances and milieu in which this violent fare is created.

3) The formal and informal influences which affect the selection and prohibition of television content.

1

It should be emphasized that the television with which the studies deal is almost exclusively television entertainment. News and other nonfictional content receives only slight attention.

The portrait that emerges of popular culture's ubiquitous medium will disturb more than a few. Whether alarm is justified, of course, is debatable. For evidence on this issue, one must look to studies of television's effects such as those reported in the other volumes presenting the research sponsored by this program. Here, we are concerned with *content*, and how it comes to be what it is, *not* with effects.

It is certain, however, that those who believe that the mass media have some effect—that they are imitated, learned from, or taken as a guide for behavior and attitudes—and believe that the mass media should contribute to social harmony will not be happy with television's portrayal of the world. If it is posited that television is a source of information about real life, despite the fictional or fantasy guise of entertainment, the lesson is that life is violent, that violence often succeeds, that moral goodness and violent behavior may coincide, and that victimization is a common occurrence. If it is posited that the portrayal of violence presents, in covert symbolism, clues about the distribution of power and influence, then the lesson is that women, nonwhites, foreigners, and persons of low socioeconomic status lack the social efficacy of white males. If it is posited that those who are portrayed as violent to a more than average degree are surreptitiously identified as those of whom one should beware, then those so adversely identified are nonwhites, foreigners, and persons of low socioeconomic status.

If children—because of limited alternatives for information and limited experience with life—are taken as a susceptible audience, there are at least two reasons to be troubled: television failed in whatever efforts it made between 1967 and 1969 to constrain violence in programs specifically directed to young children—cartoons; and the young audience for violent prime time fare ostensibly prepared for adults is not small.

In addition, those who believe that a concern for effects beyond what is represented in network censorship and monitoring should guide those who create for television will find little evidence of such concern. For many, however, what may be most troubling is the conjunction of the finding that television is filled with violence and an impression—gained from this array of studies—that for a complex of reasons violence in television content at present comes close to eluding constraint.

THE RESEARCH

Six studies make up this volume; one incorporates the separate efforts of several investigators. The principal approaches are content analysis and the interviewing of television professionals. The production and content of both television aimed specifically at children and prime time evening television are dealt with extensively. The emphasis is on the contemporary milieu of television production and recent television content. However, considerable attention is also given to long-term trends in television content and to content and trends in other media. The focus is also almost exclusively on content intended as entertainment, although one study does compare the violence reported on television news with that reported on the front pages of metropolitan newspapers.

One study provides information of a different sort by asking samples of the viewing public and of television critics to rate violence in specific television series. In addition, the American media are placed in some perspective by a set of studies that report on television content and the factors influencing it in four societies—the United States, Great Britain, Israel, and Sweden.

In brief preview:

•Gerbner analyzes in great detail one week of fall prime time and Saturday morning programming in 1969, and compares the results with his similar analyses for 1967 and 1968 prepared for the National Commission the Causes and Prevention of Violence. He deals not only with the quantity of violence, but also with its quality or character.

•Clark and Blankenburg examine the violence in television since it emerged as a major medium in 1953. They also analyze violence during various time periods in movies, television news, newspapers, and a family magazine. Results are matched against various measures of environmental violence, such as the Federal Bureau of Investigation's Uniform Crime Reports, to test the oft-advanced speculation that the media merely mirror the violence in the real world.

•Greenberg and Gordon had television critics and members of the public rate television series by their violence, thus obtaining data on what is perceived as violent.

•Cantor, who interviewed professionals producing children's programs, discusses the factors influencing the selection of content for children's programs.

•Baldwin and Lewis, also on the basis of interviews, report on how the top professionals responsible for producing adult drama perceive their role in regard to violent content, on the place of violent content in television drama, and on efforts made to control violence in television.

•Four social scientists each report on programming and production with special emphasis on violence in a different country—Gerbner, the United States; Halloran, Great Britain; Katz, Israel; and Dahlgren, Sweden—and Gurevitch provides an introductory commentary on this exploratory cross-national effort.

Together, the studies in this volume contain much more than can be covered in a single review. We will concentrate on the major findings concerning violence in television entertainment in the United States.

VIOLENCE ON RECENT TELEVISION

In "Violence in Television Drama: Trends and Symbolic Functions," Gerbner presents an elaborate account of violence in televised dramatic entertainment in 1967, 1968, and 1969 that conveys not only the facts of its occurrence but also some of its complexities. If television purveys our national myths about violence, then Gerbner offers its most complete mapping to date.

Methodology. Violence was tabulated by teams of coders, who viewed videotapes of all prime time and Saturday morning programs with fictional content shown during comparable fall weeks. A program was defined as a single story, so that in a few instances a single commercial presentation contributes more than one "program" to the analysis. For 1969, 121 programs, 72 hours of programming, and the activities of 377 leading characters were coded. Comparisons over the three years are based on program formats presented in all three years. These three-year data cover 281 programs, 182 hours, and 762 leading characters in which the 1969 share is 98 programs, 62 hours, and 307 characters. Both the comparative and full 1969 sample (although the latter is statistically more reliable because larger) lead to the same conclusions.

A warning is in order to prevent misinterpretation. Gerbner's data do not represent the totality of television. The data are intentionally confined to dramatic presentations because it is the way violence is presented in this massively popular form of fictional entertainment that Gerbner set out to study. For this reason, the terms "dramatic play" or "play" are generally used, instead of program.

As Gerbner observes, "Violence connotes a great variety of physical and mental violations, emotions, injustices, and transgressions of social and moral norms." He chose to define violence "in its strictest sense as an arbiter of power":

. . .the overt expression of physical force against others or self, or the compelling of action against one's will on pain of being hurt or killed.

This focus limits the coverage to what most would agree is "real violence." Broader or alternative definitions would have led to different findings.

The basic unit of measurement was the violent episode, defined as a scene involving violence between the same adversaries. Three primary measures were constructed: a) a program score, representing the amount of violence in dramatic plays; b) a character score, representing the degree to which leading characters were involved in violence; and c) an overall violence index, the sum of the program and character scores. Although the computation of these measures involved arbitrary assumptions and weightings, the reporting of the data is so complete that any doubts about their validity in a specific instance can be easily checked. In addition, comparisons of the circumstances and kinds of people involved in violence are made possible by a multitude of measures of the characteristics of programs and characters.

Three components. Gerbner's work has three components: a) accounts of the quantity of violence; b) descriptions of the quality or character of this violence; and, c) a theory dealing with the meaning and function of violence in popular entertainment in a modern society. The first component leads to comparisons between types of program formats, among networks, and over time. The second involves an analysis of the dramatic structuring of violence based on the time, place, and setting of violence, the agents, means, and consequences of violence, and the role in violence—doer, receiver, or both—of people of various kinds. The theory holds that television violence reflects, in the roles given various kinds of people, the norms of society with regard to power, influence, and status, and that the demonstration on a broad and popular basis of such norms is so important and necessary to the existing structure of social relations that attempts to reduce violence lead to the portrayal of these norms in sharper relief.

The data for the second are presented in the context of the theory. However, both the first and second components can be considered entirely on their own as descriptions of television fare. The theory, of course, gives violence in televised dramatic entertainment the status of an indicator and reinforcer of social structure, and thus amounts to a justification for studying such dramatized violence apart from the issue of how much is presented.

Quantity of violence

One would be remiss not to begin with a perhaps obvious warning: program content in the aggregate says nothing about exposure for an individual or a group. As Gerbner comments, "General trends in television programming are somewhat like fluctuations of average national temperature or of average barometer readings," and as every tourist has discovered these do not offer much certainty for the individual circumstance—"they do not necessarily resemble what any one person experiences, but they do indicate what the nation as a whole absorbs, and how that changes, if at all, over time." However, as Gerbner argues, what aggregate content does show are the "systems of images and messages network television as a whole releases into the mainstream of national consciousness."

The principal findings can be stated fairly succinctly:

—*The prevalence of violence did not change markedly from 1967 through 1969.* Lack of change is reflected both in the percentage of dramatic plays containing violence and in the frequency of violent episodes. In each of the three years, about eight out of ten plays contained violence, and violent episodes occurred at the rate of about five per play and eight per hour.

—*The frequency of lethal violence declined markedly and the pervasiveness of characters' participation in violence declined somewhat.* Lethal violence dropped sharply from two in ten leading characters involved in killing in 1967 to one in ten in 1968 and one in 20 in 1969. The percentage of characters involved in violence dropped from more than seven in ten in 1967 to more than six in ten in 1969; the actual number involved, however, did not change.

—*Grossly measured, violence declined.* The overall index fell about 11 percent between 1967 and 1969. This occurred despite the steady rate of violent incidents, because of the reduced proportion of characters participating in violence and the reduction in killing.

—*Violence increased in the programming directed most specifically at young children—cartoons.* Cartoons were more violent than any other category of program format—plays, feature films, action-adventure, or comedy—in 1967. In 1969, they were even more violent, and they increased their lead over other types of programs. Any decline in violence over the three years is attributable to television plays, which presumably are aimed at adults.

As Gerbner notes:

It is . . . clear that children watching Saturday morning cartoons had the least chance of escaping violence or of avoiding the heaviest. . .saturation of violence on all television.

Of all 95 cartoon plays analyzed during the three annual study periods, only two in 1967 and one each in 1968 and 1969 did *not* contain violence. The average cartoon hour in 1967 contained more than three times as many violent episodes as the average adult hour. The trend toward shorter plays sandwiched in between frequent commercials on fast-moving cartoon programs further increased the saturation. By 1969, with a violent episode at least every two minutes of all Saturday morning cartoon programming (including the least violent, and also including commercial time), and with adult drama becoming less saturated with violence, the average cartoon hour had nearly six times the violence rate of the average adult television drama hour, and nearly 12 times the violence rate of the average television movie hour.

In addition, the share of cartoons in all dramatic programming actually increased in 1969. As a result, cartoons were responsible for less than one-third of all violent episodes in 1967, but in 1969 they were responsible for more than half the total.

—*Violence varied by network, with one remaining consistently lowest and the other two varying in relative standing over the three years.* The overall violence index shows that CBS was consistently lowest. ABC, the most violent by a small margin in 1967 and 1968, declined steadily through 1969, when it was in second place. NBC declined from 1967 to 1968, and was in second place in both years, but rose in 1969 to be the most violent network. The three-year average ranking, from most to least violent, was NBC, ABC and CBS.

—*Cartoon violence varied by network, with one remaining about the same, one increasing somewhat, and another increasing markedly.* Cartoon violence on CBS in 1969 was about the same as in 1967, after an increase in 1968. CBS was the lowest of the three networks both in 1969 and in its three-year average. ABC cartoon violence increased somewhat in 1969 over both 1967 and 1968, although it had decreased between 1967 and 1968. NBC cartoon violence increased greatly in 1969—and this rise in cartoon violence was largely responsible for the network scoring as the most violent in 1969—and 1968 represented an increase over 1967, so that the three-year trend was of consistently increasing violence in NBC cartoons. The three-year average for ABC and NBC was about the same.

Comment. It is no secret that the television industry in recent years has become concerned about violence on television. The sources of this unease are easy enough to catalogue:

—the social unrest that escapes no one's attention: urban rioting, campus protests and demonstrations, the increasing rate of violent crime, the seemingly regular occurrence of bizarre mass killings, and the assassinations of President John F. Kennedy in 1963 and of the Reverend Martin Luther King, Jr. and Senator Robert F. Kennedy in 1968;

—the broad issues and problems that have led to social conflict and anxiety over our direction as a nation: racism, poverty, urban decay, pollution, and the American involvement in Vietnam;

—the general and at times intense public concern about crime and violence and the vicarious exposure of children and young persons to them in television and other media;

—the conviction on the part of many social scientists and some of the public that the portrayal of violence on television is to some extent directly responsible for some violent behavior in everyday life, especially among the young;

—the public attention drawn to the issue of violence in the media by the 1969 staff report to the National Commission on the Causes and Prevention of Violence, *Mass Media and Violence*; the hearings held by Senator John Pastore on television violence in 1969; and the hearings held by Senator Thomas Dodd on television and juvenile delinquency in 1964 and 1961.

Although there has not been unanimity—in the form either of intuitive opinion or of irreproachable scientific evidence—about any responsibility of television for widespread antisocial behavior, the industry has responded to the discomfort in many quarters over the possibility with attempts to reduce the amount of violence portrayed. The studies by Cantor and by Baldwin and Lewis make it clear that those who create our television have not been ignorant of these network efforts. The trends in television content reported by Gerbner can be viewed as reflecting the efficacy of network policy in constraining violence.

The results would seem to be ironic at best. Killing almost dropped from sight, but aggression, harm, and threat did not. Violence in prime time television plays on the whole decreased slightly. Violence in children's cartoons, however, increased. The "children's viewing hours" not only remained the most violent of all television hours, but were more violent than the ostensibly adult hours by a greater margin in 1969 than in 1967.

Quality of violence

Quantity is far from the sole attribute of television violence. Gerbner analyzes its qualitative aspects—where and when it occurs, who participates, and in what ways different kinds of people are involved—in terms of a) violent actions, and b) violence-related roles. Over the three years, 1,355 violent episodes and the activities of 762 leading characters were studied.

Violent actions. The character of television's violent actions is described on the basis of the agents, means, consequences, time, place, and setting of violence. The major findings:

—*Agents:* The proportion of nonhuman agents that inflict violence has been increasing, although violence was inflicted by humans in 70 percent of all the episodes. In general drama, nonhuman agents increased from one out of ten episodes in 1967 and 1968 to two out of ten in 1969, and in cartoons from about half in 1967 and 1968 to three-quarters in 1969.

An agent of special interest, the representative of law enforcement was portrayed as increasingly violent when he or she appeared in a violent episode. When involved, law enforcement agents were violent in 60 percent, 72 percent, and 77 percent of violent episodes in 1967, 1968, and 1969, respectively. However, their overall role was relatively minor: they appeared in one of ten of all episodes and two of ten noncartoon episodes.

—*Means:* Weapons were popular, being used in about half of all violent episodes; in cartoons the use of weapons increased from 52 to 83 percent of episodes over the three years.

—*Consequences:* Fatalities, as previously noted, decreased sharply. So did casualties. Discomfort on the part of victims was hard to detect.

Those intrigued by the tabulation of gore will find that the body count over the three years declined from 82 to 46, while the casualty count declined from 437 to 134; that fatality's share in casualties dropped from 42 to 34 percent; and that there was an injury in nearly every violent episode in 1967 and 1968 but only one in three in 1969 and a death in every two to three episodes in 1967 and 1968 but only one in ten in 1969. Throughout, however, violence was typically presented in the absence of physical suffering: "Pain and suffering were so difficult to detect that observers could not agree often enough to make the results acceptable. There was little doubt that no painful effect was shown in over half of all violent episodes."

—*Time, place, and setting:* Violence tended to occur with greater frequency when the setting was the past or the future, rather than the present; when the setting was some place other than the United States; and when the setting was remote—"uninhabited, mobile, or not identifiable." Violence was less common in small town or rural than in remote settings and least common in urban settings. Almost all portrayals of the past or the future were violent. Between 1967 and 1969, urban settings became more common in programs without violence, less common in violent programs; remote settings became more common in violent programs, less common in nonviolent programs. In short, violence tended to be excluded from the familiar.

Violence-related roles

Some of Gerbner's most intriguing findings concern the way violence is structured in regard to participants. He describes the social order of television, as delineated by violence, by identifying whether a character is violent or nonviolent, is a victim or a nonvictim, is a killer or an injurer, is killed or injured.

These findings are interesting not in spite of television being designed as entertainment, but precisely because of this. Whether or not construed as the national mythology, television is the fiction attended to most ardently by the nation.

What kind of world do television's people inhabit? Let us see:

Involvement in violence is common. Of the 762 leading characters, more than two out of three were involved in violence and about half committed violence.

Victimization is common. For every character that could be said to be violent, one and one-half could be said to be a victim of violence. As Gerbner notes, "The overriding message is that of the risk of victimization."

Retribution and punishment are common. Victims who were injured or killed in return for having been violent totalled 42 percent of all leading characters; only eight percent committed violence without subsequent injury or death.

Nonaggression is no guarantee of safety. Seventeen percent of all characters were victims who themselves had not been violent.

Violence and television action tend to be the prerogative of a male free of responsibilities. About three-quarters of all leading characters were "male, American, middle and upper class, unmarried and in the prime of life," and most male roles involved violence while only half of female roles did so. In addition, most television violence, unlike violence in real life, occurs outside close personal relationships—between strangers or slight acquaintances. Television violence also tends to be related to "a personal goal, private gain, power, or duty" and not to broad social or moral issues.

Nonwhites, foreigners, and persons of low socioeconomic status tend to inflict violence. Characters identifiable as belonging to these groups had a higher rate of committing violence than, respectively, whites, nonforeigners, and persons of higher socioeconomic status.

Ordinary work is far from portrayed as a general activity. Only five out of ten characters were clearly gainfully employed; some sort of occupational activity, paid or unpaid, was indicated for only six out of ten. In addition, the occupational breakdown favors high status jobs and enforcers or breakers of society's rules. Of the five out of ten gainfully employed, three were proprietors, managers, or professionals; one was a skilled or unskilled blue or white collar worker; and one was an enforcer of the law or social propriety on behalf of either public or private employers. Of the six out of ten with discernible activities, two represented legitimate business or industry; two, the arts, science, health, religion, and the like; and two, the population of adversaries—such as police and criminals—in the conflict of "right" and "wrong."

Women are generally portrayed as exuding sexual attraction, mates in marriage, or both; as lacking in social power and influence; and as much more likely to be the objects of victimization than men. Males appeared in a relatively wide variety of roles, but women usually appeared so as to connote sex and typically represented romantic or family involvements. Females were concentrated in the sexually eligible category of young adults, with half in this age range, compared to only one-fifth of males. Marriage was portrayed as more typically a female than a male concern —only one in three male leads was or intended to be married, compared with two out of three females.

Between 1967 and 1969, female involvement in violence dropped more markedly than male involvement. This was almost entirely attributable to the reduction in violent people among females.

Once involved in violence, women have become more likely to be victims than men. For each year, there were five victims for every four violents among men; in 1967 for women, there was an equal number of victims and violents, in 1968, four victims for three violents, and in 1969, four victims for about two violents. Men were much more likely to be violent and less likely to escape counterviolence, but they were also more likely to return violence for violence and killers outnumbered killed among them by a greater margin. What has happened over time is that the number of violents in general has been reduced, and killing by women almost eliminated, while the number of victims declined more slowly and did not decline at all among women.

Thus, the way violence has been reduced has resulted in the further subordination of the female. If the ability to be violent and to avoid victimization symbolically represents the possession of power and influence, then women were clearly depicted as less endowed than men with these assets.

One principal variable remains: *Age*. As the preponderance of males in the prime of life suggests, there were few characters on either side of these "prime" years so suitable for violent interaction. Only ten percent of the total fictional population were children, adolescents, and old people. There was very little relationship between age and involvement in violence; 60 percent of children, 70 percent of young adults, 60 percent of the middled aged, and 50 percent of older characters were involved. Over the three years, the percentage of children and middled-aged people involved in violence declined, while the percentage of young adults did not (the older category had too few for reliable trend data), with the drop for the middle aged almost entirely due to a decline in violence involving females.

Such is the social structure of violence on television. What should one make of it? One view is given by Gerbner. He essentially sees television entertainment as a national mythology in which violence has the special function of explicating the values and norms held by our society with regard to power and influence. He suggests that it is through violence that people's relative status is depicted. It shows who has power and who does not by showing who acts and who is acted upon. Aggressing represents power; victimization, subordination. The fact that television entertainment is fiction is central; it is taken, not as a mirror image, but as an idealized representation—social ideology in the garb of fantasy.

A corollary of this formulation is that efforts to reduce violence lead to the sharpening of the representation of these norms and values. The less crucial elements are abandoned, and what remains conveys the message even more explicitly. For example, since the networks decided to reduce violence, the increasing victimization of females, the increasing tendency of violence to monopolize unfamiliar locales, and the tendency of young adults (especially suitable personnel for violence) to maintain their rate of participation while other age groups decline, are all interpreted as reflecting this sort of sharpening.

All aspects of television violence are viewed as enhancing its ability to fulfil this mythic function. For example, the strong tendency for violence to be placed in the past or future, to be set in relatively uncommon surroundings, and to involve people who are not closely acquainted, are seen as devices that make violence itself less disturbing. They permit it to occur, so that it can do its symbolic job. The preponderance of mobile and economically and physically able males is viewed in a similar light. Not only do they possess attributes of high status, which fits them for the role of a doer, but they are rootless and in every respect especially qualified for action. As Gerbner remarks, "In a world of contrived and specialized relationships, violence is just another specialty: it is a skill, a craft, an efficient means to an end." Given Gerbner's perspective, the "means" is instrumental not only for the character but also for the medium's social function.

Comment. The most striking aspect of television violence—and, because violence plays such a large part in it, of television entertainment in general—is its unreality. People, relationships, settings, places, and time all depart from real life.

This has two implications. The reflection thesis, which holds that television simply mirrors the world as it is, hardly receives much support. The other is that as a guide for attitudes or behavior television can hardly be said to provide much accurate information about real life. Whether or not entertainment generally functions as a source of learning, of course, is another issue.

Gerbner's theory is undeniably heuristic. It gives meaning to the multitude of dimensions by which television violence can be described and fits them into a single, consistent framework. It also offers an explanation of one way in which popular culture serves (or disserves) modern society. However, it is not easy to test its adequacy as an explanation of why television drama and television violence are what they are.

The problem is the absence of unambiguous predictions or criteria. For example, take the contentions regarding 1) enchancement, and 2) sharpening. In the absence of a clear statement of what would and would not enhance the presentation of violence, a wide variety of dramatic elements, not all consistent and some perhaps the obverse of each other, plausibly might be interpreted as having an enhancing effect. Again, in the absence of some outside yardstick of norms and values, changes in a variety of directions and of various kinds, not all consistent and some perhaps the obverse of each other, plausibly might be interpreted as having a sharpening effect. In short, the capacity of the theory for accommodation is not at present small.

The theory also unfortunately does not explicitly treat two important issues. One is the reinforcement of values and norms. If it is their essence that television symbolically offers to the nation, one might suspect that one function of the medium is to further confirm them among viewers. Another concerns special interests. Since vested interest in these norms and values could hardly be said to be equal for all, one might also suspect that the medium would bear a special relationship to one or another social group or stratum of society. Both of these issues deal with the relationship of television to the social structure and its role in the maintenance of the *status quo*. Neither is presently dealt with other than by implication.

On these topics, the relationship between Gerbner and Cedric Clark's "Race, Identification, and Television Violence" [in Volume 5 of this series] should not be overlooked. Clark argues that television can *do* violence *to* people by what it presents. Positing that television is one source for learning about the worth of one's self and others, he designates the television medium as violent because it portrays blacks in roles that fail to enhance their self-esteem, while society's dominant group, whites, fare less badly.

Gerbner's interpretation of violence as a definer of power is consistent with Clark's contention that television conveys status, and his finding on the relative subordination of nonwhites and foreigners supports Clark specifically. Since Clark's argument presumably would also hold for other identifiable groups, such as women, Gerbner's data simply widen the range of those who, in Clark's view, are television's real-life victims.

Gerbner's description of the highly capable and rootless male as predominant on television, and his data on occupations and activities, are consistent with Clark's thesis that television specializes in images acceptable and enhancing to those already dominant in society. Gerbner's conclusions regarding sharpening are also in accord with Clark's view that television will generally tend to try to maintain its supportive relationship with the more powerful, which Clark sees as a reflection of the medium's understandable desire to maintain its own status.

Gerbner, then, gives Clark's perspective added strength and meaning, while Clark partly supplies what is missing from Gerbner's theory.

LONG-RANGE TRENDS AND OTHER MEDIA

Gerbner's data on recent television are supplemented by (David) Clark and Blankenburg in "Trends in Violent Content in Selected Mass Media." They report on violence in prime time television drama since television's beginnings as a major mass medium; they also report, on a limited basis, on violence in movies, television news, newspapers, and a family magazine; and they match measures of media violence against measures of environmental violence.

Television entertainment

Old videotapes are generally not available; even if they were, a large number could not economically be coded. The authors found a surrogate measure and tested its validity with Gerbner's comprehensive data. They coded *TV Guide* synopses for one October week for 17 years—from 1953, when the magazine was founded, through 1969—for all prime time offerings described. Violence was defined as "physical acts or the threat of physical acts by humans designed to inflict physical injury to persons or damage to property." If the synopsis contained such an act, programs were coded as violent, suggesting that only those programs in which violence was integral to the story were classified as violent.

Comparing 1967-69 trends of data from Gerbner and from *TV Guide* indicated that the surrogate measure would provide an acceptable parallel. Altogether, 982 synopses were coded.

Clark and Blankenburg find that violence declined between 1967 and 1969, a finding which is consistent with Gerbner. However, their most interesting findings are of long-range fluctuation and the relationship between violence and popularity.

The peak year for violence was 1959, when television was following the Cheyenne trail. Peaks occur in 1955 (although the dip afterwards is slight), 1959, 1963, and 1967—in short, every four years.

The percentage of programs coded as violent and the average Nielsen-rated popularity of all evening programs were significantly correlated. The frequency of programs classified as of a type high in violence ("western," etc.) correlated significantly with ratings for such high-violence programs the previous year. However, a similar relationship was not found either for low-violence programs between years or for high-violence programs within a year.

These findings—the observation of some cyclical tendency and the predictive nature of ratings for later violent content—lead the authors to speculate that television violence is responsive to the networks' search for popularity. The goal is the largest possible audience; networks copy one another; and violence has a broad appeal and a wide range of dramatic possibilities, although viewers may tire of a particular violent format. As a result, violence fluctuates in accord with signs of its drawing power.

Other mass media

To place violence on television entertainment in at least some perspective, violence was also studied in several other mass media.

Movies. A sample of 807 synopses was drawn from the approximately 7,000 in *Movies on TV* of films released between 1930 and 1969. Although the films are limited to those with some currency on television, this provides a much broader spectrum of movies than could be extracted from the prime time analysis (where films had a minor role, accounting for only 54 of the 982 *TV Guide* synopses.

Thirty-five percent were coded as violent. However, more than half of those made for television were violent. The trend has been upward since 1930, although there are considerable fluctuations from year to year. Peaks appear every four to six years. After the beginning of commercial television, the frequency of violent films was never less than 30 percent, but in the 14 years between 1937 and 1950 it was below 30 percent ten times.

The authors suggest an influence of television on movies, commenting, "It may be speculated that motion pictures became more violent in order to compete for audiences with television." They also note that holding the growth of cinematic "maturity" and "candor" responsible is not a satisfactory rebuttal, since these too could be partly attributable to competition with television.

Newspapers. Ten front pages a year, from 1927 through 1968, were sampled for each of four major metropolitan dailies: The Atlanta *Constitution*, the Chicago *Tribune*, the San Francisco *Chronicle*, and the *New York Times.* Over the 32 years, 19,264 news stories were coded; 3,386, or 18 percent, concerned violence. Violence seemed to be a stable element in peacetime, usually representing between 12 and 20 percent of front page stories. However, about half the stories were war-related, and war and nonwar stories tend to vary inversely in frequency, as if there were some vaguely understood quota on front page violence. Data on suicides and homicides in each city correlated significantly with nonwar violence on its newspaper's front page. Clark and Blankenburg conclude that newspapers do mirror violence in the real world and that violence is an integral part of news.

Television news and newspapers. Twenty-seven network evening newscasts were compared with the front pages of the same four newspapers during nine days in July, 1970, with 495 network news items and 370 front page stories studied.

The typical newscast contained more items (18) than the average front page (14). The frequency of violent items for television was 26 percent; for front pages, it was 22 percent, a statistically nonsignificant difference. Both media fluctuated in violence daily, but violence in one was not correlated with violence in the other. More of the television violence tended to involve war, probably because of the medium's national and international emphasis. About 12 percent of violent items on the newscasts included action sequences of the violence, 32 percent showed the participants or the aftermath, and the rest did not involve film or tape coverage.

The authors observe that network newscasts and front pages are similar in the quantity of violence displayed. They also note that it is uncertain whether television news should be characterized as more violent or about as violent as prime time drama. It depends on whether the news program or the news item is taken as the relevant television sequence. Every newscast reported some violence, so as a program format newscasts could be said to be more violent; however, the proportions of news items and dramatic programs coded as violent were about the same.

A family magazine. The fiction in 159 issues of the *Saturday Evening Post*, every 13th issue from 1925 and 1964, was coded for violence.

Over the 40 years, 27 percent of the fiction contained violence. It varied markedly under four different editorial reigns. It increased in the 1940's and continued high until editorship changed in 1962. Interestingly, violence in fiction was not used to win readership when the magazine began to lose money in the early 1960's. Unlike real life, death and injury by attack outnumbered casualities from accidents, with the ratio about four and one-half to one. Stories dealing with war were popular during World War II, with war accounting for two-thirds of fictional violence in 1944. However, 85 percent of fictional war deaths occurred after World War II. The authors speculate that the experience of war may have influenced the editors to turn to a high level of violence in the 1940's and afterward.

Environmental influence

The authors attempted to test the proposition that the media reflect the rate of violence in real life. For the measure of societal violence, they used the Uniform Crime Reports between 1933 and 1968, recently adjusted by the FBI for greater accuracy. The rate of violent crime declined in the 1930s, rose during the war years, remained relatively stable during the 1950's, and shifted sharply upward in the 1960's. No meaningful correlation was found with any of the media trend data. For example, the rate of violent crime in the nation was unrelated significantly to television either in the same year or in the following year, allowing for production time. The sole significant correlation is with violent movies between 1937 and 1966, and the authors doubt that movies are a medium in which immediate reflection is likely to occur.

Comment

Violence would seem to be a standard element in all media. The measures are too crude to say whether television entertainment is more or less violent than other media. Undeniably, however, its pervasiveness makes it our major carrier of media violence.

Clark and Blankenburg's most suggestive inference concerns the responsiveness of television violence to efforts to reach the largest possible audience. This would seem to make both audience tastes and broadcasters' decisions rather simplistic sources to blame for oscillations and occasional gluts in the quantity of violence presented. Instead, responsibility would seem to fall to the way in which television operates as a business enterprise in a competitive market economy. Ratings reflect audience preference among available choices; ratings guide decisions about future presentations; decisions are constrained by the accepted criterion of maximum audience size. The result is a rise in violent content whenever there is a hint that violence is especially popular.

The contention that television competition has forced movies to become more violent also fits a general theory of the responsiveness of violent content in media to the workings of the media marketplace. However, it is far from certain that the effect, if there has been an effect at all, has been in the direction of television influencing the movies. It is equally plausible, as Gerbner (In "The Structure and Process of Television Program Content Regulation in the United States") suggests, that the increasing forthrightness of the movies in regard to both violence and sex have led to greater violence on television in an effort to hold audiences.

The reflection thesis is hardly thoroughly tested with the UCR data. However, the data do make it plain that whatever television may be thought to reflect, it does not reflect shifts in violent crime. To this extent, the reflection argument is weakened.

RECOGNITION OF VIOLENCE

In "Perceptions of Violence in Television Programs: Critics and the Public," Greenberg and Gordon report on the ways violence in specific television series is rated by the public and by television critics. Their results challenge a folk belief.

Methodology. The public sample consisted of 303 Detroit residents interviewed by telephone, a 70 percent response rate; 41 percent were men, 59 percent were women. The critics' sample consisted of 43 newspaper and magazine television writers reached by mail questionnaire, 48 percent of those polled.

Sixty-five network series offered by Detroit stations were rated by both groups on a five-point scale. Half the public sample and all the critics were given a definition of violence: "By violence, I mean how much fighting, shooting, yelling, or killing there usually is in the show." The critics rated the entire list, but for ease of telephone query each public respondent was asked to rate only half the list.

Violence perceived. The principal finding is that the public and the critics agreed very closely on the relative quantity of violence in the programs. The ratings of each group led to almost the same rank ordering. An additional finding is that being given the definition did not lead part of the public to a ranking different from those who did not use the definition.

The public found *Mod Squad, Mannix, Mission Impossible, Hawaii Five-O,* and *It Takes a Thief* the five most violent series. The critics made one substitution: *Mannix, Hawaii Five-O, The FBI, Mod Squad* and *Mission Impossible* were their choices. For both groups, the 20 series given the highest violence ratings were the same. Further evidence of general social agreement about what is violent on television is given by the near perfect parallel of the rankings from men and women in the public sample.

Although there was pervasive agreement on relative standings, there were differences in the absolute level of ratings—that is, in the amounts of violence perceived. Ratings tended to decrease with age over four categories beginning with people under 30; women tended to rate the violent series as more violent than did men; and those who were given the definition gave higher ratings. This research also had an important by-product; the scoring served a number of other researchers sponsored by the Television and Social Behavior program who needed some measure of violence in programs for their own studies, and it is likely to be used even more widely in the future.

Comment. The results discredit the often heard argument that violence in entertainment is subjective, idiosyncratically perceived, and thus beyond measurement. The evidence is strong: there is close agreement between different groups—critics and public, public with and without a definition, and men and women—and there was no difficulty in differentiating among the programs (for example, the mean scores for the public ranged from 1.06 to 3.56). While violence may be conceptually elusive, the public has an implicit understanding and readily recognizes it.

BEHIND THE SCREEN

Content alone can offer a suggestive basis for speculation about the reasons for violence on television, as Gerbner, (Cedric) Clark, and (David) Clark and Blankenburg illustrate. However, we are not confined to this approach. In two studies, television professionals were interviewed. Here we can learn something of what lies behind the television we see.

Cantor focuses on children's programming ("The Role of the Producer in Choosing Children's Television Content"). Baldwin and Lewis report on the production of drama aimed at adults ("The Industry Looks at Itself"). The two studies vary in many ways, but the picture they convey is largely consistent.

Children's television

Cantor interviewed 24 men and women script writers and producers in Los Angeles who together represent nearly all the programs in production in early 1970 that were specifically aimed at children. The programs included both cartoons and live action presentations, and most were for telecasting on Saturday mornings. The factors influencing the content of children's television are Cantor's major interest.

She concludes that the networks are the principal aribiters. This is attributed partly to their explicit exercise of authority, and partly to the absence of other effective influences.

The networks are said to have power because they choose and pay for the programs. At the same time, the characteristics of mass media in general and of children's television in particular inhibit other possible influences. Feedback beyond simple popularity ratings is always hard to obtain from any mass media audience since such audiences are large and diffuse and reactions can occur only after the presentation of a finished production. Children are especially difficult to survey for any purpose at any time. There are no regularized prescreenings or trials of the television programs before general showing. As a result, audience reaction comes late; the almost sole index available of that reaction is audience size, and the almost sole impact is the elimination of programs with audiences judged to be unacceptably small.

The values and occupational milieu of those who make television for children also are a factor. Unlike the people who create programs for adults, those who create for children do not believe that they have extensive creative control. Consequently, there is no balancing influence of individual and professional values. The network is the client, and the client must be satisfied. The lonely professional value that is honored is technical quality.

None of those interviewed had had any academic training for the making of children's entertainment. Almost half had been film animators before animated cartooning declined as an occupation in the early 1960's. The rest had been involved in the entertainment business in advertising, promotion, publicity, or as writers. One-third had attended or graduated from college; several had attended art schools, and a few had not graduated from high school. In short, the milieu is a mixture of business and craft.

Cantor found widespread recognition of network interest in reducing violence, but she infers that there is very little chance that it can be substantially reduced given the present circumstances of production; the criteria of success are popularity and the holding of attention, and violence is looked upon as a successful means of achieving both. "The creators of animated programs see children as creatures whose attention spans are limited," she writes, "and they use loud banging noises and quick movements to keep the children watching."

Cantor also found indifference to possible harmful effects on children: "While the shows are in production, producers rarely consider the effects they may have on children; most believe that those considerations are the networks' responsibility, or maybe the parents', but not theirs."

Those creating programs popular with children which are shown on weekday evenings expressed a similar myopia:

> Those producing adventure stories deny that they are making shows for children, although these programs are categorized as children's programs by the National Academy of Television Arts. One producer, whose program's ratings and demographic survey data show a large number of children under ten as part of the audience, said, "We are not making a children's story. I don't think anyone in the business knows who their audience is. I think it is presumptuous of anyone to claim they know this. Kids don't know anything. They are not discerning. As long as we are on the air, I don't care."

Cantor acknowledges that a large number of factors have some influence on children's television. She sees those who create it as affected by their studios and peers, by advertisers, and by what they think they know about the attitudes of parents and children, as well as by the networks. However, she argues that the creators are largely isolated from or indifferent to influences, other than the network and that it is the network which translates the outside influences into the decisions and desires to which a creator responds. In her words, "While all the various parts of the system may influence the final product, evidence suggests that the most important influence comes from those parts of the system having direct interaction with the communicator."

Comment. The irony of Cantor's analysis is that while the networks are said to largely determine content, the desire (shared by both networks and creators) to achieve popularity is said to inhibit the success of network efforts to reduce violence. Put another way: the network seems to have the power, but not the capability.

Prime time television

In 1970 Baldwin and Lewis interviewed 48 high-level persons concerned with the production of 18 network television series judged to contain substantial violence. They report on: a) the reasons for violence; b) network censorship; and c) attitudes inside the television industry toward critics of violent content. The producers, writers, directors, and others interviewed represented all the prime time western, police, detective, and spy series offered at the beginning of the 1970-71 season. The group also included six network censors.

This report is valuable because those interviewed generally occupied key positions within the production part of the television industry. It also shows the relevance of this prime time fare to the young by providing data on the number of young people in the audiences for these programs.

Reasons for violence. Baldwin and Lewis conclude that violence is the most useful device for creating a compelling story. The television people see conflict as essential, violence as synonymous with conflict, action as the best way to hold attention, clearcut and exaggerated attributions of good and evil as facilitating easy understanding and identification, and physical jeopardy as central because it is easily perceived and understood. The principal motivating factors are the competition to win and hold the largest possible audience, the need to create quickly, the scarcity of especially innovative writers, the easy rewards of imitating what seems to be successful, and the constraints on deviation from violence imposed by the adversarial nature of action-adventure series.

The television people report that they attempt to confine violence to situations where it is essential to plot or character. They are aware of the networks' interest in restraining violence, evidenced by the practice of often shooting alternative scenes with reduced violence in case the original is rejected by network censors.

Network censorship. The networks attempt to influence production through their broadcast standards departments. Each network has a director and about eight staff members on the West Coast where production takes place. These people are referred to collectively as "the censors."

Baldwin and Lewis report that a censor can influence a program at many points, from its initiation as a story outline to its final completion. At each stage—outline, draft script, revisions, rough film, and completed film—written approval and editoral commentary is involved. Approval is always tentative until the finished product is reviewed; however, the pressure to avoid financial loss puts a premium on change at the earliest possible stage and may inhibit the harshness of later judgment.

The censors see themselves as representing the station licensees, insuring that the dramatic products they receive conform to the standards of the National Association of Broadcasters Code and the codes and policies of the individual networks. The television people, however, see them as "buffers" standing between the networks and those who would pressure them—the public, Congress, and the Federal Communications Commission.

The television people also see the censors primarily as adversaries. As one producer told Baldwin and Lewis, "The networks are specious, commercial, seeking to please, easily intimidated, and conciliatory." They believe that the censors are primarily concerned with what will be acceptable, or with taste, rather than with any possible effects of content.

This latter impression is reinforced by the absence at the time of the study of any social scientists in the censors' offices. One chief censor said of the work of social scientists on the effects of television violence, "We laugh at them. I don't see how the work accomplished so far by social scientists is of practical value."

Justifying their irritation at restraint, the television people argue that violent content is beneficial. They assert that violence accurately reflects life, and that the suggestion of violence may have a more adverse effect than complete portrayal because of the task left to imagination and the absence of perceivable suffering. They also feel that they are unfairly imposed on because news, movies, and sports are not subject to the same restraints.

The result is a rather odd game-playing situation in which the television people continually try to outguess and sometimes outwit the censor. The censors argue against self-censorship on the grounds that inventiveness and creativity may be hampered, but the writers report that they attempt to submit only "acceptable" ideas. Since the restraints are resented, these obviously often approach the unacceptable as closely as possible. "Excessive" violence is often included by the writers so that negotiations can center on the inessential. Oddly, most television people feel that some others in the industry may need restraint, but not themselves.

Attitudes toward criticism. The television people were generally unsympathetic with criticism of television violence. They rebut by citing influences on viewers other than television, other possible causes of social violence, ignored parental responsibilities, cathartic benefits, positive contributions of implied messages, and the naivete and self-interest of those who criticize.

They generally believe that television might adversely influence a "disturbed" viewer. However, they do not believe that the television industry can be concerned with this minority. For most people, they argue, social norms toward violence are the nonsituationally specific influences that really figure in most violent behavior. For the young, they specify the attitudes toward violence of adults as important influences.

They suggest that television may be a scapegoat when poverty, racial hostility, distrust of government, and alienation should be the true focus. They criticize parents on the grounds that the high ratings of certain violent programs indicate parental support and the absence of objections.

They often argue that violent entertainment is cathartic. They also often argue that television discourages violent behavior because revenge is not portrayed favorably and because violent acts are shown as immoral unless they are in self-defense, on behalf of national security, or for law enforcement. They offer the heroes of violent programs as models for emulation; these protagonists, they say, take their responsibilities seriously, use violence only when necessary, and act generally in accord with the aims (if not the narrow prescriptions) of the law. In sum, violence on the part of viewers is said to be inhibited either because of cathartic emotional release or because violence is always shown as either justified or punished.

Violence on television is also advocated as preparing the young for adulthood. This is based on the premise that violence and conflict are common in life and that advance preparation is helpful.

It is hardly surprising, then, that the television people are hostile toward government inquiries and criticism from others of violent content. They question the qualifications of those involved and ascribe to them opportunism and self-seeking.

Adult Television? The television people generally assert that they produce prime time entertainment for adults. However, Baldwin and Lewis cite Nielsen data showing that the violent prime time series represented were viewed by large numbers of young people.

The Nielsen data divided the audience into those 2-5, 6-11, and 12-17 years old. The number of viewers more than doubles between the youngest children and the 6-11-year-olds then increases only very slightly among the 12-17-year-olds. However, among even the 2-5-year-olds, viewing was substantial in absolute numbers—one program (*Gunsmoke*) had an audience of 2.7 million and seven attracted between one and two million. For the 6-11-year-olds, one program (*Adam 12*) had an audience of 4.3 million and another (*Mod Squad*) of 4.4 million; four fell between three and four million; and only one had less than one million. For the 12-17-year-olds, one (*Mod Squad*) had an audience of 4.6 million, seven fell between three and four million, and only two had less than one million.

Comment. Baldwin and Lewis make it clear that violence is not a commodity easily dispensed with in television drama. It is a solution— and quite possibly the only one feasible for widespread and frequent application—to the constraints and pressures imposed by such general professional and industrial factors of television production as economics, competitiveness, time schedules, available pool of talent, and rate of consumption of dramatic products, and by such presentational factors as the relatively limited and standardized program lengths and the mechanical placement of commercials.

Whether or not the general level and the kind of violence that has been typically presented in television drama has any justification or benefit beyond its obvious appeal as entertainment is moot. However, certain of the contentions reported by Baldwin and Lewis as being advanced by the television people are inconsistent with the available scientific evidence. There is little, if any, support for the proposition that television violence has a cathartic effect (Liebert, 1971). There is also little, if any, support for the contention that the portrayal of violence as justified, or ending in punishment, reduces the likelihood that exposure to violence will reduce any tendency on the part of viewers to behave violently. Evidence from studies done for this research program indicates that dramatic context—the motivations and consequences portrayed—has

little, if any, influence on any effects of exposure to violence on television (Leifer and Roberts, 1971); and other research suggests that viewing justified aggression increases aggressive tendencies among persons
recently frustrated (Berkowitz et al., 1963; Berkowitz and Rawlings,
1963).

UNITED STATES TELEVISION IN PERSPECTIVE

Television in the United States is placed in some perspective by four
studies introduced by Gurevitch. Each examines the structure of broadcasting, and the formal and informal controls affecting the portrayal of
violence and sex in a different society—the United States, Great Britain,
Israel, and Sweden.

As Gurevitch notes, the independent nature of the studies makes
comparisons difficult, since they differ in approach and emphasis. Nevertheless, some generalizations are justified:

—Violence and sex are widespread as issues in programming, even
when they are not explicitly acknowledged as content of special sensitivity. The concern not to offend any sector of the hetereogeneous populace
that makes up the mass audience appears to be general. Even in Israel,
where political considerations are foremost in regard to restraints on
broadcasting, broadcasters acknowledge a variety of concerns about
violence and sex, and have devised numerous criteria to guide inclusion
or exclusion.

—There is some tendency toward an Americanization of world television. The pressure leading to the use of American programs—limited
capacity for local production because of the expense—suggests that this
is almost inevitable.

—Violence was greater in American dramatic programming as a
whole than in the other three societies. However, when a program was
of a violent type, the programs produced in Great Britain tended to be
more violent. This would seem to exemplify differences in television
policy about what is appropriate to present and what is judged acceptable to audiences in the two societies.

—The extent of governmental involvement in broadcasting sets the
United States apart from the other societies. In Great Britain, Sweden,
and Israel, broadcasting is under much greater constraint by government
and other various public bodies, and broadcasting draws support from
subsidy or the licensing of receivers. In the United States, government
influence is minimal, and support is drawn from sale of advertising while
access is free after the purchase of a receiver.

Gerbner's report on United States television is especially interesting
on two counts. First, it sets forth quite clearly the mesh of economic interests, corporate broadcast structure, and application of broadcast
codes and policies that leads to what is ultimately presented, and shows

that the networks clearly dominate television programming. Second, there is the observation that the public's investment is not at all small if the contribution from set purchases and cost to consumers of television advertising are taken into account.

Comment. These studies emphasize what is obvious but easy to forget: The structure and procedures of American television are not the only means of providing a mass public with television. They also suggest that institutional fretting—of so pervasive and serious an order as to be reflected in a variety of organizational mechanisms and social norms and conventions in and around broadcasting—about content is probably inherent to television.

FINAL COMMENT

The most striking impression left by the studies in this volume is of the intractability of violence in commercial television entertainment in the United States. The evidence converges on a single point: violence is extraordinarily difficult and perhaps impossible to control within the present context of commercial broadcasting.

Between 1967 and 1969, violence to a great extent persisted despite efforts to reduce it. Although killing was largely eliminated and the proportion of leading characters involved in violence dropped, the rate of violence in television as a whole continued evenly and violence in children's cartoons increased markedly (Gerbner, 1971a).

Violence is a staple of all mass media—movies, television news, front pages, magazine fiction—and television cannot be expected to be an exception when it must compete for attention with other media (Clark and Blankenburg, 1971). Television is only special because it is so extraordinarily popular as the source of mass story telling.

Violence varies in accord with hints as to its popularity. High ratings for violent programs in one season are precursors of a greater number of programs of a violent type the next season (Clark and Blankenburg, 1971). It also seems to be favorably received by the public, because seasons high in violence tend to have higher average audience ratings (Clark and Blankenburg, 1971). As long as an audience of the maximum possible size is the criterion of success in broadcasting, violence is certain to be a persistent and common ingredient in programming.

Violence also solves a number of problems related to the craft and dramatic exigencies of television production. The job is to tell an engrossing story in a limited time span, to produce such stories quickly and regularly, and to do so at minimum cost. These demands easily take priority over inventiveness and creativity. Violence is a device that provides conflict, action, and understandable dramatic resolution, and its relative ease of application makes it ideal for these circumstances (Cantor, 1971; Baldwin and Lewis, 1971).

The result is that programming is constantly changing but in regard to violence is simply not very malleable. There is certainly no single source to blame. Audiences do indicate some desires for violence, but these desires are expressed through ratings that only indicate preference within the range of what is being offered. Television decision-makers obviously choose to present violence, but they also occupy roles that require them to present what appears likely to gain or hold the largest possible audience. Their roles require that they do not inhibit corporate advantage by failing to meet competition. This suggests that if less violence is desired, the solution lies in changes in the dynamics of contemporary broadcasting.

REFERENCES

Baldwin, T.F., and Lewis, C. Violence in television: the industry looks at itself. In *Television and social behavior*, Vol. 1 (this volume).

Berkowitz, L., Corwin, L., and Hieronimus, M. Film violence and subsequent aggressive tendencies. *Public Opinion Quarterly*, 1963, **27**, 217-29.

Berkowitz, L., and Rawlings, E. Effects of film violence on inhibitions against subsequent aggression. *Journal of Abnormal and Social Psychology*, 1963, **66**(3), 405-12.

Cantor, M. G. The role of the producer in choosing children's television content. In *Television and social behavior*, Vol. 1 (this volume).

Clark, C. Race, identification, and television violence. In *Television and social behavior*, Vol. 5 (this series). Washington, D.C.: U.S. Government Printing Office, 1971.

Clark, D.G., and Blankenburg, W.B. Trends in violent content in selected mass media. In *Television and social behavior*, Vol. 1 (this volume).

Dahlgren, P. Television in the socialization process: structures and programming of the Swedish Broadcasting Corporation. In *Television and social behavior*, Vol. 1 (this volume).

Gerbner, G. Violence in television drama: trends and symbolic functions. In *Television and social behavior*, Vol. 1 (this volume).

Gerbner, G. The structure and process of television program content regulation in the United States. In *Television and social behavior*, Vol. 1 (this volume).

Greenberg, B.S., and Gordon, T.F. Perceptions of violence in television programs: critics and the public. In *Television and social behavior*, Vol. 1 (this volume).

Gurevitch, M. The structure and content of television broadcasting in four countries: an overview. In *Television and social behavior*, Vol. 1 (this volume).

Halloran, J.D., and Croll, P. Television programs in Great Britain: content and control (a pilot study). In *Television and social behavior*, Vol. 1 (this volume).

Leifer, A.D., and Roberts, D.F. Children's responses to television violence. In *Television and social behavior*, Vol. 5 (this series). Washington, D.C.: U.S. Government Printing Office, 1971.

Liebert, R.M. Television and social learning: some relationships between viewing violence and behaving aggressively. In *Television and Social Behavior*, Vol. 2 (this series). Washington, D.C.: U.S. Government Printing Office, 1971.

Shinar, D. Structure and content of television broadcasting in Israel. In *Television and social behavior*, Vol. 1 (this volume).

Violence in Television Drama: Trends and Symbolic Functions

George Gerbner

The Annenberg School of Communications
University of Pennsylvania

This research began as the conclusion of a three-year study of violence in prime time and Saturday morning network television drama.[1] It concluded as the beginning of the development of indicators of popular cultural trends, and of a theory of the symbolic functions of television violence.

The basic findings of the three-year comparative analysis (and of a separately tabulated enlarged 1969 sample, providing a broader base for future trend studies) appear in tabular form, in Appendix A. The results may lend themselves to a variety of further analyses and interpretations. A summary and interpretation of the results comprises the text of the report. The Appendix contains a full account of analytical procedures and a description of the samples of programs analyzed.

It is obvious that television violence is communication, not violence. The implication of this simple fact is that research presumably investigating the relationships between violence and communication cannot proceed on the basis of unexamined assumptions about the extent, nature, and functions of the communication. The conventional approaches and methods of social research appropriate to the study of violent (or any other) behavior are not fully adequate to the analysis of the symbolic presentations of that behavior. Research on mass communications has the unique task of studying symbol systems and their roles in social behavior. Such specialized study is needed when the symbolic functions of the communication are not necessarily or even typically the same as the functions of the behavior they symbolize. It becomes necessary, therefore, to investigate the message of dramatic violence before attempting to find out what that message might cultivate in social conceptions and behavior. Such an investigation was undertaken in this study.

Symbolic functions are, of course, intimately involved in and govern most human activity. The social meaning of an act stems from the symbolic context in which it is embedded. The significance of a life or a death rests in some conception of personality, goals, values, and fate. Similarly, the significance of dramatic action such as violence is an organic part of symbolic structures in which the action helps define, move, and resolve dramatic situations. If the structure changes, the significance of the act will change. If the incidence of a certain dramatic act such as violence changes because of censorship or other controls, the dramatic structures may shift to accommodate the change and to preserve—or even enhance—the symbolic functions of the act.

The study of dramatic violence and its symbolic functions reveals how such a communication helps define, characterize, and often decide the course of life, the fate of people, and the nature of society in a fictional world. The fact that the fictional world is often very different from the real world and that dramatic behavior bears little resemblance to everyday actions is the very essence of the power and human significance of symbolic functions. Fiction and drama can structure situations and present action in a variety of realistic, fantastic, tragic, or comic ways so as to provide the appropriate symbolic context for some human, moral, and social significance that could not be presented or would not be accepted (let alone enjoyed) in other ways.

Interpretations will, of course, vary. But they must start from some knowledge of the time, space, characterization, plot, type of action, and other elementary facts that define the situations to be interpreted. The basic common message of television drama was seen as implicit in these definitions.

Although setting agenda and defining issues do not determine all decisions, in the long run they have a systematic and critical influence on the outcome of most decisions. Similarly, this research assumed that the almost ritualistically regular and repetitive symbolic structures of television drama cultivate certain premises about the rules of the game of life. Violence plays an important role in that game. Not only is real life violence ruled by real consequences but, more important, it is governed by the symbolic attributes that illuminate its meaning and significance. Men commit violence out of love as well as hate, avoid it out of fear as well as prudence, fall victim to it out of accident as well as weakness, and die deaths that can be ignominious as well as glorious. Dramatic violence, free from constraints of reality, calculates the risks of life and the pecking order of society for symbolic purposes. Its implicit moral and social significance governs all behavior. Its functions can define the basic premises that affect interpretations and conclusions independent of individual differences.

These assumptions guided the methodology of this research. The methods of analyzing media content were designed to investigate the aggregate and collective premises defining life and its issues in representative samples of mass-produced symbolic material. Such analysis attempts to establish the incidence and grouping of selected terms presented in the material. The analysis rests on the reliable determination of unambiguously perceived elements of communication. Its data base is not what any individual would select, but what an entire national community absorbs. It does not attempt to interpret single or selected units of material or to draw conclusions about artistic merit. The analysis is limited to those interpretations and conclusions that are implicit in the prevalence, rate, and distribution of clear and common terms over the entire sample. By depending on the reliable determination of unambiguously perceived terms and by ordering these terms along lines of theoretical and social interest, the analysis can identify symbolic structures and functions not available to any selective scrutiny or to any subjective general interpretation.

The reliability of the analysis is achieved by multiple codings and by the measured agreement of trained analysts on each usable item (see Appendix A). If one were to substitute the perceptions and impressions of casual observers, no matter how sophisticated, the value of the investigation would be reduced and its purpose confounded. Only by objectively analyzing unambiguous message elements and separating them from global personal impressions left by unidentified clues can the researcher track the symbolic functions of a specific type of dramatic action (such as violence) and provide the basis for comparison with audience perceptions, conceptions and behavior. No such relationships can be established as long as the actual common terms and their implicit symbolic functions are unknown, are derived from unexamined assumptions, or are inferred from subjective verbalizations of uncertain and ambiguous origin. By taking into account the symbolic origins of the relationships, the researcher will be able to direct attention to the most relevant behavioral and other aspects. If change is desired, an account of symbolic dynamics will also reveal what the potentials and limitations of specific program controls might be and how such changes might relate to symbolic and social structures. In other words, the next step toward understanding television violence and social behavior is to look for the *effects* of the message where the message actually is. That step was beyond the scope of this research, but some suggestions are made in the conclusions on page 39.

Violence connotes a great variety of physical and mental violations, emotions, injustices, and transgressions of social and moral norms. For this study violence was defined in its strictest physical sense as an arbiter of power. Analysts were instructed to record as violent only "the overt expression of physical force against others or self, or the compelling of action against one's will on pain of being hurt or killed." The expression of injurious or lethal force had to be credible and real in the symbolic terms of the drama. Humorous and even farcical violence can be credible and real, even if it has a presumable comic effect. But idle threats, verbal abuse, or comic gestures with no real consequences were not to be considered violent. The agent of violence could be any sort of creature, and the act could appear to be accidental as well as intentional. All characters serve human purposes in the symbolic realm, and accidents or even "acts of nature" occur only on purpose in drama.

The purpose was assumed to be simply to tell a story. Dramatic purposes shape symbolic functions in ways implicit in the distribution and arrangement of elements over a large and representative sample of stories; they do not necessarily derive from stated or implied purposes of specific plays. The basic unit of analysis, therefore, was the play, defined as a single fictional story in play or skit form.

All plays produced specifically for television, all feature films, and all cartoon programs telecast during prime time and Saturday morning on the three major national networks were included in the analysis. (If a program included more than one play, each play became a separate unit of analysis. However, trends are reported in terms of program hours as well as of plays in order to control the possibly distorting effects of a few multi-play programs.)

The study period was one full week of fall programming for each annual television season. The 1969 analysis enlarged the time period to provide a broader base for future trend studies. However, all comparative findings for 1967, 1968, and 1969 were reported only for programs telecast during the same time periods. The enlarged 1969 sample was tabulated in a separate column and is so labeled in the relevant tables of Appendix A. A description of the exact time period and an account of the representativeness of the one-week sample is found in Appendix B. An index and a calendar are listed in Appendix C.

The story defines a play, but characters act out the dramatic story. Units of analysis within the basic context unit—the play—were, therefore, leading characters and scenes of violent action. Leading characters were defined as all those who play leading parts representing the principal types essential to the story and to the thematic elements (including violence) significant to the play. Scenes of violent action were defined as those confined to the same agents of violence. Every such scene (also called a "violent episode") was considered a single unit of analysis as long as the violence involved the same parties; if a new agent of violence entered the scene, it became another episode.

Trained analysts worked in rotating pairs, with two pairs (four analysts) independently recording all observations after repeated viewings of all programs. The programs were videotaped for that purpose from network broadcasts aired during the analysis periods. The analysis procedures and the assessment of reliability determining the usability of observations are described in Appendix A. The entire three-year analysis yielded comparable samples of a total of 281 plays or 182.25 program hours, 762 leading characters, and 1355 violent episodes.

Certain items of the 1967-68 analysis, such as the "significance of the violence to the plays' plots" (included in the tabulations) and the enumeration of "acts" and "encounters," are not summarized here because of their duplication of other and more valid measures. The instrument of analysis for the 1969 study included items in the 1967-68 research (published in the previously cited report on *Violence and the Media*[2]) and new items for which previous data were reanalyzed to yield comparative and comprehensive results. The instrument is contained in a 110-page book of instructions.[3]

The text of this report presents and interprets the findings of the three-year analysis, including all comparative features added in 1969. The first major section is devoted to measures and indicators of variations in amounts of violence presented over the three years. The trends are analyzed for all programming, for networks, and for different kinds of programs. The general prevalence of violence, the rate of violent episodes, and the frequency of roles involving violent characterizations are indicated; these are also combined into composite scores and an overall violence index. A separate analysis of the distribution of violent presentations shows the contribution of each network and program type to the total volume and how that contribution changed over time. These trends illustrate the effects of program *policy* controls upon the symbolic *mix*.

The second major section deals with the structure of the symbolic world and the functions of violence in it. It describes the dynamics of violent action and the consequences of selective changes upon the setting and population of television plays. The shifting complexion of violence roles and their relationship to the temporal, spatial, demographic, and ethnographic dimensions of the fictional world define the risks of life and allocation of powers in that world, and set the stage for some final conclusions.

VARIATIONS IN AMOUNTS OF VIOLENCE OVER TIME, PROGRAMS, AND NETWORKS

The amount of violence in network television drama is essentially a matter of programming *policy*. The mix of different program formats and types and the selection of plays for each kind determine the extent and frequency of violent representations. The measures and indicators developed to compare violent representation over time, across different kinds of programs, and among the three major networks are described below. The trends and comparisons are presented in detail in Tables 1 through 66.

Measures and indicators

The amount of violence in television plays was measured in several ways. Some of these ways showed the extent to which there was any violence in the program samples. Others noted the frequency of violence. Still others showed the number of leading characters involved in violence. These measures were called *prevalence*, *rate*, and *role*, respectively.

The *prevalence* of violence in the program samples is expressed as the percent of plays, program hours, or both, containing any violence at all. This shows the likelihood of encountering (or chances of avoiding) violence in the course of nonselective viewing.

The *rate* of violence expresses the frequency and concentration of violent action in the samples. It is based on scenes of violence (violent episodes between the same opponents). The number of violent episodes divided by the total number of plays (whether violent or not) yielded the rate per all programs; the same number divided by the total number of program hours gave the rate per all hours.

Roles related to violence are those of leading characters committing violence, falling victim to it, or both. Each of these roles was separately computed; so was the percentage of those involved in lethal violence and fatal victimization.

These measures of violence are based directly on analysts' observations. They are combined to form *indicators* expressing several of the qualities measured in single summary figures. The indicators facilitate gross comparisons. However, they should be used in light of the interpretive judgments and assumptions inherent in the formulas that generated them.

Three kinds of indicators are used. Two are based on selected measures showing qualities of programs and of characterizations. The third and most general index is the sum of the first two. The two intermediate indicators are called scores. Prevalence, rate per play, and rate per hour are reflected in the *program score* (PS). This was computed as:

$$PS = (\%P) + 2(R/P) + 2(R/H)$$

In this formula, (%P) is the percent of programs containing violence, (R/P) is the rate of violent episodes per play, and (R/H) is the rate per hour. The rates are doubled in order to raise their relatively low numerical value to the importance that the concepts of frequency and saturation deserve. The rate per hour is included to reflect the concentration or diffusion of violent action in time. The formula, then, gives the greatest weight to the extent to which violence prevails at all in the programs. Secondary but substantial weight is given to the frequency of violence and to the saturation of programs with violent action.

Roles involving characters in some violence, weighted by roles involving them in killing, are expressed in the *character score* (CS). The formula:

$$CS = (\%V) + (\%K)$$

represents the percentage of all leading characters committing violence, suffering violence, or both (%V), with added weight given to the percent of those involved in killing either as killers or as victims or both (%K).

Finally, the *violence index* was obtained by adding the program score to the character score. Prevalence, rate, and role are thus reflected in the index, with program information weighing usually slightly more heavily in the balance than information derived from character analysis. Of course, all these indices are additive: if all components change in the same direction, the index accumulates the changes; if they counter to one another, the index balances them.

An examination of the trends and comparisons indicated in the findings follows. The results are presented in Tables 1-28. The basic frequencies and some additional measures are given in detail in Tables 29-66.

Trends and comparisons

General trends in television programming are something like fluctuations of average national temperature or average barometer readings; they do not necessarily resemble what any one person experiences, but they do indicate what the nation as a whole absorbs and how that changes, if at all, over time. This report of programming trends shows what systems of images and messages network television as a whole releases into the mainstream of national consciousness.

Nevertheless, overall trends can be misleading unless one knows their composition. Shifts in complex cultural manifestations are seldom evenly distributed. The complexion of the total system of messages and the specific conceptions cultivated by them is a blend of different programs, policies, and viewer selections.

Overall trends. The percentage of programs containing violence (*prevalence*) and the rates of violent episodes did not change significantly from 1967 to 1969. About eight in ten plays still contained violence, and the frequency of violent episodes was still about five per play and nearly eight per hour.

The percentage (although, as the tabulations show, not the number) of characters involved in violence declined from over seven in ten in 1967 to somewhat more than six in ten in 1969, with most of the reduction from 1967 to 1968. More substantial and steady was the reduction of lethal violence. Leading characters involved in killing dropped from nearly two in ten in 1967 to one in ten in 1968 and to one in 20 in 1969.

The violence index was 198.7 in 1967, 180.7 in 1968, and 175.5 in 1969. The drop in the violence index can be attributed to the reduction in violent characterizations, especially in killing. Total violence remained the same, but it was committed by fewer characters. Only a handful committed violence of a lethal sort. This resulted in declining character scores and violence index, but at the same time program scores remained steady over the years.

A compilation of detailed program scores, character scores, and the violence index of network programming can be seen in Tables 1 and 2.

Comparison of network indicators. Although not license holders themselves, networks dominate national television programming. Since they compete in the same markets, networks do not differ from one another as much as programs on the same network differ from one another. Nevertheless, network policies do change from time to time.

The violence index of each network was:

	1967	1968	1969	1967-69
ABC	222.3	192.9	170.0	193.4
CBS	151.0	167.1	148.7	155.2
NBC	219.6	187.3	203.8	203.4

The violence index of all network programming declined from 1967 to 1969, but NBC's rose from 1968 to 1969 (see Table 2). That rise can be attributed to an increase in program violence while character violence remained steady. CBS viewers had the best chance of avoiding violence, if they wished to. After a rise in 1968 (mostly in program violence), the index returned to slightly below its 1967 level, the lowest of the three networks. ABC, formerly the most violent, substantially reduced its dependence on video mayhem, but not quite to the level of CBS. NBC, after a reduction in both program and character violence in 1968, increased its program violence (specifically in cartoon programming), making its index the highest in 1969.

Comparison of kinds of programs. Technique, tradition, and markets shape dramatic formulas on television, each with its own violence quotient. Competition and convention tend to inhibit drastic tampering with profitable formulas. Program formats that we have analyzed separately are cartoons, feature films, and plays. These are exclusive categories; a program may be classified in only one of them. Programs were also tabulated by two additional types: crime, western, action-adventure type; and comedy type. These two are not exclusive categories; a program classified in any one of them may also be classed in others.

Cartoons, already the most violent programs in 1967, increased their lead in 1969. In fact, only plays were substantially less violent in 1969 than they had been in 1967. Feature films dropped to slightly below 1967 levels after a surge of violence in 1968. The rise in the prevalence and rate of cartoon violence was also reflected in the program scores of crime-action and comedy programs.

A more detailed record of measures and indicators by kinds of programming can be found in Tables 3-7. A comparative examination confirmed that only plays produced specifically for prime time adult television declined on all measures of violence from 1967 to 1969. It is also clear that children watching Saturday morning cartoons had the least chance of escaping violence or of avoiding the heaviest saturation of violence on all television.

Of all 95 cartoon plays analyzed during the three annual study periods, only two in 1967 and one each in 1968 and 1969 did *not* contain violence. The average cartoon hour in 1967 contained more than three times as many violent episodes as the average adult dramatic hour. The trend toward shorter plays sandwiched between frequent commercials on fast-moving cartoon programs further increased the saturation. By 1969, with a violent episode at least every two minutes in all Saturday morning cartoon programming (including the least violent and including commercial time), and with adult drama becoming less saturated with violence, the average cartoon hour had nearly six times the violence rate of the average adult television drama hour, and nearly 12 times the violence rate of the average movie hour.

While crime, western, action-adventure programs are, of course, more violent than comedy programs, an increase in program score for the former and in all measures for the latter can be attributed to the number of cartoon programs in each.

Network programming. Tables 8-22 present measures and indicators of violence for each network and selected measures for each network by cartoons, noncartoon programming, crime, western, action-adventure programs, and comedy.

ABC programs were less violent in 1969 than they had been in 1967. ABC's violence index dropped further than any other network's. All measures for the network as a whole declined, with the sharpest reductions in video killing. The bulk of the reductions, however, came from general adult programming, with cartoons and crime-action programs all remaining violent and highly saturated with violence. ABC comedy programs, unlike those of the other networks, were no more violent in 1969 than they had been in 1967.

CBS programming, the least violent, also changed the least among the networks. Its violence index combined conflicting tendencies. A rise in the prevalence and rate of violence balanced a drop in the proportion of killers, while the percentage of violents and victims remained steady. The bulk of the increase in program violence came from comedy, crime, western, action-adventure, and general adult drama. Cartoon programs in 1969 were not significantly more violent than in 1967.

NBC's 1969 violence index, although below that of 1967, was the highest of the networks. The main reason was the high concentration of violence in NBC cartoon programming, which also affected the comedy program score. An all-network record of 43 violent episodes per hour over all NBC Saturday morning cartoon hours boosted the 1969 NBC violence index to 203.8, compared with 170.0 for ABC and 148.7 for CBS.

Distribution of violent presentations

Measures and indicators do not reveal the relative amounts of material (including violent material) that each network and program type contributes to the whole. For example, if cartoons increased in violence but decreased in number, they would have less impact on the entire flow of violent representations than if their number remained steady or increased; a nonselective viewer would have less chance of finding cartoon violence, despite the fact that cartoons had become more violent.

In fact, this hypothetical example turns out to be false. Tables 23-28 present the distribution of selected measures of violence by program format, type, programming within networks, and network totals. They show what share each contributed to all programming and to violent programming each year. The figures for cartoons, for example, are:

	1967	1968	1969
Share of cartoons out of			
all programs	33.3	28.7	38.8
violent programs	38.5	33.8	46.8
violent episodes	31.6	41.1	52.6

all leading characters	25.8	21.9	33.2
those involved in violence	31.8	26.4	41.7
those involved in killing	20.0	8.0	6.3

Share by program format and type

Researchers studied the relative contributions of cartoons, plays and feature films to total programming. Cartoons' share of all plays increased, as did their contribution to violence. For example, cartoons provided 151 violent episodes in 1967, less than one-third of all such episodes on prime time and Saturday morning network plays. In 1969, cartoons' share of all violent episodes was 254, more than half of the total. Cartoons also gained in their share of characters involved in violence, despite the sharp drop in cartoon killings.

Plays decreased their share of all programming and of violent programs but increased their share of killers. With the reduction in TV killings, plays produced for television boosted their share from about seven of every ten killings in 1967 to eight of ten in 1969. Crime, western, and action-adventure programs have the greatest share of violence; they contain most violent episodes, characters, and nearly all killings. Comedies have less violence. Their share of violent programs and episodes increased, but their share of violent characters decreased. Killing disappeared from comedies. (See details in Tables 23 and 24.)

Share by networks and programs. Among the networks, CBS contributed less program violence throughout the years (1967-69) than the other networks. ABC's violence by most measures decreased, while NBC's increased.

A viewer tuned to ABC in 1969 found half of all plays cartoons; but six out of ten violent plays and episodes were in cartoons. Cartoon violence had increased in time. ABC crime drama, containing the most violence, also increased its violent representations. ABC comedy contained a larger share of all violence on that network in 1969 than it had in 1968 and 1967, but the number of comedy plays increased even more. (It should be noted again that these are not exclusive classifications. A play can be classified in more than one; the overlap with cartoons may be especially significant.)

CBS cartoons contributed an increasing share, crime dramas a decreasing share, of violence to the total on that network. CBS comedy, formerly containing much less than its proportional share of violence, increased its contribution to the total; by 1969 more than half of all plays and the same proportion of violence came from comedies (including cartoons) on CBS.

NBC cartoons and crime dramas both contributed more than their share of violence to the network total. Comedies' share increased until, as on CBS, they contained nearly half of all violence on the network. Substantiation of these conclusions can be found in Tables 25-28.

Conclusions

Strictly defined as the overt expression of physical force intended to hurt or kill, violence prevailed in about eight of every ten plays during prime time and Saturday morning network television drama. Scenes of violence were shown at the rate of five per play or eight per hour. The overall prevalence and rate of violence did not change over the years but differed by network and by kind of program. What did show a significant change were the proportion of leading characters engaged in violent action and the physical consequences of the violence. Violents committed as much violence in 1969 as they had in 1967, but they were fewer in number and their violence was less lethal. An overall drop in the composite index of violence could be attributed to selective reductions of some of its most blatant manifestations, and to a shifting of its burden within the fictional population.

What is the meaning of these changes? Amounts of violence indicate the general climate of the fictional world of television drama but reveal nothing about the nature and role of violence in that world. The symbolic functions of violence are implicit in its representation, regardless of amount; they emerge from an examination of the dynamics of violent action in its relationship to the roles and to the types of characters that populate the fictional world. In order to chart the social relevance of these symbolic fluctuations and currents, we need to know what winds blow good or ill for whom, and how they change. Varying amounts and shifting burdens of violence become meaningful only if we can determine how the selective changes alter the structure of action, and whose burden shifts whose fate in what direction.

SYMBOLIC FUNCTIONS OF VIOLENCE IN THE WORLD OF TELEVISION

An analysis of the role of violence in the fictional world of television drama illuminates symbolic functions of violence. These are not as amenable to administrative and other policy controls as is the sheer amount of violence. Symbolic functions of mass-produced violence have deep institutional and cultural roots. They cultivate dominant assumptions about how things work in the world and, more particularly, about how conflict and power work in the world.

However, changes in total amounts of violence and variations in the relative distribution of types and people of violence, may shift the balance of power in the symbolic world of television. When they do, they alter the calculus of the risks of life that provides the implicit lessons and performs the symbolic functions of violence.

Selected characteristics of two major aspects of violence in the world of television drama are examined: violent actions and the violence-related roles of the cast of characters that populates the fictional world.

Violent action

Violent acts must have agents to commit them, means to inflict them, casualties to sustain them, and scenes to contain them. Symbolic violence is also conveyed in some tone or style and is located in time, space, and setting of some significance. These characteristics of violent action in television were analyzed in all programs, cartoons, and noncartoon plays separately, and are tabulated in Tables 67-87.

Agents, means, and consequences. For each violent episode—a total of 1,355 for the three years—analysts recorded who engaged in violence, how, and with what consequences. (A violent episode was defined as a scene of whatever duration involving violence between the same opponents. A change in opponents would start a new episode.)

Human agents inflicted violence in 70 percent of all violent episodes. The proportion of human agents of violence declined somewhat over the years as that of nonhuman agents increased, especially in cartoons.

In general drama, nonhuman agents engaged in violence in one of every ten violent episodes in 1967 and 1968 and in two of ten in 1969. In cartoon episodes, nonhuman agents and causes of violence climbed from about half in 1967 and 1968 to three-quarters of all such episodes in 1969.

Agents of law enforcement played a minor but increasingly violent role in the encounters. Their part was limited to about one in every ten of all and two in ten of general (noncartoon) dramatic episodes. When they did play a role, it was violent in 60 percent of such episodes in 1967, 72 percent in 1968, and 77 percent in 1969. (The role of such agents will be discussed below under "Occupation.")

Violence was inflicted by a weapon other than the body in half or more of all violent episodes. The use of weapons increased from 52 to 83 percent in cartoon episodes, as did the incidence of violence itself and of violence by nonhuman agents. At the same time, the proportion of violent episodes taking place in a light or comic program context also increased in cartoons (from 41 to 48 percent), but decreased in noncartoon plays (from 22 to 14 percent).

The number and rate of casualties and fatalities declined sharply, as was also indicated by the results of the character analysis. Casualties were observed in half of all violent episodes in 1967 and 1968, but in only one of six in 1969. The weekly casualty count dropped from 437 to 134 in the same period. The "body count" of dead fell from 182 to 46, or from 42 percent to 34 percent of all casualties. While in 1967 and 1969 nearly every violent episode produced an injury, in 1969 three such encounters produced one casualty. Similarly, in 1967 and 1968 it took two to three episodes to produce a fatality; in 1969 it took ten.

Violence appeared no more painful or debilitating (except for the dead) in 1969 than it had before. Pain and suffering were so difficult to detect that observers could not agree often enough to make the results acceptable. There was little doubt that no painful effect was shown in more than half of all violent episodes.

Time, place, and setting. Symbolic violence was more likely to occur in remote settings than in the here and now. Plays set in the past and the future were nearly always violent and had a much higher rate of violent episodes per play than programs set in the present (about the time of production). Since all but two cartoons were violent (Table 77), the differences apply mostly to noncartoon programs. However, the rate of violent episodes in cartoon plays was also consistently highest in those set in the past.

Action in the "worlds" of television took place in the present more than half the time. But comparing all violent programs with all plays that do not contain violence, we find that the world of violence held nearly all dramatic images of the past and the future. Although the evidence is not clear-cut, it may be that reducing violence also narrows the time range of representations to the more current and familiar settings.

Location has a similar affinity with the symbolic functions of violence. When the setting of the play was partly or wholly outside the United States, violence was much more likely than when the action took place only in the United States. Foreign, international, and mixed settings contained the bulk of television violence. Consequently, the world of violence on television was much more distant, exotic, or geographically indistinct than the predominantly domestic world of nonviolence. The distribution in cartoon plays and trends was similar to that in all programs.

As in time and place, so also in social setting, symbolic violence on television sought that which was far removed from the experience of most viewers. The prevalence and rate of violence was lowest in an urban setting, higher in a small town or rural setting, and highest when the locale was uninhabited, mobile, or not identifiable at all. The rate of violent episodes per play in remote or indistinct settings was twice that per play in urban settings. The social setting of the world of violence was half the time uninhabited or unidentifiable, while the world without violence was half urban and one-third small town or rural.

A comparison of trends between violent and nonviolent programs also shows that as proportions of violent characterizations and casualties decrease, the locales of violent programs shift away from urban settings while the nonviolent programs become more urbanized. As will be observed in the discussion of illegal occupations, the probable reason is that selective reductions first eliminate those characters who do not fit within the most conventional and acceptable formats. These cuts can best be made by limiting urban violence to crime and detective plays. Thus the proportion of violence in urban settings decreases, and settings "close to home" for most viewers become more pacified. A separate check on plays set in an urban environment showed that in 1967 and 1968 seven to eight of all such plays contained violence, but that in 1969 only half did. As most plays were still violent, this shift resulted in a slight overall reduction of all plays located in an urban environment (see Table 83), a proportion that never exceeded one-third of all programs.

Selective reduction of certain features of violent representations—with other conditions of cultural production remaining the same—appears to have two major consequences. First, the changes tend to trim potentially disturbing or troublesome manifestations not essential to the traditional and ritualistic symbolic functions that violence performs in the world of television. Second, the changing proportions and shifting burdens of violent representations further tip the scales of power in the direction already inherent in the representations. Both consequences lead to a tightening and sharpening of the basic social functions of symbolic violence.

It appears that the most convenient dramatic circumstances for the smooth performance of those social functions rest in symbolic structures relatively far removed from familiar issues and direct social relevance. The apparent paradox vanishes when we recognize that dramatic violence is not behavior but a communication, a message. It can be viewed most appropriately as an element of myth in the historic sense of a moral ritual. Its lesson can have direct social significance to the extent that it can freely demonstrate the clash and resolution of personalized social values and forces. The historic role of the demonstration is to socialize real life behavior in ways that do not require violent enforcement of its norms. The ritualistic functions of violence rest on its roles symbolizing the risks of life and arbitrating man's fate in socially determined ways. These roles require imaginary situations. The situations define life so as to indicate the relative powers and fates of different groups of characters and to demonstrate how power works (or should work) in the preferred moral and social order. Such functions may be easiest to perform in settings relatively remote, unfamiliar, exotic, farcical, or whimsical, unaffected by the need or opportunity for reality-testing or other factors in the viewers' everyday experience. Most traditional rituals, myths, fairy tales, and other forms of implicit acculturation function in that way; there is no reason to assume that industrial lore must be essentially different. The implicit lessons of acts of violence, the lessons of the different risks of violence for different kinds of people assuming different power roles in the vicarious world of mass entertainment, probably emerge most clearly and sharply when relatively stylized and uncontaminated by familiar and potentially conflicting clues.

The fictional world of television and the role of violence as an integral part and often prime mover of that world are artificial, synthetic, and symbolic. They are constructed for dramatic purposes, serve institutional tasks, and condition members of society to modes of thinking considered functional to its dominant institutions. The resort to violence to perform social functions in the symbolic world appears to be inversely related to the general relevance of the plays to contemporary domestic social issues, except in ritualized conventional forms. However, a reduction in violent characterizations and gory details, combined with the apparent social irrelevance of most violent action and settings, need not weaken and may only enhance the social relevance of the collective lessons. Action and settings serve mainly to animate characters, to facilitate and frame their acting of a moral drama of direct social import. Exotic, distant, or stylized though the circumstances may be, in the final analysis it is the people—characters in action—who represent the contending values and drive home the lessons through their struggles and their fate.

The history and geography depicted in the world of television drama have been shaped by society's institutional and functional requirements. Demography and ethnography are similarly structured. The people of the fictional world must be considered; what do the winds of violence, and their changing currents, blow in their paths?

Violence roles and the role of violence

The fictional world reflects, not life, but purpose. Its time, space, and motion—even its accidents—follow, not laws of physics, but the logic of dramatic action. Its society is not a mirror but a projection of dramatic and social intent. Its people are not born but are created to serve a purpose. They do not behave as real people; they act out the purposes for which they were created.

In a fictional world governed by the economics of the assembly line and the production values of optimal appeal at least cost, action follows conventional ground rules of social morality. The requirement of wide acceptability assures general adherence to common notions of justice and fair play. The ground rules are usually expressed in clear-cut characterizations, tested plot lines, and proven formulas for resolving all issues. Problems are personalized rather than verbalized, conflicts are settled through action, and the resolutions are implicit in the outcomes.

Roles are written and parts are cast to convey images consistent with desired patterns of action in a symbolic society. Any society seems freest to those who run it; the dominant groups of the fictional world are those who can be cast in the greatest variety of freewheeling roles. A leading character will be female, for example, not on any occasion when a woman might be cast in a certain role, but typically when a romantic or family theme requires it. Similarly, age, occupation, and ethnic or other identity are used to signify thematic, value, and power attributes needed for a dramatic purpose.

Representation in the fictional world signifies social existence; absence means symbolic annihilation. Being buffeted by events and victimized by people denotes social impotence; ability to wrest events about, to act freely, boldly, and effectively, is a mark of dramatic importance and social power. Values and forces come into play through characterizations: good is a certain type of attractiveness, evil is a personality defect, and right is the might that wins. Plots weave a thread of causality into the fabric of dramatic ritual, as stock characters act out familiar parts and confirm preferred notions of what's what, who's who, and who counts for what. The issue is rarely in doubt; the action is typically a game of personality, group identification, skill, and power.

Violence plays a key role in such a game. It is the simplest and cheapest dramatic action available to signify risk to human integrity and purpose. In real life, much violence is subtle, slow, circumstantial, invisible, even impersonal. Acts of physical violence are rare, a last resort when symbolic means fail. In the symbolic world, overt physical motion makes dramatically visible that which in the real world is usually symbolic and hidden. Thus violence in drama cannot be equated with violence in the real world. Real violence is the dead end of symbolic action. Symbolic violence is one of society's chief instruments for achieving the aims of real violence without having to commit any. Symbolic hurt to symbolic people and causes can show real people how they might use—or avoid—force to stay alive and to advance their causes. The ritual of dramatic violence demonstrates the relative power of people, ideas, and values in a clash of personalized forces. To be able to hit hard and to strike terror in the hearts of one's opponents—that makes one count when the chips are down. The battered hero triumphs over evil by subduing the bad guy in the end. The last man to hit the dust confirms his own flaw of character and cause. Hurting is a test of virtue and killing is the ultimate measure of man. Loss of life, limb, or mind, any diminution of the freedom of action, are the wages of weakness or sin in the symbolic shorthand of ritual drama. What appears to be the resolution of an issue is the art of staging the demise of doomed powers and the fall of ill-fated characters. The typical plot ends by reaching a reassuring and usually foregone conclusion about who is the better man.

Several times a day, seven days a week, the dramatic pattern defines situations and cultivates premises about power, people, and issues. Just as casting the dramatic population has a meaning of its own, assigning "typical" roles and fates to "typical" groups of characters provides an inescapable calculus of chances and risks for different kinds of people. Who commits and who suffers violence of what kind is a central and revealing fact of life in the world of television drama that viewers must grasp before they can follow, let alone interpret, the play. The allocation of values and of the means of their implementation defines any social structure. Who gets (and gives) what, how, and why delineates the social structure of the world of television drama. The distribution of roles related to violence, with their different risks and fates, performs the symbolic functions of violence, and conveys its basic message about people.

The cast of characters. Casting in the symbolic world has a meaning of its own. Every member of the dramatic population is created to serve a purpose. Violence plays a role not only in ruling but also in populating the fictional universe.

Of all 762 leading characters analyzed, three-quarters or more were male, American, middle and upper class, unmarried, and in the prime of life (see Table 88). The lion's share of representation went to types that dominate the social order and to characterizations that permit unrestrained action. Symbolic independence requires freedom relatively uninhibited by real-life constraints. Less representation was allocated to those lower in the domestic and global power hierarchy and to characters involved in familiar social contexts, human dependencies, and other situations that impose real-life burdens of primary human relationships and obligations upon freewheeling activity.

Geared for independent action in a loosely-knit and often remote social context, two-thirds to three-quarters of all characters were free to engage in violence, and nearly half were free to "specialize" in violence as far as dramatic role and purpose was concerned. A separate analysis of the 1967-68 program material[4] found that violence on television, unlike real-life violence, rarely stems from close personal relationships. It usually occurs between people who do not even know each other, or at least do not know each other well. Most of it is directed against strangers or members of "other" groups and stems from instrumental purposes such as a personal goal, private gain, power, or duty, not from social or moral issues transcending individual interest. In a world of contrived and specialized relationships, violence is just another speciality; it is a skill, a craft, an efficient means to an end.

Women typically represent romantic or family interest, close human contact, love. Males can act in nearly any role, but rare is the female part that does not involve at least the suggestion of sex. Most women cast in other specialties are marked for impotence or death.

The theme of marriage in a program requires a woman lead and makes the incidence of violence less likely. While only one in three male leads in the programs surveyed was shown as intending to or ever having been married, two of every three females were married or expected to marry in the story. The number of women characters generally varied inversely with the frequency of violent characterizations. As the latter declined from three-quarters to two-thirds of all characters, the proportion of women increased from one-fifth to one-fourth. : Women's share of all leading characters in feature films (which have the highest incidence of love stories) was 47 percent in 1967, 39 percent in 1968 (when films reached a peak in violence), and 41 percent in 1969. In plays, where violence declined most over the years, the proportion of female characters climbed from 21 percent in 1967 to 29 percent in 1969. In cartoons, where violence is highest and romantic interest or family settings are rare, women played between seven and 11 percent of leading roles. In general, women's roles and fates is one of the most sensitive indicators of the distribution of power and the allocation of values that the symbolic world bestows upon its victors and victims.

Children, adolescents, and old people together accounted for only about ten percent of the total fictional population. The rest were young and middle-aged adults available to act out their fates free of family dependencies or marital entanglements. Nearly half of all females were concentrated in the most sexually eligible young adult population, to which only one-fifth of males were assigned; women were also disproportionately represented among the very young and old.

Assigning a character to a category provides the characterization (and often the setting) necessary for the solution of a special dramatic problem. But such solutions create the problem of specialists destined to seek solutions along lines of their specialities. Many of these specialties do not require professionalization or occupational activity, but some do. Gainful employment was indicated for about half of all characters; discernible occupational activity of any kind for six in ten.

Much of the "work to be done" in the world of television drama revolves around threats to and the preservation of the moral, social, and global order. We have seen before that symbolic demonstrations of power with violence as a dramatic test and arbiter are most likely to appear in relatively remote, exotic, farcical, or whimsical settings. Bringing them into familiar situations is more likely to be upsetting and offensive and to raise dangerous issues close to home, except when the potential threats can be neutralized and ritualized in the form of the conventional law-and-order formats. The symbolic functions of power are best performed, therefore, in the crime, western, and action-adventure types of plays, including cartoons. In fact, half of all leading roles in all dramatic programs were males in those categories. Their occupations and activities generally related to the game of power and provided a disproportionate number of the stock jobs and tasks of the fictional labor force.

Of the approximately five in ten characters who could be unambiguously identified as gainfully employed, three were proprietors, managers, and professionals. The fourth came from the ranks of labor—including all those employed in factories, farms, offices, shops, stores, mining, transportation, service stations, restaurants, and households, and working in unskilled, skilled, clerical, sales, and domestic service capacities. The fifth served to enforce the law or preserve the peace on behalf of public or private clients.

Type of activity—paid and unpaid—reflected the dramatic requirements and functions more adequately. The six in ten characters engaged in discernible occupational activity could be roughly divided into three groups of two each. The first group represented the world of legitimate private business, industry, agriculture, finance, etc. The second group was engaged in activity related to art, science, religion, health, education, and welfare, as professionals, amateurs, patients, students, or clients. The third group made up the forces of official or semiofficial authority and the army of criminals, outlaws, spies, and other enemies arrayed against them. One in every four leading characters acted out a drama of some sort of transgression and its suppression at home and abroad.

Sex, age, occupation, and other social characteristics quickly add up to a complex dramatic demography not dealt with in the task of this report. The investigator here deals merely with a feeling for the significance of casting in the symbolic world and of the role of violence in the creation of the fictional population. The main task was to investigate the relationships between types of violence and the social structure of the fictional population. The ethnography of the symbolic world is examined in that context.

Violence roles. We looked at different types of involvement in violence and their distribution among different types of characters. "Violents" were, of course, those who committed violence, and "nonviolents" were those who did not. Two groups of violents were (a) those who injured but did not kill, and (b) those who killed. Similarly, victims of violence were divided into (a) those who only got hurt, and (b) those who got killed. Three roles related to violence and three related to victimization define nine basic roles:

	VICTIMS who		NONVICTIMS
VIOLENTS who	(a) get hurt	(b) get killed	
	1	2	3
(a) injure	Injure another and get hurt	Injure another and get killed	Injure another with impunity
	4	5	6
(b) kill	Kill another and get hurt	Kill another and get killed	Kill another with impunity
	7	8	9
NONVIOLENTS	Get hurt but commit no violence	Get killed but commit no violence	Not involved

Tables 88-113 provide yearly figures and totals on *violents* (1-6, above); *killers* (4-6); *victims* (1,2,4,5,7,8); *killed* (2,5,8); all those *involved in any violence* (1-8); and those *involved in any killing* (2,4-6,8). Character scores (percentage of those involved in any violence plus percentage involved in any killing) are also given in the tables.

Tables 89-93 present violence roles by network and by program format and type. These findings amplify but do not modify the summary of roles and character scores presented in the first section of this report. Table 94 presents violence roles of all leading characters, and Table 95 shows the share of male and female characters in these roles. Subsequent tables group the results by demographic, social, and dramatic classifications.

The investigators attempted to report and interpret a complex structure of dramatic and power relationships implicit in the distribution of violence roles and in the dynamics of their change. These relationships and shifts compose the specific message of violence in television plays. That message is a definition of social situations that underlies all perceptions, interpretations, and uses of the material. We looked at the overall frequencies of violence roles and at the probabilities of committing or suffering violence (or both) inherent in them. We compared distributions, relative shares, and probable risks by different types of leading characters: men and women, single and married, young and old, rich and poor, selected occupations, races, nationalities, and characters were destined for a happy or an unhappy fate.

Violent people and the risks of life. Of all 762 leading characters studied during the three annual study periods, 513, or 67 percent, were involved in some violence (as violents, as victims, or as both). That left 249 not involved. The ratio of the two numbers is 2.1 to one. Thus the "average" character's chance of being involved in some violence is about twice as good as his chance of not being involved.

Of those involved, more were involved as victims than as violents. Five in ten committed some violence, but six in ten suffered. Chances of suffering violence rather than escaping it were 1.5 to one. Chances of being a violent or nonviolent were even.

The overriding message is that of the risk of victimization. For every three violents there were three nonviolents, but for every three victims there were only two nonvictims. If one had to be either a violent or a victim, chances were 1.2 to one of becoming a victim.

Violent victims—those who injured or killed and got hurt or killed in return—numbered 42 percent of all leading characters. Only eight percent committed violence with impunity, i.e. did not suffer violence in return. Thus the odds were 5.3 to one that violence brought counter violence.

Nonviolent victims—those who got hurt or killed without inflicting violence upon others—numbered 17 percent of all characters. Chances were, therefore, 2.5 to one against being victimized without having committed violence. The risk of being only victimized (suffering violence without inflicting any) was more than twice as great as the chance of committing violence with impunity. The relative probabilities suggest that few violents will escape injury or death. But nonviolents must beware, too—perhaps even more; although most (71 percent) will escape injury or death, nonviolents are twice as likely to suffer unprovoked violence as violents are likely to hurt or kill with impunity.

Dramatic characters can take—and dish out—a great deal of physical punishment, but the elimination of a leading character concludes a moral lesson. The relative probabilities of killing and being killed shift the emphasis from the risks of victimization to the efficacy of the final blow.

A three-year total of 86 leading characters (11 percent of all) were involved in lethal violence. That is more than one in ten; the probability against being involved is 7.9 to one. Killers numbered eight percent, killed were four percent, and killers who were also killed numbered one percent of all leading characters. So while, in general, more suffered than committed violence, twice as many leading characters killed than got killed in the stories; the odds in favor of being a killer rather than killed were two to one. Chances were 6.9 to one that a killer would not get killed in return. But chances were only 2.9 to one that one got killed without having killed (rather than after having killed) someone. Fear of victimization and the image of the suffering hero may be somewhat tempered by the suggestion that lethal violence will balance the score, at least for the more dominant figures of the symbolic world.

The total proportions and trends in the involvement of all characters in different kinds of violence can be seen in the "All Characters" columns of Table 94. While general involvement decreased from 1967 to 1968, the proportion of killing dropped each year. Within these overall trends, however, several currents mingled. Victims always outnumbered violents by approximately six to five, and their proportion appeared to decline more slowly. This would suggest that if violence is reduced by cutting out more violent characters than victims, each of the remaining violents hurts more people, and the ratio of victimization increases. Indeed, while the percentage of violents declined, nonviolent victims of violence remained 16-17 percent of all characters.

Killers consistently outnumbered the killed. Both killers and killed became less numerous. Fatal victimization, in general, dropped more slowly than killing. In 1967 there were four killers for every two killed; in 1969 there were three killers for every two killed. Thus the relative probability of being killed rather than killing increased, as did the ratio of all victims to all violents.

Men and women. Different and shifting roles and risks are likely to affect two unequal populations in different ways. (Table 94 shows some of these differences.) Violence was part of the roles of most males but part of only about half of all female characters. Male involvement, essential to the dramatic functions of violence, dipped slightly and uncertainly, while female involvement, often troublesome and disturbing, was cut more decisively. But a clearer look at the violence roles shows how differently the changes affected the sexes.

The drop was mostly in violent females and in male victims. The number of violent males declined only slightly, that of female victims not at all. The shifting sands of fate piled a greater burden of victimization upon women.

A look at the probabilities shows that men's chances of encountering some violence were 2.6 to one, while women had an even chance. But once they brushed up against violence, women took a greater and increasing risk of falling victim to it. The disparity was greatest when it came to "pure" violence roles—those of only committing or only suffering violence.

If a man was violent, his odds against committing violence with impunity were 6.9 to one; if a woman was violent, her odds against getting away with it were 1.6 to one. But male victims were also violents 2.9 to one, whereas female victims had only an even chance for counter-violence. Furthermore, male killers outnumbered males killed 2.1 to one. while female killers outnumbered females killed only 1.5 to one.

The reduction of violence roles intensified the differences. Most of the decline in violence was due to the reduction of the number of violents in general and to the virtual elimination of killing among women. The number of victims, however, did not decline as much, and not at all among women. So the shift was more than in amount of violence; it was also in the power position of women.

For men, there were five victims to every four violents throughout the three years, a steady ratio of 1.2 to one. For women, there was an equal number of victims and violents in 1967, four victims to every three violents in 1968, and four victims to little over two violents in 1969. Women's odds of being victimized rather than inflicting violence shifted from 1 to one, to 1.3 to one, to 1.5 to one. So a reduction in the percentage of violence roles without a reduction in either the number or the proportion of women victims resulted in changing the complexion of women's involvement in violence. In 1967 as many dished out as suffered violence; by 1969, one and one-half times as many suffered from violence as could inflict it upon others. In 1967, 17 percent of all women fell victim to vio-. lence without committing violence themselves; 17 percent of women committed violence with impunity. By 1969, the same 17 percent fell victim to unreciprocated violence, but only five percent were allowed to commit violence with impunity.

The relative share of the sexes in the distribution of violence roles reflects these shifts. On the whole, women were represented less in all violence roles. But, as has been noted, their share of victims hurt and especially killed was greater than their share of violents and killers, while the male proportions were the reverse.

The percentage of women in the entire fictional population increased slowly as the share of violent characterizations declined. The only female violence roles that increased in the same or greater proportion than the number of women in the fictional population were their share of all victims and of the killed. Women's share of all victims increased from 12 to 15 percent, and their proportion of all killed rose from six to 17 percent. The sex balance of those killed shifted from one woman for every 16 men in 1967 to one woman for every five men in 1969.

These shifts of fate and power position appeared to be the result of selective reductions in violence roles. These reductions, by following existing ground rules, only enhanced the inherent biases of the pattern. When violents were cut, they were least likely to be cut from the ranks of those whose violence was most essential for the performance of the symbolic functions and dramatic purposes of the drama: the free, the independent, the powerful. These are typically male roles. But since the more powerful and more violent also require the most victims, the less free, independent, and dramatically useful or powerful groups must supply a disproportionate share of the victims. These target groups became increasingly passive, for they absorbed most of the cut in active, aggressive violence. The pattern was not so much one of declining violence (for the overall prevalence and rate of violence did not decrease) as one of the increasing victimization and simultaneous pacification of the underdog under the impact of the more concentrated and relatively even higher levels of punishment meted out by the more powerful.

The dynamics of the sex differences in violence roles has illustrated the dynamics of power in television drama. But analysis showed that women's roles were involved both as an element and as an index of the balance of violent power in most other groups.

Young and old. Age does not affect violence as much as sex. An average of six in ten children, nearly seven in ten young adults, over six in ten middle-aged, and over five in ten old characters were involved in some violence. The level of involvement would be expected to drop most where there is least necessity for it, but remain where it is most essential to the dramatic tasks and social functions to be performed. This appeared to be true by the drop in the youngest and the steady rates in the young adult groups. The small number of old characters makes that category unreliable. The large group of middle-aged (345 for the three years) shows a decided drop in violent characterizations, perhaps greater than might be expected from the heavy and essential involvement of middle-aged characters in dramatic violence.

The role of women may be indicative of the reasons for certain configurations and trends in any category. If we examine the percent of middle-aged violents and victims separately by sex, we find that women indeed play their role more intensively in the middle-aged category than in the context of all characters. The sharp and disproportionate drop in the percentage of violent middle-aged women is clearly responsible for the marked decline shown in that age category (note tables 96 and 97).

The middle-aged contribute more than their proportional share of killers and especially of killed to the fictional population. (Old people are just more likely to be killed than younger people.) Most middle-aged violence and all middle-aged killing shifted to males. The rising middle-aged female population appeared continually to be victimized, even as they were being pacified. The marital status involved in these findings will be discussed below.

Marital status. Most interpersonal conflict and violence in life occurs in the context of the most frequent and intimate interpersonal relationships—the family. But real-life sources of violence are only tangentially relevant to their symbolic functions. When reality interferes, it is avoided or transformed. That appears to be the case with regard to the relationship of violence to marital status.

Married (and about-to-be-married) characters were less frequently involved in violence than the unmarried (including those for whom there was no indication of marital status). Violence also declined more among the married than the unmarried. Further examination indicated that a major part of the reason was the different and shifting composition of the two groups.

The unmarried lead characters were overwhelmingly male. The proportion of women among single characters never went much above two in ten. The married population, on the other hand, was more than one-third female. Violence, as we have seen, fell more rapidly as a characteristic of female than of male roles. Hence the lower level and general decline of violent characterizations was among married and about-to-be-married characters.

However, a separate examination of violence roles by sex yields some additional findings of interest. The frequency of unmarried male violence and victimization was, as would be expected, somewhat higher than that of all males, but the pattern was the same. Married male violence was substantially lower and steady.

Women were, of course, generally less violent than the men, and the difference increased over the years. But single women were much more likely to fall victim of violence than married women, and the relative rate of victimization increased. Married women, on the other hand, started from a different power position to arrive at the same relative standing.

In 1967, married women were more likely to be violents (42 percent) than victims (37 percent), and they were more violent even than married men (36 percent). But the frequency of married women violents fell from 42 percent of all married women in 1967 to 17 percent in 1969. The frequency of married women victims fell from 37 percent to 28 percent. The rates of both violence and victimization among married men remained stable.

Therefore, the largest change relevant to the trends in violence and marital status was the striking pacification of the married woman, and her relegation to the same fate of relatively increasing victimization as was the lot of all women.

In the context of the male-dominated and power- and violence-oriented world of television drama, married women have often been seen by writers and analysts as potentially disturbing and even punitive conscience-figures. The success of motherless family situation shows and of the lovable "bachelor father" types has been explained on that basis. The share of unmarried and of married characters in the different violence roles (table 101) provides further insight into the "politics" of sex and marriage in the world of television plays.

While nearly three-quarters of all male dramatic leads were unmarried, only about half of all female leads were single. So the world of the single character was largely male; it comprised most males (and the more violent males) seen in television plays. The world of married characters was one-third female; half of all women characters inhabited it. Not surprisingly, married characters were represented less and singles more in all violence roles.

But married women again played a special role. They comprised a much larger proportion of all married characters than did single girls of all single characters. Therefore, violence committed and suffered by married women was a larger proportion of all violence roles among the married than was single-girl-violence among all unmarried. Numbering 17 percent of all unmarried characters, single women committed nine percent of the violence and suffered 12 percent of the victimization of all single characters. Numbering 32 percent of the married characters, married women committed 27 percent of the violence and suffered 20 percent of the victimization of all married characters. The implication was that married women were more dangerous than single girls, and also more vulnerable. But single girls were more likely to be victims than violents, while—at least on the average for the three years—married women administered more punishment than they suffered. It has been noted before that the trend has been to pacify the married woman and to reduce, if not eliminate, this menace to male power on television.

Occupations. This study focused on four occupational categories closely related to the dramatic requirements of television and the symbolic tasks of violence. These were the challengers, the protectors, the enforcers of law and order, and (one other sizeable occupational category that does not necessarily symbolize social conflict and power but rather projects the television industry's own self-image) the entertainers. The challengers are professionals engaged in illegal business of a domestic or international nature. The protectors are members of some armed forces, and the enforcers are the agents of law and of crime detection.

The law-and-order population balance shifted slightly in favor of the enforcers, and its complexion changed toward the relative pacification of challengers. The proportion of criminals declined from ten to seven percent of all characters. Law enforcement and crime detection occupied nearly seven percent of all characters in 1967, and increased to equal or surpass the proportion of criminals. Military occupations, however, declined from over seven to less than four percent. Entertainers (comprising roles in show business, sports, mass media, and the popular arts) increased in proportion from eight to 11 percent of all characters.

Trends in violence roles, shown in Table 102, reflect falling levels of violence among the illegals, sharp fluctuations among lawmen and the military, and some overall drop in violence among entertainers. The pattern suggests that the violent activity of criminals was cut, but that of lawmen and the military ranged up and down (and, on the whole, increased in a less lethal form) in an apparently complementary fashion. When military violence fell in 1968, violence committed and suffered by police agents rose as if to fill a void on the side of the law. The proportion of entertainers involved in violence dropped, but their percentage of violent victims (those both committing and suffering violence) more than doubled. The involvement of women in illegal and entertainment occupations (the only two of the selected categories in which women were involved) played a part in the changing complexion of violence in the two groups.

A separate examination of violence roles in each group fills the gaps in the pattern. In the illegal occupations, eight of ten committed and nine of ten suffered violence in both 1967 and 1968. In those years, the number of criminals victimized without committing violence was negligible. By 1969, illegal violents declined to 54 percent and victims to 68 percent of the criminal population, but those who fell victims of violence without committing (or before having a chance to commit) violence rose to nearly one in four. The relative pacification of criminals applied to both men and women. But the few women criminals doubled in number (from two to four a week) and enhanced the effect while remaining relatively more likely to be victimized than the men. The overall picture was of a less violent and apparently less victimized criminal element, but one that was, in fact, more vulnerable to violent attack because it was less able to inflict violence upon its opponents.

Most of these opponents were, of course, their occupational counterparts—the agents of crime detection and law enforcement. Starting from a minority representation and power position, the lawmen achieved numerical equality and balance-of-power superiority. While criminal violence fell and nonviolent vulnerability rose, lawmen's violence did not decline. More important, the agents' vulnerability to violent attack and ability to inflict punishment with impunity shifted dramatically. In the year when criminal violence was highest (1968), the number of nonviolent police victims of violence (negligible the year before) shot up to one in four, then fell to one in seven in 1969. Meanwhile, the proportion of lawmen who only inflicted violence but did not suffer from it rose from 19 percent in 1967 to 22 percent in 1968 and 27 percent in 1969. Police violence of a unilateral or preventive nature appeared to have overcome the rise in police victimization. The sequence, then, might be: high criminal violence; a sharp rise in police victimization, provoking even more massive unilateral police violence; the relative pacification of criminals and their growing vulnerability to violent attack, all against the background of the massing of forces of the law.

Soldiers and entertainers provided different and contrasting patterns. Soldiers declined in number but, after a drop in 1968, increased their violent activities. (The protectors of a national order uphold a variety of foreign and domestic interests. This involves a variety of symbolic functions and yields no clear pattern without a longer and more detailed analysis.) A decline in the number and lethal activity of members of the armed forces was found, yet their overall violence fluctuated regardless of their numbers. In 1967 they appeared not much more violent, in 1968 much less violent, than the average dramatic character in television, as if they were switching from wartime to peacetime armies. In 1969, however, they led criminals and lawmen in both violence and victimization. In any case, in 1967 and 1968 no soldier was shown inflicting violence with impunity, while an occasional soldier each year became the victim of violence he did not or could not return. Unlike lawmen, most of whom were in domestic service, soldiers did not appear to gain in unpunished violence. The diffusion of armies in the world of television and the ambivalence of military life in war, peace, and peacetime war, permitted sheer victimization but inhibited roles of the unpunished (and thus usually righteous) violent soldier.

Entertainers in the fictional world occupy a special position. They project the self-image of the talent industry, provide a favorite staple of stock parts, and form the single largest peaceful occupational category. Their number roughly equals that of criminals or of law enforcers. What the illegals lost of their share of the population over the three years, the entertainers gained. As the general population became less violent, the entertainers became more violent. Starting with a mere one violent in every four, the entertainers nearly doubled their violent members even as their total involvement in violence declined. Most of the rising violence was done by characters who previously only took punishment; the proportion of victims who also inflicted violence more than doubled. On the whole, therefore, program control over violence worked to improve the power position of the fictional entertainment group. But while the men within the group became more violent and less easily victimized, the women remained relatively nonviolent and as vulnerable to victimization as were the female criminals. The increase in the number of women entertainers from four to 11 a week meant that the proportionate share of women victims of all entertainers who suffered violence tended to increase. The overall effect, then, became one of growing male pugnacity in the much-victimized entertainment world, with the burden of suffering shifting to a larger corps of female entertainers. There was no evidence to indicate whether such trends were peculiar to this occupational category or were part of a general shift in the balance of power as reflected in those parts of the fictional population that were identified with a profession and in which women played especially sensitive and potentially vulnerable roles.

The violence-related professions, while obviously highly involved in violence, did not represent most of the violence in the world of television drama. The share of each occupation in selected violence roles can be seen in Table 103. Illegals naturally inflicted proportionately more violence. But about nine-tenths of all violence and at least three-quarters of all killing did not involve criminals. The chief symbolic function of violence was moral and social, rarely legal. Recognition of the illegality of violence usually relegated the play to the limited genre of crime or courtroom drama. The 1967-68 analysis found that due process of law was indicated as a consequence of major acts of violence in only two of every ten violent plays.

The legal protectors and enforcers of the social order also engaged in violence in greater proportions than their numbers in the population would suggest, and their ratio of killers to killed was naturally more favorable than that of criminals. But entertainers, who were much less violent, claimed as large a share of all violents as did members of the armed forces and as a group contained as many victims as did all soldiers or all agents of law. Occupations in the fictional world serve functions of characterization and plot. None has the lion's share of all violence, because violence is diffused to serve symbolic functions of power in every segment of that world.

Social class. Social class, however, is a direct but delicate matter of power. Therefore, the symbolic rituals of a society—especially those rituals produced for consumer markets—rarely flaunt naked power based on class distinction alone. When they do, they are likely to be showing the ruthlessness of other times and places. Otherwise, class is a troublesome dramatic element. When class distinctions are apparent at all, they appear to be incidental to other traits, goals, and outcomes.

Television drama in America particularly blurs class distinctions, even if it cannot obscure its dynamics. The vast majority of leading characters can only be classified as members of that elastic "middle class" stretching from the well-to-do professional, entertainer, or executive through the comfortable or careless majority, to the frugal paraprofessional (nurse, reporter, detective). Many are presented outside any regular class structure (adventurers, spies, members of the armed services). Even other classes are easiest and most "entertaining" to present through middle-class eyes, as when a family of impoverished farmers become suburban millionaires, or when the wealthy exurbanite lawyer attempts to make good as a simple farmer among other simple folk.

No more than two in every ten leading roles was distinctively upper-class. Many of them played in settings far away and long ago. Their involvement in violence was greater than that of middle-class characters. Constraints on violence may have helped to shrink the upper-class population from 22 percent of all characters in 1967 to nine percent in 1969. Upper-class involvement in violence was reduced from 74 percent of all upper-class characters in 1967 to 54 percent in 1969. The middle class and mixed-class population increased in size; their involvement in violence fell much less than did that of the upper class: from 72 to 65 percent. Table 104 indicates these trends. A contributing cause may be the tendency to portray more women in the upper class than in other classes. Sex breakdown by class (available only for 1969) shows women comprising 29 percent of the upper-class population, 24 percent of the middle-class and mixed-class population, and none of the lower-class population.

Lower-class characters were few to begin with (four percent in 1967), and dropped to half or less of that number. But they were the most violent of all. Violence, victimization, or both was the lot of all but one of the 17 lower-class characters who played leading roles in the three annual samples. That one escaped involvement in 1969, accounting for the reduction that year. The three-year average rate of victimization and its margin over the rate of violence were higher among the lower-class characters than among all others.

As with upper-class and other relatively "sensitive" roles, killing by or of lower-class characters disappeared. Nevertheless, such killing as there was in 1967 and 1968 yielded a three-year average higher than that of the other classes. The ratio of killers to killed was twice as "favorable" (to killers) in the middle class as in the other classes.

Table 105 gives the relative shares of the classes in violence roles for 1967-69. The upper and lower classes represented more, and the middle class less, than their proportionate shares of characters killed.

Nationality. The nationality of a dramatic character is not an accident of birth. It is another element of the symbolic structure in which persons and actions take on particular significance. When nationality is not used for characterization, it may be assumed from the setting. When the setting itself is unclear or mixed and nationality is irrelevant to character and action, it cannot be reliably assessed. However, it was possible to differentiate the clear from the unclear and mixed cases of nationality and to divide the dramatic population into two groups: Americans and Others.

In comparing these two groups, it should be kept in mind that Americans is the clear-cut category; Others includes both foreign nationals and those for whom no nationality could be established. The image of foreigners is thus blurred by that of mixed and unclear nationals. If we assume that the nationals of the producing country might be presented in a different light from foreigners, this grouping would tend to provide a most conservative estimate of the differences.

More than two-thirds of all characters could be identified as Americans. As is shown in Table 106, a smaller proportion of Americans than' of Others engaged in violence, and the involvement of Americans declined over the years, while that of the Others did not. Over the three years, six in ten Americans but eight in ten Others committed violence, suffered violence, or both. Even greater was the difference in the "both": 36 percent of Americans, but only 57 percent of all Others, committed *and* suffered violence. In other words, foreigners and those not identifiable as Americans, as a group, were increasingly more likely to become involved in violence and to pay a higher price for it than were the Americans.

The different mix of the sexes again contributed to these findings. Nearly three in ten Americans but fewer than two in ten Others were women. A somewhat larger proportion of women contributed to the declining number of violents (and the more slowly declining number of victims) among the Americans. On the other hand, the high and persistent violence of the Others reflected, in part, the smaller proportion of women. Of course, dramatic population mix is not an independent "fact of life." It is, in fact, quite unrelated to actual population figures. But it is related to the message implicit in the symbolic functions of given groups in given settings. If the domestic group appears a little more "feminine" than the rest of the world (within a still overwhelmingly masculine structure), it is not simply because there are more women in it, but because its symbolic tasks call upon that group to perform most familiar scenes of domesticity. The Others, by comparisons, act in the more remote regions of representation and embody most of the symbolic attributes of "pure" masculinity, such as freewheeling action, mobility, and social unrelatedness. These characterizations do not lend themselves to feminine roles. (Which is why the exceptions are often disturbing and the most likely to be muted in any tightening of controls.) These factors help shape the patterns of the groups' relationships to violence.

Among the Americans both violence and victimization declined, but victimization fell more. Among the Others, the relative trends were the reverse; in fact, victimization increased in absolute terms, as well as in relation to the number of violent Others.

Table 107 indicates the shares of the two groups in the different violence roies. The Others represented more violents and victims but fewer killers. The incidence of killing dropped sharply in both groups. But the three-year balance of killers and killed favored the Americans. For every American killed, 2.6 Americans were killers. But for every Other killed, only 1.3 Other characters were able to inflict fatal violence. Like every subordinate group of characters, the Others are especially prone to victimization; as violence ebbs and killing drops, their chances of being victimized become greater. Becoming more violent does not prevent victimization; in fact, it appears to provoke it, especially when the minority group commits the violence. But the role of killer and the lethal balance—the final arbiter of power—remains a prime preserve of the dominant group.

"Reducing violence" thus becomes selective muting of its most morbid and marginal manifestations while enhancing its symbolic utility. The trimming of some commercially sensitive and dramatically problematic scenes from conventional plays works to widen the gap of differential risks in favor of the already dominant groups. The net effect is to sharpen rather than to blur the symbolic functions of violence as dramatic demonstrations cultivating assumptions about social power.

Race. Television drama presents a world of many places and races. The ethnic composition of this world intertwines with other characteristics in the total symbolic structure. Television drama's global population during the observation period was 77 percent white, 70 percent American, and 67 percent white American.

The white majority was 82 percent American, while the nonwhite majority was only 15 percent American. Of those clearly identified as Americans, 95 percent were white, while of the Others only 35 percent could be identified as white. The imbalance of the sexes between the white majority and the nonwhite minority was even more pronounced than that between Americans and Others. Almost three in ten whites but barely one in ten nonwhites were women. Yet, despite the larger percentage of women among both whites and Americans than among all others, fully half of all TV dramatic characters observed were white American males.

Therefore, the population mix of whites combines American male dominance with a substantial female representation. Nonwhites are virtually all male and mostly distant from the American social setting. Although nonwhites comprise the majority of the world's people, and non-American nationalities comprise the bulk of nonwhites, both appear in the position of minorities in the world of television. These features facilitate the development of a symbolic structure in which "whiteness" is largeley associated with American dominance and "nonwhiteness" with the bulk of "other" humanity subordinate to it. It is consistent with the implicit message of this population mix that the findings on the relationship of race and violence (Table 110) present a pattern very similar to that of nationality and violence. The figures show lower and declining engagement among whites, and higher and persisting involvement among nonwhites. The margin between the generally higher proportion of victims and lower proportion of violents was consistently in favor of whites, despite the fact that they had the higher percentage of women (who, in general, suffered more victimization than men).

Nonwhites were more than proportionately represented among violents and especially among victims, but less than proportionately represented among killers (see Table 109). However, as with non-Americans, such killing as nonwhites encountered exacted a higher price from them than from whites. For every white killed, 2.3 whites were killers. But a nonwhite was killed for every nonwhite killer. In the symbolic world of television, nonwhites suffered more and killed less than whites. But when nonwhites killed they died for it, while the white group was more than twice as likely to get away with murder—or to kill in a "good cause" to begin with.

Final outcome. The "good cause," usually embodied in a "good guy," typically leads to the hero's success and a happy outcome. Happiness is goodness on television. The "mistakes" and frailties of the hero may enhance his attractiveness, but the final demonstration of "who is the better man" usually resolves any lingering doubts about the preferred structure traits, values, and power.

Violence is more likely to be reduced where it is already relatively low—among the "happies"—than among the "lesser men," those who supply the unhappy violents and victims. This selective reduction can achieve an overall softening of potentially disturbing mayhem and leave intact, or even tighten, the essential symbolic structure.

Involvement in all kinds of violence dropped most among characters who reached a clearly happy ending in the plays. The relative distribution of violents and victims can be examined in Table 110. "Happy" violents declined most in number, while "happy" victims declined somewhat less. The victimization of the hero is, of course, a more essential dramatic element than his commission of violence—except perhaps in the end. Among the "unhappies," however, the number of violents did not decline, and the proportion of victims fell only to equal that of violents. Those who reached an unhappy fate needed not to be victimized any more—or less—than seemed "fair" to reciprocate their high level of aggression.

When the pressure is on, therefore, the "good guys" victimized by the "bad guys" become less violent (save perhaps for the final blow), while the ill-fated "bad guys" continue to get what they deserve. It is advisable to see if this differential outcome applies evenly to other groups. For example, as the general frequency of violence declined, the proportion of women increased. The percentage of women among the "happies" rose even more (from 22 percent in 1967 to 29 percent in

1969), but that of women among the "unhappies" fell from 13 to seven percent. On the basis of previously reported findings, women can be expected to be less violent but relatively more often victimized than men. Does outcome make a difference in the relative position of women? Table 111 shows that it does.

The pressures on programming that led to a reduction in the number of unhappy women characters resulted in a corresponding decline in violence among ill-fated women. There was no such decline either among men of the same fate or among "happy" women. The increase of victimization among women was left for the "happy" female population to absorb.

This suggests that the shift toward female victimization is not so much an aspect of defeat as of fear and suffering. With an increase in both the proportion of women and their rate of victimization, the complexion of the "happy" population can be expected to change.

The "happies" clearly engaged in less than their proportionate share of violence, although their ratio of killers to killed—a sign of the "final blow"—was naturally more favorable than that of the "unhappies." What, then, was the effect of rising female victimization on the complexion of the "happy" majority?

Males, of course, dominated both groups. But, as indicated in Table 113, women's share of all "unhappies" dropped by 1969 to half its 1967 percentage, and violent women practically disappeared from among those who met an unhappy end. On the other hand, as the share of women among all "happy" characters rose, and as violence among them declined, the proportion of female victims of violence increased from 12 percent in 1967 to 15 percent in 1968 and to 20 percent in 1969. This is greater than the rise of women's share among the "happies" and greater than the increase of female victims among all characters (12, 14, and 15 percent, respectively). Just like a decline in violence, then, a "happy" outcome relegates women to a less favorable treatment than that accorded the dominant male group. The unhappy world of "bad guys" becomes virtually all male, but the "happy heroes" suffer less and the "happy" heroines more than before. The world of the good and the happy appears to need an increasing number of "happy" women victims to suffer the indignities inflicted by the bad guys.

CONCLUSIONS

Violence in prime time and Saturday morning network television drama was, on the whole, no less prevalent in 1969 than it had been in 1967 or 1968. It was, however, less lethal. Cartoons were the most violent, and increasingly so. CBS programs remained the least violent, but by a decreasing margin. The proportion of violent characterizations declined, and killings and casualties dropped sharply, resulting in a general lowering of the overall violence index. The effect of *policy* and program controls was most noticeable in reducing mayhem on certain types of non-cartoon plays produced for television, in shifting some network lineups in the violence "rating game," and in altering the mix of elements in the symbolic structure.

The symbolic structure of a message system defines its own world. Differences in representation direct varying amounts of attention to what exists in that world. Dramatic focus and emphasis signify hierarchies of importance: type casting and fate accent value and power; and the thread of action ties things together into a dynamic whole. Casual, subjective, and selective interpretations and conclusions start from and rest on the basic premises of what exists, what is important, what is right, and what is related to what in the symbolic world.

The freedom of fiction permits the time, space, distance, style, demography, and ethnography of the symbolic world and the fate of men to be bent to the institutional purposes of dramatic mass production and to its rules of social morality. Violence is a pervasive part and instrument of the allocation of values and powers in the symbolic world. It touches most characters, but, of course, it does not touch them equally; sex, age, status, occupation, nationality, race, and the consequent dramatic destinies all play a role in the pattern of allocation. The pattern appears to project the fears, biases, privileges, and wishful thinking of dominant institutions onto a cosmic canvas. The changes apparent over the years shift the burdens of violence and victimization, escalate the already differential risks, skew the actuarial tables, and further load the unequal balance of symbolic powers.

The fundamental function and social role of ritualized dramatic violence is, then, the maintenance of power. The collective lessons taught by drama tend to cultivate a sense of hierarchical values and forces. The conflicts expose the danger of crossing the lines and induce fear of subverting them. Historically, such symbolic functions of myth and ritual socialized people; they grew up knowing how to behave in different roles in order to avoid, as well as to use, violence. The culture of every society cultivates images of self and of the world that tend to reduce the necessity for resorting to social violence to enforce its norms, but that also justify the frequent necessity for doing so.

Changes in the pattern are, then, equally selective. Cuts are made in areas least damaging to and most consistent with the pattern's essential features. Violence may be trimmed, but not everywhere. It may be "degoryfied" or even deglorified (for neither gore nor glory is essential to the pattern), but only in ways that serve the dramatic purposes as well as, if not better than, gore and glory. Writers, producers, directors, and censors will eliminate or soften violent characterizations that run counter to the conventional rules, that demand complexity not easily accepted (or obtained) in television drama, and that may offend commercial sensitivity to selected moral sensibilities. The net effect is not to blur but to heighten dramatic functions and to tighten the symbolic noose of social power.

The frequency of dramatic violence and the shifting ratios of victimization may have important effects on setting levels of expectation and acquiescence, and on generating a climate of fear. But the message of symbolic violence is implicit in whatever amount there is of it; the message is unaffected by overall frequencies. That message has deep roots in the institutional structure. Real acts of social violence are likely to stem from the same stresses that dramatic violence bends to its symbolic purpose. The two structures—symbolic and social—stem from the same social order and serve the same purposes in their own different ways.

This study has shown that symbolic functions rooted in social power relationships are not easily altered. It is doubtful that they can be significantly altered at all without some institutional innovation and social alteration. The evidence of change found by the investigator (mostly along lines of least resistance) suggests that even the best-intentioned program controls introduced into the same basic structures have unanticipated consequences.

It seems appropriate now to point to implications for further study and to such other considerations as the findings suggest:

1. Trend studies of longer duration and comparative scope are needed to confirm or modify and extend the findings of this research. A broader base for such comparison is reported in the tables in Appendix A on the "Enlarged 1969 Sample."

2. Some of the measures developed for this study lend themselves to a comprehensive system of "cultural indicators," yielding periodic reports on symbolic representations of theoretical and social importance. The broader the context, the more reliable and valid would be the determination of each function in the total symbolic structure. Such indicators would provide the type of information for the mass-produced cultural environment that economic indicators provide for the economy, that public opinion polling provides for reflecting verbal responses (without revealing their symbolic premises), that social indicators are proposed to provide for social health and welfare, and that ecological indicators might provide for the physical environment.

3. The effective control of symbolic violence, and the free dramatic use of its essential function to serve the aims of a democratic society, will exact a higher price than we have been willing to pay. When a society attempts to control an industrial process polluting the air only to find that its basic productive powers depend on it, a predicament of major proportions becomes apparent and demands creative and costly institutional, scientific, and technical innovation. All that can—and in time must—be done. Cheaper solutions have limited value; although they may, in the short run, alleviate selected problems, in the long run they

may only disguise a worsening situation. Symbolic production, including the portrayal of violence, when necessary, running counter to its prevailing ritualistic functions, should be encouraged. As real social relations and institutional processes change, the old symbolic rituals become dysfunctional. Indicators of cultural trends can be sensitive measures not only of what mass media produce but also of what society requires for the cultivation of its changing patterns.

4. Two other types of related research are indicated. One is of the institutional processes of creation and decisionmaking in the mass media, particularly in television. The objective would be to specify the diffuse and now largely invisible pressures and controls that shape dramatic—and probably also other—types of symbolic functions in ways that neither the decisionmaker nor the public fully realizes. The other type of related research would investigate what the symbolic functions cultivate in popular conception and social behavior. Such research would relate television exposure not to violent behavior alone, but also to definitions of social situations, values, powers, and aspirations. It would relate exposure to the means of attaining people's aspirations and to the price to be paid for the use of different means by different people. The research would proceed on the assumption, supported by the findings of this study, that symbolic violence is neither a singular concept nor a semantic equivalent for violent behavior but a function implicit in certain basic premises about life, society, and power. Television relates to social behavior as it defines the world beyond one's ken, and cultivates symbolic structures in which violence may—or may not—play an instrumental role.

FOOTNOTES

1. The 1967 and 1968 studies were conducted under contract to the National Commission on the Causes and Prevention of Violence and were included in its task force report *Violence and the Media* (U.S. Government Printing Office, 1969). The 1969 study was done under contract to the Surgeon General's Scientific Advisory Committee on Television and Social Behavior, National Institute of Mental Health, to which this report is submitted. The research reported here revamped and refined procedures, permitting both a fuller utilization of the previous studies and new information in an enriched comparative perspective.

   Thanks for support, advice, and complete assurance of the scientific integrity of the research should go to the staff of the Scientific Advisory Committee, and particularly to its director, Dr. Eli A. Rubinstein. Research associates on this project were Michael F. Eleey and Nancy Tedesco, whose competent technical assistance and collaboration made the work possible. The investigator is also grateful to

Mrs. Kiki Schiller and Mrs. Joyce Wattenberger for their skillfull assistance.
2. U.S. Government Printing Office, 1969. A task force report of the National Commission on the Causes and Prevention of Violence.
3. An 84-page listing of all items, annotated with reliability results, is available from the investigator at the cost of reproduction and shipment.
4. George Gerbner, "Cultural Indicators: The Case of Violence in Television Drama," *The Annals* of the American Academy of Political and Social Science, 1970, **388**, 69-81.

Appendix A: Tabulation of findings

Table 1: Measures and indicators: all networks, all programs

	One week's prime time and Saturday morning programs in				Enlarged 1969 sample
	1967	1968	1969	1967-69	
SAMPLES (100%)	N	N	N	N	N
Programs (plays) analyzed	96	87	98	281	121
Program hours analyzed	62.00	58.50	61.75	182.25	71.75
Leading characters analyzed	240	215	307	762	377

MEASURES OF VIOLENCE

Prevalence	%	%	%	%	%
(%P) Programs containing violence	81.2	81.6	80.6	81.1	83.5
Program hours containing violence	83.2	87.0	82.0	84.0	83.2
Rate	N	N	N	N	N
Number of violent episodes	478	394	483	1355	630
(R/P) Rate per all programs (plays)	5.0	4.5	4.9	4.8	5.2
(R/H) Rate per all hours	7.7	6.7	7.8	7.4	8.8
Roles (% of leading characters)	%	%	%	%	%
Violents (committing violence)	55.8	49.3	46.6	50.3	48.5
Victims (subjected to violence)	64.6	55.8	57.7	59.3	58.9
(%V) All those involved in violence either as violents or as victims or both	73.3	65.1	64.2	67.3	66.3
Killers (committing fatal violence)	12.5	10.7	3.3	8.3	3.7
Killed (victims of lethal violence)	7.1	3.7	2.0	4.1	2.1
(%K) All those involved in killing either as killers or as killed or both	18.8	11.6	5.3	11.3	5.5

INDICATORS OF VIOLENCE

Program score: $PS = (\%P) + 2(R/P) + 2(R/H)$	106.6	104.0	106.0	105.5	111.5
Character score: $CS = (\%V) + (\%K)$	92.1	76.7	69.5	78.6	70.8
Violence index: $VI = PS + CS$	198.7	180.7	175.5	184.1	182.3

Table 2: Summary of network and program indicators

	1967	1968	1969	1967-69
ABC				
Program score	117.6	113.5	102.1	110.4
Character score	104.7	79.4	67.9	83.0
Violence index	222.3	192.9	170.0	193.4
CBS				
Program score	84.0	98.7	92.8	92.1
Character score	67.1	68.4	55.9	63.3
Violence index	151.0	167.1	148.7	155.4
NBC				
Program score	118.3	103.8	121.0	114.6
Character score	101.3	83.5	82.8	88.8
Violence index	219.6	187.3	203.8	203.4
Cartoons				
Program score	146.3	155.8	169.4	158.0
Character score	104.8	83.0	91.2	93.3
Violence index	251.1	238.8	260.6	251.3
TV plays				
Program score	98.3	88.1	84.7	90.7
Character score	88.0	69.5	57.4	71.5
Violence index	186.3	157.6	142.1	162.2
Feature films				
Program score	97.5	126.8	103.1	109.5
Character score	84.3	108.7	65.4	84.5
Violence index	181.8	235.5	168.5	194.0
Crime, western, action-adventure				
Program score	125.9	128.1	135.2	129.3
Character score	116.0	100.0	93.2	102.7
Violence index	241.9	228.1	228.4	232.0
Comedy				
Program score	81.3	86.3	102.4	89.3
Character score	59.8	58.0	63.4	60.3
Violence index	141.1	144.3	165.8	149.6

Table 3: Measures and indicators: cartoons, all networks

	One week's prime time and Saturday morning programs in				Enlarged 1969 sample
	1967	1968	1969	1967-69	
SAMPLES (100%)	N	N	N	N	N
Programs (plays) analyzed	32	25	38	95	53
Program hours analyzed	7.00	6.92	8.67	22.59	12.17
Leading characters analyzed	62	47	102	211	146

MEASURES OF VIOLENCE

Prevalence

	%	%	%	%	%
(%P) Programs containing violence	93.7	96.0	97.4	95.8	98.1
Program hours containing violence	94.3	92.8	96.1	94.5	97.2

Rate

	N	N	N	N	N
Number of violent episodes	151	162	254	567	370
(R/P) Rate per all programs (plays)	4.7	6.5	6.7	6.0	7.0
(R/H) Rate per all hours	21.6	23.4	29.3	25.1	30.4

Roles (% of leading characters)

	%	%	%	%	%
Violents (committing violence)	72.6	66.0	70.6	54.0	67.1
Victims (subjected to violence)	83.9	76.6	85.3	82.9	80.1
(%V) All those involved in violence either as violents or as victims or both	90.3	78.7	90.2	87.6	87.0
Killers (committing fatal violence)	4.8	4.3	0.0	2.4	0.7
Killed (victims of lethal violence)	9.7	0.0	1.0	19.4	1.4
(%K) All those involved in killing either as killers or as killed or both	14.5	4.3	1.0	5.7	2.1

INDICATORS OF VIOLENCE

Program score:					
PS=(%P)+2(R/P)+2(R/H)	146.3	155.8	169.4	158.0	172.9
Character score:					
CS=(%V)+(%K)	104.8	83.0	91.2	93.3	89.1
Violence index:					
VI=PS+CS	251.1	238.8	260.6	251.3	262.0

Table 4: Measures and indicators: TV plays, all networks

	One week's prime time and Saturday morning programs in				Enlarged 1969 sample
	1967	1968	1969	1967-69	
SAMPLES (100%)	N	N	N	N	N
Programs (plays) analyzed	58	55	52	165	60
Program hours analyzed	42.50	36.58	36.58	115.66	43.08
Leading characters analyzed	159	145	176	480	202

MEASURES OF VIOLENCE

Prevalence	%	%	%	%	%
(%P) Programs containing violence	74.1	72.7	67.3	71.5	70.0
Program hours containing violence	81.2	80.6	76.8	79.6	77.0
Rate	N	N	N	N	N
Number of violent episodes	298	168	187	653	218
(R/P) Rate per all programs (plays)	5.1	3.1	3.6	4.0	3.6
(R/H) Rate per all hours	7.0	4.6	5.1	5.6	5.1
Roles (% of leading characters)	%	%	%	%	%
Violents (committing violence)	49.7	40.7	34.7	41.5	37.1
Victims (subjected to violence)	59.1	46.9	42.6	49.4	44.6
(%V) All those involved in violence either as violents or as victims or both	67.3	57.2	50.0	57.9	52.5
Killers (committing fatal violence)	15.7	11.0	5.1	10.4	5.9
Killed (victims of lethal violence)	6.3	4.1	2.3	4.2	2.5
(%K) All those involved in killing either as killers or as killed or both	20.7	12.4	7.4	13.3	7.9

INDICATORS OF VIOLENCE

Program score: PS=(%P)+2(R/P)+2(R/H)	98.3	88.1	84.7	90.7	87.4
Character score: CS=(%V)+(%K)	88.0	69.6	57.4	71.2	60.4
Violence index: VI=PS+CS	186.3	157.7	142.1	161.9	147.8

Table 5: Measures and indicators: feature films, all networks

| | One week's prime time and Saturday morning programs in | | | | Enlarged 1969 sample |
	1967	1968	1969	1967-69	
SAMPLES (100%)	N	N	N	N	N
Programs (plays) analyzed	6	7	8	21	8
Program hours analyzed	12.50	15.00	16.50	44.00	16.50
Leading characters analyzed	19	23	29	71	29

MEASURES OF VIOLENCE

Prevalence	%	%	%	%	%
(%P) Programs containing violence	83.3	100.0	87.5	90.5	87.5
Program hours containing violence	84.0	100.0	86.4	90.0	86.4

Rate	N	N	N	N	N
Number of violent episodes	29	64	42	135	42
(R/P) Rate per all programs (plays)	4.8	9.1	5.3	6.4	5.3
(R/H) Rate per all hours	2.3	4.3	2.5	3.1	2.5

Roles (% of leading characters)	%	%	%	%	%
Violents (committing violence)	52.6	69.6	34.5	50.7	34.5
Victims (subjected to violence)	47.4	69.6	51.7	56.3	51.7
(%V) All those involved in violence either as violents or as victims or both	68.4	87.0	58.6	70.4	58.6
Killers (committing fatal violence)	10.5	21.7	3.4	11.3	3.4
Killed (victims of lethal violence)	5.3	8.7	3.4	5.6	3.4
(%K) All those involved in killing either as killers or as killed or both	15.8	21.7	6.9	14.1	6.9

INDICATORS OF VIOLENCE

Program score: PS=(%P)+2(R/P)+2(R/H)	97.5	126.8	103.1	109.5	103.1
Character score: CS=(%V)+(%K)	84.2	108.7	65.5	84.5	65.5
Violence index: VI=PS+CS	181.7	235.5	168.6	194.0	168.6

Table 6: Measures and indicators: crime, western, action-adventure, all networks

| | One week's prime time and Saturday morning programs in | | | | Enlarged 1969 sample |
	1967	1968	1969	1967-69	
SAMPLES (100%)	N	N	N	N	N
Programs (plays) analyzed	64	54	63	181	82
Program hours analyzed	47.60	39.20	33.25	120.05	40.25
Leading characters analyzed	164	135	190	489	248

MEASURES OF VIOLENCE

Prevalence

		%	%	%	%	%
(%P)	Programs containing violence	95.3	98.1	96.8	96.7	97.6
	Program hours containing violence	94.3	98.7	96.5	96.4	97.1

Rate

		N	N	N	N	N
	Number of violent episodes	419	341	418	1178	559
(R/P)	Rate per all programs (plays)	6.5	6.3	6.6	6.5	6.8
(R/H)	Rate per all hours	8.8	8.7	12.6	9.8	13.9

Roles (% of leading characters)

		%	%	%	%	%
	Violents (committing violence)	72.6	65.9	64.2	67.5	63.7
	Victims (subjected to violence)	80.5	73.3	77.4	77.3	75.4
(%V)	All those involved in violence either as violents or as victims or both	89.0	82.2	85.3	85.7	84.3
	Killers (committing fatal violence)	18.3	16.3	4.7	12.5	5.2
	Killed (victims of lethal violence)	9.8	5.2	3.2	5.9	3.2
(%K)	All those involved in killing either as killers or as killed or both	26.8	17.8	7.9	17.0	8.1

INDICATORS OF VIOLENCE

	1967	1968	1969	1967-69	Enlarged 1969 sample
Program score: $PS = (\%P) + 2(R/P) + 2(R/H)$	125.9	128.1	135.2	129.3	139.0
Character score: $CS = (\%V) + (\%K)$	115.8	100.0	93.2	102.7	92.4
Violence index: $VI = PS + CS$	241.7	228.1	228.4	232.0	231.4

Table 7: Measures and indicators: comedy, all networks

| | One week's prime time and Saturday morning programs in | | | | Enlarged 1969 sample |
	1967	1968	1969	1967-69	
SAMPLES (100%)	N	N	N	N	N
Programs (plays) analyzed	44	42	48	134	60
Program hours analyzed	24.30	20.20	19.07	64.07	22.32
Leading characters analyzed	107	81	82	270	101

MEASURES OF VIOLENCE

Prevalence	%	%	%	%	%
(%P) Programs containing violence	65.9	66.7	70.8	67.9	73.3
Program hours containing violence	57.30	68.4	55.1	57.6	61.4

Rate	N	N	N	N	N
Number of violent episodes	122	134	216	472	324
(R/P) Rate per all programs (plays)	2.8	3.2	4.5	3.5	5.4
(R/H) Rate per all hours	4.9	6.6	11.3	7.7	14.51

Roles (% of leading characters)	%	%	%	%	%
Violents (committing violence)	37.4	38.3	40.2	38.5	47.5
Victims (subjected to violence)	46.7	43.2	61.0	50.0	68.3
(%V) All those involved in violence either as violents or as victims or both	55.1	53.1	63.4	57.0	70.3
Killers (committing fatal violence)	3.7	4.9	0.0	3.0	0.0
Killed (victims of lethal violence)	0.9	0.0	0.0	0.4	0.0
(%K) All those involved in killing either as killers or as killed or both	4.7	4.9	0.0	3.3	0.0

INDICATORS OF VIOLENCE

Program score: $PS=(\%P)+2(R/P)+2(R/H)$	81.3	86.3	102.4	89.3	113.1
Character score: $CS=(\%V)+(\%K)$	59.8	58.0	63.4	60.3	70.3
Violence index: $VI=PS+CS$	141.1	144.3	165.8	149.6	183.4

Table 8: Measures and indicators: ABC, all programs

| | One week's prime time and Saturday morning programs in | | | | Enlarged 1969 sample |
	1967	1968	1969	1967-69	
SAMPLES (100%)	N	N	N	N	N
Programs (plays) analyzed	35	22	34	91	39
Program hours analyzed	22.00	17.50	20.00	59.50	22.50
Leading characters analyzed	86	63	109	258	127

MEASURES OF VIOLENCE

Prevalence	%	%	%	%	%
(%P) Programs containing violence	88.6	90.9	76.5	84.6	76.9
Program hours containing violence	90.9	94.3	71.3	85.3	70.0
Rate	N	N	N	N	N
Number of violent episodes	195	111	161	467	168
(R/P) Rate per all programs (plays)	5.6	5.0	4.7	5.1	4.3
(R/H) Rate per all hours	8.9	6.3	8.1	7.8	7.5
Roles (% of leading characters)	%	%	%	%	%
Violents (committing violence)	62.8	55.6	44.0	53.1	41.7
Victims (subjected to violence)	72.1	57.1	53.2	60.5	48.8
(%V) All those involved in violence either as violents or as victims or both	82.6	66.7	61.5	69.8	57.5
Killers (committing fatal violence)	14.0	12.7	3.7	9.3	3.1
Killed (victims of lethal violence)	8.1	1.6	2.7	4.3	2.4
(%K) All those involved in killing either as killers or as killed or both	22.1	12.7	6.4	13.2	5.5

INDICATORS OF VIOLENCE

Program score: $PS=(\%P)+2(R/P)+2(R/H)$	117.6	113.5	102.1	110.4	100.5
Character score: $CS=(\%V)+(\%K)$	104.7	79.4	67.9	83.0	63.0
Violence index: $VI=PS+CS$	222.3	192.9	170.0	193.4	163.5

Table 9: Selected measures, ABC cartoons

| | | One week's prime time and Saturday morning programs in | | | | Enlarged 1969 sample |
		1967	1968	1969	1967-69	
SAMPLES (100%)		N	N	N	N	N
	Programs (plays) analyzed	13	4	16	33	18
	Program hours analyzed	3.00	1.50	3.50	8.00	4.00
Prevalence		%	%	%	%	%
(%P)	Programs containing violence	100.0	100.0	100.0	100.0	100.0
	Program hours containing violence	100.0	100.0	100.0	100.0	100.0
Rate		N	N	N	N	N
	Number of violent episodes	70	26	95	191	99
(R/P)	Rate per all programs (plays)	5.4	6.5	5.9	5.8	5.5
(R/H)	Rate per all hours	23.3	17.3	27.1	23.9	24.8
	Program score: PS=(%P)+2(R/P)+2(R/H)	157.4	147.6	166.0	159.4	160.6

Table 10: Selected measures, ABC noncartoon programs

| | | One week's prime time and Saturday morning programs in | | | | Enlarged 1969 sample |
		1967	1968	1969	1967-69	
SAMPLES (100%)		N	N	N	N	N
	Programs (plays) analyzed	22	18	18	58	21
	Program hours analyzed	19.00	16.00	16.50	51.50	18.50
Prevalence		%	%	%	%	%
(%P)	Programs containing violence	81.8	88.9	55.6	75.9	57.1
	Program hours containing violence	89.5	93.8	65.2	83.0	63.5
Rate		N	N	N	N	N
	Number of violent episodes	125	85	66	276	69
(R/P)	Rate per all programs (plays)	5.7	4.7	3.7	4.8	3.3
(R/H)	Rate per all hours	6.6	5.3	4.0	5.4	3.7
	Program score: PS=(%P)+2(R/P)+2(R/H)	106.4	108.9	71.0	96.3	71.1

Table 11: Selected measures, ABC crime, western, action-adventure

| | One week's prime time and Saturday morning programs in | | | | Enlarged 1969 sample |
	1967	1968	1969	1967-69	
SAMPLES (100%)	N	N	N	N	N
Programs (plays) analyzed	25	16	24	65	26
Program hours analyzed	18.60	12.50	12.25	43.35	12.75
Prevalence	%	%	%	%	%
(%P) Programs containing violence	100.0	100.0	100.0	100.0	100.0
Program hours containing violence	100.0	100.0	100.0	100.0	100.0
Rate	N	N	N	N	N
Number of violent episodes	170	99	154	423	158
(R/P) Rate per all programs (plays)	6.8	6.2	6.4	6.5	6.1
(R/H) Rate per all hours	9.1	7.9	12.6	9.8	12.4
Program score: PS=(%P)+2(R/P)+2(R/H)	131.8	128.2	138 0	132.6	137.0

Table 12: Selected measures, ABC comedy

| | One week's prime time and Saturday morning programs in | | | | Enlarged 1969 sample |
	1967	1968	1969	1967-69	
SAMPLES (100%)	N	N	N	N	N
Programs (plays) analyzed	13	6	16	35	18
Program hours analyzed	6.00	6.00	7.85	19.85	8.85
Prevalence	%	%	%	%	%
(%P) Programs containing violence	76.9	100.0	62.5	74.3	66.6
Program hours containing violence	58.3	100.0	39.5	63.5	46.3
Rate	N	N	N	N	N
Number of violent episodes	45	32	57	134	77
(R/P) Rate per all programs (plays)	3.5	5.3	3.6	3.8	4.3
(R/H) Rate per all hours	7.5	5.3	7.3	6.8	8.7
Program score: PS=(%P)+2(R/P)+2(R/H)	98.9	121.2	84.3	95.5	92.6

Table 13: Measures and indicators: CBS, all programs

	One week's prime time and Saturday morning programs in				Enlarged 1969 sample
	1967	1968	1969	1967-69	
SAMPLES (100%)	N	N	N	N	N
Programs (plays) analyzed	32	35	29	96	44
Program hours analyzed	19.50	20.00	18.00	57.50	24.00
Leading characters analyzed	73	79	93	245	135

MEASURES OF VIOLENCE

Prevalence

		%	%	%	%	%
(%P)	Programs containing violence	65.6	77.1	72.4	71.9	81.8
	Program hours containing violence	70.5	80.0	78.7	76.4	84.0

Rate

		N	N	N	N	N
	Number of violent episodes	111	137	113	361	232
(R/P)	Rate per all programs (plays)	3.5	3.9	3.9	3.8	5.3
(R/H)	Rate per all hours	5.7	6.9	6.3	6.3	9.7

Roles (% of leading characters)

		%	%	%	%	%
	Violents (committing violence)	39.7	40.5	38.7	39.6	49.6
	Victims (subjected to violence)	46.6	51.9	47.3	48.6	57.8
(%V)	All those involved in violence either as violents or as victims or both	53.4	59.5	52.7	55.1	65.2
	Killers (committing fatal violence)	8.2	7.6	1.1	5.3	3.7
	Killed (victims of lethal violence)	6.8	3.8	2.2	4.1	3.0
(%K)	All those involved in killing either as killers or as killed or both	13.7	8.9	3.2	8.2	5.9

INDICATORS OF VIOLENCE

	1967	1968	1969	1967-69	1969 sample
Program score: $PS=(\%P)+2(R/P)+2(R/H)$	84.0	98.7	92.8	92.1	111.8
Character score: $CS=(\%V)+(\%K)$	67.0	68.4	55.9	63.3	71.1
Violence index: $VI=PS+CS$	151.0	167.1	148.7	155.4	182.9

Table 14: Selected measures, CBS cartoons

| | | One week's prime time and Saturday morning programs in | | | | Enlarged 1969 sample |
		1967	1968	1969	1967-69	
SAMPLES (100%)		N	N	N	N	N
	Programs (plays) analyzed	10	13	9	32	20
	Program hours analyzed	2.00	3.00	3.00	8.00	5.50
Prevalence		%	%	%	%	%
(%P)	Programs containing violence	90.0	100.0	88.9	93.8	95.0
	Program hours containing violence	90.0	100.0	88.7	93.3	94.0
Rate		N	N	N	N	N
	Number of violent episodes	44	77	66	187	160
(R/P)	Rate per all programs (plays)	4.4	5.9	7.3	5.8	8.0
(R/H)	Rate per all hours	22.0	25.7	22.0	23.4	29.1
	Program score: PS=(%P)+2(R/P)+2(R/H)	142.8	163.2	147.5	152.2	169.2

Table 15: Selected measures, CBS noncartoon programs

| | | One week's prime time and Saturday morning programs in | | | | Enlarged 1969 sample |
		1967	1968	1969	1967-69	
SAMPLES (100%)		N	N	N	N	N
	Programs (plays) analyzed	22	22	20	64	24
	Program hours analyzed	17.50	17.00	15.00	49.50	18.50
Prevalence		%	%	%	%	%
(%P)	Programs containing violence	54.5	63.6	65.0	60.9	70.8
	Program hours containing violence	68.6	76.5	76.7	73.7	81.1
Rate		N	N	N	N	N
	Number of violent episodes	67	60	47	174	72
(R/P)	Rate per all programs (plays)	3.0	2.7	2.4	2.7	3.0
(R/H)	Rate per all hours	3.8	3.5	3.1	3.5	3.9
	Program score: PS=(%P)+2(R/P)+2(R/H)	68.1	76.0	76.0	73.3	84.6

Table 16: Selected measures, CBS crime, western, action-adventure

| SAMPLES (100%) | One week's prime time and Saturday morning programs in | | | | Enlarged 1969 sample |
	1967	1968	1969	1967-69	
	N	N	N	N	N
Programs (plays) analyzed	18	18	12	48	27
Program hours analyzed	11.00	9.00	5.50	25.50	11.50
Prevalence	%	%	%	%	%
(%P) Programs containing violence	94.4	94.4	91.6	93.8	96.3
Program hours containing violence	97.7	94.4	87.8	94.6	94.2
Rate	N	N	N	N	N
Number of violent episodes	99	107	76	282	195
(R/P) Rate per all programs (plays)	5.5	5.9	6.3	5.9	7.2
(R/H) Rate per all hours	9.0	11.9	13.8	11.1	17.0
Program score: PS=(%P)+2(R/P)+2(R/H)	123.4	130.0	131.8	127.8	144.7

Table 17: Selected measures, CBS comedy

| SAMPLES (100%) | One week's prime time and Saturday morning programs in | | | | Enlarged 1969 sample |
	1967	1968	1969	1967-69	
	N	N	N	N	N
Programs (plays) analyzed	16	21	17	54	26
Program hours analyzed	8.00	7.90	7.50	23.40	9.50
Prevalence	%	%	%	%	%
(%P) Programs containing violence	43.8	61.9	64.7	57.4	76.9
Program hours containing violence	37.5	49.4	62.7	49.6	70.5
Rate	N	N	N	N	N
Number of violent episodes	16	61	66	143	143
(R/P) Rate per all programs (plays)	1.0	2.9	3.9	2.6	5.5
(R/H) Rate per all hours	2.0	7.7	8.8	6.1	15.1
Program score: PS=(%P)+2(R/P)+2(R/H)	49.8	83.1	90.1	74.8	118.1

Table 18: Measures and indicators: NBC, all programs

	One week's prime time and Saturday morning programs in				Enlarged 1969 sample
	1967	1968	1969	1967-69	
SAMPLES (100%)	N	N	N	N	N
Programs (plays) analyzed	29	30	35	94	38
Program hours analyzed	20.50	21.00	23.75	65.25	25.25
Leading characters analyzed	81	73	105	259	115

MEASURES OF VIOLENCE

Prevalence	%	%	%	%	%
(%P) Programs containing violence	89.7	80.0	91.4	87.2	92.1
Program hours containing violence	87.0	87.7	93.7	89.7	94.1
Rate	N	N	N	N	N
Number of violent episodes	172	146	209	527	230
(R/P) Rate per all programs (plays)	5.9	4.9	6.0	5.6	6.1
(R/H) Rate per all hours	8.4	7.0	8.8	8.1	9.1
Roles (% of leading characters)	%	%	%	%	%
Violents (committing violence)	63.0	53.4	56.2	57.5	54.8
Victims (subjected to violence)	72.8	58.9	71.4	68.5	71.3
(%V) All those involved in violence either as violents or as victims or both	81.5	69.9	77.1	76.4	77.4
Killers (committing fatal violence)	14.8	12.3	4.8	10.0	4.3
Killed (victims of lethal violence)	6.2	5.5	1.0	3.9	0.9
(%K) All those involved in killing either as killers or as killed or both	19.8	13.7	5.7	12.4	5.2

INDICATORS OF VIOLENCE

Program score: $PS = (\%P) + 2(R/P) + 2(R/H)$	118.3	103.8	121.0	114.6	122.5
Character score: $CS = (\%V) + (\%K)$	101.3	83.5	82.8	88.8	82.6
Violence index: $VI = PS + CS$	219.6	187.3	203.8	203.4	205.1

Table 19: Selected measures, NBC cartoons

| | | One week's prime time and Saturday morning programs in | | | | Enlarged 1969 sample |
		1967	1968	1969	1967-69	
SAMPLES (100%)		N	N	N	N	N
	Programs (plays) analyzed	9	8	13	30	15
	Program hours analyzed	2.00	2.42	2.17	6.59	2.67
Prevalence		%	%	%	%	%
(%P)	Programs containing violence	88.9	87.5	100.0	93.3	100.0
	Program hours containing violence	90.0	79.2	100.0	89.1	100.0
Rate		N	N	N	N	N
	Number of violent episodes	37	39	93	189	111
(R/P)	Rate per all programs (plays)	4.1	7.4	7.2	6.3	7.4
(R/H)	Rate per all hours	18.5	24.4	42.9	28.7	41.6
	Program score: $PS=(\%P)+2(R/P)+2(R/H)$	134.1	151.1	200.2	163.3	198.0

Table 20: Selected measures, NBC noncartoon programs

| | | One week's prime time and Saturday morning programs in | | | | Enlarged 1969 sample |
		1967	1968	1969	1967-69	
SAMPLES (100%)		N	N	N	N	N
	Programs (plays) analyzed	20	22	22	64	23
	Program hours analyzed	18.50	18.58	21.58	58.66	22.58
Prevalence		%	%	%	%	%
(%P)	Programs containing violence	90.0	77.3	86.4	84.4	87.0
	Program hours containing violence	86.5	88.8	93.0	89.6	93.4
Rate		N	N	N	N	N
	Number of violent episodes	135	87	116	338	119
(R/P)	Rate per all programs (plays)	6.8	4.0	5.3	5.3	5.2
(R/H)	Rate per all hours	7.3	4.7	5.4	5.8	5.3
	Program score: $PS=(\%P)+2(R/P)+2(R/H)$	118.2	94.7	107.8	106.6	108.0

Table 21: Selected measures, NBC crime, western, action-adventure

		One week's prime time and Saturday morning programs in				Enlarged 1969 sample
		1967	1968	1969	1967-69	
SAMPLES (100%)		N	N	N	N	N
	Programs (plays) analyzed	21	20	27	68	29
	Program hours analyzed	18.00	17.70	15.50	51:20	16.00
Prevalence		%	%	%	%	%
(%P)	Programs containing violence	90.5	100.0	96.3	95.6	96.5
	Program hours containing violence	86.1	100.0	97.0	94.1	97.0
Rate		N	N	N	N	N
	Number of violent episodes	150	135	188	473	206
(R/P)	Rate per all programs (plays)	7.1	6.8	7.0	7.0	7.1
(R/H)	Rate per all hours	8.3	7.6	12.1	9.2	12.9
	Program score: PS=(%P)+2(R/P)+2(R/H)	121.3	128.8	134.5	128.0	136.5

Table 22: Selected measures, NBC comedy

		One week's prime time and Saturday morning programs in				Enlarged 1969 sample
		1967	1968	1969	1967-69	
SAMPLES (100%)		N	N	N	N	N
	Programs (plays) analyzed	15	15	15	45	16
	Program hours analyzed	10.80	6.30	3.72	20.82	3.97
Prevalence		%	%	%	%	%
(%P)	Programs containing violence	80.0	60.0	86.0	75.5	87.5
	Program hours containing violence	71.0	35.7	72.9	60.1	74.4
Rate		N	N	N	N	N
	Number of violent episodes	61	41	93	195	104
(R/P)	Rate per all programs (plays)	4.1	2.7	6.2	4.3	6.5
(R/H)	Rate per all hours	5.6	6.5	25.0	9.4	26.2
	Program score: PS=(%P)+2(R/P)+2(R/H)	99.4	78.4	148.4	102.9	152.9

Table 23: Distribution of selected measures by format

	Totals N (100%)	Cartoons N	%	TV play N	%	Feature film N	%
1967							
All programs	96	32	33.3	58	60.4	6	6.3
Violent programs	78	30	38.5	43	55.1	5	6.4
Violent episodes	478	151	31.6	298	62.3	29	6.1
All leading characters	240	62	25.8	159	66.3	19	7.9
Characters involved							
in any violence	176	56	31.8	107	60.8	13	7.4
in killing	45	9	20.0	33	73.3	3	6.7
1968							
All programs	87	25	28.7	55	63.2	7	8.0
Violent programs	71	24	33.8	40	56.3	7	9.9
Violent episodes	394	162	41.1	168	42.6	64	16.2
All leading characters	215	47	21.9	145	67.4	23	10.7
Characters involved							
in any violence	140	37	26.4	83	59.3	20	14.3
in killing	25	2	8.0	18	72.0	5	20.0
1969							
All programs	98	38	38.8	52	53.1	8	8.1
Violent programs	79	37	46.8	35	44.3	7	8.9
Violent episodes	483	254	52.6	187	38.7	42	8.7
All leading characters	307	102	33.2	176	57.3	29	9.4
Characters involved							
in any violence	197	92	46.7	88	44.7	17	8.6
in killing	16	1	6.3	13	81.2	2	12.5
1967-69							
All programs	281	95	33.8	165	58.7	21	7.5
Violent programs	228	91	39.9	118	51.8	19	8.3
Violent episodes	1355	567	41.8	653	48.2	135	10.0
All leading characters	762	211	27.7	480	63.0	71	9.3
Characters involved							
in any violence	513	185	36.1	278	54.2	50	9.7
in killing	86	12	14.0	64	74.4	10	11.6
Enlarged 1969 sample							
All programs	121	53	43.8	60	49.6	8	6.6
Violent programs	101	52	51.5	42	41.6	7	6.9
Violent episodes	630	370	58.7	218	34.6	42	6.7
All leading characters	377	146	38.7	202	53.6	29	7.7
Characters involved							
in any violence	250	127	50.8	106	42.4	17	6.8
in killing	21	3	14.3	16	76.2	2	9.5

Table 24: Distribution of selected measures by program type

	Totals N (100%)	CWWA* N	%	Comedy* N	%
1967					
All programs	96	64	66.7	44	45.8
Violent programs	78	61	78.2	29	37.2
Violent episodes	478	419	87.7	122	25.5
All leading characters	240	164	68.3	107	44.6
Characters involved					
in any violence	176	146	83.0	59	33.5
in killing	45	44	97.8	5	11.1
1968					
All programs	87	54	62.1	42	48.3
Violent programs	71	53	74.6	28	39.4
Violent episodes	394	341	86.5	134	34.0
All leading characters	215	135	62.8	81	37.7
Characters involved					
in any violence	140	111	79.3	43	30.7
in killing	25	24	96.0	4	16.0
1969					
All programs	98	63	64.3	48	49.0
Violent programs	79	61	77.2	34	43.0
Violent episodes	483	418	86.5	216	44.7
All leading characters	307	190	61.8	82	26.7
Characters involved					
in any violence	197	162	82.2	52	26.4
in killing	16	15	93.8	0	0.0
1967-69					
All programs	281	181	64.4	134	47.7
Violent programs	228	175	76.8	91	39.9
Violent episodes	1355	1178	86.9	472	34.8
All leading characters	762	489	64.2	270	35.4
Characters involved					
in any violence	513	419	81.7	154	30.0
in killing	86	83	96.5	90	10.5
Enlarged 1969 sample					
All programs	121	82	67.8	60	49.6
Violent programs	101	80	79.2	46	45.5
Violent episodes	630	559	88.7	324	51.4
All leading characters	377	248	65.8	101	26.8
Characters involved					
in any violence	250	209	83.6	71	28.4
in killing	21	20	95.2	0	0.0

*Program type classifications are not mutually exclusive.

Table 25: Distribution of selected measures of violence on ABC

	Totals N (100%)	Cartoons * N	%	CWAA * N	%	Comedy * N	%
1967							
All programs	35	13	37.1	25	71.4	13	37.1
Violent programs	31	13	41.9	25	80.6	10	32.3
Violent episodes	195	70	35.9	170	87.2	45	23.1
1968							
All programs	22	4	18.2	16	72.7	6	27.3
Violent programs	20	4	20.0	16	80.0	6	30.0
Violent episodes	111	26	23.4	99	89.2	32	28.8
1969							
All programs	34	16	47.1	24	70.6	16	47.1
Violent programs	26	16	61.5	24	92.3	10	38.5
Violent episodes	161	95	59.0	154	95.7	57	35.4
1967-69							
All programs	91	33	36.3	65	71.4	35	38.5
Violent programs	77	33	42.9	65	84.4	26	33.8
Violent episodes	467	191	40.9	423	90.6	134	28.7
Enlarged 1969 sample							
All programs	39	18	46.2	26	66.7	18	46.2
Violent programs	30	18	60.0	26	86.7	12	40.0
Violent episodes	168	99	58.9	158	94.0	77	45.8

*Classifications are not mutually exclusive

Table 26: Distribution of selected measures of violence on CBS

		Totals N (100%)	Cartoons* N	Cartoons* %	CWAA* N	CWAA* %	Comedy* N	Comedy* %
1967								
	All programs	32	10	31.3	18	56.3	16	50.0
	Violent programs	21	9	42.9	17	81.0	7	33.0
	Violent episodes	111	44	39.6	99	89.2	16	14.4
1968								
	All programs	35	13	37.1	18	51.4	21	60.0
	Violent programs	27	13	48.1	17	63.0	13	48.1
	Violent episodes	137	77	56.2	107	78.1	61	44.5
1969								
	All programs	29	9	31.0	12	41.4	17	58.6
	Violent programs	21	8	38.1	11	52.4	11	52.4
	Violent episodes	113	66	58.4	76	67.3	66	58.4
1967-69								
	All programs	96	32	33.3	48	50.0	54	56.3
	Violent programs	69	30	43.5	45	65.2	31	44.9
	Violent episodes	361	187	51.8	282	78.1	143	39.6
Enlarged 1969 sample								
	All programs	44	20	45.5	27	61.4	26	59.1
	Violent programs	36	19	52.8	26	72.2	20	55.6
	Violent episodes	232	160	69.0	195	84.1	143	61.6

*Classifications are not mutually exclusive

Table 27: Distribution of selected measures of violence on NBC

	Totals N (100%)	Cartoons *		CWAA *		Comedy *	
		N	%	N	%	N	%
1967							
All programs	29	9	31.0	21	72.4	15	51.7
Violent programs	26	8	30.8	19	73.1	12	46.2
Violent episodes	172	37	21.5	150	87.2	61	35.5
1968							
All programs	30	8	26.7	20	66.7	15	50.0
Violent programs	24	7	29.2	20	83.3	9	37.5
Violent episodes	146	59	40.4	135	92.5	41	28.1
1969							
All programs	35	13	37.1	27	77.1	15	42.9
Violent programs	32	13	40.6	26	81.3	13	40.6
Violent episodes	209	93	44.5	188	90.0	93	44.5
1967-69							
All programs	94	30	31.9	68	72.3	45	47.9
Violent programs	82	28	34.1	65	79.3	34	41.5
Violent episodes	527	189	35.9	473	89.8	195	37.0
Enlarged 1969 sample							
All programs	38	15	39.5	29	76.3	16	42.1
Violent programs	35	15	42.9	28	80.0	14	40.0
Violent episodes	230	111	48.3	206	89.6	104	45.2

*Classifications are not mutually exclusive

Table 28: Distribution of selected measures by network

	Totals N (100%)	ABC N	%	CBS N	%	NBC N	%
1967							
All programs	96	35	36.5	32	33.3	29	30.2
Violent programs	78	31	39.7	21	26.9	26	33.3
Violent episodes	478	195	40.8	111	23.2	172	36.0
All leading characters	240	86	35.8	73	30.4	81	33.8
Characters involved							
in any violence	176	71	40.3	39	22.2	66	37.5
in killing	45	19	42.2	10	22.2	16	35.6
1968							
All programs	87	22	25.3	35	40.2	30	34.5
Violent programs	71	20	28.2	27	38.2	24	33.8
Violent episodes	394	111	28.2	137	34.8	146	37.0
All leading characters	215	63	29.3	79	36.7	73	34.0
Characters involved							
in any violence	140	42	30.0	47	33.6	51	36.4
in killing	25	8	32.0	7	28.0	10	40.0
1969							
All programs	98	34	34.7	29	29.6	35	35.7
Violent programs	79	26	32.9	21	26.6	32	40.5
Violent episodes	483	101	33.3	113	23.4	209	43.3
All leading characters	307	109	35.5	93	30.3	105	34.2
Characters involved							
in any violence	197	67	34.0	49	24.9	81	41.1
in killing	16	7	43.8	3	18.7	6	37.5
1967-69							
All programs	281	91	32.4	96	34.2	94	33.4
Violent programs	228	77	33.8	69	30.3	82	35.9
Violent episodes	1355	467	34.5	361	26.6	527	35.9
All leading characters	762	258	33.9	245	32.1	259	34.0
Characters involved							
in any violence	513	180	35.1	135	26.3	198	38.6
in killing	86	34	39.5	20	23.3	32	37.2
Enlarged 1969 sample							
All programs	121	39	32.2	44	36.4	38	31.4
Violent programs	101	30	29.7	36	35.6	35	34.7
Violent episodes	630	168	26.7	232	36.8	230	36.5
All leading characters	377	127	33.7	135	35.8	115	30.5
Characters involved							
in any violence	250	73	29.2	88	35.2	89	35.6
in killing	21	7	33.3	8	38.1	6	28.6

Table 29: Network distribution of programs and hours: all networks

	1967 N	1967 %	1968 N	1968 %	1969 N	1969 %	1967 – 69 N	1967 – 69 %	Enlarged 1969 sample N	Enlarged 1969 sample %
ALL PROGRAMS	96	100.0	87	100.0	98	100.0	281	100.0	121	100.0
ABC	35	36.5	22	25.3	34	34.7	91	32.4	39	32.2
CBS	32	33.3	35	40.2	29	29.6	96	34.2	44	36.4
NBC	29	30.2	30	34.5	35	35.7	94	33.4	38	31.4
ALL PROGRAM HOURS	62.00	100.0	58.50	100.0	61.75	100.0	182.25	100.0	71.75	100.0
ABC	22.00	35.5	17.50	29.9	20.00	32.4	59.50	32.6	22.50	31.4
CBS	19.50	31.4	20.00	34.2	18.00	29.1	57.50	31.6	24.00	33.4
NBC	20.50	33.1	21.00	35.9	23.75	38.5	65.25	35.8	25.25	35.2

Table 30: Format distribution of programs and hours: all networks

	1967 N	1967 %	1968 N	1968 %	1969 N	1969 %	1967 – 69 N	1967 – 69 %	Enlarged 1969 sample N	Enlarged 1969 sample %
ALL PROGRAMS	96	100.0	87	100.0	98	100.0	281	100.0	121	100.0
Cartoons	32	33.3	25	28.7	38	38.8	95	33.8	53	43.8
TV plays	58	60.4	55	63.2	52	53.0	165	58.7	60	49.6
Feature films	6	6.3	7	8.1	8	8.2	21	7.5	8	6.6
ALL HOURS	62.00	100.0	58.50	100.0	61.75	100.0	182.25	100.0	71.75	100.0
Cartoons	7.00	11.3	6.92	11.8	8.67	14.1	22.59	12.4	12.17	17.0
TV plays	42.50	68.5	36.58	62.5	36.58	59.2	115.66	63.5	43.08	60.0
Feature films	12.50	20.2	15.00	25.7	16.50	26.7	44.00	24.1	16.50	23.0

Table 31: Crime, western, action-adventure and comedy, programs and hours: all networks

	1967		1968		1969		1967 – 69		Enlarged 1969 sample	
	N	%	N	%	N	%	N	%	N	%
ALL PROGRAMS	96	100.0	87	100.0	98	100.0	281	100.0	121	100.0
CWAA	64	66.7	54	62.1	63	64.3	181	64.4	82	67.8
Comedy	44	45.8	42	48.3	48	49.0	134	47.7	60	49.6
ALL HOURS	62.00	100.0	58.50	100.0	61.75	100.0	182.25	100.0	71.75	100.0
CWAA	47.60	76.8	39.20	67.0	33.25	53.8	120.05	65.9	40.25	56.1
Comedy	24.80	40.0	20.20	34.5	19.07	30.9	64.07	35.2	22.32	31.1

Table 32: Format distribution of programs and hours: ABC

	1967		1968		1969		1967 – 69		Enlarged 1969 sample	
	N	%	N	%	N	%	N	%	N	%
ALL PROGRAMS	35	100.0	22	100.0	34	100.0	91	100.0	39	100.0
Cartoons	13	37.2	4	18.2	16	47.1	33	36.3	18	46.2
TV plays	20	57.1	16	72.7	15	44.1	51	56.0	18	46.2
Feature films	2	5.7	2	9.1	3	8.8	7	7.7	3	7.6
ALL HOURS	22.00	100.0	17.50	100.0	20.00	100.0	59.50	100.0	22.50	100.0
Cartoons	3.00	13.6	1.50	8.6	3.50	17.5	8.00	13.4	4.00	17.8
TV plays	14.50	65.9	12.00	68.6	10.75	53.7	37.25	62.6	12.75	56.7
Feature films	4.50	20.5	4.00	22.8	5.75	28.8	14.25	24.0	5.75	25.5

Table 33: Crime, western, action-adventure and comedy, programs and hours: ABC

	1967		1968		1969		1967 — 69		Enlarged 1969 sample	
	N	%	N	%	N	%	N	%	N	%
ALL PROGRAMS	35	100.0	22	100.0	34	100.0	91	100.0	39	100.0
CWAA	25	71.4	16	72.7	24	70.6	65	71.4	26	66.7
Comedy	13	37.1	6	27.2	16	47.1	35	38.5	18	46.2
ALL HOURS	22.00	100.0	17.50	100.0	20.00	100.0	59.50	100.0	22.50	100.0
CWAA	18.60	84.5	12.50	71.5	12.25	61.0	43.35	72.9	12.75	56.0
Comedy	6.00	27.3	6.00	34.3	7.85	39.3	19.85	33.4	8.85	39.3

Table 34: Format distribution of programs and hours: CBS

	1967		1968		1969		1967 — 69		Enlarged 1969 sample	
	N	%	N	%	N	%	N	%	N	%
ALL PROGRAMS	32	100.0	35	100.0	29	100.0	96	100.0	44	100.0
Cartoons	10	31.2	13	37.1	9	31.0	32	33.3	20	45.5
TV plays	20	62.5	20	57.1	18	62.1	58	60.4	22	50.0
Feature films	2	6.3	2	5.8	2	6.9	6	6.3	2	4.5
ALL HOURS	19.50	100.0	20.00	100.0	18.00	100.0	57.50	100.0	24.00	100.0
Cartoons	2.00	10.3	3.00	15.0	3.00	16.7	8.00	13.9	5.50	22.9
TV plays	13.50	69.2	13.00	65.0	11.00	61.1	37.50	65.2	14.50	60.4
Feature films	4.00	20.5	4.00	20.0	4.00	22.2	12.00	20.9	4.00	16.7

Table 35: Crime, western, action-adventure and comedy, programs and hours: CBS

	1967 N	%	1968 N	%	1969 N	%	1967 – 69 N	%	Enlarged 1969 sample N	%
ALL PROGRAMS	32	100.0	35	100.0	29	100.0	96	100.0	44	100.0
CWAA	18	56.3	18	51.4	12	41.4	48	50.0	27	61.4
Comedy	16	50.0	21	60.0	17	58.6	54	56.3	26	59.1
ALL HOURS	19.50	100.0	20.00	100.0	18.00	100.0	57.50	100.0	24.00	100.0
CWAA	11.00	56.4	9.00	45.0	5.50	30.0	25.50	44.3	11.50	47.9
Comedy	8.00	41.0	7.90	39.5	7.50	41.7	23.40	40.7	9.50	39.5

Table 36: Format distribution of programs and hours: NBC

	1967 N	%	1968 N	%	1969 N	%	1967 – 69 N	%	Enlarged 1969 sample N	%
ALL PROGRAMS	29	100.0	30	100.0	35	100.0	94	100.0	38	100.0
Cartoons	9	31.0	8	26.7	13	37.1	30	31.9	15	39.5
TV plays	18	62.1	19	63.3	19	54.3	56	59.6	20	52.6
Feature films	2	6.9	3	10.0	3	8.6	8	8.5	3	7.9
ALL HOURS	20.50	100.0	21.00	100.0	23.75	100.0	65.25	100.0	25.25	100.0
Cartoons	2.00	9.8	2.42	11.5	2.17	9.1	6.59	10.1	2.67	10.6
TV plays	14.50	70.7	11.58	55.2	14.83	62.5	40.91	62.7	15.83	62.7
Feature films	4.00	19.5	7.00	33.3	6.75	28.4	17.75	27.2	6.75	26.7

Table 37: Crime, western, action-adventure and comedy, programs and hours: NBC

	1967 N	%	1968 N	%	1969 N	%	1967 – 69 N	%	Enlarged 1969 sample N	%
ALL PROGRAMS	29	100.0	30	100.0	35	100.0	94	100.0	38	100.0
CWAA	21	72.4	20	66.7	27	77.1	68	72.3	29	76.3
Comedy	15	51.7	15	50.0	15	42.9	45	47.9	16	42.1
ALL HOURS	20.50	100.0	21.00	100.0	23.75	100.0	65.25	100.0	25.25	100.0
CWAA	18.00	87.8	17.70	84.3	15.50	65.3	51.20	78.5	16.00	63.4
Comedy	10.80	52.7	6.30	30.0	3.72	15.7	20.82	31.9	3.97	15.7

Table 38: Prevalence of violence: all programs, all networks

	1967 N	%	1968 N	%	1969 N	%	1967 – 69 N	%	Enlarged 1969 sample N	%
ALL PROGRAMS	96	100.0	87	100.0	98	100.0	281	100.0	121	100.0
All violence	78	81.2	71	81.6	79	80.6	228	81.1	101	83.5
significant to plot	63	65.6	48	55.2	67	68.4	178	63.3	87	71.9
incidental to plot	15	15.7	23	26.4	12	12.2	50	17.8	14	11.6
ALL HOURS	62.00	100.0	58.50	100.0	61.75	100.0	182.25	100.0	71.75	100.0
All violence	51.59	83.2	50.92	87.0	50.66	82.0	153.17	84.0	59.67	83.2
significant to plot	41.17	66.4	35.17	60.0	41.83	67.7	118.17	64.8	50.09	69.8
incidental to plot	10.42	16.8	15.75	26.9	8.83	14.3	35.00	19.2	9.58	13.4

Table 39: Number and rate of violent episodes: all programs, all networks

	1967		1968		1969		1967 – 69		Enlarged 1969 sample	
	N	%	N	%	N	%	N	%	N	%
ALL VIOLENT EPISODES	478		394		483		1355		630	
Rate per all programs	5.0		4.5		4.9		4.8		5.2	
Rate per violent program	6.1		5.5		6.1		5.9		6.2	
Rate when violence is significant to plot	6.9		6.9		6.7		6.8		6.8	
Rates per all hours	7.7		6.7		7.8		7.4		8.8	
Rate per violent hour	9.3		7.7		9.5		8.8		10.6	
Rate per hour when violence is significant to plot	10.5		9.5		10.7		10.3		11.8	

Table 40: Prevalence of violence: TV plays, all networks

	1967		1968		1969		1967 – 69		Enlarged 1969 sample	
	N	%	N	%	N	%	N	%	N	%
ALL PROGRAMS	58	100.0	55	100.0	52	100.0	165	100.0	60	100.0
All violence	43	74.1	40	72.7	35	67.3	118	71.5	42	70.0
significant to plot	32	55.2	23	41.8	25	48.1	80	48.5	31	51.7
incidental to plot	11	19.0	17	30.9	10	19.2	38	23.0	11	18.3
ALL HOURS	42.50	100.0	36.58	100.0	36.58	100.0	115.66	100.0	43.08	100.0
All violence	34.50	81.2	29.50	80.6	28.08	76.8	92.08	79.6	33.58	77.0
significant to plot	28.50	67.1	20.75	56.7	21.58	59.0	70.83	61.2	26.58	61.7
incidental to plot	6.00	14.1	8.75	23.9	6.50	17.8	21.25	18.4	7.00	16.2

Table 41: Number and rate of violent episodes: TV plays, all networks

	1967	1968	1969	1967 – 69	Enlarged 1969 sample
ALL VIOLENT EPISODES	298	168	187	653	218
Rate per all programs	5.1	3.1	3.6	4.0	3.6
Rate per violent program	6.9	4.2	5.3	5.5	5.2
Rate when violence is significant to plot	8.5	5.7	6.5	7.1	6.2
Rates per all hours	7.0	4.6	5.1	5.6	5.1
Rate per violent hour	8.6	5.7	6.7	7.1	6.5
Rate per hour when violence is significant to plot	9.5	6.3	7.5	8.0	7.2

Table 42: Prevalence of violence: feature films, all networks

	1967		1968		1969		1967 – 69		Enlarged 1969 sample	
	N	%	N	%	N	%	N	%	N	%
ALL PROGRAMS	6	100.0	7	100.0	8	100.0	21	100.0	8	100.0
All violence	5	83.3	7	100.0	7	87.5	19	90.5	7	87.5
significant to plot	3	50.0	4	57.1	6	75.0	13	61.9	6	75.0
incidental to plot	2	33.3	3	42.9	1	12.5	6	28.6	1	12.5
ALL HOURS	12.50	100.0	15.00	100.0	16.50	100.0	44.00	100.0	16.50	100.0
All violence	10.50	84.0	15.00	100.0	14.25	86.4	39.75	90.0	14.25	86.4
significant to plot	6.50	52.0	9.00	60.0	12.25	74.3	27.25	61.9	12.25	74.3
incidental to plot	4.00	32.0	6.00	40.0	2.00	12.2	12.00	27.3	2.00	12.2

Table 43: Number and rate of violent episodes: feature films, all networks

	1967	1968	1969	1967 — 69	Enlarged 1969 sample
ALL VIOLENT EPISODES	29	64	42	135	42
Rate per all programs	4.8	9.1	5.3	6.4	5.3
Rate per violent program	5.8	9.1	6.0	7.1	6.0
Rate when violence is significant to plot	7.3	13.0	5.8	8.4	5.8
Rates per all hours	2.3	4.3	2.5	3.1	2.5
Rate per violent hour	2.8	4.3	2.9	3.4	2.9
Rate per hour when violence is significant to plot	3.4	5.8	2.9	4.0	2.9

Table 44: Prevalence of violence: cartoons, all networks

	1967		1968		1969		1967 — 69		Enlarged 1969 sample	
	N	%	N	%	N	%	N	%	N	%
ALL PROGRAMS	32	100.0	25	100.0	38	100.0	95	100.0	53	100.0
All violence	30	93.7	24	96.0	37	97.4	91	95.8	52	98.1
significant to plot	28	87.5	21	84.0	36	94.7	85	89.5	50	94.3
Incidental to plot	2	6.3	3	12.0	1	2.6	6	6.3	2	3.8
ALL HOURS	7.00	100.0	6.92	100.0	8.67	100.0	22.59	100.0	12.17	100.0
All violence	6.59	94.3	6.42	92.8	8.33	96.1	21.34	94.5	11.83	97.2
Significant to plot	6.17	88.1	5.42	78.3	8.00	92.3	19.59	86.7	11.24	92.4
incidental to plot	0.42	6.0	1.00	14.5	0.33	3.8	1.75	7.7	0.59	4.8

Table 45: Number and rate of violent episodes: cartoons, all networks

	1967	1968	1969	1967 – 69	Enlarged 1969 sample
ALL VIOLENT EPISODES	151	162	254	567	370
Rate per all programs	4.7	6.5	6.7	6.0	7.0
Rate per violent program	5.0	6.8	6.9	6.2	7.1
Rate when violence is significant to plot	5.0	7.1	6.9	6.4	7.3
Rates per all hours	21.6	23.4	29.3	25.1	30.4
Rate per violent hour	22.9	25.2	30.5	26.6	31.3
Rate per hour when violence is significant to plot	22.7	27.7	31.3	27.6	32.4

Table 46: Prevalence of violence. ABC

	1967		1968		1969		1967 – 69		Enlarged 1969 sample	
	N	%	N	%	N	%	N	%	N	%
ALL PROGRAMS	35	100,0	22	100.0	34	100.0	91	100.0	39	100.0
All violence	31	88.6	20	90.9	26	76.5	77	84.6	30	76.9
significant to plot	26	74.3	14	63.6	26	76.5	66	72.5	28	71.8
incidental to plot	5	14.3	6	27.3	0	0.0	11	12.1	2	5.1
ALL HOURS	22.00	100.0	17.50	100.0	20.00	100.0	59.50	100.0	22.50	100.0
All violence	20.00	90.9	16.50	94.3	14.25	71.3	50.75	85.3	15.75	70.0
significant to plot	17.58	79.9	11.00	62.9	14.25	71.3	42.83	72.0	15.00	66.7
incidental to plot	2.42	11.0	5.50	31.4	0.00	0.0	7.92	13.3	0.75	3.3

Table 47: Number and rate of violent episodes: ABC

	1967	1968	1969	1967 – 69	Enlarged 1969 sample
ALL VIOLENT EPISODES	195	111	161	467	168
Rate per all programs	5.6	5.0	4.7	5.1	4.3
Rate per violent program	6.3	5.6	6.2	6.1	5.6
Rate when violence is significant to plot	6.8	6.9	6.2	6.6	5.9
Rates per all hours	8.9	6.3	8.1	7.8	7.5
Rate per violent hour	9.8	6.7	11.3	9.2	10.7
Rate per hour when violence is significant to plot	10.1	8.8	11.3	10.2	11.0

Table 48: Prevalence and rate of violence: ABC cartoons

	1967		1968		1969		1967 – 69		Enlarged 1969 sample	
	N	%	N	%	N	%	N	%	N	%
NUMBER OF VIOLENT EPISODES	70		26		95		191		99	
ALL PROGRAMS	13	100.0	4	100.0	16	100.0	33	100.0	18	100.0
Violent programs	13	100.0	4	100.0	16	100.0	33	100.0	18	100.0
Violent episodes: rate per program	5.4		6.5		5.9		5.8		5.5	
ALL HOURS	3.00	100.0	1.50	100.0	3.50	100.0	8.00	100.0	4.00	100.0
Violent hours	3.00	100.0	1.50	100.0	3.50	100.0	8.00	100.0	4.00	100.0
Violent episodes: rate per program	23.3		17.3		27.1		23.9		24.8	

Table 49: Prevalence and rate of violence: ABC TV plays

	1967		1968		1969		1967 – 69		Enlarged 1969 sample	
	N	%	N	%	N	%	N	%	N	%
NUMBER OF VIOLENT EPISODES	119		67		53		239		56	
ALL PROGRAMS	20	100.0	16	100.0	15	100.0	51	100.0	18	100.0
Violent programs	16	80.0	14	87.5	8	53.3	38	74.5	10	55.5
Violent episodes: rate per program	6.0		4.2		3.5		4.7		3.1	
ALL HOURS	14.50	100.0	12.00	100.0	10.75	100.0	37.25	100.0	12.75	100.0
Violent hours	12.50	86.2	11.00	91.7	7.25	67.4	30.75	82.6	8.25	76.4
Violent episodes: rate per hour	8.2		5.6		4.9		6.4		4.4	

Table 50: Prevalence and rate of violence: ABC feature films

	1967		1968		1969		1967 – 69		Enlarged 1969 sample	
	N	%	N	%	N	%	N	%	N	%
NUMBER OF VIOLENT EPISODES	6		18		13		37		13	
ALL PROGRAMS	2	100.0	2	100.0	3	100.0	7	100.0	3	100.0
Violent programs	2	100.0	2	100.0	2	66.6	6	85.7	2	66.6
Violent episodes: rate per program	3.0		9.0		4.3		5.3		4.3	
ALL HOURS	4.50	100.0	4.00	100.0	5.75	100.0	14.25	100.0	5.75	100.0
Violent hours	4.50	100.0	4.00	100.0	3.50	60.9	12.00	84.2	3.50	60.9
Violent episodes: rate per hour	1.3		4.5		2.3		2.6		2.3	

Table 51: Prevalence and rate of violence: ABC crime, western, action-adventure

	1967 N	%	1968 N	%	1969 N	%	1967 – 69 N	%	Enlarged 1969 sample N	%
NUMBER OF VIOLENT EPISODES	170		99		154		423		158	
ALL PROGRAMS	25	100.0	16	100.0	24	100.0	65	100.0	26	100.0
Violent programs	25	100.0	16	100.0	24	100.0	65	100.0	26	100.0
Violent episodes: rate per program	6.8		6.2		6.4		6.5		6.1	
ALL HOURS	18.60	100.0	12.50	100.0	12.25	100.0	43.35	100.0	12.75	100.0
Violent hours	18.60	100.0	12.50	100.0	12.25	100.0	43.35	100.0	12.75	100.0
Violent episodes: rate per hour	9.1		7.9		12.6		9.8		12.4	

Table 52: Prevalence and rate of violence: ABC comedy

	1967 N	%	1968 N	%	1969 N	%	1967 – 69 N	%	Enlarged 1969 sample N	%
NUMBER OF VIOLENT EPISODES	45		32		57		134		77	
ALL PROGRAMS	13	100.0	6	100.0	16	100.0	35	100.0	18	100.0
Violent programs	10	76.9	6	100.0	10	62.5	26	74.3	12	66.6
Violent episodes: rate per program	3.5		5.3		3.6		3.8		4.3	
ALL HOURS	6.0	100.0	6.0	100.0	7.85	100.0	19.85	100.0	8.85	100.0
Violent hours	3.5	58.3	6.0	100.0	3.10	39.5	12.60	63.5	4.10	46.3
Violent episodes: rate per hour	7.5		5.3		7.3		6.8		8.7	

Table 53: Prevalence of violence: CBS

	1967 N	1967 %	1968 N	1968 %	1969 N	1969 %	1967 – 69 N	1967 – 69 %	Enlarged 1969 sample N	Enlarged 1969 sample %
ALL PROGRAMS	32	100.0	35	100.0	29	100.0	96	100.0	44	100.0
All violence	21	65.6	27	77.1	21	72.4	69	71.9	36	81.8
significant to plot	16	50.0	17	48.6	13	44.8	46	47.9	28	63.6
incidental to plot	5	15.6	10	28.5	8	27.6	23	24.0	8	18.2
ALL HOURS	19.50	100.0	20.00	100.0	18.00	100.0	57.50	100.0	24.00	100.0
All violence	13.75	70.5	16.00	80.0	14.17	78.7	43.92	76.4	20.17	84.0
significant to plot	8.25	42.3	8.00	40.0	8.34	46.3	24.59	42.8	14.34	59.8
incidental to plot	5.50	28.2	8.00	40.0	5.83	32.4	19.33	33.6	5.83	24.3

Table 54: Number and rate of violent episodes: CBS

	1967	1968	1969	1967 – 69	Enlarged 1969 sample
ALL VIOLENT EPISODES	111	137	113	361	232
Rate per all programs	3.5	3.9	3.9	3.8	5.3
Rate per violent program	5.3	5.1	5.4	5.2	6.4
Rate when violence is significant to plot	5.9	6.2	6.8	6.3	7.4
Rates per all hours	5.7	6.9	6.3	6.3	9.7
Rate per violent hour	8.1	8.6	8.0	8.2	11.5
Rate per hour when violence is significant to plot	11.4	13.3	10.7	11.8	14.5

Table 55: Prevalence and rate of violence: CBS cartoons

	1967		1968		1969		1967 – 69		Enlarged 1969 sample	
	N	%	N	%	N	%	N	%	N	%
NUMBER OF VIOLENT EPISODES	44		77		66		187		160	
ALL PROGRAMS	10	100.0	13	100.0	9	100.0	32	100.0	20	100.0
Violent programs	9	90.0	13	100.0	8	88.9	30	93.8	19	95.0
Violent episodes: rate per program	4.4		5.9		7.3		5.8		8.0	
ALL HOURS	2.00	100.0	3.00	100.0	3.00	100.0	8.00	100.0	5.50	100.0
Violent hours	1.80	90.0	3.00	100.0	2.66	88.7	7.46	93.3	5.17	94.0
Violent episodes: rate per hour	22.0		25.7		22.0		23.4		29.1	

Table 56: Prevalence and rate of violence: CBS TV plays

	1967		1968		1969		1967 – 69		Enlarged 1969 sample	
	N	%	N	%	N	%	N	%	N	%
NUMBER OF VIOLENT EPISODES	60		49		36		145		61	
ALL PROGRAMS	20	100.0	20	100.0	18	100.0	58	100.0	22	100.0
Violent programs	10	50.0	12	60.0	11	61.1	33	56.9	15	68.2
Violent episodes: rate per program	3.0		2.5		2.0		2.5		2.8	
ALL HOURS	13.50	100.0	13.00	100.0	11.00	100.0	37.50	100.0	14.50	100.0
Violent hours	8.00	59.3	9.00	69.2	7.50	68.2	24.50	65.3	11.00	75.9
Violent episodes: rate per hour	4.4		3.8		3.3		3.9		4.2	

Table 57: Prevalence and rate of violence: CBS feature films

	1967		1968		1969		1967 – 69		Enlarged 1969 sample	
	N	%	N	%	N	%	N	%	N	%
NUMBER OF VIOLENT EPISODES	7		11		11		29		11	
ALL PROGRAMS	2	100.0	2	100.0	2	100.0	6	100.0	2	100.0
Violent programs	2	100.0	2	100.0	2	100.0	6	100.0	2	100.0
Violent episodes: rate per program		3.5		5.5		5.5		4.8		5.5
ALL HOURS	4.00	100.0	4.00	100.0	4.00	100.0	12	100.0	4.00	100.0
Violent hours	4.00	100.0	4.00	100.0	4.00	100.0	12	100.0	4.00	100.0
Violent episodes: rate per hour		1.8		2.8		2.8		2.4		2.8

Table 58: Prevalence and rate of violence: CBS crime, western, action-adventure

	1967		1968		1969		1967 – 69		Enlarged 1969 sample	
	N	%	N	%	N	%	N	%	N	%
NUMBER OF VIOLENT EPISODES	99		107		76		282		195	
ALL PROGRAMS	18	100.0	18	100.0	12	100.0	48	100.0	27	100.0
Violent programs	17	94.4	17	94.4	11	91.6	45	93.8	26	96.3
Violent episodes: rate per program		5.5		5.9		6.3		5.9		7.2
ALL HOURS	11.00	100.0	9.00	100.0	5.50	100.0	25.50	100.0	11.50	100.0
Violent hours	10.80	97.7	8.50	94.4	4.83	87.8	24.13	94.6	10.83	94.2
Violent episodes: rate per hour		9.0		11.9		13.8		11.1		17.0

Table 59: Prevalence and rate of violence: CBS comedy

	1967		1968		1969		1967 – 69		Enlarged 1969 sample	
	N	%	N	%	N	%	N	%	N	%
NUMBER OF VIOLENT EPISODES	16		61		66		143		143	
ALL PROGRAMS	16	100.0	21	100.0	17	100.0	54	100.0	26	100.0
Violent programs	7	43.8	13	61.9	11	64.7	31	57.4	20	76.9
Violent episodes: rate per program	1.0		2.9		3.9		2.6		5.5	
ALL HOURS	8.00	100.0	7.90	100.0	7.50	100.0	23.4	100.0	9.50	100.0
Violent hours	3.00	37.5	3.90	49.4	4.70	62.7	11.6	49.6	6.70	70.5
Violent episodes: rate per hour	2.0		7.7		8.8		6.1		15.1	

Table 60: Prevalence of violence: NBC

	1967		1968		1969		1967 – 69		Enlarged 1969 sample	
	N	%	N	%	N	%	N	%	N	%
ALL PROGRAMS	29	100.0	30	100.0	35	100.0	94	100.0	38	100.0
All violence	26	89.7	24	80.0	32	91.4	82	87.2	35	92.1
significant to plot	21	72.4	17	56.7	28	80.0	66	70.2	31	81.6
incidental to plot	5	17.3	7	23.3	4	11.4	16	17.0	4	10.5
ALL HOURS	20.50	100.0	21.00	100.0	23.75	100.0	65.25	100.0	25.25	100.0
All violence	17.83	87.0	18.42	87.7	22.25	93.7	58.50	89.7	23.75	94.1
significant to plot	15.33	74.8	16.17	77.0	19.25	81.1	50.75	77.8	20.75	82.2
incidental to plot	2.50	12.2	2.25	10.7	3.00	12.6	7.75	11.9	3.00	11.9

Table 61: Number and rate of violent episodes: NBC

	1967	1968	1969	1967 – 69	Enlarged 1969 sample
ALL VIOLENT EPISODES	172	146	209	527	230
Rate per all programs	5.9	4.9	6.0	5.6	6.1
Rate per violent program	6.6	6.1	6.5	6.4	6.6
Rate when violence is significant to plot	7.7	7.6	7.0	7.4	7.0
Rates per all hours	8.4	7.0	8.8	8.1	9.1
Rate per violent hour	9.6	7.9	9.4	9.0	9.7
Rate per hour when violence is significant to plot	10.6	8.0	10.2	9.6	10.5

Table 62: Prevalence and rate of violence: NBC cartoons

	1967		1968		1969		1967 – 69		Enlarged 1969 sample	
	N	%	N	%	N	%	N	%	N	%
NUMBER OF VIOLENT EPISODES	37		59		93		189		111	
ALL PROGRAMS										
Violent programs	9	100.0	8	100.0	13	100.0	30	100.0	15	100.0
Violent programs	8	88.9	7	87.5	13	100.0	28	93.3	15	100.0
Violent episodes: rate per program	4.1		7.4		7.2		6.3		7.4	
ALL HOURS										
Violent hours	2.00	100.0	2.42	100.0	2.17	100.0	6.59	100.0	2.67	100.0
Violent hours	1.80	90.0	1.90	79.2	2.17	100.0	5.87	89.1	2.67	100.0
Violent episodes: rate per hour	18.5		24.4		42.9		28.7		41.6	

Table 63: Prevalence and rate of violence: NBC TV plays

	1967 N	1967 %	1968 N	1968 %	1969 N	1969 %	1967 – 69 N	1967 – 69 %	Enlarged 1969 sample N	Enlarged 1969 sample %
NUMBER OF VIOLENT EPISODES	119		52		98		269		101	
ALL PROGRAMS	18	100.0	19	100.0	19	100.0	56	100.0	20	100.0
Violent programs	17	94.4	14	73.7	16	84.2	47	83.9	17	85.0
Violent episodes: rate per program		6.6		2.7		5.2		4.8		5.1
ALL HOURS	14.50	100.0	11.58	100.0	14.83	100.0	40.91	100.0	15.83	100.0
Violent hours	14.00	96.6	9.50	82.0	13.33	89.9	36.83	90.0	14.33	90.5
Violent episodes: rate per hour		8.2		4.5		6.6		6.6		6.4

Table 64: Prevalence and rate of violence: NBC feature films

	1967 N	1967 %	1968 N	1968 %	1969 N	1969 %	1967 – 69 N	1967 – 69 %	Enlarged 1969 sample N	Enlarged 1969 sample %
NUMBER OF VIOLENT EPISODES	16		35		18		69		18	
ALL PROGRAMS	2	100.0	3	100.0	3	100.0	8	100.0	3	100.0
Violent programs	1	50.0	3	100.0	3	100.0	7	87.5	3	100.0
Violent episodes: rate per program		8.0		11.7		6.0		8.6		6.0
ALL HOURS	4.00	100.0	7.00	100.0	6.75	100.0	17.75	100.0	6.75	100.0
Violent hours	2.00	50.0	7.00	100.0	6.75	100.0	15.75	88.7	6.75	100.0
Violent episodes: rate per hour		4.0		5.0		2.7		3.9		2.7

Table 65: Prevalence and rate of violence: NBC crime, western, action-adventure

	1967		1968		1969		1967 – 69		Enlarged 1969 sample	
	N	%	N	%	N	%	N	%	N	%
NUMBER OF VIOLENT EPISODES	150		135		188		473		206	
ALL PROGRAMS	21	100.0	20	100.0	27	100.0	68	100.0	29	100.0
Violent programs	19	90.5	20	100.0	26	96.3	65	95.6	28	96.5
Violent episodes: rate per program	7.1		6.8		7.0		7.0		7.1	
ALL HOURS	18.00	100.0	17.70	100.0	15.50	100.0	51.20	100.0	16.00	100.0
Violent hours	15.50	86.1	17.70	100.0	15.00	97.0	48.20	94.1	15.50	97.0
Violent episodes: rate per hour	8.3		7.6		12.1		9.2		12.9	

Table 66: Prevalence and rate of violence: NBC comedy

	1967		1968		1969		1967 – 69		Enlarged 1969 sample	
	N	%	N	%	N	%	N	%	N	%
NUMBER OF VIOLENT EPISODES	61		41		93		195		104	
ALL PROGRAMS	15	100.0	15	100.0	15	100.0	45	100.0	16	100.0
Violent programs	12	80.0	9	60.0	13	86.0	34	75.5	14	87.5
Violent episodes: rate per program	4.1		2.7		6.2		4.3		6.5	
ALL HOURS	10.80	100.0	6.30	100.0	3.72	100.0	20.82	100.0	3.97	100.0
Violent hours	7.70	71.0	2.30	35.7	2.70	72.9	12.70	60.1	2.90	74.4
Violent episodes: rate per hour	5.6		6.5		25.0		9.4		26.2	

Table 67: Agent of violence in violent episodes

	1967 N	%	1968 N	%	1969 N	%	1967 – 69 N	%	Enlarged 1969 sample N	%
All episodes	478	100.0	394	100.0	483	100.0	1355	100.0	630	100.0
Human being	362	75.7	306	77.7	238	49.3	906	66.9	314	49.9
Animal (including cartoon animals and other animated creatures)	37	7.8	29	7.3	83	17.2	149	11.0	94	14.9
Nature, accident, mixed, unclear, etc.	79	16.5	59	15.0	162	33.5	300	22.1	222	35.2
Cartoon episodes	150	100.0	163	100.0	254	100.0	567	100.0	370	100.0
Human being	66	44.0	96	58.9	59	23.2	221	39.0	106	28.6
Animal (including cartoon animals and other animated creatures)	31	20.7	26	16.0	79	31.1	136	24.0	89	24.1
Nature, accident, mixed unclear. etc.	53	35.3	41	25.1	116	45.7	210	37.0	175	47.3
Noncartoon episodes	328	100.0	231	100.0	229	100.0	788	100.0	260	100.0
Human being	296	90.2	210	90.9	179	78.2	685	86.9	208	80.0
Animal (including cartoon animals and other animated creatures)	6	1.8	3	1.3	4	1.7	13	1.6	5	1.9
Nature, accident, mixed, unclear, etc.	26	8.0	18	7.8	46	20.1	90	11.4	47	18.1

Table 68: Use of weapon in violent episodes

	1967		1968		1969		1967 – 69		Enlarged 1969 sample	
	N	%	N	%	N	%	N	%	N	%
All episodes	478	100.0	394	100.0	483	100.0	1355	100.0	630	100.0
Weapon was used	281	58.8	184	46.7	338	70.0	863	59.3	463	73.5
No weapon was used	197	41.2	210	53.3	145	30.0	552	40.7	167	26.5
Cartoon episodes	150	100.0	163	100.0	254	100.0	567	100.0	370	100.0
Weapon was used	78	52.0	76	46.6	210	82.7	364	64.2	316	85.4
No weapon was used	72	48.0	87	53.4	44	17.3	203	35.8	54	14.6
Noncartoon episodes	328	100.0	231	100.0	229	100.0	788	100.0	260	100.0
Weapon was used	203	61.9	108	46.8	128	55.9	439	55.7	147	56.5
No weapon was used	125	38.1	123	53.2	101	44.1	349	44.3	113	43.5

Table 69: Comic context: tone of program in which violent episode appears

	1967		1968		1969		1967 − 69		Enlarged 1969 sample	
	N	%	N	%	N	%	N	%	N	%
All episodes	478	100.0	394	100.0	483	100.0	1355	100.0	630	100.0
Mostly light, comic humorous	132	27.6	142	26.1	156	32.3	430	23.7	221	35.1
Serious, mixed, unclear	346	72.4	252	73.9	327	67.7	925	76.3	409	64.9
Cartoon episodes	150	100.0	163	100.0	254	100.0	567	100.0	370	100.0
Mostly light, comic, humorous	61	40.7	84	51.5	123	48.4	268	47.3	184	49.7
Serious, mixed, unclear	89	59.3	79	48.5	131	51.6	299	52.7	186	50.3
Noncartoon episodes	328	100.0	231	100.0	229	100.0	788	100.0	260	100.0
Mostly light, comic, humorous	71	21.6	58	25.1	33	14.4	162	20.6	37	14.2
Serious, mixed, unclear	257	78.4	173	74.9	196	85.6	626	79.4	223	85.8

Table 70: Agents of law in violent episodes*

	1967 N	1967 %	1968 N	1968 %	1969 N	1969 %	1967–69 N	1967–69 %	Enlarged 1969 sample N	Enlarged 1969 sample %
All episodes	478	100.0	394	100.0	483	100.0	1355	100.0	630	100.0
Law enforcement agents play no role	418	87.4	346	87.8	431	89.2	1195	88.2	550	87.3
Law enforcement agents play some role	60	12.6	48	12.2	52	10.8	160	11.8	80	12.7
When they do play a role, it is:										
nonviolent	24	40.0	13	27.1	12	23.1	49	30.6	25	31.2
violent	36	60.0	35	72.4	40	76.9	111	69.4	55	68.8
Cartoon episodes					254	100.0			370	100.0
Law enforcement agents play no role					244	96.1			345	83.2
Law enforcement agents play some role					10	3.9			25	6.8
Noncartoon episodes					229	100.0			260	100.0
Law enforcement agents play no role					186	81.2			204	78.8
Law enforcement agents play some role					43	18.8			56	21.2
When they do play a role, it is:										
nonviolent					9	20.9			13	23.2
violent					34	79.1			43	76.8

*1969 figures meet levels of acceptable reliability for noncartoon episodes only

Table 71: Casualties in violent episodes

	1967 N	%	1968 N	%	1969 N	%	1967 – 69 N	%	Enlarged 1969 sample N	%
Violent episodes in all programs	478	100.0	394	100.0	483	100.0	1355	100.0	630	100.0
No casualties	223	46.7	194	49.2	403	83.4	820	60.5	522	82.9
Some casualties	255	53.3	200	50.8	80	16.6	535	39.5	108	17.1
Violent episodes in which the casualty count was:										
one	189	39.5	146	37.1	64	13.3	399	29.4	85	13.5
two	34	7.1	26	6.6	8	1.7	68	5.0	13	2.1
three	11	2.3	9	2.3	3	0.6	23	1.7	4	0.6
four	2	0.4	5	1.3	0	0.0	7	0.5	0	0.0
five	3	0.6	0	0.0	0	0.0	3	0.2	0	0.0
six	4	0.8	0	0.0	1	0.2	5	0.4	2	0.3
seven	0	0.0	0	0.0	0	0.0	0	0.0	0	0.0
eight or more	12	2.5	14	3.6	4	0.9	30	2.2	4	0.6
Number of individual casualties	437	100.0	371	100.0	134	100.0	942	100.0	174	100.0
Fatal casualties	182	41.6	131	35.3	46	34.3	359	38.1	58	33.3
Rate of all casualties per violent episode		0.9		0.9		0.3		0.7		0.3
Rate of fatal casualties		0.4		0.3		0.1		0.3		0.1

Table 72: Crime, science, and minority and foreign themes related to the prevalence and rate of violence: all programs

Programs containing the following themes as significant story elements	Total No. programs containing theme	% of all programs	% of all with theme	Violent programs containing theme	% of all violent programs	Nonviolent programs containing theme	% of all nonviolent programs
	N	%	N	%	%	N	%
Crime, corruption, illegality							
1967	31	32.3	29	93.5	37.2	2	11.1
1968	39	44.8	38	97.4	53.5	1	6.3
1969	43	43.9	39	90.7	49.7	4	21.1
1967 - 69	113	40.2	106	93.8	46.5	7	13.2
Enlarged 1969 sample	54	44.6	50	92.6	50.0	4	20.0
Science and technology							
1967	29	30.2	26	89.7	33.3	3	16.7
1968	24	27.6	21	87.5	29.6	3	18.8
1969	52	53.1	43	82.7	54.4	9	47.4
1967 - 69	105	37.4	90	85.7	39.5	15	28.3
Enlarged 1969 sample	68	56.2	58	85.3	57.4	10	50.0
Minority and foreign themes							
1967	30	31.3	28	93.3	35.9	2	11.1
1968	39	44.8	34	87.2	47.9	5	31.3
1969	49	50.0	38	77.6	48.1	11	57.8
1967 - 69	118	42.0	100	84.7	43.9	18	34.0
Enlarged 1969 sample	59	48.8	48	81.4	48.0	11	55.0

Table 73: Distribution of all programs by time of action

	1967 N	%	1968 N	%	1969 N	%	1967 – 69 N	%	Enlarged 1969 sample N	%
ALL PROGRAMS	96	100.0	87	100.0	98	100.0	281	100.0	121	100.0
Past	19	19.8	19	21.8	21	21.4	59	21.0	22	18.2
Contemporary (Present)	52	54.2	59	67.8	70	71.4	183	65.1	85	70.2
Future	8	8.3	5	5.7	3	3.1	16	5.7	5	4.1
Several, other	15	15.6	4	4.6	4	4.1	23	8.2	9	7.4
PROGRAMS THAT CONTAIN VIOLENCE	78	100.0	71	100.0	79	100.0	228	100.0	101	100.0
Past	19	24.4	18	25.4	20	25.3	57	25.0	21	20.8
Contemporary (Present)	39	50.0	45	63.4	52	65.9	136	59.7	66	65.3
Future	8	10.3	5	7.0	3	3.8	16	7.0	5	4.9
Several, other	12	15.4	3	4.2	4	5.0	19	8.3	9	8.9
PROGRAMS THAT DO NOT CONTAIN VIOLENCE	18	100.0	16	100.0	19	100.0	53	100.0	20	100.0
Past	0	0.0	1	6.3	1	5.3	2	3.8	1	5.0
Contemporary (Present)	15	83.3	14	87.5	18	94.7	47	88.7	19	95.0
Future	0	0.0	0	0.0	0	0.0	0	0.0	0	0.0
Several, other	3	16.7	1	6.3	0	0.0	4	7.5	0	0.0
ALL PROGRAMS SET IN THE PAST	19	100.0	19	100.0	21	100.0	59	100.0	22	100.0
Violence	19	100.0	18	94.7	20	95.2	57	96.6	21	95.5
No violence	0	0.0	1	5.3	1	4.8	2	3.4	1	4.5
ALL PROGRAMS SET IN THE PRESENT	54	100.0	59	100.0	70	100.0	183	100.0	85	100.0
Violence	39	72.2	45	76.3	52	74.3	136	74.3	66	77.6
No violence	15	28.8	14	23.7	18	25.7	47	25.7	19	22.4

Table 73: Distribution of all programs by time of action—Continued

	1967 N	1967 %	1968 N	1968 %	1969 N	1969 %	1967–69 N	1967–69 %	Enlarged 1969 sample N	Enlarged 1969 sample %
ALL PROGRAMS SET IN THE FUTURE	8	100.0	5	100.0	3	100.0	16	100.0	5	100.0
Violence	8	100.0	5	100.0	3	100.0	16	100.0	5	100.0
No violence	0	0.0	0	0.0	0	0.0	0	0.0	0	0.0
ALL PROGRAMS WITH SEVERAL OR OTHER SETTING	15	100.0	4	100.0	4	100.0	23	100.0	9	100.0
Violence	12	80.0	3	75.0	4	100.0	19	82.6	9	100.0
No violence	3	20.0	1	25.0	0	0.0	4	17.4	0	0.0

Table 74: Distribution of cartoon programs by time of action

	1967 N	1967 %	1968 N	1968 %	1969 N	1969 %	1967 – 69 N	1967 – 69 %	Enlarged 1969 sample N	Enlarged 1969 sample %
ALL PROGRAMS	32	100.0	25	100.0	38	100.0	95	100.0	53	100.0
Past	1	3.1	4	16.0	5	13.1	10	10.5	6	11.3
Contemporary (present)	11	34.4	15	60.0	28	73.7	54	56.8	35	66.1
Future	6	18.8	4	16.0	1	2.6	11	11.6	3	5.7
Several, other	14	43.8	2	8.0	4	10.5	20	21.1	9	17.0
PROGRAMS THAT CONTAIN VIOLENCE	30	100.0	24	100.0	37	100.0	91	100.0	52	100.0
Past	1	3.3	4	16.7	5	13.5	10	11.0	6	11.5
Contemporary (present)	11	36.7	15	62.5	27	72.9	53	58.2	34	65.4
Future	6	20.0	4	16.7	1	2.7	11	12.1	3	5.8
Several, other	12	40.0	1	4.2	4	10.8	17	18.7	9	17.3

Table 74: Distribution of cartoon programs by time of action—Continued

	1967 N	1967 %	1968 N	1968 %	1969 N	1969 %	1967–69 N	1967–69 %	Enlarged 1969 sample N	Enlarged 1969 sample %
PROGRAMS THAT DO NOT CONTAIN VIOLENCE	2	100.0	1	100.0	1	100.0	4	100.0	1	100.0
Past	0	0.0	0	0.0	0	0.0	0	0.0	0	0.0
Contemporary (present)	0	0.0	0	0.0	1	100.0	1	25.0	1	100.0
Future	0	0.0	0	0.0	0	0.0	0	0.0	0	0.0
Several, other	2	100.0	1	100.0	0	0.0	3	75.0	0	0.0
ALL PROGRAMS SET IN THE PAST	1	100.0	4	100.0	5	100.0	10	100.0	6	100.0
Violence	1	100.0	4	100.0	5	100.0	10	100.0	6	100.0
No violence	0	0.0	0	0.0	0	0.0	0	0.0	0	0.0
ALL PROGRAMS SET IN THE PRESENT	11	100.0	15	100.0	28	100.0	54	100.0	35	100.0
Violence	11	100.0	15	100.0	27	96.4	53	98.1	34	97.1
No violence	0	0.0	0	0.0	1	3.5	1	1.9	1	31.4
ALL PROGRAMS SET IN THE FUTURE	6	100.0	4	100.0	1	100.0	11	100.0	3	100.0
Violence	6	100.0	4	100.0	1	100.0	11	100.0	3	100.0
No violence	0	0.0	0	0.0	0	0.0	0	0.0	0	0.0
ALL PROGRAMS WITH SEVERAL OR OTHER SETTING	14	100.0	2	100.0	4	100.0	20	100.0	9	100.0
Violence	12	85.7	1	50.0	4	100.0	17	85.0	9	100.0
No violence	2	14.3	1	50.0	0	0.0	3	15.0	0	0.0

Table 75: Distribution of noncartoon programs by time of action

	1967		1968		1969		1967 – 69		Enlarged 1969 sample	
	N	%	N	%	N	%	N	%	N	%
ALL PROGRAMS	64	100.0	62	100.0	62	100.0	186	100.0	68	100.0
Past	18	28.1	15	24.2	16	26.7	49	26.3	16	23.5
Contemporary (present)	43	67.2	44	71.0	42	70.0	129	69.4	50	73.5
Future	2	3.1	1	1.6	2	3.3	5	2.7	2	2.9
Several, other	1	1.6	2	3.2	0	0.0	3	1.6	0	0.0
PROGRAMS THAT CONTAIN VIOLENCE	48	100.0	47	100.0	42	100.0	137	100.0	49	100.0
Past	18	37.5	14	29.8	15	35.7	47	34.3	15	30.6
Contemporary (present)	28	58.3	30	63.8	25	59.5	83	60.6	32	65.3
Future	2	4.2	1	2.1	2	4.8	5	3.6	2	4.1
Several, other	0	0.0	2	4.3	0	0.0	2	1.5	0	0.0
PROGRAMS THAT DO NOT CONTAIN VIOLENCE	16	100.0	15	100.0	18	100.0	49	100.0	19	100.0
Past	0	0.0	1	6.7	1	5.6	2	4.1	1	5.3
Contemporary (present)	15	93.8	14	93.3	17	94.4	46	93.9	18	94.7
Future	0	0.0	0	0.0	0	0.0	0	0.0	0	0.0
Several, other	1	6.2	0	0.0	0	0.0	1	2.0	0	0.0
ALL PROGRAMS SET IN THE PAST	18	100.0	15	100.0	16	100.0	49	100.0	16	100.0
Violence	18	100.0	14	93.3	15	93.8	47	95.9	15	93.8
No violence	0	0.0	1	6.7	1	6.3	2	4.1	1	6.3
ALL PROGRAMS SET IN THE PRESENT	43	100.0	44	100.0	42	100.0	129	100.0	50	100.0
Violence	28	65.1	30	68.2	25	59.5	83	64.3	32	64.0
No violence	15	34.9	14	31.8	17	40.5	46	35.7	18	36.0

Table 75: Distribution of noncartoon programs by time of action—Continued

	1967		1968		1969		1967–69		Enlarged 1969 sample	
	N	%	N	%	N	%	N	%	N	%
ALL PROGRAMS SET IN THE FUTURE	2	100.0	1	100.0	2	100.0	5	100.0	2	100.0
Violence	2	100.0	1	100.0	2	100.0	5	100.0	2	100.0
No violence	0	0.0	0	0.0	0	0.0	0	0.0	0	0.0
ALL PROGRAMS WITH SEVERAL OR OTHER SETTING	1	100.0	2	100.0	0	0.0	3	100.0	0	0.0
Violence	0	0.0	2	100.0	0	0.0	2	66.7	0	0.0
No violence	1	100.0	0	0.0	0	0.0	1	33.3	0	0.0

Table 76: Rate of violent episodes, by time of action

	1967	1968	1969	1967 – 69	Enlarged 1969 sample
ALL PROGRAMS	5.0	4.5	4.9	4.8	5.2
Past	9.3	7.1	6.1	7.5	6.2
Contemporary (present)	3.7	3.5	4.3	3.9	4.4
Future	6.3	5.8	8.3	6.5	9.0
Several, other	3.3	6.3	7.8	4.6	7.9
CARTOON PROGRAMS	4.7	6.5	6.7	6.0	7.0
Past	12.0	7.8	7.8	8.2	7.8
Contemporary (present)	5.2	6.1	6.4	6.0	6.4
Future	5.3	6.3	6.0	5.7	8.7
Several, other	3.6	7.5	7.8	4.8	8.2
NONCARTOON PROGRAMS	5.1	3.7	3.8	4.2	3.8
Past	9.1	6.9	5.6	7.3	5.6
Contemporary (present)	3.4	2.6	2.9	2.9	3.0
Future	9.0	4.0	9.5	8.2	9.5
Several, other	0.0	5.0	0.0	3.3	0.0

Table 77: Measures of violence by time of action: 1967 — 69 totals

	Past	Present	Future	Other
ALL PROGRAMS				
Programs containing violence (% of all programs)	96.6	74.3	100.0	100.0
Number of violent episodes	440	705	104	106
Rate per all programs	7.5	3.9	6.5	4.6
All those involved in violence (% of leading characters)	80.7	60.3	78.6	76.2
All those involved in killing (% of leading characters)	19.3	7.4	14.3	16.7
CARTOONS				
Programs containing violence (% of cartoon programs)	100.0	98.1	100.0	85.0
Number of violent episodes	82	326	63	96
Rate per all programs	8.2	6.0	5.7	4.8
NONCARTOON PROGRAMS				
Programs containing violence (% of all noncartoon programs)	95.9	64.3	100.0	100.0
Number of violent episodes	358	379	41	10
Rate per all programs	7.3	2.9	8.2	3.3

Table 78: Distribution of all programs by place of action

	1967 N	1967 %	1968 N	1968 %	1969 N	1969 %	1967 – 69 N	1967 – 69 %	Enlarged 1969 sample N	Enlarged 1969 sample %
ALL PROGRAMS	96	100.0	87	100.0	98	100.0	281	100.0	121	100.0
U.S. only	61	63.5	60	69.0	69	70.4	190	67.6	80	66.1
Several, other	35	36.5	27	31.0	29	29.6	91	32.4	41	33.9
PROGRAMS THAT CONTAIN VIOLENCE	78	100.0	71	100.0	79	100.0	228	100.0	101	100.0
U.S. only	46	59.0	46	64.8	52	65.8	144	63.2	62	61.4
Several, other	32	41.0	25	35.2	27	34.2	84	36.8	39	38.6
PROGRAMS THAT DO NOT CONTAIN VIOLENCE	18	100.0	16	100.0	19	100.0	53	100.0	20	100.0
U.S. only	15	83.3	14	87.5	17	89.5	46	86.8	18	90.0
Several, other	3	16.7	2	12.5	2	10.5	7	13.2	2	10.0
PROGRAMS SET IN U.S. ONLY	61	100.0	60	100.0	69	100.0	190	100.0	80	100.0
Violence	46	75.4	46	76.7	52	75.4	144	75.8	62	77.5
No violence	15	24.6	14	23.3	17	24.6	46	24.2	18	22.5
PROGRAMS IN SEVERAL OR OTHER SETTINGS	35	100.0	27	100.0	29	100.0	91	100.0	41	100.0
Violence	32	91.4	25	92.6	27	93.1	84	92.3	39	95.1
No violence	3	8.6	2	7.4	2	6.9	7	7.7	2	4.9

Table 79: Distribution of cartoon programs by place of action

	1967 N	1967 %	1968 N	1968 %	1969 N	1969 %	1967–69 N	1967–69 %	Enlarged 1969 sample N	Enlarged 1969 sample %
ALL PROGRAMS	32	100.0	25	100.0	38	100.0	95	100.0	53	100.0
U.S. only	14	43.8	16	64.0	25	65.8	55	57.9	30	56.6
Several, other	18	56.2	9	36.0	13	34.2	40	42.1	23	43.4
PROGRAMS THAT CONTAIN VIOLENCE	30	100.0	24	100.0	37	100.0	91	100.0	52	100.0
U.S. only	13	43.3	15	62.5	24	64.9	52	57.1	29	55.8
Several, other	17	56.7	9	37.5	13	35.1	39	42.9	23	44.2
PROGRAMS THAT DO NOT CONTAIN VIOLENCE	2	100.0	1	100.0	1	100.0	4	100.0	1	100.0
U.S. only	1	50.0	1	100.0	1	100.0	3	75.0	1	100.0
Several, other	1	50.0	0	0.0	0	0.0	1	25.0	0	0.0
PROGRAMS SET IN U.S. ONLY	14	100.0	16	100.0	25	100.0	55	100.0	30	100.0
Violence	13	92.9	15	93.8	24	96.0	52	94.5	29	96.7
No violence	1	7.1	1	6.2	1	4.0	3	5.5	1	5.5
PROGRAMS SET IN SEVERAL OR OTHER SETTINGS	18	100.0	9	100.0	13	100.0	40	100.0	23	100.0
Violence	17	94.4	9	100.0	13	100.0	39	97.5	23	100.0
No violence	1	5.6	0	0.0	0	0.0	1	2.5	0	0.0

Table 80: Distribution of noncartoon programs by place of action

	1967 N	1967 %	1968 N	1968 %	1969 N	1969 %	1967–69 N	1967–69 %	Enlarged 1969 sample N	Enlarged 1969 sample %
ALL PROGRAMS	64	100.0	62	100.0	60	100.0	186	100.0	68	100.0
U.S. only	47	73.4	44	70.9	44	73.3	135	72.6	50	73.5
Several, other	17	26.6	18	29.1	16	26.7	51	27.4	18	26.5
PROGRAMS THAT CONTAIN VIOLENCE	48	100.0	47	100.0	42	100.0	137	100.0	49	100.0
U.S. only	33	68.8	31	65.9	28	66.7	92	67.2	33	67.3
Several, other	15	31.2	16	34.1	14	33.3	45	32.8	16	32.7
PROGRAMS THAT DO NOT CONTAIN VIOLENCE	16	100.0	15	100.0	18	100.0	49	100.0	19	100.0
U.S. only	14	87.5	13	86.7	16	88.9	43	87.7	17	89.5
Several, other	2	12.5	2	13.3	2	11.1	6	12.2	2	10.5
PROGRAMS SET IN U.S. ONLY	47	100.0	44	100.0	44	100.0	135	100.0	50	100.0
Violence	33	70.2	31	70.5	28	63.6	92	68.1	33	66.0
No violence	14	29.8	13	29.5	16	36.4	43	31.9	17	34.0
PROGRAMS SET IN SEVERAL OR OTHER SETTINGS	17	100.0	18	100.0	16	100.0	51	100.0	18	100.0
Violence	15	88.2	16	88.9	14	87.5	45	88.2	16	88.9
No violence	2	11.8	2	11.1	2	12.5	6	11.8	2	11.1

Table 81: Rate of violent episodes, by place of action

	1967	1968	1969	1967 – 69	Enlarged 1969 sample
ALL PROGRAMS	5.0	4.5	4.9	4.8	5.2
U.S. only	4.3	3.7	4.2	4.1	4.4
Several, other	6.2	6.3	6.7	6.4	6.9
CARTOON PROGRAMS	4.7	6.5	6.7	6.0	7.0
U.S. only	3.8	4.6	6.4	5.2	6.7
Several, other	5.4	9.8	7.2	7.0	7.3
NONCARTOON PROGRAMS	5.1	3.7	3.8	4.2	3.8
U.S. only	4.4	3.4	2.9	3.6	3.0
Several, other	7.0	4.6	6.3	5.9	6.2

Table 82: Measures of violence by place of action: 1967 - 69 totals

	U.S. Only	Other
ALL PROGRAMS		
Programs containing violence (% of all programs)	75.8	92.3
Number of violent episodes	773	582
Rate per all programs	4.1	6.4
All those involved in violence (% of leading characters)	61.3	80.4
All those involved in killing (% of leading characters)	9.8	14.6
CARTOONS		
Programs containing violence (% of cartoon programs)	94.5	97.5
Number of violent episodes	287	280
Rate per all programs	5.2	7.0
NONCARTOON PROGRAM		
Programs containing violence (% of all noncartoon programs)	68.1	88.2
Number of violent episodes	486	302
Rate per all programs	3.6	5.9

Table 83: Distribution of all programs by setting of action

	1967 N	1967 %	1968 N	1968 %	1969 N	1969 %	1967 – 69 N	1967 – 69 %	Enlarged 1969 sample N	Enlarged 1969 sample %
ALL PROGRAMS	96	100.0	87	100.0	98	100.0	281	100.0	121	100.0
Urban	32	33.3	29	33.3	27	27.6	88	31.3	30	24.8
Small town, rural	20	20.8	30	34.5	26	26.5	76	27.7	31	25.6
Uninhabited, mobile, etc.	44	45.8	28	32.2	45	45.9	117	41.6	60	49.6
PROGRAMS THAT CONTAIN VIOLENCE	78	100.0	71	100.0	79	100.0	228	100.0	101	100.0
Urban	24	30.8	23	32.4	14	17.7	61	26.7	16	15.9
Small town, rural	13	16.6	24	33.8	22	27.9	59	25.9	27	26.7
Uninhabited, mobile, etc.	41	52.6	24	33.8	43	54.4	108	47.4	58	57.4
PROGRAMS THAT DO NOT CONTAIN VIOLENCE	18	100.0	16	100.0	19	100.0	53	100.0	20	100.0
Urban	8	44.4	6	37.5	13	68.4	27	50.9	14	70.0
Small town, rural	7	38.9	6	37.5	4	21.1	17	32.1	4	20.0
Uninhabited, mobile, etc.	3	16.7	4	25.0	2	10.5	9	17.0	2	10.0
PROGRAMS IN URBAN SETTINGS	32	100.0	29	100.0	27	100.0	88	100.0	30	100.0
Violence	24	75.0	23	79.3	14	51.9	61	69.3	16	53.3
No violence	8	25.0	6	20.7	13	48.1	27	30.7	14	46.7
PROGRAMS SET IN SMALL TOWN, RURAL	20	100.0	30	100.0	26	100.0	76	100.0	31	100.0
Violence	13	5.0	24	80.0	22	84.6	59	77.6	27	87.1
No violence	7	5.0	6	20.0	4	15.4	17	22.4	4	12.9
PROGRAMS SET IN UNINHABITED OR MOBILE SETTING, ETC.	44	100.0	28	100.0	45	100.0	117	100.0	60	100.0
Violence	41	93.2	24	85.7	43	95.6	108	92.3	58	96.7
No violence	3	6.8	4	14.3	2	4.4	9	7.7	2	3.3

Table 84: Distribution of cartoon programs by setting of action

	1967 N	1967 %	1968 N	1968 %	1969 N	1969 %	1967 – 69 N	1967 – 69 %	Enlarged 1969 sample N	Enlarged 1969 sample %
ALL PROGRAMS	32	100.0	25	100.0	38	100.0	95	100.0	53	100.0
Urban	8	25.0	7	28.0	4	10.5	19	20.0	4	7.5
Small town, rural	2	6.3	4	16.0	14	36.9	20	21.1	17	32.1
Uninhabited, mobile, etc.	22	68.7	14	56.0	20	52.6	56	58.9	32	60.4
PROGRAMS THAT CONTAIN VIOLENCE	30	100.0	24	100.0	37	100.0	91	100.0	52	100.0
Urban	8	26.7	6	25.0	4	10.8	18	19.8	4	7.7
Small town, rural	1	3.3	4	16.7	13	35.1	18	19.8	16	30.8
Uninhabited, mobile, etc.	21	70.0	14	58.3	20	54.0	55	60.4	32	61.5
PROGRAMS THAT DO NOT CONTAIN VIOLENCE	2	100.0	1	100.0	1	100.0	4	100.0	1	100.0
Urban	0	0.0	1	100.0	0	0.0	1	25.0	0	0.0
Small town, rural	1	50.0	0	0.0	1	100.0	2	50.0	1	100.0
Uninhabited, mobile, etc.	1	50.0	0	0.0	0	0.0	1	25.0	0	0.0
PROGRAMS IN URBAN SETTING	8	100.0	7	100.0	4	100.0	19	100.0	4	100.0
Violence	8	100.0	6	85.7	4	100.0	18	94.7	4	100.0
No violence	0	0.0	1	14.3	0	0.0	1	5.3	0	0.0
PROGRAMS SET IN SMALL TOWN, RURAL	2	100.0	4	100.0	14	100.0	20	100.0	17	100.0
Violence	1	50.0	4	100.0	13	92.9	18	90.0	16	94.1
No violence	1	50.0	0	0.0	1	7.1	2	10.0	1	5.9
PROGRAMS SET IN UNINHABITED OR MOBILE SETTINGS. ETC.	22	100.0	14	100.0	20	100.0	56	100.0	32	100.0
Violence	21	95.5	14	100.0	20	100.0	55	98.2	32	100.0
No violence	1	4.5	0	0.0	0	0.0	1	1.8	0	0.0

Table 85: Distribution of noncartoon programs by setting of action

	1967		1968		1969		1967 – 69		Enlarged 1969 sample	
	N	%	N	%	N	%	N	%	N	%
ALL PROGRAMS	64	100.0	62	100.0	60	100.0	186	100.0	68	100.0
Urban	24	37.5	22	35.5	23	38.3	69	37.1	26	38.2
Small town, rural	18	28.1	26	41.9	12	20.0	56	30.1	14	20.6
Uninhabited, mobile, etc.	22	34.4	14	22.6	25	41.7	61	32.8	28	41.2
PROGRAMS THAT CONTAIN VIOLENCE	48	100.0	47	100.0	42	100.0	137	100.0	49	100.0
Urban	16	33.3	17	36.2	10	23.8	43	31.4	12	24.5
Small town, rural	12	25.0	20	42.5	9	21.4	41	29.9	11	22.4
Uninhabited, mobile, etc.	20	41.7	10	21.3	23	54.8	53	38.7	26	53.1
PROGRAMS THAT DO NOT CONTAIN VIOLENCE	16	100.0	15	100.0	18	100.0	49	100.0	19	100.0
Urban	8	50.0	5	33.3	13	72.2	26	53.1	14	73.7
Small town, rural	6	37.5	6	40.0	3	16.7	15	30.6	3	15.8
Uninhabited, mobile, etc.	2	12.5	4	26.7	2	11.1	8	16.3	2	10.5
PROGRAMS IN URBAN SETTING	24	100.0	22	100.0	23	100.0	69	100.0	26	100.0
Violence	16	66.7	17	77.3	10	43.5	43	62.3	12	46.2
No violence	8	33.3	5	22.7	13	56.5	26	37.7	14	53.8
PROGRAMS SET IN SMALL TOWN, RURAL	18	100.0	26	100.0	12	100.0	56	100.0	14	100.0
Violence	12	66.7	20	76.9	9	75.0	41	73.2	11	78.6
No violence	6	33.3	6	23.1	3	25.0	15	26.8	3	21.4
PROGRAMS SET IN UNINHABITED OR MOBILE SETTINGS, ETC.	22	100.0	14	100.0	25	100.0	61	100.0	28	100.0
Violence	20	90.9	10	71.4	23	92.0	53	86.9	26	92.9
No violence	2	9.1	4	28.6	2	8.0	8	13.1	2	7.1

Table 86: Rate of violent episodes, by setting of action

	1967	1968	1969	1967 – 69	Enlarged 1969 sample
ALL PROGRAMS	5.0	4.5	4.9	4.8	5.2
Urban	2.8	3.7	2.1	2.9	2.3
Small town, rural	3.9	4.8	4.8	4.6	5.1
Uninhabited, mobile, etc.	7.0	5.2	6.7	6.4	6.7
CARTOON PROGRAMS	4.7	6.5	6.7	6.0	7.0
Urban	4.1	5.0	6.5	4.9	6.5
Small town, rural	2.5	3.8	5.6	5.0	6.2
Uninhabited, mobile, etc.	5.1	8.0	7.5	6.7	7.5
NONCARTOON PROGRAMS	5.1	3.7	3.8	4.2	3.8
Urban	2.4	3.2	1.4	2.3	1.7
Small town, rural	4.1	4.9	3.8	4.4	3.8
Uninhabited, mobile, etc.	8.9	2.4	6.0	6.2	5.8

Table 87: Measures of violence by setting of action: 1967 - 69 totals

	Urban	Small town	Uninhabited, mobile, etc.
ALL PROGRAMS			
Programs containing violence (% of all programs)	69.3	77.6	92.3
Number of violent episodes	255	346	754
Rate per all programs	2.9	4.6	6.4
All those involved in violence (% of leading characters)	55.1	62.5	80.5
All those involved in killing (% of leading characters)	7.0	13.9	12.9
CARTOONS			
Programs containing violence (% of cartoon programs)	94.7	90.0	98.2
Number of violent episodes	94	99	374
Rate per all programs	4.9	5.0	6.7
NONCARTOON PROGRAMS			
Programs containing violence (% of all noncartoon programs)	62.3	73.2	86.9
Number of violent episodes	161	247	380
Rate per all programs	2.3	4.4	6.2

Table 88: Census of leading characters analyzed

	1967 N	1967 %	1968 N	1968 %	1969 N	1969 %	1967 – 69 N	1967 – 69 %	Enlarged 1969 sample N	Enlarged 1969 sample %
All characters	240	100.0	215	100.0	307	100.0	762	100.0	377	100.0
Humans	206	85.8	200	93.0	255	83.1	661	86.7	313	83.0
Humanized animals	17	7.1	9	4.2	47	15.3	73	9.6	54	14.3
Other, unclear	17	7.1	6	2.8	5	1.6	28	3.7	10	2.7
Males	191	79.6	167	77.7	234	76.2	592	77.7	290	76.9
Females	47	19.6	46	21.4	73	23.8	166	21.8	82	21.8
Other, unclear	2	0.8	2	0.9	0	0.0	4	0.5	5	1.3
Cartoons	62	100.0	47	100.0	102	100.0	211	100.0	146	100.0
Males	56	90.3	40	85.1	92	90.2	188	89.1	129	88.4
Females	4	6.5	5	10.6	10	9.8	19	9.0	12	8.2
Other, unclear	2	3.2	2	4.3	0	0.0	4	1.9	5	3.4
TV plays	159	100.0	145	100.0	176	100.0	480	100.0	202	100.0
Males	125	78.6	113	77.9	125	71.0	363	75.6	144	71.3
Females	34	21.4	32	22.1	51	29.0	117	24.4	58	28.7
Other, unclear	0	0.0	0	0.0	0	0.0	0	0.0	0	0.0
Feature films	19	100.0	23	100.0	29	100.0	71	100.0	29	100.0
Males	10	52.6	14	60.9	17	58.6	41	57.7	17	58.6
Females	9	47.4	9	39.1	12	41.4	30	42.3	12	41.4
Other, unclear	0	0.0	0	0.0	0	0.0	0	0.0	0	0.0
Crime, western, action-adventure	164	100.0	135	100.0	190	100.0	489	100.0	248	100.0
Males	141	86.0	113	83.7	165	86.8	419	85.7	214	86.3
Females	21	12.8	21	15.6	25	13.2	67	13.7	29	11.7
Other, unclear	2	1.2	1	0.7	0	0.0	3	0.6	5	2.0

Table 88: Census of leading characters analyzed—Continued

	1967 N	1967 %	1968 N	1968 %	1969 N	1969 %	1967–69 N	1967–69 %	Enlarged 1969 sample N	Enlarged 1969 sample %
Comedies	107	100.0	81	100.0	82	100.0	270	100.0	101	100.0
Males	78	72.9	59	72.8	64	78.0	201	74.4	80	79.2
Females	27	25.2	21	25.9	18	22.0	66	24.4	20	19.8
Other, unclear	2	1.9	1	1.2	0	0.0	3	1.1	1	1.0
Networks										
ABC	86	35.8	63	29.3	109	35.5	258	33.9	127	32.7
CBS	73	30.4	79	36.7	93	30.3	245	32.2	135	35.8
NBC	81	33.7	73	34.0	105	34.2	259	34.0	115	30.5
Characters from plays in										
Past	59	24.6	56	26.1	77	25.1	192	25.2	91	24.1
Present	136	56.7	134	62.3	216	70.4	486	63.8	265	70.3
Future	16	6.7	12	5.6	14	4.6	42	5.5	21	5.6
Other, unclear	29	12.0	13	6.0	0	0.0	42	5.5	0	0.0
Characters from plays in										
U.S. only	160	66.7	147	68.4	215	70.0	522	68.5	248	65.8
Several other, unclear	80	33.3	68	31.6	92	30.0	240	31.5	129	34.2
Characters from plays in										
Urban locale	80	33.3	75	34.9	88	28.7	243	31.9	98	26.0
Small town, rural	55	22.9	85	39.5	76	24.8	216	28.3	92	24.4
Several, other, unclear	105	43.8	55	25.6	143	46.6	303	39.8	187	49.6

Table 88: Census of leading characters analyzed—Continued

	1967 N	%	1968 N	%	1969 N	%	1967–69 N	%	Enlarged 1969 sample N	%
Marital status										
Unmarried, unknown	173	72.1	152	70.7	227	73.9	552	72.4	285	75.6
Married, has been married	55	22.9	55	25.6						
Expects to marry; impending marriage	12	5.0	8	3.7						
Total married and expects to marry	67	27.9	63	29.3	80	26.1	210	27.6	92	24.4
Age of characters										
Children and adolescents	12	5.0	16	7.5	28	9.1	56	7.3	33	8.8
Young adults	65	27.1	80	37.2	89	29.0	234	30.7	104	27.6
Middle aged	113	47.1	94	43.7	138	45.0	345	45.3	170	45.1
Old	12	5.0	14	6.5	5	1.6	31	4.1	7	1.9
Uncertain, unclear, several	38	15.8	11	5.1	47	15.3	96	12.6	63	16.7
Selected occupations										
Illegal	25	10.4	19	8.8	22	7.2	66	8.7	30	8.0
Armed forces	18	7.5	8	3.7	12	3.9	38	5.0	14	3.7
Entertainers	20	8.3	15	7.0	33	10.7	68	8.9	46	12.2
Law enforcement and crime detection	16	6.7	23	10.7	22	7.2	61	8.0	24	6.4
Socioeconomic status										
Upper class	54	22.5	35	16.3	28	9.1	117	15.4	32	8.5
Middle class, unclear, other	176	73.3	177	82.3	275	89.6	628	82.4	340	90.2
Lower class	10	4.2	3	1.4	4	1.3	17	2.2	5	1.3

Table 88: Census of leading characters analyzed—Continued

	1967 N	1967 %	1968 N	1968 %	1969 N	1969 %	1967–69 N	1967–69 %	Enlarged 1969 sample N	Enlarged 1969 sample %
Race										
Whites	178	74.2	173	80.5	234	76.2	585	76.8	290	76.9
Nonwhite, other, unclear	62	25.8	42	19.5	73	23.8	177	23.2	87	23.1
Nationality										
American	156	65.0	164	76.3	211	68.7	531	69.7	257	68.2
Non-American, other, unclear	84	35.0	51	23.7	96	31.3	231	30.3	120	31.8
Outcome for character										
Happy ending	134	55.8	132	61.4	143	46.6	409	53.7	168	44.6
Unhappy ending	47	19.6	42	19.5	44	14.3	133	17.5	62	16.4
Mixed, uncertain	59	24.6	41	19.1	120	39.1	220	28.9	147	39.0

Table 89: Violence roles by network

	1967 N	1967 %	1968 N	1968 %	1969 N	1969 %	1967–69 N	1967–69 %	Enlarged 1969 sample N	Enlarged 1969 sample %
ABC										
Totals	86	100.0	63	100.0	109	100.0	258	100.0	127	100.0
Violents	54	62.8	35	55.6	48	44.0	137	53.1	53	41.7
Killers	12	14.0	8	12.7	4	3.7	24	9.3	4	3.1
Victims	62	72.1	36	57.1	58	53.2	156	60.5	62	48.8
Killed	7	8.1	1	1.6	3	2.7	11	4.3	3	2.4
Involved in										
any violence	71	82.6	42	66.7	67	61.5	180	69.8	73	57.5
any killing	19	22.1	8	12.7	7	6.4	34	13.2	7	5.5
Character score		104.7		79.4		67.9		83.0		63.0
CBS										
Totals	73	100.0	79	100.0	93	100.0	245	100.0	135	100.0
Violents	29	39.7	32	40.5	36	38.7	97	39.6	67	49.6
Killers	6	8.2	6	7.6	1	1.1	13	5.3	5	3.7
Victims	34	46.6	41	51.9	44	47.3	119	48.6	78	57.8
Killed	5	6.8	3	3.8	2	2.2	10	4.1	4	3.0
Involved in										
any violence	39	53.4	47	59.5	49	52.7	135	55.1	88	65.2
any killing	10	13.7	7	8.9	3	3.2	20	8.2	8	5.9
Character score		67.1		68.4		55.9		63.3		71.1
NBC										
Totals	81	100.0	73	100.0	105	100.0	259	100.0	115	100.0
Violents	51	63.0	39	53.4	59	56.2	149	57.5	63	54.8
Killers	12	14.8	9	12.3	5	4.8	26	10.0	5	4.3
Victims	59	72.8	43	58.9	75	71.4	177	68.3	82	71.3
Killed	5	6.2	4	5.5	1	1.0	10	3.9	1	0.9
Involved in										
any violence	66	81.5	51	69.9	81	77.1	198	76.4	89	77.4
any killing	16	19.8	10	13.7	6	5.7	32	12.4	6	5.2
Character score		101.3		83.5		82.8		88.8		82.6

Table 90: Network share in violence roles

	1967 N	%	1968 N	%	1969 N	%	1967–69 N	%	Enlarged 1969 sample N	%
All characters	240	100.0	215	100.0	307	100.0	762	100.0	377	100.0
ABC	86	35.8	63	29.3	109	35.5	258	33.9	127	33.7
CBS	73	30.4	79	36.7	93	30.3	245	32.1	135	35.8
NBC	81	33.8	73	34.0	105	34.2	259	34.0	115	30.5
Violents	134	100.0	106	100.0	143	100.0	383	100.0	183	100.0
ABC	54	40.3	35	33.0	48	33.6	137	35.8	53	29.0
CBS	29	21.6	32	30.2	36	25.2	97	25.3	67	36.6
NBC	51	38.1	39	36.8	59	41.2	149	38.9	63	34.4
Killers	30	100.0	23	100.0	10	100.0	63	100.0	14	100.0
ABC	12	40.0	8	34.8	4	40.0	24	38.1	4	28.6
CBS	6	20.0	6	26.1	1	10.0	13	20.6	5	35.7
NBC	12	40.0	9	39.1	5	50.0	26	41.3	5	35.7
Victims	155	100.0	120	100.0	177	100.0	452	100.0	222	100.0
ABC	62	40.0	36	30.0	58	32.8	156	34.5	62	27.9
CBS	34	21.9	41	34.2	44	24.9	119	26.3	78	35.1
NBC	59	38.1	43	35.8	75	42.3	177	39.2	82	37.0
Killed	17	100.0	8	100.0	6	100.0	31	100.0	8	100.0
ABC	7	41.2	1	12.5	3	50.0	11	35.4	3	37.5
CBS	5	29.4	3	37.5	2	33.3	10	32.3	4	50.0
NBC	5	29.4	4	50.0	1	16.7	10	32.3	1	12.5
Involved in any violence	176	100.0	140	100.0	197	100.0	513	100.0	250	100.0
ABC	71	40.3	42	30.0	67	34.0	180	35.1	73	29.2
CBS	39	22.2	47	33.6	49	24.9	135	26.3	88	35.2
NBC	66	37.5	51	36.4	81	41.1	198	38.6	89	35.6

Table 90: Network share in violence roles—Continued

	1967 N	1967 %	1968 N	1968 %	1969 N	1969 %	1967–69 N	1967–69 %	Enlarged 1969 sample N	Enlarged 1969 sample %
Involved in any killing	45	100.0	25	100.0	16	100.0	86	100.0	21	100.0
ABC	19	42.2	8	32.0	7	43.8	34	39.5	7	33.3
CBS	10	22.2	7	28.0	3	18.7	20	23.3	8	38.1
NBC	16	35.6	10	40.0	6	37.5	32	37.2	6	28.6
Characters in crime-adventure										
Totals	164	100.0	135	100.0	190	100.0	489	100.0	248	100.0
Violents	119	72.6	89	65.9	122	64.2	330	67.5	158	63.7
Killers	30	18.3	22	16.3	9	4.7	61	12.5	13	5.2
Victims	132	80.5	99	73.3	147	77.4	378	77.3	187	75.4
Killed	16	9.8	7	5.2	6	3.2	29	5.9	8	3.2
Involved in										
any violence	146	89.0	111	82.2	162	85.3	419	85.7	209	84.3
any killing	44	26.8	24	17.8	15	7.9	83	17.0	20	8.1
Character score		115.8		100.0		93.2		102.7		92.4
Characters in comedy										
Totals	107	100.0	81	100.0	82	100.0	270	100.0	101	100.0
Violents	40	37.4	31	38.3	33	40.2	104	38.5	48	47.5
Killers	4	3.7	4	4.9	0	0.0	8	3.0	0	0.0
Victims	50	46.7	35	43.2	50	61.0	135	50.0	69	68.3
Killed	1	0.9	0	0.0	0	0.0	1	0.4	0	0.0
Involved in										
any violence	59	55.1	43	53.1	52	63.4	154	57.0	71	70.3
any killing	5	4.7	4	4.9	0	0.0	9	3.3	0	0.0
Character score		59.8		58.0		63.4		60.3		70.3

Table 91: Violence role by program format and type

	1967 N	1967 %	1968 N	1968 %	1969 N	1969 %	1967 – 69 N	1967 – 69 %	Enlarged 1969 sample N	Enlarged 1969 sample %
Characters in cartoons										
Totals	62	100.0	47	100.0	102	100.0	211	100.0	146	100.0
Violents	45	72.6	31	66.0	72	70.6	148	70.1	98	67.1
Killers	3	4.8	2	4.3	0	0.0	5	2.4	1	0.7
Victims	52	83.9	36	76.6	87	85.3	175	82.9	117	80.1
Killed	6	9.7	0	0.0	1	1.0	7	3.3	2	1.4
Involved in										
any violence	56	90.3	37	78.7	92	90.2	185	87.7	127	87.0
any killing	9	14.5	2	4.3	1	1.0	12	5.7	3	2.1
Character score		104.8		83.0		91.2		93.3		89.1
Characters in TV plays										
Totals	159	100.0	145	100.0	176	100.0	480	100.0	202	100.0
Violents	79	49.7	59	40.7	61	34.7	199	41.5	75	37.1
Killers	25	15.7	16	11.0	9	5.1	50	10.4	12	5.9
Victims	94	59.1	68	46.9	75	42.6	237	49.4	90	44.6
Killed	10	6.3	6	4.1	4	2.3	20	4.2	5	2.5
Involved in										
any violence	107	67.3	83	57.2	88	50.0	278	57.9	106	52.5
any killing	33	20.7	18	12.4	13	7.4	64	13.3	16	7.9
Character score		88.0		69.6		57.4		71.2		60.4

Table 91: Violence role by program format and type—Continued

	1967		1968		1969		1967–69		Enlarged 1969 sample	
	N	%	N	%	N	%	N	%	N	%
Characters in feature films										
Totals	19	100.0	23	100.0	29	100.0	71	100.0	29	100.0
Violents	10	52.6	16	69.6	10	34.5	36	50.7	10	34.5
Killers	2	10.5	5	21.7	1	3.4	8	11.3	1	3.4
Victims	9	47.4	16	69.6	15	51.7	40	56.3	15	51.7
Killed	1	5.3	2	8.7	1	3.4	4	5.6	1	3.4
Involved in										
any violence	13	68.4	20	87.0	17	58.6	50	70.4	17	58.6
any killing	3	15.8	5	21.7	2	6.9	10	14.1	2	6.9
Character score		84.2		108.7		65.5		84.5		65.5
Characters in cartoons										
Totals	62	100.0	47	100.0	102	100.0	211	100.0	146	100.0
Violents	45	72.6	31	66.0	72	70.6	148	70.1	98	67.1
Killers	3	4.8	2	4.3	0	0.0	5	2.4	1	0.7
Victims	52	83.9	36	76.6	87	85.3	175	82.9	117	80.1
Killed	6	9.7	0	0.0	1	1.0	7	3.3	2	1.4
Involved in										
any violence	56	90.3	37	78.7	92	90.2	185	87.7	127	87.0
any killing	9	14.5	2	4.3	1	1.0	12	5.7	3	2.1
Character score		104.8		83.0		91.2		93.3		89.1

Table 91: Violence role by program format and type—Continued

	1967		1968		1969		1967–69		Enlarged 1969 sample	
	N	%	N	%	N	%	N	%	N	%
Characters in TV plays										
Totals	159	100.0	145	100.0	176	100.0	480	100.0	202	100.0
Violents	79	49.7	59	40.7	61	34.7	199	41.5	75	37.1
Killers	25	15.7	16	11.0	9	5.1	50	10.4	12	5.9
Victims	94	59.1	68	46.9	75	42.6	237	49.4	90	44.6
Killed	10	6.3	6	4.1	4	2.3	20	4.2	5	2.5
Involved in										
any violence	107	67.3	83	57.2	88	50.0	278	57.9	106	52.5
any killing	33	20.7	18	12.4	13	7.4	64	13.3	16	7.9
Character score		88.0		69.6		57.4		71.2		60.4
Characters in feature films										
Totals	19	100.0	23	100.0	29	100.0	71	100.0	29	100.0
Violents	10	52.6	16	69.6	10	34.5	36	50.7	10	34.5
Killers	2	10.5	5	21.7	1	3.4	8	11.3	1	3.4
Victims	9	47.4	16	69.6	15	51.7	40	56.3	15	51.7
Killed	1	5.3	2	8.7	1	3.4	4	5.6	1	3.4
Involved in										
any violence	13	68.4	20	87.0	17	58.6	50	70.4	17	58.6
any killing	3	15.8	5	21.7	2	6.9	10	14.1	2	6.9
Character score		84.2		108.7		65.5		84.5		65.5

Table 92: Program format share in violence roles

	1967 N	1967 %	1968 N	1968 %	1969 N	1969 %	1967–69 N	1967–69 %	Enlarged 1969 sample N	Enlarged 1969 sample %
All characters	240	100.0	215	100.0	307	100.0	762	100.0	377	100.0
Cartoon	62	25.8	47	21.9	102	33.2	211	27.7	146	38.7
TV play	159	66.3	145	67.4	176	57.3	480	63.0	202	53.6
Feature film	19	7.9	23	10.7	29	9.4	71	9.3	29	7.7
All violents	134	100.0	106	100.0	143	100.0	383	100.0	183	100.0
Cartoon	45	33.6	31	29.2	72	50.3	148	38.6	98	53.6
TV play	79	59.0	59	55.7	61	42.7	199	52.0	75	41.0
Feature film	10	7.4	16	15.1	10	7.0	36	9.4	10	5.5
All killers	30	100.0	23	100.0	10	100.0	63	100.0	14	100.0
Cartoon	3	10.0	2	8.7	0	0.0	5	7.9	1	7.1
TV play	25	83.3	16	69.6	9	90.0	50	79.4	12	85.7
Feature film	2	6.7	5	21.7	1	10.0	8	12.7	1	7.1
All victims	155	100.0	120	100.0	177	100.0	452	100.0	222	100.0
Cartoon	52	33.5	36	30.0	87	49.2	175	38.7	117	52.7
TV play	94	60.6	68	56.7	75	42.4	237	52.4	90	40.5
Feature film	9	5.8	16	13.3	15	8.5	40	8.8	15	6.8
All killed	17	100.0	8	100.0	6	100.0	31	100.0	8	100.0
Cartoon	6	35.3	0	0.0	1	16.7	7	22.6	2	25.0
TV play	10	58.8	6	75.0	4	66.7	20	64.5	5	62.5
Feature film	1	5.9	2	25.0	1	16.7	4	12.9	1	12.5
All violents and/or victims	176	100.0	140	100.0	197	100.0	513	100.0	250	100.0
Cartoon	56	31.8	37	26.4	92	46.7	185	36.1	127	50.8
TV play	107	60.8	83	59.3	88	44.7	278	54.2	106	42.4
Feature film	13	7.4	20	14.3	17	8.6	50	9.7	17	6.8
All killers or killed	45	100.0	25	100.0	16	100.0	86	100.0	21	100.0
Cartoon	9	20.0	2	8.0	1	6.3	12	14.0	3	14.3
TV play	33	73.3	18	72.0	13	81.2	64	74.4	16	76.2
Feature film	3	6.7	5	20.0	2	12.5	10	11.6	2	9.5

Table 93: Program type share in violence roles

	1967		1968		1969		1967 – 69		Enlarged 1969 sample	
	N	%	N	%	N	%	N	%	N	%
All characters	240	100.0	215	100.0	307	100.0	762	100.0	377	100.0
Crime-adventure	164	68.3	135	62.8	190	61.9	489	64.2	248	65.8
Comedy	107	44.6	81	37.7	82	26.7	270	35.4	101	26.8
Violents	134	100.0	106	100.0	143	100.0	383	100.0	183	100.0
Crime-adventure	119	88.8	89	84.0	122	85.3	330	86.2	158	86.3
Comedy	40	39.9	31	29.2	33	23.1	104	27.2	48	26.2
Killers	30	100.0	23	100.0	10	100.0	63	100.0	14	100.0
Crime-adventure	30	100.0	22	95.7	9	90.0	61	96.8	13	92.9
Comedy	4	13.3	4	17.4	0	0.0	8	12.7	0	0.0
Victims	155	100.0	120	100.0	177	100.0	452	100.0	222	100.0
Crime-adventure	132	85.2	99	82.5	147	83.1	378	83.6	187	84.2
Comedy	50	32.3	35	29.2	50	28.2	135	29.9	69	31.1
Killed	17	100.0	8	100.0	6	100.0	31	100.0	8	100.0
Crime-adventure	16	94.1	7	87.5	6	100.0	29	93.5	8	100.0
Comedy	1	5.9	0	0.0	0	0.0	1	3.2	0	0.0
Involved in any violence	176	100.0	140	100.0	197	100.0	513	100.0	250	100.0
Crime-adventure	146	83.0	111	79.3	162	82.2	419	81.7	209	83.6
Comedy	59	33.5	43	30.7	52	26.4	154	30.0	71	28.4
Involved in any killing	45	100.0	25	100.0	16	100.0	86	100.0	21	100.0
Crime-adventure	44	97.8	24	96.0	15	93.8	83	96.5	20	95.2
Comedy	5	11.1	4	16.0	0	0.0	9	10.5	0	0.0

Table 94: Violence roles of leading characters

	1967		1968		1969		1967 – 69		Enlarged 1969 sample	
	N	%	N	%	N	%	N	%	N	%
All characters										
Totals	240	100.0	215	100.0	307	100.0	762	100.0	377	100.0
Violents	134	55.8	106	49.3	143	46.6	383	50.3	183	48.5
Killers	30	12.5	23	10.7	10	3.3	63	8.3	14	3.7
Victims	155	64.6	120	55.8	177	57.7	452	59.3	222	58.9
Killed	17	7.1	8	3.7	6	2.0	31	4.1	8	2.1
Involved in										
any violence	176	73.3	140	65.1	197	64.2	513	67.3	250	66.3
any killing	45	18.8	25	11.6	16	5.3	86	11.3	21	5.5
Character score		92.1		76.7		69.5		78.6		70.8
Male characters*										
Totals	191	100.0	167	100.0	234	100.0	592	100.0	290	100.0
Violents	114	59.7	91	54.5	125	53.4	330	55.7	159	54.8
Killers	26	13.6	21	12.6	10	4.3	57	9.6	14	4.8
Victims	135	70.7	101	60.5	150	64.1	386	65.2	186	64.1
Killed	16	8.4	6	3.6	5	2.1	27	4.6	7	2.4
Involved in										
any violence	148	77.5	114	68.3	166	70.9	428	72.3	209	72.0
any killing	40	21.0	22	13.2	15	6.4	77	13.0	20	6.9
Character score		98.5		81.5		77.3		85.3		78.9

Table 94: Violence roles of leading characters—Continued

	1967 N	1967 %	1968 N	1968 %	1969 N	1969 %	1967–69 N	1967–69 %	Enlarged 1969 sample N	Enlarged 1969 sample %
Female characters*										
Totals	47	100.0	46	100.0	73	100.0	166	100.0	82	100.0
Violents	18	38.3	13	28.3	18	24.7	49	29.5	22	26.8
Killers	4	8.5	2	4.3	0	0.0	6	3.6	0	0.0
Victims	18	38.3	17	37.0	27	37.0	62	37.3	32	39.0
Killed	1	2.1	2	4.3	1	1.4	4	2.4	1	1.2
Involved in										
any violence	26	55.3	24	52.2	31	42.5	81	48.8	37	45.1
any killing	5	10.6	3	6.4	1	1.4	9	5.4	1	1.2
Character score		65.9		58.6		42.9		54.2		46.3

*"Other" characters, i.e. those whose sex could not be identified (all in cartoon plays), were not included.

Table 95: Share of the sexes in violence roles

	1967 N	%	1968 N	%	1969 N	%	1967 – 69 N	%	Enlarged 1969 sample N	%
All characters	240	100.0	215	100.0	307	100.0	762	100.0	377	100.0
Males	191	79.6	167	77.7	234	76.2	592	77.7	290	76.9
Females	47	19.6	46	21.4	73	23.8	166	21.8	82	21.8
Violents	134	100.0	106	100.0	143	100.0	383	100.0	183	100.0
Males	114	85.1	91	85.8	125	87.4	330	86.2	159	86.9
Females	18	13.4	13	12.3	18	12.6	49	12.8	22	12.0
Killers	30	100.0	23	100.0	10	100.0	63	100.0	14	100.0
Males	26	86.7	21	91.3	10	100.0	57	90.5	14	100.0
Females	4	13.3	2	8.7	0	0.0	6	9.5	0	0.0
Victims	155	100.0	120	100.0	177	100.0	452	100.0	222	100.0
Males	135	87.1	101	84.2	150	84.7	386	85.4	186	83.8
Females	18	11.6	17	14.2	27	15.2	62	13.7	32	14.4
Killed	17	100.0	8	100.0	6	100.0	31	100.0	8	100.0
Males	16	94.1	6	75.0	5	83.3	27	87.1	7	87.5
Females	1	5.9	2	25.0	1	16.7	4	12.9	1	12.5
Involved in any violence	176	100.0	140	100.0	197	100.0	513	100.0	250	100.0
Males	148	84.1	114	81.4	166	84.3	428	83.4	209	83.6
Females	26	14.8	24	17.1	31	15.8	81	15.8	37	14.8
Involved in any killing	45	100.0	25	100.0	16	100.0	86	100.0	21	100.0
Males	40	88.9	22	88.0	15	93.7	77	89.5	20	95.2
Females	5	11.1	3	12.0	1	6.2	9	10.5	1	4.8

Table 96: Violence roles by age

	1967		1968		1969		1967 – 69		Enlarged 1969 sample	
	N	%	N	%	N	%	N	%	N	%
Children and adolescents										
Totals	12	100.0	16	100.0	28	100.0	56	100.0	33	100.0
Violents	8	66.7	4	25.0	10	35.7	22	39.3	11	33.3
Killers	1	8.3	0	0.0	0	0.0	1	1.8	0	0.0
Victims	9	75.0	10	62.5	14	50.0	33	58.9	17	51.5
Killed	0	0.0	0	0.0	0	0.0	0	0.0	0	0.0
Involved in										
any violence	10	83.3	10	62.5	15	53.6	35	62.5	19	57.6
any killing	1	8.3	0	0.0	0	0.0	1	1.8	0	0.0
Character score		91.6		62.5		53.6		64.3		57.6
Young adults										
Totals	65	100.0	80	100.0	89	100.0	234	100.0	104	100.0
Violents	31	47.7	38	47.5	39	43.8	108	46.1	46	44.2
Killers	11	16.9	9	11.2	4	4.5	24	10.3	4	3.8
Victims	42	64.6	46	57.5	55	61.8	143	61.1	65	62.5
Killed	2	3.1	3	3.7	2	2.2	7	3.0	2	1.9
Involved in										
any violence	44	67.7	52	65.0	62	69.7	158	67.5	73	70.2
any killing	13	20.0	10	12.5	6	6.7	29	12.4	6	5.8
Character score		87.7		77.5		76.4		79.9		76.0

Table 96: Violence roles by age—Continued

	1967		1968		1969		1967–69		Enlarged 1969 sample	
	N	%	N	%	N	%	N	%	N	%
Middle-aged										
Totals	113	100.0	94	100.0	138	100.0	345	100.0	170	100.0
Violents	64	56.6	52	55.3	59	42.8	175	50.7	78	45.9
Killers	15	13.3	13	13.8	6	4.3	34	9.8	10	5.9
Victims	70	61.9	51	54.3	65	47.1	186	53.9	82	48.2
Killed	11	9.7	4	4.3	3	2.2	18	5.2	5	2.9
Involved in										
any violence	83	73.4	62	65.9	76	55.1	221	64.1	98	57.6
any killing	24	21.2	14	14.9	9	6.5	47	13.6	14	8.2
Character score		94.6		80.8		61.6		77.7		65.8
Old										
Totals	12	100.0	14	100.0	5	100.0	31	100.0	7	100.0
Violents	5	41.7	6	42.9	0	0.0	11	35.5	1	14.3
Killers	0	0.0	1	7.1	0	0.0	1	3.2	0	0.0
Victims	6	50.0	4	28.6	3	60.0	13	41.9	4	57.1
Killed	1	8.3	1	7.1	1	20.0	3	9.7	1	14.3
Involved in										
any violence	7	58.3	7	50.0	3	60.0	17	54.8	4	57.1
any killing	1	8.3	1	7.1	1	20.0	3	9.7	1	14.3
Character score		66.6		57.1		80.0		64.5		71.4

Table 97: Middle-aged violents and victims by sex

Middle-aged males	1967 (N=94) %	1968 (N=78) %	1969 (N=112) %
Violents	59.6	57.7	50.0
Victims	69.1	60.3	54.5
Either or both	77.6	68.0	63.4

Middle-aged females	1967 (N=19) %	1968 (N=16) %	1969 (N=26) %
Violents	42.1	43.8	11.5
Victims	26.3	25.0	15.4
Either or both	52.6	56.3	19.2

Table 98: Share of ages in violence roles

	1967 N	1967 %	1968 N	1968 %	1969 N	1969 %	1967 – 69 N	1967 – 69 %	Enlarged 1969 sample N	Enlarged 1969 sample %
All characters	240	100.0	215	100.0	307	100.0	762	100.0	377	100.0
Children and adolescents	12	5.0	16	7.5	28	9.1	56	7.3	33	8.8
Young adults	65	27.1	80	37.2	89	29.0	234	30.7	104	27.6
Middle-aged	113	47.1	94	43.7	138	45.0	345	45.3	170	45.1
Old	12	5.0	14	6.5	5	1.6	31	4.1	7	1.9
Violents	134	100.0	106	100.0	143	100.0	383	100.0	183	100.0
Children and adolescents	8	6.0	4	3.8	10	7.0	22	5.7	11	6.0
Young adults	31	23.1	38	35.8	39	27.3	108	28.2	46	25.1
Middle-aged	64	47.8	52	49.1	59	41.2	175	45.7	78	42.6
Old	5	3.7	6	5.7	0	0.0	11	2.9	1	0.5
Killers	30	100.0	23	100.0	10	100.0	63	100.0	14	100.0
Children and adolescents	1	3.3	0	0.0	0	0.0	1	1.6	0	0.0
Young adults	11	36.7	9	39.1	4	40.0	24	38.1	4	28.6
Middle-aged	15	50.0	13	56.5	6	60.0	34	54.0	10	71.4
Old	0	0.0	1	4.3	0	0.0	1	1.6	0	0.0
Victims	155	100.0	120	100.0	177	100.0	452	100.0	222	100.0
Children and adolescents	9	5.8	10	8.3	14	7.9	33	7.3	17	7.6
Young adults	42	27.1	46	38.3	55	31.1	143	31.6	65	29.3
Middle-aged	70	45.2	51	42.5	65	36.7	186	41.1	82	36.9
Old	6	3.9	4	3.3	3	1.7	13	2.9	4	1.8
Killed	17	100.0	8	100.0	6	100.0	31	100.0	8	100.0
Children and adolescents	0	0.0	0	0.0	0	0.0	0	0.0	0	0.0
Young adults	2	11.8	3	37.5	2	33.3	7	22.6	2	25.0
Middle-aged	11	64.7	4	50.0	3	50.0	18	58.1	5	62.5
Old	1	5.9	1	12.5	1	16.7	3	9.7	1	12.5

Table 98: Share of ages in violence roles—Continued

	1967		1968		1969		1967–69		Enlarged 1969 sample	
	N	%	N	%	N	%	N	%	N	%
Involved in any violence	176	100.0	140	100.0	197	100.0	513	100.0	250	100.0
Children and adolescents	10	5.7	10	7.1	15	7.6	35	6.8	19	7.6
Young adults	44	25.0	52	37.1	62	31.5	158	30.8	73	29.2
Middle-aged	83	47.1	62	44.3	76	38.6	221	43.1	98	39.2
Old	7	4.0	7	5.0	3	1.5	17	3.3	4	1.6
Involved in any killing	45	100.0	25	100.0	16	100.0	86	100.0	21	100.0
Children and adolescents	1	2.2	0.	0.0	0	0.0	1	1.2	0	0.0
Young adults	13	28.9	10	40.0	6	37.5	29	33.7	6	28.6
Middle-aged	24	5.3	14	56.0	9	56.2	47	54.6	14	6.7
Old	1	2.2	1	4.0	1	6.2	3	3.5	1	4.8

Table 99: Share of middle-aged women in violence roles of all middle-aged characters

	1967 Total (100%)	1967 Women N	1967 Women %	1968 Total (100%)	1968 Women N	1968 Women %	1969 Total (100%)	1969 Women N	1969 Women %
All middle-aged characters	113	19	16.8	94	16	17.0	138	26	18.8
Middle-aged									
violents	64	8	12.5	52	7	13.5	59	3	5.1
killers	15	1	6.7	13	0	0.0	6	0	0.0
victims	70	5	7.1	51	4	7.8	65	4	6.2
killed	11	1	9.0	4	0	0.0	3	0	0.0

Table 100: Violence roles by marital status

	1967		1968		1969		1967 – 69		Enlarged 1969 sample	
	N	%	N	%	N	%	N	%	N	%
Unmarried, unknown										
Totals	173	100.0	152	100.0	227	100.0	552	100.0	285	100.0
Violents	111	64.2	77	50.7	120	52.9	308	55.8	156	54.7
Killers	26	15.0	17	11.2	8	3.5	51	9.2	10	3.5
Victims	124	71.7	94	61.8	143	63.0	361	65.4	183	64.2
Killed	15	8.7	7	4.6	6	2.6	28	5.1	8	2.8
Involved in										
any violence	137	79.2	103	67.8	160	70.5	400	72.5	207	72.6
any killing	40	23.1	19	12.5	14	6.2	73	13.2	17	6.0
Character score		102.3		80.3		76.7		85.7		78.6
Married, marries, expects to marry										
Totals	67	100.0	63	100.0	80	100.0	210	100.0	92	100.0
Violents	23	34.3	29	46.0	23	28.7	75	35.7	27	29.3
Killers	4	6.0	6	9.5	2	2.5	12	5.7	4	4.3
Victims	31	46.3	26	41.3	34	42.5	91	43.3	39	42.4
Killed	2	3.0	1	1.6	0	0.0	3	1.4	0	0.0
Involved in										
any violence	39	58.2	37	58.7	37	46.2	113	53.8	43	46.7
any killing	5	7.5	6	9.5	2	2.5	13	6.2	4	4.3
Character score		65.7		68.2		48.7		60.0		51.0

Table 101: Share of unmarried and married in violence roles

	1967		1968		1969		1967 − 69		Enlarged 1969 sample	
	N	%	N	%	N	%	N	%	N	%
All characters	240	100.0	215	100.0	307	100.0	762	100.0	377	100.0
Unmarried, unknown	173	72.1	152	70.7	227	73.9	552	72.4	285	75.6
Married, marries, expects to marry	67	27.9	63	29.3	80	26.1	210	27.6	92	24.4
Violents	134	100.0	106	100.0	143	100.0	383	100.0	183	100.0
Unmarried, unknown	111	82.8	77	72.6	120	83.9	308	80.4	156	85.2
Married, marries, expects to marry	23	17.2	29	27.4	23	16.1	75	19.6	27	14.8
Killers	30	100.0	23	100.0	10	100.0	63	100.0	14	100.0
Unmarried, unknown	26	86.7	17	73.9	8	80.0	51	81.0	10	71.4
Married, marries, expects to marry	4	13.3	6	26.1	2	20.0	12	19.0	4	28.6
Victims	155	100.0	120	100.0	177	100.0	452	100.0	222	100.0
Unmarried, unknown	124	80.0	94	78.3	143	80.8	361	79.9	183	82.4
Married, marries, expects to marry	31	20.0	26	21.7	34	19.2	91	20.1	39	17.6
Killed	17	100.0	8	100.0	6	100.0	31	100.0	8	100.0
Unmarried, unknown	15	88.2	7	87.5	6	100.0	28	90.3	8	100.0
Married, marries, expects to marry	2	11.8	1	12.5	0	0.0	3	9.7	0	0.0
Involved in any violence	176	100.0	140	100.0	197	100.0	513	100.0	250	100.0
Unmarried, unknown	137	77.8	103	73.6	160	81.2	400	78.0	207	82.8
Married, marries, expects to marry	39	22.2	37	26.4	37	18.8	113	22.0	43	17.2
Involved in any killing	45	100.0	25	100.0	16	100.0	86	100.0	21	100.0
Unmarried, unknown	40	88.9	19	76.0	14	87.5	73	84.9	17	81.0
Married, marries, expects to marry	5	11.1	6	24.0	2	12.5	13	15.1	4	19.0

Table 102: Violence roles by occupation*

	1967		1968		1969		1967 – 69		Enlarged 1969 sample	
	N	%	N	%	N	%	N	%	N	%
Illegal										
Totals	25	100.0	19	100.0	22	100.0	66	100.0	30	100.0
Violents	20	80.0	16	84.2	12	54.5	48	72.7	19	63.3
Killers	7	28.0	5	26.3	3	13.6	15	22.7	4	13.3
Victims	22	88.0	17	89.5	15	68.2	54	81.8	21	70.0
Killed	3	12.0	2	10.5	1	4.5	6	9.1	2	6.7
Involved in any violence	22	88.0	17	89.5	16	72.6	55	83.3	23	76.7
killing	9	36.0	6	31.6	4	18.2	19	28.8	6	20.0
Character score		124.0		121.1		90.8		112.1		96.7
Armed forces										
Totals	18	100.0	8	100.0	12	100.0	38	100.0	14	100.0
Violents	12	66.7	3	37.5	9	75.0	24	63.2	11	78.6
Killers	6	33.3	2	25.0	0	0.0	8	21.0	1	7.1
Victims	13	72.2	4	50.0	10	83.3	27	71.1	12	85.7
Killed	1	5.6	2	25.0	0	0.0	3	7.9	2	14.3
Involved in any violence	15	83.3	4	50.0	10	83.3	29	76.3	12	85.7
killing	7	38.9	2	25.0	0	0.0	9	23.7	2	14.3
Character score		122.2		75.0		83.3		100.0		100.0

Table 102: Violence roles by occupation*—Continued

	1967 N	1967 %	1968 N	1968 %	1969 N	1969 %	1967–69 N	1967–69 %	Enlarged 1969 sample N	Enlarged 1969 sample %
Entertainment										
Totals	20	100.0	15	100.0	33	100.0	68	100.0	46	100.0
Violents	5	25.0	7	46.7	14	42.4	26	38.2	23	50.0
Killers	1	5.0	1	6.7	0	0.0	2	2.9	0	0.0
Victims	12	60.0	7	46.7	17	51.5	36	52.9	25	54.3
Killed	0	0.0	1	6.7	1	3.0	2	2.9	1	2.2
Involved in any violence	14	70.0	8	53.3	20	60.6	42	61.8	31	67.4
killing	1	5.0	1	6.7	1	3.0	3	4.4	1	2.2
Character score		75.0		60.0		63.6		66.2		69.6
Law enforcement and crime detection										
Totals	16	100.0	23	100.0	22	100.0	61	100.0	24	100.0
Violents	10	62.5	17	73.9	13	59.1	40	65.6	15	62.5
Killers	2	12.5	5	21.7	0	0.0	7	11.5	0	0.0
Victims	8	50.0	17	73.9	10	45.5	35	57.4	11	45.8
Killed	0	0.0	0	0.0	0	0.0	0	0.0	0	0.0
Involved in any violence	11	68.8	22	95.7	16	72.6	49	80.3	18	75.0
killing	2	12.5	5	21.7	0	0.0	7	11.5	0	0.0
Character score		81.3		117.4		72.6		91.8		75.0

*The occupational categories are not mutually exclusive.

Table 103: Share of occupation in violence roles*

	1967		1968		1969		1967 – 69		Enlarged 1969 sample	
	N	%	N	%	N	%	N	%	N	%
All characters	240	100.0	215	100.0	307	100.0	762	100.0	377	100.0
Illegal	25	10.4	19	8.8	22	7.2	66	8.7	30	8.0
Armed forces	18	7.5	8	3.7	12	3.9	38	4.9	14	3.7
Entertainment	20	8.3	15	7.0	33	10.7	68	8.9	46	12.2
Law enforcement/ crime detection	16	6.7	23	10.7	22	7.2	61	8.0	24	6.4
Violents	134	100.0	106	100.0	143	100.0	383	100.0	183	100.0
Illegal	20	14.9	16	15.1	12	8.4	48	12.5	19	10.4
Armed forces	12	9.0	3	2.8	9	6.3	24	6.3	11	6.0
Entertainment	5	3.7	7	6.6	14	9.8	26	6.8	23	12.6
law enforcement/ crime detection	10	7.5	17	16.0	13	9.1	40	10.4	15	8.2
Killers	30	100.0	23	100.0	10	100.0	63	100.0	14	100.0
Illegal	7	23.3	5	21.7	3	30.0	15	23.8	4	28.6
Armed forces	6	20.0	2	8.7	0	0.0	8	12.7	1	7.1
Entertainment	1	3.3	1	4.3	0	0.0	2	3.2	0	0.0
Law enforcement/ crime detection	2	6.7	5	21.7	0	0.0	7	11.1	0	0.0
Victims	155	100.0	120	100.0	177	100.0	452	100.0	222	100.0
Illegal	22	14.2	17	14.2	15	8.5	54	12.2	21	9.5
Armed forces	13	8.4	4	3.3	10	5.6	27	6.0	12	5.4
Entertainment	12	7.7	7	5.8	17	9.6	36	8.0	25	11.3
Law enforcement/ crime detection	8	5.2	17	14.2	10	5.6	35	7.7	11	5.0

Table 103: Share of occupation in violence roles*—Continued

	1967		1968		1969		1967–69		Enlarged 1969 sample	
	N	%	N	%	N	%	N	%	N	%
Killed	17	100.0	8	100.0	6	100.0	31	100.0	8	100.0
Illegal	3	17.6	2	25.0	1	16.7	6	19.4	2	25.0
Armed forces	1	5.9	2	25.0	0	0.0	3	9.7	2	25.0
Entertainment	0	0.0	1	12.5	1	16.7	2	6.5	1	12.5
Law enforcement/ crime detection	0	0.0	0	0.0	0	0.0	0	0.0	0	0.0
Involved in any violence	176	100.0	140	100.0	197	100.0	513	100.0	250	100.0
Illegal	22	12.5	17	12.1	16	8.1	55	10.7	23	9.2
Armed forces	15	8.5	4	2.8	10	5.1	29	5.7	12	4.8
Entertainment	14	8.0	8	5.7	20	10.2	42	8.2	31	12.4
Law enforcement/ crime detection	11	6.3	22	15.7	16	8.1	49	9.6	18	7.2
Involved in any killing	45	100.0	25	100.0	16	100.0	86	100.0	21	100.0
Illegal	9	20.0	6	24.0	4	25.0	19	22.1	6	28.6
Armed forces	7	15.6	2	8.0	0	0.0	9	10.5	2	9.5
Entertainment	1	2.2	1	4.0	1	6.3	3	3.5	1	4.8
Law enforcement/ crime detection	2	4.4	5	20.0	0	0.0	7	8.1	5	23.8

*The occupational categories are not mutually exclusive.

Table 104: Violence roles by class

	1967 N	%	1968 N	%	1969 N	%	1967 – 69 N	%	Enlarged 1969 sample N	%
Upper										
Total	54	100.0	35	100.0	28	100.0	117	100.0	32	100.0
Violent	27	50.0	21	60.0	8	28.6	56	47.9	10	31.3
Killer	6	11.1	4	11.4	0	0.0	10	8.5	1	3.1
Victim	36	66.7	20	57.1	13	46.4	69	59.0	17	53.1
Killed	6	11.1	3	8.6	0	0.0	9	7.7	1	3.1
Involved in										
any violence	40	74.1	25	71.4	15	53.6	80	68.4	19	59.4
any killing	11	20.4	5	14.3	0	0.0	16	13.7	1	3.1
Character score		94.5		85.7		53.6		82.1		62.5
Middle, mixed										
Total	176	100.0	177	100.0	275	100.0	628	100.0	340	100.0
Violent	98	55.7	84	47.5	133	48.4	315	50.2	170	50.0
Killer	22	12.5	19	10.7	10	3.6	51	8.1	13	3.8
Victim	110	62.5	97	54.8	161	58.5	368	58.6	201	59.1
Killed	9	5.1	5	2.8	6	2.2	20	3.2	7	2.1
Involved in										
any violence	126	71.6	112	63.3	179	65.0	417	66.4	227	66.8
any killing	31	17.6	20	11.3	16	5.8	67	10.7	20	5.9
Character score		89.2		74.6		70.8		77.1		72.7
Lower										
Total	10	100.0	3	100.0	4	100.0	17	100.0	5	100.0
Violent	9	90.0	1	33.3	2	50.0	12	70.6	3	60.0
Killer	2	20.0	1	33.3	0	0.0	3	17.6	0	0.0
Victim	9	90.0	3	100.0	3	75.0	15	88.2	4	80.0
Killed	2	20.0	0	0.0	0	0.0	2	11.8	0	0.0
Involved in										
any violence	10	100.0	3	100.0	3	75.0	16	94.1	4	80.0
any killing	3	30.0	1	33.3	0	0.0	4	23.5	0	0.0
Character score		130.0		133.3		75.0		117.6		80.0

Table 105: Share of classes in violence roles

	1967 N	%	1968 N	%	1969 N	%	1967 – 69 N	%	Enlarged 1969 sample N	%
All characters	240	100.0	215	100.0	307	100.0	762	100.0	377	100.0
Upper	54	22.5	35	16.3	28	9.1	117	15.4	32	8.5
Middle, mixed	176	73.3	177	82.3	275	89.6	628	82.4	340	90.2
Lower	10	4.2	3	1.9	4	1.3	17	2.2	5	1.3
Violents	134	100.0	106	100.0	143	100.0	383	100.0	183	100.0
Upper	27	20.1	21	19.8	8	5.6	56	14.6	10	5.5
Middle, mixed	98	73.1	84	79.2	133	93.0	315	82.2	170	92.9
Lower	9	6.7	1	0.9	2	1.4	12	3.1	3	1.6
Killers	30	100.0	24	100.0	10	100.0	63	100.0	14	100.0
Upper	6	20.0	4	16.7	0	0.0	10	15.8	1	7.1
Middle, mixed	22	73.3	19	79.2	10	100.0	50	80.9	13	92.9
Lower	2	6.7	1	4.2	0	0.0	3	4.7	0	0.0
Victims	155	100.0	120	100.0	177	100.0	452	100.0	222	100.0
Upper	36	23.2	20	16.7	13	7.3	69	15.3	17	7.7
Middle, mixed	110	71.0	97	80.8	161	91.0	368	81.4	201	90.5
Lower	9	5.8	3	2.5	3	1.7	15	3.3	4	1.8
Killed	17	100.0	8	100.0	6	100.0	31	100.0	8	100.0
Upper	6	35.3	3	37.5	0	0.0	9	29.0	1	12.5
Middle, mixed	9	52.9	5	62.5	6	100.0	20	64.5	7	87.5
Lower	2	11.8	0	0.0	0	0.0	2	6.4	0	0.0
Involved in violence	176	100.0	140	100.0	197	100.0	513	100.0	250	100.0
Upper	40	22.7	25	17.9	15	7.6	80	15.6	19	7.6
Middle, mixed	126	71.6	112	80.0	179	90.9	417	81.3	227	90.8
Lower	10	5.7	3	2.2	3	1.5	16	3.1	4	1.6
Involved in killing	45	100.0	25	100.0	16	100.0	86	100.0	21	100.0
Upper	11	24.4	5	20.0	0	0.0	16	18.6	1	4.8
Middle, mixed	31	68.9	20	80.0	16	100.0	67	77.9	20	95.2
Lower	3	6.7	0	0.0	0	0.0	3	3.5	0	0.0

Table 106: Violence roles by nationality

	1967		1968		1969		1967 – 69		Enlarged 1969 sample	
	N	%	N	%	N	%	N	%	N	%
American										
Total	156	100.0	164	100.0	211	100.0	531	100.0	257	100.0
Violent	78	50.0	79	48.2	81	38.4	238	44.8	106	41.2
Killer	20	12.8	20	12.2	6	2.8	46	8.7	9	3.5
Victim	96	61.5	83	50.6	99	46.9	278	52.4	126	49.0
Killed	7	4.5	6	3.7	5	2.4	18	3.4	5	1.9
Involved in										
any violence	108	69.2	101	61.6	116	55.0	325	61.2	149	58.0
any killing	26	16.7	22	13.4	11	5.2	59	11.1	14	5.4
Non-American and other, mixed unclear										
Total	84	100.0	51	100.0	96	100.0	231	100.0	120	100.0
Violent	56	66.7	27	52.9	62	64.6	145	62.8	77	64.2
Killer	10	11.9	3	5.9	4	4.2	17	7.4	5	4.2
Victim	59	70.2	37	72.5	78	81.2	174	75.3	96	80.0
Killed	10	11.9	2	3.9	1	1.0	13	5.6	3	2.5
Involved in										
any violence	68	80.9	39	76.5	81	84.4	188	81.4	101	84.2
any killing	19	22.6	3	5.9	5	5.2	27	11.7	7	5.8

Table 107: Share of nationality in violence roles

	1967 N	%	1968 N	%	1969 N	%	1967 – 69 N	%	Enlarged 1969 sample N	%
All characters	240	100.0	215	100.0	307	100.0	762	100.0	377	100.0
American	156	65.0	164	76.3	211	68.7	531	69.7	257	68.2
Non-American, mixed, other	84	35.0	51	23.7	96	31.2	231	30.3	120	31.8
Violents	134	100.0	106	100.0	143	100.0	383	100.0	183	100.0
American	78	58.2	79	74.5	81	56.6	238	62.1	106	37.5
Non-American, mixed, other	56	41.8	27	25.5	62	43.4	145	37.9	77	27.2
Killers	30	100.0	23	100.0	10	100.0	63	100.0	14	100.0
American	20	66.7	20	87.0	6	60.0	46	73.0	9	64.3
Non-American, mixed, other	10	33.3	3	13.0	4	40.0	17	27.0	5	35.7
Victims	155	100.0	120	100.0	177	100.0	452	100.0	222	100.0
American	96	61.9	83	75.4	99	55.9	278	61.5	126	56.8
Non-American, mixed, other	59	38.1	37	33.6	78	44.1	174	38.5	96	43.2
Killed	17	100.0	8	100.0	6	100.0	31	100.0	8	100.0
American	7	41.2	6	75.0	5	83.3	18	58.1	5	62.5
Non-American, mixed, other	10	58.8	2	25.0	1	16.7	13	41.9	3	37.5
Involved in any violence	176	100.0	140	100.0	197	100.0	513	100.0	250	100.0
American	108	61.4	101	72.1	116	58.9	325	63.4	149	59.6
Non-American, mixed, other	68	38.6	39	27.9	81	41.1	188	36.6	101	40.4
Involved in any killing	45	100.0	25	100.0	16	100.0	86	100.0	21	100.0
American	26	57.8	22	88.0	11	68.8	59	68.6	14	66.7
Non-American, mixed, other	19	42.2	3	12.0	5	31.2	27	31.4	7	33.3

Table 108: Violence roles by race

	1967		1968		1969		1967 – 69		Enlarged 1969 sample	
	N	%	N	%	N	%	N	%	N	%
Whites										
Total	178	100.0	173	100.0	234	100.0	585	100.0	290	100.0
Violent	94	52.8	81	46.8	97	41.5	272	46.5	129	44.5
Killer	27	15.2	21	12.1	8	3.4	56	9.6	12	4.1
Victim	108	60.6	86	49.7	120	51.3	314	53.7	154	53.1
Killed	11	6.2	7	4.0	6	2.6	24	4.1	8	2.8
Involved in										
any violence	123	69.1	106	61.3	138	59.0	367	62.7	180	62.1
any killing	36	20.2	23	13.3	14	6.0	73	12.5	19	6.6
Nonwhites and other, mixed, uncertain										
Total	62	100.0	42	100.0	73	100.0	177	100.0	87	100.0
Violent	40	64.5	25	59.5	46	63.0	111	62.7	54	62.1
Killer	3	4.8	2	4.8	2	2.7	7	4.0	2	3.3
Victim	47	75.8	34	81.0	57	78.1	138	78.0	68	78.2
Killed	6	9.7	1	2.4	0	0.0	7	4.0	0	0.0
Involved in										
any violence	53	85.5	34	81.0	59	80.2	146	82.5	70	80.5
any killing	9	14.5	2	4.8	2	2.7	13	7.3	2	2.3

Table 109: Share of race in violence roles

	1967 N	%	1968 N	%	1969 N	%	1967–69 N	%	Enlarged 1969 sample N	%
All characters	240	100.0	215	100.0	307	100.0	762	100.0	377	100.0
Whites	178	74.2	173	80.5	234	76.2	585	76.8	290	76.9
Nonwhites, mixed, other	62	25.8	42	19.5	73	23.8	177	23.2	87	23.1
Violents	134	100.0	106	100.0	143	100.0	383	100.0	183	100.0
Whites	94	70.1	81	76.4	97	67.8	272	71.0	129	70.5
Nonwhites, mixed, other	40	29.9	25	23.6	46	32.2	111	29.0	54	29.5
Killers	30	100.0	23	100.0	10	100.0	63	100.0	14	100.0
Whites	27	90.0	21	91.3	8	80.0	56	88.9	12	85.7
Nonwhites, other, mixed	3	10.0	2	8.7	2	20.0	7	11.1	2	14.3
Victims	155	100.0	120	100.0	177	100.0	452	100.0	222	100.0
Whites	108	69.7	86	71.7	120	67.8	314	69.5	154	69.4
Nonwhites, other, mixed	47	30.3	34	28.3	57	32.2	138	30.5	68	30.6
Killed	17	100.0	8	100.0	6	100.0	31	100.0	8	100.0
Whites	11	64.7	7	87.5	6	100.0	24	77.4	8	100.0
Nonwhites, other, mixed	6	35.3	1	12.5	0	0.0	7	22.6	0	0.0
Involved in any violence	176	100.0	140	100.0	197	100.0	513	100.0	250	100.0
Whites	123	69.9	106	75.7	138	70.1	367	71.5	180	72.0
Nonwhites, other, mixed	53	30.1	34	24.3	59	29.9	146	28.5	70	28.0
Involved in any killing	45	100.0	25	100.0	16	100.0	86	100.0	21	100.0
Whites	36	80.0	23	92.0	14	87.5	73	84.9	19	90.5
Nonwhites, other, mixed	9	20.0	2	8.0	2	12.5	13	15.1	2	9.5

Table 110: Violence roles by outcome for character

	1967 N	%	1968 N	%	1969 N	%	1967–69 N	%	Enlarged 1969 sample N	%
Happy ending										
Totals	134	100.0	132	100.0	143	100.0	409	100.0	168	100.0
Violents	66	49.3	60	45.5	49	34.3	175	42.8	60	35.7
Killers	16	11.9	9	6.8	1	0.7	26	6.4	2	1.2
Victims	76	56.7	68	51.5	71	49.7	215	52.6	90	53.6
Killed	0	0.0	0	0.0	1	0.7	1	0.2	1	0.6
Involved in										
any violence	90	67.2	80	60.6	79	55.2	249	60.9	98	58.3
any killing	16	11.9	9	6.8	2	1.4	27	6.6	3	1.8
Character score		79.1		67.4		56.6		67.5		60.1
Unhappy ending										
Totals	47	100.0	42	100.0	44	100.0	133	100.0	62	100.0
Violents	34	72.3	27	64.3	33	75.0	94	70.7	50	80.6
Killers	5	10.6	11	26.2	6	13.6	22	16.5	8	12.9
Victims	38	80.9	28	66.7	33	75.0	99	74.4	47	75.8
Killed	17	36.2	8	19.0	3	6.8	28	21.1	4	6.5
Involved in										
any violence	40	85.1	32	76.2	35	79.5	107	80.5	52	83.9
any killing	20	42.6	13	31.0	9	20.5	42	31.6	12	19.4
Character score		127.7		107.2		100.0		112.1		103.3

Table 110: Violence roles by outcome for character—Continued

Mixed, unclear ending	1967 N	1967 %	1968 N	1968 %	1969 N	1969 %	1967–69 N	1967–69 %	Enlarged 1969 sample N	Enlarged 1969 sample %
Totals	59	100.0	41	100.0	120	100.0	220	100.0	147	100.0
Violents	34	57.6	19	46.3	61	50.8	114	51.8	73	49.7
Killers	9	15.3	3	7.3	3	2.5	15	6.8	4	2.7
Victims	41	69.5	24	58.5	73	60.8	138	62.7	85	57.8
Killed	0	0.0	0	0.0	2	1.7	2	0.9	3	2.0
Involved in any violence	46	78.0	28	68.3	83	69.2	157	71.4	100	68.0
any killing	9	15.3	3	7.3	5	4.2	17	7.7	6	4.1
Character score		93.3		75.6		73.4		79.1		72.1

Table 111: Selected violence roles by sex and outcome

	1967		1968		1969	
	M	F	M	F	M	F
Happy ending N(100%)	103	30	97	33	102	41
	%	%	%	%	%	%
Violents	52.4	36.7	50.5	27.3	41.2	17.1
Victims	64.1	30.0	57.7	30.3	55.9	34.1
Unhappy ending	41	6	36	6	41	3
	%	%	%	%	%	%
Violents	78.0	33.3	66.7	50.0	78.0	33.3
Victims	85.4	50.0	66.7	66.7	78.0	33.3

Table 112: Share of outcomes in violence roles

	1967 N	%	1968 N	%	1969 N	%	1967–69 N	%	Enlarged 1969 sample N	%
All characters	240	100.0	215	100.0	307	100.0	762	100.0	377	100.0
Happy ending	134	55.8	132	61.4	143	46.6	409	53.7	168	44.6
Unhappy ending	47	19.6	42	19.5	44	14.3	133	17.4	62	16.4
Mixed, unclear	59	24.6	41	19.1	120	39.1	220	28.9	147	39.0
Violents	134	100.0	106	100.0	143	100.0	383	100.0	183	100.0
Happy ending	66	49.2	60	56.6	49	34.3	175	45.7	60	32.8
Unhappy ending	34	25.4	27	25.5	33	23.1	94	24.5	50	27.3
Mixed, unclear	34	25.4	19	17.9	61	42.6	114	29.8	73	39.9
Killers	30	100.0	23	100.0	10	100.0	63	100.0	14	100.0
Happy ending	16	53.3	9	39.1	1	10.0	26	41.3	2	14.3
Unhappy ending	5	16.7	11	47.8	6	60.0	22	34.9	8	57.1
Mixed, unclear	9	30.0	3	13.1	3	30.0	15	23.8	4	28.6
Victims	155	100.0	120	100.0	177	100.0	452	100.0	222	100.0
Happy ending	76	49.0	68	56.7	71	40.1	215	47.6	90	40.5
Unhappy ending	38	24.5	28	23.3	33	18.6	99	21.9	47	21.2
Mixed, unclear	41	26.5	24	20.0	73	41.3	138	30.5	85	38.3
Killed	17	100.0	8	100.0	6	100.0	31	100.0	8	100.0
Happy ending	0	0.0	0	0.0	1	16.7	1	3.2	1	12.5
Unhappy ending	17	100.0	8	100.0	3	50.0	28	90.3	4	50.0
Mixed, unclear	0	0.0	0	0.0	2	33.3	2	6.5	3	37.5
Involved in any violence	176	100.0	140	100.0	197	100.0	513	100.0	250	100.0
Happy ending	90	51.1	80	57.1	79	40.1	249	48.5	98	39.2
Unhappy ending	40	22.7	32	22.9	35	17.8	107	20.9	52	20.8
Mixed, unclear	46	26.2	28	20.0	83	42.1	157	30.6	100	40.0
Involved in any killing	45	100.0	25	100.0	16	100.0	86	100.0	21	100.0
Happy ending	16	35.6	9	36.0	2	12.5	27	31.4	3	14.3
Unhappy ending	20	44.4	13	52.0	9	56.2	42	48.8	12	57.1
Mixed, unclear	9	20.0	3	12.0	5	31.3	17	19.8	6	28.6

Table 113: Share of women in the violence roles of all "happy" and "unhappy" characters

	1967		1968		1969	
	"Happy"	"Unhappy"	"Happy"	"Unhappy"	"Happy"	"Unhappy"
Women as percent of all characters	22.4	12.8	25.0	14.3	28.7	6.8
all violents	16.7	5.9	15.0	11.1	14.3	3.0
all victims	11.8	7.9	14.7	14.3	19.7	3.0

Appendix B: Analytical procedures

I. Samples of Programming

Network dramatic programs transmitted October 10-16, 1969 during prime evening time (weekdays and Saturday evening 7:30 to 11 p.m. and Sunday evening 7 to 11 p.m.) and Saturday 8 a.m. to 2:30 p.m. were videotaped for the analysis. The calendar position of this sample week corresponded closely to the October 1-7 weeks of 1967 and 1968 analyzed previously. The 1969 sample, however, extended its prime time limits an extra hour, to 11 p.m., and expanded the Saturday daytime interval past noon into the early afternoon. This was done in order to secure all relevant program material and provide a baseline archive for future analyses of this sort.

Inasmuch as the 1967 and 1968 monitorings terminated at 10 p.m. and excluded Saturday afternoon, the comparisons, interpretations and trend analyses were limited to the same time periods in 1969. The 1969 results have thus been reported separately for the entire sample and for that portion which conforms to the 1967-68 parameters.

The solid-week sample has been demonstrated to be at least as generalizable to a year's programming as larger randomly selected samples. In a sampling experiment executed in connection with the 1967-68 study, a sample of 365 programs was constructed according to the parameters of the 1967-68 project's sample, except that it was drawn according to a one-program-per-day random selection procedure, for a calendar year that approximately bridged the interval between the 1967 and 1968 one-week samples* There proved to be no significant differences in proportions along the dimensions of program style, format, type and tone (as defined for the 1967-68 projects) between the experimental and solid-week samples. This is consistent with some assumptions about network programming. This week of October is located about one month into the new, or "Fall," television season. At such a time the programming schedule is generally kept more free of "specials" and preemptions to allow the audience to become familiar with the new schedule and to facilitate the preliminary audience ratings. As the bulk of the fall programs will continue into the rest of the programming year, many with summer reruns, this particular week may be considered highly representative of the ensuing year of network programming.

II. Coder Training and Instrument Revision

Thirteen graduate students were recruited for this project. Approximately ten days were devoted to familiarizing them with the preliminary recording instrument. This involved several general meetings during

---

*Eleey, Michael F., *Variations in Generalizability Resulting from Sampling Characteristics of Content Analysis Data: A Case Study*. The Annenberg School of Communications, University of Pennsylvania, 1969.

which the instrument was discussed and explained item by item. All students involved then coded three programs available on tape from the 1968 sample: "The Guns of Will Sonnett," a melodramatic western; "That Girl," a situation comedy; and "The Herculoids," a fantastic science-fiction cartoon. Subsequent general discussions illuminated practical problems experienced by the coders in this exercise, and consequent modifications were introduced into the coding instrument.

The next three weeks were devoted to further refinement, using this modified instrument and involving seven more 1968 programs: "Felony Squad," "Petticoat Junction," "Peyton Place," "The Night of the Iguana," "Wacky Races," "The Land of the Giants," "The Avengers." A second revision of the instrument arose out of the common experience of the coders' work with these additional programs. This revision constituted the final working version of the instrument.

III.   Assessment of Reliability

The entire 1969 sample was analyzed according to a procedure in which four assigned coders screened each program and then split into two assigned pairs, to separately agree on joint codings between the two partners. Each pair worked independently of the other pair, and all pairing combinations were systematically rotated by assignment. In this way, the entire sample was double-coded and submitted for reliability analysis.

The purpose of reliability measures in content analysis is to ascertain the degree to which the recorded data truly reflect the properties of the material being studied, and do not reflect the contamination of observer bias or of instrument ambiguity. Theoretically both types of contamination can be corrected, by refining the instrument and/or by intensifying coder training, or, as a last resort, by eliminating the unsalvageable variable or dismissing the incorrigible coder. Measures of reliability may thus serve two functions: as diagnostic tools in the confirmation of the recording process; and as final arbitrators of the accuracy of the phenomena's representations in the actual recorded data. In this project, reliability measures served both purposes. During the preliminary period of instrument revision and coder training, they provided direction to the problem areas in the recording process. Final measures, computed on the study's entire corpus of double-coded data, determined the acceptability of information for analysis and provided guidelines for the interpretation of data.

Agreement due merely to chance gives no indication that the data truly reflect the phenomena under observation; reliability measures in the form of agreement coefficients indicate the degree to which agreement among independent observers is above chance. In general, then,

$$\text{Coefficient of agreement} = 1 - \frac{\text{observed disagreement}}{\text{expected disagreement}}$$

Values for coefficients of this form will range from plus one when agreement is perfect, to zero when agreement is purely accidental (or perfectly random), to negative values when agreement is less than that expected, due to chance.

Four computational formulas are currently available for calculating the coefficient of agreement. These variations are distinguished by a difference function, the form of which depends upon the type of scale used by the particular variable being analyzed. For nominal scales, the difference between any two categories is equal. For interval scales, the difference between two neighboring categories is equal. For polar scales, the distinctions among scale points are finer, and the differences are more significant near the boundaries of the scale as defined by its polar opposites. For ratio scales, the distinctions among scale points are finer near zero, and the significance of the differences are relative to the zero point.*

Except for their respective scale-appropriate sensitivity to deviations from perfect agreement, all formulas make the same basic assumptions as the prototype for nominal scales devised by Scott.** Thus in the case of the binary variable, all four formulas yield identical results.

The project's double-coded sample of data was analyzed for agreement via these four coefficients, with the aid of a recently developed computer program.*** In addition to being computed for the entire sample of 1969 programs, the coefficients have also been computed separately for cartoon and noncartoon programs. And where indicated by preliminary reliability results, variables have been recoded (i.e., categories have been collapsed and/or rearranged) and renalyzed for reliability.

Variables meeting reliability criteria were selected for the analysis. Those variables exhibiting coefficients of .80 or higher were accepted as unconditionally reliable. Variables between .67 and .80 were accepted as conditionally reliable, to be interpreted cautiously. Variables below .67 were considered unreliable and excluded from the analysis.‡

IV. Data Processing

As data were recorded by the coders, it was office-checked for administrative errors and keypunched twice. The two sets of data cards were then submitted for matching by computer for verification. Mismatches

---

*Krippendorff, Klaus, *Reliability in Message Analysis*, The Annenberg School of Communications, Philadelphia, March 1970. Discusses the formulae's derivations and properties.

**Scott, William A., *Reliability of Content Analysis: The Case of Nominal Scale Coding*, *Public Opinion Quarterly*, 17:3:321-325, 1955.

***Krippendorff, Klaus, *A Computer Program for Analyzing Multivariate Agreements*, Version 2, The Annenberg School of Communications, Philadelphia, March, 1970.

‡See Eleey, *op cit.*, for a justification of the levels of acceptability according to the probabilities of Type I and Type II errors involved.

were corrected by a return to the original recording sheets. Verified data were then submitted for computerized agreement analysis to evaluate reliability. On the basis of reliability measures, variables were selected for analysis, which proceeded by a combination of standard computer programs and specific software designed for the project's needs.

Appendix C: Samples of programs

The 1969 sample of television programs for the analysis represented a departure from some sampling criteria used for the 1967 and 1968 selections. For the latter, the time periods used were: weekdays and Saturday evening—4 to 10 p.m.* Sunday evening 7 to 10 p.m.; Saturday children's programs 8 a.m. to noon. Since these parameters eliminated potentially valuable material, i.e. the prime time hour from 10 to 11 p.m., and the early Saturday afternoon children's programming, the 1969 sample was not subject to these limitations. In 1969, the Sunday time period extended from 7 p.m. to 11 p.m., the weekday and Saturday evening period from 7:30 to 11 p.m., and the Saturday daytime period from 8 a.m. to 2:30 p.m.

These additional time periods made available program slots not secured for the previous analysis. In the Calendar of Television Programs Analyzed, programs videotaped in 1969 which were beyond the scope of the previous samples, are bordered in double lines, and their serial numbers are in parentheses.

The 1969 analysis was performed on all the programs secured according to the revised time criteria. The results, however, are presented separately for the entire 1969 sample and only for those 1969 sample programs *that are* strictly comparable to the previous time constraints. In the interpretations of the results and trends, data used were based on a restricted 1969 sample to maintain the integrity of the comparisons. The enlarged 1969 sample, however, has now been secured and analyzed as a more complete baseline for future analyses.

Index of television programs analyzed, 1967-69

Serial Number of   001 = *Batman*
Program (1967)   002 = *Yellow Rolls Royce*
                         003 = *My Three Sons*
                         004 = *Felony Squad*
                         005 = *That Girl*
                         006 = *Off to See the Wizard*
                         007 = *Ironside*
                         008 = *Virginian*
                         009 = *Petticoat Junction*
                         010 = *Daktari*
                         011 = *Journey to Center of Earth*
                         012 = *Peyton Place*

---

*Programs beginning before 10 p.m. but terminating after that time were taped and analyzed in their entirety.

013 = *I Dream of Jeannie*
014 = *Star Trek*
015 = *The Man from U.N.C.L.E*
016 = *Voyage to Bottom of Sea*
017 = *Hondo*
018 = *Custer*
019 = *He & She*
020 = *Daniel Boone*
021 = *Maya*
022 = *Lost in Space*
023 = *The Invaders*
024 = *Bonanza*
025 = *Bewitched*
026 = *Accidental Family*
027 = *Flying Nun*
028 = *Second-Hundred Years*
029 = *Viva Las Vegas - CBS Friday*
030 = *Gunsmoke*
031 = *Andy Griffith Show*
032 = *Man's Favorite Sport*
033 = *Super 6-Matzanuts*
034 = *Super 6-Man from T.R.A.S.H*
035 = *Monkees*
036 = *Gentle Ben*
037 = *Magilla Gorilla*
038 = *Casper Cartoon #1 Troubly Date*
039 = *Casper #2 Goody Gremlin*
040 = *Casper #3 Wandering Ghost*
041 = *Smothers Brothers*
042 = *Smothers Brothers*
043 = *Super President - Spy Shadow*
044 = *Super President*
045 = *Super President*
046 = *Lassie*
047 = *Green Acres*
048 = *The Jerry Lewis Shoe, I*
049 = *Fantastic Four*
050 = *Fantastic Four*
051 = *The Jerry Lewis Show, II*
052 = *Super Six*
053 = *Mothers-in-Law*
054 = *Spiderman*
055 = *Second Time Around*
056 = *Tarzan*
057 = *NYPD*

058 = *Lucy*
059 = *Cimarron Strip*
060 = *Dragnet*
061 = *Gomer Pyle*
062 = *Good Morning World*
063 = *Garrison's Gorillas*
064 = *Walt Disney - The Fighting Prince*
065 = *Wild, Wild West*
066 = *Cowboys in Africa*
067 = *Peyton Place*
068 = *Family Affair*
069 = *Trouble with Harry*
070 = *Beverly Hillbillies*
071 = *Iron Horse*
072 = *Hogan's Heroes*
073 = *Shazzan-Evil Jester of Messina*
074 = *Shazzan-City of the Tombs*
075 = *Frankenstien Jr.- Smogula*
076 = *Frankenstien Jr. - Shocking Monster*
077 = *Frankenstien Jr.- Perilous Paper Doll*
078 = *Flintstones - House Guest*
079 = *Space Ghost*
080 = *Herculoids - Spider Man*
081 = *Herculoids - Android People*
082 = *Young Samson & Goliath #1*
083 = *Danny Thomas Show*
084 = *FBI*
085 = *Beagles #3 - By the Plight of the Moon*
086 = *Beagles #1 - Ghosts, Ghouls & Fouls*
087 = *Get Smart*
088 = *Rat Patrol*
089 = *Guns of Will Sonnet*
090 = *Whatever Happened to Baby Jane*
091 = *Magilla Gorilla #2 - B. Brun*
092 = *Magilla Gorilla #3 - Cat and Mouse*
093 = *Spiderman #2*
094 = *Young Samson & Goliath #2*
095 = *Space Ghost #2*
096 = *Space Ghost #3*

Serial Number of   101 = *That Girl*
Program (1968)   102 = *Julia*
                         103 = *Ugliest Girl in Town*
                         104 = *Outcasts*
                         105 = *Adam 12*

106 = *Night of the Iguana*
107 = *Mod Squad*
108 = *NYPD*
109 = *Avengers*
110 = *Here Come the Brides*
111 = *Lancer*
112 = *Ironside*
113 = *FBI*
114 = *Cat Ballou*
115 = *Green Acres*
116 = *The Good Guys*
117 = *Do Not Disturb*
118 = *Spiderman - Captured by J. Jonah Jamison*
119 = *Spiderman - Sky is Falling In*
120 = *My Three Sons*
121 = *Gunsmoke*
122 = *Hawaii 5-0*
123 = *A Man Could Get Killed*
124 = *Daktari*
125 = *I Dream of Jeannie*
126 = *Mothers-In-Law*
127 = *Land of the Giants*
128 = *Petticoat Junction*
129 = *New Adventures of Huck Finn*
130 = *Peyton Place*
131 = *Bewitched*
132 = *Beverly Hillbillies*
133 = *Peyton Place*
134 = *Wild, Wild West*
135 = *It Takes a Thief*
136 = *Here's Lucy*
137 = *Mayberry RFD*
138 = *Bonanza*
139 = *Family Affair*
140 = *Doris Day Show*
141 = *Hogan's Heroes*
142 = *Blondie*
143 = *Gomer Pyle USMC*
144 = *Journey to the Unknown*
145 = *Get Smart*
146 = *Flintstones - No Biz Like Show Biz*
147 = *The Ghost & Mrs. Muir*
148 = *Lassie*
149 = *Dragnet*
150 = *The Name of the Game*

151 = *Felony*
152 = *The Archie Show - The Circus*
153 = *The Archie Show - Jughead & the Airplane*
154 = *Gentle Ben*
155 = *Go Go Gophers - Up in the Air*
156 = *Go Go Gophers - Space Kiddettes*
157 = *Go Go Gophers - Big Banger*
158 = *Underdog - Bubbleheads*
159 = *Wacky Races - Creepy Trip to Lemon Twist*
160 = *Wacky Races - Baja Ha-Ha*
161 = *Flying Nun*
162 = *Rare Breed*
163 = *Batman/Superman Hour - 9 Lives of Batman*
164 = *Batman/Superman Hour - Can Luthor
       Change His Spots*
165 = *Batman/Superman Hour - Forget Me Not,
       Superdog*
166 = *Batman/Superman Hour - In Again Out
       Again Penguin*
167 = *High Chaparral*
168 = *Fantastic Voyage - Master Spy*
169 = *Super 6 - Thunder 8 Ball*
170 = *Super 6 - Ruin & Board*
171 = *Super 6 - Mummy Caper*
172 = *Herculoids - Tiny World of Terror*
173 = *Herculoids - Electrode Men*
174 = *Daniel Boone*
175 = *Guns of Will Sonnett*
176 = *Khartoum*
177 = *Fantastic 4 - Yancy Street*
178 = *Top Cat*
179 = *The Singing Nun*
180 = *The Virginian*
181 = *Banana Splits - Introduction*
182 = *Banana Splits - Wizard Ramizer*
183 = *Banana Splits - Danger Island*
184 = *Banana Splits - Puppet Masters*
185 = *Banana Splits - End Segment*
186 = *Banana Splits - 1st Comic Interlude*
187 = *Banana Splits - 2nd Comic Interlude*

Serial Number of   201 = *Marcus Welby, M.D.*
Program (1969)   202 = *Land of the Giants*
                     203 = *Julia*
                     204 = *Pink Panther - Prehistoric Pink*

205 = *Pink Panther - The Inspector*
206 = *Pink Panther - Bicep Beach*
207 = *Here's Lucy*
208 = *ABC Sunday Night Movie - Fantastic Voyage*
209 = *Jonny Quest*
210 = *Good Buys*
211 = *NBC Tuesday Night at the Movies -
        The Tiger and the Pussycat*
212 = *The Ghost and Mrs. Muir*
213 = *Get Smart*
214 = *The Bill Cosby Show*
215 = *Dragnet*
216 = *I Dream of Jeannie*
217 = *Bewitched*
218 = *CBS Thursday Night Movie - Inside Daisy Clover*
219 = *It Takes a Thief*
220 = *The Bold Ones*
221 = *The Survivors*
222 = *Adam-12*
223 = *Hawaii Five-O*
224 = *Daniel Boone*
225 = *Lassie*
226 = *Then Came Bronson*
227 = *Jackie Gleason*
228 = *The Bugs Bunny - 14 Carrot Rabbit*
229 = *The Bugs Bunny - Tweety & the Beanstalk*
230 = *The Bugs Bunny - War and Pieces*
231 = *The Bugs Bunny - Knightly Knight Bugs*
232 = *The Bugs Bunny - Clippity Clobbered*
233 = *The Bugs Bunny - Hillbilly Hare*
234 = *Petticoat Junction*
235 = *The New People*
236 = *NBC Monday Night at the Movies -
        By Love Possessed*
237 = *Mannix*
238 = *Lancer*
239 = *Superman - Rain of Iron*
240 = *Superman - Superboy Meets Mighty Lad*
241 = *My Three Sons*
242 = *Mayberry R.F.D.*
243 = *Chattanooga Cats - Witchy Wacky*
244 = *Chattanooga Cats - Sno Go*
245 = *Chattanooga Cats - India or Bust*
246 = *Chattanooga Cats - Any Sport in a Storm*
247 = *Chattanooga Cats - Hard Day's Day*

248 = Movie of the Week - Wake Me When the War is Over
249 = Banana Splits - Saucy Saucers
250 = Banana Splits - Danger Island
251 = Banana Splits - Jewels of Joowar
252 = Hardy Boys - Restaurant Mystery
253 = Hardy Boys - Mr. Izmeer
254 = Here Come the Brides
255 = Family Affair
256 = The F.B.I
257 = Wacky Races - Hot Race at Chillicothe
258 = Wacky Races - By Roller Coaster to Ups & Downs
259 = Mr. Deeds Goes to Town
260 = Doris Day Show
261 = That Girl
262 = Green Acres
263 = Mission Impossible
264 = Monkees
265 = Skyhawks - Untamed Wildcat
266 = Skyhawks - Trouble Times Three
267 = The Jetsons
268 = Heckle & Jeckle - Thousand Smile Check-Up
269 = Heckle & Jeckle - Don't Burro Trouble
270 = Heckle & Jeckle - Pastry Panic
271 = Heckle & Jeckle - Miami Maniacs
272 = Heckle & Jeckle - Sad Cat Basketball
273 = Heckle & Jeckle - Stuntmen
274 = Heckle & Jeckle - Darn Barn
275 = Heckle & Jeckle - Hair Cut-Ups
276 = Jambo
277 = H. R. Pufnstuff
278 = Walt Disney
279 = Virginian
280 = Scooby-do, Where Are You?
281 = Flying Nun
282 = Love, American Sytle - Love and the Doorknob
283 = Love, American Style - Love and the Phone Booth
284 = Bracken's World
285 = Gunsmoke
286 = Perils of Penelope Pitstop
287 = To Rome With Love
288 = The High Chaparral
289 = Courtship of Eddie's Father
290 = Bonanza

291 = *Name of the Game*
292 = *The Brady Bunch*
293 = *Hot Wheels - Avalanche Country*
294 = *Adventures of Gulliver*
295 = *Medical Center*
296 = *Archie Hour - Magic Bone*
297 = *Archie Hour - Visiting Nephew*
298 = *Archie Hour - Detective Jughead*
299 = *Hogan's Heroes*
300 = *Mod Squad*
301 = *Casper the Friendly Ghost - A Visit From Mars*
302 = *Casper the Friendly Ghost - Be Mice to Cats*
303 = *Casper the Friendly Ghost - Cane & Able*
304 = *Debbie Reynolds Show*
305 = *CBS Friday Night Movie - Doctor,*
       You've Got to be kidding
306 = *Here Comes the Grump: The Yuks*
307 = *Room 222*
308 = *My World and Welcome to It*
309 = *Ironsides*
310 = *Dastardly & Muttley - Operation Anvil*
311 = *Dastardly & Muttley - Cuckoo Patrol*
312 = *Dastardly & Muttley - Masked Muttley*
313 = *NBC Saturday Night at the Movies -*
       The Hell With Heroes
314 = *Beverly Hillbillies*
315 = *The Governor & J.J.*
316 = *ABC Wednesday Night Movie -*
       Divorce American Style
317 = *Smokey Bear Show - Heroes Are Born*
318 = *Smokey Bear Show - Winner & Still Chump*
319 = *Smokey Bear Show - Freddy's Big Date*
320 = *Here Comes the Grump - Wily Wheelies*
321 = *Hot Wheels - Hit & Run*

Calendar of television programs analyzed, 1967-69

Table 114: October 1-7, 1967

NBC 1967 (times 4:00 p.m. – 10:00, and 8:00 a.m. – 12:00)

	SUN. OCT. 1	MON. OCT. 2	TUE. OCT. 3	WED. OCT. 4	THU. OCT. 5	FRI. OCT. 6	SAT. OCT. 7
10:00 / 9:30	24	83	55		60	26	32
9:00 / 8:30	53	15	48 / 51	8	7	14	87
8:00 / 7:30	64	35	13		20	56	21

SAT. OCT. 7: 82, 94 (11:00); 78 (10:30); 43, 44, 45 (10:00); 33, 34, 52 (9:30)

CBS 1967

	SUN. OCT. 1	MON. OCT. 2	TUE. OCT. 3	WED. OCT. 4	THU. OCT. 5	FRI. OCT. 6	SAT. OCT. 7
10:00 / 9:30	41 / 42	68 / 31	62	19 / 47	29	2	9 / 72
9:00 / 8:30	36	58 / 30	10	70 / 22	59	61 / 65	3
8:00 / 7:30	46						

SAT. OCT. 7: 79, 95, 96 (11:00); 73, 74 (10:30); 80, 81 (10:00); 75, 76, 77 (9:30)

ABC 1967

	SUN. OCT. 1	MON. OCT. 2	TUE. OCT. 3	WED. OCT. 4	THU. OCT. 5	FRI. OCT. 6	SAT. OCT. 7
10:00 / 9:30	90	12 / 4	57 / 23	69	67 / 5	89 / 17	71
9:00 / 8:30	84	88 / 66	63	28 / 18	25 / 27 / 1	6	
8:00 / 7:30	16						
5:00 / 4:30	37, 91, 92 / 85, 86						

SAT. OCT. 7: 11 (11:00); 54, 93 (10:30); 49, 50 (10:00); 38, 39, 40 (9:30)

Table 115:   October 1–7, 1968

NBC 1968

Day	7:00–7:30	8:00	8:30	9:00	9:30	10:00
SUN. OCT. 6	129			126		138
MON. OCT. 7		125				162
TUE. OCT. 1				102		123
WED. OCT. 2		180				149
THU. OCT. 3		174		112		
FRI. OCT. 4		167			150	
SAT. OCT. 5		105	145	147		176

NBC 1968 (SAT. OCT. 5, a.m.)

8:30	9:30	11:00	12:00
	169 170 171	181 187	158

CBS 1968

Day	7:00–7:30	8:00	8:30	9:00	9:30	10:00
SUN. OCT. 6	148	154				
MON. OCT. 7		121		136	137	139
TUE. OCT. 1		111		116	132	140
WED. OCT. 2		124		122		115
THU. OCT. 3		142		122	106	
FRI. OCT. 4		134		143	179	
SAT. OCT. 5				120	141	128

CBS 1968 (SAT. OCT. 5, a.m.)

8:30	10:00	10:30	11:00	12:00
155 156 157	159 160	152 153	163 164 165 166	172 173

ABC 1968

Day	7:30	8:00	8:30	9:00	9:30	10:00
SUN. OCT. 6	127		113			117
MON. OCT. 7		109		130		104
TUE. OCT. 1		107		135		108
WED. OCT. 2		110		133		114
THU. OCT. 3		103 161		131 101		144
FRI. OCT. 4				151		175

ABC 1968 (SAT. OCT. 5, a.m.)

10:30	11:00	12:00
118 119	168	177

Table 116: October 10-16, 1969

NBC 1969

Time	SUN. OCT. 12	MON. OCT. 13	TUE. OCT. 14	WED. OCT. 15	THU. OCT. 16	FRI. OCT. 10
11:00	(220)	236	211	(226)	(284)	313
10:30	290			215		
10:00				309	291	
9:30	214		203			222
9:00	278		216 304	279	224	288
8:30		308				
8:00	225					
7:30						
7:00 p.m.						

NBC 1969 — SAT. OCT. 11:

Time	SAT. OCT. 11
12:00	276
11:30	249 250 251
11:00	
10:30	277
10:00	204 205 206
9:30	306 320
9:00	268
8:30	
8:00 a.m.	

CBS 1969

Time	SUN. OCT. 12	MON. OCT. 13	TUE. OCT. 14	WED. OCT. 15	THU. OCT. 16	FRI. OCT. 10
11:00	(263)	260	315	(223)	305	(237)
10:30				218		
10:00						234
9:30		207 242		295		262
9:00			314		299	241
8:30		285	238		210	227
8:00	287			255	213	
7:30						
7:00 p.m.						

CBS 1969 — SAT. OCT. 11:

Time	SAT. OCT. 11
2:30	(267)
2:00	(209)
1:30	(239,240)
1:00	(257,258)
12:30 p.m.	(264)
12:00 / 11:30	296 297 298
11:00	280 286
10:30	
10:00	310 311 312
9:30 / 9:00	228 233
8:30 a.m.	

ABC 1969

Time	SUN. OCT. 12	MON. OCT. 13	TUE. OCT. 14	WED. OCT. 15	THU. OCT. 16	FRI. OCT. 10
11:00	208	(282) (283)	(201)	316	(219)	
10:30		221	248			254
10:00						
9:30	256	235		307	217	259
9:00			300	289	261	292
8:30	202			281	212	
8:00						
7:30						
7:00 p.m.						

ABC 1969 — SAT. OCT. 11:

Time	SAT. OCT. 11
12:00	294
11:30	265 266
11:00	252 253
10:30	293 321
10:00	
9:30	243 247
9:00	317 318 319
8:30	301 303
8:00 a.m.	

Selected Aspects of Television Programs Analyzed, 1967-69

Explanation of Codes:

Number:	Refer to Index of Television Programs Analyzed for serialized list of program titles.
No. Violent Acts:	The number of violent actions observed to have occurred in the program.
Format:	1 = cartoon 2 = TV play 3 = feature film
Type:	1 = crime 2 = western 3 = action-adventure 4 = other
Tone:	1 = comedy 2 = serious, other

Number	No. Violent Acts	Format	Type	Tone
1	3	2	1	1
2	2	3	3	2
3	0	2	4	1
4	4	2	1	2
5	4	2	4	1
6	14	2	3	2
7	4	2	1	2
8	2	2	2	2
9	4	2	4	1
10	3	2	3	2
11	12	1	3	2
12	1	2	4	2
13	1	2	4	1
14	12	2	3	2
15	14	2	3	2
16	21	2	3	2
17	12	2	2	2
18	11	2	2	2
19	0	2	4	1
20	11	2	3	2
21	10	2	3	2
22	6	2	3	2
23	4	2	3	2
24	15	2	2	2
25	0	2	4	1
26	0	2	4	1
27	0	2	4	1
28	0	2	4	1
29	5	3	4	2
30	3	2	2	2
31	0	2	4	1
32	0	3	3	1
33	1	1	3	1
34	2	1	3	1

Number	No. Violent Acts	Format	Type	Tone
35	5	2	4	1
36	4	2	3	2
37	5	1	3	1
38	2	1	4	1
39	9	1	4	1
40	2	1	3	1
41	0	2	4	1
42	1	2	4	1
43	5	1	3	2
44	6	1	3	2
45	4	1	3	2
46	0	2	4	2
47	2	2	4	1
48	1	2	4	1
49	8	1	3	2
50	5	1	3	2
51	1	2	4	1
52	0	1	1	1
53	2	2	4	1
54	4	1	3	2
55	16	3	1	1
56	15	2	3	2
57	3	2	1	2
58	0	2	4	1
59	20	2	2	2
60	1	2	1	2
61	0	2	4	1
62	0	2	4	1
63	11	2	3	2
64	7	2	3	2
65	15	2	2	2
66	3	2	3	2
67	0	2	4	2
68	0	2	4	1
69	0	3	1	2
70	0	2	4	1
71	13	2	2	2
72	2	2	3	1
73	2	1	3	1
74	4	1	3	2
75	1	1	3	1
76	2	1	3	1
77	4	1	3	1
78	7	1	4	1
79	7	1	3	2
80	4	1	3	2
81	6	1	3	2
82	6	1	3	2
83	5	2	4	1
84	5	2	1	2
85	6	1	1	1
86	4	1	4	1
87	13	2	3	1
88	7	2	3	2
89	3	2	2	2
90	6	3	3	2
91	5	1	4	1
92	5	1	3	1
93	3	1	3	2

Number	No. Violent Acts	Format	Type	Tone
94	6	1	3	1
95	8	1	3	2
96	6	1	3	2
101	1	2	3	1
102	0	2	4	1
103	4	2	3	1
104	5	2	2	2
105	1	2	1	2
106	7	3	4	2
107	8	2	3	2
108	3	2	1	2
109	11	2	1	2
110	1	2	2	2
111	11	2	2	2
112	3	2	1	2
113	5	2	1	2
114	17	3	2	1
115	7	2	4	1
116	1	2	4	1
117	1	3	4	1
118	3	1	3	2
119	5	1	3	2
120	0	2	4	1
121	7	2	2	2
122	6	2	1	2
123	15	3	3	2
124	3	2	3	1
125	0	2	4	1
126	0	2	4	1
127	4	2	3	2
128	0	2	4	1
129	3	2	3	2
130	0	2	4	2
131	3	2	4	1
132	1	2	4	1
133	0	2	4	2
134	7	2	2	2
135	2	2	3	2
136	1	2	4	1
137	0	2	4	1
138	7	2	2	2
139	0	2	4	1
140	0	2	4	1
141	0	2	3	1
142	0	2	4	1
143	0	2	4	1
144	2	2	4	2
145	4	2	3	1
146	0	1	4	1
147	0	2	4	1
148	1	2	4	2
149	1	2	1	2
150	2	2	3	2
151	6	2	1	2
152	4	1	4	1
153	2	1	4	1
154	2	2	4	2
155	1	1	3	1

Number	No. Violent Acts	Format	Type	Tone
156	8	1	3	1
157	3	1	3	1
158	13	1	3	1
159	12	1	3	1
160	8	1	3	1
161	6	2	4	1
162	10	3	2	2
163	13	1	3	2
164	5	1	3	2
165	4	1	3	1
166	3	1	3	2
167	3	2	2	2
168	3	1	3	2
169	5	1	3	1
170	5	1	3	1
171	3	1	3	1
172	5	1	3	2
173	9	1	3	1
174	10	2	3	2
175	8	2	2	2
176	10	3	3	2
177	15	1	3	2
178	6	1	4	1
179	4	3	4	2
180	8	2	2	2
181	2	2	4	1
182	15	1	3	2
183	5	2	3	2
184	12	1	3	2
185	2	2	4	1
186	0	2	4	1
187	1	2	4	1
201	0	2	4	3
202	12	2	3	3
203	0	2	4	1
204	8	1	3	1
205	8	1	1	1
206	11	1	3	1
207	1	2	4	2
208	7	3	3	3
209	11	1	3	3
210	6	2	4	1
211	3	3	4	2
212	0	2	4	1
213	3	2	3	2
214	0	2	4	1
215	0	2	1	3
216	6	2	4	2
217	0	2	4	1
218	4	3	4	3
219	8	2	1	3
220	5	2	1	3
221	4	2	3	3
222	6	2	1	3
223	10	2	1	3
224	10	2	2	3
225	0	2	4	3
226	6	2	3	3

Number	No. Violent Acts	Format	Type	Tone
227	9	2	4	1
228	7	1	3	1
229	9	1	3	1
230	8	1	3	1
231	10	1	3	1
232	8	1	3	1
233	5	1	3	1
234	0	2	4	1
235	5	2	1	3
236	2	3	4	3
237	3	2	1	3
238	3	2	2	3
239	9	1	3	3
240	1	1	3	2
241	0	2	4	1
242	4	2	4	1
243	6	1	3	1
244	9	1	3	2
245	9	1	3	2
246	8	1	3	1
247	6	1	3	1
248	6	3	4	1
249	5	1	3	1
250	9	2	3	3
251	12	1	3	3
252	5	1	3	3
253	8	1	3	3
254	9	2	2	2
255	0	2	4	1
256	10	2	1	3
257	14	1	3	1
258	12	1	3	1
259	1	2	4	2
260	0	2	4	1
261	0	2	4	1
261	0	2	4	1
262	2	2	4	2
263	8	2	3	3
264	4	2	3	1
265	2	1	1	3
266	2	1	1	3
267	6	1	3	1
268	9	1	3	1
269	10	1	3	1
270	1	1	3	2
271	8	1	3	1
272	5	1	3	1
273	12	1	3	1
274	1	1	3	1
275	3	1	3	1
276	3	2	3	2
277	12	2	3	1
278	7	2	4	3
279	9	2	2	3
280	9	1	1	1
281	0	2	4	1
282	1	2	4	1
283	2	2	4	1

Number	No. Violent Acts	Format	Type	Tone
284	3	2	4	3
285	4	2	2	2
286	20	1	3	2
287	0	2	4	2
288	3	2	2	2
289	0	2	4	1
290	8	2	2	3
291	7	2	1	3
292	0	2	4	2
293	1	1	3	3
294	9	1	3	2
295	1	2	4	3
296	0	1	3	1
297	4	1	3	1
298	5	1	1	1
299	2	2	4	2
300	4	2	1	3
301	4	1	3	1
302	7	1	3	1
303	4	1	3	1
304	1	2	4	1
305	7	3	4	2
306	7	1	3	2
307	0	2	4	2
308	2	2	4	2
309	4	2	1	3
310	8	1	3	1
311	10	1	3	1
312	4	1	3	1
313	13	3	3	3
314	1	2	4	1
315	0	2	4	1
316	0	3	4	1
317	3	1	3	1
318	8	1	3	1
319	5	1	3	1
320	11	1	3	1
321	3	1	1	3

Trends in Violent Content in Selected Mass Media

David G. Clark
and
William B. Blankenburg

The University of Wisconsin, Madison

During the 1960s, when presidential commissions, scholars, and critics examined the mass media in connection with violence, civil disorder, and other national distresses, they often concluded with a plea for continuing studies of media content (National Advisory Commission on Civil Disorders, 1968; Baker and Ball, 1969). Existing studies of relevant content, while solid and intriguing, tended to be short-range and not readily comparable with one another (Greenberg, 1969). Additionally, content analyses of some kinds of media—mainly broadcast—have been limited because the content is ephemeral.

The present study attempts to provide longitudinal information on violent content since 1925 in several American media: network television entertainment, motion pictures, a popular magazine, four leading daily newspapers, and network television news programs.[1] A fairly typical definition of violence was applied in all cases: physical acts or the threat of physical acts by humans designed to inflict physical injury to persons or damage to property.

While most research on media violence has sought to determine whether violent content affects the social environment, this study concentrates on the reverse: how the environment, especially "real-world" violence, may have affected media content. The process is apparently circular: long- and short-range conditions in the real world influence the media, and the media in turn affect real life. Just how these effects take place and interact is a complex and only partly answerable question; the researcher's necessary artifice is breaking into the hen-and-egg circle.

The circle is demonstrated by a "contagion of violence" theory proposed by Berkowitz and Macaulay, who suggest that a series of reactions may take place in many people who see mass media depictions of violence: aggressive ideas and images may arise in the mind of the viewer or reader; if inhibitions are not evoked and if the observer is ready to act violently, open aggression may result; the aggressive reactions may subside quickly but may reappear if the observer encounters other stimuli associated with aggression. Berkowitz and Macaulay (1970) suggest that the media-borne violent event may have a "relatively long-lasting influence." They cite the case of an Arizona schoolboy who murdered four women and a child and later said he had gotten the idea after hearing about the Speck (Chicago nurses) and Whitman (Texas Tower) mass murders a few months earlier. Analyzing the FBI's Uniform Crime Report data on violent crimes, Berkowitz and Macaulay found extraordinary jumps in criminal aggression following the John F. Kennedy assassination and the Speck killings.

In short, the theory is one of imitative or reflexive behavior in which a real event inspires a media event which may in turn inspire another real event. If the theory were natural law, society would have collapsed long ago in a resonation of violence. Criminal violence *has* increased since the 1930s (and phenomenally in the 1960s), but there have been periods when violence in the U.S. was likely to be greater than it is today (Levy, 1969). Intervening naturalistic and normative factors prevent a cataclysm; some people, for example, never receive the violent message, some don't understand it, and some (most, one hopes) inhibit themselves from imitating the event.

The contagion-of-violence theory implicates the media in a process of violence. Mass communicators confess their participation in such a process even as they excuse it. Both journalists and entertainers say that in their roles they hold up a mirror to society, and that they are not culpable for what the mirror reflects. Journalists in particular claim this mirror function as valid in their role as the "watchdog of society." There may also be some psychological validity to the reflection thesis: mass communicators are, after all, quite human and subject to being affected by violence.[2] Perhaps the effect of media violence on them is to engage them in a sublimated kind of violence—reporting the event in journalistic or dramatic form.

The mass communication process is hardly that simple, of course. Economics influences the media, and so do diverse professional, social, and official pressures. This study considers these various forces, as well as "real" violence, in its look at the media as affected by the environment.

FBI statistics on violent crime in the United States from 1933 onward were among the environmental data acquired. These statistics describe trends in real violence against which media violence can be compared.

ENVIRONMENTAL VIOLENCE

The difference between an event and a report of an event is especially distinct to the victim of a crime, as psychiatrist W. Walter Menninger (1968) illustrated: "I recall my own reaction—when working in the prison, where I could be detached in considering intellectually the difficult backgrounds of the inmates—but when one broke into *my* home on the prison reservation and stole something which belonged to *me*, I wasn't quite so 'understanding' and dispassionate."

However, victims and nonvictims alike are led to expect some correspondence between real life and media life, both in news media, whose proprietors profess to hold up a mirror to the world of events, and in dramatic works that espouse "realism." The mirror (or reflection) thesis offered by the media contains both a motivation for and a defense of violent content.

Because of the presumed connection between media and real violence, the historian of communicated violence must inspect aggression in the real world. For his study of 150 years of political violence in America, Levy (1969) content-analyzed 6,000 issues of newspapers published between 1819 and 1968. But if the press is to be regarded as the dependent variable—as the reflection thesis suggests it should—independent sources of data on real violence are needed. For better or worse, these sources must be either the Uniform Crime Reports (UCR) of the Federal Bureau of Investigation or individual city police statistics.

In the late 1920s, the International Association of Chiefs of Police felt a need to compile and exchange statistical information on crime. In 1927 the organization divided crime into seven categories for compilation and in 1930 it asked the FBI to serve as a clearinghouse for those data. The first Uniform Crime Report was issued in 1933. Today the FBI collects its raw data from law enforcement agencies whose jurisdictions encompass nearly 95 percent of the U.S. population. The reliability of the contributing agencies has been uneven, and one author has called the UCR data "easily the most suspect statistics published under the imprimatur of the U.S. Government" (Graham, 1969). While the Reports may be generally uniform (the classes of crime have been expanded to nearly 30, but seven serious, or "index" crimes are still featured as bellwethers), their adequacy is in doubt. In 1965 the Commission on Law Enforcement and Administration of Justice sponsored a survey that revealed severe underreporting of some kinds of violent crime. For example, personal injury crimes may be as much as 50 percent underreported; rape reports are probably even more discrepant (President's Commission on Law Enforcement, 1968).

Despite problems of reliability and validity, the UCR figures remain the best national data on environmental violence, and the FBI has taken steps to improve reporting and tabulation procedures. Inspector Jerome J. Daunt, chief of the Uniform Crime Reports section of the FBI, has provided the authors with 1933-68 index crime data that were recently adjusted by the Bureau for greater reliability. From these have been extracted figures for what are generally considered crimes of violence: murder, forcible rape, robbery, and aggravated assault. Table 1 presents these data, and Figure 1 converts them to graphic form.

The UCR data disclose a declining rate of violent crime in the 1930s, followed by an increase during the war years and relative stability in the 1950s. In the 1960s, the trend was sharply upward.

With the exception of the first years recorded, the picture drawn by these data is one of a chronic increase in violent crime. However, within this general trend are fluctuations; there is some evidence that violent crime is rhythmic and that the present period is not the highest in U.S. history (Graham, 1969; President's Commission, 1968; Levy, 1969). Violence during the Reconstruction and western frontier eras may have been greater. The question is clouded, of course, by the lack of early statistics.

VIOLENCE IN TELEVISION ENTERTAINMENT

A parent told us of his child, I think about seven years old, who came to him and said, "Why do they kill all these people on the shows?" Meaning Westerns in this case. He said he told him "Because they are bad men." He asked, "What do they do?. . .Do we always kill bad men?" (Testimony before Senate Subcommittee on Juvenile Delinquency, June 5, 1954.)

The answer to the child's question, based upon this study, would be: nearly always, and for reasons that have little to do with good or evil. Ample evidence from the history of the media indicates that violence

Table 1: Rates per 100,000 population of four violent crimes, 1933-68,
Uniform Crime Reports data

Year	Murder	Forcible rape	Robbery	Aggravated assault	Total
1933	7.7	3.7	93.9	48.4	153.6
1934	6.1	4.0	74.3	46.9	131.3
1935	7.0	4.4	61.1	44.2	116.7
1936	7.1	5.1	49.9	44.4	106.5
1937	7.0	5.3	53.3	42.3	107.9
1938	6.6	4.5	52.4	41.1	104.6
1939	6.6	5.3	48.5	42.6	103.0
1940	6.5	5.2	46.4	42.2	100.3
1941	6.5	5.3	42.8	43.4	98.0
1942	6.4	6.1	46.6	53.9	113.0
1943	5.5	7.4	44.6	51.3	108.8
1944	5.6	7.9	43.6	57.1	114.2
1945	5.9	8.9	54.2	62.5	131.5
1946	6.9	8.7	59.4	67.0	142.0
1947	6.2	8.5	55.8	69.3	139.8
1948	5.9	7.6	51.9	70.5	135.9
1949	5.3	7.2	54.8	70.7	138.0
1950	5.3	7.3	48.7	71.6	132.9
1951	5.1	7.5	46.8	68.3	127.7
1952	5.3	7.1	51.5	75.2	139.1
1953	5.1	7.3	54.9	77.9	145.2
1954	4.8	6.8	57.6	77.3	146.5
1955	4.7	8.0	48.2	75.1	136.0
1956	4.7	8.5	46.7	76.7	136.6
1957	4.6	8.4	49.6	78.1	140.7
1958	4.6	9.3	54.9	78.8	147.6
1959	4.8	9.3	51.2	81.5	146.8
1960	5.0	9.4	59.9	84.7	159.0
1961	4.7	9.2	58.1	84.4	156.4
1962	4.5	9.3	59.4	87.3	160.5
1963	4.5	9.2	61.5	91.0	166.2
1964	4.8	11.0	67.9	104.5	188.2
1965	5.1	11.9	71.3	109.5	197.8
1966	5.6	12.9	80.3	118.4	217.2
1967	6.1	13.7	102.1	128.0	249.9
1968	6.8	15.5	131.0	141.3	294.6

has been prescribed as a cure for weak casts, weak plots, and weak positions in audience ratings. Eric Barnouw (1970) notes a running list of comments between the headquarters of the American Broadcasting Company and the producer of *The Untouchables*, one of the most violent television series ever aired. "I hope," said New York, "that you will give careful attention to maintaining this action and suspense in future episodes. As you know, there has been a softening in the ratings. . ." The producer passed the message along to a subordinate: "You'd better dictate some scenes of action. . .or we're all going to get

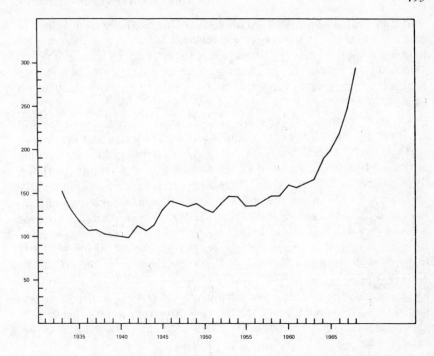

Figure 1:   Rate per 100,000 population of four violent crimes, 1933-68, Uniform
Crime Reports data.

clobbered." The National Broadcasting Company's *Producer's Showcase* files contain this memorandum, from the producer of a 90-minute
live drama series, about an upcoming 1956 production of Somerset
Maugham's "The Letter": "Since the casting on THE LETTER is no-
ticeably weak, I am afraid that we will loose [sic] our audience very
quickly unless they are exposed to some excitement." His proposed
solution was an opening scene "ending with Siobhan McKenna standing
over the prostrate body of her lover and firing her revolver into him."[3]

Almost every viewer has his or her own memory of a violent television episode, and some have recorded their impressions or cataloged
acts of aggression. Charles Sopkin (1968), in his painful memoir of a
week's viewing, recalled a rash of stairway deaths in soap operas. He
concluded, "I realize now that when a writer wants to eliminate a character he pulls the rug out from under him, as it were, and dumps him
down a flight of stairs."

In an article appearing in the fall of 1968, The *Christian Science Monitor* reported finding 254 incidents of violence (including 71 murders, suicides, and killings) during 75 hours of the first week of the new television
season. A one-week violence census was conducted in October 1960
during 100 hours of weekday programming, broadcast 4 to 9 p.m. from

four San Francisco outlets. Among other things, the census found 12 murders, 16 major gunfights, 21 persons shot, 21 other violent incidents with guns, and 37 hand-to-hand fights (Schramm, Lyle, and Parker, 1961). Such enumerations are familiar fare at Congressional hearings on media violence, where even the networks put forth their own tabulations of aggression.[4]

The most comprehensive content analysis of television violence was performed for the National Commission on the Causes and Prevention of Violence by a team headed by Dr. George Gerbner of the Annenberg School of Communications of the University of Pennsylvania (Gerbner, 1969). Gerbner's team coded entertainment programs offered by the three networks between the hours of 4 and 10 p.m. weekdays and Sunday, 8 and 11 a.m. and 7 and 10 p.m. (Eastern time) Saturdays, for the week of Oct. 1-7 in 1967 and 1968.

Gerbner defined violence as "physical or psychological injury, hurt, or death, addressed to living things. Violence is explicit and overt. It can be verbal or physical. If verbal, it must express intent to use physical force and must be plausible and credible in the context of the program. Idle, distant, or vague threats; mere verbal insults, quarrels, or abuse, or comic threats with no violent intent behind them are *not* to be considered violent."

Observing tapes of network programs, Gerbner's group recorded the nature, frequency, participants in, and milieu of violence in fictional presentations with storylines.

Gerbner found some kind of violence in 81 percent of all programs analyzed. (A "program" in his study could include a separate story within a larger offering, such as a skit within a variety show; an "episode" was a scene of violence within a program.) Almost every crime, western, action-adventure, and cartoon program contained some kind of violence, and two-thirds of the comedy programs contained violence as defined. The survey results showed no decline in percentage of violent programs from 1967 to 1968, but the rate of violent acts per play declined from 11.1 to 10.5.

A decline from 1967 to 1968 in percentage of violent programs was noted when the Gerbner group applied a more conservative criterion, *violence significant to plot* (that is, violence that is integral with the story), rather than *any kind of violence*. In 1967, 65.5 percent of all programs contained violence significant to plot, while the figure for 1968 was 56.3 percent.

Although rich in data, the Gerbner study does not look at pre-1967 television violence. Thus, while it shows that in some respects 1968 violence was lower than 1967 violence, it does not show how both 1967 and 1968 compared with, say, 1965 or 1966.

The major problem researchers face in establishing long-term trends in televised violence is the ephemeral nature of the broadcast medium.

A large number of early television dramas were presented "live"—requiring a good deal of production ingenuity but leaving no visual record. Some were filmed directly or kinescoped, but not all of these films have been preserved, and those which were saved are not readily accessible. Even after videotape recording was introduced, not all programs were taped and not all tapes were preserved. Gerbner, for example, was unable to examine a 1967 *Captain Kangaroo* program; evidently the tape had been destroyed.

It is also difficult to meld existing one-time-only studies into a cohesive analysis of trends in violent content, not only because of different definitions, but also because the various investigators have chosen different indices of violence. As Greenberg (1969) points out, some count acts and some count hours of violence. Others record the number of programs containing violence out of all programs offered, and some choose to examine fashions in programing—the fluctuating percentage of action-adventure programs, for example. Gerbner (1969) took all these approaches, but covered only two years of programming. The present study examines the percentage of programs judged to contain vioence, and the frequencies of various types of programs offered by the networks.

A partial solution to the problem of reconstructing lost program data can be derived from Gerbner's operational definition of violence integral to a program: "The criterion used to measure 'significance to the plot' was whether or not the violence, regardless of type or amount, would have to be noted in a one-page summary of the play." Even though visual records of programs may not exist, brief written summaries do remain in the form of program synopses. The most extensive collection of these synopses is, of course, in the more than 900 issues of *TV Guide* that have been published since its first issue in April 1953. If it can be shown that *TV Guide* synopses are valid and reliable indices to violent content, then we have an accessible source of longitudinal data.

Violence coded from synopses

Inspection of *TV Guide* confirmed that violence is indeed disclosed in synopses. For example, the summary of an *Ironside* crime drama read: "Two attempts on Mark's life spark an investigation by Chief Ironside. But the case is complicated when the gunman hired for the job is slain."

The next step was establishing a definition of violence and a coding routine and assessing the reliability of synopsis coding. We used a definition of violence we had applied to other media analyses: physical acts or the threat of physical acts by humans designed to inflict physical injury to persons or damage to property. Coders were told that the synopsis must strongly imply such violence before the program could be judged violent. (This definition was not identical to Gerbner's, but the two contained similar elements; one difference is that Gerbner's was restricted to injury to "living things," while ours included intentional damage to property.)

In a preliminary test, two coders independently judged 115 *TV Guide* synopses of evening entertainment programs that had storylines. Excluded were sports, news shows, and variety programs that did not contain skits. The coders agreed on the coding of 90 percent of the synopses; a more conservative index of intercoder reliability, Scott's (1955) pi coefficient, yielded a figure of .79.

The synopses were selected from Philadelphia area editions of *TV Guide* for October 1-7, 1967 and 1968—the locale and period of Gerbner's study. Thus, using synopses, we coded most of the programs that the Gerbner team had coded audiovisually. However, we were interested in evening shows (8-11 p.m. Eastern time), and for that reason the two samples were overlapping rather than identical.

The disagreements between the synopsis coders were resolved by a check coder, and the consensus was then tested for agreement with Gerbner's "violence significant to plot" data. The "synopsis" and "direct" coders agreed on 68 of 78 programs coded in common, or 87 percent. (Scott's pi coefficient was .73) In another test of agreement, the Gerbner and *TV Guide* violence dichotomies were subjected to tetrachoric correlation, with the result rt = .94. A comparison of findings from direct and synopsis coding for the same programs is shown in Table 2.

Table 2: Violent programs out of all programs coded: Direct coding and synopsis coding for the same programs, 1967 and 1968

	1967	1968	Both
Direct	46.3%	37.7%	42.3%
Synopis coding	39.0	29.7	34.6
	(N=41)	(N=37)	(N=78)

The direct-coded percentages of violent programs for the two years (42.3 percent) is considerably lower than the 81 percent attributed earlier to the Gerbner findings. The discrepancy is due largely to the fact that Table 2 reflects only those programs coded in common and excludes late afternoon shows that are exceedingly prone to violence. The percentages yielded by direct coding are also reduced by the "violence significant to plot" criterion. Though in general agreement with direct coding, synopsis coding yields a still lower percentage of violent programs, as might be expected in view of the brevity of synopses. Violence indexed via synopses may be inherently low.   Of the ten disagreements between direct and synopsis coders, seven arose over comedy programs, and the other three were over programs in the categories of general drama, western, and crime. Comedies that mix humor and action—such as *Hogan's Heroes* and *Get Smart*—are particularly difficult to code for violence, and violence in all comedies may be underestimated in synopsis coding.

Satisfied that there was a reasonable relationship between direct and synopsis coding, we acquired copies of *TV Guide* for an early week in October for each of the years 1953-69 and instructed coders—two for each year—in the appropriate procedure. All synopsized programs broadcast between 8 and 11 p.m. (Eastern time) and that had storylines were coded. Most of the *TV Guides* were from Milwaukee, but the 1953 issue was from the New York Metro edition, and the 1954, 1955, 1967 and 1968 issues were from Philadelphia. Thus the programs of prime network outlets in Milwaukee, New York, and Philadelphia were surveyed. Programs broadcast between 7 and 10 p.m. Central time were surveyed in the Wisconsin editions. Some unavoidable variation may owe to this geographic disparity; however, the selected weeks were within the network "season," and local programing during those hours appeared to be minimal. The first October week is thought to be fairly representative of the season's programming (Eleey, 1969).[6]

Questions can be raised about whether *TV Guide*'s program summaries have been consistent over the years. The programming department of that publication was closely questioned on this point, but the responding executive preferred not to give detailed answers because of "competitive considerations." He did offer the opinion that the magazine was "an accurate reflection of the television medium" and that "the program listings are hopefully objective reports on program content and in no way constitute an attempt to influence that content." Inspection of synopses of long-running series suggests that *TV Guide*'s synopses have not changed greatly over the years. Comparison of different editions for the same week suggests that only minor changes are made in synopses between areas, and only then for the purpose of fitting copy to available space. *TV Guide* in the 1970s looks remarkably like *TV Guide* in 1953.

Altogether, 982 synopses from 17 October weeks of *TV Guide*, 1953-69, were coded for violence in programs that began between the hours of 8 and 11 p.m. (Eastern time). Overall agreement of the 34 coders on the violence variable was 86.8 percent, and the Scott coefficient was .64. Table 3 presents the findings by year and by network. These data are presented in graphic form in Figures 2 and 3.

These data confirm some familiar impressions. Television violence appears to be cyclic; violence was especially prevalent during the late 1950s when the video cowboys claimed much of the range; after 1967 the networks made a greater effort to reduce violence.

Figure 2 shows that the highest proportion of violent programs occurred in 1953, but it also shows that this was only one of several peak years. If 1955 can be considered a crest, then peaks can be noted at four-year intervals, in 1955, 1959, 1963, and 1967. It might, therefore, be hypothesized that an upturn in violence will be perceptible in the early 1970s. However, even if we grant high validity to the present data, 17 years may not be a sufficiently long time period for gauging cycles of TV violence; the 1955 and 1963 summits may appear to be foothills to the researcher in 1985.

Table 3: Percentage of violent programs by network, 1953-69,
as derived from TV Guide synopses

Year	All networks			ABC			CBS			NBC		
	Vi	N	%	Vi	N	%	Vi	N	%	Vi	N	%
1953	10	52	19.2	0	7	0.0	7	22	31.8	3	23	13.0
1954	10	59	16.9	2	13	15.4	6	22	27.3	2	24	8.3
1955	17	63	26.9	7	15	46.7	7	25	28.0	3	23	13.0
1956	13	52	25.0	6	14	42.9	3	19	15.8	4	19	21.1
1957	21	67	31.3	5	17	29.4	5	26	19.2	11	24	45.8
1958	23	62	37.1	8	16	50.0	6	22	27.3	9	24	37.5
1959	28	68	41.3	15	25	60.0	5	25	20.0	8	18	44.4
1960	22	69	31.9	8	23	34.8	5	26	19.2	9	20	45.0
1961	13	63	20.6	5	22	22.7	1	23	4.3	7	18	38.8
1962	11	49	22.5	4	18	22.2	5	18	27.8	2	13	15.4
1963	14	48	29.2	7	15	46.7	3	21	14.3	4	12	33.3
1964	17	61	27.9	4	24	16.7	5	22	22.7	8	15	53.3
1965	11	62	17.7	4	23	17.4	2	18	11.1	5	21	23.8
1966	13	56	23.2	4	21	19.0	2	18	11.1	7	17	41.2
1967	20	53	37.7	10	18	55.6	4	19	21.1	6	16	37.5
1968	16	50	32.0	9	15	60.0	3	19	15.8	4	16	25.0
1969	10	48	20.8	4	16	25.0	3	19	15.8	3	13	23.1
Totals	269	982	27.4	102	302	33.8	72	364	19.8	95	316	30.1

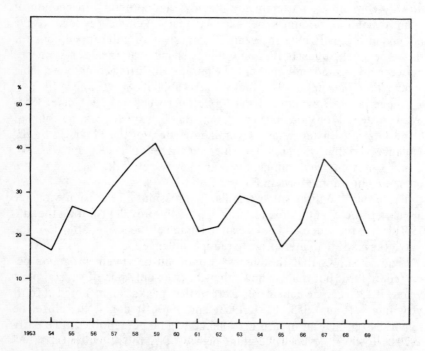

Figure 2: Percentage of violent programs, three networks combined, 1953-69,
as derived from *TV Guide* synopses.

Televison violence may be cyclic for several reasons. Environmental violence exhibits peaks and valleys, so realistic and topical drama might be expected to follow that pattern. Periodic critical outcries against excessive violence may inspire a reduction in violent programs. Viewer affection for violent programs waxes and wanes, and the networks adjust their offerings accordingly.

The expectation that media violence follows environmental violence finds little support. Rank-order correlation of violent years on television and in the real world as charted by the Uniform Crime Reports is only .18. Lagging television one year behind the environment (comparing 1959 television violence with 1958 environmental violence because of the lead time required to prepare a season's schedule) does not improve the correlation: $r_s = .14$. Because network headquarters are in New York City, a correlation was sought between television violence and New York environmental violence. That city's homicide and suicide data, substituted for the UCR national figures, showed virtually the same lack of correlation.

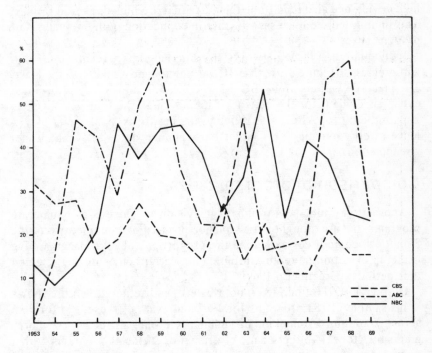

Figure 3: Percentage of violent programs by network, 1953-69, as derived from
TV Guide synopses.

The theory that criticism reduces violent programming has some face validity, especially if the critics represent governmental power. A Senate subcommittee on Juvenile Delinquency held hearings on television violence in 1954, 1961, and 1964. The National Commission on the Causes and Prevention of Violence was appointed in June 1968 and conducted hearings on the media that fall and winter. Again it is difficult to ascertain a relationship. Figure 2 indicates that after two of these years violence increased and after two it decreased. The means of measurement we used did not determine whether the forms and frequencies of violent acts within programs were moderated; the historical evidence examined later in this paper, however, strongly suggests that the networks were in some way affected and that they may have moderated their methods of treating violence, if not their devotion to it as prime program content.

The assumption that violence varies with ratings also finds some support. During the years 1956-69 (excluding earlier years when a total audience, rather than average audience, rating was made by the A. C. Nielsen Company), the product-moment correlation between percentages of violent programs derived from *TV Guide* and mean Nielsen ratings for all evening programs was $r = .534$, $p < .025$. In short, the years that are high in violence also tend to be the years that are high in overall ratings. This finding will be discussed further in connection with an analysis of program types.

Individually the three networks also fluctuated in percentages of violent programs (Figure 3), with ABC varying the most and CBS the least. The mean deviations are: ABC, 15.5; CBS, 6.0; and NBC, 12.0. Some cycling is evident for the network data, although the four-year cycle is apparent only for ABC. Interestingly, the networks' peak years of violence rarely coincide. This might be explained as a follow-the-leader phenomenon.

Comparison of program types

Another way to assess trends in television violence is to enumerate programs that are thought to be violence-prone. For example, two of the Senate subcommittees examined the proportions of total programming made up of action-adventure programs in certain cities during selected time periods. (Greenberg, 1969).

Gerbner (1969) found 118 crime, western, and action-adventure shows in his sample of 183 programs for 1967 and 1968; of these, 114 (or 96.6 percent) contained some kind of violence. Gerbner also categorized programs by "tone"—either comic or dramatic. Of the 44 programs with a comic tone, 66.4 percent contained some kind of violence. The "violence significant to plot" criterion would lower those percentages.

Through the courtesy of the A. C. Nielsen Company we acquired relevant portions of the first October Nielsen Television Index reports for the years 1952-69. These reports provide mean data from two consecutive weeks early each October. Among other things, Nielsen reports the number and mean rating of evening (6-11 p.m. Eastern time) programs

Table 4: Types of programs, 1952-69: their ratings and frequencies

Type	Ratings and number of programs by year																	
	1952	1953	1954	1955	1956	1957	1958	1959	1960	1961	1962	1963	1964	1965	1966	1967	1968	1969
General (Rating) Drama (N)	29.8 18	26.8 18	23.8 24	23.7 38	20.8 26	19.8 17	18.8 14	20.2 9	16.2 10	17.7 9	17.3 21	17.2 19	17.6 11	16.3 15	18.0 6	16.7 6	16.7 6	17.2 8
Suspense, mystery	27.7 17	26.4 14	20.7 12	24.0 6	20.4 9	19.7 15	21.7 6	17.5 22	15.9 23	15.0 23	14.2 11	14.7 5	16.2 6	18.2 5	17.0 9	17.0 9	16.7 14	18.1 9
Situation comedy	32.2 16	25.8 25	23.3 27	25.0 27	22.4 20	19.8 20	22.5 17	20.1 16	18.3 20	16.4 30	18.2 27	21.2 22	21.6 33	18.7 35	18.3 27	19.5 20	19.7 21	16.8 28
Western drama	24.1 4	19.2 5	19.2 4	20.6 7	20.8 7	25.7 9	26.6 18	22.6 28	18.8 29	18.2 20	19.9 11	20.9 5	21.9 4	20.2 9	17.8 8	16.2 8	18.4 8	19.2 6
General variety	33.3 13	28.8 17	33.4 14	30.2 14	19.3 19	19.6 11	19.5 23	18.9 23	17.2 15	17.3 13	20.7 17	16.6 24	17.6 15	16.6 17	17.3 10	19.8 10	18.4 15	18.2 16
Talent variety	27.4 3	28.2 3	21.2 2	17.4 3														
Musical variety	26.7 4	22.2 3	21.4 4	22.6 6														
Other musical	16.3 4	20.6 4	15.5 7	12.5 4														
Quiz & audience participation	22.7 15	19.6 20	20.8 17	20.5 20	20.9 16	24.3 11	19.7 14	17.1 10	16.9 9	19.0 7	17.0 8	20.4 6	17.2 5	17.1 4	15.1 3			12.6 3
Sports	21.4 10	17.0 10	15.0 10	17.7 4														
Feature film															21.8 5	24.2 6	20.2 7	19.8 8
Adventure					17.8 10	16.8 10	17.0 11	12.3 4		11.2 5	12.7 4	16.3 2	22.5 3	18.8 7	17.0 11	16.8 6		

Table 4: Types of programs, 1952-69: their ratings and frequencies—Continued

Ratings and number of programs by year

Type	1952	1953	1954	1955	1956	1957	1958	1959	1960	1961	1962	1963	1964	1965	1966	1967	1968	1969
Other					14.3	16.7	17.2	13.4	10.4									
					15	15	6	6	12									
Informational										11.0	6.3	11.1	9.2	9.6	9.0	9.6	11.1	11.3
										5	6	4	15	6	6	6	6	6
Science fiction															17.0	15.3		
															3	3		
Mean rating:	27.5	24.2	22.6	23.3	19.8	20.0	20.8	19.1	16.7	16.3	17.2	18.0	17.9	17.4	17.2	17.8	18.0	17.2
Total number:	104	119	121	129	122	108	109	118	118	112	105	87	92	98	88	74	71	84

within selected categories. The frequency and relative popularity of certain types of programs can be seen in Table 4.

The table does not enumerate all the programs that appeared every evening; local programming is necessarily excluded, and some cells are empty because Nielsen lacked a sufficient number of programs of that type to calculate a valid rating.. Additionally, the ratings for the years 1952, 1953, 1954, and 1955 are somewhat inflated because they reflect estimates of the total number of television homes reached any time during the program. Ratings from 1956 onward are estimates of the percentage of TV households tuned in during the average minute of the program—a more conservative estimate.

In 1956 Nielson also changed some program categories. Music and variety were combined, and an adventure category was broken out of general drama. An "other" category, previously allied with music, also came into use. Westerns, which until 1954 had been grouped with children's programs, went adult in 1955. Much later, in 1966, when the networks began heavily broadcasting prime time movies, a feature film category was added.

In 1956 Nielsen also separated the frequencies and ratings of programs of different duration. Table 4 combines ratings and frequencies of programs regardless of length; the transformation is the responsibility of the authors, not of the A. C. Nielsen Company. (Average audience ratings of 30- and 60-minute programs of the same type do not differ greatly, except for variety shows.)

Of the major categories, situation comedy has been the most densely populated with a mean of 23.9 programs per year over the period 1952-69; general variety had a mean of 15.9 programs per year, general drama had 15.8, suspense and mystery had 11, and western drama had 10.6.

The categories in Table 4 can be regrouped according to their suspected tendencies toward violence. The assignments are necessarily somewhat arbitrary and intuitive. As in previous studies, the likely candidates for a "high violence" group are the categories of suspense and mystery (which includes crime), western, adventure, and science fiction. The categories of situation comedy, variety, music, quiz, and information are usually considered low in violence. The remaining categories are hard to dichotomize and therefore comprise an intermediate grouping of programs that are believed to have mixed tendencies toward violence: general drama, feature films, sports, and miscellany. Tables 5 and 6 present the results of this regrouping, and Figure 4 gives a graphic summary of the percentages of programs in each group.

Slightly more than half of all programs fall into the low violence group, and 11 of the 18 years contain more low violence programs than mixed and high violence programs combined.

The earlier finding that ratings appear to vary with violence suggests that violent programs are more popular than pacific programs. A little support for that inference can be derived from Table 5. High violence

Tabel 5: Types of programs grouped by tendency to contain violence: ratings and frequencies, by year

Ratings and number of programs

Tendency[a]	1952	1953	1954	1955	1956	1957	1958	1959	1960	1961	1962	1963	1964	1965	1966	1967	1968	1969
High																		
Rating	27.0	24.5	20.3	22.2	19.5	20.4	22.7	19.8	17.5	15.9	16.4	17.6	19.4	19.3	17.2	16.5	17.3	18.5
Number	21	19	16	13	26	34	35	54	52	48	26	12	13	21	31	26	22	15
Mixed																		
Rating	26.8	23.3	21.2	23.1	18.4	19.3	18.3	17.5	13.0	17.7	17.3	17.2	17.6	16.3	19.7	20.5	20.2	18.5
Number	28	28	34	42	41	32	20	15	22	9	21	19	11	15	11	12	7	16
Low																		
Rating	28.1	24.4	23.8	23.6	20.9	20.9	20.5	18.9	17.6	16.4	17.5	18.4	17.7	17.1	16.6	17.9	18.0	16.4
Number	55	72	71	74	55	52	54	49	44	55	58	56	68	62	46	36	42	53

Table 6: Percentage of programs in each group, by year

	1952	1953	1954	1955	1956	1957	1958	1959	1960	1961	1962	1963	1964	1965	1966	1967	1968	1969
High	20.2	16.0	13.2	10.1	21.3	31.5	32.1	45.8	44.1	42.9	24.8	13.8	14.1	21.4	35.2	35.1	31.0	17.9
Mixed	26.9	23.5	28.1	32.6	33.6	29.6	18.3	12.7	18.6	8.0	20.0	21.8	12.0	15.3	12.5	16.2	9.9	19.0
Low	52.9	60.5	58.7	57.3	45.1	38.9	49.6	41.5	37.3	49.1	55.2	64.4	73.9	63.3	52.3	48.7	59.1	63.1

aThe "tendency" groupings are assigned as follows:
  High violence: Suspense and mystery, western, adventure, science fiction.
  Mixed violence: General drama, feature films, sports, and miscellaneous.
  Low violence: Situation comedy, variety, music, quiz, and information.

programs for the years 1956-69 have a mean rating of 18.4 compared to 18.2 for low violence programs. The mixed group, which contains informational programs, is lowest in mean ratings.

Indirect methods compared

Comparing the curve of high violence programs (Figure 4) with the curve of synopsis-coded violence in Figure 2 reveals similar descriptions of trends in television violence. The product-moment correlation between the two sets of data is significant: $r = .507$, $p < .025$. The two descriptions are not in perfect agreement, however; the curve of high violence programs in Figure 4 has two summits, centering on 1959-61 and 1966-67, rather than the four peaks in Figure 2. But those two major peaks do coincide in the two figures. Most discrepant are the low points in the data on program types in 1955 and 1963-64—periods when coded violence was relatively high. The discrepancies can be at least partially explained by contributions of codable violence made in those years by programs in the putative low and mixed violence typologies.

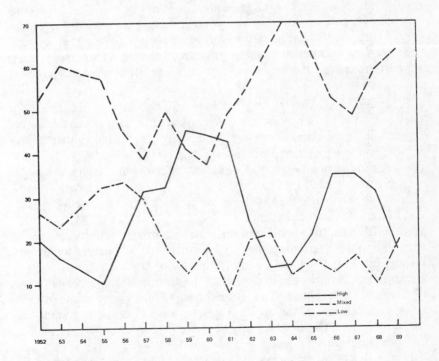

Figure 4: Percentage of high-, mixed-, and low-violence types of programs, 1952-69.

The future validity of indirect methods of assessing violence on television is dubious in light of a 1970 article that quotes television producers as saying that acts of violence are being abbreviated or eliminated but that threats of violence remain. One producer said, "We talk a great deal about the Apache menace. And we do a lot of nervous rides through Apache territory waiting for them to swoop down out of the hills. We try to get the boys through before the Apaches strike" (Finnegan, 1970). If indeed television elects to turn to more threats than acts of violence, then content analysis will have to become a great deal more subtle.

Violence and the ratings

We noted that tends in environmental violence and in television violence have little in common and that television—as determined from synopses—is more closely associated with prime time ratings. We also examined ratings in relation to the types of programs offered each year.

Table 5 shows that as the mean ratings of the violent types fluctuate, so do the number of programs of that type. But the variations are not synchronous: for the period 1956-69, there is no correlation between ratings and the number of high violence programs offered in the same year $(r = - .19)$. However, the ratings and frequencies do correlate when the number of high violence programs is lagged one year behind the ratings $(r = .494, p < .05)$. As the ratings for westerns, for example, go up, the next year the number of western programs goes up. (This finding may support the charge of copycatting that critics so often level at the industry.)

However, a similar relationship between ratings and programming does not hold for low violence programs, either in the same year or lagged one year behind. Thus high violence programming appears to be volatile and low violence programming relatively stable. Over the years the range in the number of high violence programs has been quite large —from a low of 12 in 1963 to a high of 54 in 1959, and the statistical variance of the number of high violence programs is two and one-half times that of the low violence group.

At first glance, the volatility of high violence programming might seem to be due to the alternating hunger and satiation of the action-loving audience. In 1959, when the violent types of programs were most numerous, their mean rating began to decline. But the apparent decline in popularity may be deceptive. The rating for high violence programs in 1959 (19.8, down from 22.7 the previous year) is a mean of individual ratings for 54 programs. Obviously, many of those were aired at the same time, and even the most sanguinary fans could not watch them all. In that light, the 19.8 mean rating may be remarkably high, considering the dilution of the audience. The audience may have gorged but was not satiated.

Low violence programming is also subject to internecine competition, yet it does not reflect the same variability in the number of programs offered. High violence programming may be more variable because of economics, conscience, or both.

The differing variabilities of violent and less violent programming may relate to the nature of the television medium. The most elementary kind of entertainment that television can purvey—and the most broadly suited to the living room—consists of one or more voluble entertainers in a plotless, largely spontaneous (and inherently nonviolent) program. Stand-up comedy, quiz shows, music, and variety shows have been television staples from the beginning and have commanded faithful audiences. But if television executives seek to widen their entertainment audiences, they (like the entrepreneurs of other media) have available the tools of sensationalism—with the partial exclusion of sex. It would be surprising if they did not seize these tools with varying degrees of enthusiasm and tenacity. Music, comedy, and talk remain as basic content, and action drama becomes a frosting to be applied in various forms and quantity.

Much of this discussion suggests that writers of television drama may have been taught how to make their scripts violent and at the same time acceptable to the various forces—in the audience, in government, and in the industry itself—which help shape programming. Since nothing breeds imitation faster than success, most of this instruction has probably been implicit, though explicit demands for violence are occasionally made. A survey of the papers of 32 television playwrights conducted at the Mass Communications History Center of the State Historical Society of Wisconsin revealed only 20 references to violence in more than 500 boxes of documents.[7] Although this group of writers contained few who specialized primarily in violent shows, television writers during the period studied (the late 1940s through the early 1960s), seem not to have spoken (on paper) one way or the other about violence.

A similar search was conducted in the National Broadcasting Company's program procurement files, also held at the State Historical Society of Wisconsin. The Continuity Acceptance Department, NBC's policing organ charged with enforcing adherence to the network's self-regulatory code as well as to the National Association of Broadcasters' code, had much to do with the ultimate forms program violence took. When the network censors expressed concern, to judge from the NBC example, it was invariably directed at toning down the dramatic treatment of violence expressed. Continuity Acceptance Reports (a mimeographed circular distributed to key persons at NBC from the early 1950s through 1960) show most of the censors' attention devoted to sex in dramas and commercials, not to violence. Mattress and brassiere commercials and other possible "taste" problems, especially in comedy shows, drew most of the attention. Similar priorities were also evident in public complaints to the Federal Communications Commission. An analysis of recorded complaints during 75 days in the spring of 1951 showed 73 complaints about crime and horror programs, 255 complaints about the advertising of alcoholic beverages, 221 about with "indecency," and 128 about presumed false or misleading advertising.[8] When Congressional committees met to consider the possible bad effects of radio and television, witnesses from temperance organizations usually far outnumbered those from other nonbroadcasting groups.

Even the continuity acceptance practices at NBC, which pioneered efforts at setting up program standards as early as 1927, appear at times to have been directed at calming the fears of sponsors who worried about repercussions from violence that an audience might find objectionable. In answer to a sponsor's representative's inquiry about the violent opening planned for the 1956 *Producer's Showcase* presentation of "The Letter," the NBC continuity acceptance chief wrote a reassuring note: "We at NBC have given every reasonable attention possible to the more adult and realistic aspects of this material as they reach those of our viewers who comprise the family viewing circle." He went on, "My very genuine view is that the shock opener is very definitely compensated for by the material that follows and ought to bring no material criticism except from those who may take it out of context and totally miss the point of the entire production."[9] He was correct in his assumption; no complaints were noted. Despite the violent opening, "The Letter" ran poorly in the ratings behind *I Love Lucy*.

NBC appears to have followed a management philosophy of checks and balances. Those persons in charge of program procurement and production were free to encourage violence implicitly and explicitly; they were subject to the checks applied by the Continuity Acceptance Department, which enforced standards according to its perceptions of audience acceptance. This system may have had at least two flaws: Audience taste or acceptance may not have been an appropriate measure of the potential effects of violent content; and the Continuity Acceptance Department, not being an independent check on programming, appears to have ruled with the network's interest ahead of the public's interest.

The censors consistently toned down the explicitness of violence but did not seriously question the violence itself, apparently for pragmatic and somewhat cynical reasons. The continuity Acceptance Report for November 5, 1954, contained this justification for censorship:

> One of the recent *Dragnets* (October 28) cleared on the coast over a year ago. . .seemed a little too brutal in the light of current Senatorial interest in so-called violence on television. . .Hence you'll note why in the two temperings just mentioned above the intent of the censorship action is to cut the length and degree of mayhem.

But there were other reasons for "tempering" besides "current Senatorial interest," the report noted. Going beyond just the amount of violence needed to establish conflict "inevitably seems to result in sadism, sensationalism, and, to make this brief, [it is] what brings an audience criticism and hurts the company's, the talent's, and the client's public relations."[10] The possibility that violence might have an effect other than indignation on the audience was not considered.

If, as some psychologists have recently suggested, unrealistically treated violence gives children misconceptions about what it means to hurt or to be hurt, networks may be accused of doubly stimulating violence: through overemphasizing it as a solution to problems and underemphasizing its seriousness. Although attention to realism has been offered as a defense of violence, some kinds of reality were consistently edited out of scripts, no matter what intentions the writers had. This example a 1955 NBC Continuity Acceptance Report shows how one censor distinguished between the act of violence and its aftermath:

> p. 13 sc 15 — Corpse with bullet hole in forehead. Keep it a medium long shot and show no gore.
> p. 25, sc 28—Officer starts examining corpse, do not show him peering into wound, feeling skin, etc.[11]

The lessons of these censorship and programming policies could not have been lost upon the writers. Violence was an acceptable and easy method of quickly establishing dramatic conflict. The networks encouraged it, as the testimony of NBC vice president Charles R. Denny in 1952 before a Congressional subcommittee shows:

> ...We...seek to strike a proper balance which does not destroy realism, but avoids effects which would shock or alarm a normal listener or viewers...I invite your attention...to pages 5 and 6 of the NBC Code....When properly presented, programs of this type educate against crime and delinquency.... (Subcommittee of the Committee on Interstate and Foreign Commerce. 1952).

The National Association of Radio and Television Broadcasters encouraged violence, as its president, Harold E. Fellows, testified at the same hearings:

> Mr. Chenowith: Would it be your observation, Mr. Fellows, that the crime and mystery plays have been overplayed just a little,...by both radio and television?...
> Mr. Fellows: Well, one of our big sources of programming, one of the great networks, has only seven per cent of its programming time in crime and mystery plays.
> Mr. Chenowith: I think we heard from some witnesses that it was about ten per cent.
> Mr. Fellows: that may be in some instances, sir.
> Mr. Chenowith: You think ten per cent is not too much, then?
> Mr. Fellows: I certainly don't if that is what the public wants. They may want 30 per cent.

And the viewers encouraged it. They watched, and they did not often complain.

VIOLENCE IN MOTION PICTURES ON TELEVISION

Much has been written about the effects of television on the motion picture industry. It is also worth noting that movies affected television: not only were the aesthetics and techniques of film instructive to the new medium, but movies also became a significant part of television content.

The investigators sketched trends in violence in televised motion pictures by using the same methods applied to other television entertainment.

Part of the analysis of television entertainment relied on *TV Guide* program summaries, and televised movies were coded along with other programs. Of the 982 synopses coded, 54 described motion pictures. Fifteen of the 54 movies, or 27.8 percent were judged to contain violence. This percentage is nearly identical to that for all television programs.

The available issues of *TV Guide* contained only a fraction of the thousands of films sold to television. (The exact number of such films is probably unknown.) However, about 7,000 movie synopses are available in *Movies on TV*, which syndicates television program notes to newspapers (Scheuer, 1969). This collection provides an opportunity to assess a larger body of films and to seek trends in violence. The limitations of synopsis coding in evaluating television entertainment programs also apply to movies. A further problem is that no independent criterion, such as direct coding from a screening, is available as a test of validity of coding from film synopses. Nor does *Movies on TV* summarize every movie ever made; it concentrates on those films having some currency on television.

A sample of 807 synopses was drawn from *Movies on TV*, and each was coded for violence as previously described. Other variables, including year of original release and quality rating (one to four asterisk "stars"), were also recorded. Intercoder agreement on violence was .90, and the Scott pi coefficient was .76.

Of the 807 movies (whose release dates span the years 1930-69) evaluated through synopses, 284, or 35.2 percent, were judged to contain violence.

Table 7 charts the percentage of violent films among all those coded for the years 1937-66. Earlier and later years do not appear because the number of films was judged insufficient; only those years for which at least ten synopses were found appear in the table. Figure 5 discloses great fluctuation in the yearly percentages, some of which probably owes to the small size of the sample. There is a general upward trend in violence, and the percentages of violent movies for the years 1937-66 correlate with the UCR violent crime data for the same years ($r = .58$ $p < .005$). While tantalizing, this correlation is probably fortuitous. Of all mass media, movies may be the least constrained to reflect the real world; their makers have often been accused of inhabiting a dreamland. It would be equally difficult to conclude that increased violence in the real world is a function of increased violence in films, if for no other reason than that movies are chronically losing attendance. In the years 1929-68 while expenditures on broadcast receivers, records, and musical instruments increased 89.13 percent, motion picture admissions declined 64.5 percent.[12]

Table 7: Percentage of violent films by year, 1937-66[a],
as derived from Movies on TV synopses

Year	Vi	N	Percent
1937	3	12	25.0
1938	1	12	8.3
1939	5	18	27.8
1940	3	22	13.6
1941	4	23	17.4
1942	9	21	42.9
1943	3	16	18.8
1944	6	16	37.5
1945	4	19	21.1
1946	1	12	8.3
1947	8	16	50.0
1948	11	28	39.3
1949	5	19	26.3
1950	9	34	26.5
1951	10	29	34.5
1952	11	31	35.5
1953	17	33	51.5
1954	9	24	37.5
1955	13	42	30.9
1956	13	32	40.6
1957	18	40	45.0
1958	16	39	41.0
1959	12	35	34.3
1960	17	44	38.6
1961	9	25	36.0
1962	11	34	32.4
1963	21	37	56.8
1964	12	30	40.0
1965	7	13	53.8
1966	6	15	40.0

[a] Year of first theater release. Only those years for which
ten or more films were found are presented.

The trend in percentages of violent films does not correlate with the
percentages of violent television programs. Some cycling in movie violence can be seen on a four- to six-year basis if one takes as peak years
1942, 1947, 1953, 1957, and 1963.

Movies on TV rates each film on the basis of one (poor) to four (excellent) "stars." Violent and nonviolent films are not distinguished by this
quality rating. The mean number of "stars" for the violent films was 2.5,
for the nonviolent 2.6.

In 1970, the Audience Development Department of Katz Television, a
national advertising representative for television stations, issued a
Track Record of films released to network television from mid-Sep-
tember 1961 through April 5, 1970 (Katz Television, 1970). The publication indicated each film's thematic type (e.g., western), theatrical release date, television play dates, network purchaser, and Nielsen rating.
Katz also noted whether each movie was made for television or originally shown in theatres.

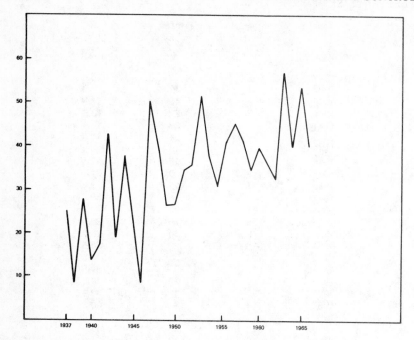

Figure 5: Percentage of violent films, release dates 1937-66, as derived from *Movies on TV* synopses.

Thus the Katz data permit an examination of movie types similar to that conducted earlier of television program types derived from A. C. Nielsen Company reports. The Katz movies typologies are similar to those Nielsen applies to television programs; the categories can be grouped according to their presumed tendencies toward violence, as in Tables 5 and 6.[13] The results of a grouping of 1961-70 televised films appear in Tables 8 and 9.

The ratings presented in Table 9 are the mean national Nielsen audience estimates, by year, for the first network showing of the films in each group by year. Several of the movies have been shown many times on television, both by the networks and through syndication. Subsequent showings usually win lower ratings.

Movies generally enjoy good ratings, averaging one or two points higher than regular television programs within each type. Their frequency has understandably increased over the ten-year period. (The totals for 1961 and 1970 are artificially low because in each case Katz summarized only part of the year.) Unlike the number of high violence television series, the number of violence-prone films does not appear to be related to rating performance.

On the whole, low violence motion pictures received slightly higher ratings than the more violent types. Table 10 presents mean ratings by type and by network.

SELECTED MASS MEDIA 213

Table 8: Types of movies grouped by tendency to contain violence: mean ratings and frequencies by year of release on television

Ratings and number of movies

Tendency	1961	1962	1963	1964	1965	1966	1967	1968	1969	1970
High										
Rating	20.0	18.0	18.1	19.2	20.3	20.4	20.5	19.2	19.5	19.7
Number	8	38	38	35	36	45	52	56	63	37
Mixed										
Rating	18.2	16.3	18.2	18.3	19.8	20.1	20.7	20.9	17.8	20.7
Number	3	11	25	21	26	32	51	40	43	11
Low										
Rating	20.2	19.7	19.6	19.7	19.7	20.5	21.2	20.0	19.1	18.4
Number	5	9	12	18	44	54	70	44	55	14

Table 9: Percentage of movies in each group, by year

	1961	1962	1963	1964	1965	1966	1967	1968	1969	1970
High	50.0	65.5	50.7	47.3	34.0	34.3	30.1	40.0	39.1	59.7
Mixed	18.8	19.0	33.3	28.4	24.5	24.4	29.5	28.6	26.7	17.7
Low	31.3	15.5	16.0	24.3	41.5	41.2	40.5	31.4	34.2	22.6

Table 10: Movies released to television, 1961-70:
frequencies, percentages, and ratings of high-, mixed-,
and low-violence types by network

Types	Network			
	ABC	CBS	NBC	ALL
High				
Number	129	76	198	403
Percentage	43.3	34.7	42.1	40.8
Mean rating	18.2	19.8	20.2	19.5
Mixed				
Number	81	69	110	260
Percentage	27.2	31.5	23.4	26.3
Mean rating	18.4	20.7	19.5	19.5
Low				
Number	88	74	162	324
Percentage	29.5	33.8	34.5	32.8
Mean rating	18.6	20.7	20.6	20.1
Totals				
Number	298	219	470	987[a]
Mean rating	18.4	20.4	20.2	19.7

[a]This total is less than 996 because the Katz data lacked
ratings for nine films.

Table 10 indicates that nearly half of the films broadcast during 1961-70 were aired by NBC, while CBS showed the fewest. These two networks received very similar ratings for their films. ABC, which has been consistently the weakest in overall program popularity, also trailed in its film ratings.

What is most striking about Table 10 is the distribution of movie types among the networks. Table 3 showed that ABC had the highest proportion of programs containing violence; ABC was followed closely by NBC and at some distance by CBS. The networks appear to demonstrate similar values in selecting movies. However, the differences in proportions of movies types among networks approach but do not reach statistical significance at the .05 level: $X^2 = 7.96$ at 4 df.

Of the 996 movies, 408 (or 41 percent)were in the high violence group. This percentage is notably higher than the 26 percent of general television programs during 1952-69 that fell into the same grouping. This discrepancy may be due not so much to the tastes of the networks as to certain differences between the two media. The motion picture medium does not have a place for quiz, information, and variety content. These three types of programs are by nature in the low violence category; if television programs of these kinds were removed from the period of 1952-69, the proportion of high violence programs would rise to 37.3 percent, which approaches the 41 percent for movies.[14]

Not all films shown on television were originally released to theatres. During the 1960s some movies were produced for initial release on television. (Film critics have been generally contemptuous of these offerings, which are usually put together rapidly and feature second-magnitude stars. However, movies of this kind offer several advantages to the networks: the "made-for" films can be touted as "premieres"; they arrive tailored for television's time requirements; they can serve as pilot programs; and the networks themselves can sponsor their production and thereby control costs and content.) Of the 996 films listed by Katz, 89 were made expressly for television. NBC aired 48, ABC 36, and CBS five. The made-for-TV movies appear to have inherited violent tendencies from both media, as Table 11 suggests. More than half these films fell into the high violence group, and the difference in proportions between television and theatrical films is statistically significant ($X^2 = 18.35$ at 2 df., $p < .001$).

Table 11: Comparison of movies made for television
and for theater

Tendency	Originally made for		
	Television	Theater	Combined
High			
Number	49	359	408
Percentage	55.1	39.6	41.0
Mixed			
Number	29	234	263
Percentage	32.6	25.8	26.4
Low			
Number	11	314	325
Percentage	12.3	34.6	32.6
Totals			
Number	89	907	996
Percentage	100.0	100.0	100.0

Whatever the critics may think of made-for-TV movies, such films do succeed with the audience. The mean rating of the 89 made-for-TV movies was 20.3; the mean rating for all others was 19.6.

Katz also tabulated 25 "all time top rated network feature films." "The Wizard of Oz" has enjoyed such repeated success that it appears seven times among the 25 top draws. Table 12 reproduces the Katz list with the lesser six appearances of "Oz" removed. Of the top 18 tabled, eight were in the high, six in the mixed, and four in the low violence categories; these proportions are not greatly different from those of all films. However, a disproportion is apparent in the distribution of the top 18 among the three networks. CBS, which showed the fewest films overall, had ten in the top 18, while ABC had five and NBC three.

Table 12: Top-rated network feature films, as of 1970, compiled by Katz Television, Inc.

Title	Producer/Distributor	Net	Playdate	Day	Rating[a]	Type[b]	Original release
1. *The Birds*	Universal	NBC	1-6-68	Sat	38.9	Dra/Sus	1963
2. *Bridge on River Kwai*	Col Screen Gems	ABC	9-25-66	Sun	38.3	War	1957
3. *Wizard of Oz*	MGM	CBS	12-13-59	Sun	36.5	Music	1939
4. *Born Free*	Col Screen Gems	CBS	2-22-70	Sun	34.2	Dra/Adv	1966
5. *Cat on a Hot Tin Roof*	MGM	CBS	9-28-67	Thu	32.2	Drama	1958
6. *My Sweet Charlie*[c]	Universal	NBC	1-20-70	Tue	31.7	Drama	1970
7. *Great Escape* (2-part)	U.A.A.	CBS	9-14,15-67	Thu	31.2 Avg.	War	1963
8. *McClintock*	U.A.A.	CBS	11-3-67	Fri	31.2	Western	1963
9. *Ballad of Josie*	Universal	NBC	9-16-69	Tue	31.1	Western	1968
10. *The Robe*	20th Century	ABC	3-26-67	Sun	31.0	Dra/Rel	1953
11. *Lillies of the Field*	U.A.A.	CBS	3-24-67	Fri	30.0	Drama	1963
12. *Your Cheatin' Heart*	MGM	CBS	4-5-68	Fri	29.7	Drama	1964
13. *Gidget Goes Hawaiian*	Col Screen Gems	CBS	3-31-66	Fri	29.6	Comedy	1961
14. *Five Branded Women*	Paramount	ABC	1-6-67	Fri	29.4	Drama	1960
15. *Roustabout*	Paramount	ABC	1-3-68	Wed	29.1	Drama	1964
16. *Hombre*	20th Century	ABC	1-25-70	Sun	29.1	Western	1967
17. *P.T.109*	Warner	CBS	1-13-67	Fri	29.1	War/Bio	1963
18. *Cat Ballou*	Col Screen Gems	ABC	10-2-68	Wed	28.8	Comedy	1965

[a]National Nielsen.
[b]Katz categories.
[c]Made-for-TV movie.

Discussion

Determined from a sample of synopses, the percentage of violent motion pictures has shown a general upward trend since the late 1930s. The fluctuation by year is considerable, but peaks do appear at four- to six-year intervals. About 35 percent of the synopses sampled were of films judged to contain violence.

The trend in percentage of violent films does not correlate with the percentage of violent television programs, but it does correlate with UCR environmental violence data. Peak years can be noted in 1942, 1947, and 1953, suggesting some relationship with World War II and the Korean War. The peak years of 1957, 1963, and 1965, however, are not easily related to wartime. More suggestive, perhaps is the fact that after the advent of commercial television, the number of violent films never dropped below 30 percent per year, while during the years 1937-50 (inclusive) the percentage was below 30 ten times. We may speculate that motion pictures became more violent in order to compete for audiences with television. It may be argued that the violence was part of a maturation of films in which they became more candid, but this "maturity" may also be a function of television competition, which removed the "family" audience and cleared the way for more vigorous expression.

Grouped according to their thematic types, movies released to television between 1961 and 1970 exhibited a greater proportion of so-called high violence than did prime time television entertainment programs. This may be due to the presence on television of certain kinds of content not suited to motion pictures—quiz and variety shows, for example. The networks acquired violent types of motion pictures in roughly the same proportion that they exhibited violent entertainment programs. Films made expressly for release on television are more often of the high violence type than are theatrical films.

VIOLENCE IN A FAMILY MAGAZINE'S FICTION

Together with radio and film, mass magazines were a major source of pretelevision family entertainment. Foremost among the family magazines was the *Saturday Evening Post*, which was once described by journalism historian Frank Luther Mott as "the great American nickelodeon. It must be generally agreed that the *Saturday Evening Post* is as American as the public school, the big department store, the television network program, the hot dog and the ice cream cone" (Mott, 1957).

The *Post* was virtually a member of every family that received it, much as television would later be. And like television's, the *Post*'s closeness to its audience was not accidental. The *Post* pioneered that indispensable tool of the modern network, the ratings system. In 1911 the Curtis Publishing Company established the first marketing research organization in the United States, and a portion of that research was conducted for editorial guidance. After 1942, when Ben Hibbs became editor, research on reader tastes became important to the editorial staff, and many modifications in the *Post*'s content and format during the 1940s and 1950s resulted from survey research (Peterson, 1964). Although Hibbs argued that "you can't edit a magazine by arithmetic," he acted on research indicating that reader interest in World War II remained high even after the end of hostilities (Ludeke, 1948).

Purchased by Cyrus H. K. Curtis in 1897 and edited by George Horace Lorimer from 1899 to 1937, the *Post* was enormously successful, in circulation terms, throughout its life. Even in its dying years, the *Post* did not want for an audience. Lorimer firmly installed themes of homely Americanism and the romantic pursuit of material wealth in *Post* fiction, and the magazine "became the reflection of a middle-of-the-road America" (Emery, 1962). Lorimer's successor in 1937, Wesley W. Stout, carried on that tradition until 1942, when he was succeeded by Hibbs. Hibbs shared the conservative outlook, but modernized the magazine in appearance and used more (and shorter) articles. He customarily included two serials in each issue; these tended to be detective stories or westerns (Mott, 1957). Hibbs retired at the end of 1961, with the *Post*'s circulation at about 6.2 million—or 3 million more than when he took over. Ironically, this was the first year that the parent Curtis Company failed to turn a profit. Hibbs was followed by Robert Fuoss, Robert Sherrod, Clay Blair, Jr., and William Emerson.

The *Post* died in 1969 of multiple causes—corporate mismanagement and lack of support from Madison Avenue are most often cited—but loss of reader loyalty was not one of them. If anything, the *Post* had too many subscribers in its final years (about 6.5 million), and its production costs were too high to permit an attractive advertising rate. One of its last acts was an attempt to lop off more than three million subscribers who were thought to be laggard consumers.[16]

This excommunication of loyal patrons was infinitely more outrageous to readers than violent content had ever been. Although an occasional sensitive reader might fault the *Post* for excessive gore in its fiction, the magazine escaped the widespread criticism of blood and thunder that was visited upon some of its contemporaries and eventually upon television. Yet the *Post* and its brethren were not devoid of violence. In his study of sex and violence in the print media, Otto (1962) found that family magazines contained an average of 12 incidents of violence per issue.

Forty years of the *Saturday Evening Post*, from 1925 through 1964, were systematically sampled by the researchers. This period covers more than half of the life of the *Post* under Curtis and includes several changes of editorship, a great economic depression, two wars, and the growth of radio and television. Environmental violence during the period was also analyzed by the Uniform Crime Reports.

The first issue sampled—February 14, 1925—was randomly selected, and every thirteenth issue thereafter was examined, for a total of 159 issues. All fiction stories, including novelettes, serials, and short stories, were coded for presence, kind, and frequency of violence as previously defined. Altogether, 1,032 individual stories were analyzed. Accompanying illustrations were not coded. Intercoder agreement on violence was 91 percent.

Table 13 summarizes the general findings on violence in *Post* fiction over 40 years. These data are presented graphically in Figures 6 and 7.

Three indices of violence in the *Post*—percentage of stories with violent themes, percentage of stories found to contain violence, and frequency of violent acts within violent stories—suggest that the magazine's fictional violence was highest during Hibb's tenure in the 1940s and 1950s. Neither the trends in percentage of violent stories nor the rate of violent acts per story correlates with the Uniform Crime Reports violent crimes for the period 1933-64.

Violent themes

The lowest percentages of war, mystery, crime, police, and western stories appeared near the beginning and end of the 40-year period—during Lorimer's and Stout's editorships and those of Hibbs's successors in the 1960s. Overall, the mean percentage of stories having these themes was 44.6 percent. The peak years for violent types of fiction were 1944, 1950, 1952, and 1959. In 1944, war stories contributed two-thirds of the thematically violent fiction; after World War II, war fiction dropped off sharply but did not disappear. Its place was taken by other violent types of stories.

Violent stories

Each story was coded for the presence or absence of violent incidents. The percentage of stories containing violence was 26.9 percent for the 40 years. The percentage of violent stories during each editor's tenure was: Lorimer (1925-36), 21.8 percent; Stout (1937-41), 15.9 percent; Hibbs (1942-61), 34.3 percent; and Fuoss, Sherrod, and Blair (1962-64), 20 percent.

A reflection-of-environment theory might explian why Hibbs presented the highest percentage of violent stories; eight of his 20 years were during wartime. But the two highest years, 1949 and 1958, came well after the two wars.

Violent acts

Another measure of violence in the *Post*, the frequency of violent acts in stories containing at least one such act, is a rough index of intensity.

Table 13: Violence in the *Saturday Evening Post*

Year	Violent types[a]	Violent stories[b]	Violent acts[c]
1925	30.2 percent	20.9 percent	2.44 percent
1926	28.6	19.0	1.75
1927	35.0	17.5	1.43
1928	34.2	28.9	2.09
1929	35.1	29.7	1.55
1930	27.8	16.7	1.83
1931	26.7	20.0	2.00
1932	23.1	11.5	1.33
1933	42.9	25.0	1.71
1934	45.5	22.7	2.00
1935	33.3	33.3	1.44
1936	56.0	16.0	2.00
1937	40.7	.1	1.00
1938	50.0	.1	1.00
1939	41.7	20.8	1.00
1940	42.3	19.2	2.80
1941	48.0	32.0	2.25
1942	50.0	26.9	3.57
1943	41.7	16.7	2.50
1944	66.7	33.3	2.88
1945	41.7	33.3	1.88
1946	40.0	28.0	2.57
1947	50.0	30.8	1.87
1948	45.8	41.7	2.50
1949	46.2	57.7	2.40
1950	68.0	48.0	2.58
1951	57.7	46.2	2.92
1952	68.0	36.0	2.22
1953	60.0	36.0	3.44
1954	60.0	40.0	2.40
1955	50.0	33.3	1.25
1956	47.8	39.1	2.00
1957	55.2	17.2	2.60
1958	52.6	52.6	2.10
1959	68.0	28.0	3.29
1960	45.5	22.7	2.60
1961	50.0	20.0	3.50
1962	58.3	25.0	3.33
1963	16.7	16.7	1.00
1964	28.6	14.3	1.00

[a]Percentage of stories that dealt predominantly with war, mystery, crime, police, adventure, or the American West, out of all stories.

[b]Percentage of stories containing at least one act of intentional death or injury out of all stories.

[c]Mean number of violent acts per story, in stories that contain any violence.

Here, too, violence is high in Hibbs's era, with the exception of the mid-1950s. These rates fluctuate considerably, but generally the fluctuation occurs within a higher range after 1940 than before. The increase is about one incident per story. During Hibbs's editorship, the mean rate of violent acts per violent story was 2.55; during the preceding 17 years it was 1.74.

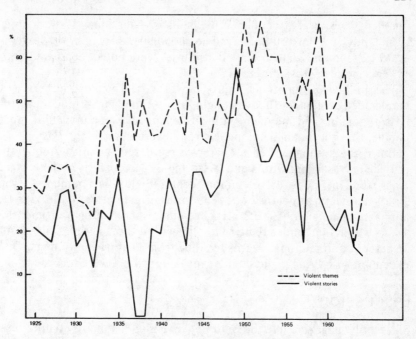

Figure 6: Percentage of violent stories and violent themes in the
Saturday Evening Post, 1925-64.

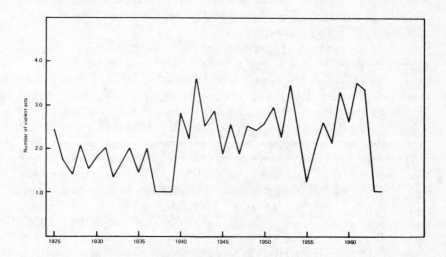

Figure 7: Mean number of violent acts within violent stories in the
Saturday Evening Post, 1925-64.

Although injurious accidents far outnumber felonious assaults in real
life, the world of fiction has a different perspective. Of the *Post* stories

sampled, 26.9 percent contained incidents of intentional death or injury and only 10.9 percent portrayed accidental death or injury. Altogether, 627 intentional violent deaths or injuries were noted, compared with 143 accidental deaths or injuries.

The method of intentional injury most favored by *Post* authors was barehanded combat—usually fist fights. The second most frequent method was torture and mayhem with miscellaneous weapons; third most popular was gunshot and knifing. No rapes were found in the *Post*.

But if the author wished a character murdered, he most frequently provided an assailant with a gun. Assorted of war comprised the second most frequent mode of intentional death. Eighty-five percent of the *Post*'s fictional war deaths occurred stories printed after World War II, although the number of war stories had diminished. During wartime, the *Post*'s war fiction tended to be romantic; later it turned grim. Only about 15 percent of intentional deaths resulted from beatings or knifings. One execution was found in the sample, and no lynchings were recorded.

Discussion

A family magazine like the *Saturday Evening Post* has by nature less violence than, say, men's magazines, but it does not eschew violence in its entertainment. The *Post*, which won a large following among middle class Americans and systematically studied their reading preferences, regularly presented aggression in its fiction. Its violence was lowest in the 1930s, increased sharply in the 1940s, and continued generally high until the magazine's terminal years.

General economic conditions are not clearly related to fictional violence. The several recession periods since 1929 found the amount of fictional violence in the *Post* varied. When Curtis first failed to show profits in the 1960s, violent fiction was not a tool of recovery; the *Post* resorted to "visual excitement" and remodeled its format; at the same time it sought quality fiction from established authors—whose characters were often embroiled in psychological rather than physical conflict.

The increase in *Post* violence in the 1940s recalls the contagion of violence theory cited in the introduction to this paper: affected by the awesome violence of war, *Post* authors and editors may have been stimulated to make their own output more violent. The trends in Post violence do not correlate with domestic crimes of violence as indexed by the Uniform Crime Reports. It might be argued that the enormity of war violence would necessarily affect media executives more profoundly than would scattered domestic violence, which rises gradually and from which executives are fairly well insulated. If war violence influences fictional violence, some delay may be involved; the two peak years in percentage of violent stories came four years after World War II and five years after the Korean War. Discussing their theory, Berkowitz and

Macaulay did suggest that some delay is possible, although it is doubtful that they anticipated a lag that could be measured in years. In the case of magazine fiction, a rather long delay in violent reaction might well occur, given the lengthy lead time required for magazine production and the fact that many authors' careers were interrupted or delayed by the war. Then too, after a period of shock and relief at war's end, the audience may have expressed renewed interest in violent fiction. Berkowitz and Macaulay noted a sudden drop in violent crime immediately after the John F. Kennedy assassination and Speck killings and then a sudden increase. It is known that *Post* researchers discerned public interest in World War II well after 1945 and that Hibbs then purchased General Eisenhower's diaries and Admiral Halsey's life story and commissioned a profile of General MacArthur.

The editors of the *Saturday Evening Post* were virtually autonomous; within the limits of their own taste, the availability of material, and their perceptions of audience interest, they could shape *Post* content largely as they wished (Peterson, 1964; Friedrich, 1970). Because Hibbs became editor at almost the same time the U.S. entered World War II, it is difficult to say whether the violence of war had an elaborate effect on his choice of fiction or whether he simply took over with a greater zest for violent stories than Lorimer and Stout.

For whatever reason, the *Post* did present a higher level of violence in the 1940's than before, and it maintained that level for much of the rest of its life. The audience was not repelled by it—and may indeed have asked for it. By the time television arrived, the *Post* and other mass magazines had helped set the midcentury agenda for family entertainment, and that agenda included a large portion of violence.[17]

VIOLENCE ON THE FRONT PAGE

Of all the media, the newspaper may be closest to the stuff of everyday existence. Indeed, the newspaper's most important justification in a democratic society, in the view of editors, critics, and readers alike, is that it reflects an accurate and timely picture of the environment. A mirror or reflection theory moved Levy (1969) to analyze 6,000 issues of the Washington *National Intelligencer* and the New York *Times* from 1819 to 1968 and to argue that the trends he found in newspaper content did fairly accurately reflect political violence in America during those years.

Newspapers do reflect such major violent events as political assassinations, and, given the nature of news values, the reflection thesis seems valid, although some studies have raised a few doubts. Deutschmann (1959) found great variations in violent content among New York City dailies that were, presumably, mirroring the same environment, and Davis (1951) found no relationship between change in the crime rate in Colorado and the amount of crime coverage in four Colorado dailies during a two-year period. Lincoln Steffens (1931) cheerfully confessed that as a reporter he once created a crime wave in New York simply by writing up a disproportionate number of ordinary crimes.

To provide the reflection theory with a longer-range test and to compare newspapers with other media, the investigators sampled the front pages of four leading dailies for the period between January 1927 and December 1968. The newspapers sampled were the Atlanta *Constitution*, Chicago *Tribune*, New York *Times*, and San Francisco *Chronicle*. These four may not be typical, but they are major successful morning dailies which had competition during the full span of the sampling period. They are geographically diverse, they are influential in their regions, and as a group they offer some variety in editorial outlook.

The sampling period contained a large enough variety of social, economic, and political events that consistent discrepancies between environmental violence and newspaper treatment of that violence became apparent. The beginning of the period corresponds roughly with the rise of radio as a competitor. While the time span is lengthy, it is not so long that what might be called the "news ethic," the definition of news applied by reporters and editors, has changed substantially.

The front page is a newspaper's showcase. Even though street sales of newspapers have dropped to a point where it is no longer necessary for headlines to scream at readers, the tradition of placing the most vital (and salable) news on the front page remains. Page One is the "prime time" of a newspaper and receives more care and planning than any other page. If a newspaper is inclined to be sensational, sensation will begin on the front page.

Ten dates were randomly selected and the newspapers of those dates for each year of the period were examined: February 14, March 3, April 2, May 9, June 3, June 15, July 5, August 11, September 3, and December 24. Nine months were netted in the sample, and over the 42 years the days of the week were fairly evenly distributed.

The coding units were front-page news or feature items at least two paragraphs long. No attempt was made to code beyond the front-page portion of a continued story, and the length in column inches was not recorded.[18] The types of violence reported were coded: death, injury, property damage, discussion of violence, and threat of violence. The latter two categories included articles that interpreted the implications of recent violence or warned of potential violence. The definition of violence used in other portions of the study was also applied here. Where more than one type of violence was reported in the item, the more severe type was coded (death over injury, injury over property). For each violence item the coders noted whether the event occurred in a war or nonwar context. They also coded the location of the item on the page (lead story, other stories above the fold, and stories below the fold), the origin of the item (local, other U.S., or foreign), and the reporting agent (wire service, syndicate, or the paper's own staff). Intercoder agreement was 94.2 percent on the violence dichotomy and 76.3 percent on the major violence categories.

A total of 19,264 items was derived for the four newspapers over the 42 years. Of these, 3,386, or 17.6 percent, were judged to contain violence. The mean number of violence items per front page was 2.3. The findings by newspaper on violence appear in Table 14.

Table 14: Summary of violence on the front pages of four newspapers, 1927-68

Year	Atlanta Mean items	Chicago Mean items	New York Mean items	San Francisco Mean items	All four Mean items	Percentage of stories containing violence
1927	2.9	2.7	2.0	2.6	2.5	21.4 percent
1928	1.9	1.5	1.3	2.5	1.8	13.8
1929	2.3	1.7	1.5	1.6	1.8	14.4
1930	2.1	2.4	1.4	1.8	1.9	14.1
1931	2.0	1.7	1.3	1.7	1.7	11.6
1932	3.6	2.3	1.9	2.7	2.6	19.9
1933	1.7	1.7	1.2	3.0	1.9	13.2
1934	3.0	1.8	1.6	2.7	2.3	16.9
1935	3.0	2.4	2.3	2.8	2.6	19.3
1936	2.9	2.2	1.5	3.5	2.5	18.2
1937	3.0	1.7	2.2	2.9	2.5	19.0
1938	1.8	1.8	1.5	2.9	2.0	15.8
1939	1.2	1.7	2.1	2.2	1.8	14.9
1940	3.3	2.9	3.6	2.5	3.1	27.6
1941	4.0	1.9	4.0	3.6	3.4	28.0
1942	4.9	3.6	4.8	3.6	4.2	37.1
1943	3.9	2.4	3.6	4.9	3.7	30.3
1944	5.1	3.8	5.1	5.6	4.9	36.8
1945	5.7	3.6	4.0	4.4	4.4	32.2
1946	1.6	2.0	1.9	1.6	1.8	10.7
1947	1.9	1.3	1.3	1.0	1.6	7.1
1948	2.6	1.8	1.1	1.4	1.7	11.1
1949	2.4	1.7	1.1	1.3	1.6	10.5
1950	1.7	1.4	1.5	1.8	1.6	13.5
1951	2.2	2.1	1.6	1.7	1.9	15.5
1952	1.7	1.3	1.1	1.7	1.5	8.4
1953	1.8	1.5	2.0	1.6	1.7	12.8
1954	1.5	2.2	1.2	2.0	1.7	12.9
1955	2.0	1.4	1.9	2.3	1.8	12.3
1956	1.9	1.8	1.8	2.2	1.9	13.9
1957	1.7	1.6	1.2	1.9	1.6	10.0
1958	2.3	1.2	1.8	2.1	1.9	13.5
1959	2.5	2.1	1.6	2.7	2.2	15.8
1960	2.0	1.8	1.8	2.2	1.9	14.4
1961	1.9	1.9	2.1	2.1	2.1	14.8
1962	1.3	1.7	2.0	1.6	1.4	12.1
1963	2.4	2.0	1.8	2.0	2.1	15.5
1964	2.6	1.7	2.3	2.1	2.2	17.1
1965	2.8	3.2	2.4	2.9	2.8	23.6
1966	2.4	2.4	2.4	2.4	2.4	19.2
1967	2.4	3.0	4.5	3.4	3.3	28.0
1968	2.4	1.6	3.3	2.2	2.4	21.8
Total	2.5	2.1	2.2	2.5	2.3	17.6 percent

The four newspapers did not differ greatly from one another in their reporting of violence. The San Francisco *Chronicle* and Atlanta *Constitution* contained the highest average number of violence items per page, the Chicago *Tribune* the lowest. However, the *Tribune* also had the fewest total items per front page, and its percentage of violence is the highest, at 21.1 percent of all items. The *Chronicle* carried 20.5 percent violent items, the *Constitution* 18 percent and the *Times* 16.7 percent.

The data reveal that except during the World War II years, violence has been a fairly stable ingredient of the front page. Only a handful of the approximately 1,600 front pages lacked at least one item containing violence. Only one non-World War II year, 1967, had an average of more than three violence items per front page (see Figure 8). The trend in percentage of violence items out of all front-page items (Figure 9) shows a similar stability.

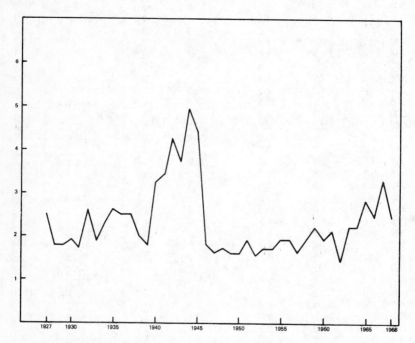

Figure 8: Mean number of violent items per front page, four newspapers, 1927-68.

There is some reciprocity between the amounts of war and nonwar violence reported on the front page. When the percentage of items devoted to war-related deaths by year is arrayed against that for nonwar deaths (see Figure 10), an inverse relationship is apparent, and the negative correlation is significant: $r = -.47$, $p < .005$. As war death items increase, nonwar violent death items decrease but do not disappear. Perhaps some civilian violent death stories are moved to the inside pages of the paper.

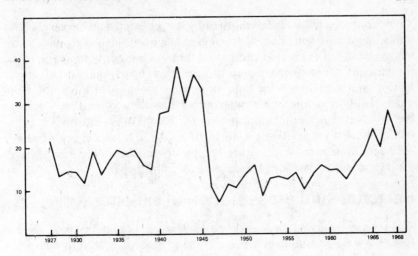

Figure 9: Percentage of violent items of all items, front pages of four newspapers,
1927-68

The great increase in the number of violence items during World War
II lends some support to the reflection thesis. A more sensitive test is a
comparison between local violence and what is reported. No statistics
are available on total violence within a community; only certain kinds of

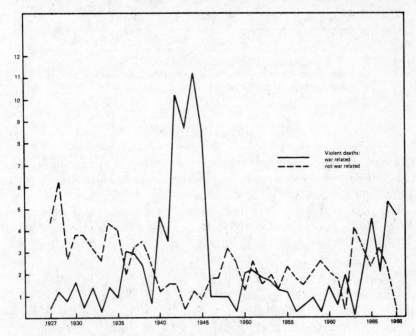

Figure 10: Percentage of war-death items and nonwar death items out of all
violent items, four front pages, 1927-68.

violence are systematically recorded by law enforcement agencies. Two kinds that are—homicide and suicide—have been fairly well documented by officials. Data were acquired on these two kinds of violence in the primary environment (county or city) of each newspaper.[19] This information was paired with the data on nonwar violent deaths on the front pages. In three of the four newspapers, significant correlations beyond the .01 level were found: Chicago, r= .40; New York, .41; and San Francisco, .40. Only the Atlanta *Constitution* (r = .16) appears not to have reflected the tendency to feature local violent deaths on its front page. The stories may have appeared elsewhere in the paper.

Selection and presentation of violence

Most violent events have some news value, but some kinds of violence have more value than others. The magnitude of war as news is indicated by the fact that 45.7 percent of all items judged violent were war-related, and most of those derived from World War II.

Table 15: Percentage of violence items by category[a]

Category	Items	Percent
Death	1182	34.9 percent
Discussions of violence	759	22.4
Threats of violence	638	18.8
Damage to property	455	13.4
Injury	335	9.9
Miscellaneous	17	.5
Total	3386	99.9 percent[b]

[a]If a story reported more than one kind of violence, it was assigned to the more severe category, in the following heirarchy: death, injury, damage, discussion.

[b]Rounding error.

Some indication of the relative importance of different kinds of violence stories is given by Table 15, which shows death stories to be most frequent. Property damage stories appeared more often than injury stories, but both of those were outnumbered by stories that discussed the implications or possibilities of violence.

The placement of violence items shows the importance of violence as news. More than twice as many violence items began on the top half of the page as on the bottom half. About 20 percent occupied the lead (upper right) position. The four newspapers did not differ greatly from one another in their placement of violence items, as Table 16 indicates.

Nor have the newspapers changed significantly over the 42 years in their placement of violence items; since 1927 the top half has been the locale of about 70 percent of front-page violence items. During World War II (1941-45), the percentage of lead-position stories reporting violence averaged 27.7 percent, the highest of any five-year period. In 1946-

Table 16: Percentage of violence stories in front-page positions, by medium

Placement	Medium				
	Atlanta *Constitution*	Chicago *Tribune*	New York *Times*	S.F. *Chronicle*	Total
Lead	17.5%	18.9%	21.5%	22.0%	20.0%
Other top half	45.5	52.2	49.5	46.0	48.2
Bottom half	37.0	28.9	29.0	32.0	31.8
Total	100.0%	100.0%	100.0%	100.0%	100.0%

50 that figure dropped back to 20.4 percent, which is close to the average for the entire 42 years.

Authorship of front-page violence stories was about equally divided between staff writers and other sources (mainly wire services) for all four newspapers combined. However, there were considerable differences in authorship among the newspapers, as shown by Table 17.

Table 17: Percentage of total violence items by source

Newspaper	Source			
	Staff	AP	UP/UPI	Other
Atlanta *Constitution*	27.6%	54.0%	11.8%	6.6%
Chicago *Tribune*	62.1	29.6	4.6	3.7
New York *Times*	75.6	17.7	6.0	0.7
San Francisco *Chronicle*	39.0	41.9	11.1	8.0

The *Times* and *Tribune* staffs produced the majority of their papers' violence items, while the smaller *Constitution* and *Chronicle* relied more on the wire services, especially for foreign news.

Discussion

This study finds support for the position that newspapers reflect the violence of the real world. The cataclysmic violence of World War II is clearly mirrored in the number of front-page violence items and percentage of violence stories in all four newspapers. In three of the four newspapers a correlation was found between local deaths and suicides and front-page violent death stories.

Typically at least one item concerning violence (but fewer than three) appears on the front page. In peacetime the number of violence stories on the front page usually averages between 12 and 20 percent of all front-page stories. It is almost as if a quota of violence exists for the front page—a quota that may derive without cynicism from the professional goal of balancing classes of stories competing for page one space. Within the quota is sufficient latitude to accommodate the value of reflectivity: bigger violence stories may drive out the lesser, as the negative correlation between war and nonwar death stories suggests.

VIOLENCE IN TELEVISION NEWS

It is easy to charge the news media with inspiring violence (Berkowitz and Macaulay, 1970). One has only to point to the widespread demonstrations that followed the invasion of Cambodia and the campus deaths in Ohio and Mississippi in May 1970. Few of the demonstrators directly witnessed the events; most learned of them through news reports, the most graphic of which appeared on television.

To defend the news media is also easy: the demonstrators were reacting to the event, not to the report, and the messenger shouldn't be blamed. Television newsmen share this attitude with their colleagues in the print media.

Still, no news medium escapes the responsibility of choosing from among a wealth of reportable events. The constraint is especially heavy on the television news director, whose air time is even more limited than the newspaperman's space. Additionally, the television newsman knows that visual reports of violence are well suited to his action-oriented medium and that his own status depends to some extent on ratings. Greenberg (1969) speculates that "violence in entertainment feeds into the news department. Television executives know what sells in entertainment programming, and the desire exists to get it into the news, to 'spice up' the news." But weighed against this temptation are journalistic standards which television newsmen profess as ardently as any newspaperman. Television news, therefore, is worth comparing for violence both with newspapers and with television entertainment. Just how much violence appears in a typical network newscast? What emphasis is it given?

In an effort to answer these questions, data were derived from 27 network evening newscasts of nine days in July 1970. Because there is no convenient long-term surrogate source for analysis of television news content—no *TV Guide* synopses, for example, the newscasts were coded directly from the air. The following findings are therefore distinctly exploratory and in no sense longitudinal.

The sampling period from July 16-31 contained a variety of news events; no single story commanded inordinate attention. The major stories included hearings held by the President's Commission on Campus Unrest, Israeli-Arab raids across the Suez, the war in Southeast Asia, a general economic malaise, and the Manson murder trial. The anchormen were Frank Reynolds and Howard K. Smith, ABC; Walter Cronkite, CBS; and Chet Huntley and David Brinkley, NBC.

The unit of analysis was the broadcast news item, and the variables of interest included the presence or absence of violent content as previously defined, the use of graphics, and the length and placement of news items.

Comparable data were gathered from the front pages of four daily newspapers (the same dailies whose front pages we analyzed) for the same dates. The findings on violence are summarized in Table 18.

Table 18: Percentage of violent items on network newscasts and front pages of four newspapers, nine days in July 1970

Day and date	Networks				Newspapers[a]				
	ABC	CBS	NBC	All 3	Atl	Chi	NYC	Sfo	All 4
Th 7-16	36.8%	41.2%	23.8%	33.3%	18.2%	0.0%	18.2%	10.0%	12.5%
M 7-20	23.1	20.0	25.0	22.9	16.7	14.3	30.0	30.0	23.1
Tu 7-21	18.8	33.3	19.0	23.1	30.0	44.4	7.7	18.2	23.3
Th 7-23	46.7	38.9	19.4	31.3	27.3	33.3	25.0	11.1	24.4
M 7-27	30.8	37.5	16.7	27.7	23.1	20.0	22.2	20.0	21.4
Tu 7-28	45.5	10.0	12.5	18.2	27.3	42.9	16.7	40.0	30.0
W 7-29	15.8	26.3	4.0	14.3	18.2	40.0	0.0	30.0	20.9
Th 7-30	43.8	28.0	16.7	28.8	25.0	10.0	16.7	9.1	14.6
F 7-31	46.2	42.1	27.8	38.0	50.0	22.2	7.7	22.2	24.4
All days	33.3%	30.5%	17.9%	26.3%	25.8%	25.3%	15.4%	21.1%	21.6%
Total N	135	164	196	495	97	79	104	90	370

[a]The Atlanta *Constitution*, Chicago *Tribune*, New York *Times*, and San Francisco *Chronicle*.

A total of 495 network news items and 370 front-page stories were examined. The typical newscast contained about 18 items; the typical front page contained about 14. The proportion of items containing descriptions of violence was 26.3 percent for television and 21.6 percent for newspapers. We noted that in the 42-year newspaper sample the mean percentage of front-page violence was 17.6 percent. In 1968, the last year of the longer study, the newspaper figure was 21.8 percent. A 1963 study of Los Angeles television news and four newspapers found that television news devoted 17.5 percent of its items to "crime, major accidents, and disasters," while the newspapers devoted 13.2 percent of their stories to those categories; "defense" news was counted elsewhere (Lyle and Wilcox, 1963). In yet another analysis, the president of ABC News reported that from September 1, 1967, to August 30, 1968, only nine percent of the items broadcast by his organization "were even remotely associated with violence."[20]

Although the network news programs contained a higher percentage of violence items than did the front pages, the difference is not statistically significant ($X^2 = 2.48$ at 1 df.). Both media fluctuated from day to day in percentage of violence, but no correlation was found over the nine days. Aside from the shortness of the time period, the lack of correlation may owe to different territoriality (for one thing, newspapers invariably contain a component of local news) or to deadlines that prevent same-day coverage of events. A future study might allow a one-day lag for morning newspapers.[21]

Among the three networks, the highest percentage of violence items was presented by ABC, which also had fewer (and longer) items. NBC had the lowest percentage, but also the greatest total number of news items. At the same time, NBC broadcast the lowest actual number of violence items, 35; ABC broadcast 45 violence items and CBS broadcast 50. The difference in proportions of violence items among the networks is significant ($X^2 = 12.17$ at 2 df., p<.005).

The New York *Times* carried the lowest percentage of front-page violence items among the four newspapers, as it had in the 42-year study. The other three papers changed ranks somewhat.

Newspapers and newscasts are somewhat distinguishable in their attention to war-related violence. Of all the violent items on the 27 newscasts, 49.2 percent related to war; among the violent stories on the front pages, 36.3 percent were war-related ($X^2 = 3.38$ at 1 df., p <.10). Television's greater proportion of news devoted to national and international affairs may account for the difference.

Accompanying illustrations

All news media have been accused of covering the sensational at the expense of the serious; one critic has asserted that "given a choice between a 30-second report about a budget item being approved and a 30-second film about a local accident, most television stations show the accident footage. . . ." (Fang, 1968). On the other hand, the president of CBS News has testified that he issued a series of memoranda to his newsmen that "emphasized time and time again. . .that very often a word is worth a thousand pictures."[22] Table 19 shed some light on whether TV news tends to go for the visual jugular.

Table 19: Percentage of items accompanied by illustrations

Items contain	Media				
	ABC	CBS	NBC	3 Nets	4 Newspapers
Violence	51.1%	42.0%	40.0%	44.6%	25.0%
No violence	51.1	35.1	34.8	38.9	19.0

In the 27 newscasts, 40.4 percent of all items were accompanied by film or videotape of the event. (Many other items were supported by maps or other graphic art, but only motion material was counted as illustration for television items.) Items about violence were more often illustrated than nonviolent items (44.6 to 38.9 percent), but the difference is not statistically significant either for the combined data or for the individual networks. Of all films or videotapes accompanying violent items, only seven (or 12.1 percent) showed the act of violence itself. Usually the aftermath or the participants were shown.

A newspaper is not a visual medium in the same sense that television is, so it is not surprising to find fewer illustrated news items on front pages. Of the newspaper stories containing violence, 25 percent were illustrated; of nonviolence stories, 19 percent were illustrated. The difference is not significant. Of the illustrations accompanying violence stories, only 15 percent showed the act of violence. Like the networks, the newspapers tended to illustrate violence items more often than other items, and the inclination was slightly stronger for newspapers than for the networks.

Display of violence

The displays of violence on television and in newspapers were compared by noting the number of violence items beginning above the fold on front pages and among the first half of broadcast items. This yielded "top and bottom" ratios for the media; the percentages appear in Table 20.

The two media are distinguishable on this variable. In the case of television, 63.1 percent of the violence items appeared among the first half of all items presented, and the disproportion is significant ($X^2 = 9.11$ at 1 df., p $<.005$). On the front pages, 54.1 percent of all stories began above. This difference is not statistically significant.

Table 20: Percentage of items appearing in the top and bottom of the daily report

Items contain	ABC		CBS		NBC		3 Nets		4 Newspapers	
	Top	Bot	Top	Bot	Top	Bot	Top	Bot	Top	Bot
Violence	39.4	26.6	35.3	25.3	24.0	11.5	32.0	20.1	23.4	19.1
No violence	60.6	73.4	64.7	74.7	76.0	88.5	68.0	79.9	76.6	80.5
	100	100	100	100	100	100	100	100	100	100

Emphasis on violence in television news was also examined in terms of length of items. Although the coders did not formally time each item, they did note whether an item ran longer or shorter than one minute. The percentage of violent items by length is indicated in Table 21.

Table 21: Percentage of items by length of item[a]

Items contain	ABC		CBS		NBC		3 Nets	
	−1	1+	−1	1+	−1	1+	−1	1+
Violence	31.1	35.1	27.1	35.3	16.9	19.4	23.5	29.9
No violence	68.9	64.9	72.9	64.7	83.1	80.6	76.5	70.1
	100	100	100	100	100	100	100	100

[a]−1 = less than one minute in length.
1+ = one minute or longer.

Of all items, 43.2 percent ran for more than one minute and 56.8 percent for less than one minute. Violent items tended to run longer than nonviolent items, but the disproportion was not significant. Among violent items, 50.8 percent ran for less than one minute and 49.2 percent for more than one minute. The respective figures for nonviolent items are 58.9 and 41.1 percent.

Discussion

Every newscast contained some violent content; in that sense news programs are considerably more violent than the general run of television entertainment, which had a 27.4 percent rate of violent programs. However, if individual broadcast news items are regarded as "programs" in their own right, then the 26.3 percent of items containing violence becomes similar to the entertainment figure.

The newscasts seem to have much in common with the front page. The term "electronic front page" seems apt (Harney and Stone, 1969). The percentage of violent items on newscasts (26.3) is not significantly different from that on front pages (21.6). Although newscasts naturally use more accompanying illustrations than do newspapers, the apportionment of illustrations between violence and nonviolence is quite similar in the two media. Television news does tend to give higher placement to violent items than do newspapers (to the extent that the two media are comparable on placement), but television news does not automatically provide greater length for violent items than for other items.

Some natural differences between the two media, especially in visual impact, may make television news seem more violent. But the measurements made here indicate great similarities between network newscasts and front pages.

SUMMARY AND CONCLUSIONS

This study of trends in violent content has revealed considerable differences among the sampled media in the degree to which violence has been employed. Television violence has fluctuated greatly over time. Newspapers rather closely reflect levels of environmental violence. A mass circulation magazine lagged behind major violent periods in its own attention to violence as content. Motion pictures have been increasing in violence over the years.

These and other findings may be subject to varying interpretations. Yet the findings present some indications of what will come, based on what has been. Media proprietors and others who establish and influence policy in these areas need to consider not only the evidence, but also what it may mean.

As measured by content analysis of program synopses, violence in television entertainment fluctuates considerably over the long term. The lowest rate of violent programs during the period 1953-69 was 16.9 percent, recorded for 1954; the highest was 41.3 percent in 1959. The percentages of violent entertainment programs do not correlate with Uniform Crime Report data on violence in the U.S., on either a direct or a delayed basis. They do correlate with other data.

Violence on television appears to run in four- or five-year cycles, and the audience ratings do correlate positively with the percentages of violent programs. As violent types of programs gain popularity, their numbers increase until they become so directly competitive that their ratings are diluted, until the audience tires, or until public and official criticism makes itself heard. Programming officials have long been concerned about the effects criticism might have on them and on their advertising clients. Network machinery has worked to moderate both the form of violence and, to a lesser degree, its extent, for short periods until other factors (chiefly competition) begin to start the new cycle. The audience appears to have a high tolerance—if not affinity—for violence. The wider fluctuations in number of violent type programs than of other kinds suggests that networks regard violence as good bait, while such programs as variety and comedy are basic content and hence less variable in number.

Motion pictures released to television, also coded from synopses, likewise fluctuate widely in violence and have displayed a general upward trend since the 1930s. This trend does correlate, probably fortuitously, with UCR crime data. After commercial television became widespread in the early 1950s, the number of violent films remained at a high level, never dropping below 30 percent. Increased violence in films may have been a response to the competition of television.

Television seems to be equal to the challenge of motion picture violence; movies made expressly for television (fairly recent phenomena) are more likely to be violent than the earlier films made for theatrical release, and made-for-TV films win generally better ratings than those originally shown in theatres.

The *Saturday Evening Post* regularly employed violence in its fiction from 1925 to 1964, reaching a peak in percentage of violent stories in 1949. A second major peak is noticeable in 1958. When the *Post* and its parent corporation fell on hard times in the 1960s, there was no apparent resort to violence in fiction. Perhaps none was needed; circulation was still strong and fiction by then had largely given way to "sophisticated muckraking" and flashy design. No correlation was found between rates of violence in the *Post* and the UCR data. Some relation between *Post* violence and the real world is suggested by a rise in violent themes and violent acts in stories in the early 1940s. However, these rates continued at a high level after the war, possibly as a result of the war's effect upon editorial and audience tastes or because Ben Hibbs, who acquired the editorship in 1942, brought with him a taste for physical conflict in fiction.

The trend in percentage of violent stories on the front pages of four leading daily newspapers, 1927-68, similarly discloses a large increase during World War II but also a reversion to a low level after the war. The mean number of violent items per page by year follows a similar course. Newspaper violence fluctuates less than does violence in the entertainment media, and the rates of civilian and war violence appear to reciprocate on the front page, suggesting that a kind of quota exists. Such a quota may not be rigorously imposed by editors (although newspapers like other media have been accused at various times of sensationalism) and may relate to a desire for "balanced" content. World War II demonstrates that the quota is flexible enough to permit reflection of increased environmental violence. For three of the four newspapers, the amount of front-page nonwar violent death items correlated with the rates of homicides and suicides for their immediate areas.

Television network newscasts were also analyzed for a brief period and were compared with front pages of four newspapers for the same days in the summer of 1970. The percentage of violence items on the newscasts was not significantly different from that on the front pages. As might be expected, television news accompanied more stories with illustrations than did newspapers. Television was more inclined to illustrate violent stories than nonviolent, but newspapers also shared this inclination. Television news tended to give higher display to its stories than newspapers did. On television, violent items were more likely to be lengthy than were nonviolent items, but the difference in proportions was not great.

Table 22: Summary of percentages of violence by medium

Medium	N Violent	Total N	Percent violent
Network television prime time entertainment, from TV Guide synopses, 1953-69	269	982	27.4%
Motion pictures, from Movies on TV synopses, 1930-69	284	807	35.2
Saturday Evening Post fiction, 1925-64	278	1032	26.9
Front-page news items, four dailies, 1927-68	3386	19264	17.6
Network television newscasts, nine days, July 1970	130	495	26.3

Table 22 summarizes the findings on percentage of violence by medium, and Figure 11 compares trends in media violence for the years surveyed. The trend lines are separated for the sake of convenience, and indices on the vertical axis are omitted.

Although present-day television entertainment, motion pictures, and front pages may seem bathed in violence, there have been periods in their recent history when media were higher in aggressive content. Because violent content fluctuates, the recession of violence exhibited in the late 1960s is probably temporary. Broadly viewed, the trend across all media has been upward

This is not to argue that the levels of violence must remain high. All the media possess machinery for controlling content and therefore can regulate violence according to editorial or artistic merit, critical consensus, or competitive need. In the entertainment media, this ability to regulate does not often appear to operate in specific relationship with real-world violence. The news media, however, can make a fair claim to reflectance. The wide fluctuations in entertainment violence and the demonstrated ability to regulate its quantity and quality argue that its use is largely a matter of choice.

If violence is elective, then the entertainment media could make a choice for less, not more. After all, media violence has had valleys as well as peaks. It is worth noting that CBS remained competitive during the 1960s while offering a comparatively low percentage of violent programs.

But the media also have the option of more violence, and this option has certain merits for the entertainment media, especially television. Violence allows conflict to be quickly established or resolved; it is visual

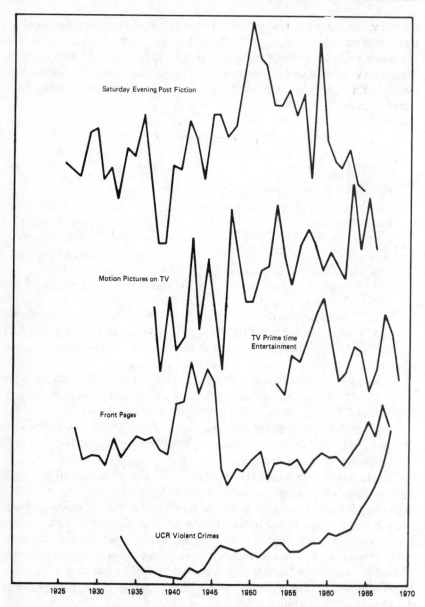

Figure 11: Violent content: a comparison of media.

and understandable; it is attractive to large segments of the audience. Other defenses of violent content include: conflict and violence have appeared in the finest literature and art throughout history; freedom of expression is infringed by proscriptions on violence; violence can demonstrate strength in heroes and punishment for villains; there is indeed violence in the real world, and to ignore it in drama is in effect to lie.

Unless equally formidable reasons for reducing violence present themselves—and taste does not appear to be sufficient—the entertainment media may be expected to continue their brisk pursuit of aggression.

FOOTNOTES

1. The investigators acknowledge the National Institute of Mental Health for its research support in the preparation of this study for the Surgeon General's Scientific Advisory Committee on Television and Social Behavior. Thanks are also due to Inspector Jerome J. Daunt of the Uniform Crime Reports division of the Federal Bureau of Investigation; Dean George Gerbner of the Annenberg School of Communications of the University of Pennsylvania; *TV Guide*; the A.C. Nielsen Company; the Audience Development department of Katz Television; the Mass Communication History Center of the State Historical Society of Wisconsin; Professor Harry P. Sharp and Mr. Charles Palit, Wisconsin Survey Research Laboratory; and the many graduate students at the University of Wisconsin who served as coders.

2. Greenberg (1969) proposes that the aggression and frustration spawned in the competitive milieu of the television industry may express itself in violent content.

3. National Broadcasting Company papers, Series E-1, Box 3, State Historical Society of Wisconsin, Madison, Wisconsin.

4. Testimony of Charles R. Denny, vice president of NBC, Harold Fellows, president of the National Association of Broadcasters, and Geraldine Zorbaugh, secretary and acting general counsel of ABC, before a subcommittee of the House Committee on Interstate and Foreign Commerce, in June, September, and December 1952. Testimony of Merle S. Jones, vice president of CBS-TV, before the Subcommittee to Investigate Juvenile Delinquency of the Senate Committee on the Judiciary, October 19, 1954. Testimony of Joseph Heffernan, president of NBC, before the Senate Subcommittee to Investigate Juvenile Delinquency, April 6 and 7, 1955. See also Greenberg, 1969.

5. The question of what constitutes prime time is somewhat vexing. The networks regard 7:30-11 p.m. Eastern time as "prime." In the Central time zone, primacy arrives an hour earlier, even if the viewers don't. Gerbner (1969) referred to his selected hours of 4-10 p.m. Eastern time as "prime time," thus excluding such 10 p.m. programs as *Mannix*. The A.C. Nielson Company, over the years, has variously referred to prime hours as simply "evening," "evening 6-11 p.m.," or as "evening 6-7:30; 7:30-11."

6. In this connection Gerbner has commented, "The solid-week sample has been demonstrated to be at least as generalizable to a year's programming as larger randomly selected samples."

7. The authors are indebted to Mrs. Carolyn Bernhardt for conducting this search.

8. The FCC complaint data were aired during the 1954 Senate hearings on juvenile delinquency. An analysis of network censor comments, 1954-56, shows that only 12.2 percent related to violence (Winick, 1968).

9. NBC Papers, Series E-1, Box 3.

10. NBC Papers, Series B-9, Box 4.

11. NBC Papers, Series B-9, Box 4.

12. Based on average expenditure per U.S. household in constant dollars. Data courtesy of Scripps-Howard Research and Dr. Maxwell McCombs of the University of North Carolina School of Journalism.

13. As with the Nielsen data, the authors take responsibility for grouping the typologies according to presumed tendencies toward violence. Neither Nielsen nor Katz goes beyond simple descriptions like "comedy," "adventure," etc.

14. The movie figure reduces to 39.6 percent if made-for-TV films are excluded (see Table 11). Made-for-TV films make a disproportionate contribution to the high violence grouping.

15. See Peterson, 1964. The president of Alfred Politz Research, Inc., a firm which conducted readership studies for the *Post* in its final years, once suggested that the magazine obtain some *Bonanza* television scripts and convert them into short stories. (See Friedrich, 1970.) Though the editors recoiled in horror, such evidence suggests that at the top levels of Curtis there was a blurring of perceived distinctions between television and mass circulation magazines. Directors of Curtis implicitly recognized the magazine's functional similarities to television when they appointed the former executive vice president of the National Broadcasting Company as president of the publishing firm during the *Post's* death throes.

16. See Friedrich (1970) for an account of the *Post's* waning days; Friedrich was the magazine's last managing editor. The story is also told, from different perspectives, by Goulden (1965), Culligan (1969), and Ackerman (1970).

17. The number of crime articles in general magazines more than doubled between 1947 and 1957, according to Ellison and Gosser (1959).

18. Item-counting correlates well with the more laborious measuring of column inches. See Budd, Thorp, and Donohue (1967).

19. The authors are grateful to Albert Hester for his valuable contribution to this task specifically and to this section of the paper generally.

20. Testimony of Elmer Lower, president of ABC News, before the National Commission on the Causes and Prevention of Violence, December 20, 1968. Available in Briand (1969).
21. Another consideration for future research is the possible cycling of violence news within the week. Preliminary examination of the present limited data suggests that both media tend to be lower in violence content in the middle of the week than at either end.
22. Testimony of Richard Salant, president of CBS News, before the National Commission on the Causes and Prevention of Violence, December 20, 1968. Available in Briand (1969).

REFERENCES

Ackerman, M. *The Curtis affair.* Los Angeles: Nash Publishing Co., 1970.

Baker, R., and Ball, S. (Eds.) *Mass media and violence:* a report to the National Commission on the Causes and Prevention of Violence. Washington, D.C.: U.S. Government Printing Office, 1969.

Barnouw, E. *The image empire.* New York: Oxford Press, 1970.

Berkowitz, L., and Macaulay, J. The contagion of criminal violence. Department of Psychology, University of Wisconsin, 1970 (mimeo).

Briand, P.L. (Ed.) *Mass media hearings,* a report to the National Commission on the Causes and Prevention of Violence. Washington, D.C.: U. S. Government Printing Office, 1969.

Budd, R.W., Thorp, R.K., and Donohue, L. *Content analysis of communication.* New York: Macmillan, 1967.

Culligan, M. *The Curtis-Culligan story.* New York: Crown, 1969.

Davis, F.J. Crime news in Colorado newspapers. *American Journal of Sociology,* 1951, **57,** 325-30.

Deutschmann, P.J. *News-page content of twelve metropolitan dailies.* Cincinnati: Scripps-Howard Research, 1959.

Gerbner, G. The television world of violence. In Baker, R., and Ball, S. (Eds.), *Mass media and violence.* Washington, D.C.: U.S. Government Printing Office, 1969.

Eleey, M.F. Variations in generalizability resulting from sampling characteristics of content analysis data: a case study. The Annenberg School of Communications, University of Pennsylvania, 1969.

Ellison, J., and Gosser, F.T. Nonfiction magazine articles: a content analysis study. *Journalism Quarterly,* 1959, **36,** 27-34.

Emery, E. *The press and America.* (2nd ed.) Englewood Cliffs, N.J.: Prentice-Hall, 1962.

Fang, I. *Television news.* New York: Hastings House, 1968.

Finnegan, J. When nonviolence hurts. *TV Guide,* 1970, **18,** No. 25, 8.

Friedrich, O. *Decline and fall.* New York: Harper & Row, 1970.

Goulden, J.C. *The Curtis caper.* New York: Putnam, 1965.

Graham, F.P. A contemporary history of American crime. In Graham, H.D., and Gurr, T.R. (Eds.), *The history of violence in America.* New York: Bantam Books, 1969.

Greenberg, B. The content and context of violence in the mass media. In Baker, R., and Ball, S. (Eds.), *Mass media and violence.* Washington, D.C.: U.S. Government Printing Office, 1969.

Harney, R.F., and Stone, V.A. Television and newspaper front page coverage of a major news story. *Journal of Broadcasting*, 1969, **13**, 185.

Katz Television. *Track record of feature films on networks.* (4th ed.) New York: Author, 1970.

Levy, S. G. A 150-year study of political violence in the United States. In Graham, H.D., and Gurr, T.R. (Eds.), *The history of violence in America.* New York: Bantam Books, 1969.

Ludeke, H.C. The role of research in the editorial reconversion problems of a magazine. *Journalism Quarterly*, 1948, **25**, 213-17.

Lyle, J., and Wilcox, W. Television news—an interim report. *Journal of Broadcasting*, 1963, **7**, 157-66.

Menninger, W.W. The roots of violence—some implications for the mass media. Paper presented at the convention of the Association for Education in Journalism, Lawrence, Kansas, August 1968.

Mott, F.L. *A history of American magazines.* Vol. 4. Cambridge, Mass.: Harvard University Press, 1957.

National Advisory Commission on Civil Disorders. *Report.* New York: Bantam Books, 1968.

Otto, H.A. Sex and violence on the American newsstand. *Journalism Quarterly*, 1962, **40**, 19-26.

Peterson, T. *Magazines in the twentieth century.* (2nd ed.) Urbana, Ill.: University of Illinois Press, 1964.

President's Commission on Law Enforcement and Administration of Justice. *The challenge of crime in a free society.* New York: Avon Books, 1968.

Scheuer, Steven H. (Ed.) *Movies on TV.* New York: Bantam Books, 1969.

Schramm, W., Lyle, J., and Parker, E. *Television in the lives of our children.* Stanford, Calif.: Stanford University Press, 1961.

Scott, W.A. Reliability of content analysis: the case of nominal scale coding. *Public Opinion Quarterly*, 1955, **17**, 321-25.

Sopkin, C. *Seven glorious days, seven fun-filled nights.* New York: Ace Publishing Corp., 1968.

Steffens, L. *The Autobiography of Lincoln Steffens.* New York: Harcourt, Brace & World, 1931, 1958.

Subcommittee of the Committee on Interstate and Foreign Commerce, House of Representatives, U.S. Congress. *Hearings, investigation of radio and television programs.* 82nd Congress, Second Session.

Washington, D.C.: U.S. Government Printing Office, 1952.
Winick, C. Censor and sensibility: a content analysis of the television censor's comments. In Larsen, O. (Ed.), *Violence and the mass media*. New York: Harper & Row, 1968.

Perceptions of Violence in Television Programs: Critics and the Public

Bradley S. Greenberg and Thomas F. Gordon
Michigan State University

The mass media critic has multiple roles and many interests—some vested, others less so. He reports to his readers on current trends in the industry; he evaluates new program offerings; he speculates about the impact of media presentations; often he pontificates on what should be, in contrast with what is. The critic's target may be his readers, the industry, or perhaps his fellow critics. In the United States, media like movies and television have regular critics; others, like newspapers, radio, and magazines, have irregular critics or none at all.

The link the critic serves between the public and the communication industry may be crucial. In theater, for example, there has long been speculation about the presumed power of the New York critics in determining the financial success or death of stage plays. Some empirical support exists for this proposition (Leitner, Moss, and Tannenbaum, 1963). With regard to television, however, no such proposition exists. No single geographical viewing area can guarantee a program's success. One can only speculate about what influence, if any, the television critic has on either the television industry or its viewers. Newspaper reader studies show that television columns are among the most widely read features. *TV Guide* is this country's largest paid circulation magazine, although its critical commentary is sparse.

The present study focuses on perceptions of television programs by professional critics and viewers. The question it posed is the extent to which the critic "sees" or characterizes programs in a way similar to that of his viewers. More particularly: how much violence does the television critic perceive in television programming, in comparison to the amount perceived by viewers?

Violence in the media is an issue of far-reaching social interest. Scientific studies, philosophical essays, presidential, commissions, federal agencies, and congressional inquiries have examined (and are currently scrutinizing) the question of the impact of television violence on the viewer.[1] There has been particular concern for the young viewer (Baker and Ball, 1969).

Mass communication literature abounds in content analyses which document the frequency of violent acts and episodes on television (Greenberg, 1969). In all these studies, the investigators define what is labeled as violent. An alternative approach is using the television critic fraternity and the American viewing public as self-definers of violence. To what extent is a given program called violent by the critics and, separately, by the viewers? This approach is demonstrated in the present study.

What does one expect, in terms of comparability of judgment, from these two groups—the professional viewers and the fans? The typical critic espouses a strong sense of social responsibility, writes that the airwaves belong to the people, and is concerned about programming in the public interest. We anticipated that the critics would be more intense about and sensitive toward the level of violence in television programs than would the public. An initial hypothesis was: *Critics will rate programs as more violent than will viewers.*

The full range of prime time programming encompasses 60-70 television programs available weekly between 7:30 and 11 p.m. However, many programs are virtually void of violence by most definitions. The subset of programs to which critics or viewers may attribute some moderate or strong degree of violence should be considerably smaller. According to our reasoning, there should be high agreement about which shows are more or less violent. A second hypothesis was: *Ordering of programs from most to least violent will be highly correlated for the critics and the public.*

In addition to critic-public comparisons, we anticipated certain subgroups differences within the public in terms of perceived violence and actual viewing behavior. These subgroup differences would be based on the sex and age of the viewer. Men and women in this society typically are differentially socialized toward violence as a mode of behavior or as a mode of acceptable behavior. Little girls generally are taught to coax and persuade, not to hit or aggress, not to be tough; boys are taught about self-defense, about not being sissies, about standing up to attackers. With this rationale, the third hypothesis was: *Women will judge programs as more violent than will men.* Given the greater affinity toward violence which presumably comes in the male's development toward manhood, a related hypothesis was: *Men will more regularly watch more of the violent programs than will women.*

Counterpart hypotheses were tested with respect to different age groups of viewers. Young viewers raised on a greater diet of television violence, it was reasoned, would be more likely to condone violence as an acceptable mode of behavior. Thus they would rate any given act or episode of violence less severely. We tested this inference: *Older viewers will judge programs as more violent than will younger viewers.* (A contradictory rationale, of course, would suggest that older adults, more experienced with both mediated and "real-life" violence, would be less severe in their judgment of televised violence.) In parallel fashion, the younger viewers, more accustomed to televised violence and perhaps more entertained by it, might be expected to watch more of it: *Younger viewers will more regularly watch more of the violent programs than will older viewers.*

The hypothesized sex and age subgroup differences imply a negative relationship between regular watching of certain television programs and the amount of violence perceived in those programs. We reasoned that the more often an individual watched a given show, the less likely he would be to perceive or admit that it was a program of considerable violence. Three plausible bases exist for this premise. For one, the general norm of our society today is opposed to aggressive violence where the intention is to deliberately harm others. Hence, adults who admittedly engage in heavy viewing of what others characterize as violent content may justify their television behavior by labeling the content as less violent or nonviolent. These viewers would "see" less violence. A second rationale originates with the nonviewers. To the extent that they are antagonistic toward programming which they believe features violence, they may avoid watching such shows. In this manner, they may then be prone to judge what they do not watch as more violent. A third premise reverts to the most frequent viewer of violence. Perhaps he has been so jaded by the acts he has seen that he is less inclined to judge repetitive "normal" acts of mayhem as very violent.

This study did not permit the direct testing of these different—if not contradictory—theoretical suppositions. On all counts, however, the regular viewer of violence was expected to differ from the irregular viewer in how much violence he "sees." This hypothesis was tested: *Perceived amount of violence in programs is negatively correlated with the regularity of viewing of those programs.*

This speculation led us to include one additional variable—a definition of violent content. If asked to define what is meant by violence, some people will talk of shootings, others of yelling, still others of debasing cultural values or aesthetic standards. Hence, asking viewers (or the critics) to judge how much violence is in a given show is inviting a myriad of personal definitions and frames of reference. On the other hand, imposing a single definition created by an academician or critic or producer may be even more arbitrary. We presented half the public viewers with a single definition of violence and gave none to the other portion. The definition used was: "By violence, I mean how much fighting, shooting, yelling, or killing there usually is in the show."

This definition seemed to encompass the majority of definitions that had been used by content analysts in prior studies of media violence. Given this response set for the meaning of violence, it was hypothesized: *Viewers receiving this definition of violence will perceive more violence in television programs than viewers not receiving this definition.*

METHODOLOGY

A sample of viewers and a population of critics were interviewed, the first by telephone and the second by mail. Comparable information was gathered from each group about how much violence they thought was present in major network television programs. Viewing data were also obtained from the public sample.

Public survey. 500 telephone numbers were drawn randomly from the 1969 Detroit area telephone book. Eight trained interviewers made long distance calls to the designated numbers during March 23-27. They attempted to interview a man at the first number called, a woman at the second, and so on; the final sample consisted of 41 percent men and 59 percent women.

Of the 500 original telephone numbers, 48 were disconnected and 20 reached respondents who could not speak English, were virtually deaf, were partially blind, and so on. Of the remaining 432 usable telephone numbers, 303 interviews were completed (a 70 percent completion rate). There were 102 refusals and 27 numbers which did not answer after a minimum of three callbacks.

Critics survey. Questionnaires were mailed (air mail special delivery) on March 27, 1970, to 90 newspaper or magazine television critics. The critics were asked to rate the programs on the scales provided and to return the forms in the air mail special delivery envelopes enclosed.

Of 90 forms sent out, 53 replies were received, 43 of which contained completed questionnaires. There were four written refusals and six incomplete forms.

Public survey. Interviewers used two 33-program listings. Programs had been randomly assigned to the two listings, and interviewers systematically varied the starting point within the list for each interview. To every other subject, the interviewer gave this definition of violence: "By violence, I mean how much fighting, shooting, yelling, or killing there usually is in the show." Each respondent rated 33 of the 66 television programs offered in Detroit by the three commercial networks from 7-11 p.m. The programs were on stations WJBK-TV (Ch. 2, CBS), WWJ-TV (Ch. 4, NBC), and WKYZ-TV (Ch. 7, ABC). One show (*Passage to Adventure*), which was a local rather than a network offering, was deleted from our analysis. Some network shows offered elsewhere in the country (for example, *Adam-12* and *Medical Center*), were not carried by the Detroit network affiliate.

To reduce the interview length, three programs were excluded on the basis of low violence ratings in a similar study conducted in the Detroit area: *Ed Sullivan, Kraft Music Hall,* and *Lawrence Welk* (Gordon, 1969). *Anniversary Game, Newlywed Game, Truth or Consequences,* and *Let's Make a Deal* were excluded because they were game shows.

A five-point scale was used to rate the amount of violence in each show, according to whether it contained "a lot" of violence, "quite a bit," "some," "not much," or "none at all." Each respondent was asked if "there is or is not violence on . . ." the show. If he stated that there was violence, he was asked, "Would you say there is a lot, quite a bit, or some?" If he said there was no violence, he was asked, "None at all, or not much?" After rating each program on the violence scale, the respondent was asked whether he watched each show "almost all the time, now and then, or not at all."

Of 123 men, 61 received one program listing and 62 the other; 56 were given a definition of violence, and 67 were not. Of 180 women, 88 received one program listing and 92 the other; 87 were given a definition of violence, and 93 were not.

Critics survey. The critics rated each of the 66 programs on the same violence scale used by the public. Amount of viewing was not asked. Each critic was asked to rate the programs according to the definition of violence given to the public sample. They were also given an opportunity to present their own definitions of violence and to rerate the programs using that definition if they wished. Nine gave self-definitions of violence.

RESULTS

Two general analyses were made. The first compared the program judgments of the critics with those of the public sample. The second focused on subanalyses of the public sample, looking at both program ratings and program viewing behaviors. This second analysis made possible comparisons among age groupings, between men and women, and between watchers and nonwatchers.

The critics and the public

Perceived violence in 65 network programs was obtained for both the critics and the public sample. Means were computed for each program. (The entire set of means is in Appendix A.) The mean scores were converted to ranks—with a rank of 1 representing the show of maximum violence and 65 representing the show of minimal perceived violence. The sets of ratings for these two groups were correlated .86 (p <.001). There was virtual unanimity between the critics and the public about where the violence was to be found.

Table 1 presents these data for the 20 most violent programs. The top shows named by 20 critics were identical with the 20 named by the viewers. The five most violent shows (in order) for the public were *Mod*

Table 1: 20 most violent programs*

Public		Program	Critics	
Mean	Rank		Rank	Mean
3.56	1	Mod Squad	4	3.65
3.37	2	Mannix	1	3.91
3.35	3	Mission: Impossible	5	3.55
3.24	4	Hawaii Five-0	2	3.81
3.23	5	It Takes a Thief	9	3.39
3.19	6	The F.B.I.	3	3.79
3.16	7	Gunsmoke	6	3.49
2.98	8.5	High Chaparral	8	3.46
2.98	8.5	Dragnet	19	2.78
2.95	10	Ironside	14	3.00
2.90	11	Bonanza	12	3.11
2.88	12	The Virginian	11	3.19
2.77	13	The Name of the Game	13	3.05
2.69	14	Land of the Giants	7	3.47
2.67	15.5	Lancer	10	3.32
2.67	15.5	Death Valley Days	15	2.97
2.58	17	The Bold Ones	17	2.96
2.51	18	Then Came Bronson	20	2.65
2.43	19	Daniel Boone	18	2.91
2.38	20	Paris 7000	16	2.96

* Mean program differences within the public or within the critic samples which exceed .5 may be interpreted as statistically significant beyond the .05 level. Differences between the two groups which exceed .4 also warrant that interpretation. The number of respondents per show is in Appendix A.

Squad, Mannix, Mission Impossible, Hawaii Five-O, and *It Takes a Thief.* For the critics, the five most violent (in order) were *Mannix, Hawaii Five-O, The FBI, Mod Squad,* and *Mission: Impossible.*

For this set of 20 shows, the critics' ratings of perceived violence were higher for 19 of the 20 shows (p <.001 by sign-test). Beyond the top 20, there was no consistent difference in the pattern of perceived violence.

For each of 16 shows, the critics perceived significantly more violence than did the public sample: *Mannix, The FBI, Lancer, Hawaii Five-O, Hee-Haw, Carol Burnett, High Chaparral, Land of the Giants, Paris 7000, Daniel Boone, Here Come the Brides, World of Disney, Laugh-In, I Dream of Jeannie, Red Skelton,* and *Lassie.*[2]

Violence and viewing in the public

The analyses focused on subgroup differences within the public sample in terms of perceived violence, amount of actual viewing, and the relationship between the two. The main data were individual program ratings and indices constructed from individual program judgments.

Violence ratings. Two forms of the questionnaire were used. Each contained half the master list of network programs.[3] Within these forms, a random group of 143 respondents was given this definition of violence from the interviewer: "By violence, I mean how much fighting, shooting, yelling, or killing there usually is in the show." The remaining 160 respondents were given no definition of violence.

Respondents receiving this definition rated 42 of 65 programs more severely than those who did not (p <.05). Seventeen of the 20 most violent programs did not vary. For 33 programs, the correlation between program ratings with and without definition was .90; for the other 32 it was .91. Thus, presenting a definition of violence served to cue more perceived violence within this sample of citizens.

There was no overall tendency, across the 65 programs, for men and women to differ in the amount of violence they perceived. However, of the 25 programs judged as most violent by both sexes (the same 25 for men and women), women viewers perceived more violence in 23 (p <.01). Where more violence in general was judged to exist, the women were likely to label these offerings as even more violent.

This tendency is further demonstrated by a violence index we constructed as a summary measure. For the six shows judged most violent by the entire sample, we summed the violence ratings as a single index, labeled the Perceived Violence Index (PVI).[4] For the men in this study, the mean PVI was 2.92; for the women, it was 3.19. This difference, tested by t-test, was statistically significant beyond the .01 level.

Not only did men's and women's choices of the 25 most violent programs correspond; their ordering of the shows by amount of violence was also similar. The correlation between men and women for rated violence in the 65 programs was .88 (p < .001). We found striking agreement about what is violent, but differences in judgments of the quantity of violence.

To examine age differences, we used five age categories: under 30; 30-40; 41-49; 50-59; and 60 and over. These categories were determined empirically by segmenting the overall distribution into five equivalent age groups.) The younger viewers were most likely to judge the 20 most violent programs as more violent; the older viewers were most likely to judge these programs as least violent. The relationship was linear and significant, as tested by a Friedman two-way analysis of variance ($x^2 = 35.8$. df, = 4, p < .001). Appendix B contains the categorical means for these 20 programs.

Table 2 provides further confirmation. It presents the mean PVI indices for each age category, indicating a difference among age groupings that is significant beyond the .0005 level. This relationship between age and perceived violence is counter to what we hypothesized.

To measure the similarity of program ordering, we computed a correlation among the top 20 programs, using the coefficient of concordance as a measure of association. This correlation was .73; again, we found high agreement in terms of ordering the violence in programs, and a reliable difference in amount of perceived violence.

Table 2: Perceived violence index by age

	Under 30	30-40	41-49	50-59	60+
Mean PVI	3.32	3.32	3.08	2.73	2.83
Source of variance	Mean Square		F		
Between categories	430.5	4	6.16	< .0005	
Within categories	69.9	293			

Viewing patterns. Viewing *per se* is of little concern in this study. More precise estimates of program viewing may be obtained from commercially available audience data. But since the interest of the present study is in the relationship between viewing and perceived violence, some viewing findings seem appropriate. Viewing data were derived for each program by asking each respondent whether he watched a particular program "almost all the time," "now and then," or "not at all."

Table 3 presents the 20 most violent programs, together with their rank in viewing for this sample. The violent programs ranged from the second most popular show (*Bonanza*) to the least watched show (*Paris 7000*). Overall, the most violent programs were no more or less watched than the less violent shows. (The average viewing level for the 20 programs was a rank of 33.3; the average viewing level for all 65 programs was 32.5.)

Men were more likely than women to watch 31 of the 65 programs; women were more likely to watch the other 34. However, men claim they are more often in the audience for 16 of the 20 programs of maximum judged violence and for 18 of the top 25 violent shows. Both trends are significant (p < .05).

Table 3: 20 most violent programs
by viewing level

Violence rank	Program	Watching rank
1	Mod Squad	27
2	Mannix	25
3	Mission: Impossible	9
4	Hawaii Five-0	42
5	It Takes a Thief	21
6	The F.B.I.	12.5
7	Gunsmoke	17.5
8.5	High Chaparral	43.5
8.5	Dragnet	32
10	Ironside	14
11	Bonanza	2
12	The Virginian	27
13	The Name of the Game	41
14	Land of the Giants	54.5
15.5	Lancer	57.5
15.5	Death Valley Days	36
17	The Bold Ones	53
18	Then Came Bronson	48
19	Daniel Boone	39
20	Paris 7000	65

Viewing of shows for the various age groups in the sample did not differ consistently across all shows. There also were no reliable differences in viewing of the 20 most violent programs between younger and older respondents.

The relationship between perceived violence and viewing behavior. We hypothesized a negative association between the amount of violence one attributes to a given television program and the frequency with which one watches such programs. For example, we postulated that a frequent watcher of a violent show like *Mannix* would describe that program as less violent than would a less frequent viewer.

Several segments of our data bear on this proposition. First, for each of the 65 programs we correlated the judged violence of the program with the viewing data of each respondent. Of these correlations, 53 of 65 were negative. This tendency is overwhelmingly in the predicted direction (p < .001), although few correlations for individual programs were sizable.

Second, we ranked the mean viewing scores for the programs and computed the rank-order correlation between viewing and ranked average violence score. This correlation was negative but trivial.

Finally, for each program we divided the sample into "watchers" (defined as those who watched almost all the time or now and then) and "nonwatchers." For each program, we compared the mean judged violence for the watchers and nonwatchers. The nonwatchers rated 43 of 65 programs as more violent (p < .05). For the 20 most violent programs, watchers and nonwatchers split evenly, each judging ten of the shows to be more violent.

Therefore, we found inconclusive support for the predicted relationship. By some tests, regular viewers of violence were less likely to see as much violence in those shows as irregular viewers; with other measures, no relationship was obtained. In no case was there any empirical suggestion that watching violent programs was accompanied by more frequent assessments of violence in these shows.

SUMMARY AND DISCUSSION

In terms of the original hypotheses, the data support these conclusions:

1. Among the 20 shows judged most violent by the public sample, the television critics considered 19 even more violent. For the remainder of the network programming, the critics did not differ from the public in their violence estimates.

2. There was unanimity between the critics and the public about which 20 shows were the most violent. The correspondence in program rankings between the two groups correlated .86.

3. Giving a definition of television violence led to consistently larger estimates of program violence by the viewers.

4. Women viewers perceived more violence than did their male counterparts in the most violent television programs; the men saw more violence in the less violent shows. Men also were more likely to be regular viewers of the more violent programs.

5. There was partial support for the hypothesis that the amount of violence perceived in television programs was negatively correlated with regularity of watching those programs; the more frequent viewers judged the programs as less violent, and vice versa.

The proposed hypothesis with respect to age differences in perceived violence received countersupport. Rather than finding that the older viewers perceived more violence in television programming, we found that the younger age groups consistently and significantly rated the program offerings as more violent. The locus of the differences was in the under-40 and over-50 groups. There were no age differences with respect to viewing patterns.

Speculation about reasons for the age differences in violence perception is based on two sets of premises. As a caveat in the original hypothesis, we suggested that the older adults might be somewhat jaded in their assessment of television violence compared with the "real-life" violence they had experienced. Thus, their discount of the magnitude of the television violence would be greater. An alternate interpretation could begin with younger viewers. Among the youngest we find the contemporary peace movement a central interest; one decade beyond are young men and women with growing families to protect. It is possible that people in these age groups show a greater sensitivity to the potential personal consequences of victory and make more acute assessments of television violence. Such speculations await subsequent verification.

Perhaps a more critical question is raised by the distinctive differences in perceived violence between those who do and do not regularly watch televised violence. If, indeed, the perception of televised violence is largely the fantasy behavior of those who do not watch programs which they believe contain violence, then the level of general public concern may be too high. If, on the other hand, the regular watchers of such programming have been inoculated against "seeing" violence or against admitting its existence, then the level of concern may not be high enough. The origin of this difference demands to be ferreted out both theoretically and practically.

Subsequent research on this issue might well deal with some experimental paradigms. Given controlled exposure to violence maintained at a relatively constant level from program to program, does a viewer make more neutral assessments over time? Given controlled exposure to violence, which is increased according to some empirical criteria from program to program, does the new level of violence receive higher violence judgments? Or is the incremental violence necessary in order to maintain the prior judged magnitude of violence?

One may, as well, wish to examine other background factors which predispose an individual to perceive violent content. For example, it would be possible to posit social class and/or race as critical factors in the propensity to "see" violence. Citizens whose environs contain more frequent exposures to "real-life" violence may deem television violence less violent.

This study begs the question of what it is in the programs that is being perceived as violent. To what extent are the women reacting to the same scenes or acts of violence as the men? The differences in the amount of violence being seen may be attributable to more severe judgments of the same acts, or to one group's labeling as violent acts which are ignored by other subsets of viewers. Some may be reacting to implicit violence, others only to explicit vignettes; some may be reacting more to verbal clashes, others primarily to physical acts of aggression. The content cues used by the viewers have not been studied elsewhere, nor has the present research served to clarify such issues.

Finally, the initial query dealing with the potential influence of the critics' views on the public remains unanswered. Do viewers follow critics' reports on new and old programs; are such programs watched or not watched on the basis of such professional judgments? The best guess may be that, as is the case with other media selections, the viewers' prior dispositions toward different programming predict current habits. Yet some violent shows succeed and others fail—often in spite of the critics' beliefs. Indeed, the critics perceive more violence in television than the viewers do. The relationship between such perceptions and the program content or the public preference is indeterminate.

FOOTNOTES

1. The research upon which this publication was based was performed pursuant to Contract No. HSM 42-70-32 with the National Institute of Mental Health, Health Services and Mental Health Administration, U.S. Department of Health, Education, and Welfare.
2. For each of three shows—*To Rome with Love, Room 222,* and *My World and Welcome to It*—the public's violence ratings were significantly higher than the critics'. For this number of programs, the difference could be attributable to chance.
3. Overall violence ratings for the two forms did not differ; therefore, subsequent analyses ignored the split-half program listings.
4. The six programs were different for the two halves of the sample which received different program listings. For each viewer, the scores for the top six programs were summed, then divided by the number of programs of the six for which ratings were given.

REFERENCES

Ball, Sandra J., and Baker, Robert K. (Eds.) *Mass media and violence: a staff report to the National Commission on the Causes and Prevention of Violence.* Washington, D.C.: U.S. Government Printing Office, 1969.

Gordon, Thomas F. An exploration into television violence. *Educational Broadcasting Review*, 1969, **3**, 44-48.

Greenberg, Bradley S. The content and context of violence in the mass media. In Baker and Ball (Eds.) *Mass media and violence.*

Leitner, M.A., Moss, S., and Tannenbaum, P.H. Who makes the play run? *Journalism Quarterly*, 1963, **40**, 375-77.

Appendix A: Critic and public program ratings

	Public (N=303)	Program	Critics (n=37-43)
n	Mean		Mean
108	3.56	Mod Squad	3.65
112	3.37	Mannix	3.91
124	3.35	Mission: Impossible	3.55
101	3.24	Hawaii Five-O	3.81
111	3.23	It Takes a Thief	3.39
124	3.19	The F.B.I.	3.79
128	3.16	Gunsmoke	3.49
102	2.98	High Chaparral	3.46
120	2.98	Dragnet	2.78
117	2.95	Ironside	3.00
133	2.90	Bonanza	3.11
117	2.88	The Virginian	3.19
89	2.77	The Name of the Game	3.05
79	2.69	Land of the Giants	3.47
67	2.67	Lancer	3.32
107	2.67	Death Valley Days	2.97
69	2.58	The Bold Ones	2.93
85	2.51	Then Came Bronson	2.65
109	2.43	Daniel Boone	2.91
79	2.38	Paris 7000	2.96
95	2.27	Get Smart	2.24
61	2.10	Bracken's World	2.17
75	1.87	Room 222	1.49
97	1.85	Here Come the Brides	2.32
124	1.81	Hogan's Heroes	2.07
105	1.61	Marcus Welby, M.D.	1.91
130	1.56	World of Disney	2.04
74	1.40	Love, American Style	1.39
67	1.36	My World and Welcome To It	1.09
63	1.35	To Rome With Love	1.07
129	1.34	Lassie	1.88
116	1.33	Laugh-In	1.79
103	1.33	Bill Cosby	1.12
118	1.30	Dean Martin	1.28
86	1.28	The Ghost and Mrs. Muir	1.20
109	1.27	Mayberry R.F.D.	1.08
65	1.26	Tim Conway	1.24

83	1.24	The Governor and J.J.	1.11
123	1.24	Red Skelton	1.51
129	1.23	Beverly Hillbillies	1.25
130	1.22	Jackie Gleason	1.38
73	1.22	Pat Paulsen	1.26
65	1.20	Nanny and the Professor	1.12
115	1.18	Here's Lucy	1.30
112	1.18	The Flying Nun	1.17
85	1.18	Debbie Reynolds	1.39
118	1.18	Julia	1.14
127	1.17	Bewitched	1.15
107	1.17	Tom Jones	1.07
114	1.17	Doris Day	1.11
88	1.17	Brady Bunch	1.14
104	1.16	I Dream of Jeannie	1.46
120	1.15	That Girl	1.14
118	1.14	Green Acres	1.14
87	1.14	Englebert Humperdinck	1.02
127	1.13	Petticoat Junction	1.16
122	1.12	Johnny Cash	1.07
116	1.11	Jim Nabors	1.13
112	1.10	Glen Campbell	1.05
		The Courtship of Eddie's	
78	1.09	Father	1.02
120	1.09	Carol Burnett	1.29
137	1.07	My Three Sons	1.02
126	1.07	Andy Williams	1.19
92	1.07	Hee Haw	1.31
129	1.06	Family Affair	1.02

Appendix B: Violence rating by age for 20 most violent programs

	Age categories				
	<30	30-40	41-49	50-59	60+
Mod Squad	3.633	3.455	3.687	3.600	3.000
Mannix	3.406	3.520	3.375	3.167	3.263
Mission: Impossible	3.355	3.483	3.324	3.200	3.333
Hawaii Five-O	3.200	2.375	3.267	3.222	3.053
It Takes A Thief	3.531	3.308	3.103	3.071	2.700
The FBI	3.240	3.500	3.050	2.833	3.240
Gunsmoke	3.517	3.167	3.238	2.840	3.034
High Chaparral	3.000	3.391	3.083	2.214	2.900
Dragnet	3.115	4.583	3.200	2.214	2.900
Ironside	3.222	3.045	2.937	2.500	2.571
Bonanza	3.138	3.000	2.912	2.565	2.862
The Virginian	3.192	2.941	2.737	2.700	2.571
Name of the Game	3.278	3.000	2.500	2.720	2.800
Land of the Giants	2.769	2.789	3.100	2.417	2.530
Lancer	2.875	2.000	2.667	2.667	2.083
Death Valley Days	2.750	2.682	2.667	2.500	2.895
The Bold Ones	2.667	2.615	2.636	2.650	2.630
Then Came Bronson	2.529	2.476	2.526	2.300	2.571
Daniel Boone	2.520	2.421	2.733	2.769	2.200
Paris 7000	2.687	2.750	2.000	2.000	1.500

The Role of the Producer in Choosing Children's Television Content

Muriel G. Cantor

American University

The principal concern of mass media research during the past several decades has been the effect of media content on the audience. Those who create for television—and particularly those who create through the film medium—have been neglected by the social scientist. Only recently has interest increased in those who "manufacture" television news and entertainment. In process or recently completed are studies of U.S. television script writers (Moore, in progress), television newscasters (Gans, 1966, 1966c, 1970), television series producers (Cantor, 1969), and television communicators in Great Britain (Hulmos, 1969).

Although these studies vary in their foci and their methods of gathering data, each emphasizes the relationship of an occupational milieu and a professional group to the content produced. Gans (1970) found that newsmen determine what is broadcast as news principally from media considerations, professional judgments, personal and professional values, and audience reactions. Blumler (1969), in a study of television producers in Britain, found their output determined by competing pressures from several sources: organization rules and policies, perceptions of the audience, and the producers' own attitudes. I found that producers making dramatic television series are influenced by their own personal values and by their orientations to their audience, the network, and their colleagues (Cantor, 1969).

A few studies have dealt with creative persons and technicians employed by commercial enterprises: dance musicians (Becker, 1963), studio musicians working in Hollywood (Faulkner, 1968), commercial artists (Griff, 1960), Hollywood starlets (Peters, in progress), and newspapermen (Breed, 1952, 1955). These studies have examined the way such creators function in organizations when their freedom and autonomy are limited by their occupational milieu and by the audience for whom they are creating.

Although much of the controversy about the effects of television has centered around the content of programs made specifically for children, no one has studied the producers and writers of such programs. The present paper is a report of an attempt to find out how producers and writers select content for commercial television films designed for the young audience (aged two to 11), how they function in the milieu of commercial television and filmmaking, and how they perceive the process of content selection in relation to their audiences.

Audience feedback (the return of information to the communicator about the message) is a major concern whenever the audience cannot make its desires and criticisms known immediately and directly to the communicator because of the nature of the medium and the special characteristics of the younger audience. Because the communication process is essentially a transaction between the communicator and the receiver, the nature of this transaction and its influence on the communicator is a major problem to an observer of all communication—whether face to face or through the mass media. The problem is complicated in mass media research by the number of steps a message goes through before it reaches the intended audience; feedback is indirect and often obscure. How the audience affects a communicator operating in a complicated setting, like the producer of filmed television shows, cannot be easily determined. The present study tried to determine how producers perceive the process of selecting program content in relation to their two audiences: those who control the occupational and organizational setting (which determines what will be shown on the air), and the viewing audience (which ultimately decides the success or failure of a program).

The information on which this report is based was obtained in interviews with 24 men and women involved in either production or script writing of filmed commercial television shows made especially for children and usually broadcast on Saturday morning or during the evening hours. Among them, these 24 were involved in work on nearly all the children's programs in production during early 1970 and on some family-audience programs as well. (See Appendix A for a detailed description of the respondents and of the way they were found, contacted, and interviewed; see Appendix B for the interview outline.)

The programs on which the respondents worked can be placed in four categories: (1) animated cartoon series with continuing characters and with each episode a complete story in itself (usually appearing on a weekly basis); (2) animated cartoon specials; (3) live-action film series (usually appearing in the early evening and made for family audiences); and (4) live-action specials.

THE PROGRAMS AND HOW THEY ARE SELECTED

The largest group of programs aimed at children are the animated cartoon shows which personify animals or animate human subjects. A second group is built around one or more live animals in primarily adventure-type stories. A third type of program is the western adventure geared to a young audience. Some programs do not fit any general category. Several are pure fantasy. One is an anthology with a variety of themes, which uses both animated and live-action episodes.

The major time period allotted to children's programming by the national commercial networks is Saturday morning. A glance at the Saturday television schedules in cities which are outlets for all three major networks will show that starting as early as 7:30 or 8 a.m., programming is aimed mainly at the young audience. A few shows are reruns of evening series from former seasons, but most are made to be shown on Saturday mornings and have been made within the past few years.

Saturday morning has been devoted to children's programming for some years, but only within the last two or three years has that time period become important to both producers and advertisers. The producers of Saturday morning shows consider the period "prime time," comparable to the evening time slots aimed at the general or adult audience. At the time these interviews were being conducted, the networks were also showing their concern with this time period by appointing special officials to head children's programming; formerly such programs were among the responsibilities of a daytime program division.

Approximately 12 hours of television time are available for the Saturday morning children's programs under discussion—four hours on each network. The time available is relatively limited and a number of these hours are devoted to reruns, so the actual number of new shows produced is small, but it is growing. As each network becomes more concerned about children's programs, it tends to contract for new films rather than continue to use old adult evening shows and cartoon features originally made for movies.

The Saturday morning shows, usually animated (although several are live-action), have short segments; stories are usually completed in ten minutes, rather than the 24 minutes used for evening shows. Each half-hour program is divided into two ten-minute stories, with ten minutes used for commercial advertising.

The three networks operate in a similar manner when they determine the number of segments to be produced for a series. When a series is purchased from a production house or an independent film producer, the producer signs a contract to make 17 half-hour episodes (or 34 segments). The network usually guarantees that each of the 17 episodes will be used six times over two years. Occasionally it will guarantee eight showings in three years. After the initial run of two or three years, the network might request several new episodes of an especially popular program to spice up the offerings.

Most of the programs appearing on the air on Saturday mornings are filmed in Los Angeles, but they are rarely filmed in the large Hollywood studios. Most are made in studios owned or rented by the independent companies which produce the films. Animated shows can be filmed in a small space, so a new producer can usually find adequate space for the artists and film work relatively cheaply and remain independent of the large Hollywood production companies. An ordinary suite of offices can often be used as a studio.

Although a producer of Saturday morning shows makes less money per program sold than does a producer of an evening film series, he is able to build a larger audience through word-of-mouth and good critical reviews. Evening television, while more lucrative, is also more risky.[1] The profit is smaller for children's programs, and the number of hours available for broadcasting them is smaller, but once a series is sold, the chance of failure is practically zero. Not only may such a series build an audience, but it is also more likely to be syndicated after being used a number of times by the network. Some children's shows can be revived often because their character is timeless and their audience changes constantly.

Three major and several small independent companies now share the 12 hours of Saturday morning children's programming. The three large companies make all types of animated films—not only the cartoon programs but also animated titles used in live drama for both television and films. A large portion of these companies' operations involves making animated commercial advertisements.

The market for the work of these independent production companies has been sharply reduced in recent years. At one time such companies would have made animated feature films, but almost no animated films are being bought and shown at this time. (The producers still try to sell the major studios ideas for full-length animated films like those the Disney studio made so successfully in the past, but as a source of ongoing revenue that path is now closed.) Another past product—the short cartoon films which used to be part of the film packages sold to theater owners—is also a vanished genre.

So the primary market for these studios' products is television, and the primary buyers are the networks. Once in a while an advertiser will contract directly for a program and syndicate it in various cities throughout the country. (One show, refused by the networks, was later syndicated by a leading toy manufacturer and was very successful, playing in 103 cities for several years and still being shown in 42 cities.) Such shows, however, are not as profitable for the producer as those purchased by the networks because the syndicating company takes so much of the profit.

Programs are created, according to the information from the producers interviewed, in three major ways. (1) A network creates an idea and gives it to a studio to develop. The studio is then responsible for each episode based on the idea. (2) The studio creates an idea and sells it to the network. If it sells, the development of the episodes is handled by the studio's writers and animators with network approval. (3) The studio buys a property (story or idea) from someone outside and develops it into a presentation to the networks. Well-known books or characters are examples of such properties.

In each of these three processes, the studio or production company develops ideas into programs; the ideas come from many places. Often they come from shows already on the air; the film and television industries call this process a "spinoff." New characters and plots introduced in a segment of an established show can become a new series with an identity of its own. The network itself may pick up a subsidiary character in a regularly scheduled show and contract for a new series based on it; more often, the new character is introduced in a deliberate attempt by the studio to attract network interest.

Ideas for the shows on which a production company is working may have come from a variety of sources or from only one—the networks. One of the three large production houses produced two series for the 1970-71 season. Both came from ideas given to the company for execution by the network contracting for their production. The production company had submitted about 12 new show ideas, but none met with network approval. The network wanted to use the talent and facilities of this company, however, and gave its ideas to be developed by the company's staff artists and writers.

Most production companies generate their own ideas each season. A typical company is owned and operated by two men (one of whom has been an animator since the beginning of his career). The partners come up themselves with ideas they like, or they find properties they like and translate them into usable form for animated film series or specials. Rarely, they purchase a famous author's idea; when they do, they may ask the author himself to participate in the process of translating the idea from story idea to story board (a series of cartoon drawings which present the characters and some dialogue).

But no matter where the ideas come from, the network must approve of them or the show is not likely to get on the air. If a network likes a story idea, it will contract with a production house for a more detailed development of the idea. If the idea is for a live-action program, the networks usually want a pilot film. (If the idea is a "spinoff," the pilot film is not required, because the regularly scheduled program presents the new material.) The pilot film is often pretested or previewed at one of the theaters operated for this purpose by the networks or by advertisers.

For animated programs, few pilot films are made. The shows are bought by the networks on the basis of story board presentations. Voices may also be recorded to give the networks some idea how the characters will sound. (Only little-known independent houses are forced to make an entire film before it is sold.) Animated shows are usually pretested by showing a series of drawings to children and recording their verbal reactions.

One producer described the whole selling and selection process:

> Early in September we come into the network with 25 or 30 ideas. Generally an idea is represented by a page or two of written material and possibly a sketch or two of the characters that will be involved in a potential series. If the networks are interested in what you have to show them, they will enter into a development deal with you. They will put up x number of dollars to develop a story board and have you record voices and characters. The well-established houses do not have to make pilot films. The networks know the quality of their work; they are only interested in content and what the idea is. My partner and I sit around and develop ideas and characters and hand them down to the staff. After the story board and voices are recorded we go back to the network with the finished product. This is usually about now (January). If they like what we did, we get a purchase order for 17 episodes. If not, too bad—no sale.

If producers are interested in making specials, they may go through the same process with the advertisers who buy and sponsor these special programs. They will often deal with the advertising agencies who handle the accounts of the cereal and toy manufacturers who sponsor the largest number of children's programs. But as the costs of program production rise, fewer and fewer advertisers take the risk of commissioning programs themselves.

At this stage of the production process, the producers consider only the networks and advertisers as the audience for whom they are creating and developing ideas. The kinds of programs popular with the networks in a particular year are uppermost in their minds. Although they know that children are the target audience, they also know that it is the networks (and particularly the network programming officials) who must be satisfied. Shows that never pass this stage, this audience, will never get the chance to be popular with children.

If a production house is willing to invest its own money in a program, the show can be conceived, developed, and translated to the drawing board and film without the approval of an advertiser or a network. But few houses are willing or able to do this often because of the money involved in the process. There is very little chance that a show made as a "speculation" will ever get on the air. One or two "specials" made this way have been bought by either a network or a studio, but they are rare cases. Only very successful producers, or those just starting out in independent production who need to advertise their skill and craftsmanship, can risk the expense of producing a whole program without some support from the networks or advertisers.

The production companies depend on the networks not only to finance the creation of shows, but also to approve all stories and scripts which fill the segments and episodes of a series or anthology. For every show idea sold, 34 segments are to be made for a Saturday morning series; 26 or more are made for an evening show. The scripts for each episode are written by staff or freelance writers. The producer of the show is the first to approve a story or script, and he often gives writers ideas. But no script for an individual episode goes into actual film production—regardless of whose idea created it—without approval from the network. Although approval must be obtained throughout the production process, it is probably most crucial at this stage of developing a series.

NETWORK POLICY AND PRODUCTION: THE FIRST AUDIENCE

Network policy and norms about content vary from year to year with the networks' perceptions of the "mass audience" and the social climate. In 1966 Sam Blum, writing in *The New York Times*, noted that

Saturday morning television programming for the 1966-67 season would be almost "totally a matter of cartoon superheroes beating the brains out of supervillains" (Blum, 1969). Television critic Neil Compton (1968) considered the Saturday morning children's cartoon shows an oasis of wit and sophistication in the earlier part of the 1960s but says these shows were replaced by morally repellent pseudoscientific space fantasies by 1966. The nature of children's programming has changed radically once more since then, according to both television schedules and the respondents in this study. The policy change this reflects has had some effect on the producers of specifically children's programs, and a much greater effect on the producers of family-audience programs.

Since the 1968 assassination of Robert Kennedy, there has been an outcry against violence on television; as a result, content has shifted away from space shows and superhero stories. The networks have been especially careful not to buy shows whose basic premises are violent. More comedy and music are available now than several years ago. Because of the success of *Sesame Street* with the critics, the networks have been increasingly interested in programs which might have educational value for children. One producer related that a show which he could not sell to the networks several years ago (it was considered "too soft") was being reconsidered for network presentation. Another producer who made a syndicated "education" show said he had been approached by one network and asked to make additional episodes for Saturday morning broadcast.

To remain in production, a producer must be able to conform to the changing directives of the networks. Those producers who are committed to particular artistic and ethical values have trouble remaining in the commercial field. One well-known producer of a series presently on the air left the field of children's programming because he could not reconcile what he considered the networks' lack of social conscience with his own ideas of good craftsmanship and content. But he is an exception. Most of the producers interviewed seemed willing to go along with network directives, and nearly all those producing animated shows were pleased with the networks' new attitudes toward violence. At least one believed that nonviolent cartoon shows were actually more challenging and demanding:

> You get sick doing that crap. We *had* to do it for two years because that is what the network wanted. For a while, from every studio, all programs were the superhero variety. We were glad when this phase ended because it had created a preponderance of violence. . . .We are now using our brains coming up with ways of doing things that do not rely on smashing, hitting, and banging. . . .Now we are enjoying our work—have for the last year and a half. Much more than we did the year and a half before that.

Producers of shows specifically for children

Reactions to the networks and to network control of stories, while not the same among all producers, varied little among those making shows specifically for the children's audience. Those making animated films had little trouble conforming to the network policy. They considered themselves primarily businessmen making films rather than creators of ideas. Their business is making animated films for a number of clients— of whom the networks are only a part (although a significant part). Two of the production houses make animated titles for films and live-action television series. All three of the largest studios make animated commercials, and one makes educational films for classrooms. Two smaller companies make the animated segments of *Sesame Street* in addition to their commercial offerings. These animation houses please a number of customers and have little trouble following network directives. When the network presents them with series ideas they are able and willing to carry them out.

The producers making shows with live animals also had few problems with the networks, because their shows were considered "educational" rather than amusement. One exception was *Lassie*, a show which mixed live-action and adventure and whose cast contained one animal. But because its essential ingredient is not the animal but rather the type of story, it is more accurately considered a "western."

Producers for Disney Productions, who are involved in the production of both animated and live-action animal and nature shows, had little trouble conforming to network policies. Because the ratings for their programs have always been high and because their themes are consistently the same, Disney producers had no serious doubts about their work. Two of the shows they had sold to the networks were record successes both in ratings and in time on the air, and the Disney company is one of the few left in Hollywood which successfully produces both theater films and television series and specials. In both areas it is relatively successful compared with other production companies.

The studio employs seven producers (three of whom were interviewed), and although some are assigned to theatrical projects and others to television production, the philosophy behind their work is essentially the same. Disney films, whether for television, educational purposes, or theater, are similar. The studio is well known for a certain type of product which may or may not get critical acclaim, but which has a high success record and a low network control record. The philosophy of the producers is the philosophy of the studio: nothing that would be controversial, either politically or socially, is allowed. While there has been some discussion by intellectuals of the fear that some Disney adventure stories can generate in children, there has been little in the studio's offerings that violates network policy. The studio's science education offerings, and those focusing on animals in their natural habitats, have been accepted and approved by the networks with only minor changes.

One producer making an animal show is working on this type of program for the first time. He reports little trouble with the network. On his show, live animals portray humans. "They do everything people do," says the producer. "They wash, dress, get into trolley cars, etc." The show's theme is a bumbling detective and his girl friend, who have various adventures each week. The show is a comedy; according to the producer, it contains "absolutely no violence which is unnecessary to the plot." But the idea for the show came from a theatrical film short which had been made several years earlier and had been shown to adult audiences with a feature-length film. As a result, there was some network concern about the sophistication level of the show. According to the producer, however, the network had been very cooperative and supportive in their reactions to program scripts. (At the time of the interview, about half the 34 episodes sold had been filmed, though none had been broadcast.) His only problem, he said, came from the Humane Society, which by law has a representative on the set watching the way the animals are handled.

Producers of shows for the family audience

Those making the western adventure shows which are directed at the family audience and broadcast in the evening, had more problems with network interference than did the children's producers. Two of the producers interviewed, for example, worked on shows which had been on the air for a number of seasons. When, at the beginning of the 1969-70 season, they were informed by the networks' censorship offices that violence would have to be curtailed in their programs, both thought this would be no problem; they considered their shows basically nonviolent. The networks thought otherwise, and the two, who had experienced no interference in past seasons, found their shows being scrutinized in what both considered an arbitrary manner.

These producers protested network interferences because they insisted that their programs did not use violence for its own sake and that the "action" sequences in the shows were there because they were dramatically necessary. "How are you going to have an adventure if nothing is threatening?" one asked. Both insisted that the networks had formerly been too lenient with others and that the censorship offices were now going overboard in their search for violence. One told a story about an episode he was producing:

> First I fought with the network over the basic script. The story demanded that several people be killed when a bridge had to be blown up. This was a Revolutionary war story. How can you show war without killings? That would be more dishonest than making war nonviolent. Finally they allowed me two killings—new rule: two killings in an episode. After that was settled and I thought the script was approved, I got a phone call from the network. They were upset because my main character was carrying powder to blow up a bridge. Listen, they said, we are upset about him carrying that powder. Could he find it when he arrives at the bridge—have it cached there? The implication is that the story is violent by nature because he is going to blow up something. I told them I had been shooting for a day and a half—I have already established that they are carrying powder—nothing I can do about it now. You know the networks are moral only up to a point. They are not going to spend any money reshooting. OK. That settled it.

In refusing to change the scene, the producer said he was committed to certain principles of dramatic writing: the mission had to be clearly stated in the first few minutes of the play. The audience had to know what was to be accomplished and how the characters would accomplish this mission. That, to him, was the essence of the suspense involved in such drama. There could be no suspense if the audience did not know from the beginning what was going on. The producer believed this had nothing to do with violence, and he appealed to the network vice president. It was one of seven such appeals he made during the 1969-70 season; during the 1967-68 season, he had made only one. Of the seven situations, the producer reported that he had on several occasions been able to convince the network to do the script according to the original directions and dialogue; on the other occasions, he had to yield to the network in order to get the show on the air.

During this producer's first few years with the program, he reported, his situation had been very different. The networks always had the right to approve all scripts, but they usually accepted his material, and he was able to operate within a framework he could accept. He had credited the networks with the ability to delegate content decisions to artistically and technically capable people. In 1967 he had told an interviewer:

> I haven't found any traditional things that everyone writes about—sponsor pressure or network pressure. They would like to have the best possible show —and they have never said or done anything (with one or two minor exceptions) that I felt in any way impeded my creativity. We are doing the best possible show we can do considering the time and money we have to do it with. The network has never turned me down on a script. Sometimes they like some scripts better than others, but it is always a matter of conversation. When they don't like something, I say what can I do to make it better? Sometimes I accept what they say, sometimes I don't. I have inherited a successful show. I have become spoiled. Another show on another network may not be as good. I have no problems.

But this producer's relationship with the network (like that of many of his colleagues) had changed drastically by 1970. What brought about this change? According to the producer, the viewers' reactions to his show had not changed. The letters the program received were mostly complimentary and its ratings were high.

The producer believed that the 1969 hearings before the Senate subcommittee on communications had made the difference in the networks' attitudes: "Now comes the situation where Senator Pastore has put the president of the network on the stand. Presidents of networks are not used to being pushed around. Now everyone is overreacting. Now the networks are telling the producers how to produce, the directors how to direct, the writers how to write."

In order to stay with his program, the producer had to redefine his role and, although he fought the networks on specific points, for his purposes he no longer had the autonomy he once had.

It is possible, of course, for producers to argue specific points, and even to win occasionally, but their day-to-day operations rest on the premise that all ideas for stories depend on network approval and that all stories, characters, music, and settings must be submitted for network approval before production can begin on an episode.

(On the other hand, the networks are dependent to a large extent on the ideas and skills of the studios and production houses. There are a limited number of people who are able to animate and who are trained in television and film techniques. Even the producers of *Sesame Street* deal with the same studios which already produce the Saturday morning shows to obtain the animation and some of the writing for their educational "commercials." The originators and producers of *Sesame Street* maintain the same kind of control as the networks do over commercial programs—final script and art approval—but they too are dependent for story ideas on the creative studio people who write and animate.)

It has been reported that producers of children's programs believe they are "the decision makers and though they welcome consultation and endorse research, control is properly in their hands" (Shayon, 1970). Not one of the producers interviewed for this study believed he had true creative control. The people who work in film television understand and, in most cases, generally accept network power and control. The networks may not choose to exercise this control, but it must always be considered by producers—whether they are thinking of series concepts, story ideas, or specific scripts. These interviews, at least, show that producers, particularly those of animated film series, either actively approve changes in network policy or (more often) passively accept them. Most respondents reported no trouble from the networks in response to questions about freedom and autonomy (see Appendix

B), but the quotations in this paper show that most producers either learn network policy and give the networks what they want or share the networks' beliefs about what is proper entertainment for children.

THE VIEWERS AND PROGRAM CONTENT: THE SECOND AUDIENCE

Because of the inability of the viewing audience to feed back direct reactions to the producer, the viewers may be the least important reference group the producer considers when he determines program content. Once a children's show is sold, there is little or no chance it will be cancelled, even if viewers do not like it. Because only 17 episodes (34 short segments) are made, all are often completed before even one can be shown on the air. Therefore, there can be no chance for audience feedback, and the viewing audience's effect on the producer during production is minimal, if any.

Children's shows are often pretested or previewed before purchase. However, this is not really a satisfactory method of discovering audience reactions, because only still pictures of the characters are shown to the audience. The pictures are presented so that children can voice approval or disapproval; according to the respondents, children under these circumstances are most apt to like characters with which they are already familiar. If Gulliver and Goldilocks are presented among a group of new characters, for example, they will get the approving votes. Several producers were critical of this practice; it gives them no clues about what children would like to see.

But the viewers are still the audience the producer hopes ultimately to please. If a series becomes a success with its audience (as measured by the Nielsen survey), both the producer and the production company reap many financial benefits. They can use the characters to merchandise clothing and toys. Phonograph records of the program's music can be sold. (One producer said a record featuring the musical group in his series had sold over one million copies.) Most important, once a producer or a production house has had one success, the networks are more likely to contract within them to develop new ideas and to make more programs.

Because the viewing audience is large and distant, direct feedback to the producers is slight. Nielsen ratings provide the most constant source of information about the audience. But producers do have some conceptions about their audiences—conceptions more often stereotyped than thoughtfully drawn. These preconceptions are derived from several sources. Popularity ratings of the types of shows which have been on the air in previous years give the only complete picture of the audience. Another source is direct contact with children and their parents, either from letters or from the highly personal interactions producers have with their own children and those of friends.

Ideas about the audience can also be obtained from the ratings and from other marketing research done by the networks and by advertisers. Audience "demographics" are most important to the advertiser who wants to make sure that a program is reaching a target audience. Toy and cereal manufacturers are not as interested in characteristics like ethnicity, income, and geographical distribution as are advertisers for the evening programs. More important to them are audience size, age, and sex. Advertisers (and producers) assume that parents in the United States indulge their children. If children cajole, parents will buy the products. Thus the audience the advertiser wishes to capture is children who are verbally capable of convincing parents to buy their products and who may even have spending money of their own. Because the ratings suggest that the older children in a family control the television set, advertisers see younger children as captive to the programs their older sisters and brothers want to watch.

Advertisers will gear their commercials to the sex they think most likely to favor a program. Adventures, westerns, and space fantasies will contain many commercials for "masculine toys." Comedies and rock-and-roll programs will contain more ads for "feminine toys."

Producers also accept stereotyped sex roles in writing programs for young audiences. Boys or adult men are always the leaders in a story, regardless of the major orientation of the program, and a girl or woman usually acts as his helper. If the show has a villain, this pattern is repeated, although it is not uncommon to find a major villain portrayed as a woman, especially in space fantasies. (In alien cultures women are leaders of society as well as villains, but not in middle-class America.)

The creators of animated programs see children as creatures whose attention spans are limited, and they use loud banging noises and quick movements to keep the children watching. The animated commercials that appear in the breaks between cartoon segments are made by the same people; they use the same techniques to keep the children from leaving the sets during commercials. (Some producers even think their commercials are often made with more care and are more interesting than the regular programs.)

While the shows are in production, producers rarely consider the effects they may have on children; most believe that those considerations are the networks' responsibility, or maybe the parents', but not theirs. Respondents told the interviewer that the networks hire psychologists to study whether or not shows have negative effects. (If not true, this might be a defensive belief.)

The producers also believe that adverse audience reaction to violent programming caused the networks' new emphasis on nonviolent shows. Respondents commonly reported that after Robert Kennedy's death, mothers all over America wrote thousands of letters to the networks protesting the violent types of programs which were appearing on television. Producers themselves did not receive these letters, but they believe that the networks did. (In contradiction, they also commonly believe that parents never watch television on Saturday morning. They see Saturday morning television, especially among lower- and middle-class viewers, as a babysitter.)

All this is part of a folklore which has grown up around, and influences the production of, morning programming. Of course, there is very little evidence for this folklore. Few producers have personally received unfavorable letters about their programs—at least, they did not admit to receiving letters in quantity. Parents' uses of and reactions to Saturday morning programming have never been studied, as far as these producers knew.

Producers' knowledge about the mixed-age audiences for evening programs and specials is more sophisticated. Even so, producers of such shows are apt to use personal values about entertainment or the reactions of friends and family, rather than more general feedback from the viewing audience, to determine whether their programs are being well-received. Like the Saturday morning producers, they often use the Nielsen ratings as their best measure of success; the ratings determine whether or not the networks will keep programs on the air.

Those producing adventure stories deny that they are making shows for children, although these programs are categorized as children's programs by the National Academy of Television Arts. One producer, whose program's ratings and demographic survey data show a large number of children under ten as part of the audience, said, "We are not making a children's story. I don't think anyone in the business knows who their audience is. I think it is presumptuous of anyone to claim they know this. Kids don't know anything. They are not discerning. As long as we are on the air, I don't care."

Even when producers of evening programs receive direct critical feedback in letters, they tend to rationalize or ignore the content because such comments are considered idiosyncratic. The same producer had received a semicritical letter shortly before he was interviewed. A section of the letter read:

> I am not in the habit of writing to television producers regarding their programs, but in this case I feel I must drop you a line regarding last night. My six-year-old daughter is a viewer for the past couple of years. Needless to say we have been through many adventures, trials and tribulations, but I have never seen her as shaken as during last night's program. Not only did she cry her eyes out during the show; I had to keep reminding her during the evening that it was only a story and that (animal character) in several weeks' time would be fine. She also was worried her own pet would suffer a similar mishap.

The producer's reaction to the letter was to disclaim responsibility for the emotional health of young viewers. Parents should see that their children are not frightened or in any way affected by what is on the air, he said:

> You cannot have it bland—sometimes it has to be upsetting. How can we do it to your kids? What do you mean how can we do it to your kids? We are doing something for entertainment; that is our only purpose. If we are not entertaining the kid we are failing. The entire thing of throwing the burden on us because the kids cry—this is wrong and unfair. If a parent has the child enjoying our program—which they do—then it is the parent's responsibility, when it is brought to a point that the parent is worried, to see that in an honest and realistic way this is dealt with.

This producer is representative of most of those working on all types of children's programming. Their concern about the effects of their programs is negligible. Four producers were exceptions, however; they expressed concern in various ways. One thought the networks should spend more money on psychological research. Another was no longer producing for commercial television because of the kinds of programs being broadcast, even though he saw that there had been a shift away from violence. He considered the level of children's shows still so low that children could not benefit in any way from viewing them. He also protested the lack of freedom to create and was disturbed about the fact that he might be forced to work in a medium where the intelligence level required to produce a product was minimized.

Two other producers had publicized their opinions about children's programming. One was an animator who had had limited success in producing. He showed the interviewer several newspaper clippings which quoted him as saying that the low-level programming (whether or not it was violent) was an improper use for a medium which could be a great social force to enhance the intelligence and capabilities of a whole generation of children. He was generally opposed to network television, regardless of its content, because of the commercial aspects of the programs. He believed that when well-known personalities sell products to children, their shows themselves lose their credibility.

The other producer who made his views public is extremely successful in both adult and children's programming, working primarily in live-action shows and using animals in many of them. His major concern was the effect television programs might have on the minds of children. He thinks that the television industry has definitely not met its responsibilities in several areas: first, to find out what television does to the minds of children, and second, to use its facilities to make children more loving rather than more violent. This man was so concerned about the power of television to mold the minds of the young that he actually suggested that no child under six should be allowed to watch television. Part of his concern was with program content, but another part was with the hypnotic ability of the medium itself, regardless of its content.

Some newer shows are making a special effort to present educational messages to children in the form of entertainment. These messages stress good manners, racial tolerance, and the irrelevance of physical differences. (Of course, the "good guys" still win when there is conflict, and because the characters are rarely presented in shades of gray, there is never any sympathy for "bad guys.") One producer, whose shows were on the air for the first time in 1970, said he was glad to have a chance to improve television through entertainment, because he believed the function of the medium should be to entertain rather than to inform (a commonly held belief among those producing for children):

> Some children's shows have been violent for violence's sake, as you probably already know. Here we can be funny, entertain—not hurt anyone. For instance, we have one scene where (the main character, an animal) shaves. The kids love that. We discovered people laugh when they see animals do things people do. We really hope this program will uplift the kids in certain ways. Certain messages are there. For instance, the main character always brushes his teeth after each meal. And we worry and talk a lot about safety. No one ever goes into a car without fastening his seat belt. But we don't have any strong messages, nothing controversial. We don't want to antagonize anyone.

THEORETICAL CONSIDERATIONS

Critics have frequently argued that the popular arts (defined here as the art forms presented through the mass media) have become just another profit-making opportunity for the businessmen who run the media and that these men use their power to impose their ideas of entertainment on the audience. These critics also claim that, for the most part, creators of these popular arts become spokesmen for those in charge of the system rather than remaining independent. This criticism can be found in scholarly journals as well as in publications for popular consumption (see Gans, 1966b, for a review of the criticism). Television in particular is a target for this kind of analysis. A main theme was expressed by Walter Lippman (1959): "While television is supposed to be free, it has, in fact, become the creature, the servant and, indeed, the prostitute of merchandising."

Critics claim that innovation and creativity are discouraged because the primary function of the medium (as seen by those in control) is to sell air time to advertisers and not to educate, change, or liberate the viewers. They assert that it is the profit motive which essentially structures the content and that the men who write, direct, or otherwise create television programs have their course of action decided by others rather than by their own talent and integrity.

While this view is polemic, the questions it raises are essentially sociological. The effect of social structure on workers, artists, and technicians has been of concern to sociologists since Marx. Much of the recent work in this area examines the intellectual, scientific, and professional functioning of those who once were occupationally autonomous but who became employed by organizations and bureacracies (see Kpalan, 1965). A few previously mentioned studies have considered creative persons and technicians as employees of large commercial enterprises. But only a few of these studies are interested in the effect of the social structure on the actual content of what is produced. Gans (1957, 1966c, 1970), Breed (1952), and Becker (1963) in particular are concerned with "audience effects" as they have been defined in this paper. These studies focus to a greater or lesser degree on the ways communicators operate within a social milieu. Because research has separated the audience from the communicator, the communicator, the message, and the audience are seen as existing often without any relationship to one another.

The problems of feedback and audience effects on the message are aspects of the communication process commonly neglected by sociological research. Social psychologists and some sociologists assume that the nature and significance of communications are determined in large part by the expectations of communicators and audience, which tend to be reciprocally related. They suggest that writers, broadcasters, and political speakers all select what they are going to say in terms of their beliefs about the audience (Riley and Riley, 1959). Pool and Shulman (1964) state that the "audience, or at least those about whom the communicator thinks, thus play more than a passive role in communications." Bauer (1958, 1963) has been particularly interested in audience effect, claiming that the audience has much control over what to read, listen to, or watch. However, he also notes, "Communicators committed strongly to the subject matter may 'distort' their image of the prospective audience to bring it more in line with either their own values or the content of incoming information and thereby reduce the 'audience effect' " (1958). Essentially, Bauer views communications as a transactional process in which both audience and communicator take an important initiative.

Audience effects on the communicator are not easily determined in the mass communication situation. Communicators, as John and Matilda Riley (1959) point out, must be seen as operating in a social setting, as part of a larger pattern, as people who send messages in accordance with the expectations and actions of others in the same system. The television producer's system is complex. It consists of the organization or studio producing his films, the network and advertisers who buy the films, and the general audience which eventually views the films. Because the producer has little direct contact with the large viewing audience, it appears that much of his direct feedback comes from the organizations buying the films; he sends his messages in accordance more directly with their desires than with those of an ultimate viewing audience which is unknown to him.

The networks, in turn, have a number of audiences *they* must consider when they select programs: the viewing public, the Federal Communications Commission, the political climate as reflected in Congress and the White House, the Interstate Commerce Commission (which has already investigated the networks several times), and pressure groups (ethnic and others) in the society at large. While all the various parts of the system may influence the final product, evidence suggests that the most important influence comes from those parts of the system having direct interaction with the communicator.

Most studies point out that the message communicated is determined by a combination of factors, by artistic and professional considerations as well as the social, economic, and political norms that develop within organizations (Larson, 1964). Professional considerations are usually defined in two ways: commitment to the value of freedom and autonomy in the decision-making process, and commitment to certain craft standards about filmmaking and drama. The two are related, in that to be truly creative one should have the freedom to choose content considered excellent and of high quality.

Television producers are found to vary in their degree of commitment to the value of control from the hiring organization (Cantor, 1969). There are several modes of adaptation for producers who operate in the system as it now exists. At the extremes, they can conform to network policy by denying a conflict of values, or, if they cannot conform, they can quit producing. Those who adapt neither by conforming completely nor by quitting, but rather by trying to deviate from known policy when possible, are seen as more committed to professional values and more likely to consider the standards of their colleagues than those producers who conform without deviation. The conclusion of the 1969 study was that the primary audience series producers have in mind when they select content is made up either of their professional and artistic colleagues, of the organization that will be buying their materials, or of the viewing audience as determined primarily from the rating service and market research.

The producers in the present study did not believe that they had creative control; in most cases, they generally accepted network power. Few used their own colleagues for rewards and appraisals. Thus professional colleagues were not a primary audience for these producers of children's programming.

The reality of the marketplace at this time is that if a producer wishes to make television shows to be shown on commercial television, he must please two audiences: first the buyers of the film; eventually the viewers. But the buyer necessarily becomes the most important audience. No program can ever be judged by the general audience unless it first pleases a buyer—in most cases, a network.

There are other reasons why pleasing the viewing audience is a secondary consideration. The direct ways of expressing approval or disapproval—letter writing or face-to-face contact with members of the audience—do not represent the large, heterogeneous audience that television programs command; the indirect measures like market research and rating services tell nothing about audience reactions to program content. Since television shows appear on the air long after they are made, they could not be changed to reflect audience feedback in any case. The only direct feedback is from the network representatives who watch each step of the production process. Thus especially for children's programming, the network itself is the primary audience; the content is directed to its desires and mandates.

Although an interview type of study cannot be rigorous, the present study can lead to the conclusion that the critics of television have been correct in declaring that producers of children's shows probably reflect the values of the business organization hiring them. Several questions remain unanswered. It is not possible to determine in this type of case study which of the producers' values are similar to those of the business interests. To find out we must study the network system to determine the ways (who, how, and what) decisions are made at that higher level.

The evidence does suggest that those who do not cooperate in the commercial milieu cannot become successful producers and writers for television, and must leave the medium either by choice or through neglect when their values are found to be discordant with those of the organization.

The content of children's shows has changed several times in the last decade; many of the same producers who made sophisticated social criticism cartoons at the beginning of the 1960s, then made the superhero shows and space fantasies, now make the rock-and-roll and comedy shows. As each new trend sets in, new men are also recruited whose talents and values tend to fit the programming in demand. (This might explain why those new to producing children's television shows have so few complaints about the networks; their first shows fit the needs of the networks at a time when more "educational" and comedy programs are in demand.)

Greenberg (1970) has suggested that the men who write, produce, and direct television films operate under conditions of high tension and aggression, and that this might account for the intense level of dramatic output. The question he raises is certainly an empirical one which cannot be answered by a case study method. Other studies may be able to determine whether or not the working conditions for television's creative people are more highly charged than those of other creative people whose products are less violent in nature—musicians and artists, for example.

Some of the evidence in the present study is not in agreement with Greenberg's speculation. The producers are not restricted to violent content; they can and do make educational and often highly artistic programs for commercial television, films, or public television. The production companies observed in this study have a variety of films in production, ranging from polar coordinates on a graph to a nonviolent detective story. The evidence indicated not only that the men who make violent films are able to make nonviolent ones, but that they prefer to.

The highest priority in future studies should be given to the decision-making processes of the networks themselves. Only when this process has been examined can the important questions about who determines content be answered. The present study must conclude that the networks determine the content of children's programs. *How* they make their decisions, what publics they try to satisfy, and which publics are thereby denied access to the kinds of programs they want are still open questions, which could be subjected to research.

If the networks must function so as to try to capture the largest possible audience (as has been so often suggested), they may be unable to basically change program content without losing a large part of their anticipated viewing audience. If true audience direction of television content is desirable, perhaps Gans's (1966b) suggestion of "aesthetic relationism" (forcing various public tastes to identify their own aesthetic standards) should be explored.

A final comment should be made about the effects of the programs under consideration. When more is learned about these effects, it may be that neither audience control nor network control is desirable for programs directed at children. The producers interviewed for this study would prefer to have the networks or parents take responsibility for the final effects of their programming efforts. The networks, because of their desire to sell products and please advertisers, seem to be concerned primarily with the size of the audience. Parents cannot be expected to have the sophistication to evaluate the short-term as well as the long-term effects of programs on their children.

The present series of interviews indicates that what is now a vacuum in control of programming for children could be filled by child specialists. Although we would not consider turning the school curriculum over to network officials or filmmakers, we have allowed children's television programming to remain almost completely in their hands. Their general unconcern (with a few notable exceptions) for the welfare of their final audience points to the necessity for considering new policy-making procedures in this area.

FOOTNOTES

1. When a production house or a producer sells an evening show to the network, the contract is for 11 or 13 episodes (half a season) with an option for the same number to finish a season. There is no guarantee that a series will finish a season; even if it does, there is no guarantee that it will be renewed for the following year. When a series fails, does not finish the season, or is not renewed for the following year, it is shelved and not used again. Thus there is no chance that it will build an audience and be revived. Because of the high cost of prime time series production, such programs are financial failures unless enough episodes are rerun either during the daytime by the networks or in the evenings by local stations who purchase the series from a syndicating company. Syndication requires at least a two-year supply of films—preferably more, because the more episodes made and shown on prime time, the more likely the series is to make a profit for its producer.

REFERENCES

Bauer, R. The communicator and his audience. *Conflict Resolution*, 1958, **2**, 66-76.

Bauer, R. The initiative of the audience. *Journal of Advertising Research*, 1963, **3**, 2-7.

Becker, H. Careers in a deviant occupational group. *Outsiders: studies in the sociology of deviance*. New York: The Free Press, 1963.

Blum, S. Who decides what gets on TV and why. *Social profiles in the U.S.A. today*. New York: Van Nostrand Reinhold Company, 1970.

Blumler, J.G. Producers' attitudes toward television coverage of an election campaign: a case study. The *Sociological Review monograph*, 1969, **13**, 85-116.

Breed, W. The newspaperman, news, and society. Unpublished PhD. dissertation, Columbia University, 1952.

Breed, W. Social control in the newsroom. *Social Forces*, 1955, **33**, 226-335.

Cantor, M. Television producers: a sociological analysis. Unpublished PhD. dissertation, University of California at Los Angeles, 1969.

Compton, N. TV specials. *Commentary*, 1968, **45**, 69-71.

Faulkner, R. Hollywood studio musicians: their work contingencies in the film industry. Unpublished PhD. dissertation. University of California at Los Angeles, 1968.

Gans, H. The creator-audience relationship in the mass media. In Ro-
senberg, B., and White, D.M. (Eds.) *Mass culture*. New York: The
Free Press, 1957.   ·

Gans, H. Broadcasters and audience values in the mass media: the im-
age of man in American television news. Paper prepared for the
Mass Media Research Committee of the Sixth World Congress of
Sociology, Evien, France, 1966.

Gans, H. Popular culture in America: social problem in a mass society
of social asset in a pluralist society. In Becker, H. (ed.) *Social problems: a modern approach*. New York: Wiley, 1966(b).

Gans, H. The shaping of mass media content: a study of the news. Paper
presented at the meeting of the American Sociological Association,
1966(c).

Gans, H. How well does TV present the news? *The New York Times
Magazine*, January 11, 1970, pp. 30-35, 38.

Greenberg, B. The content and context of violence in the mass media. In
Baker, R.K., and Ball, S.J. (Eds.) *Mass media and violence:* a report to the National Commission on the Causes and Prevention of
Violence. Washington, D.C.: U.S. Government Printing Office,
1969.

Griff, M. The commercial artist. In Stein, M.R., Vidich, A.J., and
White, D.M. (Eds.) *Identity and anxiety*. Glencoe, Ill.: The Free
Press, 1960.

Halmos, P. *The Sociological Review monograph: the sociology of mass
communicators*, 1969, **13.**

Kaplan, N. Essay review: professional scientists in industry. *Social
Problems*, 1965, **13,** 88-97.

Larsen, O.N. Social effects of mass communications. In Faris, R.E.L.
(Ed.) *The handbook of modern sociology*. Chicago: Rand-McNally
and Company, 1964.

Lazarsfeld, P.R. Some reflections on past and future research in broadcasting. In Steiner, G. *The people look at television*. New York:
Alfred A. Knopf, 1963.

Lippman, W. The problem of television. *The New York Herald Tribune*, October 27, 1959.

Moore, J. *The Hollywood writer*. In progress.

Peters, A. *The early careers of the Hollywood actress*. In progress.

Pool, I., and Shulman, I. Newsmen's fantasies, audiences and news-
writing. In Dexter, L.A., and White, D.M. *People, society and mass
communications*. New York: The Free Press, 1964.

Riley, J.W., and Riley, M.W. Mass communication and the social system. In Merton, R.K., Broom, L., and Contrell, L.S. (Eds.) *Sociology Today*. New York: Basic Books, 1959.

Shayon, R.L. Media mystification. *Saturday Review*, October 17, 1970,
p. 51.

Appendix A: Method and sample

Interviews took place during January 1970 in Los Angeles, California. Beause children's programs are made primarily in the Los Angeles area, it was possible to talk to most of the people directly involved in producing the bulk of commercial offerings specifically directed to the young audience and made in the film medium. Several commercial programs videotaped for the children's audience were not included in the study. These shows are usually made outside the Hollywood area, and the writers and producers who work with videotape face different problems from those of film producers and writers. Feedback to workers in videotape is more immediate from the viewing audience. They might be expected to be more responsive than film producers to their audience.

The sample consisted of 20 producers and four writers. The interviews were sought by formal letters to those producers with shows listed as "in production" by *Daily Variety* (Western edition) on December 5, 1969. Response to the letters was excellent; all but one of the interview requests were granted. (The one producer who refused an interview had no shows actually in production. Because he did not intend to make any more shows for children, he thought he could contribute little to the study.)

Some producers not only gave interviews, but suggested other colleagues not listed in *Variety* whose shows were in production or who were preparing to produce programs for the 1970-71 season. Several producers also invited the interviewer to view the making of animated cartoons and live-action films. It was also through the cooperation of the producers that I was able to interview four contract writers as well. (This sample was not representative; not enough writers and artists could be contacted in the time available.)

The three major production "houses" then making the majority of the animated cartoon shows on the air were contacted and interviews obtained from their staff members or producers. Represented in the sample are those working in large live-action studios making shows for children and those working in several smaller independent companies making either animated or live-action films. It is possible that one or more small animating studios with shows on the air in some cities during the 1969-70 season had finished production by December 5, 1969, and were missed by the survey (*TV Guide*, for example, lists two shows on the air in Los Angeles and Washington, D.C., produced by companies other than those interviewed for the study.) It is impossible to know when these shows were produced because of the nature of programming for the Saturday morning time slot.

The studios contacted, and the programs they produced, are:
Disney Productions (*The Wonderful World of Disney*)

> Sid and Marty Krofft Productions (*H.R. Pufnstuf*)
> Ivan Tors Films (*Jambo*)
> Twentieth Century-Fox Television (*Daniel Boone*)
> Wrather Corporation (*Lassie*)
> Fred Calvert Productions (Children's Television Work-
>   shop)
> DePatie-Freleng (*Pink Panther, Here Comes the
>   Grump, Goldilocks*)
> Filmation Associates (*Archie Comedy Hour, Sabrina,
>   The Teenage Witch, The Hardy Boys, Superman,
>   Batman*)
> Hanna-Barbera (*The Banana Splits Adventure Hour,
>   Scooby Doo, Where Are You?, Perils of Penelope
>   Pitstop, The Cattanooga Cats*)
> Pantomime Pictures, Inc. (*Hot Wheels, Sky Hawks*)
> Sandler Burns Marmer Productions (*Sam Simian*)

Most of the interviews were tape recorded. Two producers objected to the use of the recorder but did allow notes to be taken. All respondents were asked the same questions so their answers could be compared. Each interview was replayed and coded the day it was obtained. A diary was kept of the interviewing. This paper, although mainly based on the interviews, also contains information from the diary, some documents, and other sources.

The group of people interviewed cannot be considered a representative sample of all those who create film television shows for children. They also cannot be considered an occupational group, although certain features are common to their background and training. As a group of people who influence television content, they are certainly important, however, in understanding the process of content selection.

They ranged from 33 to 65 years of age. Their experiences in the entertainment media were surprisingly similar considering the range of ages represented and the history of film and television production. Ten were animators before becoming producers; of these ten, seven had taken their early training with the Disney studio as apprentice artists, usually doing minor animation jobs and story boards for theatre cartoon films. The other three animators had worked for other large studios—particularly Warner Brothers—in similar capacities. They were at different stages of their careers when the large studios stopped making animated motion pictures in the late 1950s and early 1960s. Most went into production on their own or with help from the parent studios; several left the studios to work for smaller independent companies before venturing on their own.

Those who had not been animators had a variety of work experiences, ranging from publicity to college teaching, but all had been on the periphery of the entertainment business as advertising men, promoters or publicists, or writers before going into film production. Two of the live-action series producers had been writer-producers, and one had been a film editor. The fourth was new to the entertainment field but had been and still was making live-action commercials for television. A fifth producer had been a puppeteer.

Their education was more varied; the live-action producers were generally the best educated. Four of the five were college graduates, and one had done graduate work. Most of the former animators had had no college training. Several (not all) had gone to art schools. One-third of the total group (eight) had some college education. This college group contained several of the older members of the sample as well as several of the younger. A few of the 24 did not graduate from high school. The group as a whole was less educated than the Hollywood film producers the interviewer studied earlier (Cantor, 1969), but they are comparable to other groups in entertainment who have been studied.

None was trained in an educational institution to make films for children. A common complaint among those interviewed was that institutions train people to become cartoonists, not animators. Although in reality a number of colleges and universities do give courses in animating for films, the producers believed that there is no place but on the job to learn the craft and to learn to make children's films in particular.

Because most of the respondents were craftsmen, they showed more concern over the art (the drawings) than over the story in the cartoons they made. The sample consisted of men who saw themselves either as businessmen providing entertainment or as artists primarily concerned about the craft aspects of their occupation.

Appendix B: Interview schedule*

Topic I. Present Situation
  1. What is your present title?
  2. What duties go with that title?
  3. Do you consider this your major occupation? (If not, what is your major occupation?)
  4. Who is your employer?

Topic II. Training and Work Record
  5. In what year did you start working in television?
  6. What was your first job in television?
  7. Have you worked steadily in television since that time?
      If yes, can you list the jobs you have held in the industry?
      If no, how much time have you spent in the industry since you started?
      a. What jobs have you held in the industry since that time?
      b. What jobs outside the industry during that time?
  8. How did you get started in the industry?
  9. How did you become a producer? (Not asked of writers)
  10. How would someone become an animator or writer at this time?

Topic III. Ambitions and Satisfactions or Dissatisfactions
  11. All things considered, how do you like working in television generally?
  12. Is there another occupation you would like to have other than the one you now have, either in or outside the industry? Why?
      a. To put it another way, what are your ambitions?
      b. Is your present job a step towards those ambitions?
      c. What would you like to be doing five years from now?

Topic IV. Comparison of Television with Other Media.
  13. What are the assets and liabilities of television as compared with other media? For instance:
      a. Does television give one as much chance for creativity as other media? By other media, I mean movies, radio, writing novels or articles, the theater, etc.
      b. Is there more or less security in television compared to the other media?
      c. What advantages does working in television have, in comparison to other media?
      d. What disadvantages does working in television have, in comparison to other media?

---

*Modified from interview schedule used in 1969 study (Cantor)

     e. (If not mentioned), do you have more autonomy or free-
       dom in television compared to other media that you have
       worked in?

     f. (If not mentioned), has network policy changed in that
       two years?

14. Do you have any particular gripes with working in television?

Topic V. The Audience

15. What kind of an audience views the show you are now on?
     a. Ages
     b. Sex

16. Does this audience differ from audiences for other shows of
    which you have been a part?
     a. If yes, how do you know this? In what ways?
     b. If no, how do you know what kind of audience views the
       show?

17. Do you have much direct contact with audience such as letters,
    telephone calls or through travels?

18. (If applicable), is the audience for show different from two years
    ago? If yes, in what way or ways?

Topic VI. The Shows and Stories

19. How is a new series or show chosen for viewing?

20. How are ideas for series developed?

21. When choosing a script for this series, how do you go about it?
    (What is wanted here is their concepts of the process.)

22. From newspaper and magazine accounts of television, there
    seems to be a concern with network and advertising interference.
    How much pressure do you get from either source when you are
    working? Can you give any specific examples?

23. Several people have spoken of television by "committee." What
    does this mean? Are there better ways (or possibly different
    ways) of producing television shows? What might they be?

24. Can you describe the show (shows) you have on the air? The plot,
    characters, etc.

Topic VII. Politics and Political Behavior (Data not relevant here)

25. Are you active politically?

25. Did you vote in the California gubernatorial election in1966?
     a. If yes, would you mind telling me who you voted for?
     b. If no, ask why. If not resident in California, find out if he
       voted in last gubernatorial race in his home state?

27. What is your party preference? If none, which party do you gen-
    erally support?

28. Do you consider yourself a liberal, moderate, conservative?

29. What do you think about *one* government sponsored or subsi-
    dized TV channel?

Topic VIII. Communication Behavior (Data not relevant here)
30. What newspapers do you read regularly? List any others:
31. If not mentioned: Do you ever read *Variety* or *Hollywood Reporter*? Yes - How often? No - Why?
32. What magazines do you read regularly? If not mentioned: Do you read such magazines as *TV Guide*, the movie magazine?
33. Is there a special columnist or critic that you read regularly either in the magazines or newspaper? If yes, ask why?
34. In an average week, how many hours do you spend listening to the radio?
35. What kind of program do you listen to? Do you have a favorite station?
36. In an average week how many hours do you spend watching TV?
37. What kinds of programs do you watch? Do you favor one network over another?
38. Is there a particular time of the year you may watch more TV? Why?
39. How often do you go to the films? What kind   films do you prefer?
40. Do you watch television specifically made for children?

Topic IX. Organizations (Data not relevant here)
41. To which guilds or related organizations do you belong?
42. Do you attend meetings of the organization? How often? If yes, or no, why or why not?
43. Have you ever held an office in any of the above organizations? Why one? What office? How long?
44. If not, would you like to hold an office? Why?
45. If yes (presently an office-holder), why are you holding that office? Why did you take the office?

Topic X. Social Background
46. What is or was your father's usual occupation? (Or that of the person by whom respondent was raised.) Please describe his main work activities.
47. What was the last grade he completed in school?

Grammar School *Jr. & Sr. High School* *College*   *Grad School*
1 2 3 4 5 6   7 8 9 10 11 12   Fr So Jr Sr   1 2 3 4 5
Trade School?   Business School?   Other (specify)?

48. What was the last grade you completed in school?

Grammar School *Jr. & Sr. High School* *College*   *Grad School*

1 2 3 4 5 6   7 8 9 10 11 12   Fr So Jr Sr   1 2 3 4 5

Trade School?   Business School?   College major?
Other (specify)?

49. What was the last grade your wife completed in school?
    Grammar School   *Jr. & Sr. High School*   *College*   *Grad School*
    1 2 3 4 5 6   7 8 9 10 11 12   Fr So Jr Sr   1 2 3 4 5
    Trade School?   Business School?   Other (specify)?
50. Do you have a religious preference? No? Yes? May I ask what it is? (Get denomination if possible)
51. May I ask your approximate age?
52. Are you single? Married? Separated? Widowed? Divorced?
53. Income: Approximately_____
54. Does income vary much from year to year?
55. What neighborhood do you live in in Los Angeles?
56. Where were you born? (City or town, state, country)
57. How long have you lived in Los Angeles?
58. Spouse's occupation, if any:
59. Was wife (husband) ever connected with the industry (or a related one)
60. Do you ever discuss business problems with your spouse?
61. Are there any comments about working in television that you'd like to add to what we're covered? If never mentioned, ask what respondent thinks is the purpose or function of television made especially for children.

Sex:
Race:
Date:
Name of Show:

Appendix C: Letter

THE AMERICAN UNIVERSITY
WASHINGTON, D.C. 20016
COLLEGE OF ART & SCIENCES,
DEPARTMENT OF SOCIOLOGY

December 30, 1969

NAME

ADDRESS

Dear Mr._____:

I will be in the Los Angeles area for a few weeks as a Consultant for the National Institute of Mental Health which is conducting a study on the subject of television and social behavior. One fundamental problem being explored is how content is created and selected for children's programs. In order to find out it is desirable to interview people who are especially knowledgeable about such matters. I am therefore contacting both you and _____.

Within the next week, I will telephone to see if such an interview is possible. At that time, I would be glad to answer any questions you might have on the objectives of the study. Your consideration of this request is much appreciated.

Sincerely yours,

Muriel Cantor, Ph. D.
Professor of Sociology

Violence in Television: The Industry Looks at Itself

Thomas F. Baldwin and Colby Lewis

Michigan State University

This study examined violence in television action drama from the broadcast industry's point of view.[1] The primary data came from the producers, writers, and directors who put the violence in entertainment television and from the network censors who set the limits. Specifically, we wanted to determine the industry's: (1) beliefs about what constitutes violent content; (2) reasons for using violence as an ingredient of popular drama; (3) guidelines, self-imposed or other-directed, for determining the degrees and kinds of violence which might be used; (4) perceptions of the child audience within the general audience; and (5) notions about the possible effects of televised violence on children and about ways in which such effects might be mitigated.

Program identification

We first identified the network television entertainment series in production for the 1970-71 season that were most likely to contain violence. Series carried over from the 1969-70 season were chosen for their degrees of violence, as rated by a general sample of viewers and by 43 newspaper and magazine television critics (Greenberg and Gordon, 1970). The returning series among the 15 most violent programs as rated by both the public and the critics were included. New programs, not on the air at the time of the study, were analyzed for violence potential from network promotional literature and from program descriptions provided by advertising agency personnel who had seen pilots or outlines.[2]

The programs selected were:

Adam-12	Ironside
Bonanza	Mannix
Dan August	Men from Shiloh
The FBI	Mission: Impossible
Four-in-One	Mod Squad
Gunsmoke	The Most Deadly Game
Hawaii Five-O	Name of the Game
High Chaparral	Silent Force
The Immortal	Young Rebels

In this report, these programs will be collectively referred to as action-adventure series. The list includes all the prime time commercial network western, police, detective, and spy series on the air at the beginning of the 1970-71 season. The programs were intended either for families or for adults with the anticipation that some children would be exposed. Most programs in each series would be shown twice on a network and then syndicated for subsequent showings by local stations.

The list does not include all television programming which may contain some sort of violence. It does not include newscasts, documentaries, specials, feature films, comedies, variety shows, and general drama. News programs, whose violence content is factual or real, present a dimension entirely different from fictional violence and should be analyzed separately. Specials are assembled by ad hoc production teams whose policies and practices about violence would not be established. Most feature films are not made for television and reflect the standards of another medium. Comedy and variety shows contain little serious violence. General drama programs may include some violence, but not consistently and often in more subtle forms than outright physical violence. We also excluded programs especially designed for children (Cantor, 1970) and syndicated programs which generally are more dated and less likely to represent current practices and values than programs filmed for the next season.

Respondents

We attempted to interview the person most responsible for the content of each listed program—the producer or executive producer with day-to-day working control and general policy responsibility—as well as writers and others involved in the production process. At least one producer was interviewed for 17 of the 18 series. (For the other program, we interviewed a production company vice president with general policy responsibility but not daily involvement.)

Each producer was asked to identify the writers who worked on programs for his series. Many of the writers had credits for several of the series. Among them, the writers interviewed had written scripts for all but two of the listed series. (The producers had done much of their own writing for those two series.) Some of the program writers were staff members with other titles in the production companies assigned to produce the programs—associate producer, story editor; but most were freelance writers. All the producers interviewed had also been writers of action-adventure television at some time in their careers, so the writer's prespective was well represented.

The four directors had worked on several of the listed programs. Two of them were also writers, and one was also a leading actor in a series. The series director, although he does not originate the action, has some control over its audial and visual dimensions.

The columnist we interviewed has written extensively about the issue of violence for the daily entertainment industry newspaper *Variety*. The six censors included the West Coast heads of the broadcast standards departments for each of the three commercial networks, one New York vice president for network standards, and two standards editors.

A total of 48 individuals were interviewed, including ten executive producers, 13 producers, 13 writers, four directors, one post-production chief, one columnist, and six censors. Two of the writers and one of the censors were women; the rest were men. (A list of the respondents by name is in Appendix A.)

Procedures

All interviews were conducted in the Los Angeles area between June 21 and July 20, 1970. Both interviewers are professors in the Department of Television and Radio at Michigan State University and have professional backgrounds in broadcast journalism, public relations, advertising, television station management, communication research and theatre and television production.

Both interviewers participated in all but two interviews. Notes were transcribed by one researcher within a few hours after each interview and reviewed by the other. Respondents were promised anonymity to encourage candid and free responses.

A letter explaining the purpose of the study and the general nature of the questioning had been sent to each producer. Each was then telephoned and an appointment arranged. During the phone call, the producers named their writers and directors, who then received similar letters. None of the individuals contacted refused an interview; one person was never reached.

An interview outline, but not a rigid set of questions, was prepared. This structure allowed maximum freedom of response and enabled us to probe as needed. The major questions concerned the respondents' definitions of violence; the reasons why their programs portrayed violence; their approaches to violence in the programs; the feasibility of using alternatives to violence; the feasibility of methods to counter alleged effects of violence; their perceptions of youthful members in the audience; their perceptions of industry standards about violence; and their knowledge of the audience. (A more detailed outline is in Appendix B.) Most question areas were covered in each interview. The interviews averaged two hours and ranged from one to four hours in length.

Our aims in interviewing were three: to attempt to specify why there is violence on television; to analyze the censoring of violence by the networks; and to give the industry an opportunity to respond to criticism of television violence.

NETWORK PROGRAMMING AND PRODUCTION

The three commercial networks distribute most of the evening television programs seen in American homes. Other programming sources serve a comparatively insignificant audience (in terms of size).

These programs reach affiliated stations by wire or microwave relay, either simultaneously or with adjustments for time zone differences. Most programs are series with a continuing cast and situations which create and serve an established set of audience expectations. The network provides 22 to 26 programs a year per series, rebroadcasting some.

These programs may reach a secondary audience through syndicated distribution. In the United States, syndicated reruns of network shows are broadcast independently by local stations during the daytime, early evening, or late evening hours. Many series are also syndicated in other nations. One producer estimated an audience of 400 million people for each program in his series.

The network and its affiliated stations are interdependent. The network has the most attractive programs for a mass audience; the affiliate has a license to broadcast the programs, usually on a VHF channel. Most affiliates are independent of the networks except for a small number owned and operated (0-and-0) by the networks. The five 0-and-0 VHF stations licensed to each network—the maximum number allowed any one owner—contribute greatly to the network's profit and serve extremely large audiences because of their major metropolitan locations. However, since each network has some 200 affiliates, the 0-and-0 stations are a small proportion. The affiliates exercise important controls over program content.

Program ownership and control

The networks own a few programs outright and have a financial interest in almost all the programs they distribute. They help underwrite the production of most programs, beginning with the initial program concept. Advertisers no longer own network programs or exercise much direct control over content because of the trend toward multiple rather than single sponsors for each program. In the 1969-70 season, 96 percent of network prime time advertising was sold on a participating basis (Herrick, 1970).

Network control of television programming has been well publicized recently. The Federal Communications Commission has taken some tentative steps toward diminishing the networks' monopoly and expanding the opportunities for independent and new producers. Producers we interviewed who mentioned this issue were unanimously disturbed by network programming power but had no faith in the FCC measures to curb it. Most felt that the emergence of cassettes (inexpensive program recordings for replay through home receivers) would provide sufficient opportunities for new creative thrusts and for specialized audience interests.

The character of television programs is determined by the three networks' notions of what will appeal to large numbers of people, sell products or services for advertisers, and not jeopardize the valuable licenses or the good will of affiliates by creating a negative audience response.

Demographics

In the business of television, simple audience totals have now given way to "demographics", an analysis of the make up of an audience. Almost every producer said the networks hoped to reach certain categories of people more than others. These categories were mainly married adult 18-49 year-olds in the higher educational and income brackets.

Many of the action-adventure programs selected for this study were in demographic trouble. Westerns in particular, as well as some police and private eye shows, have a tendency to attract too many older people—from an advertiser's point of view. Producers of such programs have been asked to "fix" the demographic problem, but they admit they don't know how. In at least one case a younger character was introduced for the new season. Some producers feel that more "action" may be necessary, but that approach is limited by recent sanctions on violence.

Whether the new interest in demographics will eliminate some of the action-adventure series, change the nature and amount of action, or bring in new types of leading characters remains to be seen. Several producers said they thought all these things might happpen.

The youth audience

Most producers of action-adventure series did not believe children or young people viewed their programs in significant numbers. However, these programs reach audiences of such size that hundreds of thousands of viewers may not be significant in their terms. The producers of current westerns, for example, said, "The children's audience is almost nonexistent." "The children find the 'drama westerns' dull and nonrelevant."

Most producers of shows scheduled at 10 p.m. believed the late hour excluded children viewers. One producer acknowledged a large youth segment from preteenage through the teens. His police show was originally planned for a late hour, but the network asked if it could be tailored to fit an earlier time slot. This posed no problem for the producer if he excluded such adult themes as sex crimes. Another producer with young leading actors reported a significant audience of "kids aged 12 and under who are attracted by projection of older brother heroism."

Some producers of early evening action-adventure series noted that they were scheduled opposite such "small-children" shows as *Lassie*, *Disney* and *Wild Kingdom*. They assumed the child audience was lost to the competition. Only one show was designed to attract children.

Table 1 presents the Nielsen audience estimates, during two weeks in October 1970, of children in the 2-5, 6-11 and 12-17 age categories for each of the programs we studied. There is a substantial child audience for television action-adventure programs at all evening hours. For instance, in the combined 2-11 age categories, the audience is less than one million for only one program and in excess of six million for two others. A weeknight program at 10 p.m. attracted over two million in this age group; a weekend program in the same time period attracted more than three million.

Network departments

The networks' programming departments procure and supervise the production of entertainment programs. Programming department representatives review all scripts and script revisions and view films at various stages of completion. The programming department men exercise a certain amount of creative control over program content. ("The producer used to have authority," said one producer. "Now he has to have constant approval from the network. Obviously, you can't buck the network liaison man.") The main goal of this control is to assure the largest possible audience for the program in the proper demographic categories.

The broadcast standards departments are the network censors. Each department's primary function is to protect from public criticism and government sanction the network, its parent company, the affiliates and the associated executives. In entertainment programs this department watches for obscenity, profanity, sadism, and violence. It is also concerned with the way controversial issues are treated and with the accuracy of dramatized versions of contemporary problems. Broadcast standards editors review story outlines, scripts and script revisions, rough film cuts, and the final film.

Program preparation

The production of a network series begins with a program idea; the idea is gradually expanded in treatment as it passes various levels of network interest. The program may be scheduled and go into production on the basis only of a lengthy narrative description of the idea itself and the reputation of the producer and star. But that is rare. More commonly, a pilot program is developed. The pilot may be aired as a two-hour television movie in order to gauge initial audience reaction and to recoup some of the pilot's production cost. Some television series ideas, pilots, and story ideas are shown to test audiences by research firms. The results are fed back into the creative process.

The producing company which makes a film series is based in Los Angeles. Many are television units of the Hollywood feature films studios. Others operate by renting studio and office space from the big film studios and using studio crews and equipment. The networks also have facilities for their own production of television films.

Most program series have both an executive producer and a producer. The executive producer is most difficult to define. He is usually the person who put the original program idea into production. He may also be responsible for one other series and be working on new program development at the same time. Usually he maintains only general policy control over a program series. The day-to-day work necessary to get each episode on film is handled by the show's producer, who brings together story, cast and crew. He is responsible for the series continuity; in that function he may be aided by a story editor or associate producer (Cantor, 1969).

The writer is brought into the production from outside but may write several episodes for one series in a given year. His role was described by one writer:

> A writer is shown a pilot to learn about the lead players and format. The producer will discuss any changes that have been made since the pilot. There's also a printed pool sheet that describes the lead characters and their backgrounds. The writer talks with the producer about story areas he has in mind. Then he may proceed with a narrative synopsis (divided into teaser, three acts, and epilogue). Then there's a story conference. Next, the first draft, followed by another meeting, which may include deciding how to shorten the script to prescribed time. Then the second draft, after which the producer is entitled to a polish.

The producer was probably once a writer. He looks out for new story material or old stories adaptable to his program. Often he gives story lines to a writer to develop. Many writers come from radio, general circulation, magazines or pulp magazines, transfering their experience rather easily to TV.

The production company buys all rights to the script and can make any changes it thinks desirable or that are suggested by the network. If a script is changed beyond acceptability to the original writer, he may request that a review board of his union, the Television Writer's Guild, consider the matter. If they uphold his complaint, the script will carry his pseudonym which is registered for that purpose. Rarely, however, does a writer follow his script beyond the final polish to finished film. By then, he is working on something else.

The television film director is brought in by the production company to translate a script into a 48-minute film with one week of preparation and six days of shooting. Because of the time pressure, he must stay very close to the script and try not to cause any problems for the producer with the network programming or standards people. At the same time, the director has a creative responsibility for the audiovisual treatment of the script; his handling of action scenes may significantly affect audience perceptions.

Actors also may contribute to the content of a television series. The big stars in established series have enormous power. Production team members may serve at these actors' pleasure. Yet they apparently have very little direct influence over the nature of violence in the programs. At most, some may lay down a general policy of keeping within "good taste," while others occasionally ask for more physical scripts.

The final production step is actually called postproduction. All the elements of the film then come together. Both picture and sound may be adjusted at this stage to affect the nature of the action. Sometimes producer and network concerns about violence are accommodated in the postproduction process.

PROGRAM CREATORS' CONCEPT'S OF "VIOLENCE"

"Is it usual for you to think about violence when you are creating your programs?" The producers, writers, and directors who answered this question revealed that the term "violence" was not indigenous to their crafts, as were such other terms as "conflict" or "action beat." However, since the pressure has increased on the networks to tighten their control of violence in program content, the word has entered their professional vocabularies.

As to how often it enters their professional minds, testimony varied. One producer confessed, "I don't really know what the word by itself means. It isn't discussed much in the industry." Others said they had devoted much thought to the subject. At least one of them had written an article about it. Some had been quoted on the subject in trade papers. A number had participated in discussions of the subject at professional meetings. What seemed to keep violence in the thoughts of many was their resentment at being blamed as a major cause of violence in American society and their belief that censorship was imposing unreasonable restrictions on their creative expression. But concern about the social effects of their programs was also evinced by all respondents.

When the producer said he didn't really know what the word 'violence" meant, he was alluding to the difficulty of pinning the term down to a single definition without regard for context. Only three general definitions were volunteered by those interviewed. A writer said that violence was "injury or threat of injury." One producer called it "aggressive action taken with intent to harm some other human being." Another said, "It's premeditated cruelty to other human beings, no matter what form it takes; it's not necessarily physical."

In general, however, violence was viewed as a relative concept. As one producer stated, "It's not the act, but what the act means to the beholder." What is violence to one person, for example, may be heroism to another, he continued:

> There are fifteen or more kinds of violence—the police battling with the Chicago demonstrators. . .a man driving his wife insane without touching her. . .a fifteen-year-old Negro girl in Selma, Alabama, being spat upon by whites. . .and, of course, the calculated, sanctified violence that's going on in Vietnam.

Vietnam also lay behind another producer's question:

> Before we lay all the blame on TV, how do we explain the actual violence—the use of napalm, for instance—that we condone? If it's fact, seemingly it's *not* violent. If it's fiction, it *is* violent.

Two respondents observed that whether or not an action sequence on television was judged to be violent could depend on the style of presentation. The traditional barroom brawl of Western films, for example, could hardly be taken seriously because of its stylized "choreography" and the relish shown by its contestants. They were engaging, as one of the speakers described it, in "the happy mayhem of folk violence."

One producer refused to believe that every exhibition of physical force on the tube could be construed as violent:

> The use of physical force isn't the thing Pastore was talking about: Nobody considers *Family Affair* a violent show, and I don't think anybody called it violence on that show when Buffy beat up another kid.

In line with this producer's attitude, some dictionaries define violence as "an *unjust* or *unwarranted* exertion of force or power." Several respondents considered it warranted to defend oneself or society when attacked and to use force when enemies of society could not be apprehended by peaceful means.

Another distinction came from a producer-writer:

> For me, "violence" has a loaded, negative meaning. When writing scripts, I think in terms of "conflict" and avoid the kinds and treatments of conflict that are negative and objectionable.

Virtually all the program creators shared this attitude and practice. For example, they claimed to restrict their use of violence to the requirements of plot and character delineation, avoiding its introduction or purely sensational effect. They said they avoided the kinds of violence which their audiences would consider repugnant, which would leave child spectators emotionally disturbed, or which would instruct people in the manufacture and use of unusual weapons.

VIOLENCE IN HUMAN LIFE

"Why is there violence in your programs?"

One answer given by virtually every program creator was that "in limiting the expression of violence, we would be going against truth to life."

> Violence is inherent in human behavior. Anger which seeks an outlet has been present in the human condition from the Bible onward.

> Should we stop our eyes and ears and pretend that we live in a fantasy world where everything is nonconflicting?

Several respondents stressed that television did not introduce Americans to violence. As one put it, "The U.S. has always been a violent country; there's been a great deal of rage in this country at all times." One of these times—the 1870's in the west—was described by the producer of a western series as "the most violent period in the history of the nation." His ability to represent it as such was being hampered, he felt, by network restrictions.

Contemporary criminal violence and civil disturbances were mentioned by the producers of police and private eye shows. One declared, "There's not one-hundredth as much violence on TV as there is in the society." Besides entertaining people, he said, his new series aimed to wake them up to the malignancy of organized crime. In his opinion, "The critics who raise a furor about the portrayal of violence on television are playing ostrich, pretending that the cancer doesn't exist instead of trying to understand it."

If drama is to help man understand himself, it requires the freedom to explore the darker as well as the lighter sides of human nature. And the dark is not limited to criminal types. "All of us," a writer said, "are vulnerable to outbursts of violence or near violence. Even our so-called nonviolent youth must make a tremendous effort to remain nonviolent."

Will reason ever prevail over violence? This question, asked in some interviews, drew negative replies:

> I don't think man is basically built to live in peace and harmony. No animal can do this, either.

> Man's mind is connected to his stomach, his groin, and his fists. It does not float five feet above his body. Violence, therefore, cannot be eradicated.

Questioned about their attitudes towards the tenets of Ghandhi or Joan Baez, the respondents showed little faith in nonviolence as a total way of life. A producer said:

> I don't believe in sweet reasonableness in all situations. If the Jews were to give back land to the Arabs, the Arabs would still try to get them out altogether. If you want to survive in some cases, you're going to have to fight. For example, American labor wouldn't have gotten anywhere without violence.

Other comments were:

> If a man is shot at, should he not shoot back? The moral question is not the kind of violence used, but what provokes it.

> If people who break society's code resist the law, we have to use violence to suppress them. In doing so, we are in the mainstream of American morality, which is no different now in that respect than it's been for years.

> A person has to stand up for what seems to be in his best interests and those of humanity.

Another respondent answered:

> Our country still demands that you defend it and believes that there are times when you need to defend yourself. I don't think we should distort the truth. The government wants kids to think there are values worth fighting for, and that's basically what the leads on our show are doing. We'd do things differently if this were a Gandhi-like country. But since it's not, when our leads are threatened by violence, they should react the way our society works.

Most people in that society don't believe in knuckling under in all circumstances. "Isn't violence part of the national tradition?" asked a writer. "Don't we smile with patronizing pride when our kid has his first fight? Show me the father who doesn't ask, 'Who won?'"

Winning is important to people. To better their situation they must resort to aggression, trying to make it serve constructive rather than destructive ends. The writer making this point said he had been obliged to fight his way past objections to his becoming a writer. To advance from the city tenement of his childhood to his present home on Malibu Beach, he had had to cross the line between force and violence countless times.

"To get where I am," he said, "I've had to resort to intellectual violence, economic violence, and emotional violence."

One director said he had also known violence from personal experience with it:

I've lived with it in bunkhouses when going out on cattle drives. I've seen violence in saloons, brought on by drunkenness or jealously over a girl. I've kicked the shit out of other people.

This man would find the expulsion of violence from drama utterly false and incredible. Another respondent summed up the matter: "If television glosses over the fact that violence exists, it will lose its credibility."

VIOLENCE IN DRAMA

Whether or not a play aims to make illuminating statements about human life, its form is designed to stimulate and then relieve arousal in an audience. Thus it ties in with basic behavioral patterns of the human organism. That organism constantly tries to achieve a condition of favorable stability, one in which it feels fulfilled, secure, certain, and free of tension. Such stability, however, is constantly being upset by pressures on the organism from its internal drives (needs or wishes) or from its awareness of external circumstances which may satisfy or frustrate those drives. These pressures arouse the organism to a state of alert attention and responsive action, which is experienced as a feeling of stimulation and vitality. This is the state of "arousal" which drama aims to induce by artificial means.

In actuality, arousal is often a product of man's orientation drive. Like other higher organisms, man seeks to stay oriented to his environment, remaining alert to possible or actual sources of danger and opportunity. To a greater degree than that manifested by other animals, man has the curiosity and daring to explore his environment for these sources of opportunity and danger. While seeking security, he has come to deliberately expose himself to insecurity and to tolerate the consequent arousal—even to enjoy it, under certain conditions. He seems to welcome physical or mental uncertainty (as in risk-taking and problem-solving), if he feels his arousal will remain within tolerable limits and will be followed by relief and perhaps by some other gratifying reward ((Bertyne, 1960). Watching drama satisfies these needs and is also recognized to be a vicarious experience, stimulated by make-believe.

Three principal purposes seem to be served by watching drama. People become better oriented to the external world by watching the way the characters in the drama react to various situations. They experience arousal, perhaps as compensation for the relative lack of stimulation in one's ordinary life. And they experience relief from tension.

Drama serves the first of these purposes to the extent that its characters and situations resemble those of the actual world. The other two purposes are served by dramatic form. In conventional dramatic form, the characters are involved in some unstable situation—usually one of conflict, which develops to a crisis. Then a crucial encounter between the conflicting forces "resolves" the issue and establishes a new state of equilibrium.

The form of the drama is designed to stimulate in the audience an experience of excitation followed by relief, this experience being carried forward on a current of curiosity or expectation. The audience is aroused by the introduction of unusual situations to which it must adjust and by other novel elements like surprises and situation reversals which generate uncertainty by conflicting with the viewer's expectations. The conflict between protagonist and antagonist arouses the viewer by inducing an internal conflict between two incompatible response tendencies. The viewer may also be aroused by suspense—a state of conflict between his belief and his disbelief regarding the outcome of events. Plot complications serve to delay that outcome and magnify its urgency, thus building up tension in the viewer and frustrating its discharge. When sufficient pressure has been accumulated, a quick, decisive resolution of the conflict releases the pressure swiftly and strongly to provide maximum gratifying relief.

Such radical change, occurring suddenly, is an effective dramatic device, whether it is used to arouse by introducing uncertainty or to relieve arousal by a return to certainty. Strong contrast between characters is also effective, both because it maximizes the possibility of their dynamic interaction and because it makes the characters register on the spectator with maximum impact. The drama must capture the spectator's attention with stimuli strong enough to activate his responses; this can be done by exaggerating the characters and their actions and by stripping irrelevant details from them.

Another way to involve the spectator is to present characters and situations with which he can identify because the psychological drives which they exhibit are similar to his own. When they are, he is the more readily aroused by the characters' strivings, moved when they are frustrated, and relieved when they succeed. Sometimes the drives with which the spectator identifies are those which he himself has been unable to satisfy. If they are satisfied in the drama, the viewer's tensions about them may find a temporary, gratifying release.

Release from tension can occur whenever the imaginary world of the drama seems more reassuring than the spectator's own. Mass audiences seem to want such reassurance—especially the sense of order, justice, and security which they derive from a decisive, happy ending. More sophisticated audiences may be willing to forego the immediate reward of such an ending. They may prefer a more accurate delineation of life's complexities and frustrations. Sophisticated audiences can be reached through their concern with intellectual certainty and uncertainty. Mass audiences seem more responsive to sensory stimuli and to those which activate the more basic biological drives, such as those concerned with sexuality, aggression, and defense.

Despite this distinction, drama is not concerned with intellectual abstractions. It presents the errors and frailties of individual human beings under the influence of strong desires and emotions. These people usually exert force to gain their ends and at times rise to vehement self-expression. Drama, then, presents many opportunities for violent content. When "violent" is used to mean "marked by strong mental excitement; vehement; passionate," it is very close to what is often meant by "dramatic." And when "violent" means "characterized by extreme and sudden force," it is describing a technique often used to achieve dramatically striking effects.

Conflict, crisis, and resolution

When asked why there was violence in his programs, rarely did a respondent fail to point out that violence permeates the Bible, mythology, folk tales, and epics. Especially he would stress that violence has always been an ingredient of drama.

Said one producer:

> Violence and drama are almost synonymous. There is violence in *Oedipus*, *Medea*, *Kyd*, *Marlowe*, *Hamlet*, *Macbeth*, and, to jump to modern times, *Winterset*. True, you can do a play without violence — *The Death of a Salesman*, for example — but I defy anyone to produce twenty-six dramas a year without a good deal of violence.

Another producer reminded his academic interviewers that there were violent dramas on Public Television: "*The Andersonville Trial* was one of the most verbally violent plays I've ever witnessed, and in *Ethelred of England* there were six or seven deaths on the screen."

Why, the respondents were asked, is there such a close association between drama and violence? Almost all answered with references to "conflict," as in the following statements:

> The basis of drama is conflict — internal, external, emotional, and physical.

> Drama is conflict of interest and desire.

> Good drama is based on conflict which erupts in violent emotion.

Such opinions derive from the critic Ferdinand Brunetiere (1906), who wrote:

> Drama is a representation of the will of man in conflict with the mysterious powers or natural forces which limit and belittle us; it is one of us thrown living upon the stage, there to struggle against fatality, against social law, against one of his fellow-mortals, against himself, if need be, against the ambitions, the interests, the prejudices, the folly, the malevolence of those who surround him.

Another theorist, William Archer (1962), has objected that conflict is not common to all drama. He argued, for example, that Othello and Desdemona, rather than struggling against Iago, "are like people sliding down an ice-slope to an inevitable abyss." Archer submitted that "the essence of drama is crisis," that "a play is more or less rapidly developing crisis in destiny or circumstance." Nevertheless, he admitted that "many dramas—perhaps most—do, as a matter of fact, turn upon strife of one sort or another," and "for a sufficient account of the matter, we need go no further than the simple psychological observation that human nature loves a fight, whether it be with clubs or with swords, with tongues or with brains."

A conflict of tongues or brains does not lead necessarily to physical injury or destruction, as two of the respondents observed: "Drama is conflict, but conflict is not violence"; "Conflict is accompanied by suspense and tension, but not necessarily by violence."

Engri (1960), in a book on dramatic writing which connects conflict with destruction, says the protagonist must want something "so badly that he will destroy or be destroyed in the effort to attain his goal." He and the antagonist are "united to destroy each other." The book explains, however, that destruction does not necessarily mean the death of a person, but can be the "death" of some dominant quality of a character or of some human relationship. Thus Ibsen's *A Doll's House* ends with the destruction of Nora's docility and of her union with Helmer.

Conflict, then, involves destruction, but not necessarily biological destruction. It means a fight, but not necessarily with fists or guns. It opens the door to physical violence, but need not let it in.

What about crisis? According to a dictionary, a crisis is "a decisive or vitally important stage in the course of anything" or "the point in a play or story at which the hostile elements are most tensely opposed to each other." This, of all times, is the one most conducive to vehement dialogue and forceful action which will decide the outcome "once and for all." For an audience, this is the point of highest tension. A common dramatic technique is to work up the spectator's desires, his anticipation, his uncertainty until they generate a tremendous potential charge which demands release. His satisfaction at the end of the play often depends on the high "voltage" of this charge and the suddenness of its release.

The release is accomplished by the resolution of the conflict. To make this resolution swift and decisive, violent action is a convenient device. One respondent observed:

> Without some kind of violence, you couldn't resolve the show. Instead of being able to hold a protracted court trial, you need to end the show in a couple of minutes.

An actor said:

> There must ultimately be some kind of physical settlement. The audience doesn't *see* a jail sentence. It will feel emotionally cheated and complain, "Christ, what a dead ending that was!"

Physical violence, in other words, makes for a visual and exciting conclusion.

Mortal violence is sometimes convenient for tying up all loose ends. The conflict definitely is over if the opposing team ends up dead. And one doesn't have to take the edge off the ending by explaining what happened to so-and-so if he dies too. Nevertheless, all dramatic crises do not involve physical struggle or have lethal resolutions. Like conflict, crisis and resolution open the door to physical violence, but need not let it in.

VIOLENCE IN ACTION-ADVENTURE DRAMA

Some other reasons for violent content are suggested when one considers the specific kind of drama represented by most of the programs in question. This genre, which is usually referred to as "action-adventure drama," caters to two of the purposes of drama cited in the last section at the expense of the third. It clearly aims to promote both excitation and release from tension, but it accomplishes these aims by avoiding an accurate depiction of reality. As diversion for the mass audience, it avoids intellect-taxing analyses of life's complex phenomena. One producer said, "My function is not to teach, but to entertain." Or, in the words of a director: "I earn my living as an escape artist. I don't send you fellows to school; I get you out of school." Many respondents classified action-adventure programs as sub-species of "escape drama." Although they did not define escape drama in so many words, they would perhaps agree that it aims to help the average viewer escape temporarily from his own cares or boredom by absorbing him in a more gratifying imaginative experience.

Excitation and release from tension

The experience of escape drama is gratifying because it includes both excitation and relief from tension. It is interesting to note that the means used to promote one of these gratifications also promote the other. For example, escape programs give temporary relief to people's actual tensions by not reminding them of their own troubles. As a writer remarked:

> To see a father take out his frustrations on his innocent kid might teach us some valuable lesson about our own conduct, but it would be too close to home to make rewarding escapist fare. It would make the viewers squeamish, and they would tune it out.

A story editor reported:

> My father always says, "I don't want to see other people's troubles." And I do think people get disturbed by seeing a person in a hospital bed with a coronary. They'd much rather watch blazing guns; then they know it's unreal.

The viewer escapes from the world of his own tensions into a world of tension which is artifically induced, whether by blazing guns or other means. This imaginative world is different from his own and provides more latitude for exciting situations. One of the subject programs was set during the American Revolution and four others in the American West of the nineteenth century. Another featured "impossible" missions in Graustarkian environments. A series in preparation at the time of the interviews introduced a leading character with regenerative blood and immunity to disease and decay. A police show planned to open with "some bizarre event and the reaction to that event"—for example, "A priest enters a confessional; we see the flash of an ice pick, then the priest's dead body." Various series (so their writers reported) try to use as their locales "far-out places like Hong Kong." For the final shootout, said one writer, "you look for a preferably unusual environment—a basement full of machinery or whatever."

In their real lives, people experience a certain amount of tension from their inability to gratify certain drives or wishes. By identifying with the characters and milieus of escape drama, they can vicariously assume roles otherwise denied them. Watching *Mannix*, as a writer pointed out, the viewer can face danger bravely, assert himself boldly and decisively, race his car through the big city, be the playboy bachelor, and frequent unique locales. "In *Gunsmoke*," claimed a director, "the viewer hopes he can behave as Matt does." This may be, whether one agrees with the producer who viewed Matt Dillon as "the greatest gun in the West" or admires other qualities in him described by the aforesaid director:

> Matt Dillon, as played by Jim Arness, has quiet strength, a Christlike quality — poise, dignity, and grace in the face of total disaster. He's an ox-like man, but tender and chivalrous in his dealings with women. He satisfies the woman who says, "Hold me firm, but treat me gentle."

Generalizing about the action-adventure hero, a producer explained:

> He must succeed againt all the evil in the world. He does it nobly and cleanly, like a quarterback in a football game. People enjoy their vicarious involvement in the game and love to identify with someone they respect.

The deeds of such heroes help to relax the tensions of their viewers by reassuring them, as one respondent said, that "evil will be conquered by good." Most of the heroes of these programs are protectors of society and champions of the underdog. One producer described the western as "a morality, concerned with helping the underdog and people in trouble." There are also champions in nonwesterns; for example, the leads in *Mod Squad* were described as "young people's watchdogs." And every law enforcement series reassures. As one respondent said of *Gunsmoke:* "Consider the fifty million people a week who watch a dedicated, intelligent Dillon risking his life to protect society, and you'll have to conclude that more good is done than evil." That Dillon risks his life and comes through unharmed is also reassuring. As a writer explained: "I identify with the hero who goes through danger and survives —if *he does*, maybe I will."

Several respondents stated that release of tension also could result from situations in which the hero is goaded to the point where he erupts: "The western is a fairy tale of everyman getting back at whatever's bugged him all these years. It's a release." One of the new programs was going to specialize in providing this kind of release:

> Our guy should appeal to the average "little man" who bears resentments against the person who got ahead of him in the line or beat him to the seat in the bus. The more our guy is pushed, the more the audience should identify; and then, at one point, our guy will explode, try to break out. The little guy likes violence of this kind because he so seldom reacts effectively against the sources of his own irritations.

In action-adventure drama, the contrast between good and evil is very pronounced. To establish the hero's nobility, there must be evil of a high degree for him to overcome. To establish his braveness, there must be danger of a high degree emanating from the source of evil. The greater the danger that the hero weathers, the more reassurance the story gives the viewer that goodness can prevail and survive. The greater the aggression, the more chance (presumably) for the viewer to vicariously vent his own aggressive urges. The more pronounced the extinction of evil, the more assurance for the viewer that these aggressive tendencies which he fears in others and mistrusts in himself have been exorcised. These are prevalent assumptions within the industry.

Such assumptions would seemingly account for the black-and-white treatment of many of the subject programs. According to one of the interviewed writers, a principal reason why the network canceled *Cimarron Strip* was that "the hero was not all good and the villains were not all bad." The writer also stated:

> In one of my scripts, I had a character of some complexity; you loved him, but knew he'd destroy himself. A network executive didn't like this. He telegraphed: "Black heavy, lead kills"—which meant: "Make the villain all bad and have the hero kill him to give the audience a sense of fulfillment."

The violence of adventurous action

Besides polarizing good and evil, action-adventure programs exhibit other evidences of simplistic treatment. The typical program is boldly drawn for easy, forceful comprehension. It tends to show exaggerated people in exaggerated situations. "Each scene," said a writer,"should produce black-and-white excitement, be easily perceivable, use simplified language, hit things on the nose." Observing that this kind of drama is viewed with only partial attention, a producer stated that its style "has to be simpler, less involved, more peaceful. It cannot be subtle." A story editor said that "In a Western, people want a simple, straightforward action story with a hard-driving motor." (The motor, he explained, was conflict.) A writer declared that "The average person comes home at night and, if given a choice between serious drama and escapist fare, he'll take the latter for diversion that won't require him to think too hard.''

In the simplistic formula of action-adventure drama, there is little room for ambivalence and qualification. According to a director, *Then Came Bronson* failed to satisfy sufficient viewers because "every show ended in theory and debate." The successful action-adventure hero knows what he is supposed to do and does it. He leads his audience into a world of simple feeling and direct emotion, away from the complexities of civilization. He leads away from confused, mind-tensing intellectual problems, which do not attract large audiences. "The clash of ideas category of drama won't hold an audience long." This statement by a producer calls to mind the line delivered by the exasperated Manager in Pirandello's play, *Six Characters in Search of an Author:* "You've got to understand that you can't go on arguing at your own pleasure. Drama is action, sir, action and not confounded philosophy."

As one of the terms in the title "action-adventure drama," the meaning of "action" is of interest. In dramatic production it has various connotations. Sometimes it means what one of the writers called "plot action—things happen; one thing triggers another." In some plays, the action may consist of changes of character or of understanding which are accomplished primarily through dialogue. In the programs we studied, however, action can mean the opposite of dialogue:

> To be or not to be. . .should I or shouldn't I? To have a person wrestle with a problem before acting may be objected to by the network executive because it slows down the action. The writer has to give the person time to do this mental wrestling, but he's also expected to keep the show moving. The people running the networks have found out that action shows — with less talk — are what people want to see.

The producer of one highly rated series said he can get away with what he calls "soul scenes":

> We do have a quotient of interior soul-searching materials. The network used to ask, "Do you think they'll stay through all that talk?" The network people are against polemics that take pages of dialogue, but they let us do them because they're working.

Despite this exception, there was a preponderance in the subject programs of almost reflexive action, of action accomplished without the amount of prior deliberation which would prevent a rapid succession of deeds. Such a succession is what one writer meant by action. "It comes," he explained, "from the speed with which your story progresses, from the number of incidents which take place and the speed with which they happen." This is probably what one of the producers meant when he described his show as "action-filled." An action-adventure program is given to deeds rather than deliberation and to physical rather than sedentary pursuits. Such a program features men of action. As a writer observed, "Producers are afraid of male stars wearing lace pants, so if it's a cerebral story, it must be presented in action terms."

There are two implications in this quotation. One is in the reference to "cerebral." The viewer cannot see cerebral processes—yet seeing is important for. as Spottiswoode (1957) observes. film "is first and foremost a visual medium." The raw material of film "is not the mental world of concepts and beliefs. But because these are the mainsprings of human action, the filmmaker must search for the physical things and events in which this inner life manifests itself." So cerebral action must be converted into physical action.

The second implication—suggested by the writer's reference to "lace pants"—is that, for the male leads in such shows, the physical action must be broad and forceful—hard-driving, not softened by "effeminate" sentiment.

"Hard" and "soft" were words used by some respondents to distinguish two contrasting types of dramatic stories. A producer-writer said he had authored the first soft story for telev;sion, about two parents getting divorced and their son's consequent devastation. In a soft piece, he explained, the emphasis is on feeling, and character relationships count over plot. A "hard" piece is an action piece which stresses situation rather than characterization and sentiment.

Action-adventure programs incline toward the hard category. This was exemplified by one writer's comments on the kind of scripts she'd been allowed to write:

> There's no real feeling, as between man and woman — and no real feeling connected with violence. We don't see the grief that goes with the loss. There's no reaction on the part of the person who did it — in *Mannix*, for instance. No one throws up. There's no room to spend a tear. They think they can't sell beer to people who cry.

Justification for the lack of feeling came from the producer of a western series during a discussion of nonviolent youth. The "peace children's" ideal of compassion was not applicable, he said, in the survival situations on his show:

> In one show, the rancher next door runs out of water. Is our guy obligated to share his if there's not enough for two? In a Western, one has the latitude to say, "No." Our guy first has to take care of himself. In a modern drama, the "no" man would have to be a heavy. In the Western, he can be a hero. *He's* not hurting the other guy, because the other guy didn't have water to begin with.

The action-adventure program also exhibits the second characteristic of hard stories—emphasizing situation more than character. A team of writers explained:

> We haven't been permitted in five years to do a real character. What you end up with, therefore, are pseudocharacters. You can't make them grow or change— particularly the regulars on the series—and you can't alter their relationship to the other regulars on the show. And if you create a character in a one-time spot, he may run away with the show and dim the lustre of the principals. Anyway, by the time you involve all of the characters and get the plot going, there's no time left for slowly building a characterization. The result is apt to be an hour's worth of running and jumping.

Situation, the writers explained, is a predicament which does not depend on character relationships. Another respondent furnished an example: "There's a fight for the gold. The marshal has to take the wounded man back for medical aid, but meanwhile the bad guys are escaping." In drama—especially action-adventure drama—a situation is frequently a predicament in the sense emphasized by dictionaries: "especially, an unpleasant, unfortunate, or trying position, condition, or situation."

To describe a dramatically effective situation, a word used frequently in the interviews was "jeopardy." Defined by a dictionary as "hazard or risk of loss or harm; peril; danger," jeopardy obviously belongs in an action-adventure story—"adventure" being "a hazardous enterprise; an undertaking of uncertain outcome." It is jeopardy to the hero, to the community he protects, to the underdog he champions, or to their property, which normally serves as the principal means for creating dramatic tension.

This jeopardy or peril need not be physical. Respondents cited, for example, the threat to a Mafia leader of losing the love of the person from whom he needs love most, or the threat to a politician of exposure for a shady act. Usually, however, the peril *is* physical. As a producer explained, "A program which is physically exciting will succeed; gentler programs in the action-adventure category have failed." Said a writer, "Physical danger is the easiest to recognize and is preferred by men viewers."

Some respondents noted that, although physical, the jeopardy need not be the result of human aggression. To support this, they cited a downhill race between two freight wagons or men swirling in water in a tunnel. In these examples physical injury or the threat thereof is caused by human agents. Usually, however, the agents *are* human. One of the interviewed writers explained that there are four possible areas of conflict for writers to treat:

Man against nature. "This is usually too expensive for TV."
Man against God. "Too intellectual for TV."
Man against himself. "Too psychological, and doesn't leave enough room for action."
Man against man. "This is what you usually end up with."

When men are in conflict and when physical jeopardy is needed to produce excitement, the result is violence or the threat of violence.

Several respondents spoke about the threat of violence. Sometimes they wanted to point out that, although the possibility of violence might exist in one of their programs, the violence never actually occurred. One example was an episode at an airport, where one local gangster was going to meet another arriving by helicopter, and FBI men aimed to arrest them. Much of the program action consisted of preparation for the arrest: clearing airport patrons off an escalator in the terminal and replacing them with FBI men, who intended to make their capture there without a struggle. In this case, the producer explained, "The threat of violence can be more exciting than the violence itself." Another respondent observed, "We are more terrified by anticipation than by what we actually see." One of the great creators of dramatic tension is suspense. Cocking the weapon, so to speak, charges up excitement; pulling the trigger discharges it.

Other respondents pointed out that suspenseful action did not necessarily have to be resolved by violence. Among them was the producer who explained, "Action can be movement—a chase, whether resolved by a gunfight or not, or the theft of the Liberty Bell." But he added, "We do have to deal with the heavy; we can't resolve everything nonphysically in an action show." This observation agrees with a writer's comment about the hero's dealings with the heavy: "If he doesn't beat the hell out of him, I want my money back!"

Of the various kinds of peril, the most exciting is mortal jeopardy. Life is the most precious possession a hero has to risk. For the audience, this risk stimulates the greatest fear and anxiety. It is also the strongest evidence of the hero's commitment to achieving or defending whatever he values. That mortal jeopardy has popular appeal was claimed by a story editor. He had begun his career by writing for pulp magazines. During that apprenticeship:

> I found that there were two areas where material was endless and the audience was constant: One of these was police stories. The police carried guns. Mortal jeopardy was what interested people most. The other area was Western stories. Here also, a man could wear a gun.

Another indication of the presumed appeal of mortal jeopardy comes from one of the guidelines which one producer said was followed by the program development section of the network to which he furnished programs. This guideline stipulated that a protagonist should hold a job which included power over life and death. This would explain the prevalence on television of policemen (including western lawmen), doctors, criminal lawyers, and members or allies of the armed services.

Virtually all the producers interviewed said they rejected violence unless it was motivated by plot or character. When this policy was mentioned to one of the writers, she responded: "That's like saying, 'I never put cotton in a wagon that's not prepared for cotton — but I never use anything but a cotton wagon.'" The milieus chosen for action-adventure programs, in other words, are those where violence can logically occur. The roles chosen for the most active program characters are those which may appropriately engage in violent action. As heavies, they initiate the violence; as heroes, they are expected to suppress the violence, by violent means if necessary.

"We aim to avoid unmotivated killing or injury," said one producer, "But what is motivated and what is not?" This question can set one speculating that the most extreme kinds of violence can be motivated if one premises a sufficiently lawless situation or a sufficiently ruthless heavy.

Violent actions result from violent premises. A "premise" carries the meaning of its Latin antecedent, *pre-missus:* "something set forth beforehand." As such, it determines what may logically follow. In drama, it sets up promises which the dramatist must keep. As two respondents explained:

> There is an old adage that when you bring a gun on stage you must fire it. Violence depends on the premises you start with, the implications of which you must fulfill.

> You can't disappoint the dramatic expectations of the audience. Introduce a bomb, and they expect it to go off. As an end to certain dramatic situations, if the good guy simply puts handcuffs on the bad guy and says, "I'll see you in court," the audience will feel dramatically cheated.

Another respondent stated, "The degree of violence at the end of the script must be proportionate to the amount of provocation or previous harrassment." A strong hero can be a premise for particularly pugnacious heavies. A producer with Matt Dillon in mind declared, "A man who slaps another man is not a suitable antagonist for the greatest gun in the West."

Trouble is in store for the action-adventure series which fails to fulfill the expectations it creates. A director stated:

> *Bronson* failed because it promised rough stuff but didn't deliver it. People who watched it have asked me, "What's wrong with this guy? He never lets the bastard have it and he never lays anybody."

If a program purports to represent a given genre, it must conform to the premises—live up to the promises—of that genre. A writer explained, "In a western, audiences expect big virile men in conflict." According to an actor, "The audience generally tunes in westerns for the excitement and escape of the Old West, of good guys taking care of bad guys." A producer said, "The private-eye show is violence-prone because the principal is a loner, outside the law, with nothing to protect him except his own wit and strength." Classifying most television dramatic series as melodrama, another respondent stated, "The audience enjoys seeing the bully get beat; the hero has to get away from his adversaries; hence violence is necessary to the plot." Less violence, however, may be expected from some program types than others. "On *Ironside*," said a person associated with that series, "violence is limited because it's an intellectual deduction show. If I were doing *Felony Squad*, I might treat it differently."

The treatment of violence may vary from series to series. The amount and degree of violence may also vary from series to series, and from program to program within a given series. But there is bound to be violence of some sort when series are premised, as the subject series are, on such conditions as war, social upheavals, crime, and the untamed frontiers. It seems incontestable that these conditions are intentionally selected because they permit physical jeopardy—jeopardy which is the result of violence and which may lead to more violence to satisfy the dramatic needs of climax or crisis and swift resolution.

The excitement of danger and the reassurance which comes when the danger is allayed are the principal means by which the action-adventure program serves its audience. Eliminating the danger would destroy the action-adventure genre altogether. Disassociating that danger from violence, threatened and actual, would so emasculate the genre as to make it no longer functional.

VIOLENCE TO ATTRACT THE MASS AUDIENCE

> Filmmaking for television is a business of merchandising and profit making. We are manufacturing a product and we want it to attract the largest possible audience, short of prostitution.

That statement by a producer raises the question: "How important is violent program content as a means to attract that largest possible audience?"

A few respondents thought the successful program needed to restrict its violence and provide other appeals. The viewers of one western did not approve of too much violence: "The public protested four years ago when *Bonanza* was hardened at the request of a sponsor. The mail now approves of keeping it sweet." In consequence, the producer of another western series reported that *Bonanza* was sometimes called "the *One Man's Family* of TV." He went on to point out, however, that "action gunplay Westerns" have not lasted on television. *Wyatt Earp* and *Have Gun Will Travel*, he said, got tiresome: "Everyone over the age of ten has seen all the shootouts he needs."

The same producer said that his series puts its audience into identifiable human situations, so that they felt "this could be them." The series does something with its people "so you care what is happening to them." For example:

> A gunfighter isn't applicable to many people; he's something they're living with every day. In one of our scripts, the daughter of a successful businessman falls in love with a wild young cowboy and tries to convert him to the image of her father. But he is incapable of fitting this straightjacket and assuming a businessman's values. The story is the working out of this dilemma.

Programs in the series do include the threat of violence and use violent climaxes. But the producers spoke against random violence, advised that violence alone could not win an audience, and recommended that it be saved for important events.

Most of the respondents were more positive about the appeal of violence to the mass audience. One producer stated:

> The audience wants and approves of violence under certain conditions. For instance, in *Bad Day at Black Rock*, Spencer Tracy takes punishment from a guy, and takes it and takes it — and all the audience is with him when he finally gives

the guy a judo chop. What the audience wants we try to give, in a medium where you must attract at least fifteen million, and ten million is a failure.

According to another producer, violent content serves a public need:

> Psychologists would say that, if we didn't give people violence on TV, they would seek it elsewhere. These action shows, they say, fulfill a need. If TV does not provide escape, the audience will find escape elsewhere.

Expressing a similar opinion, a director stated:

> People need to watch a certain amount of aggressive action to get release and escape. Note that, now violence has been soft-pedaled in television drama, it has come out more strongly in films for theatre showing.

Other respondents noted the drawing power of such films as *The Wild Bunch, Our Man Flint,* and *Bonnie and Clyde.* But nonviolent films can also draw large audiences, as a producer pointed out:

> I saw *Easy Rider* and despised most of it, while recognizing that it reflects the concerns of young people. The violence at the end is ghastly in a visually disturbing way. Rednecked bigots blow the long-haired kids off their motorcycle, which turns over and over and explodes. This was last year's box office hit— along with *Love Bug,* which is diametrically opposed in nature.

The audience for violent movies presumably coincides to some degree with the fans of action-adventure television programs. According to several respondents, these fans expect violence from the programs and, if their expectations are not satisfied, will turn away from them. One person recalled that "when Desi Arnaz followed instructions to take the violence out of *The Untouchables,* the ratings slipped and they had to put the violence back in." A producer whose police show attracted forty million said, "If the show changed to a non-action show, it would begin to fail; so violent action is necessary." Another producer stated flatly, "Water down the action and you don't get an audience." "Action," to this producer, meant violent action.

One writer contended that networks view violence as a saleable commodity. On one hand, he said, the networks are extremely sensitive to criticism, but, "although the networks will draw in when criticized, they'll expand when you let them. They'll reach for violence because of its economic good. In three years or less, we'll be back to the amount of violence in *The Untouchables.*" One of this writer's recent scripts, he said, was conceived as a "mental chess game":

> A British officer poses as a potential defector in order to capture Lafayette. Move and countermove make this a cerebral game with a lot of suspense. But it's hard to convince some people that suspense, confrontation, and conflict of interest are enough to give you good drama. I was told, "Here's a good place where they can jump each other." So they've added a scene where Lafayette fights with the British officer and one of them falls in the river. They can do that, since their company owns the material outright.

This writer thought that violent programs were an inevitable consequence of the commercial broadcasting system:

> We aren't going to get rid of violence until we get rid of advertisers. The advertiser wants something exciting with which to get the audience. Violence equals excitement equals ratings. As the population has grown, the number of TV viewers has not increased proportionately, so 'tougher stories' is the word today.

But two other writers reported that producers had never asked them to make their scripts more violent. And according to one producer, company ownership of scripts sometimes gave him a chance to moderate by rewriting whatever excessive violence a writer might have included in his script.

Most of the producers and writers believed along with the networks, that violence is a saleable commodity in both the domestic and the foreign market. A number of respondents mentioned the reaction to American television programs in foreign countries, where their distribution is syndicated by the networks. One producer said his series was hearing complaints from abroad: "Europeans have begun to feel that the programs have become Pablum." A writer said, "People in England, France, Spain, Denmark, and Italy like violence in their shows and think that ours are dull."

THE VISUALIZATION OF VIOLENCE

Violence has so far been considered mainly a function of the script. But the script is not the sole determinant of violence in the finished program. What the viewer sees is not the script, but an arrangement of camera shots which record selected aspects of a performance. Although the script serves as a basic guide for the final product, it is subject to interpretation by the editor who puts the shots together and by the director who supervises the staging and the shooting.

This study sought to learn how the director and editor influence the viewer's impression of violence through their visualization of it. What techniques do they use for picturing violence? How much latitude do they have to make something seem more violent than was contemplated by the script?

The director's latitude

The director on set is in control. He is God. The producer cannot interfere—although he can make changes by editing.

This was the most outspoken statement of the director's autonomy. It came from a prominent producer who has been in the business for many years. Another producer thought that the director should be given creative freedom within certain limits. Most of the producers stated, however, that the director had very little latitude regarding his depiction of violence.

"The director is tightly bound to the script," they said, or: "It's the company's picture," or: "The director is only hired for a given show and can be fired. . . He is a visitor for four or five shows and wants to come back, so he doesn't want to cross us."

Several respondents mentioned that a good director will shoot protection shots which can be substituted during editing for any shots that are objected to as excessively violent. If a direct view of a violent action is judged to be objectionable, the protection shot can suggest that same action by indiret means. If a shot which covers the violent action is criticized for being too long, the protection shots will be cut-ins (close shots of certain details of the action) or cut-aways (shots of corollary subjects, bystanders, or other aspects of the immediate environment). By inserting such shots, the film footage covering the main action can be shortened without apparent jumps in its continuity.

Not all directors, however, will shoot protection shots without being asked to. According to one producer, "Some directors are more inclined to stressing violence than others. Some directors will protract fights, or dwell on a dying man's eyes, or pump blood out of a wound. In this respect we have to watch. . ." He named one of the directors interviewed for this study. During his interview, that director was zealous to maintain his creative independence:

> I'm directing a whodunit, which starts in the teaser with the murder of a beautiful 25-year-old woman in her apartment. How I choose to show her murder, that's my job, that's why I'm hired. I feel restricted by the way the show's producers and the network executives come to me with their interpretations of how it should be done. They talk around it, hint at it. Finally they say, "Shoot it your way, but better make a protection shot of her hand on the phone. Have it clench and relax; then leave some time for the audience to hear the dial tone." I never do a protection shot unless it's requested, or unless I consider the indirect way more effective for telling the story. I wish it would stop with my decision and that my judgment would be trusted.

This plea was one the researchers had heard before; it had come from some of the writers and producers. All three—writers, producers, and directors—want maximum creative freedom, yet are subject to having their work altered by others. As a writer's script may be altered by a rewrite man, a director's visual treatment may be altered in the cutting room. To modify the violence in it, however, the editors must have alternative material to substitute for an objectionable length of footage. One director told us his method of preventing such modifications: "I may shoot something in such a way that they have only one choice—which isn't good, because that way I'm working negatively."

A script may suggest the action only in rather general terms, leaving the director to work out the details. In one series, demolitions were set off rather frequently. The producer had cautioned the director about these demolitions: "I want it exciting and visual, but our kids aren't there to kill people—a couple of extras, maybe, but not a lot of bodies going up into the air." (The expendability of extras figured in a theory which the producer explained as follows: "The impression of violence depends on the way it's handled. It will seem violent if you roll a body into camera with open mouth and eyes, but shoot a few extras and nobody cares.")

When the director is not warned, he may take liberties with the script. These may alter the impression about violence which the producer is trying to create. The producer of another series explained that he tried intentionally to make violence look ugly. Hence, in one script, a victim was supposed to be shot three times and to twist and turn as he fell. The three shots (needed to establish that the assassin killed out of hatred) were produced by the director as prescribed, but:

> The twists and turns were eliminated by the director because he didn't think they looked right and hadn't been briefed on the reason for them.

A director may also influence the impression of violence by amplifying what the script prescribes. Mindful of this possibility, a team of writers stated:

> We have just written a script in which a man gets knocked out. One blow is specified in the script. Will the director, we wonder, turn it into a fight?

Some directors will go further than others in depicting the effects of violence. They may have "corpses" keep their eyes open, or use makeup to stimulate blood and mutilation. (One producer remarked that makeup artists who customarily worked on feature films had to be restrained when they were assigned to work in the more heavily censored television medium.)

Directors can regulate how much a violent subject is emphasized. Greater emphasis can be obtained by shooting the subject so that it fills the frame and is isolated from competing objects of attention. Distance, on the other hand, can weaken the violent impression. One producer said a kidnapping had been made acceptable to the censor by shooting it from so far away that "one could merely perceive that some kind of struggle was going on."

How much stress a director places on a violent subject can depend on what he perceives to be the point of the action at a given moment. For example, after explaining the use of squibs and blood sacs to simulate gunshot wounds, a director explained his camera treatment of such a wound in a feature film he had recently completed:

> There is one squib when a guy is shot in the leg, but we see no blood spattering in closeup. When he falls in the water, panchromatic blood colors the water, but we don't make a study of it because that isn't the story at that moment; the story is the struggle to get out of the water.

The same director mentioned other ways of emphasizing violent action. One was a method used by actors to emphasize a punch:

> People wouldn't see a real punch, it happens so fast. So you draw hand way back before the punch—what John Wayne calls "picking cans off the shelf."

The director admired Japanese director Kurasawa's technique for pointing up a combat with samurai swords:

First, the suspense of Hayakawa and his opponent, poised with lofted swords. . .then yell! strike!! Then high-speed camerawork to slow the fight down.

Another writer mentioned slow motion and described its use in a sequence on *Ironside:*

Mark is advising a person not to try to escape in a car from the authorities. This scene is intercut with slow-motion pictures of a thief who, at that moment, is running away from the cops and getting shot down. There is dramatic irony in the intercutting, and the slow motion increases violence by intensifying the falling thief's grimace.

Does slow motion intensify or moderate the impression of violence? One interviewee said that the networks were encouraging producers to self-censor scenes "either by minimizing the violence in them or, recently, by shooting them in slow motion like a ballet, as if they weren't really happening. But in at least one censor's opinion, the scene becomes more violent by stretching it out."

A director can suggest lethal action in various ways without actually showing it. The producer whose leads to blow up a camp said that the filmed result of the detonation "is a visual impression of destruction, but in terms of fire, people running with buckets, horses rearing, and that sort of thing." A common method of avoiding showing the actual killing is to show the weapon and the victim in separate shots. Thus, "A priest enters a confessional. We see the flash of an ice-pick, then the priest's dead body."

A somewhat overworked means of avoiding showing the death agony is to frame only the victim's hand. Another solution is to cut away just before the act of killing. This does not necessarily minimize the violence, however, as one producer pointed out: "To show a man pointing a gun at his own head, then cut away and hear an explosion, is violent."

Another producer described how one can cut away to a substitute action which conveys an impression of violence by association:

A soldier for the Mafia, who's to be killed for fouling up, is left facing his executioner's tommy gun. He cries out a last appeal to his boss, who is walking away towards an elevator door. The elevator doors close as the boss leaves the scene. Then we cut to a silhouette target on a firing range. It's splattered suddenly with bullets. The view widens to show a military instructor with his trainees.

The violent sequence may be performed off camera altogether. This, as some of the interviewees noted, may intensify rather than diminish the violent impression:

In *My Name is Manuelete*, heavies beat a boy behind the drawn curtain of an open window. Blow. . ."No, I didn't tell them anything". . .Two more blows. Then the boy rushes out and the Mod Squad arrives. This off-scene treatment is probably more disturbing than a view of the actual beating.

So thought a writer. Another example came from a censor:

> In another script, a woman was to be pulled by her hair across a room and then thrown roughly onto the floor. When I disapproved of this on camera, the director did it behind some file cabinets, and the public thought that the girl was raped.

The caution of network censors may backfire when they prohibit violent action from being shown directly on camera. So it would appear, at least, to judge from a sequence screened for the researchers courtesy of the producers of a private-eye show. In one scene, the private-eye drops in at a disreputable night club to question the proprietor. He crosses the public room, where a stripper is performing to the beat of insinuating music in light which changes color as gelatines revolve in front of a spotlight. He enters the proprietor's office. On the inside wall, there is a window through which the proprietor can observe the public room. In that office, the private-eye is beaten up by two of the proprietor's hired thugs.

According to the producers, the network would not let that beating be shown on camera:

> What they approved instead was a shoddy, fierce climax of intercutting between shadows of the beating projected on a wall, the proprietor looking through his window at the stripper, the stripper's act under the changing colored lights, and closeups of the revolving color wheel—all of this accompanied by the crescendo of a tom-tom drum, as the camera shots get closer and come more quickly, building up to a more violent result than what they cut out.

When the sequence was projected for them, the researchers agreed that it was indeed a violent result.

Staging, camera, and editing technique

The montage just described demonstrates how subject matter can be reinforced by staging, camera, and editing techniques to create an impression of violence. Indeed, such techniques can create an impression of violence whether the subject depicted is inherently violent or not. If the reader needs to be convinced, he has only to watch the montage which, at the time of this report, was used with the opening titles of one of the subject programs, *Hawaii Five-O*. In that montage, no one is injured, nothing is damaged, yet the impression created is one of violent excitement. And the techniques used to create that excitement are frequently the same as those used in the private-eye beating sequence.

No attempt will be made here to present an exhaustive inventory and analysis of these techniques. Some techniques must be mentioned, however, as examples. The respondents did not mention these techniques. The researchers observed them by watching their programs. These included:

Swift camera or subject movement to create urgency or increase the force of an action.

The sudden appearance of a totally different subject on the screen, arousing the viewer through his need to adjust to it unexpectedly.

Radical changes in the screen size of a subject, effected, for example, by rapid movement towards a wide-angle lens, which may be located close to the floor or ground. Also effected by camera zooms.

Separation of antithetical elements into different, alternated shots, to emphasize their disjunction or disagreement.

Impelling the subject towards the viewer or the viewer towards the subject to produce maximum participation of the viewer in the action.

The creation of disequilibrium or uncertainty by such devices as flashing lights, wavering focus, lurching camera, and tilted or revolving camera angle.

Obtaining a crescendo of excitement through progressively closer shots and accelerated cutting between shots.

Repetition of a strong-weak-strong-weak insistent effect, such as made by a police car's flasher.

Giving special emphasis to a sequence by some unique, contrasting treatment such as slow motion or the effect of jerky stop motion, created by the periodic elimination of film frames.

Sensory stimuli so strong and so freed from competing stimuli that they dominate one's attention completely.

Any sharp contrast and sudden change—in lighting, color, or any other medium.

OTHER VIOLENCE INPUTS

Violent impressions can also be augmented by the orchestration of sound. For example, the effect of the private-eye beating sequence owed much to the acoustical quality and crescendo of the tom-tom drum. Only one of the interviewees, a censor, mentioned the use of sound to intensify violence:

Either the original editor or someone else from this office views the first trial at the lab, without commercials, but after music and sound have been added. We do this because a sound like squealing tires can increase the violence, or a music sting may need to be superimposed on top of a too horrendous scream.

Screams, squeals, shrieks, shots, and sirens all have the power to excite the senses violently and directly, almost without reference to the story situation which provokes them. So also with blasts and booms!

A writer who considered action-adventure drama to be an obviously synthetic—rather than realistic—form hoped that censors would allow violent sounds to be orchestrated for dramatic effectiveness. "For example," he explained, "the audience enjoys the sound, the explosiveness of five shots instead of just the one a censor may allow. For theatrical effect, for dramatic release, the censor's "just one shot" is dysfunctional."

Influence of the leading performers

Another question asked by the interviewers was, "How much influence on the degree of violence is exerted by the leading performers?" The one actor interviewed did not think that violent action was necessary to bolster his image. But some of the producers and writers had different experiences with other actors:

> (P_____) has told me, "It's too talky. I want to do something." An actor is apt to think, "The success of the show is due to the changes I made in the script. I threw out all the bad lines. And after all, they're tuning in to see me." If the star has an image of himself, he will try to force the image into the script. There's one actor I know with a "young Errol Flynn" image. His suggestions gave a script more violence and more sex. "It will sell better," he said, "and I could get into that scene."

(A few producers have remarked that the tempering of violent action by the networks was reducing the employment of stuntmen. Stump (1970) reports that the Stuntmens Association (SAMP-TV) has hired psychiatrists and behavioral psychologists "to help plead its case.")

Influence of the protagonist

The only example of influence by a protagonist concerns *Gunsmoke*. Some episodes do not feature and sometimes do not include the principal male character. The researchers were told that "More violence can occur in the 'big Jim shows,' in which Jim Arness, playing Matt Dillon, is prominent. This is because Matt functions as a lawman who deals in violence."

Topping the previous episode

There is a tenet in show business that material must be progressively stronger in effect in order to maintain the viewer's interest. Relating this tenet to violence, an interviewee observed:

> When the second moon walk was televised, nobody watched. A similar problem confronted the producers of *The Untouchables*. "Last week you killed

three men; what are you going to do this week?" So the producers began to
lean more heavily on the violence.

Program length

Action shows are designed to fit either thirty- or ninety-minute time
slots. Which of these lengths is more conducive to violent content?
Most replies to this question were like the following:

> In a one-and-a-half-hour show you need less violence than in a half-hour one.
> You have more opportunity to work with mystery elements, suspense, and in-
> triguing characters.
> _____
> The half-hour show has a primary emphasis on action. The hour-and-a-half
> format allows you to do something with your people, so the viewer will care
> what is happening to them.

The only dissenting opinion came from the story editor of a western
series:

> The longer the program, the more action is possible; the more you can open it
> up to raiding parties, bounty hunters, and such like.

Competition in the same slot

One interviewee volunteered the observation that "This fall, the fact
that three action shows—_Four-in-One, Dan August,_ and _Hawaii Five-0_
—are competing at 10 p.m. may accelerate their violent content."
The researchers asked the producer of one of these shows whether he
agreed with this observation. His answer was, "I'll keep my style according to my nature." Then, naming one of the competing producers,
he said that that producer "by his nature will be more aggressive."
A producer who did not consider his series to be violent observed:

> It's better business to avoid what others are doing. Because there's no clear-
> inghouse between the networks, you can find violence all over the schedule.
> "Everybody died tonight on TV." For us to copy that is not good business.

Reception conditions

Three of the interviewees mentioned something about the way in
which television programs are received in the viewers' homes. One of
them, a writer, was conscious that television receiving sets made the
picture very small:

> The small screen detracts so much from drama. It makes people seem papier-
> mâché. Scenes which come out with punch on the large screen in a studio
> projection room don't carry on the tube, so we have to hypo things up to com-
> pensate.

A producer was asked how violence got into his programs. He began his answer by indicating another condition of television reception:

> Attention in TV is not focused as when one pays to go to the theatre and sits in a darkened house, watching the screen. In TV there are distractions to overcome. These can be overcome by drama—that is, by characterization and conflict, not necessarily violent.

Another producer also referred to the distractions which accompany television viewing:

> There'll always be a market for action drama on TV. Television is viewed with only part of your attention. Therefore, the style of a television drama has to be simpler, less involved, more forceful. It cannot be subtle. This is not a matter of audience intelligence, but because the conditions under which people view television reduce their acuity and discrimination.

These dozens of factors work to increase the violence in television programs. But there are also influences concerned with removing violence from programs or keeping it within certain limits. These are the purview of the network censors.

THE CENSORSHIP OF VIOLENCE

The networks exercise their protective responsibility toward viewers through their broadcast standards departments. In a home medium with its pervasive coverage and ready accessibility to children, the censor is the moral and ethical gatekeeper for the network and for parents.

The term "censor," as applied to broadcast standards personnel, has a derogatory connotation for some people. It is not used here in that sense, but because it is the common industry term to describe a specific set of functions. Further, the official titles are cumbersome (e.g., Director of Broadcast Standards and Practices). Another term in use for those functions, "editor," overlaps with other roles in the production process and is not as descriptive.

Censors for this study's programs are located in Los Angeles where the programs are produced. Each network has a director and about eight standards editors in its West Coast offices. Each director answers to a vice president for broadcast standards in New York, who reports directly to the network president.

The censor function

The censor sees himself as "acting on behalf of the licensees, assuring them that the network programs fed to them conform to the National Association of Broadcasters Code and meet uniform network stand-

ards.'' Producers and writers are more likely to describe the function as
a buffer between the public, the F.C.C., and Congress on the one hand
and the network and corporate executives on the other. The censor is to
protect the executives from troublesome and costly criticism. The censors' procedures, similar for all three networks, were described by one
network's standards director:

> Our involvement begins when we get an outline in writing or a phone call from
> the producer following his discussion with a writer. After reading the outline
> (from 1 to 15 pages) our editor cautions about possible troublesome areas.
> Then comes at least one draft. Depending on the show, the producer, and the
> studio, there may be as many as five drafts or only one and a few revised
> pages. The same editor then screens the rough cut to note whether his suggest-
> ed modifications nave been complied with, or whether the director has added
> something, or whether a movie makeup man (unused to television practices)
> has splashed blood over everything. Then, either the original editor or some-
> one else from this office views the first trial at the lab, without commercials,
> but after music and sound have been added. Since we warn that "This scene
> can only be approved on film," all producers and directors make great efforts
> to achieve an acceptable program.

Thus, censors go about the task in a formal way with written approval
and editorial notes at several stages in the production; with the story
outline, the first script draft and all revisions, rough cut, and completed
film. (A sample set of approval forms is in Appendix C.)

Approval at each stage is a matter of economics and efficiency. Required changes must be made before the production process goes too
far. One censor emphasized the importance of the outline approval: "Some ideas which have an undercurrent of violence should be cut
off at this time." Since the Robert Kennedy assassination, one network
has assigned censors to accompany film crews on location, "to approve
as they shoot—advise the director on the set." This makes it possible to
make changes conveniently. Once the crew leaves the location, reshoot-
ing expenses are prohibitive.

The censors protect themselves in the earlier phases of approval by
calling attention to every possible point in a script which might be objectionable in the final film, depending on the way it is filmed. It then is the
producer's responsibility if the film is objectionable to the censors.

Approval is always tentative until the finished film is screened.
Changes at that point are a serious creative, economic, and administrative problem for producers. Revisions in unacceptable scenes may disturb the dramatic structure and continuity or vitiate a dramatic point.
Changes are also costly. To bring in a production crew and highly-paid
actors, at daily rates, to reshoot a short segment could put a show far
over its budget. The extreme penalty, of course, would be to have a
whole film rejected. Reflecting on this danger, one producer said, "We'd

never get so far out of line as to risk having a picture rejected." To have an entire show rejected, as in one reported instance, is about a $200,000 disaster. Censor disapproval of a finished film may be appealed all the way to the television network president. (Of the three such appeals described to us, the score was Censors 2, Producers 1.)

The high cost of change may influence the final censor decision. Speaking of problem producers, one standards director said,

> Once in a while we have a tough producer who can't accept modifications. He'll shoot what he wants to do anyway, then tell you he has no more film. Or he'll start shooting before he submits the rewritten page. So we have to know about things like the costs of redubbing lines or extending the shooting schedule. We may let a line go by because our objection doesn't outweigh what it would cost to reshoot it.

The censor's evaluation comes in the form of a page-by-page, scene-by-scene itemization. For example:

> Page 8, Scene 15: If seen at all, the woman's body should not be "grotesquely sprawled." Acceptability of this scene will be subject to its appearance on film. Any actual showing of the body must be minimal and not sensationalized.[3]
> Page 15, Scene 19: This should be carefully handled to avoid showing the ceremonial dagger actually piercing Kurtis's finger causing the single drop of blood to fall.[4]

Such judgments are first made by the censor assigned to a series. He or she works full time reviewing scripts and films for three to five television series. At one network, combined judgments are sometimes used, with multiple readings of scripts (Baker and Ball, 1969).

Where the censor is told by the chief censor to be cautious, he may be extreme. The network standards directors review scripts and films appealed from producers. A chief censor said, "When matters are appealed to me, I overrule my editors about 50 percent of the time. They know that I accept the responsibility for that and for everything that goes out of this office."

Some producers also indicated that censor suggestions and decisions are negotiable, based as they are on uncertain criteria and an abstract judgment of public tolerance:

> We never let the network decide, if we can help it—not for conscience's sake, but for effective operating procedure. We fight them as hard as we can in regard to their absolutely asinine decisions. You can get away from the rules by going to the top. It's useless to argue with a shop girl, so you go to the store manager. I call the boss and say, "Would you like to hear what your people are doing? Isn't that asinine?" And he's likely to agree.

> The higher you appeal up the ladder of censors, the more you're allowed to do until at a high level you reach a man who throws you back to the page-bov with whom you started.

> If I don't agree with the local man (West Coast censor), I can go up the line; and the man at the top isn't completely inflexible.

One producer felt it was important to raise questions occasionally about standards that have been internalized in the system and not re-evaluated:

> When you don't agree with the law, you push. If you have a question or want to push, you call (West Coast censor). If he can't answer, he may have to go back to New York. The question may not have been considered in a long time.

One writer wondered whether there was a coherent executive policy in network control of violence. He mused whether the corporate bureaucracy left too much opportunity for misinterpretation and arbitrary independent decisions that eventually become part of the informal code:

> Network continuity acceptance people here are henchmen who carry out orders from higher administrators. There may be a lack of communication in this chain. The guy at the top's instruction "Let's have less violence" can evolve into "Let's not kill anybody" without his knowing. We ought to pursue the question: "Who's really censoring American television?"

The identity and authority of the censor was also questioned by two directors:

> When they tell you to change something and you ask, "Who's pressing for this?" there's never any particular man. It's always "they."

> That guy "they" is a fantastic character in my life. "They" won't allow it. And the "they" keeps going up the ladder. Like in the military, the private puts the blame on the corporal, the corporal on the sergeant, etc.

It should be made clear, however, that the censor does represent the company—his network. His decisions evolve from experience with the company (an average of 22 years for censors in one network) and reflect established company policy.

In addition to network surveillance of television programs, the National Association of Broadcaster's Television Code Authority monitors the programs of all three networks and, by agreement prescreens some programs of ABC and NBC. According to the Code Authority, in 1968 this "broadcast self-regulatory activity was stepped up in response to public anxieties." If the Code Authority staff monitor believes that there is a failure to comply with Television Code Sanctions on the depiction of violence, a formal monitoring report is submitted to the Code Authority Director. In most cases, the program is rescreened and discussed with the affected network and/or the Code Authority Director. Findings of noncompliance with the Code result in deletion of challenged footage, revisions, cautions as to future parallel treatments, and the Code Authority request of the network that personnel affected be put on notice as to the Code Authority position.

In the case of prior-screened programs, recommended changes may be made before airing. Revisions suggested for monitored programs can be reflected in any subsequent rerun or the program can be withdrawn.

By raising questions, suggesting revisions and issuing warnings, the Television Code Authority exercises a direct influence on portrayals of violence and contributes to the informal casebook that governs the industry.*

* Correspondence (June 11, 1971) from Stockton Helffrich, Director, The Code Authority, National Association of Broadcasters.

Standards and programming

The network programming departments also assign a representative to each series. This is a liaison function with the producers. Its ultimate goal is to maximize the success of the series in terms of its desired audience. The network program department people and censors have to work together, but not always with a single purpose. At one network, the program representative and the censor assigned to a show read the script together. In a scene of questionable violence, they call in the chief censor and the program production head.

As one chief censor put it: "Programming steps on the gas; broadcast standards steps on the brake." Referring to the networks' awareness of the public interest in violent action, one writer said, "A show may not be as gutsy as they'd like it to be, so they'll say, 'this was a kind of dull one, boys'—as if they wished you might have had more success in overcoming their censor." One chief censor admitted that they work in an "adversary system with the programming department," but the same man said:

> Sometimes the programming people will say "Put in more excitement." There are ways to produce excitement without violence, but it's hard work. If the program people equate violence and action, they're against the policy of the company. (Network president's) policy is: "We will not use violence to grab audiences."

Another censor said his program department "can say *no* to something we have approved but they can't say *yes* to something we have objected to."

Self-censorship

Another aspect of the censoring mechanism is the self-censorship on the part of producers and writers, which operates without any immediate administrative action by the censor because it is based on long experience with prior censor decisions. As a matter of efficiency, it is essential for writers and producers to anticipate the censor's reaction and thereby screen out potentially troublesome material at the conception stage. After a few years in television, the self-censorship is automatic. As one associate producer/writer said, "I don't get an unacceptable idea anymore." Another writer said, "There are unseen fences, never discussed; after being pulled back a few times, you know instinctively how far to go." Another said, "We writers are so brainwashed we precensor ourselves."

Some story premises can lead to objectionable kinds of violence. According to one producer:

> We know there are areas of conflict we don't want to be in, and so we avoid a script, the premise of which cannot be completed truthfully without invading these areas. In deriving the 24 stories we do in a season, we've abandoned as many as 15 scripts, 30 outlines, and other discussion points because, if we followed their line, we'd end up with wholesale prostitution or a St. Valentine's Day massacre.

Some producers fear that self-censorship in the conceptual process retards creativity and urge writers to throw off preconceptions of censor response. They acknowledge, however, that it probably doesn't work very well.

As the producers admitted, their own permissiveness and the permissiveness of the censors at the conceptual level probably do not counteract self-censorship. Telling a writer to "write freely" is likely not a sufficient approbation to work against a conditioned attitude:

> The average television writer is atrophied by sanctions. I tell writers "forget the censors, write your story," but that only half works.

Even the censors are concerned about self-censorship. Censors from two networks mentioned this issue:

> I'd just as soon they'd write freely and let us censor them.

> We tell the producer in sincerity—don't self-censor—try us—you may be able
> to do it. We don't want bland little stories. Although we often overreact it is
> not with the intent to destroy.

The economics of the system also encourage self-censorship. The writer's fee is fixed. He must deliver an acceptable script. In the interest of his own time he must minimize rewriting. Nor can he afford to leave the producer with problems after he has delivered his polished script; if he does so, he risks falling out of favor. One writer said, "The producer wants a show that won't give him too much trouble with the network." And a producer seconded that with, . . ."To find a permissable substitute for what is disapproved causes intolerable delay."

The requirements for censors

Who are the censors? What is their background? How do they become qualified for their sensitive positions? What are their motivations? These are important questions to ask if one is to understand the internal monitoring system of the networks.

There is no school for television censors—no academic or experiential background that relates directly to the function. Program practices department executives said they looked for people who: are meticulous in detail; have a basic knowledge of television production ("so they can understand what the producers' problems would be in making the changes they recommend"); are worldly ("We look for a person who's well read and knows all the jokes in every language, who's experienced in life"); are college-educated; are diplomatic; and have a sense of public sensitivity ("They have to be able to sense how long the average person can endure some uncomfortable effect without protesting its unpleasantness").

Outside his own network, a censor seems to have three major clients: the producers, the network's station affiliates, and the audience (sometimes represented by the government). The censor's goal is to maintain harmony with each client.

If a censor is television-wise and diplomatic, he can maintain good relations with producers. One censor said a measure of his effectiveness is "...to have a policy editor work with a producer and still be invited out to his pool."

One high-ranking censor considered protection of station affiliates his major function: "Station managers are on the line reacting to what the public says. Station manager letters influence me more than anything."

Public response is obviously a concern. The censor must be both worldly and sensitive:

We are guided by our own families' reaction. We pay attention to the FCC and other watchdog complaints. We go by our past experience with audience complaints.

_____

It's a scary medium. They (public) pick you up quickly when you make a mistake.

A producer said, "Censorship regulations of networks are motivated by fear of Washington and the FCC, also by worry about the Bible Belt. Advertisers are liable to be scared by tiny pressure groups."

The censor's goal, then, seemed to be to work smoothly and efficiently in the production process and to avoid direct public criticism or criticism coming through station affiliates and government agencies.

The censor and social effects of television violence

It was difficult to find serious concern among censors for the social effects of television violence. Even when the matter was approached directly, we did not get affirmative evidence of strong concern. The head of the Television Information Office says the industry has attempted to

. . .reduce both the amount and intensity of violence depicted in television—not because there is any evidence that this will have a salutary effect on levels of violence in the society but rather because there appears to be sufficient public concern to warrant such a change.[5] (emphasis supplied)

A director said, "Censors are not basically motivated by any great social conscience. They are motivated, rather, by what will be acceptable." He added:

The motive of the network people is to stay in business, to keep their jobs; and their job is keeping that show on the air. They're trying to pacify federal agencies, religious groups, educational groups, moral critics of all kinds who are coming at them—and still put together entertainment which people will enjoy enough to keep them in business.

Two writers made similar points:

The networks are extremely sensitive to criticism. They've taken a public trust and turned it to commercial advantage. They worry when a sponsor gets a letter from a viewer saying, "I'm not going to buy your toothpaste because there's too much violence on your show." They don't dare offend anybody; their main concern is don't make waves.

_____

The networks are quite frightened by Washington. Their fear is concerned with protecting their O-and-O (owned and operated) stations and retaining their affiliates. It's a billion dollar industry. They must protect what they have. So they tend to react hastily and impulsively.

The work of social scientists who have raised questions about the effects of television violence is not taken seriously by censors. One chief censor said, "We laugh at them. I don't see how the work accomplished so far by social scientists is of practical value." A colleague of the same censor elaborated:

> Child psychologists' reports flow in occasionally, but they're not generally related to the specifics of our work. The studies of the effects of violence on children don't give us sufficient ability to generalize. They're a beginning step. But we've been a little ahead of them, especially in cartoons, in doing what they've proposed. Science takes too long. We can't apply the guidelines from the commission report (Commission on the Causes and Prevention of Violence) specifically, only in general. But we store such things for future use.

Another network censor said the company's director of social research "sometimes aims things our way, but we don't have much direct contact with him. When we face a specific case, I'd have to say we make an arbitrary judgment, based on seat-of-the-pants, guts feeling plus whatever literature is available."

In the West Coast censor offices there are no staff psychologists, psychiatrists, sociologists, child development specialists, or criminologists, although these kinds of people are consulted occasionally. The censors do try to keep abreast of the social science literature relating to television effects, whether or not they find it of much use. Two standards directors had read and circulated the staff report to the National Commission on the Causes and Prevention of Violence (Baker and Ball, 1969). The third did not know of the report before it was mentioned in the interview.

All the censors referred to a report prepared for the three networks and the National Association of Broadcasters Television Code Authority (Heller and Polsky, 1969). In this report, Heller, a professor of psychiatry, and Polsky, a professor of law and legal medicine, attempted to synthesize the findings of the behavioral sciences in forming a set of guidelines for evaluating television violence. Some censors also mentioned reprints and summaries of research and speeches by social scientists which were circulated by the Television Information Office.

INDUSTRY ATTITUDES TOWARD CENSORSHIP

Among producers, writers, and directors, reactions to censors and censorship ranged from willingness to admit a constructive contribution, through passive acceptance, to an unwilling and combative adversary relationship.

Some producers acknowledged that censors forced them to find more imaginative themes and to develop character in place of situational excitement and violent conflicts:

> Sometimes these restrictions are challenging. "How can I show tension in a fresh way without a punch in the gut?"

The antiviolence thing has done some good in one way: in order to get attention, you have to have a better story; you have to reach more.

We started as an action western, but since the furor about violence, it has become an anthology of stories with deeper psychological penetration, but with the look and feel of a western.

Censorship does have one good result. It forces you to do more with character pieces.

One producer welcomed the perspective of the censor as a check on his own:

Making a length of film is the work of many minds; it benefits from cross-pollenization. And I'm not infallible; everyone needs a certain amount of supervision. Everyone needs the perspective of another man's point of view.

Some producers find it either fruitless or inconvenient to become frustrated or embattled with censors:

There's no use arguing with Continuity Acceptance. You may not agree, but they've got a job to do. And by the time they react you're busy with something else, with no time to spare for brouhaha.

But a more militant posture was taken by quite a few others. Censors were called "assholes," "idiots," "cookie-cut network executives," "page boys," "shop girls," and "small people." Their decisions were referred to as "illiterate," simplistic," "asinine," "ludicrous," and "stupid."

The censor, of course, is the scapegoat for resentments against the network policy he enforces.

Censorship and the dramatic climax

Violent incidents usually come at climactic points in television drama. That the censor interferes at those points is a source of irritation for many creative people. Specific incidents of creative frustration seem to come from what the producer or writer thinks is a censor's inability or unwillingness to perceive the dramatic dynamic and story meaning:

In one of our few shooting deaths, the guy dies like a dog in an alley. The whole script pointed to it. The guy was a loser for a lot of reasons. He thought that with a lot of money his problems with his wife would disappear, he'd own a $300 suit, he could be seen in good restaurants. But he was just as bad off with his illicit money as he was before. Maitre'd's have a way of sizing up whether you're genuine. A girl rolls him. In the end a fatal shot puts a hole through his $300 suit. Dying, he puts a finger in the hole of the suit; it's his last concern. An absolutely necessary device to play off his character—but the network said we couldn't do it.

A script received a tentative OK from the network, but with multiple cautions. It concerned a survival school in the Air Force with a simulated enemy capture situation. It showed how a man going through training is exposed to excessive hardship and brutality to help him survive in enemy country. But the network said, "Don't make the military look like they're hurting our boys." So we had to reshoot and recut, and came out with a lollipop which missed the point entirely.

We pit two worthy adversaries: the police officer lead and a young giant, a friend of the police officer, who refuses, gun in hand, to surrender to the law. Out of his friendly concerns for the man's own good, the police officer, at the cost of danger to his own life, struggles to disarm the man and force him to turn himself in. The more violent the struggle, the greater the evidence of the police officer's concern. But continuity acceptance would not condone a struggle long enough to make the point, and the result was a compromise, eminently unsatisfactory to both parties.

Censors admit that they sometimes damage key parts of a script. They are aware that "the most suspect thing is placed at the high point, like the burlesque comic who always used to drop his pants at the climax of his act." Another censor said, "Sometimes when we get through, the script is lousy and we acknowledge that. But we call ourselves 'creative editors'—we try to show them how to do it better."

The people on the production side respond negatively to the censors' self-image of creativity:

The censors are not creative people. To reason with them is like trying to tell a blind man what blue is. A foolish suggestion from them can ruin the play. They have a genius for picking the pivotal scene and saying, "That goes." I resent their flyspecking against my creativity. I'm being told what the public wants and how a scene should go by someone who got an A in English composition back in Kalamazoo.

Questioning the censor's judgment

Many producers and writers resented the substitution of the censor's taste and judgment for their own:

What is dramatic action? What is violence? These decisions are best left to the picture maker. Self-censorship is better than guardian censorship. Some of the guardians are not equipped to make these judgments. And the networks lose sight of the public and how they react. How is a picture judged? It is screened for seven or eight network continuity people and a number of agency people representing the multiple sponsors watching with drinks in their hands.

Several producers and writers questioned the ability of the censors to interpret public standards. One producer gave two examples. Although they do not deal with violent episodes, they illustrate the point:

> In one show, Petry comes home with his wife from the hospital and is convinced they have been given the wrong baby, that there's been a switch with an unseen woman in the next hospital room, whose name they know is Peters. So Petry phones Peters and demands, "We want our baby." Peters says he'll come over to talk about it. Soon the doorbell rings, and in walks a black father!

> Program Practices refused to let me do it. I finally got their consent to try it on a preview audience and promised not to release it if there were any objections from that audience. So it was screened in the A.S.I. testing house, where we also passed out 1000 questionnaires. The questionnaire respondents called the show most elevating because it showed both the black and white families living in the same middle class neighborhood and because the black man had dignity and control whereas the white was the exasperated one.

> In another show, we had two nuns composing a song they wanted the star to record. Program Practices kept this off the air. Then along came *Dominique*.

The creative people were eager to emphasize their own sincerity in attempting to work within the limits of good taste. Almost every producer and writer mentioned his own family—young children or grandchildren—suggesting that he would not foul his own nest:

> The people who work in the medium bring to it their own good will. The implication that we are guilty of irresponsible and diabolical behavior is terribly mistaken. We consciously attempt to do the best we can within the limits of our individual differences and talents. Oh, come on fellows, none of us are trying to corrupt the very children we have and hold dear!

While almost all producers and writers had faith in their own good taste, many would not say the same for their colleagues. Censorship is necessary for the others, some seemed to be saying:

> "Most producers have come out of films. They aren't as responsible or talented as the new crop of television producers who have come to their jobs with a college education. They can't differentiate between legitimate and gratuitous violence."

> I myself wrote scenes about gaffing hooks to get a foot in the door. And I wonder if producers are really socially responsible. If they thought it would sell, they'd make it.

> I do think there is need for network censors, because only 10 of 80 producers are objective.

Producers have implicit faith in their own taste, but are not sure about the others. Perhaps none is able to be objective about his own work. When one is administratively, economically, professionally, and creatively tied to a particular script treatment, it is not easy to see it as objectionable on any grounds, especially when objective criteria are difficult to establish.

THE CENSOR'S CRITERIA

The censor's criteria for editing violence are not easily determined. Where there are written codes, they are so broadly stated that the individual censor's interpretation is needed. This interpretation is often meaningful only in the context of a particular script for broadcast at a particular time in a series with its special set of characters and audience expectations. Nonetheless, a few generalizations emerge from extensive talking with censors and producers, writers and directors. We will reproduce the codes which are the common basis for the censorship of violence by all three networks, discuss the importance of the context for violence in making editorial decisions, and finally describe what seem to be the most commonly understood criteria among all parties in the production process.

Codes

All networks refer to the National Association of Broadcasters *Television Code* (1969) as a general guide. The Code is voluntarily subscribed to by many television stations and the commercial networks "to maintain a level of television programming which gives full consideration to the educational, informational, cultural, economic, moral and entertainment needs of the American public to the end that more and more people will be better served."

Under "Responsibility Toward Children," the Code says:

It is not enough that only those programs which are intended for viewing by children shall be suitable to the young and immature. In addition, those programs which might be reasonably expected to hold the attention of children and which are broadcast during times of the day when children may be normally expected to constitute a substantial part of the audience should be presented with due regard for their effect on children.

Such subjects as violence and sex shall be presented without undue emphasis and only as required by plot development or character delineation. Crime should not be presented as attractive or as a solution to human problems, and the inevitable retribution should be made clear.

Exceptional care should be exercised with reference to kidnapping or threats of kidnapping of children in order to avoid terrorizing them.

Material which is excessively violent or would create morbid suspense, or other undesirable reactions in children, should be avoided.

Particular restraint and care in crime or mystery episodes involving children or minors should be exercised.

Under "General Program Standards," the industry is advised:

The presentation of cruelty, greed and selfishness as worthy motivations is to be avoided.

The use of animals both in the production of television programs and as part of television program content, shall at all times, be in conformity with accepted standards of humane treatment.

The presentation of techniques of crime in such detail as to invite imitation shall be avoided.

The presentation of murder or revenge as a motive for murder shall not be presented as justifiable.

Suicide as an acceptable solution for human problems is prohibited.

Sex crimes and abnormalities are generally unacceptable as program material.

The "NBC Radio and Television Broadcast Standards and Practices" booklet which is circulated to all producers makes this statement:

Whether in terms of human conflict or cruelty to animals, violence should never be presented for its own sake, for shock effect or as an audience stimulant and should never be carried to excess. Depictions of violence can be justified as an expression of conflict only to the extent essential to the advancement of plot or the depiction of characterization.

The censors admit that these standards are not definitive. Terms like "presented with due regard for their effect," "shall be presented without undue emphasis and only as required by plot development or character delineation," "exceptional care," "material which is excessively violent," and "conformity with accepted standards" serve little purpose in day-to-day editorial decision-making, nor do they permit concrete resolution of arguments with producers or critics. The standards director from one network said, "As references, we have three file drawers full of various kinds of rules and regulations. We have the NAB Code and the (network) Policy Book, but they don't teach anyone anything (about the censor's function)."

On the specification of network guidelines, another censor stated, "Our own policies are not written down, since they have to be responsive to the context of particular programs and to changes of public attitude."

The role of context

The importance of context was mentioned by the other network censors. One said:

You can't judge these things (violent acts) separately out of context. Their effect depends on their position and, most importantly, on the total impact of the show. The total impact depends on the nature of the dramatic moment of the show and on the series' image in the public's expectation. Thus, in its total impact, *Gunsmoke* is not a violent show.

Another said, "We look at total concept," adding that, "often when the story is loaded with violence and is sadistically oriented, you can't get rid of the sadistic overtone by taking out the violent scenes." He cited a show, never aired, in which a manhunt with dogs was central to the theme. The dogs eventually destroyed the man. Even though the violent action was off-camera and other changes were made, it was the censor's opinion that a sadistic, violent theme remained and no amount of post hoc fixing could remove that orientation.

One producer acknowledged the censors' attention to context:

> The (network) censors are interested in cumulative effect. Two damns may not matter, but six give an overall effect to a show. It's the same with killing. If the overall piece has a feel of warmth—a communion between people—the audience doesn't think, "I've just seen a violent show." It's a question of loading.

Not all producers and writers agreed that the censors are sensitive to context:

> They censor with no regard to context. It makes no difference to them what the story says.

> The censors look only at the obvious and they look at it out of context. Their card of rules says such things as, "There must not be more than three punches," or "There must not be blood from the mouth." This approach is totally wrong.

> Continuity (broadcast standards) skims the scripts looking for words like "shot" or "man falls." Nothing else seems to bother them. But they are *very* vigilant about these. They say they don't want to be, but they *have* to be, that pressure from Washington is too heavy. They may have a certain amount of pressure, but also there's no one in a position to make a decision except those who can easily get fired, so it's safer for them to say no to everything.

Counting violent acts

The networks sometimes place a limit on the number of blows in a fight or number of shots in a gun fight, a policy which would seem to refute their expressed interest in the context and overall impact. One censor explained that this practice was mainly a communicative convenience and did not mean an arbitrary statistical standard:

> We do count punches and killing to the extent that we mention that knocking a guy out will only take three blows. We use numerical values just to make a point. It is an effective way to communicate the point but I cringe at every report that uses numbers.

The fact that networks do refer to numbers has stimulated some interesting rumors about elaborate statistical criteria for violence:

> On (a network) it's reported they have a point system. A punch in the nose will cost you so many points, etc. You're allowed so many points total. You can spread them out or bunch them up, but when you've used them all, that's it.

> Some acts of violence are given a higher value number by the censor than others—like carbohydrates in a diet.

Other producers claimed they could bargain with violence. The assumption in this ploy is that every script loses some "action" at the hands of the censors. If you start with what you want, you will end up with less: "The easiest way to deal with a censor is to load it with things you know they'll take out, leaving what you want."

One network keeps a running tally of violent incidents in all shows. A looseleaf notebook labeled "violence" sits in a prominent place on the Broadcast Standards Director's desk. Violence is defined as "the overt use of force with intent to harm or kill." Such acts are counted because the network

> . . .has to answer to the government and the public on the subject of violence. People are likely to ask, "How much time do you devote to action programs, and how much violence is in them?" So I keep statistics on the amount and kind of violence in our programs.

This record-keeping offers some protection to the network. If someone claims that violence is increasing, the network can examine its records and refute the charge.

Despite the codes and counting, censors claim that, in the final analysis, violence "gets us into a gray area and requires subjective judgment at all times." This gives rise to certain anxieties—and sometimes to anger—among producers who seek objective guidelines:

> I find the Continuity Acceptance people reasonable, but they have a simplistic, illiterate attitude toward what the problem is. One of the biggest problems is that no one knows what the guidelines are, so we proceed with trial and error as we go along.

Established guidelines

Some guidelines are generally recognized by censors, producers, writers, and directors associated with all three networks. They seem to be context-free in the sense that they apply across the board, without regard to program type, story line, "total impact," or time of broadcast.

Gratuitous violence. One such guideline is the sanction against excessive violence—or, as more specifically labeled, gratuitous violence. This is defined by the three network's censors in these ways:

> What we are after principally is gratuitous violence, included to titillate the audience more than is required by the story.

> Excessive violence (when put in only for shock value and does not move the story ahead—is not properly motivated, is gory, shocking and sensational) is prohibited.

> When violence is without character or reason; when someone perpetrates violence of this kind without being identified for the audience as a sadistic man.

In the producer's jargon, gratuitous violence translates as "not motivated by story or character," hence "inserted purely to produce cheap excitement." One producer explained, "When the violence is dramatically necessary, the audience simply asks itself, 'What's going to happen next?'" When the violence is not motivated, it calls attention to itself as "violence for the sake of violence." Violence is also gratuitous when it is "more intense or more prolonged than is required by the story." It is "a statement beyond the needs of the point, that's laid on for audience stimulation." To illustrate, one person cited an episode of *The Untouchables* in which the heavies ("bad guys") shot a man, riddled the corpse with tommy guns, and then dumped a truckload of garbage over it. Violence of this sort is no longer acceptable, the networks claim. It is considered a breach of craftsmanship by all producers, writers, and directors; cheap and crude, a creative copout. "There's never an instance," several respondents said, "where, if the show is flat, we say, 'Let's jazz it up with violence.'"

Imitability by children. Another rule widely understood and accepted is the prohibition of acts which might be imitated by young children with serious effect:

> In one script, cab owners independent of the syndicate were supposed to be fighting back with fire bombs, but we didn't want to be teaching young people how to make Molotov cocktails. In another script, at a dry cleaning plant, heavies who were interrogating the leading lady were scripted to put a plastic cleaning bag over her head. But we didn't want to risk showing a kid how to do that to his little sister.

Child jeopardy. A third specific sanction relates to child jeopardy. Anything which might terrify a child is not permitted in early hours and must be treated circumspectly in the late evening:

> We (network standards department) look seriously at child jeopardy, partly because it's revolting, partly because we do not want child viewers to be terri-

fied. In cases where kidnapping is necessary to the story, we do not want to show terror on the part of the child. Because we don't really know what the child viewers' reaction would be, we play it safe.

The censor rides hard on violent content in (show). I've just finished a script on karate, which has the desired quality of emotional excitement without bloodletting. At one point, the karate man is going to abduct a child, but the network won't allow him to touch her. Perhaps a clever director can produce a semblance of this.

Female jeopardy. It might be said that violence against women is also given special consideration—"women are not roughhoused."

A conflict in one show required that a woman be hurt and that the only doctor available is a drunken, despised character who's accused of previous malpractice in the Andersonville prison camp. The network won't let the woman be shot, or squashed by a rearing horse. But it does approve having the horse hit her into a post so the post injures her.

In a period show about San Quentin: Women there were badly treated. Starvation. Lack of facilities. One insane prisoner chained 25 years in the yard....(lead), as one prisoner, chases another women to kill her and, in original script, throws a wet sheet over her. The network censor labeled the sheet "too violent," so a pile of crates was upset on the woman instead.

Heavies make passes at a blind girl, threaten her with a poker. She runs out into the night, pursued by one of them—and Program Practices says the girl is not to appear *unduly alarmed.*

Indian jeopardy. Paradoxically, today serious violence may not be done to Indians—at least not in the early evening. Referring to a western aired at 7:30 p.m., a writer/director for a later-hour western said:"(They) can do less than we can. When an Indian is shot off a horse, they can't cut away from him until you've seen him get up and walk away." This was confirmed by a staff member of the early show:

No one can be killed when 600 rounds are fired in an Indian attack. So everyone who's shot has to be shown getting up and running away.

Another producer said, "Your Indians have to decide to give up before a fight."

Consequences of violence. Another standard is the prohibition of "excessive evidences" of violence, such as the immediate consequences of violent acts. A producer, recalling a composite of previous censor reports, quoted, "Excessive evidences of violence should be eliminated: no scream when the victim falls; puffed-up face is offensive; in scene 42 don't wish to see blood."

Death. Finally, "the dead must have their eyes closed." This is the most specific and perhaps the only absolute sanction applied.

Double standards

Many producers and writers of action-adventure television are disturbed by what they consider to be different sets of criteria for other types of programs, like movies, sports, and news:

> The networks have a double standard operating as to what they'll allow on TV —or maybe a triple one. We can't show suicide, but it's all right for Hedda Gabler to shoot herself with the general's pistols. Then, the feature pictures obviously have greater latitude than we're allowed for our programs.

> The networks have a double standard operating as to what they'll allow on TV —or maybe a triple one. We can't show suicide, but it's all right for Hedda Gabler to shoot herself with the general's pistols. Then, the feature pictures obviously have greater latitude than we're allowed for our porgrams.

> *Mannix* is censored, while (that network's own station) airs *The Wild Bunch* with blood, knives in eyes, and brains scattering.

Whether there are different criteria remains speculative. Because many of the criteria applied to violence in television entertainment are tenuous, attempts at comparison are premature.

Dysfunctional effects of censorship

Many producers and writers speculated about the potentially dysfunctional effects of devious methods used to avoid the full-screen portrayal of violence. They hypothesized about individual powers of imagination to fill in detail. Closure supplied by the viewers, especially the imaginative child, may be more vivid, shocking and memorable than the cleverest stunts *on* camera:

> The incident (an off-camer fight) is still there, as witnessed by the cut and blood on the face. The scene that the audience may invent can be more violent than what actually occurs. We are terrified by the unseen, by the anticipation, more than by what we actually see. I wonder whether this shouldn't be considered when playing to children, since they are more imaginative than adults.

Circumventions of direct violence suggest the possibility of a more violent effect. Once of these was the intercutting between shadows of a fight, a sensuous stripper, and colored lights, all scored with the throb of a drumbeat. Another was the allusion to the murder of a mobster by showing the victim enter an elevator with his executioners—then a quick cut to a human silhouette at a military firing range being blasted by gunfire. The producers of both these scenes felt they were more violent than direct visualization would have been.

However, censors do look for symbolic or implied violence: "A sadistic tone can come from off-camera or indirect showing of violence. We are aware of that and we do not allow it." Another censor admitted making mistakes occasionally: "When we hear only the grunts of a brutal fight which takes place off screen, it may be more acceptable to let the viewer see that one of the fighters isn't killed by the other." The subtle question of effect on the viewer, given his own perceptive and cognitive processes, is as yet unanswered.

INDUSTRY RESPONSES TO CRITICISM

Questions about the effects of television on children led many of the industry respondents to discuss children's entertainment values and their perceptions of television. Some respondents described what they considered the curious appetite of children for violence and mortal jeopardy, their willingness to put themselves into synthetic, fearful situations. Fear that is kept within tolerable limits and dispelled before the end of the performance they said, can be a legitimate dramatic emotion. One producer noted that in such plays as *The Golem* and *A Night at an Inn* "we find the age-old terror that's related to violence, the atavistic fear that somebody's outside the cave." Others cited childrens' literature like *Hansel and Gretel*, *Bambi*, *Tom Sawyer*, and *Jack and the Bean Stalk* ("when we come to the giant grinding your bones my boy wants to hear that again"). One producer said:

> Violence is a catharsis for kids. It's no accident that there's violence in fairy tales. Kids love the creepy feeling they get from grisly fairy tales and horror movies. It's a way they learn to deal with a portion of their evironment.

The creators of action-adventure for television believe in the child's ability to distinguish between television stories and reality. In the opinions of virtually all those interviewed, the violence of escape drama is so obviously synthetic that it is no more likely to induce immoral conduct in society than is the violence in accepted action-adventure fiction like Stevenson's *Kidnapped* or *Treasure Island:*

> Children know about violence from their own experience and are able to distinguish television dramatized violence as make-believe.

> I don't think that the violence in televised drama can inure a child to see people as objects. He knows that his brother screams and his mother bruises.

> The medium is artificial. It deals with action that is artificial. My theory is that people know what they see on the tube is different from what happens on the street.

> My kids know the violence they see on *Gunsmoke* is make-believe and what
> they see on a newscast is real.

The western, in its period, stylized mode, is presumed to be especially
recognizable as fiction:

> Kids know that television drama is contrived make-believe. One day I went
> home in wardrobe with "blood" on my shirt where an arrow had been "sticking
> into me." My aged seven daughter asked me about it. "I was killed today," I
> told her. "You were not," she said, "When you're shot, it just makes a little
> hole in front, and the blood flows out behind."

A child's perception of violence was evaluated by some respondents:

> Kids can make the distinction when they begin (at age 7 or 8) to understand
> that violence can cause pain. When they begin to have intimations of mortality
> —realize that life will some day end—they acquire a horror of violence. When
> they do know what violence is, they can distinguish whether it is actual or fic-
> tional.
>
> _____
>
> According to psychiatrists, children don't think in terms of burning flesh and
> screams of a dying woman when *Hansel* and *Gretal* push the witch into the
> oven. Violence first appears real to them when they actually see someone hit,
> cut, bleeding, or run over by a car.

These comments admit that there may be some confusion of television fantasy with reality by children. But the industry people maintain
that the discrimination becomes clear quite early in life when the effects
of violence have been experienced in various ways. By this time, they
claim, the normal child has also learned the appropriate social sanctions
against violence.

Violence in society

The respondents felt that children cannot long be insulated from the
violent character of their society. Many producers and writers were
quick to point out that the society condones violence which is more serious and less justified than is ever seen on television. A producer noted,
"It's better to recognize that violence didn't come out of the last five
years in the United States, that it's always been a violent country, that
one's not being brought up in a time that's suddenly gone mad." There
seemed to be a strong and bitter resentment of the paradox which con-
demns fictionalized violence on television and accepts war in Vietnam
and cigarette smoking:

> To examine violence where the end result is a dead body on television glosses
> over the point. This evades the culpability of a whole society which permits
> wars.
>
> _____
>
> Exploring the effects of violence on my program is a sliver as compared with
> manifestations of violence in the total society. My program is fitted between
> cigarette advertisements, which are murder weapons, and other commercials
> which ask, "Madam, are you going to be attractive in bed?" There's reality to
> these commercials. There's a fantasy to what I do.
>
> _____
>
> Television alone isn't responsible for teaching violence. Agnew recommends
> violence by supporting the shooting in Cambodia. Television and motion pic-

tures are fall guys for a sick society. It's easier to point the finger at them than look at Agnew, and Vietnam, and poverty.

All these statements implied that adult or societal attitudes toward violence exercised a much greater influence on children than did television drama. Some stated this idea directly:

> We've been a violent society in the Western World for a long time. It's ridiculous to expect television to educate people out of violence when no one else is trying to do it.

One writer said, "TV writers are not as bright as you would think; they do much less invention, far more reporting. So if you would like less violence on TV, commit less." A producer thought violent solutions to fictional problems could be traced to the premise that our way of life is worth defending, with violence if necessary: "If the government changed its military policy, we'd have a few stories where people would try to solve their problems without violence; and some would succeed and some would fail." In other words, these respondents said, the society seems to have institutionalized violence as a problem-solving technique. It is part of the national psyche, and television is true to it.

Several said that children develop their notions about violence from their own reality, as well as from what they see on television. Asked, "If kids see Hoss Cartwright hit someone, will they conclude that hitting is effective?" One producer answered, "They find that out on the playground."

Evidence about effects

Many producers and writers lamented the lack of concrete evidence on the effects of violence in television entertainment. They cited contradictory opinions and experiment of various social scientists:

> Nobody has been able to make a definite statement about the effects of televised violence. I'd assume the matter has reached a dead end. I'm surprised that there haven't been control groups and controlled scientific studies of it.

> I have to believe it is possible to design objective studies. Right now, however, what literature is there to read? I've tried a social scientist (network) who doesn't offer much.

Two producers were critical of research methodology. One implored researchers to conduct longitudinal field experiments:

> To investigate a hypothetical, psychological action without a control group is absolutely insane. Observations should be long range. You can't generalize the real effect of violent content by merely measuring the immediate increase of adrenalin.

The second challenged his own ability to make generalizations about effects and posited that the response to violence is infinitely multidimensional:

> Any producer who makes an unqualified statement about the effects of violence is arrogant. Its effects are finite only so far as the persons watching are finite.

Several were willing to accept conclusive evidence:

> If you do come up with conclusive evidence that what I'm doing is bad for so-
> ciety, I want to know about and comply with it. No one wants to exploit a na-
> tional weakness or aggravate a national illness.

Sanitized violence

In the absence of complete evidence, television people must make some speculative judgments to satisfy their own consciences and meet operating needs. One of the more controversial areas is the treatment of the consequences of violence. Some respondents suggested that the painful results of violence are underplayed and that the effect is sanitizing, even glamorizing, violence. Television violence is quick and clean, the hypothesis goes; therefore, children do not become aware of the agonies such violent behavior creates. One writer said:

> If our kids actually saw violence as it is, they'd adjust to it more normally.
> The farm kid sees sex and birth and death among the farm animals and is in tune
> with his environment. But our public is seeing violence without the smell and
> tawdriness of it. The Virginian never has an arm taken off. The Mod Squad kids
> never get deaf or punchy. Violence to the heavy is not realistic either.

Another writer agreed:

> There's no real feeling connected with violence. We don't see the grief that
> goes with the loss. There's no reaction on the part of the person who did it. No
> one throws up. There's no room to spend a tear.

Instead of dispatching the heavy with a single gunshot and cutting away to another scene, an alternative might be to blow away part of his body, have him writhe in pain, focus on his empty eyes in death, take reaction shots of his grieving widow and kids, and at the same time show the remorse of the lawman, detective, cowboy, or soldier who did the killing. Such a version would show the pain of injury or death and portray the reaction of others for whom the dramatist has created an empathic identity.

Many respondents said they attempted to emphasize reactions and to display the compassion of the hero—if for no other reason than "to promote audience empathy, to make the audience care." A producer recalled a specific incident: "A little boy sees his grandfather shot and gets very sick; you see him find out what violence is. We don't avoid showing the suffering violence causes people"

As a matter of format and treatment, some series emphasize the dramatic effects of violence. One producer described the chase format of his program which often follows a criminal act, "but we only show the jetsam from the act, the effect of violence, which we believe has more dramatic impact than showing the violence." Another series always ends with the tragic aftermath:

> After the third act comes an epilogue when the man is being led in or making a
> statement. You may see his tearful wife. You may feel sorry to see the human
> culprit defeated and think, "There, but for the grace of God, go I."

In the western, the remorse of the hero is a vital aspect of the tradition:
"All heroes regret doing what they have to do; this is part of the western
dramatic tradition."

A few respondents said they would also make the pain of violence
more realistic if they were allowed to. A producer remarked, "I would
like to show that violence is painful and death is final. I'm for anything
that reflects the truth of any given situation." A chief censor for one
network had contemplated writing a directive with that view, but abandoned the idea lest he be misunderstood:

> I would like to see more of the painful consequences of violence (*hurt* and *af-
> ter effects on people*) but find it difficult to explain. If I were to put that into a
> memorandum to producers, I would be in trouble. It is a matter of judgment
> and degree. I tried to write a brief statement about it but it would take a thesis
> to describe what I mean, so I let it go.

To the majority of producers and writers, however, showing the
"hurt" of violence on the home screen is distasteful. Special effects
used in recent motion pictures (wires jerking the victims backwards and
packets of "blood" on performers exploding on cue by concealed
electrical circuits) are too "repulsive" for television, they say. On *their*
programs, gunshot victims promptly fall forward or slump down in place
lowering their eyelids in death. One man said, "I don't want to document what happens when a guy is shot by a .45. I'm not trying to instruct
anyone in the horrors of anything." A majority thought a display of the
specific effects of violence was simply bad television drama. It would
turn away the audience they so carefully cultivate:

> We caution writers and directors against unnecessary exhibition of repulsive
> material. To make a heavy seem ruthless, you don't have to have him eviscer-
> ate someone and eat his vitals. To sicken an audience is not drama.

Some felt that the violence in real life was too horrible for escape television:

> As escape, television can carry realism only so far. The characters on a police
> show are rough and tough, but they can't show the public the way the job is
> really done, which would make *The Wild Bunch* look like a Sunday school
> picnic. If you showed the public that, you wouldn't be making escape enter-
> tainment; you'd be telling them there isn't a Santa Claus.

In a program about the Mafia, the producer wouldn't show an actual
incident from his source material in which gangsters broke children's
arms against a curb. Nor would he show the murder in which Mafia
mobsters drove a gaspipe up their victim's anus. "Out West in 1873,"
said the producer of a western series, "they would hang people not nec-

essarily by snapping their necks, but by strangling them or dropping them off bridges to tear off their heads." From a different producer came a more contemporary example: "A script about the My Lai massacres would be too...repugnant."

Such examples were accompanied by statements that there was no place on television for the depiction of savagery, sadism, or brutality. The producers would not open their scripts to characters who were morbidly disposed to inflict suffering and who were indifferent to, or took pleasure in, the pain and distress of others. They condemned the brutality of killing innocent people and the violence which goes with saying. "I don't like 'em, so wipe 'em out." There were some allusions to the relationship between sadism and sexual perversion. When asked what kind of violence he prohibited from his programs, a producer answered: "Sadomasochistic, exhibitionistic shit to appeal to the lowest possible, common, freaky, sexual drives of people."

Thus the self-imposed limits on those who create escape entertainment preclude "instructing anyone in the horrors" of violence, although there are a few, including a censor, who think that, in some instances, television should be doing exactly that. Showing the less immediate and physical consequences of violence—compassion for victims, remorse, grief—is more acceptable. What's more, it's considered a good drama.

Triggering effects

A major fear of those concerned with the effects of television violence is that such acts may trigger violent behavior in an emotionally disturbed viewer. That fear is heightened by the emerging knowledge of the numbers of American children who are disadvantaged, who suffer from unstable or parentless homes, poverty, insecurity, and discrimination.

A few respondents refused to believe that television could trigger the disturbed to felony or murder: "No one's going to tell me that Harvey Oswald or Sirhan Sirhan watches an episode of *Felony Squad* and then goes out and kills somebody."

One writer firmly stated that it was possible for television episodes to set off violent behavior. Two others said they had seen it happen in connection with other media. One of the writers, then an actor, went to a juvenile gang meeting while researching a part. He observed that the gang had been "triggered" by the film *Blackboard Jungle*. They had stolen two cars and raped a girl—"had a real cool evening." Another writer suspected triggering: "I once wrote a story, 'The Midtown Bomber,' for the *Saturday Evening Post*, in which the manager of a department store is blackmailed with a threat to bomb the store while customers are in it. I was shocked to read later that someone tried the same thing and I wondered whether he'd been influenced by my story."

Most of the respondents acknowledged the risk of television triggering the disturbed. One producer speculated at some length about the kind of content that would "tip the deranged"—stories that use eerie themes, perversity, or sadism or that play on childhood feelings of anger and fear of the dark. He listed as examples *One Step Beyond* in which a man with a knife stalks someone all day, *Psycho* (based on a perverse crime), and an episode of *Hawaii Five-O* (in which a man, to disguise his identity as his aunt's murderer, kills others and stabs himself). Some producers and writers indicated that they they stayed away from bizzare acts of violence which could be imitated by disturbed people.

Several expressed a conviction that seriously unstable people would easily find a stimulus for antisocial behavior, whether or not television were available. Others pointed out the difficulties of monitoring and eliminating all potential triggering stimuli:

> An unstable person should be protected from shock material of any kind, not only from violence in television, but from the excitement of Aaron Copeland's *Rodeo*, or Frederick Remington's *Dash for Cover*, or the agonizing of Pagliacci.

> Christmastime in the ghetto triggers people—when a toy is advertised for $15.95 and there ain't no way to buy it. People living in terrible conditions see on television what others have.

Four producers mentioned that it would be unfair for television to cater to a small minority of disturbed people:

> That's bit like saying, "Don't sell liquor to Indians," or "Don't sell liquor at all." Certain people will be triggered by violence, whether they get it on television or wherever. So should we stop up our ears and pretend that we live in a fantasy world where everything is nonconflicting?

> To remove what might adversely affect a few would be like prohibiting medications because of a side effect which they may have on one person out of 7,000. Follow this line of reasoning and we'd stop giving prescriptions; we'd stop doing all kinds of hazardous things; we'd stop driving our automobiles.

> We certainly can't censor society and its expressions from fear that these will trigger irresponsible persons.

> You can't modify all programming to leave only shows like *Bewitched* on the possibility that a few disturbed people will be triggered.

They pointed out that the stimulation of abnormal behavior, by television or anything else, was symptomatic of serious personal problems. Respondents were concerned that public chastisement of television drew attention away from more fundamental causes:

Perhaps we do run the risk that television will sometimes influence people who are already inclined to release their hostility in a violent manner. But people with such tendencies show signs of their condition, which should be reported and watched.

Are kids from unstable environments triggered by television violence? Their not having parents is a more serious problem!

Catharsis

Some respondents thought that, contrary to stimulating disturbed people to antisocial acts, television may have a calming effect. They endorsed the classical catharsis theory. In his *Poetics*, Aristotle claimed that incidents in a tragic drama which aroused pity and fear would effect a catharsis or purgation of these emotions. [7] The respondents advanced similar claims for violent content:

> The basic question seems to be: Is television violence symptomatic or causomatic of violence in society? Does it incite a viewer to sadism of his own making, or is it a release and ventilation of his aggressive tendencies? I'm inclined to take the latter view. If the viewer identified vicariously with the program (and kids do identify strongly), catharsis should result. And that, after all, is what writing is all about: the transmitting of personal feelings into an object of general concern.

> Human culture is a thin shield superimposed over a violent core. It's better to crack it fictionally than to see it explode in the streets. Exposure to properly presented conflicts which result in violence acts as a therapeutic release for anger and self-hatred, which are present in almost everybody.

One person went so far as to say, "You can argue that TV *reduces* violence, because it vents the viewers' emotions and relaxes their tensions."

Public responsibilities

Some television is not for children. As one writer noted, "I've written thrillers that weren't for five or six year olds." His plea for more parental responsibility in monitoring children's viewing was echoed by several other writers and producers. A censor related her own experience:

> I used to be bothered by Saturday matinees when Desdemona was tied to the railroad tracks, so my mother arranged for my music lesson on Saturday afternoons. Today's mothers don't acknowledge that kind of responsibility; instead, they expect television to be a baby sitter for them.

One asked that the responsibility at least be shared:

> You don't have to watch the whole schedule. You can always turn off the set and read. And as for the cumulative effect on kids, parents should be responsi-

ble that their kids don't get saturated. There's a responsibility in the home at
least equal to ours.

Respondents argued that it would be inappropriate for all television to
be pitched at the level of a five-year-old; television is already critized for
offering too much Pablum. "The schedule should allow an opportunity
to see all kinds of things, ranging from Jacques Costeau to *The Wild
Bunch.*" A certain amount of family control is imperative, they said.

For the most part, television series are true to the format established
in the first episode. Producers take special care not to violate audience
expectations. They believe the parent has adequate opportunity to deter
children from adult series if they make the evaluative effort. The producers acknowledged a parallel task for the television industry, to provide
"adequate warnings, so the audience can be selective." That parents do
not exercise this responsibility is somewhat irritating to producers and
writers.

Some felt that the public already polices television content. Program
ratings could not be sustained without public approval:

> I don't think too many of the public disapprove of what we're giving them
> now. You don't get a rating by offending the public. The public is policing us,
> in its own way. And remember that to stay in business on TV we have to be
> approved by at least 12 million persons.

> No one comments about violence in *Ironside.* The public continues to watch it.
> They wouldn't put up with it if they seriously objected to it, any more than
> they put up with shoddy merchandise.

Where these respondents admitted public objection to violence, they
questioned the ability of the public to understand and articulate the
objections:

> If challenged, the public would probably be hard put to specify just what it
> objects to . . It's mirroring the headlines in magazines and newspapers, which
> find good copy in stories about youth being ruined—especially when they can
> accuse television, with which they are in competition.

> The public's been conditioned to say there's too much violence. It doesn't
> know the real facts. Facts are a short commodity. I don't know what they are
> myself, and it's my business.

> In the last three years we've had only three letters saying there was too much
> violence as against 50 complaining there was not enough action—but none of
> these was very articulate.

Attitudes toward government investigations

The respondents had much to say about inquiries into television violence as fostered by governmental committees. Their statements are

presented here without comment, in fairness to the stated intent of that portion of our questioning.

A number of respondents referred to the methods of government inquiry:

> Nobody looks good before one of those committees. They tape a whole evening of your programming and edit together out of context all the incidents considered objectionable and say "Look at what you're doing to the American public," making you look like a fool. Anyone who goes before a Senate investigation committee loses his citizenship status.

> The Pastore investigation seems exceedingly simplistic. One must view the question in terms of the attitude and thinking of the people who receive the programs. One must also measure the violence in relation to its purpose.

> When Bobby Kennedy was assassinated, President Johnson wondered in a public speech, "Could it be because of television?," whereupon all three networks toughened their standards and stripped violence from films which were already made.

> Pastore oversimplifies—which is natural for a politician, using the rhetoric to stir up the public.

The qualifications of government officials to make judgments about the effects of television was doubted: "What does Senator Pastore know, in comparison with my 25 years in this business? What gives him the impression that people watch what they enjoy and are then destroyed by it?" Others questioned the officials' motivations:

> Pastore and others like him should understand their own failure to improve the slums, improve educational opportunities, and get out of Vietnam is a much greater failure to improve society than that of television. I think Pastore knows this. He's not so stupid as to think that television created Sirhan Sirhan. He's got an issue—like Joe McCarthy. It's a nice way to get reelected.

> Violence on television is being used as a political tool. Let us use the medium to tell the truth, not try to make it acceptable to ax-grinders who use it to further their ends of the moment.

> I have no doubt that the networks made a deal with Pastore that, if he would support automatic renewal policy, they would put the lid on sex and violence. . . .Although Pastore is quiet on sex and violence now, no doubt he'll be back to it when he's up for reelection.

> Pastore is a publicity-oriented fool with a limited, dogmatic approach. To make TV a scapegoat for the ills of our society is preposterous.

The constitutionally-guaranteed freedom of television is diminished by government investigations, some respondents maintained:

> To discuss violence with Senator Pastore would be to concede his point that the government has a right to censor. But the government has no right to decide what is right and what is wrong with society. It has no right to dictate to private industry. It has no right to legislate morality, certainly in the arts. If the government does control these matters, the result will be like that in Hitler's Germany.

POSITIVE ASPECTS OF ACTION-ADVENTURE
PROGRAMS

The action-adventure program with violence may have redeeming social values. Its violence may speak *against* violence. Its fictional violence may help prepare children for reality. The series heroes are decent
people, condemning violence and using self-restraint. Socially significant information and moral messages are carried in the themes.

Respondents made all these claims.

Violence as substantive content

Violence is often the substantive content of television action programs. The theme is the immorality and maleffect of violence. In accord
with established morality and television standards, violence to persons
or property is evil and begets tragedy, except when it is used in self-defense, national defense, and law enforcement.

The western is the classic case in point. In some stories decent people,
including the hero, encounter the heavies who are established as evildo-
ers through recognizable conventions of appearance and language. It
isn't necessary to develop the heavy's character. He quickly commits a
violent act, motivated by his inherent evil. The hero ultimately provides
the retribution, bringing home the message that: "To provoke violence
is destructive; it gets you killed. Violence begets violence."

Revenge is often a theme. The western hero attempts to exercise a
civilizing restraint on quick-tempered, revengeful neighbors. In a *Gunsmoke* episode, an ex-gunfighter starts a crusade of revenge against men
who, given shelter by his pregnant wife, raped her. (She then ran out
into the snow and died.)

> To justify his revenge, the husband quotes Exodus 21:22: "If men strive and
> hurt a woman with child. . .and if any mischief follow, then thou shalt give life
> for life, eye for eye, tooth for tooth." But Doc tells him, "If you twist words
> enough, you can make them say anything—but before you make the Bible justi-
> fy killing without a hearing by judge and jury, you'd better take a long, hard look
> at yourself." The program is saying that revenge is an empty and terribly de-
> structive passion, and that violence is destructive because it breeds violence.

In some stories, characters are not inherently bad or revengeful, but
they struggle with themselves over violent or selfish impulses. A series
of minor incidents and moral lapses may impel them toward a disastrous
climax. This was said to be the most prominent theme in *Gunsmoke:*
"Take a tiny transgression, a little evil, and find how that escalates into a
major tragedy."

A script in another series has some "heavy" thoughts about war. The
writer said:

We are trying to make statements that war is not fun. In one scene, a group of people are conjecturing about which one of them is the intended assassin of George Washington. Our guys draw away from the rest, and one says, "Listen to us, so ready to suspect one another. See what war can do to people." And another says, "It's sad there was no other way for us than war, and strange that man, for all his intelligence, has never been able to invent a lasting peace." A heavy thought. Hope it isn't cut out, but the producer could say that it isn't the time for them to be sitting around talking.

Themes about violence carry over to the contemporary series with clearly identifiable contemporary issues. *Mannix* sometimes includes a message with its exciting action. For example:

One of our shows (about a soldier who killed unarmed peasants in Korea) makes the judgment that war brutalizes, and says to the Army, "Leave the soldier with some humanity. Nothing justifies killing innocent people."

A script called "Peace Now, Arley Blau" was cited to show the involvement of *Mod Squad* with contemporary issues and values. In it:

The nonviolent son of a general is jailed as a draft evader. His father slaps him and is then wretchedly sorry. In prison, the boy is subjected to taunts and harassments, which he takes without reprisal. But finally, when another person's life is endangered, the non-violent hero in a real rage leaps to his defense and slugs a guard. Then he says, "Are you satisfied now?" He rejects his own act of violence, even though it has saved someone's life.

A campus violence show on *Dan August* "tries to leave the idea that you don't solve a lot by burning down an administration building and shooting a professor."

The respondents' point in citing such episodes was to suggest that children may learn useful lessons about violence from their viewing. They may assimilate the conventional cultural values about violence. One producer claimed that the national morality teaches kids there are some values worth fighting for and that there are times when you need to defend yourself. He believed that television reflects these demands that the country makes on its citizens.

Another producer said he didn't think you could always turn the other cheek to violence but that, in television, "you can take the profit out of violence and, as with power, try to use it judiciously, carefully, and benevolently." One program attemtps to relate violence to human rights. The producer said, "If you usurp any man's rights—even his parking space—you are doing him an injustice. The police officer's efforts—and violence, if you will—are exerted to guarantee these rights."

A few respondents talked about the potential of television to convey such messages. A producer said:

If television does a responsible and adult job of telling it as it is, kids will respect the medium enough to take the morality we preach because they believe the source. If television glosses over the fact, that violence exists, it will lose its credibility.

Another said:

> TV editorializes, propagandizes, by inducing the audience to accept the values
> it promotes. The effect of TV violence on the public will depend upon what at-
> titude the producers take with regard to it. Programs can and sometimes do say
> editorially, 'Isn't it too bad we've come to this, that we have to resort to vio-
> lence.'

In addition to presenting message themes about violence, some respondents proposed that the exposure of children to televised violence
is functional to the extent that it prepares them to cope with reality:

> Conflict is important for children to grow up with. It's part of their life.

> I'd be concerned about people saying, "Make a drama that leaves violence out
> completely," or, "Don't put on shows about war." We don't want our kids to
> walk out innocently into the world—into a meatgrinder.

> Kids shouldn't be brought up to think that nothing is going to happen to them.

One respondent wondered whether children in the insulated environment of the suburbs might be handicapped when they left that shelter.
Television could provide a balance, he said:

> Exposure to violence in childhood is not a bad idea. Maybe there should be a
> police show for kids. Ghetto children are exposed to violence unknown to other
> children. Because they have to live with it and it's so hateful, they might be less
> influenced by it than other kids who haven't encountered it. People who grew up
> in a tough ghetto situation regard others who didn't as patsies, naive and easy to
> use.

The character of the hero

In addition to themes that speak against violence, the action-adventure series presumably portray heroes who set a worthy example. Television superheroes are endowed by their creators with godlike qualities.
They are omnipotent, magnanimous, but sometimes stern: "When Hoss
Cartwright hits someone, it's like the hand of God; the someone deserves
it." Or you have "dedicated, intelligent Matt Dillon risking his life to
protect society." "The example set by Mannix is to be brave and com-
passionate."

One western producer said his show "has a deep hold on the public;
its basic morality and honesty apparently represent something Americans would like to believe in." Westerns, another producer said, are
about fairly decent people, who come out fairly well in the end. The
town in his series is a nice town. Its people don't lynch. The main characters like and trust one another:

> We tell writers not to make them behave as petty persons, making shallow and
> unworthy judgments, since we need to maintain their nobility. If youngsters
> emulate what they see on the screen, they should emulate this example of good
> conduct.

A writer said audience acceptance is risked if the hero is not strong and virtuous in line with these standards:

> If you don't have a character stand up for what seems to be in the best interests of himself or of humanity, you've destroyed your viewers' willing suspension of disbelief, their escape, their entertainment. And so you've done harm; you haven't accomplished anything.

The attitudes of the main characters toward violence is carefully regulated: "We take care that the protagonists don't have a flip attitude toward death as though it doesn't matter whom you killed as long as they were bad guys." Another made the same point about property: "We say that property rights are reasonable. Mannix and the Cartwrights are fighting for good, including protection of property." The countercharacter of the antagonist is also important. It permits the heroes to play against them with their own exemplary attitudes:

> We don't feel the violence of the Cartwrights against oppressors is wrong. The Cartwrights are decent-minded. They're concerned about what happens to their neighbors, to Negroes, to Chinese. They're against bigotry and prejudice. The evil men they encounter are narrowminded men.

Certain rules of behavior are upheld:

> Mannix is no bully. He seldom grabs the heavies. He usually controls his temper—which is useful as contrast to when he really blows. Mannix never initiates violence or uses it as a means of getting anything. He reacts violently only when provoked, and these reactions could be legally justified as self-defense. He sometimes uses vocal violence—"Get your hoods off me." He is an extension of the arm of the law, licensed and bonded.

> Dan August gets a warrant, plays by the book even when frustrated. Interrogation scenes are not brutal. He doesn't grab and push people. He doesn't break the law. He may bend it (e.g., be away to avoid receiving a subpoena), and he may sometimes ignore orders (e.g., may not take a vacation in order to continue the case).

> McGarret acts within the framework of the law. He will come with a search warrant—but if a junky refuses to open the door, he will kick it in.

> Matt Dillon has never shot unless shot at, and always calls a warning first.

The attitude of the lead toward the use of violence, it was said, is one way he maintains his role as protagonist:

> It's good that the audience sees the good person triumph. What makes him good is that he uses violence as a last resort. If he used it first, he would be as evil as the antagonist and you'd have antagonist vs. antagonist instead of antagonist vs. protagonist.

Other message themes

The action-adventure program can be a vehicle for messages of significance to children which are not concerned with violence, we were told.

Gunsmoke started as an action western, but since the 1968-69 furor about violence, it has become an anthology of stories with deeper psychological penetration. Ministers were now commending it as a "morality play" useful to them in their duties.

Bonanza "takes an occasional jab" at prejudiced and narrow-minded people. It is assumed that likeminded people in the audience may "adjust their moral attitudes more to the times and become more tolerant."

> We did a show about the Weary Willies, who were the "flower children" of the times after the Civil War. Maybe we've loaded the show somewhat in their favor, but we hope that our audience will feel that these people have at least a right to live. . . .The audience is greatly composed of the Silent Majority; it's nice sometimes to give them a jab. We got reactions from them to a show we did about Negroes. One letter said, "No white man would beat up a black boy. For showing a lie like that, your director should be hung by his testicles"—which is a good comment on anti-violent morality.

Some producers of police, detective, and "watchdog" programs also cited their efforts to say something about human nature and social problems. For example:

> To say that *Ironside* is popular programming doesn't mean that it has nothing to say. Three or four times a year, it does a thesis piece with a strong message. One viewer writes that he's found twenty-two of our shows which have something to say besides, "Crime doesn't pay." The writer, a cripple, identifies strongly with Ironside; and the way *Ironside* influences this man's life makes us conscious that what we do concerns and affects people's lives.

"Uptown in Eden," an *Ironside* episode concerned with teenagers and marijuana, has received a commendation and is being widely used by schools and youth organizations and, in one instance, for police education. What it tells the teenager is: Marijuana is against the law. If you're caught with it, you'll be busted, and being busted will mess up your life. The question of whether marijuana should be legalized is something else. There are ways you can use to change the law in this country. Meanwhile, just don't get yourself arrested. Another episode, "The Machismo Bag," shows Chicanos in the large cities as a degraded minority, self-destructive, ashamed of their heritage, badly in need of a pride-creating nationalistic movement.

Dan August programs have been involved in the problems of Chicano laborers and their employers: with a penal institution that, because of a budget cut, is faced with freeing a killer in a society that hadn't cared enough; and with draft card burners who aren't bad kids but don't want to go to Vietnam. One man associated with the program said, "We like to think some of the shows do contribute to knowledge and treat problems with compassion."

These are the industry's beliefs about how the nature and use of violence in their programs can be justified. How much is strong belief and how much is *post hoc* rationalization remains to be evaluated. Some portion, certainly, is a function of the industry's limited ability to generate original or varied ideas and issues.

VIOLENCE AS A SUBSTITUTE FOR IDEAS

Earlier in this report, we named three functions of drama. Two of these—arousing audiences and relieving their tension—are clearly served by action-adventure programs. The third function is orienting people to their environment, helping them understand the world in which they live and helping them transact with it beneficially. Drama has served throughout history as a mirror in which people examine themselves, their institutions, and their values. It is possible for drama to perform this service and still be entertaining, still engage attention agreeably. To be entertaining, it does not always need to provide escape from life.

This, at least, is the feeling of many persons who object to violence in television drama. It is likely that many of them accept the violence in *Medea* or *Hamlet* while criticizing the violence in action-adventure series. It is possible that some are irritated not so much by violence *per se* as by its occurrence in situations which are stereotyped or which provide little insight into human values and social institutions.

According to some critics, violence is all that is left when programs are expunged of meaningful ideas. One producer has written:

> When ideas are unusable and the conflict of dramatic forces must be resolved in the triumph of clearly acceptable, publicly approved sentiments, why not reduce the conflict to its simplest possible form: lawlessness and the law, the black hat and the white hat? (Gordon, 1959)

Those words were echoed in 1970 by a television writer:

> The so-called action shows have at their core a vacuum which can only be filled by violence. They are not about real questions; they are not about real people; they are not about real situations. The only possible controversy is through violence and therefore the supply of violence on TV will remain constant as long as there is a constant number of so-called action shows. They have nowhere else to go with these shows.[8]

Readers may wish to judge the truth or exaggeration of these allegations by their own experience of watching some of the programs in this study. The study itself seems to indicate that there is sufficient truth in the allegations to merit serious consideration. We have already reported statements from respondents that action-adventure programs are mainly limited to "clearly acceptable, publicly approved sentiments" and, that on the whole, they present synthetic rather than realistic char-

acters and situations. A majority of the situations, if not violent in themselves, appear to be in the story as an outcome of violence or as preparation for it. A majority of the characters are selected and delineated in
order to support a violent situation, whether as perpetrators, victims,
protectors, or dramatic foils.[9]

Much the same things can be said about the program ideas. Action-
adventure programs do make statements about human life. On the
whole, however, these appear to be statements about violence and about
people who are involved with violence. This restriction leaves many
other more peaceful or constructive areas of human life unexamined.

This problem was recognized in some interviews, and a few respondents suggested reasons for its existence. One reason commonly advanced was the need of commercial programs to attract the largest possible audience of potential customers for the advertisers' products.
"Anything with content is usually anathema to the large audience," said
one producer.

Another was trying to circumvent this frustration. "We're constantly striving to escape the common denominator," he said, "and not
make it all meaningless." A third producer sounded more discouraged.
"If television continues to cater to the largest common denominator,"
he concluded, "there'll never be anything but pap, and that not as interesting as it should be."

Some respondents recognized that always serving the mass audience
meant leaving significant minority audiences unserved. A writer said
that television drama "is not meeting the requirements of many people,
but I don't think commercial broadcasting will change in this respect.
The problem may be helped, however, by the introduction of cassettes." A producer thought that pay television might also help to solve
the problem:

> If a million persons each paid one dollar for a program, you suddenly wouldn't
> have to create programs for the twenty or forty million. Perhaps commercial
> broadcast TV could then do what it does best: be a window on the world. Dra-
> ma would presumably move to pay-TV and cassettes.

He also predicted future influences on programming from the generation
which is now of college age: "I think the situation is encouraging. These
kids are not settling for the status-quo; they're asking why. They're not
so hung-up. As the coming audience, they'll create things for themselves."

But what about the present audience? One writer wondered whether
the viewers might not be receptive to something more relevant to actual
human experience than action-adventure programs provided:

> Wouldn't we perhaps discover that the public is as intelligent as any of us? I
> have an idea that the public would support an honest story, told well, without
> violence, and dealing with a problem with which they could identify. I've gotten
> interested responses to one of my scripts from women with alcoholic husbands.

> We don't always have to feed them the story where all they feel is, "Oh dear, they're going to die in the desert. An Indian's going to shoot them."

There was a problem, however. The writer doubted that the networks would go along with substantial experiments in this direction: "The networks are not really concerned with upgrading the product. They package what will sell. I resent their having creative control."

Another writer shared this resentment:

> With the network in charge, there's too much economic power in the hands of too few. There are too few alternatives. Things tend to fall into the same patterns. Three men in the country, essentially, decide what we're going to see.

In these decisions a producer had little faith. Asked whether paying higher fees to writers would result in better scripts, he answered:

> Yeah, better maybe—but we wouldn't get anything different, no bigger breathing hole for the human spirit. The network doesn't like to rock the boat, to tamper with what works. The network people aren't creative. The old studio bosses, for all their faults, had some love for filmmaking. But all the network people do is line up the programs on their long table and juggle them against the competition, asking, "What will work best against that?" instead of, "What are we going to do?" The network is run by salesmen. It's their business *not* to *love* the process of making a film.

Many respondents stated that the networks' fear of government reprisals and of losing audiences, affiliates, and advertisers cause them to shy away from areas of program content which might possibly give offense. According to one producer, this fear has combined with a tendency to say, "Hey, people are watching that; let's put on more like it."

> The result has been to inundate the schedule with shows like *Petticoat Junction*. It's safer to put on situation comedy, which doesn't antagonize anybody because they're all laughing.

Another result has been censorship. Censorship of any kind of content may indirectly encourage programs which have nothing much other than violence to deal with, because it limits the program creators' freedom of expression. When networks are frightened into muzzling their program creators, society is the loser because it is denied exposure to matters of public concern. "Censorship is a crown of thorns," one producer complained. "Besides the thorns of sex and violence, there's the thorn of controversial subject matter. I once did a program for *Mr. Novak*, hopefully to increase public awareness about venereal disease among teenagers—but the program never got on the air."

A writer gave some examples of currently important topics which he knew he could not "get away with." These included: the little man's fear of big government; how a big corporation runs by itself; the results of life being too easy, such as men and women getting bored with each other and seeking multiple marriages; and labor-management negotiation.

A few respondents thought that more significant program content might result from the networks' increasing attention to demographics. They were trying to narrow their target to that specific segment of the public that comprised the most likely customers for a given sponsor's product. A producer hoped that

> the time may come when the networks will say, "We don't care if we're not number one if we deliver the audience for the product." Then the customers for Lincolns hopefully won't be watching *He-Haw* and *Beverly Hillbillies*.

The producer who had failed to clear the *Mr. Novak* program was also hopeful:

> It's true that we live by the only crap game in town (the Nielsen ratings) and that the sponsor wants to get the biggest bang for his buck. But *Novak* would succeed now with the findings and growing emphasis on demographics. Although the spectrum for some programs stretches across the largest possible audience, there's getting to be room for enough kinds of programs to scatter-hit all the buyers.

Although large audiences rejected significant content, one producer thought that they could be attracted to it by the right vehicle. Such a vehicle he hoped he'd found in a series which he was producing for the coming season about young lawyers who donated their services to the disadvantaged. The series would contain more meaty themes, he said, than could have been placed on the air three years ago. "TV's pendulum is now adjusting from an excess of pap," he thought. "Not all of the new shows will survive; but if one or two of them succeed, it will trim the ship, balance it a bit."

Nevertheless, it was not proving easy to develop the series about the young lawyers:

> Every time we try to tell the stories they get into, it scares somebody. There'll be no public awareness of some important societal issues if the networks are discouraged from treating them. You don't find too many editorials about them. *Mr. Novak* was canceled for *My Mother the Car* and *Please Don't Eat the Daises*—and that's what will happen again if the networks keep getting beaten up enough.

Despite the cautious and commercial orientation of the networks, and despite having to appeal to a mass audience, several producers said they felt that some of their work had something important to say. Recall that one respondent, after describing a number of his program themes, concluded, "Shows like these are recognized as the great ones. A show that has something to say about the human condition is the better for it."

That all shows could not be equally as great was blamed by some respondents on the pressures of turning out products in quantity within a restricted time. Said one prducer: "We're constantly trying to do something good and fresh, but that's hard with the number of shows we have to do. Considering that we're turning out 26 a season, we're lucky if we get ten satisfying ones." But he added:

> Compare that record to Broadway, where maybe six out of a season get good reviews. TV has far from ideal opportunities to give the care and attention we'd like—but, considering that, we do a remarkable job. Every night, somewhere in the schedule, there's something exceptional for an audience to see.

Exceptional programs, however, require superior writing. Lack of talent, one producer said, "keeps us from achieving programs with the better kind of conflict, such as *The Treasure of the Sierra Madre* or *The Bridge Over the River Kwai.*

Is there a dearth in television of writers who have fresh and important things to say? One of the story editors thought there was:

> Members of the Writers Guild say they want to write more meaningfully, but I don't know if more than a dozen of them are that good. The true writer usually doesn't say, "I want to write a *Mannix.*" Some older men just write TV, but somewhere along the line they missed something; they probably didn't have the ability to write the things you consider yourself a writer for.

The craft of action-adventure script writing hardly seems to encourage the original expression of important creative ideas. Even the author of a pilot script may be asked to adapt it from an extant film or literary work, to revive an idea used previously on television, or to copy elements of a successful format on another network. Networks are cautious about material which has not previously been done successfully. Hence it appears that many writers draw their stories from stock rather than fresh observations of life. According to one, "Since 1949, I've told every story that can be told many times."

After the pilot has been developed and tested, writers must conform to its format. They must fit the allotted program length and divide the story into the customary segments (those for an hour show being an opening "teaser," three acts, and an epilogue, with "cliffhangers" or situations of high suspense, at the end of at least the teaser and second act). They must suit the series's geographic location, its historical period, and the characteristics of its principals, which must remain the same from week to week. The longer the format is on the air, the more difficult it is to come up with fresh ideas. "By the three hundredth episode," asked a producer, "what can you say?"

A writer often cannot wait until inspiration strikes. He must have ideas when there is a market for them and when (if a producer wants his services) he is called in to "talk story." He must be able to write according to more than one format. "To survive," one respondent explained, "one must be able to write almost anything"—which in his case had included "*Martin Kane, Loretta Young,* Westerns, *Kildares,* and macabre comedy for Boris Karloff."

There are further restrictions on the writer's originality. According to a story editor, he must write what the public expects, based on his experience of what has worked before and on his consciousness of indicators of changing taste. He must also conform to the tastes of the producer and the executive producer. "Commercial freelance writers," said the story editor, "are less interested in the audience than in the man they want to buy their material." When one or more of the principals on the series are influential, they too must be taken into account; the script must be one they are eager to play in because it supports their images and gives them sufficiently prominent roles.

The writer must be willing to have his material rewritten by someone else or to rewrite it himself. One explained:

> This being a new show, we have people coming out of the woodwork to say how it should be treated. People are nervous about it. A lot of money is involved. The head of production sees the dailies and rough cuts and wants to lighten the show up. Network Standards and Practices comments, of course. So does the network liaison man, who'll even analyze the scripts line by line. The writer's submission is read by everyone and then sent back to him to incorporate everyone's suggestions. Also concerned are the head of television for the West Coast and even a man or two in New York. Then the director comes in—and if he wants changes, we go through the chain all over again.

When the producer hires a writer, he is not necessarily looking for a creative genius. As one respondent observed, "A script by a genius may contain a scene twenty-five minutes long that can't be edited." Instead, "the producer looks for writers who can meet their deadlines and give him material that he can shoot in six and a half days, within his budget, and without any trouble." By "trouble" the speaker meant chiefly objections from the network censors. (The respondents have already pointed out that good writers do not get unacceptable ideas.)

Another requirement of the action-adventure writer is speed. The time allowed from assignment to polished script generally varies from three to six weeks. (In contrast, one writer reported that contributors to the defunct *Playhouse 90* anthology series used to be given as long as six months.) For maximum income, a writer has to move briskly from one job to another. For one respondent, this meant not following his scripts through production and editing and not bothering about Broadcast Standards's evaluations. "By the time they react," he said, "you're busy with something else, with no time to spare for brouhaha." A second writer cited another pressure. "We aren't so well paid," she stated, "that we may not have to work on four simultaneous assignments, all taken on at the beginning of the season when most of the assignments are made. The pressure takes some of the joy out of creativity and makes the job less of an art than a craft."

For another writer, the word was not "craft" but "hackwork." Her concern was not so much with speed as with the limitations imposed on her originality: "Any time you are assigned to work up pretested story ideas and are supposed to give people what it's thought they want to see, quality goes down. This is hackwork." She also cited another barrier to creativity: "You rarely get a chance to say anything in your scripts. Occasionally, you can sneak in a point of view—*if* the public already accepts it." Consequently, she and her husband, who also wrote action-adventure scripts, intended to move out of Los Angeles and devote their talents wholly to books and other types of literature. Another writer hoped that his career in television was only temporary. "I feel compromised by the medium in the content I can deal with," he explained. "I'm anxious to get into feature pictures. They offer more freedom to do and say anything I want."

One can speculate that some dramatic writers never try to enter the field of action-adventure program writing because of some of the conditions described in this section. It is to be expected that the genre will attract the kind of writers who can accomodate to its conditions and reject the rest, so it is not surprising that most of the writers we interviewed seemed contented with their occupation and with the remuneration they could obtain from it. One complained about being prevented from entering some significant subject areas, but he concluded, "The writer has a living to make, so he won't buck these restrictions too much."

Obviously there are skillful writers who comply with the conditions under which commercial network television series are produced. The question remains, however, whether these conditions are conducive to that kind of writing which has consistently important things to say, over the broadest possible range, about the genuine problems, delights, and goals of human life. With more of that kind of writing, violence, when used, might well be more widely perceived and accepted by discriminating people as one means of increasing understanding of the human condition.

FOOTNOTES

1. The research upon which this report is based was performed pursuant to Contract No. HSM 42-70-32 with the National Institute of Mental Health, Health Services and Mental Health Administration,

U.S. Department of Health, Education, and Welfare. The principal investigator is Dr. Bradley S. Greenberg.

The authors and the project director gratefully acknowledge the interest and generosity of the television producers, writers, directors, and network standards people who participated in this study. All of them had given serious forethought to our subject. Most of them sacrificed two or more hours of their time at the height of the production season.

We have attempted to be faithful to their meaning in every instance. However, we take full responsibility for supplying the context in which their thoughts appear.

Thanks also to Cynthia Alspaugh, Barbara Burakoff, and Cheryl Smith for their secretarial services at the various stages of preparation of this manuscript.

2. Home Testing Institute, "Program Popularity Poll," T6651 170., Manhasset, Long Island, New York.

3. Broadcast Standards Department, National Broadcasting Company. *Four In One:* Night Gallery, "The Diary," June 23, 1970.

4. Broadcast Standards Department, National Broadcasting Company. *Four In One:* Night Gallery, "Togetherness," June 23, 1970.

5. Roy Danish, speech to the National Council on Family Relations, Chicago, 1970. Reported in *NAB Highlights*, October 12, 1970.

6. The same program was mentioned, independently, by a writer: "I wrote an episode about a chain gang which was intended to carry a message against violence. The boss of the gang loosed dogs to chase anyone who escaped and kill him. You never saw them kill anyone. But you could sense they'd got their man when the barking stopped. The network found it preferable for another human being to do the killing; a dog was too vicious."

7. Incidentally, all who use this argument have missed the opportunity to cite the fact that Aristotle acknowledges violence as an integral component of the tragic plot. After discussing the two other components, he writes, "A third part is suffering, which we may define as an action of destructive and painful nature, such as murders on the stage, tortures, woundings, and the like." (translation by Ingram Bywater)

8. Richard M. Powell, testimony on behalf of the Writers Guild of America (West) before the Federal Communications Commission, Washington, D.C., July 22, 1969.

9. A dramatic foil is a character who sets off another character or a situation by contrasting with it.

REFERENCES

Archer, W. *Play-making.* New York: Dodd, Mead & Company, 1926.

Baker, R.K. et al. The views, standards, and practices of the television industry. Appendix to Baker and Ball, 1969.

Baker, R.K., and Ball, S.J. (Eds.) *Mass media and violence: a staff report to the National Commission on the Causes and Prevention of Violence.* Washington, D.C.: U.S. Government Printing Office, 1969.

Berlyne, D.E. *Conflict, arousal and curiosity.* New York: McGraw-Hill, 1960.

Brunetiere, F. *Etudes critiques.* Vol 7.

Cantor, M.G. The role of the producer in choosing children's television content. In *Television and social behavior,* Vol. 1 (this volume).

Cantor, M.G. *Television producers: a sociological analysis.* (Doctoral dissertation, University of California at Los Angeles) Ann Arbor, Mich.: University Microfilms, 1970. No. 70-8121.

Engri, L. *The art of dramatic writing.* New York: Simon and Schuster, 1960.

Gordon, S. Traitor to my class. *Mass Media.* New York: The Ford Foundation, 1959.

Greenberg, B.S., and Gordon, T.F. Perceptions of violence in television programs: critics and the public. In *Television and social behavior,* Vol. 1 (this volume).

Heller, M.S., and Polsky, S. The television portrayal of violence: recommendations and guidelines. The Code Authority, National Association of Broadcasters, 1969. (Summarized in: Heller, M.S. and Polsky, S. Television violence: guidelines for evaluation. *Archives of General Psychiatry,* March 1971.)

Herrick, C. Sponsorship dilemma: single program or participation. *Nielsen Newscast,* 1970, **19,** No. 3, 3.

National Association of Broadcasters. *The television code.* (14th Ed.) 1969.

Spottiswoode, R. *Film and its techniques.* Berkeley and Los Angeles: University of California Press, 1957.

Stump, A. What became of the wild bunch? *TV Guide,* 1970, **18,** 46.

Appendix A: List of respondents

Margaret Armen, writer
Philip Barry, producer *(The Silent Force)*
Harve Bennett, producer *(Mod Squad)*
Dorothy Brown, director, Broadcast Standards and Practices, Western
     Division, American Broadcasting Company
James Byrnes, writer
William Cairncross, postproduction chief *(Mannix)*
Cy Chermak, executive producer *(Ironside)*
Richard Collins, producer *(Bonanza)*
Thomas Downer, Jr., director, Program Practices, CBS Television
     Network
Robert Duncan, writer
Wanda Duncan, writer
Jon Epstein, producer *(The Young Rebels)*
Morton Fine, producer *(The Most Deadly Game)*
Leonard Freeman, executive producer *(Hawaii Five-0)*
Norman Glenn, vice president, Music Corporation of America
Ivan Goff, producer *(Mannix)*
Walter Grauman, executive producer *(The Silent Force)*
John Hawkins, associate producer *(Bonanza)*; writer
Richard Irving, executive producer *(The Name of the Game)*
David Kaufman, reporter and columnist, *Daily Variety*
Thomas Kersey, Broadcast Standards and Practices, Western Division.
     American Broadcasting Company
Fernando Lamas, director
Mike Landon, writer, director, and actor
Bruce Lansbury, producer *(Mission: Impossible)*
Sheldon Leonard, television production executive
John Mantley, executive producer *(Gunsmoke)*
Harold Medford, writer
Winston Miller, producer *(Ironside)*
James Moser, writer
John Moxey, director
Gerard Petry, director, Broadcast Standards, National Broadcasting
     Company
Frank Price, executive producer *(The Virginian, Men from Shiloh)*
Ben Roberts, producer *(Mannix)*
Mark Rodgers, associate producer *(The Silent Force)*
Sy Salkowitz, writer
Philip Saltzman, producer *(The FBI)*
Donald Sanford, writer
James Schmerer, producer *(The High Chaparral)*

Melville Shavelson, president, Writers Guild of America (West)
Anthony Spinner, producer *(Dan August)*
Samuel Taylor, Jr., Program Practices, CBS Television Network
Tony Thomas, associate producer *(The Young Rebels)*
Robert Totten, director, writer, and actor
Herminio Traviesas, vice president, Broadcast Standards, National
    Broadcasting Company
Jack Webb, executive producer *(Adam-12)*
Mark Weingart, associate producer *(The FBI);* writer
John Wilder, writer
Tony Wilson, executive producer *(The Immortal)*

Appendix B: Interview outline

Audience data

(Established program) Broad description of audience attracted
(New program) Broad description of audience expected

Definitions of violence

Its meaning for interviewee
Working definition for interview: "Overt expression of force which results, or is intended to result, in injury or destruction"
Extent to which program can be said to exhibit violence in terms of definition

Why program portrays violence

How and where the ideas for violent action originate
Importance of violence to dramatic structure as an audience stimulant
Importance of violence to reflect human life and, in particular, the nature of American society
Any reasons connected with the nature of production and reception of television
Importance of violence for commercial competition with other TV offerings

Approaches to violence in the program

In general, are there good ways to be violent
In general, are there bad ways to be violent
What is most violent thing program has ever portrayed
Are there guidelines concerned with:

Kind of injury which may be inflicted—by whom and for what purposes
Visual consequences (e.g., painful consequences, gore)
Off-camera or obscured violence
Balancing of violence with moral messages
Other relevant guidelines

Feasibility for program of using alternatives to violence

Nonphysical predicaments, such as economic perils or social sanctions
Nonviolent verbal conflict resolution
Threats of harm without payoff
Other alternatives

Feasibility of suggested ways to counter alleged harmful effects of violence

Warning by dialogue cues, preprogram announcements, etc., that violent behavior is antisocial and unacceptable
Depiction of the repelling consequences of violent acts
Punishment in close proximity to the act
Other possible palliating means

Perception of youthful members in the program audience

Consciousness of their extent
Awareness of youthful viewing reactions as differing from those of adults
Influence of young viewers on writing and filming
Reaction to specific criticisms of the effect of TV violence on children:

"Good guys" and "bad guys" alike use violence to solve problems and achieve goals, suggesting that violence is normal, even admirable behavior—thus reducing viewers' inhibitions and increasing the probability of their violent behavior.

Painful consequences of violence are underplayed, deemphasized, "sanitized."

TV teaches children to:

approve of the use of violence to solve problems
perceive that violence is a more effective means of solving problems
be more willing to use violence

Television has encouraged youth ("the TV generation") to employ violence.
There are grounds for believing that TV violence triggers acts from people who are maladjusted and mentally unstable. There

are a good many children (and adults) whose sociopsychological normality is dubious, whose family life is less than happy, and who are living in communities that are far from stable. There is ample reason for concern about the probable behavioral impact of broadcasting to audiences of this soort such programs as *Mannix, High Chapparal, Mod Squad,* ... just to mention a few.

Perception of industry standards concerned with violence

Extent of interviewee's agreement with standards of network
Agreement with TV Code
Other significant influences (e.g., by advertisers)
Consciousness of standards during writing and shooting
Gray areas in standards
How does interviewee learn standards
Future: more rigid or more liberal

Additional comments by interviewee

Anything he would like the public and government to understand concerning violence in television programming

Appendix C: Censor's Review Forms

HPR 10 REV. 69   **SHOOTING SCRIPT REVIEW**

American Broadcasting Company
DEPARTMENT OF BROADCAST STANDARDS AND PRACTICES   •   WESTERN DIVISION   •   HOLLYWOOD

Dorothy Brown, Director

STUDIO_____   DATE_____

CONTACT_____   SHOOTING DATE_____

PROGRAM TITLE_____   EPISODE TITLE_____

The above indicated shooting script, received this date, has been reviewed by the Department of Broadcast Standards and Practices under current ABC broadcast standards.

Kindly forward such revisions as are necessary to effect the modifications requested below. If revisions are acceptable upon receipt by the Department of Broadcast Standards and Practices, no supplementary review will be forthcoming.

This review does not constitute a Broadcast Standards approval of subsequent script changes or changes in method of treatment in production. A separate screening report will be issued upon viewing the Rough Cut film. *Kindly advise me at such time as this episode is available for Rough Cut/First Trial screening. Final approval is based on viewing the completed film.*

COMMENTS (Confidential):

_____
EDITOR
DEPARTMENT OF BROADCAST
STANDARDS AND PRACTICES

HPR 114 REV. 69

ROUGH CUT SCREENING REPORT

American Broadcasting Company

DEPARTMENT OF BROADCAST STANDARDS AND PRACTICES • WESTERN DIVISION • HOLLYWOOD

Dorothy Brown, Director

STUDIO_____   DATE_____

CONTACT_____ _____   RELEASE DATE_____

PROGRAM TITLE_____   EPISODE TITLE_____

The Rough Cut of the above titled episode was screened for compliance with the Department of Broadcast Standards and Practices requirements on date of_____ .

This report is applicable only to the Rough Cut as screened. Caution: Please advise me of any extensive editorial revisions after this date. Changes could possibly effect the continuing acceptability of this episode, and therefore must be re-screened for final approval.

A separate screening report will be issued upon viewing the 35mm First Trial (Answer Print). Final approval is based on viewing the completed film.

COMMENTS:

_____
EDITOR
DEPARTMENT OF BROADCAST
STANDARDS AND PRACTICES

Table 1: Audience size for study programs*
(rounded to nearest 1,000)

	Time	Day	Ages 2-5	Ages 6-11	Ages 12-17
Adam 12	8:30	Sat.	1,186,000	4,300,000	3,444,000
Bonanza	9:00	Sun.	755,000	2,961,000	3,668,000
Dan August	10:00	Wed.	379,000	1,216,000	908,000
The FBI	8:00	Sun.	1,155,000	3,845,000	3,444,000
Four-in-One	10:00	Wed.	254,000	602,000	1,408,000
Gunsmoke	7:30	Mon.	2,679,000	3,722,000	2,094,000
Hawaii Five-0	10:00	Wed.	453,000	1,843,000	3,200,000
High Chapparal	7:30	Fri.	1,437,000	1,695,000	1,419,000
Immortal	10:00	Thurs.	96,000	1,032,000	1,734,000
Ironside	8:30	Thurs.	1,150,000	2,469,000	2,885,000
Men from Shiloh	7:30	Wed.	1,251,000	2,588,000	2,567,000
Mod Squad	7:30	Tue.	1,728,000	4,361,000	4,607,000
Most Deadly Game	9:30	Sat.	222,000	1,081,000	861,000
Mission: Impossible	7:30	Sat.	1,738,000	3,047,000	3,514,000
Mannix	10:00	Sat.	490,000	2,740,000	3,607,000
Name of the Game	8:30	Fri.	429,000	1,400,000	1,012,000
Silent Force	8:30	Mon.	897,000	1,671,000	2,420,000
Young Rebels	7:00	Sun.	940,000	2,678,000	3,153,000

*   Source: Nielsen Television Index, Second Report for October 1970 (two weeks ending October 24, 1970).

The Structure and Content of Television Broadcasting in Four Countries: An Overview

Michael Gurevitch

The Hebrew University of Jerusalem
The Communications Institute

The four reports assembled here represent both the benefits and the difficulties involved in cross-cultural research. Inasmuch as the four studies constitute an attempt to look at the same phenomenon—the presentation of violence and sex on the television screen in four different countries and its relationship to the organizational structure and to the broadcasting philosophies of four different television services—it does, indeed, constitute a comparative cross-national study. However, the common denominator, as it emerges from the four reports, is limited to a general theme, rather than an agreed and explicit research design.

Garry (1970), in an introduction to a series of studies designed to evaluate the reactions of children and young people in five countries to a Czechoslovak television program for children, highlights this difficulty. He argues that while "the assumption. . .that a uniform design could be developed and executed in all five countries. . .is not impossible. . .(it) would require a 'workshop' in which the researchers reached a common understanding of the various aspects of the research design." He adds that arriving at a common understanding "was not possible in the limited time available for face-to-face meetings; and curiously, correspondence widened rather than lessened the gaps." In attempting an overview of the four reports of the present study, I can only echo Professor Garry's sentiments.

I could point out a number of reasons why it is difficult to consider these four case studies a truly unified cross-cultural study. To begin with, no agreed research design was ever evolved by the participants. The only agreed baseline was an attempted look at the same phenomenon in the respective countries. It is not surprising, therefore, that each of the participant researchers viewed the problem according to his own research interests. Moreover, the social, cultural, political, and historical circumstances which surround the broadcasting operation in each of these countries are sufficiently different to seriously curtail the possibility of a comparative evaluation, unless a very strict design were adhered to. This is most dramatically manifested in the empirical part of the reports—the content analysis of television's output, in which differences in the scope and quantity of output alone render comparative analysis impossible unless these differences are taken into account and compensated for before the content analysis operation begins. This was not done in the present study; and consequently, a meaningful comparative evaluation of the content analytic findings becomes extremely difficult. Last, but not least, the tenuous contacts between the participants while the research was carried out and the reports were written inevitably resulted in some misunderstandings and in uneven contributions, which varied in scope and in emphasis on various issues and problems.

This overview, therefore, will not attempt any comprehensive comparative evaluation of the findings. Rather, it should be seen as one observer's view of some of the issues raised in the general study. It deals first with the institutional part of the reports and then with their empirical, content analytic section.

THE INSTITUTIONS

The broadcasting institutions described and analyzed in these reports represent different concepts and different systems of ownership and control. While they do not reflect the entire spectrum of existing systems of broadcasting control, they do range from the American commer-

cial, privately owned system, through the Swedish and the British examples of a public corporation and a public authority, to the Israeli system
of broadcasting controlled by a public authority which, however (as the
Israeli report describes it), is "perhaps more closely tied to government" than the British Broadcasting Corporation, on which it is modeled. To complete the spectrum of systems of broadcasting control, an
example of a broadcasting service directly controlled by the state should
have been included. Nevertheless, the range represented in the reports
seems to be wide enough to allow some tentative generalizations about
the relationship between the structure of ownership and control and the
broadcasting output of these different institutions.

All the organizations described here are essentially self-regulating.
They also claim to be guided by a sense of "public responsibility." Be-
neath these superficial similarities, however, considerable differences
can be detected. The roots of the system of self-regulation accepted by
American broadcasters are to be found, as the American report puts it,
in "the fear of government-enforced standards of programming, of
stricter public regulation of commercial message content, and of destructive internecine industry warfare." This system constitutes a "flexible
instrument" which serves to "help protect the common interests of the
industry and its chief patrons, to cultivate its publics, and to preserve its
markets" by steering it through "paths of least turbulence." Israeli
broadcasting, on the other hand (if indeed it can be viewed as being at
the other pole of the spectrum embraced by the four case studies),
seems to be regulated and controlled by an authority and a system of
codes which is much more attuned to political considerations and much
more openly supportive of the leadership role of government. The in-
between examples of the Swedish and British broadcasting systems can
perhaps be seen as purer cases of institutions regulated by their own notions of "public responsibility," in a less adulterated and abused sense
of this concept.

This is not to argue that the British or the Swedish services are more
(or less) publicly responsible than the other two examples included here;
it is only to say that they seem to be somewhat freer of the myriad anxieties which characterize the American commercial system on the one
hand and (on the other hand) the acceptance of a subordinate self-image
vis-a-vis the government which characterizes the Israeli system. Thus,
while, structurally at least, three of the four systems described here—the
Swedish, the British, and the Israeli—manifest considerable similarities,
and while initially all four systems accept self-regulation as the best
means of protecting their autonomy, in practice the way in which the
codes and regulations governing their program output operate seems to
emphasize their differential status in society and their differential positions vis-a-vis the various constellations of "power roles" and pressure
groups in the societies in which they operate. The formal structure of

control therefore seems to be a weak predictor of the true nature in which the systems of codes and regulations actually operate.

What, then, determines the operative nature of these codes? While the answer to this question has a direct bearing on the immediate problem with which this study is concerned—the presentation of violent and sexual contents on the screen—it raises the wider question of the differential sensitivities which these institutions manifest toward different issues in their societies (or what the Israeli report describes as a "scale of sensitive subjects"). Generally, it seems justified to argue that the different sensitivities reflected in the codes and regulations reflect the sensitivities and the areas of concern of the national cultures which these organizations serve, rather than the broadcasters' specific structures of ownership and control. Thus the sensitivity of the American and (perhaps to a somewhat lesser extent) the British broadcasting organizations to the issues of sex and violence are probably a reflection of the sensitivity displayed toward these issues by the Western middle-class culture which these organizations serve and promote.

Israeli broadcasting, on the other hand, is primarily sensitive to issues of military security and to other social and political issues which stem from the specific social composition of Israeli society and the political structure of its government—to which, as has already been suggested, Israeli broadcasters are closely attuned. Thus the lower position of sex and violence on the "scale of sensitive subjects" with which Israeli broadcasting is concerned stems largely from its preoccupation with other issues which it considers more immediately pressing. At the same time, Israeli media must be sensitive to these issues both because of their self-designated role as an instrument of nation-building (a role which stresses the educational importance of their programming) and because of their audience considerations, especially their preoccupation with the image of Israeli culture they project to their Arab audiences.

Very little information in the Swedish report illuminates the extent to which the presentation of sex and/or violence reflects the degree to which different cultures take either of these issues for granted—in other words, the extent to which broadcasters can assume a high level of tolerance toward either of these issues in the national or the cultural consciousness. Regrettably, discussion of the characteristics of national cultures is almost inevitably reduced to the use of cliches and stereotypes. Simplistic as they sound, however, these notions were not unimportant when the concerns of this present study were formulated. The designers of the study seem to have assumed that American television, for example, will be saturated with violence but shy away from sex precisely because violence is assumed to be an accepted part of American culture while sex still constitutes a sensitive theme in American middle-class culture. Swedish television, on the other hand, was assumed to be not overly concerned about the display of sex but more worried than

American television about the presentation of violence. We have no evidence in the American or Swedish reports to either support or disprove this stereotypical assumption. A worthwhile task for future research in this area should therefore be to identify the hierarchy of sensitivities within different societies and cultures, and then attempt to relate this hierarchy to the prevalence of sensitive themes in their cultural products.

The British report makes an additional point about the operative impact of codes and regulations, especially as they pertain to the presentation of violence and sex. Its authors argue that, to a great extent, the planning, production, and purchase of programs is relatively free of considerations related to the specific issues of violence and sex. Considerations of audience appeal, availability of resources, and "adequate" program mix are paramount in the decision-makers' minds. Immediate concern with the adequacy of presentation of violence and sex incidents will emerge only when specific incidents included in the programs violate the boundaries of what will be taken for granted by the social consensus. British broadcasters, then, are concerned with the exceptional rather than the routinized presentation of these themes.

Broadcasting organizations in most countries are engaged in promoting and buttressing these cultural "hierarchies of sensitivity," but these organizations also employ creative people who are interested in the medium's possible role as cultural innovator. Thus the broadcasting organizations are caught between pressures from the audience's cultural consensus on the one hand and from their own creative personnel on the other.

All broadcasting organizations need to respect and remain within the audience consensus in order to maintain the allegiance of viewers and the support of the society's ruling institutions. At the same time, the broadcasters must satisfy the needs of their creative personnel to experiment and probe at the boundaries of this consensus. Like every organization which faces such a dilemma between "order" and "freedom," broadcasting organizations set up rules which compromise between the two forces: the system of codes and regulations. Ideally, this system should perform the dual function of maintaining the institution's autonomy vis-a-vis political and other social institutions by ensuring the "ordered" professional behavior of its personnel, while at the same time maintaining for them as much creative freedom as possible. In practice, both the dilemma and its resolution take different shapes in the different organizations described in this study. Of the four case studies, the British report pays more attention to this problem than do the others. It would seem, therefore, that the different ways in which the systems of codes and regulations function to maintain simultaneously both the broadcasters' autonomy and their character as "creative organizations" should be taken up in greater detail in future research.

All four reports provide fairly detailed descriptions of the formal structures of the broadcasting organizations analyzed, as well as of their formal codes and regulations. These are generally supplemented by information gathered in the course of interviews with top decision makers. However, this kind of analysis seems to give excessive representation to the view from the top; this should at least be supplemented by a view of the decision-making process as seen by other echelons involved in production. Even that procedure would not necessarily tell the full institutional story. What seems to be required is a series of production case studies conducted by close observation and designed to elicit the specific processes by which decisions are made, how they percolate down to the production staff, and how they are implemented or adapted by creative personnel and then fed back to the higher echelons by various means.

THE CONTENTS

The purpose of analyzing the contents of television in this study is, as Gerbner puts it, to tap "what systems of images and messages television as a whole releases into the national consciousness." This seems to be a tall order, and it is rather doubtful that the content analytic work reported in these studies can actually claim to have accomplished or even approximated this task—not because of the quality of the content analytic work reported, but because of the complexity and ambitiousness of the undertaking. The following discussion will comment on some of the methodological problems which reduce the comparability of the content analytic findings reported, will attempt a limited comparative presentation of the data, and will summarize some of the theoretical problems involved in achieving the difficult goal proposed by Gerbner.

Only two of the four reports (the British and the Israeli) contain sections describing the content analysis of one week of televisin output in these countries. The American content analytic study was conducted as a separate project over the last three years, covering a large amount of material and carrying the analysis to great lengths. Its findings are reported elsewhere in this volume. The Swedish researchers did not conduct a quantitative analysis of the content they viewed; they felt, after viewing the material, that "there was so little violence and sex that an elaborate schedule became meaningless."

The most obvious methodological problem is the discrepancies between the types of programs which have been viewed and analyzed in the different countries, the methods of data collection, the kinds of analysis which have been carried out, and the methods of presenting the findings. If we wish in the future to be able to draw comparative conclusions, all of these aspects will have to be standardized.

A second problem, which becomes clear when an attempt is made to review the findings comparatively, is the different amounts of television material broadcast in the different countries. The largest amount is, of course, provided by American television. Because of the unique structure of American television, it is almost impossible to estimate the total number of television hours made available to the audience unless one first specifies the geographical area. British television provides, on the whole, over 200 hours of television per week on three channels, BBC 1, BBC 2, and ITA (Independent Television Authority). Of this total, the British researchers watched a total of 98 hours on two channels during the week and analyzed and coded approximately 75 percent of what they watched. Swedish television provides a total of 68 hours of viewing per week on two channels; the researchers considered approximately 17 and one-half hours of fiction material valid subject matter for their content analysis. Israeli television, the youngest of the services studied, broadcasts a total of approximately 28 hours a week on one channel only, of which about 75 percent are in Hebrew and the rest in Arabic.

While the sheer volume of material made available to the audience does not directly affect the possibility of a comparative analysis, it has indirect implications for this problem, since an increase in the number of broadcast hours usually affects the distribution of the types of programs broadcast: when more material is broadcast, the distribution is likely to be tipped in favor of programs easily available and readily accepted by the audience, like crime series, thrillers, and similar shows which contain a great deal of violence. Thus the percentage of programs containing violence seems to be directly affected by the capability of different television services to maintain a balanced programming diet. Future research will have to take cognizance of this problem and suggest a procedure for tackling these differences in a way which will render the separate findings from each country more conducive to a comparative evaluation.

Another aspect of this problem is the balance between locally produced and imported materials broadcast. Both Swedish and Israeli television, for example, rely rather heavily at present on imported material. (Almost two thirds of Sweden's second channel output is imported material; Israeli television currently fills about half its total broadcasting hours with foreign material.) American and British television, on the other hand, with their much richer facilities and larger resources, are capable of producing a much larger percentage of their total material. These differences in balance have particularly serious implications for "the systems of messages fed into the national consciousness." The predominant position of American television material on the international market threatens to turn television in smaller countries into mere offshoots of American television. Broadcasting organizations which use a preponderance of American or other foreign material might lose their relevance for the cultures they were set up to serve. Their status as "feeders" of the "national consciousness" might become questionable.

SOME COMPARATIVE FINDINGS

Despite discrepancies between the types of materials analyzed in the different countries and the types of analyses, which were carried out, it is still possible to present a very limited comparative summary of some of the basic "measures of violence" in television's content which were included in the separate reports.

However, several discrepancies should be noted:

1) The American data is derived from Gerbner's report in this volume and is based on his "1969 enlarged sample." It is therefore approximately two years older than the data described in the British and the Israeli reports.

2) Since the American report did not include any data on sexual contents, and since the analyses of this data in the British and Israeli reports differ markedly, no comparative summary of that data is presented.

3) The computations carried out on the Israeli data differ in some ways from the analysis of the American and the British material; consequently, in a few instances no comparable figures to the British and the American figures could be presented for Israeli television. The Swedish report did not include any quantitative analysis of Swedish television's content, so no information on Swedish television could be included here.

American television not only provides the largest amount of viewing material; it is also highest in violent content. By all measures, American television contains considerably more violence than British television. Israeli television, with its very great dependence on imported material for its fictional contents, seems also to be higher in violence than British television, though not as high as American television. Table 1 presents these figures.

The amount of violence varies by format, style, or theme of the programs (Table 2). The format containing most violence is the cartoon. This is true both on American and on British television. (The Israeli report does not provide separate figures for cartoons, even though the programming schedule for the week analyzed included a half-hour of cartoons). All cartoons shown on British television (BBC only) contained violence; the percentage of cartoons containing violence shown on American television is 98.1. Feature films were also high in violence in all three countries. Seven of eight films analyzed in the American report, and eight of ten shown on British television, included violence; on Israeli television all three films shown during the sample week contained at least one violent episode. Comparable figures can be gleaned on vio-

382 MEDIA CONTENT AND CONTROL

Table 1: Selected measures of violence in American, British, and Israeli television (all fictional programes)

	American	British	Israeli
No. of programs analyzed	121	79	10
No. of hours analyzed	71.75	54.9	– –
Measures of Violence			
programs containing violence	83.5	55.7	90.0
% program hours containing violence	83.2	61.6	– –
No. of violent incidents	630	222	38
Rate per program	5.2	2.81	3.8
Rate per hour	8.8	4.04	– –
% of programs with major character involved in violence	66.3	46.8	– –
% of programs with major character committing violence	48.5	41.8	– –
Program score	111.5	69.4	– –

Table 2: Selected measures of violence by format and style

	American	British	Israeli
Cartoons			
No. of programs	53	6	– –
% of programs containing violence	98.1	100	– –
Rate of violent incidents per program	7.0	4.67	– –
Rate of violent incidents per hour	30.4	33.73	– –
Feature films			
No. of programs	8	10	3
% of programs containing violence	87.5	80	100
Rate of violent incidents per program	5.3	7	4
Rate of violent incidents per hour	2.5	4.12	– –
Style			
Comedy			
No. of programs	60	28	– –
% of programs containing violence	73.3	42.9	– –
Rate of violent incidents per program	5.4	1.79	– –
Rate of violent incidents per hour	14.51	3.37	– –
Crime, western, action-adventure			
No. of programs	82	21	4
% of programs containing violence	97.6	100	100
Rate of violent incidents per program	6.8	7.29	6.5
Rate of violent incidents per hour	13.9	7.95	– –

lence in programs labelled "Crime, western, action-adventure" and in the "comedy" category (which includes cartoons).

The category of cartoons, which contain violence almost by definition, is higher in violent content than the category of "comedy" (to which cartoons, as has been noted, contribute a high rate of violence). It should be noted that the percentage of programs containing violence in the action-adventure category and the rate of violent incidents per program in that category are higher for British television than for American television. The latter, however, broadcasts four times as many programs of this category as British television and almost twenty times as many as does Israeli television with its very limited schedule.

American television introduces violence not only to the American home screen, but also to other countries when its materials are exported. Those American programs which have been shown on British and Israeli television contribute more violence to the screen than do locally produced programs in these countries. Table 3 compares the programs shown on British and Israeli television by their origin. (No analysis by origin of programs exists in the American report.)

Table 3: Selected measures of violence on British and
Israeli Television, by origin of the programs

	U.S. originating	U.K. originating	Israeli originating
British TV			
No. of programs	24	53	– –
% of all programs	30.4	67.1	– –
% of programs containing violence	75	45.3	– –
Rate of violent incidents per program	5.17	1.66	– –
*Israeli TV**			
No. of programs	14	8	21
% of all programs	31.1	17.7	46.6
% of programs containing violence	85.7	50.0	9.5
Rate of violent incidents per program	1.21	1.75	0.19

* Includes also nonfiction programs (but excludes news programs). No analysis by origin is available for fictional programs only.

It is interesting to note, however, that those British programs shown on Israeli television are higher in "rate of violent incidents per program" than are American programs, though fewer of them contain violence. Those British programs which do contain violence apparently contain, on the average, a larger dose of violent incidents than do the American programs imported by Israeli television.

In general, then, one may safely conclude that, on the basis of the data presented in these reports, American television programs come out highest on almost all measures of violence. This obviously results in large amounts of violence on American television screens; it also means that the importation of American television material to other countries usually results in an increase of the amount of violence on their screens. However, the fact that British-made programs of this genre are no less violent than their American counterparts suggests that the prevalence of certain genres, rather than the country of origin of the program, is the critical variable in the diffusion of violence on the screen.

THEORETICAL CONSIDERATIONS

The question of the feasibility of conducting a cross-cultural content analysis also raises basic theoretical issues. The British study attempted to tackle some of these problems empirically, by supplementing the content analytic report with additional material designed to compare the content analytic findings with audience perceptions of the same material. By doing this, the British study pointed to one of the procedures by which the problems might be handled.

In order to move from the simplest form of content analysis—counting the frequency with which particular units of content occur, to the level suggested by Gerbner—tapping the systems of images and messages which are fed into the national consciousness—at least three problems have to be solved satisfactorily: 1) moving from describing units of content to describing recurrent structures in the content; 2) establishing a degree of equivalence between the meaning attributed to these structures by the content analyst and the meanings attributed to it by different individuals and groups in the audience; and 3) establishing the extent to which we can locate and identify in the audience's perception of media messages a shared universe of meanings corresponding to the shared symbolic environment provided by the media.

The problem of attributing specific meanings to the content analyzed in these studies becomes even more acute because of the cross-national character of the study. Even if we assume that we can tap the meanings of the contents and generalize about their universality in one society, it does not necessarily follow that we can attribute such universality of interpretation to audiences in different and varied cultures. While it is true that one of the remarkable characteristics of television is that television screens almost all over the world project not only similar but (to a large degree) *identical* messages, there is very little evidence to suggest that this globally shared symbolic environment generates a globally shared universe of meaning. Indeed, if we are to go by the evidence of cross-cultural study, the opposite is probably more likely.

A further question which ought to be raised is that of the scope of the themes analyzed in the present study. Perhaps instead of looking at sex and violence, we should attempt to elicit the underlying structure which shapes the patterns of human relationships as they are conceived of and presented on television. Are sex and violence merely instances of human interaction perceived as power relationships? If that is the case, perhaps the scope of themes analyzed should be widened to include other manifestations of these relationships. Indeed, what seems to be required is an attempt to identify the structure underlying all the themes presented on television; only then can we hope to arrive at some more comprehensive system of "cultural indicators."

A truly valid and comprehensive system of cultural indicators, however, would have to take into account the entire range of messages released into the national consciousness by television, by other media, and by other forms of communication. It would also have to perceive the relationship between the media, on the one hand, and culture and the "national consciousness," on the other, as a dynamic one. Both feed into each other and act on each other. Some theory about the nature of this interaction can then also act as theoretical underpinning for the proposed system of cultural indicators.

The Structure and Process of Television Program Content Regulation in the United States

George Gerbner

The Annenberg School of Communications

University of Pennsylvania

Television is a prime cultivator of common images and patterns of information among large and heterogeneous publics that have little else in common. These images and patterns form a major part of our symbolic environment. They help socialize members of society to the prevailing institutional and moral order.

Different societies organize their major symbol-making activities, and particularly their braodcasting systems, along different lines; each attempts to be functional to its own requirements. In the United States, three major commercial networks and their affiliates dominate broadcasting. Public television plays a minor complementary role: providing services that broadcasters consider worthwhile but not profitable.

The Preamble to the Television Code of the National Association of Broadcasters (the chief industry organization) reminds station owners of their sweeping responsibilities under the law. Not only is the television broadcaster as license holder legally responsible for the programming of his station, the Preamble warns, but he is "obligated to bring his positive responsibility. . .to bear upon all who have a hand in the production of programs, including networks, sponsors, producers of film and live programs, advertising agencies, and talent agencies."

Going even further, the Preamble specifies the broadcaster's "accountability" for fulfilling the special needs of children's, community, educational, and cultural programming and for the "acceptability," "decency and decorum," and "propriety" of their choices for "every moment of every program":

> Television and all who participate in it are jointly accountable to the American public for respect for the special needs of children, for community responsibility, for the advancement of education and culture, for the acceptability of the program materials chosen, for decency and decorum in production, and for propriety in advertising. This responsibility cannot be discharged by any given group of programs, but can be discharged only through the highest standards of respect for the American home, applied to every moment of every program presented by television.

How does American television fulfill the solemn and exacting responsibilities it has proclaimed for itself? No one can possibly know or easily discover. There is no definitive study, no theory based on objective investigation, no systematic surveillance, and no mechanism of accounting for the substance of the services for which "television and all who participate in it are jointly accountable to the American people." Program content control and regulation are private affairs. They are protected by the First Amendment to the U.S. Constitution from government intervention and thus also from public scrutiny. Consequently, and rather shockingly, in probably no area of significant social policy are far-reaching decisions made with as little systematic, reliable, cumulative, and comparative information brought to bear on the decision-making (and on its public policy implications) as in the sphere of the common culture.

Such attempts as have been made to assemble the needed information have been stimulated mostly by Congressional, Presidential or other governmental inquiries into matters of special concern at a particular time. This study is no exception. But our purpose is merely to point the way toward a broader and more sustained comparative investigation. This report is an attempt to collect a few facts, observations, and suggestions based on public documents, published sources, and interviews with knowledgeable informants to provide the context in which recent research on televised sex and violence can be placed in a social and institutional perspective.[1]

THE SCOPE OF AMERICAN TELEVISION

In the first quarter of 1971, 892 active channels telecast programs to over 60 million homes. A year earlier, there were 677 stations; sixteen years before, 411. All but about four percent of American homes have television and use it an average of over six hours a day. It has been calculated that the people of the United States already spend approximately half as many hours with radio and television as they spend in all kinds of paid work put together. The patronage—by which we mean guardianship and funding—that supports this service was divided between advertisers, who paid in 1971 about $3.5 billion for sending messages over the air, and the public, who paid some $3.8 billion in new sets alone for receiving them.

Table 1 shows that 78 percent of all active channels were private

Table 1: Active U.S. TV channels as of February 1, 1971

	VHF	UHF	TOTALS
Private (commercial)	511 86%	185 62%	695 78%
	73%	27%	100%
Public (noncommercial)	85 14%	111 38%	196 22%
	43%	57%	100%
TOTALS	595 100%	296 100%	892 100%
	67%	33%	100%

commercial corporations; 22 percent were public corporations. Of all private stations, 73 percent were Very High Frequency serving large established markets, while only 43 percent of the public stations were VHF. Or, to look at it another way, of all VHF channels on the air (67 percent of all channels), 86 percent were commercial and 14 percent public, while of all Ultra High Frequency (UHF) channels (33 percent of all channels), 27 percent were commercial and 57 percent public.

The number of individual license holders reflects an FCC rule limiting the number of stations a single corporation may own. About 25 percent of all commercial stations are owned in groups of five or more. However, 82 percent of all commercial stations are owned by or affiliated with one of the three major networks. NBC owned and affiliated stations number 39 percent of the total, CBS stations 34 percent, and ABC stations 28 percent. This group of 572 network stations dominates commercial television programming in the U.S.

Public television stations, licensed as "noncommercial, educational" broadcasters, are interconnected by the Public Broadcasting Service; PBS distributes programs produced by a few major production centers, member stations, and foreign sources. All public channels are individually operated by local and state educational systems, colleges, universities, and community organizations. In addition to PBS, six regional networks provide interconnection or program exchanges for member stations. Twenty-one state networks also help stations exchange services and primarily instructional programs.

SOME POWER ROLES AND FUNCTIONS

No established theory of organization, decision-making, or policy formation accounts for the complex interplay of forces governing television programming and the shaping of program content. I shall follow and develop earlier suggestions (Gerbner, 1969) for a classification of power roles and functions affecting content. It is evident that in cultural production, as in any other mass production and distribution involving high stakes and broad impact, the analysis of control processes must focus upon the distribution and exercise of power.

The groups which have some stake in and influence, authority, or power over the choice and shaping of content include: the authorities who confer licenses and administer or enforce the laws; the patrons who invest, subsidize, or otherwise fund the operation in return for services rendered; other organizations, institutions, and loose aggregations of people (publics) that require attention, services, protection, or cultivation; the corporate management that regulates, supervises, and develops programs; the auxiliary industry groups and associations that provide services, raw materials, and protection; the creative talent, experts, and technicians who actually form the symbolic content and transmit the signals; and the colleagues and competitors whose solidarity or innovation help set standards and maintain vigilance.

These groups represent *roles* that can exist in any combination of persons and whose functions and powers vary widely. We shall not analyze or describe them here further except to suggest that a full study of these functions and powers should systematically observe all critical incidents that require the exercise of leverage and the application of sanctions. It is these acts, sporadic as they may be, that set the lines of power and authority for the routine control and regulation of program content.

We shall briefly note the role of authorities, patrons, organizations and publics in the control process, and then examine in greater detail the formal structure and informal dynamics of two decisive management functions: program regulation and program development.

Authorities

The Communications Act of 1934 established the Federal Communications Commission (FCC) and authorized it to grant exclusive licenses to broadcast in assigned geographical areas and to renew them for three-year periods if that still served the "public interest, convenience, and necessity." These terms were never clearly spelled out, and the FCC and the courts have been reluctant to use their contested powers to set program standards. The "fairness doctrine," upheld by the Supreme Court, sought to safeguard some diversity in the presentation of public policy issues, but no such doctrine exists for general programming. Antitrust laws and other devices have sought to maintain some multiplicity of forums, but with little success. Network domination, multimedia ownership, advertising concentration, and the trend toward conglomerates all tended to erode such multiplicity. Also, as Barron (1969) has observed, "diversity of ideas, not multiplicity of forums, is the primary objective of the First Amendment."

The Supreme Court's landmark *Red Lion* decision has held that "freedom of press from governmental interference. . .does not sanction repression of the freedom by private interests." But public authority has not yet found a way of holding private power in check in matters of general program content, except by stimulating industry self-regulation.

Organizations and the public

The general public continues to view in ever-increasing numbers whatever is on the air. During prime time evening hours, over 64 percent of all American homes use television. An average home uses television six hours 18 minutes daily. In one day, television reaches almost 81 million adults—66 percent of all Americans 18 and older—and an uncounted number of children.

Every study shows that television is the most massive magnet of public attention in history. Berelson (1964) surveyed cultural content in various forms and found commercial television and fictional and dramatic material in the lead. Imaginative representations of life and the world in the form of plays, films, exhibition of talents and personalities, and documentary presentations form the basic appeal of television as a cultural medium.

For the services of this medium, viewers pay no fee or license. They have, however, invested many billions of dollars in receivers (43 percent of homes in color); in 1970 alone, $3.8 billion was spent on new sets. In addition, viewers (and nonviewers paid an indirect television subsidy of about $3.5 billion in 1970—that is, all consumers paid about $3.5 billion more for the goods and services they purchased because of advertising costs to the companies they bought from.

The direct patronage of the viewing public in the form of payment for receiving sets does not confer upon the public the power to shape program content or to apply sanctions other than those of consumers. The indirect public subsidy paid through television advertising confers power over programming upon the advertising and broadcasting corporate managements. These managements' relations with the public are exactly what the terms suggest: public relations.

This means that there is active competition for public attention, favor, and program and product support without any allocation of power over programming to representatives of the public—in or out of the government. Nevertheless, during the past 20 years a number of civic and private organizations have brought pressure to bear on the shaping of program content. The National Association for Better Radio and Television has lobbied against violence and published program studies and critiques since the early 1950s. More recently, the National Citizens Committee for Broadcasting was formed to lobby on public policy issues, and Action for Children's Television (ACT) began to direct attention to programs and commercials aimed at children. The civil rights and consumer movements have generated both organizations and a growing sense militancy in urging scrutiny of television. The technological innovations of cable television offers the possibility of greater public access and selectivity in programming.

These and other pressures are reflected in the process of program regulation and development. But the main function of the public for the broadcasters is to serve as a commodity he can measure, package, and sell to the patrons who directly subsidize television broadcasting.

Competition among networks takes the form of management strategy for expanding the share of viewers or of markets of certain types for certain programs and products. For example, CBS recently produced for its advertisers a color wheel showing "Where the girls are." The wheel's perimeter lists 91 types of products. Inside, five little windows show product buying by demographic categories, indicating that women aged 25 to 64, for whom many CBS daytime programs are designed, buy more than do women in the 18 to 49 bracket, standard for other media statistics. NBC's management then pointed out that *its* daytime schedule attracts 2,960,000 women 25-64 (against 2,830,000 for CBS), winning a majority for eight out of its 12 daytime programs against their CBS competitors (*Variety*, February 24, 1971).

Patrons and client relations

Media patrons are those who directly invest in or subsidize media operations in exchange for economic, political, or cultural benefits. Clients are media that provide such benefits in exchange for discretionary patronage. Media patrons may be banks, advertisers, other corporate or civic organizations, religious or military bodies, or governments. The principal types of patrons and the major client relationships determine the role of media management in the power scheme of every society. Patron-client relationships also delineate the mass media's approach to most issues and problems, and permeate the climate of communicator decision-making.

In U.S. television, the principal client relationship is between the large national advertisers and the networks. Television revenues come primarily from the sale of access to the airways to advertisers; television delivers to the advertisers the time and attention of the publics it has assembled through its programming. The rates for the delivery of public time and attention depend on the size (and often on the type) of the audiences delivered. The value of this service ultimately depends on how the purchases, good will, votes, and other economic, political, or cultural services obtained affect the patron's share of the market, his competitive position, and his future prospects.

U.S. advertisers paid, for all such services to all media, about $20 billion in 1969. Television, second only to newspapers, received $3.5 billion (18 percent of the total); magazines were a poor third with only eight percent, and radio fourth with 6.5 percent of the total.

National advertisers, footing nearly $7 billion of the $20 billion total media bill, provided 44 percent of all television revenues, compared with 21 percent of magazine, 16 percent of newspaper, and seven percent of radio income. Furthermore, the top 100 national advertisers provided 63 percent of all television income in exchange for the time and attention of TV's massive and heterogeneous audiences. The same group of national advertisers paid only 16 percent of magazine income and nine percent of newspaper income. Two-thirds of television advertising was accounted for by the manufacturers of food, toiletry, drug, soap, tobacco, and automotive products. The top 25 network advertisers accounted for 54 percent of all network television billings in 1969, with three giant soap companies alone claiming 14 percent of the total.

The advertiser's chief leverage is logistical. He can cut back or terminate his sponsorship, or shift to another time, program, station, network, or medium. The accumulated experience of such sanctions guides network executives in setting programming policy. Substantive demands of advertising patrons are codified by the network censor's office and sometimes by the sponsoring agencies themselves. Most of these comments and codes pertain to the commercial messages or to the protection of product or client interests in the programs. Some, however, are more sweeping. General Mills, one of the Big Ten network sponsors, ruled that "The moral code of the characters in our dramas will be more or less synonymous with the moral code of the bulk of the American middle class as it is commonly understood...." Other provisions in the 22-point General Mills code were: "Where it seems fitting, the characters should reflect acceptance of the world situation in their thoughts and actions, although in dealing with war, our writers should minimize the 'horror'aspects. . . . Men in uniform should not be cast as heavy villains or portrayed as engaging in any criminal activity." And: "There will be no material on any of our programs which could in any way further the concept of business as cold, ruthless, and lacking all sentiment and spiritual motivation" (*Variety*, October 26, 1960).

The FCC inquiry which brought to public attention the existence of advertiser leverage over program content also heard testimony from an executive of Screen Gems, the largest supplier of television films who said that "advertisers' contracts with the nets give them control over taste and policy. . . . If discussions did not resolve differences, the advertisers would have the final say" (quoted in *Advertising Age*, October 17, 1960). Some advertising agency officials testify to close supervision of program material from inception to final airing, while others claim a hands-off policy. In general, broadcasting executives interviewed say they work harmoniously with agency personnel in the common quest for large and quiescent audiences in the mood to support the sponsors' interests, activities, and products.

The basic cost of producing a prime time half-hour averages about $100,000. A major one-minute commercial may cost as much or more to produce and air. Most advertisers are content to leave the responsibility for program content to the networks and stations, retaining "only" the power of the purse.

Limited advertising budgets and the growing standardization of television program production has tied the medium increasingly into an assembly-line operation with its principal client relationships serving as the main transmission belt. After hearing the testimony of many of those whom the television industry holds obligated to bring positive responsibility to bear upon the production of programs and whom the industry holds "jointly accountable to the American public," the FCC's Office of Network Study (1965) concluded:

> . . .the policies and practices of network managers. . . tended to substitute purely commercial considerations based on circulation and 'cost per thousand' for considerations of overall service to all advertisers and to the various publics, as the dominant motives in the plan and design of network schedules. In other words, network television became largely a 'slide rule' advertising medium principally motivated by a commercial concept. . . .

One-sided as that indictment may be, and qualified as it should be by obvious exceptions, there is little or no alternative to this system in the present structure of American television—except perhaps in the public sector, which, however, provides more of a complementary than an alternative service.

Public television was traditionally supported by state, municipal, and educational funds and by foundation grants. The Corporation for Public Broadcasting (CPB) was created by the Public Broadcasting Act of 1967 to serve as a national organization acquiring and distributing both Federal and private funds throughout the public broadcasting system. The

CPB supports the Public Broadcasting Service and provides program grants to several production centers.

In the first year of its operation, CPB received $5 million in Federal funds; during 1970 it acquired $15 million, and in 1971, $23 million. Many CPB programming grants to production centers are coordinated with Ford Foundation program grants to the same centers and stations. Of the $8.1 million PBS budget for 1971, $1 million originated in a Ford grant to the CPB for network publicity.

In two decades, the Ford Foundation has spent over $200 million on public broadcasting. In 1970, Ford distributed $18 million, an amount roughly equal to that spent by CPB throughout the entire public broadcasting system for the same year. During 1971, as increased Federal funds were appropriated for CPB and as Ford began to withdraw from its leadership role, the Foundation will be surpassed for the first time and the Corporation will emerge as the major source of funds for public broadcasting.

Public patronage has been miniscule compared with private patronage. The client services performed by public television have been largely those that would not perform profitable consumer services for private corporate patrons. The mainstream of American television is commercial, and the main decisions affecting American culture are made by the corporate managements of the commercial networks.

PROGRAM REGULATION

Fears of government-enforced standards of programming, of stricter public regulation of commercial message content, and of destructive internecine industry warfare are the chief reasons for self-regulation in broadcasting. Standards imposed from outside would couple authority with power to apply sanctions that might interfere with the present conduct of client relationships from which broadcasters derive their income. A recent FCC suggestion for more active and publicly supervised enforcement of the industry's own Television Code was greeted with an outburst of defiant opposition from the industry that adopted the Code.

On the other hand, codes administered by industry-appointed censors and industry-financed boards are flexible instruments. They help protect the common interests of the industry and its chief patrons, to cultivate its publics, and to preserve its markets. The function of the trade associations, the networks, and the various self-censorship boards is to act as radar guiding the fleet, to help spot storm and trouble ahead, to chart the currents, and to calculate the paths of least turbulence for the most and biggest ships.

The storms that led to the adoption of the Hollywood Production Code in 1930 and to its more definite enforcement since 1934 were predominantly of a moral character. Just as, in the late nineteenth century, rapid mass printing led to the adoption of obscenity laws, so, in the 1930s, the movies (and, in the 1950s, television) became suspected of "vulgar" and other immoral influences. The rising storm of outside censorship and criticism over alleged "blue material," and threats of religious boycott and federal action convinced the major movie producers, banded together in a trade association, that it was time to act.

The Production Code drew upon a prior list of "Don'ts and Be Carefuls" which had attempted to codify the most damaging bans and deletions of government censors. The list was supplemented by reasoning and explanations which bore the imprint of collaboration between Martin Quigley, prominent trade publisher and Catholic layman, and the Reverend Daniel A. Lord, a trained moralist with an interest in the theater.

The resulting document—which, with minor changes, guided until recently the production and distribution of most movies in the United States—was moralistic in character. Forty percent of the lines of the code pertained to matters of sex. The rest dealt with crime, brutality, suicide, murder, drug addiction, religion, executions, liquor, surgery, childbirth, cruelty to animals, and respect for flags, institutions, and people of all nations and races.

Fear of censorship because of sexual allusions overshadowed most other sensibilities. The wording of the Code, in effect until 1956, contained the following proscription under the heading of "Profanity": "No approval. . .shall be given to the use of words and phrases in motion pictures including. . .Nuts (except when meaning crazy)."

The broadcasting codes, once modeled after the motion picture Production Code, have come to reflect the legal status and broad scope of radio and television in the life of the community—much different from the status of movies. Sex and conventional morality are not the codes' main preoccupations. They also contain sections on children's programs, "community responsibility," public issues, political affairs, and the "advancement of education and culture."

Network censorship began in the mid-1930s. The "broadcast standards" departments were originally commissioned to make common-sense decisions about the acceptability of verbal content ("continuity"). Departments of Continuity Acceptance, Editing, and finally Standards and Practices were established for each network and some larger stations to formally perform the functions of internal censorship.

The National Association of Broadcasters adopted industry-wide standards of practice for radio in 1937. The Television Code became effective in 1952. Both were composites of existing network codes. By 1971, the NAB Radio Code had been revised 16 times, the Television Code 15 times.

NAB and network standards

The specifications that follow the sweeping declarations of the NAB Television Code Preamble are broad provisions whose application depends on current interpretations of such terms as "valid," "significant," "challenging concepts," "undesirable meanings," "excessive or unfair exploitation," "decency," "good taste," "delicacy," and "impropriety." The definition and application of these terms in concrete and specific communication situations is the day-to-day task of the Code Authority. If a violation occurs and neither numerous nor important people object to it, the terms may be defined in such a way as to do away with the violation by bringing the practice within standards of acceptability. One expression of this operational elasticity is the Code's intricately worded statement on advertising:

> In consideration of the customs and attitudes of the communities served, each television broadcaster should refuse his facilities to the advertisement of products and services, or the use of advertising scripts, which the station has good reason to believe would be objectionable to a substantial and responsible segment of the community. These standards should be applied with judgment and flexibility, taking into consideration the characteristics of the medium, its home and family audience, and the form and content of the particular presentation.

Guidelines of "acceptability" boil down to assumptions of nonobjec-. tionability to "a substantial and responsible segment of the community." Within those limits, and subject to the qualifications of good faith and pure motives, the Code encourages the presentation of "adult themes":

> It is in the interest of television as a vital medium to encourage and promote the broadcast of programs presenting genuine artistic or literary material, valid moral and social issues, significant controversial and challenging concepts and other subject matter involving adult themes. Accordingly, none of the provisions of this Code, including those relating to the responsibility toward children, should be construed to prevent or impede their broadcast. All such programs, however, should be broadcast with due regard to the composition of the audience. The highest degree of care should be exercised to preserve the integrity of such programs and to ensure that the selection of themes, their treatment and presentation are made in good faith upon the basis of true instructional and entertainment values, and not for the purposes of sensationalism, to shock or exploit the audience or to appeal to prurient interests or morbid curiosity.

NAB Code provisions on sex and violence

On material relating to sexual expression, the Code contains the following provisions:

> Profanity, obscenity, smut and vulgarity are forbidden, even when likely to be understood only by part of the audience. From time to time, words which have been acceptable, acquire undesirable meanings, and telecasters should be alert to eliminate such words.

> Illicit sex relations are not treated as commendable.

Sex crimes and abnormalities are generally unacceptable as program material. The use of locations closely associated with sexual life or with sexual sin must be governed by good taste and delicacy.

The costuming of all performers shall be within the bounds of propriety and shall avoid such exposure or such emphasis on anatomical detail as would embarrass or offend home viewers.

The movements of dancers, actors, or other performers shall be kept within the bounds of decency, and lewdness and impropriety shall not be suggested in the positions assumed by performers.

Camera angles shall avoid such views of performers as to emphasize anatomical details indecently.

A variety of Code provisions pertain to the presentation of murder, suicide, horror, cruelty, and morbid detail in news:

The presentation of murder or revenge as a motive for murder shall not be presented as justifiable.

Suicide as an acceptable solution for human problems is prohibited. . . .

The use of horror for its own sake will be eliminated; the use of visual or aural effects which would shock or alarm the viewer, and the detailed presentation of brutality or physical agony by sight or by sound are not permissible. . . .

Excessive or unfair exploitation of others or of their physical or mental afflictions shall not be presented as praiseworthy.

The presentation of cruelty, greed and selfishness as worthy motivations is to be avoided. . . .

Good taste should prevail in the selection and handling of news:

Morbid, sensational or alarming details not essential to the factual report, especially in connection with stories of crime or sex, should be avoided. News should be telecast in such a manner as to avoid panic and unnecessary alarm.

As a special "Responsibility Toward Children," broadcasters are told:

Such subjects as violence and sex shall be presented without undue emphasis and only as required by plot development or character delineation. Crime should not be presented as attractive or as a solution to human problems, and the inevitable retribution should be made clear. . . .

Exceptional care should be exercised with reference to kidnapping or threats of kidnapping of children in order to avoid terrorizing them. . . .

Material which is excessively violent or would create morbid suspense, or other undesirable reactions in children, should be avoided.

Particular restraint and care in crime or mystery episodes involving children or minors should be exercised.

Network codes

CBS uses the NAB Code without further amplification or modification. ABC reproduces the NAB Code (as well as pertinent statutes and government regulations) in its large loose-leaf handbook of Standards and Policies, and adds a 77-page section of its own provisions. Many of these duplicate or expand upon the NAB Code provisions. None refers to or gives additional detail about sex or violence in programming.

NBC publishes its own printed handbook of Broadcast Standards and Practices, supplementing the NAB Code. Struggling with the same creative and interpretive problems as did the framers of the NAB Code, the NBC censors developed similar language with respect to general guidelines, sex, and violence:

There are two general standards to be considered in judging programs for broadcast acceptability: (1) Is the subject matter acceptable? (2) Is the treatment consonant with good taste?

Recognizing the subjective nature of these two questions, the criterion used in reviewing programs is whether they would be regarded as acceptable in subject matter and treatment by a normal viewer under normal circumstances.

NBC believes that the proper application of these standards should not preclude the presentation of programs of genuine artistic or literary merit dealing with valid moral and social issues even though they may be challenging or controversial, or present realities which some people might wish did not exist. The test is whether such material is treated with dramatic integrity, rather than for purposes of sensationalism; and whether it seeks to develop genuine moral and artistic values, rather than to shock or exploit audiences or appeal to prurient interests or morbid curiosity. . . .

Aspects of Sex. All of these—such as costuming, adultery and divorce—should be treated with intelligent respect and due regard for normally acceptable standards of behavior.

Violence. Whether in terms of human conflict or cruelty to animals, violence should never be presented for its own sake, for shock effect or as an audience stimulant and should never be carried to excess. Depictions of violence can be justified as an expression of conflict only to the extent essential to the advancement of plot or the depiction of characterization.

ADMINISTRATION OF THE CODES

The NAB Code is the broadest of all television codes. But (except perhaps in its scrutiny of commercial claim substantiations) the NAB Code Authority is long on authority but short on power. It is dependent on voluntary subscriptions and cooperation. It cannot screen much material with its limited staff (smaller than that of any of the network censors). Although it has the ultimate right to suspend (not used in nearly ten years) it lacks the power to enforce compliance.

The network censors can review and screen all broadcast material repeatedly from conception to airtime. They can exert influence and apply sanctions either directly or, if necessary, through the network's corporate structure. What network censors lack in formal authority they make up in power.

How the NAB Code works

The National Association of Broadcasters' Television code is administered by a Television Code Review Board of nine members, appointed for two-year terms by the NAB President from among member station executives and subject to confirmation by the NAB general Television Board.

The Television Code Review Board is authorized and directed:

> (1) To recommend to the Television Board of Directors amendments to the Television Code; (2) to consider, in its discretion, any appeal from any decision made by the Code Authority Director with respect to any matter which has arisen under the Code, and to suspend, reverse, or modify any such decision; (3) to prefer formal charges,looking toward the suspension or revocation of the authority to show the Code seal to the Television Board of Directors concerning violations and breaches of the Television Code by a subscriber; (4) to be available to the Code Authority Director for consultation on any and all matters affecting the Television Code.

The actual implementation of the NAB Code falls to the Television Code Authority Director and staff. The Code Authority Director is also appointed by the President of the NAB, subject to the approval of the Board of Directors. He is instructed:

> (1) To maintain a continuing review of all programming and advertising material presented over television, especially that of subscribers to the Television Code of NAB; (2) to receive, screen and clear complaints concerning television programming; (3) to define and interpret words and phrases in the Television Code; (4) to develop and maintain appropriate liaison with governmental agencies and with responsible and accountable organizations and institutions; (5) to inform expeditiously and properly, a subscriber to the Television Code of complaints or commendations, as well as to advise all subscribers concerning the attitudes and desires program-wise of accountable organizations and institutions, and of the American public in general; (6) to review and monitor, if necessary, any certain series of programs, daily programming, or any other program presentations of a subscriber, as well as to request recorded material, or script and copy, with regard to any certain program presented by a subscriber; (7) to reach conclusions and make recommendations or prefer charges to the Television Code Review Board concerning violations and breaches of the Television Code by a subscriber; (8) to recommend to the Code Review Board amendments to the Television Code.

The NAB Code is also a membership organization. There are two kinds of membership, with two apparent degrees of adherence to the Code.

Anyone broadcasting or holding a station construction permit in the
U.S. may become a regular subscriber to the Code by paying a fee and
upon the approval of the NAB's Television Board of Directors. The
Television Board grants "to each subscribing station authority to use the
'NAB Seal of Good Practice,' a copyrighted and registered seal to be
provided in the form of a certificate, a slide and/or a film, signifying that
the recipient thereof is a subscriber in good standing to the Television
Code of the NAB." Such subscription remains in force as long as the fee
is paid or until it is suspended by the Television Board of Directors upon
charges preferred by the Code Review Board and after a lengthy and
complicated quasijudicial procedure.

The other kind of membership is called "affiliate subscriber." Such
membership needs to be approved only by the Code Review Board,
which has the power to grant to each affiliate subscriber "authority to
use a copyrighted and registered seal and declaration, in a manner approved by the Television Code Review Board, identifying the individual
firm or corporation as an affiliate subscriber to the Television Code of
the NAB. Such authority shall not constitute formal clearance or approval by the Television Code Review Board of specific film programs
or other recorded material."

What, then, do the status of "affiliate subscriber" and its "seal and
declaration" signify? The only hint the published rules and regulations
give is that "the conditions and procedures applicable to subscribers
shall not apply to affiliate subscribers." What appears to be a wide loop-
hole permitting membership and seal without adherence to standards
or clearance by the Code Review Board is explained by the Code Authority as applying only to film producers (mostly on the West Coast)
whose completed products are subject either to network clearance or to
subsequent review by the West Coast branch of the NAB Code Authority.

Another type of "second-class membership" under active NAB consideration would bring a number of nonsubscribing stations into the fold
by permitting them more time to broadcast messages than is approved
for the regular members. About 65 percent of commercial stations, including all network and large independent stations serving major markets, are regular subscribers to the Code. There are an additional 23-25
affiliate subscribers. It is the view of the Code Authority that most non-
member stations do follow content standards but do not wish to or cannot afford to comply with commercial time limitations. Most of the non-
subscribers are small independent UHF stations competing with large,
network-affiliated VHF operations. Typically such stations have small
audiences and weak signals. To remain solvent, they are forced to exceed Code commercial time standards, thereby failing to qualify for the
Seal. The NAB director feels that it would be in the public interest, as
well as that of the industry, to accord associate status to those stations

that meet Code standards in all respects other than that of the regular commercial time limitation.

The director sees the Authority's chief task as urging and assisting members, affiliates, and other producers and advertisers to avoid violations of standards (most of which occur in the commercial area) and to ask for sanctions as a last resort. At any rate, there have been no suspensions in nearly ten years. In the last major charge preferred against members (in the matter of deodorants), the Board decided in favor of the subscribers' deviations and changed the interpretation of the Code.

The NAB Code Authority

The office of the NAB director is in New York. The Authority also maintains offices in Washington and in Hollywood. Besides the director and his staff assistant, the New York office consists of a manager, an assistant manager, five editors, and four secretaries. The Hollywood office has a manager, an assistant (both editors) and secretarial help. In Washington there are two managers—one for the radio code, the other for television, an assistant television manager, two or three television monitors, and three of four radio monitors. The work of the monitors is largely checking station observance of time standards.

While the Authority is responsible for reviewing programs and commercials on both radio and television, the majority of its work is with television, and the greatest portion of that work has to do with commercials. Because of the volume of broadcast material, the Code Authority can review or monitor only a small sample of programs and commercials, and mostly in a *post facto* fashion. The exceptions are in areas of unusual pressure or current sensitivity. For example, in 1971 all toy commercials were reviewed before they were broadcast. This procedure reflected pressures on the television industry by ACT and other groups protesting the use of children's programs for commercial purposes. In 1968, in the wake of the Martin Luther King and Robert Kennedy assassinations, the Television Code Review Board ordered the Code Authority to increase its scrutiny of the incidence and portrayal of violence in television programs. The authority had previously spent roughly 15-20 percent of its time on program matters; the percentage was increased to about 35 or 40 as a result of the Board's order. The increased attention to violence lasted for close to two years. Then, with the growth of interest in consumer rights and toy advertising, and given the same limited budget and staff, the Authority's involvement with commercials has returned to its former high level.

In areas other than its current "critical" concerns, the Code Authority lets the networks perform the active prior screening; it deals with problems brought to its attention after they are broadcast. Since the networks conduct day-to-day total clearance, the Authority prefers to remain free to work on broader problems of Code interpretations and on the troublesome area of commercial regulation.

Since 1968, the Code Authority has been urged by Senator John O. Pastore and others to become more involved in active prebroadcast screening of programs. Both the Authority and CBS have resisted this suggestion, fearing that more power behind the Code Authority might hurt the long-run interests of the industry. ABC and NBC have not been as strongly opposed, and both have been submitting pilots of new series to the Authority for screening prior to the beginning of new seasons.

Most of the problems coming before the Authority, however, are still in the area of commercials. Private individuals and organized groups deliver a steady stream of complaints to the Authority. Advertisers often object to the claims of competitors. One network may complain about another, or seek the Authority's assistance with a problem it has been unable to resolve with an agency or a producer. Occasionally, too, a broadcast station group will call attention to network programs or commercials which it thinks questionable in light of the group's own standards.

The industry is always more beset with trouble pertaining to advertising than to programs. The clamor from advertisers and agencies to go beyond the limits of the acceptable, the legal, and the credible makes the review of commercials the Authority's chief task. While the validity of claims is studied with increasing care by the Authority, certain flexibility is developing with regard to the types of products which may be allowed. A few years ago feminine deodorant sprays, for instance, were banned. Today they are commonplace, and the Authority is considering proposals to advertise tampons and sanitary napkins. The director foresees the day when contraceptive commercials will be accepted.

The NAB finds it both necessary and convenient to be active in the commercial areas and to remain removed from program review. The Code Authority director, himself a former network censor, has often stressed the need to let broadcasters respond with great flexibility to the constantly changing tastes and tolerances of society.

CBS Program Practices

The Columbia Broadcasting System's Office of Program Practices is headed by a vice president who reports directly to the president of the network. The office is independent of any other department of the network, and relates to other departments through the top executive of the corporation.

The Office has a staff of about 40 in two divisions—one for commercials, the other for general programs. A staff of editors in each division is responsible for day-to-day script and film screening. Most of the commercial editors work in the New York office; the majority of the program editors are based in Los Angeles, where most programs are made.

All commercials and programs (excluding news and most sports) are scrutinized by the editors before broadcast. In fact, the editors are involved at every step of the production process, beginning with early program discussion and ending with the finished film or tape.

The process follows a regular pattern which has been in effect at CBS for over a decade. An editor is assigned to work with a given program. In preliminary discussion with the producer and writers, the editor will make suggestions about potential problems. The first draft of the script is submitted to the editor, who completes a blue form listing suggested deletions or changes. Each version of the script is read and thus annotated by the editor.

When a script is returned to the producer with a pink form, it is cleared for filming. When a rough cut of the show is available, the editor screens it and submits yellow evaluation forms to the producer until an acceptable version is cleared for broadcast.

Once a program is completed, the editor sends a synopsis to all CBS affiliate stations. A particular program may be previewed for a local station. The local station owner as license holder has the ultimate responsibility under the law for what is broadcast.

While the vast majority of editor criticisms are followed by appropriate script and film changes, some 10-15 percent of the issues raised by the editors are settled by the division supervisor or by the chief of the Office of Program Practices.

CBS follows the NAB Code and has no formal written guidelines of its own. The Office claims that it interprets the NAB Code more severely than the Code demands and that, accordingly, CBS feels little pressure from the NAB. Indeed, the vice president heading the Office sits on the NAB Television Code Review Board. Memoranda from the NAB most often are concerned with commercials and are directed more to the advertising agency preparing the commercial than to the network.

While the major pressure on editors has been the growing concern about commercial claims for products, a perennial problem in program content is "the aggregate of violence." Sex and other issues appear from time to time, but violence persists as the single greatest problem for CBS Program Practices editors: "The writers avoid sex, but go the violent route because of greater social tolerance [for violence]." Editors feel that there is a pattern permitting more violence, which runs in four-year cycles. The Office maintains a monthly record of the number of acts of violence, the treatment of various professions and minority groups, the amount of liquor, drug and tobacco use, and other sensitive subjects in network programs.

ABC Policies

The American Broadcasting Company's Standards and Policies Handbook (March 1969 Revision) gives this description of the operation of that network's censors:

> In exercising its responsibility, the Department of Broadcast Standards and Practices follows a detailed series of steps to assure conformity with the American Broadcasting Company's policies as well as standards set forth by the National Association of Broadcasters' Radio and Television Codes.
>
> ABC maintains a staff of editors in New York and Los Angeles to read and screen all radio and television material for network broadcast except for News, News Documentary, and Sports Events which are under their own jurisdiction.
>
> The Department of Broadcast Standards and Practices operates independently of the ABC Radio and Television Networks so that there is in effect a system of 'checks and balances' in determining the acceptability of program material.
>
> Editors are trained and, when experienced and competent, are given the responsibility of applying the standards to each program broadcast. Theirs is the challenging work of reviewing and commenting on material which on the one hand will permit and encourage genuine, artistic and literary material which covers significant and controversial concepts involving adult themes while preserving the integrity of such programs and ensuring that the treatment and presentation are made in good faith on the basis of instructional and dramatic values.
>
> . . .Programs of the public forum or question and answer type in the public information field and quiz and audience participation programs in the entertainment field for which continuity cannot be prepared before broadcast are subject to the same ABC policies and standards as are programs with written continuities, and the ABC Director or other designated representatives assigned to the program will be responsible for enforcing the policies on such programs. ABC reserves the right to cancel any program which does not comply with the accepted policies and procedures of the Company. All material used in pre-broadcast performances or "warm-ups" shall be in conformity with ABC policies and standards and the ABC Director or other designated representative will be responsible for enforcing such policies.

Although it is stated that Standards and Policies "operates independently of the ABC Radio and Television Networks," the office is, of course, an integral part of ABC's corporate structure, and acts through its executive hierarchy. Each of the office's three departments—Literary Rights, Script Routing, and Clearance—reports to the director, who is in turn responsible to the vice president of the Broadcast Division, who is the chief assistant to the executive vice president of ABC, Inc. The total editing staff numbers 41, with 27 based in New York and 14 in Los Angeles.

All commercials and non-news or sports programs are scrutinized by the Office of Standards and Practices. The process of program review at ABC is similar to that at CBS, with a series of colored forms guiding program development and acceptance.

Fundamental program policy is governed by the assumption that "People don't want relevance; they want to be entertained. They want to take off their shoes and relax." The Office tends to encourage entertainment themes unencumbered by overt political, racial or moral issues.

NBC Broadcast Standards

The National Broadcasting Company launched a Department of Continuity Acceptance in 1934. Its "standards of taste and propriety" were the first codified, and served as a model—along with the Motion Picture Code—for the NAB Radio Code. Now the Department of Broadcast Standards, it is described in the NBC booklet of *Radio and Television Broadcast Standards and Practices* as "still dedicated to the same goal: to maintain conduct befitting an invited guest in the home."

NBC's own account of that operation is contained in the introduction to its Standards and Practices codebook.

> The direct responsibility of interpreting and applying these NBC Broadcast Standards and of proposing new of modified standards is assumed by the Department of Standards and Practices, which reports directly to management and is headed by a Vice President who supervises the Director of Broadcast Standards and the Director of Practices. The staff consists of editors and assistants in New York City and Burbank, California.
>
> The broadcast Standards Department concerns itslef with the actual content of all material—program and advertising—broadcast by NBC. (The only exception is programs produced by NBC News whose content is separately reviewed by the NBC News Division.)
>
> Broadcast Standards enlists the expertise of other NBC departments as well as outside authorities for assistance in the application of specialized provisions of this Code of Broadcast Standards. A similar function for local originations of the NBC Owned Stations is performed by specially designated station personnel who maintain liaison with the Broadcast Standards Department and are guided by the same NBC policies.
>
> The Practices Department is largely investigatory, concerning itself with background facts of reliability and fairness. For example, it is responsible for insuring that conditions under which contestants compete on game shows conform to the requirements set forth under Specific Rules And Practices. It assures that conformance by fact-finding prior to the actual program, monitoring during the broadcast, and spot checking after completion of the broadcast.

The Vice President in charge of the Department reports to the Executive Vice President who administers NBC's Corporate Information Division and who reports in turn to the President of NBC. As with the other networks, the Department of Broadcast Standards is independent of such major network offices as programming and sales.

The department is smaller than those of the other networks. It has a total staff of 28 editors, secretaries, and supervisors on both coasts.

While violence is considered a problem—"television glamorized violence," and "its consequences are not shown"—the major program concerns seem to be with language: "A single 'hell' or 'damn' gets hundreds of letters." The NBC editors operate under a philosophy that television must follow, not lead, that it cannot generally initiate greater cultural and moral flexibility in the society: "As cinema follows the novel, so must television follow film."

Movies: the Trojan horse

If that is true, a sharp escalation in television violence may be around the corner. "NEW TIDE OF FILM GORE RISES" was the front page banner headline in the trade paper *Variety* on June 2, 1971. "Graphic gratuitous violence seems to have replaced sex as the newest film industry ploy to lure patrons away from their television sets," noted the report on new movies and those in production.

What will the television industry do to lure them back? Censors believe that the competition will be reflected in changing standards. The standards of television will remain stricter than those of the more selectively viewed and harder to control films, but they must change in the same direction. Movie trends pave the way for the acceptability of the same type of material for television at a later time. At any one time, films are subjected to the stricter standards of television, but they also test and stretch those standards. An editorial entitled "Comment on the Times," in the February 22, 1971 issue of the trade magazine *Advertising Age* observed signs of change—if indeed it is a change.

> A movie called *Madigan* appeared on NBC-TV the other night. It was a chase film in which no character seemed—you should excuse the expression—virtuous; a film in which the cast was given to murder, adultery, "unusual" sex habits, brutality, bribery, you name it—and most of it portrayed or explicitly suggested right there on the screen. Not the kind of thing, you'd imagine, for the living room. But opposite of what you suppose: NBC-TV got not a single complaint.

Just what the trend is and why are graphically described in the *Variety* report cited above. The story also reflects filmmakers' views on what happens when their product gets on television, and the long-term business prospects for violence as "an integral part of American entertainment."

> Explicit sex and violence are two things still taboo on U.S. television, but the major films companies are attempting to avoid the more graphic shores of sex and thus stay clear of the Motion Picture Assn.'s X rating. Despite denials that tag, in the vast majority of cases, is given on the basis of sexual content. No film in memory has been given an X because of violence, although 'The Wild Bunch' was threatened with one and minor cuts were made. The majors are relatively safe with violence, however . . . . What happens when these films eventually turn up on television is another matter. When *The Dirty Dozen* was shown recently, so much of the brutality was cut that it was sometimes impossible to tell who was doing what to whom. And even *Ben-Hur* was trimmed of a few gory moments for its television debut.

Filmmakers usually excuse their overindulgence in gore by saying it shows the real effects of bullets, knives etc. and does not make brutality pretty. Admittedly the old style war films in which U.S. Marines died gallantly without shedding a drop of blood or even messing their hair painted a glossy indeed, but one has only to hear the audiences cheering and giggling at the spurting blood of late to wonder about all those good intentions. In a recent interview, director Sam Peckinpah said of the audience reaction to *Wild Bunch* violence, "I rubbed their noses in it. . .they loved it."

Psychologists, especially those dealing with children, find all this disturbing and ultimately symptomatic of a society weaned on a Puritan tradition of sexual repression. In many other countries, American films are censored more because of their violence than their sexual content. In this U.S. however violence is somehow more socially acceptable than overt sexual activity. Ask most middle American mothers whether they would prefer their sons to participate in a barroom brawl or indulge in group (heterosexual) sex, and there's little doubt what the majority would answer. Violence as titillation thus seems an integral part of American entertainment now being capitalized upon by the major filmmakers and distributors. The MPAA in being lenient towards such films, merely reflects social attitudes.

PROGRAM DEVELOPMENT

The basic management power to select and develop programming rests with corporate executives in charge of network program departments and their subdivisions. The popular notion of television program directors on the search for ideas is deceptive. Program executives might just as well be called Vice Presidents in Charge of Suppression, not because they are against innovation (although many others claim that they are), but because they are inundated with ideas, most of which are not new or, if new, are too costly, impractical, or troublesome.

The few that are chosen represent an investment, a gamble, a fragile commodity to be sold to top management, sponsors, and stations. The program executives' chief tasks are to select as few new programs as possible; oversee their development, cost, treatment, and ratings as closely as possible; use them as widely as possible to realize all potential earnings from the investment; and keep them as long as they continue to hold their own in the competition for patrons and publics.

Creative people with something to contribute to the endless hours of television programming over hundreds of channels can sell to only three major ultimate buyers: ABC, CBS, and NBC. The networks usually buy all program rights, including syndication to independent and foreign stations, and they own or control the bulk of U.S. and much of world television programming—from choice of themes, writers, and actors, through all script revisions, to the actual filming or taping of the show.

In the 1950s, a time now referred to as the "Golden Age of Television," FCC figures record that over half of network evening fare was devoted to independently produced programs. Writers, directors, and stars of live and even filmed programs exercised influence virtually unknown today.

Today more than 93 percent of all prime time programming is reported to be under direct network control from conception to airtime. The economies of scale that result from assembly-line production, the apparent cost-effectiveness of ritualistic repetition of tried formulas, and the legal and political challenges facing broadcasters have forced the issue of supervision, power, and control of what goes on the air.[2]

Writers' complaints

Even though the networks originate little in the way of program ideas or themes and depend almost entirely on outside talent, the creators of programs typically have no legal or financial leverage or responsibility in the decision-making process. Subject to the currents and cross-currents of management, production company, and advertiser relationships, writers generally do as they are told. At premium are the handful of "professionals" who "know" without even being told, and who turn our reliable and trouble-free scripts on the assembly line. One network censor was reported to have said to Steven Roberts of The New York Times (July 27, 1969):

> There's a tremendous amount of self-censorship, not only by network executives but by writers and producers as well. They don't want to commit money to a property that might get into trouble, so they don't even bother with something different.

A writer of half-hour shows stressed the element of time (both playing time and time for writing) as precluding adequate development:

> Okay, so you have 23 minutes to establish your exposition, to delineate your characters, work to your climax with as much action as possible, and bring your tale to a thrilling and moral conclusion. Oh yes, you must provide suitable breaks for commercials, too. You use as many shortcuts as possible: you want to paint a 'bad' guy or someone outside the social norm quickly and simply. You fall back on a sterotype of some sort which presumably your audience will understand without full explanation. If shingles or hives connoted social aberration, I imagine they would be as common as escapees from prisons and asylums. The run-of-the-mill half-hour TV film is as stylized as the Japanese Noh Play.

Examples of positive prescription are rare because of the early involvement and totality of the supervisory process. The published hearings of the Dodd Committee on "Television and Juvenile Delinquency" (1965) record claims that sex and violence were injected into programs to boost lagging interest without boosting program cost or level of sophistication. But it is safe to say that seasoned writers rarely need such advice. In fact, a frequent complaint of the censors is, "Why can't those hacks write something different?"

NETWORK MANAGEMENT

Management practices related to program development and control are similar at the three networks. Nevertheless, shifts of emphasis and different ways of expressing similar policies become evident in the account each network gives of its own operation. These shifts and differences indicate the range of options and alternatives that the structure of American television provides for program development.

ABC: "keep producers in line"

Nearly all program ideas emanate from the program suppliers. More than one hundred ideas are discussed seriously with the network's Program Development office each year. Of these perhaps 50 are eventually presented in the form of written proposals or outlines. After further discussion with the suppliers, the network may settle on ten to 15 of these program ideas to be scripted and produced as potential series for the new season.

In this process of program selection the networks are moving away from the pilot film concept. The reasons are primarily economic. It costs the network $500,000-800,000 to produce a one-hour pilot. If (as often happened), as many as 15 pilots were prepared and then only five to seven were used, the networks would have thrown away six to eight million dollars from which it got little if any return. Instead, the network plans to use in some way most of the program ideas approved for scripting. Few are developed as disposable pilots. Rather, a one-to-two-hour movie is developed around each program idea. This movie is then viewed by network officials during the spring before the new season. If it is found suitable for expansion into a series, the company that produced it is given a contract to provide a full portfolio of episodes related to the program concept. If not deemed suitable for series development, the program is then scheduled for a single screening as a movie of the week. This screening may be used as a further test for the program's potential as a series. In any case the program is sold and screened, and some return on the original Development Office investment is made.

The network used to be somewhat removed from the process of production after the series was approved. Involvement was limited to a simple determination of the program's ratings and the decision whether or not to continue the series. Now, however, the script of each episode is reviewed by the Nighttime Programming staff and discussed with the series producer. This procedure allows the networks to "keep producers in line" and to insure that the program concept bought in the spring continues to be developed in the fall.

The more creative producers and directors seek to develop new ideas and to enlarge on actor talents. Over a period of time they may wish to mold a program in a direction different from that originally approved. A comedy, for instance, may become more serious or satirical; an action-adventure program may attempt to become more dramatically sophisticated. But, because "the way to succeed in television is to generate audience flow" (the maintenance of high audience ratings throughout an evening's schedule), the network programmers want individual episodes of particular programs to be generally the same week after week, so that the viewer will get what he expects. Too much variety within a series, it is felt, will lose viewers not only for the particular program, but for the entire evening.

The program executives at ABC feel little pressure from their Office of Broadcast Standards. "I can count on the fingers of one hand the number of times I received complaints from the Office last year .... I can't say that it's one of my pressing problems." This seeming lack of pressure at the executive level is not meant to imply that the ABC Standards Office does not make its wishes known. But most of its efforts are handled at a lower level, between Standards Office editors and the production supervisors.

The few warnings that have come through to the higher staff level have had to do with excessive violence in the early prime time hours (when many children are assumed to be viewing), questions of taste, and sometimes questions of safe, exemplary behavior on the part of actors ("Are seat-belts fastened when characters get into automobiles?").

CBS: conscious of Practices code

Of the hundreds of program ideas considered each year, ten to 30 are developed as pilots. For the past two years, CBS, like ABC, has attempted to insure that its pilot films will be usable whether or not they lead to full series.

The CBS Department of Programs employs more than 30 people. Three or four senior executives consult and make the major decisions in all areas of the department's interest.

The CBS Programs Department appears to be keenly conscious of the network's Program Practices Division. Memoranda and verbal comments flow constantly among the top executives as well as at lower echelons. The comments of the Practices Office are generally noted and usually followed. They are typically questions of tone: "That scene is questionable as to the plot needs of the sex" or "Is that much violence necessary at that point?"

The process of individual program creation is similar to those of the other networks. Once a series is scheduled, a program staff member reviews each script and works with the producer to get what the network originally saw in the program. The position of the program staffer during reviews of an episode is often that of mediator between the Program

Practices editor and the contracting company producer. While conscious of the network's legal and public relations interests in observing sex, violence, and other Code provisions, the programmers are usually ex-producers themselves whose jobs depend on keeping ratings high and costs low.

Except for ratings and the Program Practices comments, the Programs Department has little contact with the outside: "Letters to networks are a myth." Seldom are organized groups heard from or considered. The programmer's job is simply to create the most attractive schedule he can. His chief considerations are the relative size of the audience compared with the relative cost of the program.

NBC: "the audience can have a love affair"

Like those of the other networks, the NBC Programs Department is split between the East and West Coasts. The work of the California office is largely devoted to the process of supervising the production of programs. The New York office carries the major administrative responsibilities, oversees program and schedule development, and coordinates the programming process with the sales department and the advertising agencies.

The process of program selection at NBC is no different from that of the other networks. Most new ideas originate with the production companies. About 18 months prior to a new season, several dozen written program treatments are considered. Shortly thereafter, 12 to 20 program outlines are approved for scripting. Like its competitors, NBC is no longer preparing many disposable pilot films. The network does not even solicit many more initial scripts than it is likely to approve for production; a script can now cost $25,000. Program ideas going into production are generally made into television movies. Two-thirds of the new programs in the NBC 1971-72 schedule have come from the movie format, most of them having already been presented on NBC's World Premiere Movie program.

It is the view of the program staff that the movie format allows much greater control over subsequent series development. From the movie can be drawn a "bible" of characterizations, scene settings, plot conditions, and so on. These help the NBC program supervisors to oversee the work of the production company's producers, writers, directors and actors. With the original one- or two-hour movie and the related written program guide, the network finds it can elicit a greater consistency among the various episodes of the series. Consistency is closely allied with the condition that leads to the success of a program: "the ability of the producer, writer and actors to create a character or set of characters with whom the audience can have a love affair."

The NBC Programs Department maintains routine contact with the network's Office of Broadcast Standards. The vast majority of problems raised are settled without controversy. Program executives confirm that a special measure of scrutiny at NBC is reserved for language. In any case, few censorship problems rise above the level of the daily work of the individual program supervisors and editors.

At all three networks, the audience is blamed for the repetitiveness and banality of much network programming. But none of the program offices maintains much direct contact with the public or with any outside groups. Since most comments deal with issues of taste in programming or with the accuracy of commercials, they are steered to the Broadcast Standards offices. Few viewers offer comments on the substance of a program. In fact, the only time large responses are received is when a program of longstanding popularity is cancelled, or when the networks are embroiled in a political controversy. Vice President Agnew's 1969 remarks in Des Moines elicited 70,000-80,000 individual letters, calls or other responses to NBC alone (75 percent supporting Mr. Agnew). "Nobody writes to say what's good about Bonanza." The ratings assume the role of the only regular guide to audience response.

SUMMING UP

A television executive said "There are only two types of audience demand: the cry that 'You throw Herbie Glotz off the air' and the demand that 'You carry more programs like that last one.' That's all." Surveys confirm that the majority of even well-educated viewers have few general complaints or creative suggestions to offer. Television is a medium of mass appeal, although the responsibility for program development and control is concentrated in relatively few hands.

The Federal Communications Commission and the NAB Code Review Board have authority but little effective power. Power stems from the chief client relationships between major national advertisers and the managements of the three national networks.

That basic structure determines the process of program control and development and shapes symbolic content. In a fictional world governed by the economics of the assembly line and the "production values" of optimum appeal at least cost, symbolic action follows conventional rules of social morality. The requirements of wide acceptability and a suitable environment for the sponsor's message assure general adherence to consumer values and to common notions of justice and fair play. The issue is rarely in doubt; the action is typically a game of skill and power.

Sex and violence play critical and somewhat antithetical roles in such a game. Sex gives a promise of human relatedness, even if the relationship may be exploitive. Violence signifies a break in human relatedness matic device available to indicate who is the better man in a clash of personalized forces.

With their emphasis on frequency and explicitness rather than on the substance of what violence demonstrates about life, the codes are public relations instruments whose applications protect and enhance the social and commercial functions of programming. The pressures toward standardizing and streamlining program production, with greater executive supervision over the creative process, also promote the ritualistic nature and institutional functionality of the representations. It is in that context that studies of the representations of sex and violence and their effects in cultivating norms of life can best be viewed.

FOOTNOTES

1. Facts and figures are from the *Broadcasting Yearbook*, the *Television Factbook*, the FCC annual Reports, and various corporate annual reports unless otherwise specified. Views cited come from interviews, correspondence, or other recorded personal comments, unless otherwise specified. The assistance of Willard Rowland (who bears no responsibility for this report) is gratefully acknowledged.

2. A dramtic illustration of why and how the issue of control was forced in one celebrated instance, and an account of how it was settled, came from the former CBS senior vice president for programming—the man responsible for signing, supporting, and then cancelling the Smothers Brothers comedy program:

   "I put the Smothers Brothers on the air. Tommy Smothers pioneered social satire and was a terribly important influence in the broadcasting world. No program hurt me more personally and professionally than the cancellation of that program, and I was part of the cancellation.

   "Tommy was out in the vanguard. His neck was out. He was anti-Vietnam before it was popular. He was anti-Nixon before it was correct. But all that was not so bad. He had one big problem. Tommy blew it because of one thing. One thing ruined it for me, for the network, and for himself, and practically destroyed his career.

   "A week before we cancelled we were in Washington. Senator Pastore, who was Chairman of the Committee in charge of the Federal Communications Commission, wanted to establish a system whereby everything would be submitted ahead of time to the NAB code, before it was put on the air. CBS was the one network which said no. We will decide what goes on our air. Now, I had problems with most of Tommy's shows. Tommy would stick in things that he knew wouldn't get by. I once left in a whole sketch where a guy got the tablecloth caught in his zipper. He really thought it wouldn't get by; I didn't think it was so bad, I got a million pieces of mail that thought it was disgusting. He said, "I thought you were going to take it out!" You know, it works both ways.

"The show was renewed on a Friday night at five of five when our option was up. But we told Senator Pastore that we would show the tapes to our stations ahead of time. It is the function of every local station to determine whether they want to carry the show. I called Tommy the following Wednesday morning and said, "Tommy, give me the tape because we have to show it to the stations." Wednesday afternoon I'm panicky. I said we have to show it. He said, "You tell the stations that if they don't want to carry it that's fine. But I don't want you guys to touch the tape."

"I'm not going to give up the right, the network will never give up the right to edit and be responsible for everything going out on our air. We have certain rules and regulations and we are going to live by them. Now at that point the lawyers are sitting by and that was one of the most depressing Thursday nights of my whole career. The President of the network said to me, "Where's the tape?" And I said, "I don't have it." And he said, "When are you going to get the tape?" And I said, "I don't know." And in that office at nine o'clock that night a wire went out and cancelled the Smothers Brothers.

"He crucified himself when he didn't have to. Certainly the conservative forces were fighting to keep the Smothers Brothers off the air. But we had renewed him on the Friday before so there was no question that we were looking for an excuse to dump him. But that was the one line if he stepped over he had to get hit. Because the stations will see those tapes ahead of time to decide for themselves, and we will not sumbit our tapes to the NAB in Washington. The affiliates shall have the final say in the decision-making process. And Tommy decided that he wasn't going to give us the tape. Now, since then Tommy has told me that he gave us the tape, that CBS saw it, he said a million things. And I tell you, as God is my judge, we never got the tape."

REFERENCES

Barron, J. An emerging First Amendment right of access to the media? *George Washington Law Review*, 1969, **37**, 487-89.

Berelson, B. In the presence of culture. *Public Opinion Quarterly*, 1964, **28**, 1-12.

Federal Communications Commission Office of Network Study. *Second interim report.* Docket No. 12782, 1965, 535.

Gerbner, G. Institutional pressures upon mass communicators. *Sociological Review* Monograph No. 13, 1969.

Television Programs in Great Britain: Content and Control

James D. Halloran and Paul Croll

Centre for Mass Communication Research, University of Leicester

In reading this report it is essential to bear in mind the scale and limitations of the project. The main purpose of the report is *not* to provide a detailed, comprehensive description and analysis of television program control and program content in Great Britain. Our main hope is that the report should serve as one of four working papers which, when studied together, will hopefully enable their authors to select salient areas for incorporation into an agreed, cross-cultural research design along these lines.

The limitations inherent in such an approach and the short cuts that have been taken in carrying out the work will soon become apparent.

415

But the reader also needs to be warned on one other score. Even if the work reported in these pages were not part of a pilot study, and even if it presented a far more systematic, thorough and comprehensive coverage of television control and content than it does, it would still be misleading to judge it in isolation.

Our own research approach at the Centre for Mass Communication Research (and fortunately we are not alone in this approach) requires us to treat mass communication as a social process, and this implies that the various stages in this process must be studied within the appropriate social contexts. This means that the social context of the creation and the reception of the content as well as the content itself should be incorporated into the analysis.

We need to ask, "How does the content come to be like this?" We cannot assume that the perceptions and intentions of the producers coincide with the pictures that emerge from content analysis. The study of the television production process is not without its problems, as we shall see, and for those who consider the main area of interest to be the relationship between content and audience, such a study might not be thought necessary. However, if we are interested in control over areas of media content, the everyday working procedures and definitions of the people actually producing the material must be examined.

We need to know about the forces and pressures from inside and outside the institution that impinge upon the production process. To quote George Gerbner, we must try "to illuminate the complex web of power roles that governs the collective image making of a culture—to discover how that web is woven into the fabric of institutional relationships and to grasp, for the first time, the dynamics of leverage that move communicators and through them modern society."

Moreover, broadcasting institutions have not developed, nor do they exist, in isolation. Television is related to other institutions; to study it as though this were not the case could be extremely misleading.

Television may be an all-pervasive medium; it may dominate the climate of the mass produced symbolic environment, and it may, through its provision of messages and images, *make possible* more shared perspectives and common assumptions than ever before. But provision and availability is one thing; interpretation, use, and end product is another. The nature of the relationship between the two is an empirical question, and even at the level of latent meanings, implicit definitions, and basic assumptions it is both dubious and dangerous to infer "effect" from content without taking into account a wide range of other variables. We shall return to this matter in our concluding remarks.

The individual member of the audience or public, like the broadcaster, does not live in isolation; consequently, he too must be studied in terms of the relevant situations, relationships, and interactions. We may talk of situationally based cultures as well as of media relayed cultures; the relationship between the two is what we should be studying.

One final point in this introduction has to do with the already mentioned emphasis in this pilot study on sex and violence. As social scientists, whilst accepting the obligation to address ourselves to problems of social concern, we also claim the right to refuse to accept these problems at face value—or as defined by others. Yet it could be argued that in our approach to this pilot study we have more or less taken the conventional approach, and have failed to challenge the givers.

Is it sex and violence, as normally defined, on which we should be concentrating? It is possible that in our search for nipples and four-letter words we might miss out on the real problems. Perhaps we should be looking at media content and how it is controlled at greater depth in terms of the significance of the relationships within which the "incidents" occur or with regard to implicit values or symbolic representations of such things as power, authority, exploitation, love relationships and so on. This is another question to which we will return in our final section.

TELEVISION IN GREAT BRITAIN

Great Britain has two separate television systems: the British Broadcasting Corporation (BBC) and the Independent Television Authority (ITA).

The constitution of the BBC

The BBC is a public corporation established by Royal Charter and operating under license. Its object is to provide a public service of broadcasting for general reception at home and overseas.

The corporation received its first charter on January 1, 1927, and although this has been renewed four times, its constitutional position has remained largely unaltered over the years. Subject to the terms of its charter and of a license granted by the Postmaster-General (now Minister of Posts and Telecommunications), the Corporation has undivided responsibility for the conduct of its broadcasting services.

The charter defines the BBC's functions and responsibilities, but almost its only reference to programs is a remark in the preamble, where the Sovereign takes note of the "widespread interest. . . taken by Our Peoples in the broadcasting services and of the great value of such services as means of disseminating information, education and entertainment." As the Director General of the BBC recently remarked, "Our only stated obligation in the charter and therefore our central responsibility is to serve the public."

The BBC is neither state-owned nor government-run, and it is not controlled by a minister or ministry. It is not a commercial concern seeking to make a profit for distribution to shareholders; it must apply the

MEDIA CONTENT AND CONTROL

whole of its income solely to promoting its objects. It is set up in a way recommended by the Crawford Committee, which reported in 1926 that broadcasting in the United Kingdom should be conducted by a public corporation "acting as Trustee for the national interest." Consequently it is administered as a nationwide service under public control through a body *not directly* responsible to Parliament.

It seems to be generally accepted that this method of administration, coupled with the license fee system, has enabled the BBC to combine that degree of public control which safeguards the general interest with a freedom from day-to-day intervention by the political machine.

The Corporation consists of a chairman, a vice-chairman, and ten governors. Among the members of the Board of Governors (all appointed by the Queen in Council) are three national governors selected for their knowledge of affairs in Scotland, Wales, and Northern Ireland respectively. With that exception, no governor is chosen as a representative of any particular section or interest. The governors, who are engaged primarily in other occupations, are not called upon to make broadcasting their sole concern. They work through a permanent executive staff headed by the director-general, the chief executive officer of the BBC. They are usually appointed for five years, receive a fee, and meet regularly once a fortnight.

Formal restrictions on the BBC's program output are four:

1) It is prevented from obtaining funds by on-the-air advertising without government permission. This prohibition is a formality, because the BBC has already insisted that truly comprehensive public service broadcasting is impossible in a system financed by advertising.

2) It is required to broadcast any announcement when so required by a minister of Her Majesty's government. In practice, government announcements of any importance find their way into news bulletins as a matter of course; others are broadcast in announcement periods by informal arrangement between the department concerned and the news and presentation staff of the BBC.

3) It is required to broadcast an impartial daily account, prepared by professional reporters, of the activities of the Parliament. The BBC is also under obligation not to use subliminal techniques, not to express editorial opinions on current affairs or matters of public policy, and to treat controversial subjects with impartiality.

4) The Minister of Posts and Telecommunications has a formally absolute veto over BBC programs. In practice, this has always been treated as a reserve power; the governors have had absolute freedom in the handling of day-to-day matters, including programming.

Independent television

Independent television in Great Britain is a federal system made up of a nonprogram-producing Authority and fifteen program-producing companies.[1]

We have seen that the BBC is a public service institution. Independent Television would claim to be both public service and commercial. Sir Robert Fraser, ex-director general of ITA, has referred to "the great successful political compromise of creating a system of private enterprise under public control." It is said by those in the system that an outside investigator would be struck, not so much by the commercial character of ITV, but by the extensive powers and duties of the public authority under which it operates. The Authority is meant to be more than a watchdog; it is required to be involved in the positive processes of program planning and the formulation of program policy. This calls for a close liaison between the Authority and company program staffs.

It is possible to view the Authority as a sort of middleman between producer and viewer, with certain duties and obligations which the law spells out quite clearly. These legal provisions have the general effect of making the Authority answerable to public and Parliament for the content and nature of all the programs transmitted by Independent Television, no matter who produces them.

Parliament created the Independent Television Authority in August 1954 for ten years, then extended its life for another twelve years to 1976. Its overall purpose, as defined by the 1964 Television Act, is to provide public television services of information, education, and entertainment. The four main functions of ITA may be summarized as:

Selecting and appointing program companies. Fifteen companies operate in ITA's fourteen areas, obtaining their revenue from the sale of advertising time and paying a rental to the ITA and a levy, based on net advertisement revenue, to the Exchequer. No income is received from license fees or other public funds.

Transmitting the programs. The ITA builds, owns and operates the transmitting stations. Forty-seven VHF 405 line transmitters reach 98.7 percent of homes, fifteen VHF 625 line transmitters reach over two-thirds of homes with the combined color/black and white picture (early 1971).

Controlling the program output. The creative content of the programs is the concern of the companies, but the ITA has to ensure that the output of each company provides a proper balance of information, education, and entertainment.

Controlling the advertising. To ensure that in frequency, amount, and nature advertisements accord with the Television Act and the rules and principles laid down by the Authority.

The Authority, as constituted by Parliament under the 1964 Act and as amended by the Minister in 1969, consists of a chairman, a deputy-chairman, and nine members. They are appointed by the Minister of Posts and Telecommunications, and three of the members have as their special care the interests of Scotland, Wales, and Northern Ireland.

The ITA would maintain that it applies stringent conditions to ensure that program companies comply with the requirements of the Act, that they produce a balanced output of programs of high quality, that control remains within the U.K. and does not change without the ITA's approval, that the companies remain completely independent of one another (as to both finance and control), and that due regard is paid to the particular character of the areas which the regional companies serve.

The Authority has general responsiblility for the institutional shape of the system, and the refusal to renew contracts is of course its ultimate sanction. This sanction has been used, and, although the decision not to renew seemed to cause some surprise at the time, the Authority's position and powers are clear. Program contracts have a finite term and are not automatically renewable. (A decision not to reappoint an existing company need not be regarded as a censure of that company. The Authority's duty is to choose the applicant group whose appointment, it deems, will be in the best interests of Independent Television.)

FINANCE

The BBC

According to Barrie Thorne (Controller Finance BBC), speaking in 1970, the BBC's financial state, when examined in the appropriate historical perspective, is extremely sound:

> The BBC has acquired gross some £85 million of assets, financed solely out of income. No loans. No debentures. No share issues. Their value is based on cost, not market price, and it does not therefore take account of the very large appreciation in some of its real estate holdings, both in London and elsewhere.

However, that is only one way of looking at the financial picture. The BBC has never had any large reserves, although it is arguable that if the government had allowed bigger ones to be accumulated for future capital expenditure, the combined license fee could have been lower and stable for longer periods. It is important to note that with the exception of the war years, the Treasury has retained some of the license income every year between 1927 and 1961. Over these years £100,000,000 contributed by the license holder has been retained by the government and may be considered "lost" to broadcasting.

The BBC has always attempted to pay its way (although it appears to be anticipating a period of continuous borrowing in the 70s), and it claims that it has always endeavored to ensure that "program aspirations must be met and left uninhibited." Still money has never been plentiful, and according to Barrie Thorne liquidity is likely to become one of the main problems in the future.

Thorne maintains that the BBC's affairs are kept under fairly constant government scrutiny. In the postwar period the Corporation has appeared five times before the Public Accounts Committee and twice before the Estimates Committee of the House of Commons. A special committee composed of senior government officials examined the BBC's finances in 1964, and there have been regular discussions with the Post Office and Treasury since that time. Two official committees—the Beveridge Committee in 1949 and the Pilkington Committee in 1960—considered the BBC's finances as part of a comprehensive review of broadcasting in the United Kingdom.

Both these reports may be regarded as milestones in the history of the BBC. The Beveridge Report recommended that the BBC should continue to be responsible for all broadcasting, but the government of the day subsequently allowed the introduction of a competitive, commercially financed television system.

This competition led to a substantial increase in costs, and it is from this time—the mid-1950s—that the old order began to change. By 1957, television had supplanted radio as the main source of broadcast entertainment in the evening, and progressively very large increases in expenditure were needed. The Corporation spends nearly £100 million per year, of which television's share is nearly £70 million.

The development of a second television network, the introduction of color, the expansion in educational and regional broadcasting, extensions in radio, and the increasing complexities in production have combined to produce drastic changes in the financial situation in recent years. But, according to Thorne, no immediate finance was provided to adequately meet these developments. "Throughout the sixties there was continued uncertainty of government action about the timing and the amount of increases in the licence fee." Whether this uncertainty produces more problems than the anticipated borrowing remains to be seen.

Lord Hill, in his foreword to the 1971 handbook, drawing attention to the financial problems of the Corporation, states that the BBC is in the business of being creative and "without business, without money there is no creativity." He quotes from the *Guardian* of 3 September 1970:

. . .obviously financial pressure can be inhibiting. Public service broadcasting in Britain has been most praised for its independence. But can we be sure it is still as independent as it ought to be? That is the question to be asked when judging what is the proper sum for the licence fee.

In examining, as we propose to do in this paper, the control of subject matter in BBC programs, we shall have to consider, albeit briefly, the relationship between the Corporation and its public. Not the least important aspect of this relationship is the question of the license fee, or perhaps more specifically the question of increases in the fee. Attitudes toward the Corporation, its policies, and its products are bound to be influenced by these financial considerations.

This is the place neither for a full examination of BBC finances nor for an assessment of recent reorganization within the Corporation, but two points are worth mentioning. Two of the outcomes of the recent Mc-Kinsey investigation were an increased emphasis on cost effectiveness and a move away from what some people saw as a traditional financial paternalism, toward a wider participation in budgetary affairs within the Corporation. As far as programs are concerned, the financial control now operates on a total cost basis. The producer is now in a position to know what all his decisions will cost. Management at all levels is directly involved—from managing director through network controller. It is intended in the long run that producers should be free, so far as possible, to spend their expenditure as they wish on the different items comprising their program budgets.

However, these changes are not seen by all as an unmixed blessing. It has been argued that the new system could mean that although the individual producer has more opportunity for fuller participation, perhaps in one sense even more freedom, this could be more than offset by the fact that he cannot easily escape from the day-to-day implications of financial stringency.

Independent television

The income of Independent Television, apart from the overseas sale of programs, comes from the sale of advertising time. The companies obtain their revenue from the sale of advertising in their own areas. They pay a rental to cover the cost of the ITA in administering the system and in operating its national network of transmitters.

In addition to normal company taxes, the program companies must pay an Exchequer Levy on a sliding scale related to their advertising receipts. It was the operation of this levy, this particular aspect of public control, that led Sir Robert Fraser in October 1970 to speak of something which had become "so burdensome as to threaten the balance between private enterprise and public control." He went on to ask whether Independent Television would be allowed to be commercial enough, and be able to retain the financial margins it needed to fulfil its public service role and responsibilities.

In his foreword to the ITV GUIDE 1971, the new Director General, Brian Young, states that the current financial climate is bad, partly because of the levy and high costs. (Company profits declared in mid 1971, however, suggest that the situation is improving and that at least some of the independent clouds appear to have a silver lining.) In the Annual Report and Accounts for 1969-70 we read that:

> The start of color television meant a substantial increase in costs, both in capital and revenue. There has been no compensating increase in income for Independent Television, because the amount of color viewing is still below the level at which adjustments in advertising rates could be made for this reason.

Indeed, far from an increase in income the summer and autumn of 1969 saw the start of a fall in the amount spent on television advertising which became even more acute as the winter drew on. On top of this the industry was feeling the impact of the increase in the rate of levy announced in the Budget of 1969, which came into operation on 1st July 1969 and which was designed to increase the yield by an extra £3m. or so in a full year. The combination of these factors meant that for virtually the whole of the year under review there was great financial uncertainty in the system. Following representations by the Authority to the Minister of Posts and Telecommunications, the Minister announced on 16th March 1970 a reduction in the rate of the Levy, effective from 15th April 1970, estimated to reduce the yield in a full year by some £6m. At the same time it was announced that the costs and revenues of the program companies would be referred to the National Board for Prices and Incomes.

The reduction in the Levy provided relief at a time when it was urgently needed if a serious threat to programs was to be avoided. This was action in the short term. With a continuing downward trend in income on the one hand and rising costs on the other, it was apparent that there was more than a short-term problem, and the reference to the Board was seen as providing for an independent and authoritative examination in the light of which consideration might be given to the further measures needed for long-term financial stability. Even with the reduction in Levy, the total surplus of all the companies for the year to the end of July 1970 was estimated to reach only about £4m - £5m before tax, while the forecast position for the following year to July 1971 was that, without any further change in the Levy, the system as a whole might do little more than break even.

As pointed out in the last Report, the Authority's financial position is in the long run directly affected by the general financial health of the program companies. While the companies are reasonably prosperous, the Authority can secure the money it needs to maintain and extend its transmissions. When they are less prosperous, the Authority has to consider whether the total rental that it needs is a sum which can reasonably be borne by the companies as additions to their other expenditure. It was considerations of this kind which led the Authority to forego throughout the year a general increase in rental, which would have had to be paid by all companies, of nearly six percent.

The companies' financial problems had no visible effect during the year on the overall standard of the programs. However, it may be that the immediate effect of shortage of money is not to be found in what appears on the screen but in what does not appear. The capacity of any television service to raise its standards depends not only on the talents of its creative personnel but also on the ability at management level to underwrite fresh enterprise and experiment. Advances in television can only be nurtured in an atmosphere that permits the taking of calculated financial risks.

It is important to note in this connection that in recent years, with the levy and the recession in advertising, the surplus program production of earlier years could no longer be afforded. Tighter economic planning became necessary, and this was not unconnected with the formation of the Program Controller's Committee. This is a vitally important committee with the basic tasks of ensuring that there is always a core of network programs available to all companies and that this core is of the right sort of mix to meet ITA requirements—without undue waste and with financial justice between the companies.

It has been said that Independent Television only works satisfactorily in a time of economic surplus in the industry and that in times of economic stringency it has a tendency to look like a second-rate BBC. It just fills the slots. Availability of surplus production, so it is argued, means choice. This also means waste but, granted the system, so it is argued, one needs to be wasteful to be good. You can't be wasteful when the economic screws are on. Moreover, the risks, without which good programs are unlikely to be produced, cannot be taken.

It is a fundamental principle of the Television Act 1964, as of the original Act of 1954, that the programs should not be provided or sponsored by advertisers. They are obtained by the Authority from independent program companies under contract. The advertiser has no share in program production and no say in program decisions: these are matters for the broadcasters—that is to say, for the program companies and the Authority. There are two provisions in the Television Act for this total distinction between programs and advertisements. The advertiser's role is limited to buying time in television for the insertion of his advertisement, just as he buys screen time in the cinema or space in a newspaper or magazine.

It is, however, important to remember that although the advertiser's role may be limited in this way, the overall influence of advertising on program content need not be confined to this form of direct influence.

It seems to be quite widely accepted within the industry that the system proceeds smoothly and without much argument on this basis. Some of the popular imported programs do owe their existence to advertisers who have "sponsored" them in their country of origin, but for British viewers these programs have been bought and broadcast on the decisions of one of the broadcasting bodies and not on the decisions of advertisers.

There are over forty Acts of Parliament that restrict, control, or otherwise affect advertisements in Britain. In a sense, one of the most generally powerful of these Acts is the Television Act. It gives to a public board (the Independent Television Authority) the duty and the power: "to exclude from television any advertisement that could reasonably be said to be misleading" and "to decide as to the classes and descriptions of advertisements and methods of advertising that should be excluded from television."

As regards the unacceptable classes and methods of advertising, the Act requires the Authority to consult with the Minister of Posts and Telecommunications, from time to time, and to carry out any directions that he may feel the need to issue in these fields, over and above anything the Authority itself, with his concurrence, may propose to do. Thus, through the Television Act, the Authority is one of the country's official instruments of consumer protection.

The Authority fulfils its obligations in this area at two levels. First, it is concerned with the general principles and draws up and publishes a code to govern standards and practice in advertising. This it does in consultation with its Advertising Advisory Committee, a Medical Advisory Panel, and the Minister of Posts and Telecommunications. Secondly, in cooperation with the program companies, the Authority's advertising central staff examines the advertisements in relation to the rules before they are accepted for broadcasting.

STRUCTURE AND ORGANIZATION

The BBC

The director general of the BBC is the link between the Board of Governors, which determines policy, and the Board of Management, which applies that policy. The Board of Management can also help to shape policy by means of professional advice given to the governors by directors.

The Board of Management is composed of ten directors and the director general. Three of them, the managing directors, are directly responsible for the Radio, Television and External Broadcasting Services respectively; a fourth, the editor of News and Current Affairs, holds direct responsibility for all domestic news services and has editorial control over domestic current affairs programs.

Engineering, Personnel and Finance are each represented on the board, and one of its members, the director of Public Affairs, has among his responsibilities that of representing the BBC's policy to its public and the views of the public to the BBC.

The BBC is a large and complex structure. The total labor force is now nearly 25,000, 15,000 of whom work in television. There is little reliable information available to the public on how the organization really works, but according to a recent article in the *Times*:

> A tremendous number of decisions are taken by this widely variegated group of people without reference to higher authority. A somewhat subdued McKinsey man confessed late one night to Mr. Huw Wheldon, Managing Director

of Television, that they had been unable to narrow the number of decision-takers in television to fewer than 1,500—normally they expected in an organization with a £70m. a year turnover like BBC television to be able to reduce the number to between 12 and 15.

Consequently, the tone of the organization, apart from major policy pronouncements by the Director General—evolves like Conservative leaders of old. The myriad checks and balances, the proliferation of meetings, the rivalries between personalities, all go to producing a lifestyle which eventually manifests itself on the television screen and on radio.

It percolates up and down a long chain of command which has drawn comparisons with a feudal structure. Indeed the enormously influential middle management—the heads of groups responsible for say, current affairs, drama, light entertainment—are often referred to as "the barons," each zealously and jealously guarding his own particular domain. In television they have to account for considerable sums of money: drama's budget is about £7 1/2m., light entertainment £5 1-2m., features £3 1-2m., news £3 1-2m., outside broadcasts £3 1/2m. The "barons" are former producers who have been promoted into virtually fulltime administrators. There are grey areas in which there is overlapping, particularly between current affairs and features, and there are suggestions that these should be "policed" by higher management to prevent friction.

Sometimes senior staff will get a direction of the kind which Huw Wheldon gave a few months ago: ". . .I should be glad to get from plays, current affairs, documentaries, and features, a little more delight and a little less insight. As it seems to me, we have been just a little too heavy on insight recently. I am sick and tired of being preached at. I hope as the months pass away we can move a touch towards delight and a touch away from sermonizing."

But how does it move upwards? Mr. Arthur Hutchinson, Head of Talks and Current Affairs, Radio, explained: "One must remember the BBC has sacred cows, but things do change. One can push and push but drip, drip is a more accurate description. You may have been putting a point of view to someone until it is a dead duck as far as he is concerned but when eventually a new man comes along with an empty slate you may strike lucky. There is also the interaction between personalities."

This interaction is on display at its best at the weekly program review meetings which is probably one reason why outsiders are never allowed to attend. Mr. David Attenborough, Controller of Television Programs, and Mr. Gerry Mansell, Controller of Radio Programs, chair these meetings at which executives and senior staff will thrash out the past week's programs with the Radio Times as the agenda.

If one really wishes to understand the structure and organization of the Corporation and its system of control, then attendance at these and other meetings would be an essential part of a wider overall research approach.

ITA

Under the director general, the headquarters staff (about 800) is divided into five main divisions: Program Services, Administrative Services, Engineering, Finance, and Information.

Program Services, under the deputy director general (Program Services), is responsible for the whole range of the output of Independent Television in both the program and the advertising fields, its control and supervision.

The Program Department deals with the approval and supervision of programs in relation to matters such as balance, quality, good taste, and decency, and the maintenance of political impartiality; and to detailed matters such as the administration of control of hours of broadcasting and the requirements concerning foreign material.

The Advertising Control Department deals with the whole range of advertising on television and is responsible for ensuring that the strict control provisions which apply to advertisements are observed.

The Research Department is responsible for obtaining, by audience research, knowledge of the state of public opinion about Independent Television programs. The Regional Offices also form part of this division.

Administrative Services, under the deputy director general (Administrative Services), consists of two departments. The Secretariat, under the Secretary of the Authority, is responsible for the conduct of the business of the Authority and for the contractual relations with the program companies. The Secretariat also services the General Advisory Council, the Standing Consultative Committee (which constitutes the formal link between the Authority and the program companies), and the advisory committees which assist the Authority on advertising, education, and religion.

The Establishments Department is responsible for all personnel and establishment matters, including the welfare of staff and the office administration, accommodation and services. It is also responsible for trade union liaison and negotiation.

The Finance Division, under the head of Finance, is responsible for the Authority's internal financial controls and procedures, e.g., budgetary control, preparation of forward estimates of income and expenditure, and submission of regular financial returns to the Authority. It is also responsible for advising the Authority on matters of financial policy and on the financial aspects of general policy.

The head of Information is responsible for the provision of information to the public about the Authority's activities, and is assisted in this work by specialists dealing with publications, press relations, and exhibitions.

PROGRAM POLICY AND CONTROL

The BBC

Accounts of the policies and operations of the BBC rarely pay enough attention to the part played by the Corporation's governors, and perhaps this is one of the reasons why the role of the governors appears to be frequently misunderstood. As Lord Normanbrook (an ex-chairman of the Board of Governors) has stated:

> Constitutionally the Board of Governors *is* the BBC. It holds the legal title to all BBC property, it determines policy, and it controls personnel. It takes the final decisions on all major questions of management and on all matters of controversy (political, religious, or cultural) which may arouse strong feeling in Parliament or among large sections of public opinion.

The Board has all the responsibilities normally associated with the board of any large organization, including "an unfettered discretion" in the appointment of the director general and senior management officials. The Board is an integral part of the BBC; it is the final source of decision, not only on general policy, but also on specific issues which are of sufficient importance to call for decisions at the highest level within the Corporation. It is important to remember that a decision taken by the Board is a decision taken within the Corporation and should not be regarded, as it sometimes is, as an intervention from outside.

It is tempting to oversimplify and see the Board as responsible for policy and the management as responsible for execution. But in reality the policy and executive functions can be closely interrelated at practically all levels.

Lord Normanbrook states:

> In the executive processes points of difficulty are constantly being thrown up which seem to suggest the need for modification of existing policy, or possibly call for the formulation of new policy; and these points, if they are not susceptible of immediate solution, have to be referred upwards for decision at higher levels in the hierarchy. Equally, policy cannot sensibly be formulated in vacuo: it needs to grow out of the experience gained in administration and should be capable of continuous adjustment in the light of that experience. All this means that, in the BBC, as in other large organizations, no hard and fast line can be drawn between a body of persons concerned only with formulating policy and another body concerned only with carrying it out. Minor decisions of policy must necessarily be taken below Board level, if only because of the need for speedy executive decision. And, conversely, the Board cannot deal solely in generalities and must address itself from time to time to particular questions, even though they may have no general application, just because they are in themselves of outstanding political or public importance. Points of

importance are referred up the hierarchy, and at each stage in the chain of command the person responsible must decide whether this is a point that he can settle himself or whether it is one that should be referred still higher. Skill in taking such decisions is born of experience, which may sometimes be bitter. But it is by this process that the most important questions find their way up for ultimate decision at the top; and within the BBC the ultimate level of decision, even executive decision on matters of the first importance, is the Board of Governors, or, in a matter of urgency, the Chairman acting under the authority delegated to him by the Board.

Codes, vetting procedures, and formal rules and regulations tend not to be favored by the Board of Governors. Generally, these have been seen as concentrating on the letter rather than on the spirit of rules, as being potentially stifling of creativity, and as having little practical value as guides to action. In any case (and this is often argued by the BBC), no Board of Governors, whole time or part time, could possibly control the vast output of the BBC in detail. Quite apart from other important consequences it just would not be practicable. According to Lord Normanbrook:

> The nature of this broadcasting is such that a large measure of discretion must inevitably be left with individual producers and with those exercising immediate supervision over their work. What can be done, and is done, is to encourage producers to refer upwards for guidance in any case of doubt: to reinforce that encouragement by adverse comment and criticism when mistakes are made: and to ensure that Heads of Output Departments and the Controllers above them are vigilant in passing guidance downwards, as and when it is required, as well as encouraging those below them to refer upwards for advice. *This process is essentially one of editorial control by retrospective review.* It is a constant flow of comment and criticism, praise and blame, which goes on continuously at all levels within the Corporation. This constant exchange of views and ideas is, through its continuity, designed to develop among producers a sense of what is right. Program staff are required to apply their own judgment to particular problems, but they do so within a framework of general guidance arising from the continuing discussion of individual programs by themselves and by their seniors up to and including the Board of Governors itself.

The Board is anxious that its function should not be seen as purely negative. It likes to think that it gives praise as well as, and perhaps even more often than, blame. It also claims to take initiatives and to exercise a general influence by frequent informal meetings with groups of staff. However, in general the control which the Board exercises is largely by retrospective review.

Some people outside the Corporation evidently think that the Board is not active enough, but there are those within the Corporation who take the opposite viewpoint. They appear to be apprehensive that "the guardians" will become overzealous in response to the ill-informed activities of pressure groups.

Is the Board much more active now than it used to be? Is it tending to exercise more control and take more initiative; if so, how, why, and to what purpose? These are questions which, in addition to being of interest to the broadcaster, are central to the researcher who wishes to study program control. However, we are unlikely to obtain adequate answers to these questions from official documents and statements, or even from personal accounts of their experiences by those who have occupied or are currently occupying positions within the Corporation. These sources are not without value, but in most institutions there tends to be a predictable gap between what people say they do and what they really do. If we wish to gain an adequate understanding of the mechanisms of control, we shall have to use other methods of research, including participant observation.

Whatever the true picture, there seems to be a general impression that the Board is more active now than it used to be. The name of the present chairman of the Board, Lord Hill, is known to more people than were the names of some of his predecessors. This, of course, could be due to the greater degree of controversy which surrounds broadcasting today. People within the Corporation seem split on this question of whether there is more control now than there used to be. Perhaps not surprisingly, those lower down the ladder seem to have more doubts and fears than those at the top. As far as can be ascertained, the "official" position is that there has been little change in the function and activities of the Board in recent years.

Nevertheless, in July 1968 the governors did produce a note under the title "Broadcasting and the Public Mood." The following quotations from this document may reasonably be taken as representing their current position with regard to some of the central issues of this paper.

It is not surprising that today the interaction between the public mood and the BBC is a somewhat uneasy one, because a country disturbed and divided inevitably has the BBC on the rack. If the BBC is accurately to reflect the world in which it lives (and that is part of its job) then it must accept the assaults of those who accuse the Corporation of inventing or aggravating the factors they would prefer not to take into account.

We have to work within the whole perspective—the whole society. We cannot accommodate ourselves to a particular trend of public thinking at the expense of our corporate programme responsibilities. So what are these responsibilities? Always remembering that the BBC's broad principles must remain consistent throughout recurring national alarms and political excursions, we have to decide what deductions the BBC should draw from the contemporary scene. Should it be content to mirror what it believes it sees? It cannot editorialize—but should it moralize? It may be useful to consider two categories of programs—News and Current Affairs, and Drama.

Facts are sacred. It is the BBC's basic responsibility to report the facts as it finds them. Giving bad news is as much a public service as giving good news. The messenger cannot be blamed if he does not always bear glad tidings. Yet, even in news, the BBC has its problems. The television set is in the living room and any member of the family may be watching. There are times, therefore, when we may feel justified in not using a particularly shocking film about, say, the war in Vietnam. It may be wiser not to give gruesome details of a child murder in early evening bulletins. When the news is bad, we should be scrupulously careful not to appear to relish the contemplation of the unpleasant or the unwelcome.

What is the BBC's responsibility in drama? Basically, the BBC is (and should be) an enlightened patron of the arts, providing the conditions and the atmosphere in which creative people can work. Inevitably this involves some risks. The artist is not willing to be harnessed to other people's morals. He does not see it as his function to operate within the limits of contemporary taste or convention. By his nature, he is in danger of offending, particularly when he probes around the outer edges of acceptance with the object of increasing man's understanding of himself. At the same time, he may conceivably yield to the temptation to shock for meretricious effect.

Standards of taste are always changing. It is difficult to assess at any given time exactly what is and is not good taste. Nevertheless, the BBC has a definite obligation to the public not willfully or unncessarily to depart from a standard of good taste. At the same time the BBC has a responsibility to achieve for the creative artist the maximum amount of freedom consistent with this obligation. Its judgment, therefore, has to operate on a most delicate balance of responsibilities to audiences, writers, and subjects. There are separate obligations to each, and the BBC has the responsibility of judging each obligation for itself. Occasionally —however infrequently—the existence of these obligations may involve some limitation of the artist's freedom.Nevertheless, it is a limitation we should always be reluctant to impose.

Many people have little capacity to take large doses of anxiety and gloom. Never to undertake plays in which such emotions dominate would be to deny to television dramatists the opportunity to comment on our times and would turn our dramatic output into a succession of reassuring palliatives. On the other hand, to allow the pessimistic and the sordid to overwhelm our dramatic output would present an unbalanced view of the world and alienate the sympathy of our viewers. A balance must be struck.

The problem is particularly acute in sexual matters. No aspect of human behaviour is surrounded by more sensitivities. Whenever we deal with it we must somehow reconcile the dramatist's need to express himself with the nature and susceptibilities of our audience, a large proportion of whom are deeply offended by overt references to our portrayals of sexual behaviour. Total license is impossible and few would wish it otherwise.

The question is at which point the line should be drawn. Among the many factors we must consider are the necessity and validity of the action or reference within the context of the play. Another is the quality of the writing and production. Ineptitude can render unacceptable what skill and sensitivity can make acceptable. Similar considerations apply to the use of swear words. They must never be included in dialogue carelessly, automatically, or unnecessary. If they are present then their existence must be relevant to the theme and bring a reality or quality to the play which justifies their being there.

Back in 1920, Lord Reith warned that 'He who prides himself on giving what he thinks the people want is often creating a fictitious demand for lower standards which he will then satisfy.' The BBC is aware of this danger. Yet it is often asserted that the BBC is tending to destroy established moral standards while putting nothing in their place. However unjustified, this kind of criticism raises the question: is it part of the BBC's obligation to urge higher or different moral standards? Part of the answer is that we already provide a platform for those equipped to advocate higher moral standards. Another part is that we accept the role of encouraging higher standards of appreciation, discrimination, and knowledge in all fields. We also maintain in our religious broadcasting the policy of the 'Christian mainstream.' Perhaps we should provide more such platforms, especially aside from religious broadcasting. Again, should we ourselves actively promote an acceptance of certain moral standards? The answer must be that, even if we so wished we are not equipped to define such standards for others. On the other hand, it is no part of our responsibility to appear to deride, or despise, or destroy, merely because they are traditional or conventional, the moral standards to which sections of the public are attached. There are people who are deeply hurt by the intrusion into their homes of what they believe to be the BBC's amoral or antimoral attitude. We should take care not to offend such people needlessly. If we do not pursue a traditional line, we should not cultivate or appear to cultivate a 'permissive' one. We cannot be neutral on moral values. We know that hatred, cruelty, intolerance, and indifference to human misery are bad, and that love, kindness, tolerance, and truthfulness are good.

It is worth adding that, even though we decline the role of moralizer, we do nevertheless exercise a commanding influence by our acts of selection — selection of script, author, producer and director, actors and actresses. Inescapably this selection is the BBC's responsibility and is exercised according to the standards of the selector.

We have seen what the Board has to say, but we are bound to wonder whether such statements are adequate guides to practice. Hatred, cruelty, and intolerance may be considered bad, but what in specific program terms are so regarded? Policy is one thing, practice is another.

Obviously, no matter how hard they tried, the governors could not communicate directly with all or even a substantial minority of the Corporation's staff. Consequently, those in between, the executive or management, form an important link in the communication process.

In this paper we can do little more than ask questions about how the governors and the BBC staff see one another and how they communicate with one another, and hope that someday independent researchers will be able to try and find the answers. But one thing is clear, even at this stage: in this system, a great deal depends on the sharing of opinions and concerns at every level of the Corporation.

A code of practice on violence in television programs (perhaps soon to be reviewed in the light of new research) has been in existence since 1960, but it is generally regarded as having a limited applicability.

In addition to the code, there are also ground rules for the handling of sexual themes and drugs and warnings about programs likely to disturb. Producers have been warned about the reconstruction of events and the

mixing of reality and fiction. Director-General Charles Curran has this to
say on the last point:

> We warn producers against the risks of being tempted to reconstruct events or
> to mix reality with fiction. They must decide, if they do this, how much warning
> must be given to the viewer of the fact that it is being done. Warning there must
> be, because we are concerned with the state of good faith between the producer
> and the viewer. That must never be violated. The viewer must know within what
> convention the producer is working, and if it is not obvious he must be told.

According to R. D 'A Marriott, former Assistant director of BBC
Radio, one of the judgments that has to be made is whether a writer is
using potentially offensive material seriously and sincerely for a genuine
literary or dramatic purpose or whether he is dragging it in for its own
sake, the latter not usually difficult to recognize:

> It is our practice also to look at the total effect of a work rather than to apply
> rules regardless of context. For example, thriller and murder plays have their
> own special conventions. Coarse language may be necessary to establish and
> give reality to a character. Violence and cruelty may be a necessary part of a
> dramatic situation, and evil of any kind may be an incidental part of a work
> whose whole character is unquestionably moral.

> The general aim therefore is to keep our policy and practice as flexible as possi-
> ble. We have obviously taken note of the much greater permissiveness in con-
> temporary society, and things are certainly broadcast which would not have
> been thought acceptable a few years ago. In spite of this, and in spite of the very
> large output of radio programs in this area, there are relatively few criticisms on
> the score of their being shocking, offensive, or immoral.

Some five years ago Huw Wheldon (then controller of Programs Television, now managing director of Television) stated that control over the
subject matter of programs in the BBC was a process in which the assumptions, opinions, and experience of many of its servants are involved. He emphasized that censorship should be seen as part of a process rather than a single act, and that the system of control was really "a
set of practices and relationships which permeated the whole organization up and down and through and through."

In practice, according to Wheldon, the crux of the matter had to do
with responsibility and reference. Describing "reference," he stated
that the general intention to produce, say, a play emerged out of past
experience, possibilities seen, the recognition of a particular and individual talent, or the recognition of new technical potentialities. The intention emerged vaguely out of the incessant exploration of professional
possibilities and personal experience by writers and directors and designers. This intention was then developed specifically in a series of dia-

logues in which several people were variously concerned. All those involved, according to Wheldon, brought to the new project, in that degree which suited their main concern, a responsible sense of what is due to and required of them as public broadcasters. That is, they are aware of but do not prejudge the possible difficulties. A project is finally and decisively launched when it has been developed and costed in detail by the head of Plays and agreed to formally and fully by the channel controller.

The departmental head, his project approved, puts a producer or producers on to the series. The producer approaches writers. A writer suggests or submits an idea suitable to the previously agreed general intention, style, and budget of the group of plays concerned. The producer then commissions a first treatment, finds a suitable director, and seeks agreement from his departmental head to the commission. Wheldon regards both producer and director as being intimately involved in the play from the point of view of their separate responsibilities. One of their main concerns he sees as making sure that the writer is fulfilled and encouraged. *"Their other main concern — their public broadcasting responsibilities — is an inbuilt one, only articulated when difficulties arise."* Should difficulties arise the director handles them. The producer agrees, disagrees, or himself initiates points for special consideration. Control over the subject matter is exercised. The writer is involved. At this point, if there are issues on which they are puzzled, when varying responsibilities, artistic and public, seem to contradict, then the matter is referred to the departmental head, or higher. Reference is obligatory in matters of serious dispute or matters of doubt."

Wheldon also argues that it is possible to mount a television program in secret; designers, script writers, performers, and studio staff surround any production, and elements thought to be doubtful become the subject of general comment or query. Underlying this practice "there is, in broadcasting, the constant and inextinguishable awareness that the audience consists of family groups quite commonly seeing a program as a family group in their own homes." This means that the BBC has to occupy a middle group; and according to Wheldon the concept of the "middle ground" leads one to the concept of "balance," which is regarded as central to the Corporation's control of its subject matter.

Balance is not just a matter of presenting two sides to every question, however:

It has to do with truth and coverage — it has to do with an intelligent effort to make sense of all the facts, however difficult, and not just some of them. It does not preclude the idiosyncratic, or the unusual, or the unconventional; on the contrary. But it will tend to emphasize a totality rather than a partiality. "Balance" also does not preclude attacks and passion and lampoons and deep convictions in given programs. But it precludes " a BBC line" as a whole. Balance also precludes pornography and propaganda in any program. That both are increasingly difficult to define with any measure of unanimity in a splintered society is, of course, true; but equally, what can be so described is remarkably recognizable.

"Balance," or truth, also assumes and must assume that the state of public opinion is not at one and unchanging.In these times when previously held common assumptions are no longer commonly held, when society is undergoing stress and strain of which we are all aware, when generations seem so widely separated, the idea of "balance," of coverage and truth, is one that weighs ever more deeply upon all those responsible for programs.

In his submission Wheldon goes on to state that "control over subject matter" should not be dissociated from "control over the treatment of given subject": "Treatment is all. Hamlet is about incest, murder, revenge, suicide; it is about violence and about sex. It is possible to transmit Hamlet. It is also possible to make an offensive program about buttercups which during its making would come up against the system of editorial control described above, or even prove untransmittable."

Wheldon confirms that it is questions of tone rather than questions of material which to him constitute the most baffling side of editorial judgments in television. In general he feels that the processes of editorial control are more akin to similar processes in large newspapers than they are to the machinery of censorship in the theatre and the film industry, and he asks whether subediting and editorial decision should be regarded as acts of censorship: "Newspapers act within the laws of libel and obscenity, and are tempered by the necessity to maintain an editorial policy and a relationship with their readers. The BBC acts similarly."

It is worth noting that Wheldon more or less confines himself to drama; throughout the general debate on program control there are relatively few specific references to feature films, imported series, etc. Yet it is arguable that, at least as far as violence is concerned, these are the types of programs where the greatest vigilance is required.

One gathers, however, that the code is rigidly applied in these areas also and that the head of the film purchasing department is extremely well-informed and closely involved in program policy. As far as feature films are concerned, the need in most cases to attract large family audiences may be an additional safeguard. However, it would be interesting to know more about the factors that govern the importing of series and cartoons, including those that are shown in time slots normally associated with children's programming.

For the BBC, the concept of "public service responsibility" is at the very heart of this matter. Wheldon writes:

If the BBC is to provide the country with the best television service of which it is capable, then it must be in a position to attract the good minds and talents of the country. It must, as far as humanly possible, be the country speaking for and to itself. The principles underlying editorial control are based deeply on the assumption that the finding, securing, and encouraging of all those creative and wayward and surprising talents that go into making television programmes is a major part of the Corporation's responsibility to the public. It means taking chances into the unknown with a view to having a future. This aim, to have a good reputation which attracts fine talents, and in turn to succour and develop those talents, is one that will often seem to come up against the equally strong aim to provide a seemly and responsible public service. It is the work of editorial control to make them lie together, selling neither one nor the other of them short.

Not surprisingly, public service responsibility is also a recurring theme in Charles Curran's talk and public statements. According to Curran freedom and responsibility is what works:

> The price of freedom is, of course, responsibility exercised by the man who claims to be free, and I have no real fear that our creative staff in the BBC are unaware of this requirement. . .We are concerned reflectors of the world we live in, responsible in our freedom and balanced because we live by balance and perspective, and we are lost without them.

There is no lack of conviction, confidence, certainty (some people might even say arrogance) in these statements. According to Charles Curran, the professional standard of the Corporation is excellence. Moreover, according to both Curran and Wheldon, the lapses and mistakes of the Corporation are few, although some recent research suggests that over one-third of a national sample saw or heard things on BBC television which they considered offensive. This by itself (although there is other supporting evidence) does not mean a great deal, but it is worth mentioning if only because the BBC with its certainty often gives the impression of being its own judge and jury. Could excellence be whatever the Corporation does? One sometimes gets that impression from the official pronouncements. An outsider may be forgiven if he refuses to accept all the BBC statements at face value. He may even suggest an independent assessment.

ITA

The statutory duties of the Independent Television Authority in relation to programs are both general and specific. Generally, the Act states that the Independent Television service, like the BBC, shall be for "disseminating information, education and entertainment." It is also the duty of the Authority "to ensure that the programs broadcasts by the Authority in each area maintain a high general standard in all respects, and in particular in respect of their content and quality, and a proper balance and wide range in their subject-matter, having regard both to the programs as a whole and also to the days of the week on which, and the times of day at which, the programs are broadcast; and to ensure a wide showing for programs of merit."

More specifically, the Authority is required to satisfy itself "that nothing is included in the programs which offends against good taste or decency or is likely to encourage or incite to crime or to lead to disorder or to be offensive to public feeling; that all news is presented with due accuracy and impartiality; and that due impartiality is preserved as respects matters of political or industrial controversy or relating to current public policy."

In particular, the Authority is required by the Act to draw up a code giving guidance "as to the rules to be observed in regard to the showing of violence, particularly when large numbers of children and young persons may be expected to be watching the programs."

In order to ensure that these requirements are observed, the Authority needs to have from the contractors reasonable advance information about programs; the Television Act gives the Authority power to get it. All program schedules must be drawn up in consultation with the Authority; when complete, they have to be submitted to the Authority for approval. In its contracts with the program companies, the Authority must also stipulate that details of program content (and, where required, full scripts) will be provided. As a last resort, the Authority has in reserve the power to give directions to a company about the inclusion or exclusion of any particular item from a program schedule.

The Authority possesses considerable powers and is of necessity involved in program planning and the formulation of program policy. However, the interesting questions have to do with the manner of control—the way in which the powers are used and the nature and degree of the Authority's involvement in program planning and formulation.

A memorandum from the director-general to the Joint Committee on Theatre Censorship in 1966, referring to the ITA's executive arrangements, had this to say:

> The Authority itself regularly discusses and makes decisions about broad questions of program policy, and also deals from time to time with general or especially difficult *ad hoc* issues related to the subject-matter of programs which are referred to it by the staff.

> The principal members of the staff concerned with the day-to-day oversight of program matters are the director-general, the deputy director program services, the head of program services and the senior program officer. Additionally there are specialist members of the staff concerned with educational programs, religious programs and news and current affairs programs.

> The senior program officer has first sight of the routine advance information supplied to the Authority by the companies about their drama output—single plays, series plays, and serials. He is specially concerned with the application of the code of violence, with the content of programs designed for children and with ensuring, under the Authority's "family viewing policy" that, so far as possible, programs up to 9 p.m. contain nothing likely to be harmful to children.

Committees are an important feature of the ITA structure. For our present purposes the most important subcommittee of the Authority is the Program Schedule Committee, set up by Lord Hill (ex-chairman of

ITA) to meet the statutory requirements of the 1964 Act. It meets four times a year (the Authority meets monthly except in August) to approve the companies' schedules.

The Authority presides over a committee known as the Program Policy Committee, on which all the companies are represented and which is regarded as the principal channel for making known to the companies the Authority's views on program policy and for establishing the main trends on which detailed planning proceeds. Its work is closely linked with that of the Network Program Committee, which is the main instrument of the companies for working out the basic network schedules and arranging cooperation between them in program matters: a representative of the Authority sits on this committee. The Network Program Committee deals with forward planning, takes decisions on the basis of subcommittee representation, and could prepare company representations to the Authority. It deals with all sorts of intercompany and general broadcasting business, has its own secretariat, and on the program side now operates through a number of subcommittees (Children's, Religious, etc.).

A further body, the Standing Consultative Committee, which meets monthly under the chairmanship of the director-general, takes questions of program policy between the meetings of the Program Policy Committee. At lower levels, there are all kinds of operational committees through which day-to-day decision-taking passes.

There is also regular consultation between the companies individually and the Authority. The Authority has recently required the program companies to review their individual internal arrangements for the control of program content and to provide precise descriptions of these arrangements to the Authority.

A company lays out its intended weekly pattern of broadcasts in schedules which are issued once every three months and submitted to the Authority for approval. This periodic approval of schedules is required by the Act. Therefore, one of the main tasks of the Authority's known requirements about balance of programs, the timing of particular series, and similar matters of program content have been observed in the proposed schedules and in the amendments to those schedules that are also proposed from time to time. The approval of program schedules and amendments is given on the basis of reports submitted by the staff to the Authority's Program Schedule Committee, with whom they are discussed; subsequent recommendations are made by the Committee to the full Authority.

Although schedule approval takes place at regular intervals, the development of program plans is a continuous process that goes on throughout the year. This means that Authority staff must keep in touch with the chief executives and program controllers of all the companies by means of attendance at the various committees and by less formal personal contacts.

There is no single time in the evening at which the broadcasters can be certain that there are not substantial numbers of young children in the audience. Children have their own programs in the hour or so preceding the early news bulletin, and it is the practice in Independent Television to assume that large numbers of them continue to watch thereafter. The Authority seeks to ensure that the programs shown in the early evening period should not be unsuitable for children. As the evening advances, more adult material is introduced and so the burden of responsibility for deciding what programs children should watch is progressively transferred to the shoulders of the parents.

Let us illustrate the process by looking at the way in which an imaginary summer schedule might be planned. Much work on this would have already been done in the previous year because, of course, writing, planning and recording of major television series now takes a minimum of one year and can take very much longer. Decisions would also have been taken within the program companies about what they were going to offer. The program controllers would, at the end of the winter or the beginning of the spring quarter, begin to slot this into some kind of coherent schedule.

However, their room for maneuver is limited. There are certain basic Authority requirements which they cannot alter without Authority permission. In some cases this would require literally months of negotiation (e.g., a proposal to shorten the midevening news and restore it to 9 o'clock).

They do not begin, therefore, with a blank sheet of paper, but with one into which are already written certain "givens"—for example, *News at Ten*, documentaries, two plays, two major current affairs programs, *The Weekend Special*, children's programming, closed period. Into blank spaces they would have to write what they know is currently available from the production companies. Some of this, made up of major network productions from the five majors, will be in agreed ratios between the companies. There are also usually varying amounts of additional programming on offer. The controller will make use of this additional programming according to his own knowledge of his audience and his own understanding of what constitutes a balanced schedule. In addition, the companies still have to make programs for their own regions. (The Act says, "A suitable proportion of the matter calculated to appeal specially to the tastes and outlook of the persons served by the station.") Occasionally some of these can be offered for network use as well. The Authority's staff will at this stage formally have been made aware of the main features of the outline schedule and, not infrequently, have made comments and suggestions which influence the later form. The outline does not cover a whole week's broadcasting—for example, feature films are used locally, and so are many film series; such local programs as *ATV Today* or Thames's *Today* are written in.

These schedules are then submitted to the Authority's staff, who can, and regularly do, make points about them. This happens in two ways. There is a formal statistical examination of the schedules to ensure that they are within the permitted hours of broadcasting, that not too much imported material is used in and out of peak hours, and so on. They are also examined in terms of balance—e.g., not too much clustering of similar kinds of material and so on. At this stage only the schedules of the Big Five would be available, but copies would find their way to the regional companies who would likewise, usually in consultation with the Authority's regional officers, be clothing the network skeleton.

After staff discussions on individual points with the program companies, the schedules are formally submitted to the program schedule committee of the Authority for its approval. They will be accompanied by staff commentaries drawing the committee's attention either to new developments or to points on which the staff seek guidance.

The Authority states that three factors are always present in the appraisal of a proposed program schedule:

1) Control of the relative proportions of different classes of program (such as are likely to contain scenes of conflict or "strong action," for example).

2) The avoidance of undue concentration of several examples of the same kind of strong action material at particular times in the week.

3) The observance of the established family viewing policy, which requires that programs considered unsuitable for children should not be shown before approximately 9 p.m. A producer of a studio production is briefed by the program planners about the time of day for which his program should be made suitable. In the case of film series or feature films, it is usual to rely, in the first instance, on the judgment of the companies as to the most suitable timing: early evening, eight o'clock, or after nine.

The companies themselves do the initial sorting and selecting of feature films. Originally they used to buy them independently; each company would negotiate independently with the distributors in this country for the American films. Now they tend to be bought for and on behalf of the network by a Granada official who has specialized film knowledge. But even so, although rights are acquired for the network, each company will schedule the films as it thinks fit. All films and film series (not just imported ones) are classified or certified in three ways. They're suitable for transmission either any time, after 8 p.m., or after 9 p.m.

From all accounts there are not many disputes over the classification system. The main reason for this has been attributed by some to the general "play safe," "offend no-one" policy of the independent system. People in business do not wish to make or buy something that is in danger of being left on the shelf. No doubt a general understanding develops as to what is acceptable and what is not. As one might expect, the main problems centre around violence, sex, and language.

The concept of family or home viewing figures very prominently in ITA thinking as manifested in official documents and pronouncements. It is also worth noting what has already been implied, namely that with regard both to films and other programs, it is not in the companies' commercial interests to be too far out. One further point of interest in this area is that whereas sex in the cinema can attract audiences, this need not be the case with television. Violence may attract, but there seems to be a feeling in Independent Television that sex on the smaller screen could be a loser. There are, in fact, more complaints from the public about sex and bad language than about violence.

A rather different system applies in the case of the programs— plays or series—produced by the Independent Television companies themselves. There are no arrangements for the automatic submission to the Authority of full scripts. The system of control is concerned with both content and timing and would appear to rest primarily on the practice of regular consultation between company and authority.

The producing company sends a synopsis of each play or episode to the Authority in advance of production. If the staff of the Authority has any doubts or questions, these are normally put to the company orally at an appropriate level. More often than not, these doubts are resolved simply by the supply of further information. Where this is not so, there will usually be discussion with the company, which may lead to agreement to take no further action, to agreement that the company will itself take certain action, or to a request for a full script or a preview of the program, or both. In the last resort the Authority may issue an instruction to withdraw the program or an instruction to present it only after deletions have been made, but final directions of this kind are rarely necessary.

Occasionally the Authority or the Authority's staff is asked to preview a program in order to assist a company to resolve doubts which a company may itself entertain. People in the creative process themselves may also make representations to the Authority, either directly or through an association to which they belong. The Authority claims that it does not refuse to consider any representations from whatever source they come, provided its formal relationship with the managements of the program companies is not prejudiced.

As a result of this continuing process of examination and inquiry, there have inevitably been some occasions when the Authority has had to intervene in drama and documentary programs so as to ensure that the Act is observed. But, according to the ITA, such interventions are rare in relation to the totality of the output, and they have never been on such a scale or of such severity as could be said to "hamstring creative artists." As we shall see later, not all creative artists would accept this statement.

With the exception of the code on violence, the Authority has published no document describing the criteria it adopts in exercising control
over the subject matter of its programs. Nevertheless, from time to time
the Authority discusses with the companies standards of practice in relation to the production of particular classes of programs, and these discussions sometimes lead to the circulation of agreed notes for guidance.
All transmissions are monitored by ITA staff, and each month the Authority considers a report from the staff on programs, or incidents there-
in, which have aroused criticism. Companies are notified of any retrospective judgments reached by the Authority about the content and
presentation of drama and other programs. It has always been the aim of
the Authority that the initial responsibility for observing the provisions
of the Act and for observing the Authority's known policies should be
taken by the companies themselves as part of their contractual obligations.

According to Lord Hill (in 1966 when he was still Chairman of ITA),
about ten percent of plays might possibly raise some initial query. In a
three-year period, he said, the Authority had insisted on alterations
being carried out in about a half-dozen instances. But this doesn't tell us
very much about how the system really works. As we have seen, initiatives can come from either side; difficult problems may be ironed out in
the early informal exchanges between company and Authority. People
get used to the patterns of the organizations in which they work. They
soon find out what is likely to be accepted and what rejected. They come
to accept the ground rules and to anticipate reactions. The fact that Authority action is required in few cases may be the surest indication that
everyone has learned and internalized the rules.

Both sides if one may use this term, get to know each other and learn
by experience. It is not a matter of drawing up black lists (although
some may disagree), but if an ITA program officer sees the synopsis of a
certain type of play coupled with the names of a known writer and director he sees the warning light and no doubt acts accordingly.

The official position is still that no formal code, no statement of principles, can of itself be more than a point of reference; it must be supplemented by measures to ensure its observance. Although, as we have already seen, the program initiatives lie with the program companies, they
are required by the Television Act to make known their plans in advance
to the Authority by submitting program schedules for its approval. Over
the years this procedure has been developed by experience into an in-
terlocking system of checks and controls.

A Working Party on Violence in Television Programs (on which the
Authority, the companies, and the General Advisory Council are represented) is at present preparing a new code. It seems unlikely, however,
that this Working Party will wish to produce anything more specific than
what exists at present. In the last resort in all controversial areas, the

program maker must accept responsibility, and the general advice as always will probably be, "If in doubt leave it out".

Lord Aylestone, in a recent talk entitled "Television and Public Taste," illustrates the general approach in dealing with the question of blasphemy.

What better answer to this problem can you find than the one which the Authority has arrived at — *not to ban the use of the word* absolutely *but to ask company managements, and all those concerned* with the *creative side of television, to think carefully before using it, and not to use it trivially or carelessly?* This, you will notice, is a position some way away from that of those who argue that there are absolute standards (usually their own) from which no deviation is possible, but equally far away from those who would argue that there are no inhibitions left, that total freedom is the only possible stand for the creative artist today.

I would occupy much the same middle ground if our subject were sex or bad language. I would occupy not very different ground if I were brought into the argument between those who say that television is a major factor in corrupting youth (they would find precious little evidence for that) and those who maintain that it has no influence at all, because we just don't know enough yet to be confident that is true. Television cannot allow itself to be used simply to reflect the embalmed taste of the nineteen-thirties, never involving itself in the ecstasies and the agonies of the seventies about sex and violence, never employing the language of the ordinary people, and the extraordinary people, with whose lives it is involved. I repeat that what it must do is try and keep in step with what people want to say, on the one hand, and what people find acceptable to hear on the other.

To see how this thinking is reflected in action, some passages from the ITA Annual Report of 1969-70 are cited below:

The treatment of events in Northern Ireland, as indeed that of continuing students unrest and other events during the year, raised for the Authority and ITN the general problem of the extent to which the presence, anticipated or actual, of the television camera at potentially violent events, can itself act as a catalyst or even stimulus to violence. Another related problem was seen in the direct visual presentation of violent events to the general viewer. Here the Authority and ITN, whilst quite clear that it is the function of a television news service to report what has happened unsensationally but accurately, take the view that particular discretion needs to be exercised in bulletins shown in the early part of the evening when children are likely to be viewing. In the course of the year the Authority and Ulster Television, after previewing the material, decided against the transmission of three programmes in Northern Ireland, taking the view that the contributions from persons of extreme attitudes which each contained could well at the time in question have exacerbated an already dangerous situation. These decisions were directly related to part of clause 3 (1) (a) of the Television Act which requires the Authority to satisfy itself that nothing is included in the programs which is likely to lead to disorder.

One of the most significant series of the year in a number of ways was Granada's *Big Breadwinner Hog.* The program attempted, on the basis of a great

deal of research in the East End of London, to describe the kind of gang warfare that had been going on there for some years previously. Most of those
involved in the program saw it as something of a social duty to tell the audience about this, albeit within the framework of a clearly fictional program. The
first episode showed in use and in convincing detail the weapons employed
within this gang warfare. In the Authority's view there was an error of judgment in the degree of violence thus put before the viewer. The Authority
viewed all subsequent episodes before transmission and decided, after the
fourth episode, that the series would be better shown late at night. There was
considerable public reaction and it was disappointing, but no doubt salutary, to
see that of the very many correspondents who complained about the series,
few gave any thought to the motives which had prompted its production. The
assumption was made, as it often gratuitously is, that television was interested
simply to make programs that glorified violence. On the other hand, a research
survey, carried out later with a random sample of the population, indicated
that few people thought that *Big Breadwinner Hog* would attract anyone to
violence. The questions that remained with the Authority were two. First, a
production which aims to expose the bestial subhumanity of organized crime
needs to be of quite outstanding excellence in writing and performance if it is
to carry the heavy load of crude violence that such an intention requires. Did
Big Breadwinner Hog, despite its occasional technical brilliance, really come
up to such a standard? Secondly, how far is it possible for a television production like this to make it plain to the mass audience that it is not simply telling a
story, but trying at the same time to imply a social comment?

A second problem has arisen. During the year the Authority has had to exercise a restraining influence on language and innuendo in some programs. Undoubtedly broad humor, not to say healthy vulgarity, has been a continuing
strand in the comic tradition of all cultures. Moreover there has undeniably
been a considerable change over the past two years in what is publicly acceptable as humor and socially suitable language. The Authority is not seeking to
return to standards which were appropriate fifteen years ago. It is important
that the comedy scriptwriter should have as much freedom as his colleagues
working in the serious drama, but the writer's craft remains a disciplined one,
even for television and particularly in comedy where large effects are often
achieved with small means.

ITA's program companies

So far, using mainly official sources, we have examined in a relatively
superficial way the approaches to program control by two differently
structured broadcasting institutions in Great Britain. Even recognizing
that this is only a pilot, exploratory exercise, it still has been done in a
manner that must be regarded as biased — in fact, as top-heavy. The ratio of official statements to statements from the shop-floor in these pages
is a clear indication of this. Moreover, in the case of the independent
system, we have concentrated on the Authority and on its relationships
with the companies; little has been said about the nature of the companies and how they operate. Yet this is a vital aspect of the total picture
and would certainly need to be covered in any research project which
addressed itself comprehensively to the question of program control.

As far as the companies are concerned, whilst accepting that no two are alike, we could try to redress the balance a little with the help of Denis Forman, joint managing director of Granada Television, (although recognizing that once again the statements come from the top).

In a contribution he made to a 1969 symposium on the Structure of Broadcasting in Manchester, Forman maintained that Granada's structure could only operate in a company which was employing in the region of 1,000 to 1,500 people, and would not be appropriate for such large organizations as the BBC. He went on to say that the structure had been evolved by instinct and that instinctive reactions to events had resulted in certain methods of doing things and a certain manner or style of operating. He felt that these instincts were peculiar to a particular group of people, and were different from those which would have guided another similar but different group of people doing the same job. In that way the structure of Granada was unique.

Speaking of the generation of program ideas, Forman stated that "sometimes the generation was involuntary, almost a reflex. 'This is the sort of thing we must do' or 'This is a good idea, we must do it.' " He accepted that another kind of generation was forced upon the Program Committee in that sometimes they had an obligation to the network, the public, the ITA, or other companies. In such cases the generation was not "involuntary" and it was necessary to find a program to meet the bill. He seemed to think a great deal of time was spent doing this. He saw Granada as a company operating under a system of dual control:

> In most television companies, matters of fundamental program policy are resolved at the Board; in most companies those people who make programs are responsible to the Board. But I found that in Granada there was a Program Committee, running parallel to the Board, and with a direct responsibility not just to the Board but to the Public. This Program Committee was composed of eight people, all program executives, who were its constant members. Whereas the Granada Board was responsible upwards to Granada Group, and downwards to the heads of the administrative departments, the Program Committee was responsible upwards to the public and downwards to the directors, producers and other creative people who make programs. . . .
>
> Now it might seem a touch irresponsible that the program-making branch of a company is in no way responsible to its Board. Yet Granada appears to have solved this problem, as it seemed to me, by the simple and rational expedient of having more than half the Board on the Program Committee, including most of the more senior executive members of the Board. I looked into the records and discovered that no decision of the Program Committee had ever been questioned by the Board. The reason you will have already grasped. If the Board wanted to query what was happening in the program area they would then be raising questions about the conduct of half their own members, including the Chairman and the two Joint Managing Directors. . . .
>
> Both bodies have their responsibilities, but the interesting point is that each group conducts its affairs independently. The Program Committee has, for

instance, its own external relationship with the ITA; the Board have a different relationship towards the ITA, and on quite separate matters.

Forman went on to claim that there was genuine person-to-person contact on the creative side of Granada, and that there was a program responsibility to an Executive Producer, running parallel to an individual responsibility between an individual member of the Program Committee and each of the 60 individual producers and directors. He also claimed that he had discovered that when major reviews or decisions had to be taken, there was a wide base for discussion in the meetings between the Program Committee and the creative men and women concerned:

> When there was a review of drama, or of drama series, I found that all the producers and directors who were directly interested in drama, perhaps fifteen or twenty, would occasionally meet with all the Program Committee for a considerable length of time. So in addition to the person-to-person direct contact, in addition to the subgroups, each run by an executive producer, there were also wider program consultations held from time to time.

> Granada was also characterized by fluidity. If you were to take three members of the Program Committee, and assess their main interests as, let us say, drama and comedy, and the next one's main interest as journalism, and a third member were to have an equal interest in all three, I found that individual producers and directors, according to their own interests, from year to year worked to and with different members of the Committee. A drama director or producer might work for any one of three of the executives on the Committee: equally with a comedy producer. A journalistically-inclined producer might work for almost any one of the Committee. Departmentalisation, in the sense of rigid hierarchies, did not exist.

Commenting of the flow of ideas reaching the Program Committee, Forman tells us that the number of ideas which come from outside the company is exceedingly small. However, apparently a large number of ideas come from people who know the company, who know people in the company, or who work for the company. Perhaps not surprisingly, the company's own program staff is the major source of ideas:

> Once these ideas reached the Program Committee, a large number of them were rejected and the remainder were considerably transformed, except in those rare cases where the first concept had a clarity and a shape so obviously right that it could not, or should not, be amended or adapted. I found, too, that there was a certain body of opinion, both within and without the Program Committee, which swung from one area of interest to another from time to time, and from year to year, with its point of focus centering variously on political, social, or dramatic ideas. This background swing of ideas and opinions tended to generate programs.

The total picture

This picture of television as projected by some of its senior practitioners in both broadcasting institutions is not one that every viewer would immediately recognize. "High standards," "splendid quality," "vehicle for creativity," "overall excellence" are not the words that one automatically associates with current television fare. These pages have included many examples of apparent certainty and confidence (perhaps even over-confidence and arrogance) on the part of broadcasters. There is no lack of conviction, although the reader may be conscious of a lack of supporting evidence for the many claims that have been made. The feeling that broadcasters like to be advocate, judge, and jury in their own case may have been strengthened.

However, it would be naive not to expect the apparent arrogance, the justifications, and the rationalizations from such highly involved people in such visible and vulnerable positions. The relationship of the broadcasting institutions to other institutions in society and the nature of the socialization process in the broadcasting institutions make such public attitudes almost inevitable. These apparently wider questions are not without relevance to the problems of program control.

We have talked about the sources of program material both inside and outside the broadcasting institutions, the methods of selection and rejection, the importance of contacts and relationships, the types of criteria employed, the belief that some things are immediately recognized as being "obviously right," and so on. On several occasions attention has been drawn to the importance of informal exchanges among people occupying different focal positions as well as to shared perspectives, common experience, and mutual understanding.

This is the essence of the control process. The importance of historical, economic, political, constitutional, and wider organizational factors needs no further stressing here, but to confine the study of program control to the relatively formal framework of the operation, vital though this undoubtedly is, would be inadequate.

It is the whole network of relationships and interactions that we are called upon to examine. Who are the people, both inside and outside the company, who produce most of the ideas? What are their values and expectations? What are their relationships with the gatekeepers? Who are the gatekeepers? What is the nature of the filtering process? Who and what is encouraged? What other pressures and constraints are present? These are just a few of the questions to which we must address ourselves as we study the nature and the mechanisms of program control. We are not likely to obtain the answers to these questions simply by studying organizational charts or the type of policy statements and official documents so frequently quoted in this paper.

The sources used have tended to be biased in a top-heavy manner. This point needs to be stressed, even though the messages from these sources have been critically reviewed in this paper. In a paper such as this, it is neither possible nor necessary to attempt to balance all sides,

but it is important to record that not all those connected with broadcasting speak with the same official voice.

Writing in the magazine *Censorship* some years ago, Wilfred Greatorex, a well-known television script-writer, had this to say:

> "We never censor," said the (ITA) spokesman. "We edit." But wasn't this
> what the program-making company was paying me to do? "We re-edit."

> The ITA's technique of censorship is to create a climate of fear in the produc-
> ing companies, who depend for the extension of their licenses on the say-so of
> the ITA. It has its fifth column planted inside the companies, a sort of human
> early-warning radar system. What qualifications these people have is not clear,
> though a capacity to twitch easily is essential. The twitchworthy things they
> look for are lapses of taste, political dodginess, sex, violence and swearwords.

> At the ITA itself the full-blown censors see advance synopses of programs
> drafted by the program makers, and it is not unknown for these to be couched
> tranquillisingly to disalarm the fretful. If in doubt the censor calls for the script
> and "makes suggestions", or he calls for a preview of the show—a simple
> process almost all prerecorded. The image of grown men sitting in darkened
> offices monitoring television pictures created by others with ten times their
> creative talent would be Kafkaesque if it weren't so tragic. In the end, such
> are the rules of the game, the program makers — writer, director, producer —
> are usually the last to hear of a clamp-down. In my own case I was told about
> it by newspapermen seeking my views.

> The ITA displays as arrogant a contempt for the Great British Public as it does
> for the programme makers. The G.B.P. must be protected, mollycoddled, co-
> cooned from the world of ideas where truths can be disturbing and facts un-
> pleasant. The G.B.P., in other words, is not to be trusted.

"The time has come," writes Greatorex, "to turn the searchlight onto
the watchdog of Independent Television. The watchers up there in the
ITA need watching." We can certainly agree with him there— although
we would want to turn the spotlight on the writers as well and not just on
their formal statements. We hope he would agree.

In the same volume, R. Vernon Beste (then deputy chairman of the
Writers' Guild of Great Britain and chairman of the Guild's Censorship
Appeals Committee) had this to say:

> While the Authority exercises an overall censorship, it has no direct contact
> with the writers who are commissioned and paid by the contractors. But not all
> the bans in commercial TV come from the ITA exercising its statutory powers.
> The Contractors themselves censor material idiosyncratically, and words,
> phrases, subjects and even forms that are acceptable to one company may be
> anathema to another. Thus the contractors' willingness to cooperate was es-
> sential to any censorship procedure agreed to by the Authority.

> Censorship in ITV is therefore very confused. For every time the ITA applies
> the clamp there are many more where the contractor blue-pencils things the
> Authority would pass. And they are very jealous of their right to do it.

As commercial firms their first duty is to their shareholders and some of them have a very weak concern for the public service aspect of their licenses. They prefer to play safe, to skulk well back from the frontiers of public opinion rather than risk offending someone by adding to their compass. This attitude is not confined to material they produce themselves. By refusing to buy programs they consider "advanced" they seek to impose it on all network productions. At the other end of the scale, more liberally oriented contractors are inhibited from clashing too harshly and consistently with the ITA lest they jeopardize the future of their licenses.

The Authority later agreed that the fundamental criterion in evaluating questions of censorship in television drama should be the seriousness of the writer's intention and that decisions in this area should be communicated and justified. Apparently at that time the position with the BBC was regarded as reasonably satisfactory on these scores.

This question cannot be examined simply in terms of one side being right and the other being wrong. People occupy different positions and play different roles. Situations are diagnosed and remedies and solutions put forward in terms of these positions and roles—and it is just this that we need to include in our study.

Stuart Hood, having worked in both BBC and ITV, is in a particularly suitable position to compare both systems. He writes:

There is within the BBC not only no written code but no formal machinery of censorship. The policy is to encourage producers or directors to make their own decisions, referring any problems upwards in case of doubt. Program control is, therefore, in the vast majority of cases exercised by post-mortems—a fact which explains the number of occasions on which the BBC apologizes for what has appeared on the screen. These apologies are sometimes justified, sometimes mere attempts to placate particular interests. In cases where difficult decisions have to be made on political, moral, religious or other grounds, the decision may be passed upwards through the hierarchy to end up with the Board of Governors. The system has obvious advantages. It allows great freedom to the individual producer or director. Its drawbacks are that much—no one can tell how much—may be smothered at birth because of timidity at lower levels in the organization; on the other hand, the moment a program reaches the Board of Governors the judgments passed on it tend to reflect the extreme sensitivity of that body. No governing body willingly exposes itself to unpleasantness or difficulty. But, given these reservations, program-makers in the BBC enjoy great freedom—too much in the eyes of many politicians and moral reformers—and their liberty is much envied by their counterparts in ITV.

The companies, for their part, wishing to avoid clashes with the Authority, have set up their own watchdogs. Most of the large companies have a system of program clearance—a supervisor who, while not directly interfering in the making of programs, is empowered—indeed enjoined—to call the attention of the producer or director to points which might cause the Authority to object. The manner in which this duty is performed varies according to the personality of the men or women in the post. They are not, however, generally regarded with favor by the program-makers—although their powers are limited and not mandatory. They may be—and in some cases are—of considerable help to producers in suggesting how to present a program to the Authority and avoid censorship by them.

The waste of time and energy involved in arguing with men and women who
have themselves no program experience is greatly resented by those involved on
the creative side. . . . It is the censorship of the ITA which is felt by the men
and women who work on programs in Independent Television to be the most
frustrating element they have to deal with in their daily work.

This, then, is the other side of the picture. However, we are not likely
to obtain a satisfactory view of the total scene merely by examining
statements from different sides. We must be able to observe the process
in action, and this means full access to media institutions.

THE BROADCASTING INSTITUTIONS AND THE PUBLIC

The BBC

The BBC has always claimed to attach great importance to its relationship with its public. There are many aspects to this relationship (a-
round £500,000 per annum is spent on publicity), but according to Kenneth Lamb (director of public affairs), "the interaction between the
BBC and its public depends, overwhelmingly, inescapably, rightly, on
the BBC's programs, not on its other relations with its public."

It is argued that the license fee system brings broadcasters and public
together in a direct relationship and impels the BBC to ask itself the
question, "What ought we to be doing to serve the public better?" One
assumes that the BBC must listen to what the public has to say, and
there are several ways both formal and informal by which it can do this.

Over the years various advisory bodies have been established. Most
of these are specialist bodies (educational, religious, etc.), but the body
with the widest terms of reference is the General Advisory Council. This
Council is called upon to advise the BBC "on all matters which may be
of concern to the Corporation or to bodies or persons interested in the
broadcasting services of the Corporation."

Kenneth Lamb claims that the importance the BBC attaches to this
Council is indicated by the fact that its quarterly meetings are attended
by the Chairman of the BBC, the director-general, and members of both
the Board of Governors and the Board of Management. Reports on the
proceedings of the General Advisory Council are invariably heard and
considered by the Board within 24 hours of the Council's meetings. The
General Advisory Council is a confidential body (its discussions are private), and the BBC clearly wishes it to remain so. Although its members, no more than 60, serve and speak as individual members of society
rather than as the delegates of other bodies or professions, they reflect a
wide range of interests and public activities. They are, of course, appointed by the Corporation. The appointments are on a part-time basis
for a five year period.

The BBC's aim in creating the Council was to "secure the constructive criticism and advice of representative men and women over the whole field of its activities." It also hoped that members of the Council "would use their influence in helping towards a fuller understanding of the BBC's problems and policy on the part of the general public." Amongst the issues which in the last year or two the Council has discussed — some on its own initiative, some on the BBC's—have been the depiction of student unrest, children's television, science and the future of society, training for broadcasting, and the portrayal of violence on television.

The fact that the Council's proceedings are confidential carries with it the disadvantage that, active and valuable to the BBC though the Council may be, little can be said publicly about the nature of the advice it proffers. Even less can be said about how the advice was received and what action, if any, followed. To some people the alternative of treating the Council as an open and public forum may appear attractive, but according to Lamb there are good reasons why this alternative has not been adopted. Under the BBC's charter the Board of Governors ("trustees of the national interest") is established as the final, unitary authority in the BBC. Such a body as the GAC can therefore only be advisory. It is argued that for the GAC or any other body to duplicate the Board's role, or to act independently of the BBC in publishing its views, could only lead to a weakening or confusing of responsibility and would be bound to derogate from the ultimate public accountability of the governors for all the BBC's actions and decisions.

There are many, including some who have served on the Council, who regard the whole advisory structure as a facade, a mere pretense at public consultation. Naturally, the BBC deny that this is the case, and official spokesmen are always ready to cite instances when the Corporation has acted on the advice given to it by the GAC. Obviously there is no way, short of research, that will enable us to make an accurate assessment of the role of the GAC.

The most significant recent development in the advisory system has been the appointment during the past year of an advisory group on the social effects of television. One of its functions is to offer the BBC advice on how the results of all the relevant research in this field might be applied to the direct needs of program-makers. It is not exclusively concerned with violence but, granted the present climate, it seems likely that this issue will loom large in its discussions. This body will no doubt be particularly interested in relevant research projects at present being undertaken by the BBC and other institutions. It is hoped that the proposed redrafting of the code of violence will be able to benefit from the results of this research.

According to the BBC Handbook, the Corporation has always recognized that it must keep in touch with public opinion. But, so it is said, this cannot be done by simply being open to any representations made to it, important though these representations are. The BBC itself accepts that it has an active role to play by deliberately and systematically collecting what it considers to be relevant information. This collecting is performed by its own Audience Research department, which attempts to find out about the public's tastes and habits, how much viewing or listening is taking place, and what people think of the programs they see or hear.

Side by side with these continuous studies, the Audience Research department also undertake several types of *ad hoc* investigations. These may involve anything from discovering public opinion on a single point—such as a proposed change in the timing of a broadcast—to a study of the audiences for one particular type of output, such as local broadcasting.

Audience Research may also be called upon to forearm the producer of, say, a documentary program with information about the public's existing stock of knowledge of his subject, or to measure the extent to which his efforts to widen it have been successful. But, so it is claimed, in every case the object is the same: to collect information which is representative and reliable, as a basis for evaluation or decision-making by those concerned. It is also claimed, although supporting evidence is not presented, that the results from all this research play a valuable part in future program decisions.

Needless to say, there has been no systematic study of the way in which this information is used as a basis for evaluation or decision making. Once again we are reminded of the gap that can and often does exist between the availability of information on the one hand and its use on the other. It is one thing to know that information about public opinion is sought and is available; it is another, entirely different, matter to know how is used (if at all) once it has been obtained.

In addition to all this deliberately sought information, the BBC receives nearly 1,000 letters each day from viewers and listeners. These letters cover a wide range of topics, and less than one-third of them are complaints. It is claimed that these letters are answered or acknowledged and taken seriously, even though it is recognized that the complaints often cancel each other out, that letter writers tend to be unrepresentative, and that some may reflect the interests of pressure groups.

People in their letters are more inclined to object about sex and bad language than about violence. Probably a relatively recent trend in public reaction, this trend is also supported by independent research results.

Yet in recent years the Corporation appears to have been more concerned with violence than with sex and bad language.(It is worth mentioning in this connection that although violence is difficult enough to
codify and regulate, it is relatively simple when compared with sex,
however that may be defined.)

Increasingly over the past few years, many voices, including those
from sources normally regarded as liberal, have been raised in favor of
establishing some sort of public watchdog or broadcasting council. The
BBC, however, has shown little enthusiasm for any such development.
The Corporation maintains that the present system of handling complaints could not be improved upon by an outside body and that those
who argue for a Broadcasting Council do so without giving thought to
the question of such a Council's responsibilities. The Board of Governors is the responsible body, and its responsibilities include the handling
of complaints. What more is required?

Independent television

The General Advisory Council is often referred to as a "broadly representative body." Its responsibilities are: "to keep under review the
programs of Independent Television and to make comments to the Authority thereon; to advise the Authority on the general pattern and content of programs; and to consider such other matters affecting the Independent Television service as may from time to time be referred to it by
the Authority."

The Council normally meets at quarterly intervals. It chooses subjects
which it wishes to discuss; specific matters are also suggested by the
Authority for its consideration. Sometimes there are special viewing
sessions, and special papers are prepared for it by the Authority's staff.
These papers normally consist of an exposition of the problems involved
in particular aspects of Independent Television programs and an account of Authority thinking on specific issues.

The minutes of the General Advisory Council are circulated to the
Authority, which considers them and takes note, in particular, of any
formal resolutions passed by the Council. The Authority's reactions to
points raised by the Council and action taken as a result are reported
back to the Council. Senior members of the Authority's staff, including
the director general, attend its meetings as observers to give information, to answer questions, and to hear at first hand the full discussion by
the Council of the matters before it. This, so it is claimed, provides for a
direct exchange of views between the Council and the staff responsible
for advising the Authority and for executing its policy.

During 1969-70, the General Advisory Council met on four occasions; according to the official report, the subject which most occupied
its attention was the depiction of scenes of violence on television. Its

consideration of this subject started in May of 1969 when the Authority asked the Council for its views on a controversial eight-part serial, *Big Breadwinner Hog*, which was then running and whose nature served to bring important aspects of the problem of violence sharply into focus.

The Council returned to the question of violence more generally at later meetings. At a meeting in January 1970 it discussed that section of the report of the United States National Commission on the Causes and Prevention of Violence which referred to violence in television entertainment programs, as well as other research work in this field.

It is reported that the Council, in a wide-ranging discussion, considered, not only violence in fiction programs, but also its inclusion in news programs. It expressed itself as broadly satisfied with the ITA system and standards of control over scenes of violence, though there was criticism of individual programs. It rejected the idea that all scenes of violence should be excised from factual programs in which their inclusion was justified by their significance as news. It felt, however, that too often violent scenes were shown without sufficient factual background.

As a result of these discussions and the public interest which existed in this subject, it has been retained upon the Council's agenda. In subsequent discussions with the Home Office, the Authority intimated intention of forming a special working party to consider further this important subject; it would be composed equally of Authority, General Advisory Council, and program company representatives. The working party would concern itself generally with the problems attendant upon the portrayal of violence in television programs and would also concern itself with such matters as whether any changes are desirable in the Authority's Code on Violence, procedures for the scrutiny and approval of program content, the certification of acquired programs, and the use to be made of audience research.

The Authority saw the working party as providing a direct link between the Council, companies' program planners, and those in the Authority responsible for its supervisory responsibilities over programs and as constituting an important development in the system of program control.

According to the ITA, another important topic considered by the Council during the year was the inclusion of material in programs which some— and sometimes many—viewers found offensive. Included in this category are plays about sexual themes or those containing scenes of explicit sex, the use of swear words or coarse phrases either in a serious context or in comedy programs, and broad or suggestive jokes.

The Advisory Council has no executive power, but it has the power, should there be a serious difference of opinion with the Authority, to publish its own conclusions. It has never exercised this power. Needless to say, there has been no independent assessment of the operation of the Council, and it is easy to be cynical about this body and to talk of facades and window dressing in the same way some people do about the BBC General Advisory Council. There are those within the ITA, however, who think the Council might well serve a useful function—although this might be quite other than its name would imply. It has been said that it keeps the professional staff on their toes. If questions are asked and papers have to be prepared, there is an opportunity for a constant examination of policy. Again, whether this examination really does take place or what other functions are served by the Council are questions that can only be answered by more systematic and searching probes than have hitherto been carried out.

Viewers write letters about Independent Television programs, but there is no "central registry" here as with the BBC. Some of these letters (not very many except in exceptional circumstances) are addressed to the Authority and others to the various companies.

ITA also conducts its own research operations. A market research organization goes out at regular intervals and interviews a sample of the population. According to Lord Aylestone, though the main theme of the surveys changes from time to time, series of questions about taste are always included:

> Invariably, there is a proportion, usually rather less than one in four, which claims to have been offended. Then when we pursue the question a little, and ask for examples of offensive material, that proportion equally invariably drops sharply—usually to about five per cent. This may reflect the fact simply that people have bad memories: but it may equally reflect the fact that although some people find it not difficult to voice a general criticism that is abroad, they find it much more difficult to give evidence from their own experience. Obviously, if we see the proportion of offended people rising from one survey to another, we try to find out why. We discuss it internally, and with the program companies.

Other research which attempts to assess the enjoyment and appreciation of programs is conducted, and individual programs are also put under the microscope.

The ITA also uses other methods to bring it into more direct touch with some sections of the audience. One is the conferences arranged by Regional Officers, mainly with women's organizations up and down the country. It must also be recorded that the Authority maintains close contact with organizations concerned with research into the effects of mass media. It was the ITA's financial grant of £250,000 in 1963 to the Television Research Committee which led to the establishment of the Centre for Mass Communication Research at Leicester University. The studies which have been undertaken and published by the Centre have been carefully considered by the Authority—particularly with reference to its responsibilities in the area of the control of violence on the screen. In the support of independent research, the Authority has a better record than the BBC. But, with the Authority, as with the BBC, little is known about the influence of research results within the institution.

As mentioned earlier, there appears to be more audience unease about sex and bad language than about violence. It also appears that it is the offensive word, the incident, the scene that gives the offense, not the story, message, or moral. The overall implication of a program could be quite insidious or trivial, but this would not lead to as many complaints as would four-letter words, frontal nudity, a nipple, or instances of specific sexuality.

It is not possible in this paper to deal at length with research into attitudes towards the media, although we have in fact covered this elsewhere. But we do need to stress that concern about the media can only be examined adequately against the background of a wide range of other factors, including other concerns, expectations, ability to comprehend, and general value orientations. It is also worth noting that a study covering these and other relevant factors would call for a much more sophisticated approach than those normally associated with audience research departments.

THE PROGRAMS AND THE AUDIENCE

The BBC

The BBC has two channels. The normal limit of BBC program hours (fixed by the Minister of Posts and Telecommunications) is 53 1/2 hours a week for BBC-1 and an extra 450 hours a year for outside broadcasts, and 32 hours a week for BBC-2 and an extra 225 hours a year for outside broadcasts. Certain categories of programs, such as religious programs, school and educational broadcasts, programs for the deaf, and charitable appeals are not counted against the basic allowance of hours.

The BBC maintains that the program output of the two national networks (BBC-1 and BBC-2) is the product of joint planning so that alternatives can be offered to the viewer. (In 1970 half the sets installed in people's homes were equipped to receive BBC-2 as well as BBC-1.) The BBC say it is important, therefore, to have as many program junctions as possible, so as to avoid overlapping. The program planners are said to aim at positive alternatives: for instance, the choice might be between a serious documentary on BBC-1 and a light entertainment show on BBC-2: sport on BBC-1 and drama on BBC-2. Occasionally, BBC-2 will devote the bulk of the evening to one program—an entire opera, such as Mozart's *Idomeneo* or an evening of professional tennis. The claim is that on BBC television viewers have a real choice. In the course of a day, it is estimated, more than 26 million people in Britain watch one or more BBC television programs.[2]

In February 1970, the average amount of time each person in the U.K. devoted to viewing BBC television was about eight hours per week; in August of the same year, BBC viewing averaged six hours 40 minutes.

Table 1 gives a breakdown of the programs transmitted by the BBC in 1969-70. The content categories are those normally used by the BBC, but they are not particularly useful for our purposes.

Table 1: Content of television network programs,
53 weeks ended 3 April 1970

	Hours			
	BBC-1	BBC-2	Total	%
Talks, documentaries and other information programs	621	469	1,090	16.5
British and foreign feature films and series	619	438	1,057	16.0
Outside broadcasts	613	217	830	12.6
Presentation material	336	295	631	9.5
Drama	350	178	528	8.0
Light entertainment	318	155	473	7.1
Children's programs	357	88	445	6.7
News, weather, and other news programs	196	210	406	6.1
School broadcasts	376		376	5.7
Further education	247	76	323	4.9
Sports news and reports	122	87	209	3.2
Religious programs	143	10	153	2.3
Music	31	61	92	1.4
	4,329	2,284	6,613	100.0
Programs in Welsh language carried by network transmitters	108		108	
	4,437	2,284	6,721	
Presented by London	3,641	2,039	5,680	
regions	796	245	1,041	
	4,437	2,284	6,721	

Of the 4,437 hours on BBC-1, 1,047 hours were in color.
Of the 2,284 hours on BBC-2, 1,880 hours were in color.

In the "drama" category, some interesting regular audience figures (from the point of view of the subject matter of this paper) are: *Softly Softly* 12 million viewers, *Z Cars* 8.7 million, *Doomwatch* 7.8, *Wednesday Play* 4.9 million, *Troubleshooters* 7.7 million, *The Expert* 9.3 million. The last two are August viewing figures, the others February viewing figures. In the "films" category, *The Virginian* attracted 12 million viewers in February, and (according to figures provided by ITA) *A Man Called Ironside* (an imported series) was viewed in 6.75 million homes in March 1970. As far as BBC output is concerned, it is worth noting that the category "British and Foreign feature films and series" accounts for 16 percent of all network programs. This is the second largest category, but it is not one which receives a great deal of attention in BBC official statements and publications.

Independent television

The annual report of the Independent Television Authority for 1969-70 states that the Authority ensures that the output of each program company provides a proper balance of information, education, and entertainment. The ITA may also require specific periods of time to be allocated to special classes of programs such as education, religious programs, news, documentaries, and programs serving local tastes and interests.

The permitted hours of broadcasting are limited by the Minister of Posts and Telecommunications. In each of the 14 Independent Television service areas, about 70 to 75 hours of programs were transmitted in an average week. Within this total were considerable variations in the programs to be seen in different parts of the country, because each program company included a proportion of programs calculated to appeal to viewers in its own area. However, the overall weekly pattern of programs and the balance between different program categories remained substantially the same in all Independent Television areas. Table 2, taken from the 1969-70 Annual Report, shows the average weekly program output on Independent Television during 1969-70.

Table 2: ITV program output: weekly average, year ended 5 April 1970

	Duration Hrs.	Mins.	Proportion %
News and news magazines	7	19	10
Documentaries and news features	4	31	6
Religion	2	30	3
Adult education (including repeats)	2	08	3
School programs (including repeats)	5	07	7
Children's programs:			
(a) informative	1	22	2
(b) entertainment	5	08	7
Plays, drama series, and serials	15	51	22
Feature films	8	37	12
Entertainment and music	9	47	14
Sport	9	19	13
Other outside broadcasts	– –	29	1
	72	08	100

Note: The output of school and adult education programs during term-time is considerably higher than shown in the above table, which is the average over the whole year including the holidays.

There is little logic in the generally accepted classification of television programs. The above table shows that some program categories are defined in terms of program form, some in terms of content, some in terms of intended audience, and some even in terms of program purpose. The difficulty is compounded when one tries to make clear division between "serious" and "nonserious" programs—a distinction which appears to matter very much to both BBC and ITA. It is obviously important to them to be seen winning (or at least to be making progress in) the fight against trivialization.

According to the annual report, on the average evening during March 1970, over 60 percent of television homes were already watching one or another of the main services by 6-7 p.m. This meant about ten million out of a total 16 3/4 million television homes able to watch both ITV and BBC-1. Between 10 and 11 p.m., the number of homes viewing was still over nine million. The evening plateau of viewing is in the period between 7 and 10 p.m., when about 66 percent (or 11 million) television receivers are turned to one or another of the services. Nevertheless, as Table 3 shows, the evening audience is much more evenly distributed over the five hours from 6-11 p.m. than is sometimes supposed. The figures refer to a typical week in March 1970.

Table 3: The distribution of the evening TV audience*

| | Percentage of homes viewing | | |
	ITA	BBC	Total
6—8 p.m. (early evening)	35	28	63
8—10 p.m. (middle evening)	37	29	66
10—11 p.m. (late evening)	33	19	52

* Note: Figures from the BBC Audience Research Department would be kinder to its parent body. As mentioned earlier the two institutions use different research methods and basically provide answers to different questions

On average, in March 1970 in each of the three main evening time segments, over nine million homes had sets switched to Independent Television. In terms of the overall balance of programs the period may therefore be reasonably considered as a whole. From 6 p.m. until 11 p.m., 28 percent of the time was on average devoted to "serious" programs. During the period from 6 p.m. to the close of transmissions, the proportion was 30 percent.

Bearing in mind the apparent importance of this serious/entertainment distinction, it would be interesting to find out whether classification along these lines had any bearing on the way sex and violence were treated.

Each week during 1969-70, the 15 program companies together were providing for the Authority's transmissions a total of about 124 hours of programs produced in their own studios. This production accounted for about 52 to 55 hours out of the weekly total of about 70 to 75 hours transmitted in each service area. The remaining programs were British film material made for television or the cinema (much of which was produced by subsidiaries of the program companies or in association with them) and foreign recorded programs, which during the year accounted for 13.4 percent of the total transmission time over the whole Independent Television system. There is an upper limit of 14 percent for all foreign material, and no company may show more than five British feature films per fortnight. The companies' own production during 1969-70 is analyzed by program categories in Table 4.

Table 4: Program production, weekly average, year ended 5 April 1970

	Duration		Proportion
	Hrs.	Mins.	%
News and news magazines	38	20	31
Documentaries and news features	13	48	11
Religion	8	52	7
Adult education	3	13	3
School programs	3	22	3
Children's programs:			
(a) informative	1	42	1
(b) entertainment	9	47	8
Plays, drama series and serials	10	-	8
Entertainment and music	13	59	11
Sport	19	24	16
Other outside broadcasts	1	21	1
	123	48	100

During 1969-70, the Independent Television program companies produced a total of 6,500 hours of programs from their own studios; a number of others were produced by subsidiaries, or in association with them.

At the end of March 1970, over 98 percent of the total population (55 million people) lived within reach of the transmissions from the Authority's stations. Over 48 1/2 million people in over 16 1/2 million homes, representing over 90 percent of all homes in areas covered by Independent Television, had television sets able to receive Independent Television.

During the year ended 15 March 1970, 55 percent of the total time spent watching television in homes able to view both BBC and Independent Television was spent watching Independent Television. The average evening audience from 7:30-10:30 p.m. for ITV programs was 6.8 million homes in the four weeks ended 15 March 1970; audiences for the most popular programs exceeded 18 million people.

Many factors affect the size of the audience for different television programs. In addition to the general popularity or the perceived quality of a program, the number of people viewing it is determined by such variables as the day and time of transmission, the programs preceding and following it, the attractiveness of programs available on the other channels, and the overall "channel-loyalty" of the audience.

THE DESIGN OF THE CONTENT STUDY
Selection of programs

The raw material for the content study was the broadcast material of BBC-1 and ATV (the Midlands independent television company) between 4 p.m. and 11 p.m. during the week of 24-30 April 1971. The limited time and resources available for the study prevented the analysis of a wider selection of television material. A study of American television has suggested that a "solid week" sample will be as representative of a year's programming as a larger, randomly selected sample.[3] It was not possible to carry out an equivalent study on British television. The BBC material analyzed is virtually identical to that broadcast nationally. ATV like all the independent companies, broadcasts a mixture of network and nonnetwork material; however, the programming "mix" is very similar in all regions.

This procedure yielded 79 fiction or drama programs. Fifty-six news, documentary, and current affairs programs were also coded. The remaining 41 sport, variety, and miscellaneous programs were not coded. Programs which overlapped the time limits were included in the analysis.

Units of analysis

The major content dimensions studied were violence and sex; the units of analysis were the program, the violent incident, and the sexual or romantic relationship. Following Gerbner,[4] *violence* was defined as

> Physical or psychological injury, hurt or death addressed to human beings (or in the case of cartoons, animals with human characteristics). Violence is explicit and overt. It can be verbal or physical. If verbal it must express intent to use physical force and must be plausible and credible in the context of the program. Idle distant or vague threats, insults, quarrels or abuse are not violent.

A *violent incident* was defined as

> a scene of whatever duration in which violence is committed and which involves the same agent or group of agents and the same receiver or group of receivers. Thus a fight and a battle scene would both be one violent incident. A fight between two people in the course of which a third person joins in would be two violent incidents.

Programs were defined as a discrete time slot rather than, as in the Gerbner studies, as a single dramatic story. There were no cases of multistory programs; in the case of serials broadcast more than once a week, it was not felt possible to determine where one story ended and another began.

A program was coded in terms of the amount and type of violence it contained, the relevance of violence to the plot and to the outcome of the program, the kind of characters involved and certain themes of the program, and information about program type and format, time of transmission, and so on. The programs were also coded in terms of whether or not certain sexual relationships and incidents occurred.

Incidents were coded in terms of the type and seriousness of violence, the type of people involved, the relationships between the people involved, and the outcome of the incident.

A sexual or romantic relationship was coded in terms of its type, its outcome, and the degree of sexual explicitness with which it was presented.

The coding instruments for violence were based on those used by Gerbner, and many of the variables were reproduced exactly. As well as providing comparable data, this meant that it was possible to concentrate on variables which had achieved high reliability and provided useful and discriminating data. However, new variables were also included. There was no comparable study on which the coding instrument for sex could be based.

Recording the data

The material was coded by a team of eight observers who had been trained to use the coding schedule and who had been pretested for idiosyncracies or misinterpretations of the categories.

Each program was coded by a single observer, except for 26 programs taken at random, which were coded independently by two observers to provide reliability tests.

Information such as time and date of broadcast and origin of the programs was coded separately by the researchers.

Reliability

The reliability coefficient used was Scott's coefficient of agreement. [5] Only variables which reached a reliability of at least 0.67 were included in the analysis.

Problems of analysis

Where there are several different, but related, levels of analysis (programs, program hours, incidents, participants in incidents), these differences and relationships should be kept in mind when interpreting the figures. Comparisons for programs may give different results from those for program hours, especially for very short programs like cartoons or very long ones like films. Some of the information coded for incidents comes from the program in which they occur and is therefore not independent between incidents. Participants in one incident (instigator, receiver/reciprocator) may also be participants in another incident in the same or a different role. Thus observations of roles in violent incidents are not independent for individuals but only for incidents.

In all cases, raw numbers are given in the tables; normally percentages are also given. In some cases percentages have been calculated on the basis of very small numbers; obviously these should be interpreted with care.

Programming in the sample week

During the week studied, 176 programs were broadcast on the two channels within the 4 p.m. and 11 p.m. time limits. (This time period for two channels over seven days amounts to 98 hours, but there were times when one or both channels were broadcasting. Programs which overlapped the time limits were also coded.) Of this total, 79 were fictional or dramatic programs occupying 54.9 program hours. 39 of these (23.1 hours) were on BBC, and 40 (31.8 hours) were on ATV. There were 56 news, current affairs, and documentary programs accounting for 23.9 hours. Of these, 33 (14.4 hours) were on BBC and 23 (9.5 hours) on ATV. There were also 41 sport, variety, and miscellaneous programs which were not coded.

The results from the analysis of news, current affairs, and documentaries are reported later; the following description of programming and of violence refers to fiction and drama programs only.

Tabe 5 describes the programming "mix" in terms of origin, style, and format of programs. Sixty-seven percent of the programs were home-produced, the remainder being imported, mostly from the United States (30.3 percent). Films accounted for 12.6 per cent of programs and 31.0 per cent program hours; cartoons for 7.5 percent of programs and 1.5 percent of hours; and plays for 7.5 per cent of programs and 11.5 percent of hours.[6] Programs coded as "crime, westerns or other action-adventure" accounted for 26.8 percent of the programs and 35.1 percent of the program hours; comedies for 35.4 percent of programs and 27.0 percent of hours; and noncartoon comedy for 27.8 percent of programs and 25.5 percent of hours. (All the cartoons were also coded as comedies.)

All programs were coded for categories of format: film, play, domestic serial, and series; for categories of style: crime, western, action-adventure, and cartoon; and for tone: comic and serious. These categories have been rearranged in the tables and are probably better regarded as various dimensions of program type with some overlap between categories. Plays and domestic serials do not in practice overlap any of the other categories. All the cartoons were also coded as comedies.

As Table 5 shows, programming on the two channels was very similar in terms of these program categories. The most important difference is that the BBC broadcast 11 domestic serial episodes (with more than one episode a week) compared with the BBC's two.

Table 5: Fictional programming on BBC—1 and ATV.

		BBC	ATV	Both
Origin				
	U.K.	25	28	53
		(64.1%)	(70.0%)	(67%)
	U.S.	12	12	24
		(30.7%)	(30.0%)	(30.3%)
	Other	2	0	2
		(5.1%)		(3.7%)
	Total	39	40	79
Format				
	Film	4	6	10
		(10.2%)	(15.0%)	(12.6%)
	Cartoon	6	0	6
		(15.3%)		(7.5%)
	Play	4	2	6
		(10.2%)	(5.0%)	(7.5%)
	Domestic	2	11	13
	serial	(5.1%)	(27.3%)	(16.4%)
	Other	23	21	44
		(59.0%)	(52.3%)	(53.7%)
	Total	39	40	79
Style				
	Crime, western,	11	10	21
	action-adventure	(28.2%)	(23.0%)	(26.6%)
	Comedy	18	10	28
		(46.1%)	(25.0%)	(35.4%)
	Comedy (not including	12	10	22
	cartoons)	(30.7%)	(25.0%)	(27.8%)
	Total programs	39	40	79

Programming is much less uniform when the origin of programs is considered. Imported material is a great deal more likely to consist of crime, western, or action-adventure programs than is British-produced material. Of the American programs, 37.5 per cent are of this type, as are all the "other" imported programs (only two); only 18.8 per cent of British material is of this type. American programs are also much more likely to be films: 80 percent of the films shown were American and five of the six cartoon programs came from the U.S. Of the British programs, only 3.7 percent were films and 1.8 per cent cartoons. These differences in the distribution of program types have consequences for the distribution of violence.

THE DEGREE AND DISTRIBUTION OF VIOLENCE IN TELEVISION DRAMA

The data contain several measures of the degree of violence in programs. The simplest of these are the percentage of programs and the percentage of program hours containing violence. These can be interpreted as measuring the extent or prevalence of violent material. The frequency or rate of violence is measured by the average number of violent incidents per program or per program hour. Gerbner suggests a program score which combines these measures.[7] This score is obtained by:

$$\text{Program score} = \begin{array}{l}\text{Percent programs} \\ \text{containing violence}\end{array} + 2 \times \begin{array}{l}\text{(Rate of incidents per} \\ \text{program} + \text{Rate of} \\ \text{incidents per hour)}\end{array}$$

There are also measures based on the percentage of programs depicting fatalities and the percentage of programs with a major character involved in and committing violence.

In Table 6 these programs are tabulated by channel, time slot, origin of program, and various aspects of format and program type. In this way we can compare these categories in terms of the violent material they contain.

Of the 79 programs coded, 44 (or 55.7 percent) contained violence. These occupied 33.8 hours (or 61.6 percent) of the total program hours. Within this time there were 222 violent incidents, 2.81 per program or 4.04 per hour. Fatal violence occurred in 19 programs, 24 percent of the total. In 37 programs (46.8 percent), a major character was involved in violence either as a perpetrator or as a victim, and in 33 programs (41.8 percent), a major character committed violence. Of the violent incidents, 196 were deliberate rather than accidental and 196 were shown on the screen.

Program scores are summarized in Table 19. The program score for all programs was 69.40.

Violence is not evenly distributed across channels, time slots, and types of programming. Table 6 shows that in the week studied 27 BBC programs contained violence (69.2 per cent of all programs on BBC). This compares with 17 ATV programs, or 42.5 percent of the ATV output. BBC contained 123 violent incidents and ATV 99; the channels had program scores of 86.14 and 53.68 respectively.

Country of origin also made a difference in the amount of violence. Seventy-five percent of American-made programs contained violence, and these had a program score of 96.88. In contrast, 45.3 percent of British programs contained violence, and their program score was 54.02. Both of the "other" imported programs were violent; these had a program score of 134.1.

Violence decreased late at night. Programs starting before 6 p.m. and between 6 and 9 p.m. had very similar amounts of violence, but violence declined in programs commencing at or after 9 p.m.

Table 6: Degree and distribution of violence in TV fiction

	No. of programs	% containing violence	Violent incidents Rate per program	Rate per hour	Program score
All programs	79	55.7%	2.87	4.04	69.40
BBC	39	69.2	3.15	5.32	86.14
ATV	40	42.5	2.48	3.11	53.68
Origin:					
U.K.	53	45.3	1.66	2.70	54.02
U.S.	24	75.0	5.17	5.77	96.88
Other	2	100.0	5.00	12.05	134.10
Time slot:					
Before 6 p.m.	34	58.8	2.50	5.86	75.52
6–9 p.m.	34	58.8	3.09	3.60	72.18
After 9 p.m.	11	36.4	2.91	2.84	47.90
Type *					
Film	10	80.0	7.00	4.12	102.24
Cartoon	6	100.0	4.67	33.73	176.80
Play	6	50.0	1.00	0.95	53.90
Domestic serial	13	23.1	0.23	0.51	24.58
C C,W, A/A	21	100.0	7.29	7.95	130.48
Comedy	28	42.9	1.79	3.37	53.22
Comedy (not cartoons)	22	27.2	1.00	1.57	32.34
Crime, western, action=adventure					
BBC	11	100.0	6.09	7.96	128.10
ATV	10	100.0	8.60	7.94	133.08
U.K.	10	100.0	5.60	6.86	124.90
U.S.	9	100.0	9.67	8.48	136.30
Other	2	100.0	5.00	12.05	134.10
Films only					
BBC	4	75.0	6.50	3.90	95.80
ATV	6	83.3	7.33	4.26	106.48
Comedy only					
BBC	18	55.6	2.56	6.42	73.56
ATV	10	20.0	0.40	0.52	21.84
BBC (not cartoons)	12	33.3	1.50	2.84	41.98

* These categories are not exclusive; C,W, A/A and comedy overlap certain of the other categories.

Despite these findings, the type of program was much more important than the channel or country of origin in accounting for the amount of violence the programs contained; differences between channels and origins are largely explained by this factor.

GREAT BRITAIN
467

The most violent type of program is the cartoon. All cartoons contained violence, and the rate of incidents per hours was a particularly high 33.73. The program score for cartoons was the highest for any type of program: 176.8. The only measure of violence on which cartoons were low was the number of fatalities; none of the cartoon incidents was fatal.

Films were also high on violence; 80 percent of them contained violent material—an average of 7 incidents per program and 4.12 per hour, resulting in a program score of 102.24. This contrasts with plays, 50 percent of which contained violence but which had rates per program and per hour of only 1 and 0.95. The program score for plays was 53.9. Serial episodes contained even less violence and had a program score of 24.58.

Table 6 shows the degree of violence in two more categories of programs. The merged category of crime, western and other action adventure programs is second only to cartoons as a violent type of program. All the programs in this category contained violence—a total of 153 incidents, 7.29 per program or 7.95 per hour. This gives a program score of 130.48. In contrast, comedies have a much lower score, 53.22; when cartoons are removed from the comedy category this drops to 32.34.

When we cross-tabulate these categories of program type by channel and country of origin, it is apparent that the violent content of types of programs is uniform across channel and origin. Programs characterized as crime, western, or action-adventure contain similar amounts of violence whether they are on BBC or ATV, whether they are from Britain, America, or elsewhere. Films also have similar amounts of violence on both channels. Comedy is one area in which BBC remains more violent. However, when cartoon programs (which are all comedies, all violent, and all on BBC) are removed from the comedy category, this difference is considerably reduced.

In general, then, differences in the amounts of violence across channels and origins of programs can be explained by differences in the programming mix rather than differences in the levels of violence in the same kinds of program. The BBC's higher violence socre is largely attributable to the fact that six cartoon programs were shown on BBC in the sample week while there were none on ATV, and that ATV had a much higher proportion of serial episodes, which are normally nonviolent.

American imports were far more likely to consist of the type of programs where violence is most often found. The action-adventure category accounted for 37.5 percent of U.S. programs and for only 18.8 percent of British material. Films and cartoons were also much more heavily represented in American than in British programs.

An alternative method of looking at differences in the violence content of various program categories is to see how the total violence content is distributed over the categories. We can calculate that the action-adventure category contains nearly half the total of violent programs and nearly seven in ten of the violent incidents, even though it only accounts for 26.6 percent of the total number of programs. Action-adventure programs and cartoons between them account for over 80 percent of the total number of violent incidents.

THE NATURE OF VIOLENCE IN TELEVISION DRAMA

We have discussed the amount and distribution of violence in television drama. By examining the nature of this violence, how it is presented, where it takes place, its outcome, and its participants, we may be able to describe the place of violence in television drama and some of the symbolic functions it may perform—in defining social power, distributing rewards and punishments, or suggesting the appropriate, expected, or desirable consequences of certain sorts of behavior.

Type, presentation, effects

Most of the violence on television in the week studied was deliberate physical violence; as Table 7 shows, this accounted for 165 (or 74.3 percent) of the incidents studied or 74.3 percent of the whole. Serious threats comprised another 31 incidents and accidental violence a further 26. Serious programs contained 172 of these incidents and comedies 50. Not surprisingly types of violence are unevenly distributed among serious and comic programs. Thirty-two percent of the violent incidents in comedies were accidents compared with less than six percent of those in serious programs. Accidents are of course not "accidental" in TV drama and are a staple component of comedy.

Most of the violent incidents were shown on the screen (88.3 percent) rather than implied or described (11.7 percent). Again there are differences between serious and comic programs. Virtually all the violent incidents in comic programs were shown on the screen (98.0 percent), while 14.5 percent of those in serious programs were implied or described. Over all the programs, 196 incidents (or 88.3 percent) were shown on the screen and 26 (11.7 percent) were implied or described.

Most violence caused some pain or injury. Nearly as many incidents resulted in death for one or more of the participants (47) as resulted in no physical harm (55). A further 103 incidents were between these extremes and resulted in some pain or injury.[8]

All the deaths occurred in serious rather than comic programs. The incidents in serious programs were slightly more likely to have no effects; as a consequence, incidents in comic programs were much more likely to involve some injury short of death. (Unfortunately the distinction between major and minor injuries proved unreliable.) The higher proportion of incidents not involving injury in serious programs is a result of the fact that serious threats are much more likely to occur in these programs.

Table 7: Type, presentation, and effects of violence

	Serious programs	Comic programs	All programs
Type of violence			
Deliberate violence	131	34	165
	(76.2%)	(68.0%)	(74.3%)
Threat	31	0	31
	(18.0%)		(14.0%)
Accidental violence	10	16	26
	(5.8%)	(32.0%)	(11.7%)
Presentation			
Shown on screen	147	49	196
	(85.5%)	(98.0%)	(88.3%)
Implied or described	25	1	26
	(14.5%)	(2.0%)	(11.7%)
Effects			
None	45	10	55
	(26.2%)	(20.0%)	(24.8%)
Some injury	67	36	103
	(39.%)	(72.0%)	(46.4%)
Death	47	0	47
	(27.3%)		(21.2%)
Unclear	13	4	17
	(7,6%)	(8.0%)	(7.7%)
All incidents	172	50	222
	(100%)	(100%)	(100%)

These differences between serious and comic programs reflect the differing functions of violence in serious programs and comedies. Another indicator of this is that in 25 percent of comedy programs containing violence the violence is incidental to the plot, while in only 6.2 percent of serious programs containing violence is the violence incidental to the plot.

Location, date, setting

Gerbner suggests that the symbolic functions of violence are performed best in unreal or exotic environments, were the constraints of familiarity and realism are absent. It is certainly true on British as well as American television that a disproportionate amount of violence takes place in faraway times, places, and settings. This raises the question: just what are these symbolic functions, and how does their performance depend on the relevance of their context to real life problems and situations?

In Table 8 we see that, while 53.2 percent of the programs take place in Britain, only 36.4 percent of violent programs and 21.2 percent of violent incidents do so. This pattern is reversed for programs taking place in North America or "other" locations. Of all programs, 29.1 percent take place in North America, while 55.9 percent of violent incidents are located there. Of course, American-made programs which are likely to be located in America are more likely to contain violence than British-made programs.

Table 8: Location, date, and setting of violence

	All programs	Violent programs	Violent incidents
Location			
Britain	42 (53.2%)	16 (36.4%)	47 (21.2%)
North America	23 (29.2%)	17 (38.6%)	124 (55.9%)
Other	14 (17.7%)	11 (25.0%)	51 (23.0%)
Date			
Pre-1900	6 (7.6%)	5 (11.4%)	58 (26.1%)
1900–1945	11 (13.9%)	8 (18.2%)	31 (14.0%)
1945–present	58 (73.4%)	27 (61.4%)	113 (50.9%)
Future	4 (5.1%)	4 (9.1%)	20 (9.0%)
Setting			
Urban/suburban	42 (53.2%)	19 (43.2%)	91 (41.0%)
Countryside	12 (15.2%)	8 (18.2%)	60 (27.0%)
Uninhabited	5 (6.3%)	4 (9.1%)	16 (7.2%)
Mixed, other	20 (25.3%)	13 (29.5%)	55 (24.8%)
Programs set in modern Britain	33 (41.8%)	10 (22.7%)	30 (13.5%)
Total	79 (100%)	44 (100%)	222 (100%)

Programs set in the present or recent past are less likely to be violent than those set in the past or the future. Only 27 of the 58 programs set between 1945 and the present were violent, while 13 of the 17 set in the past, and all the four programs set in the future, were violent. Put another way: 73.4 percent of the programs were set between 1945 and the present, while 50.9 percent of the violent incidents were set at this time. Inevitably this pattern is reversed for programs set before 1945 and in the future.

This tendency for violence to occur in unfamiliar environments is repeated, though less dramatically, when we consider the physical settings of programs and violent incidents. 53.2 percent of programs are located in urban or suburban settings, while 41.0 percent of the violent incidents occur in these settings. This is reversed for the countryside, where 15.2 percent of the programs are set but where 27.0 percent of the incidents occur. Uninhabitated settings also have a disproportionate amount of violence, though both the differences and the number of programs are small.

This process is seen again when we look at programs set in modern Britain. Of the total of 79 programs broadcast, 41.8 percent are set in modern Britain. Of the 44 violent programs, 22.7 percent are set in modern Britain, but of the 222 violent incidents, 13.5 percent, or 30 incidents (less than one incident per program) are set in modern Britain (less than one incident per program are set in modern Britain (Britain since 1945). For programs set elsewhere, the rate of incidents is 4.2 per program. Violence is therefore disproportionately likely to occur in an environment with which most of its viewers have no experience and with which they are only to be familiar only through television. The familiar world of personal experience is much less likely to contain violence.

Weapons and context

In a majority of violent incidents, some sort of weapon was used. Threats comprised 15.8 percent of the nonaccidental violence, the body (fist, foot, etc.,) was used in 28.6 percent, and in 65.8 percent of nonaccidental violence (or 129 incidents) a variety of weapons was used. Rifles or pistols appeared in 21.9 percent of incidents, military weapons (bombs, tanks) in 3.6 percent, stabbing instruments in 10.7 percent, and clubs or truncheons in 5.1 percent[9]. The most deadly weapons were rifles and pistols; 53.5 percent of incidents in which they were used resulted in death, and a further 30.2 percent in some injury. Stabbing instruments were close behind, with 52.4 percent deaths and 23.8 percent injuries.

Violence took place in a variety of contexts, as Table 9 shows. Criminal acts of violence accounted for 50 incidents (or 25.5 percent of nonaccidental violence and law enforcement for a further 19 incidents (9.7 percent). There were 16 incidents (8.2 percent) in the context of war and 11 incidents (5.6 percent in the context of violence within the family. "Other personal violence" such as revenge was the largest category—61 incidents or 31.6 percent of the total. Incidents in the context of war

Table 9: Weapons used and context of violence by effects

		Effects			
Weapons	None	Major and minor injury	Death	Unclear	Total
Threat only	28 (90.3%)*	0	0	3 (9.7%)	31 (100%)
Body	5 (8.9%)	44 (78.6%)	2 (3.6%)	5 (89.%)	56 (100%)
Rifle, pistol	5 (11.6%)	13 (30.3%)	23 (53.5%)	2 (4.7%)	43 (100%)
Military weapon	2 (28.6%)	2 (28.6%)	0	3 (42.9%)	7 (100%)
Stabbing instrument	5 (23.8%)	5 (23.8%)	11 (52.4%)	0	21 (100%)
Club, truncheon	1 (10.0%)	8 (80.0%)	1 (10.0%)	0	10 (100%)
Context					
War	4 (25.0%)	2 (12.5%)	7 (43.8%)	3 (18.8%)	16 (100%)
Civil strife, riot	1 (50.0%)	1 (50.0%)	0	0	2 (100%)
Criminal	18 (36.0%)	19 (38.0%)	13 (26.0%)	0	50 (100%)
Law enforcement	4 (21.1%)	10 (52.6%)	3 (15.8%)	2 (10.5%)	19 (100%)
Family	1 (9.1%)	6 (54.5%)	3 (27.3%)	1 (9.1%)	11 (100%)
Other personal	14 (22.6%)	28 (45.2%)	11 (17.7%)	9 (14.5%)	62 (100%)
Other	9 (25.0%)	21 (58.3%)	5 (13.9%)	1 (2.8%)	36 (100%)

* Percentages are calculated horizontally.

were the most deadly, 43.8 percent resulting in death, followed by the
family (27.3 percent deaths), and criminal violence (26.0 percent). Other
personal violence (17.7 percent of incidents fatal) and law enforcement
(15.8 percent) were less deadly.

Participants in violence: roles and outcomes

The 196 nonaccidental incidents yielded 392 participants, two for each
incident. A participant may be an individual, a group of individuals, or a
group. A particular individual or group may appear in more than one incident and may have different roles (instigator/receiver, winner/loser) in
different incidents. This has the effect of inflating the figures for people
involved in violence and giving most weight to those involved in most
violence. It also has the effect of damping down differences between
(for instance) particular individuals who are instigators only and those

who are receivers only, as other individuals who figure variously as in-stigators and receivers appear in both sets of figures.

This procedure is justified both by the absence of data on individuals as such and by the fact that the violent incident is the unit of analysis. The figures on (for instance) outcomes or moral status are not independent for individuals, and there is no comparable data for individuals not involved in violent incidents. The figures refer to participants in violent incidents treated as independent occurrences.

Table 10: Participants in violence

	Instigator	Reciprocator	Receiver	Mixed	All
Relation to plot					
Incidental	17	3	22	14	56
	(9.8%)	(5.7%)	(18.3%)	(30.4%)	(14.3%)
Minor essential	70	15	37	14	136
	(40.5%)	(28.3%)	(30.8%)	(30.4%)	(34.7%)
Major essential	86	35	61	18	200
	(49.7%)	(66.0%)	(50.8%)	(39.1%)	(51.0%)
Sex					
Male	150	47	92	36	325
	(86.7%)	(88.7%)	(76.7%)	(78.3%)	(82.9%)
Female	11	1	18	4	34
	(6.4%)	(1.9%)	(15.0%)	(8.7%)	(8.7%)
Unclear	12	5	10	6	33
	(6.9%)	(9.4%)	(8.3%)	(13.0%)	(8.4%)
Relation to law					
Ordinary citizen	90	28	88	26	230
	(52.0%)	(52.8%)	(73.3%)	(56.5%)	(58.7%)
Law enforcement officer	8	5	4	6	23
	(4.6%)	(9.4%)	(3.3%)	(13.0%)	(5.9%)
Semilaw enforcement	15	10	10	4	38
	(8.7%)	(18.9%)	(8.3%)	(8.7%)	(9.7%)
Secret service	0	0	1	0	1
			(0.8%)		(0.3%)
Criminal, outlaw	60	10	17	10	96
	(34.7%)	(18.9%)	(14.2%)	(21.7%)	(24.5%)
Moral status					
Good	58	31	50	19	158
	(33.5%)	(58.4%)	(41.7%)	(41.3%)	(40.3%)
Bad	79	13	31	11	134
	(45.7%)	(24.5%)	(25.8%)	(23.9%)	(34.2%)
Neutral, mixed, unclear	36	9	39	16	100
	(20.8%)	(17.0%)	(32.5%)	(34.8%)	(25.5%)
Total	173	53	120	46	392
	(100%)	(100%)	(100%)	(100%)	(100%)

Of the 196 incidents, 173 had a clear instigator; in 53 of these the vio-lence was reciprocated, and in 120 it was not.

Most of the participants in violence had roles essential to the plot (defined as a role which would need to be included in a one page summary of the plot). Fifty-one percent played major roles essential to the plot, 34.7 percent played minor roles essential to the plot, and only 14.3 percent played roles incidental to the plot. In the absence of data on the relevance to the plot of violent incidents, this gives us an indication of the centrality and importance of violence to the programs in which it occurs.

In incidents where it is unclear who is the instigator, the participants are more likely to be incidental to the plot; reciprocators are the least likely to be incidental characters and are most likely to be major characters. Two-thirds reciprocators are major characters essential to the plot while half of the instigators and receivers are essential. Reciprocation is a major form of participation in violence for heroes and is typically associated with this kind of character.

Table 11: Outcomes and moral status of "good" characters

	Instigator	Reciprocator	Receiver	Mixed	All
Immediate outcome					
Winner	43 (74.1%)	19 (61.3%)	11 (22.0%)	10 (52.6%)	83 (52.5%)
Loser	5 (8.6%)	4 (12.9%)	30 (60.0%)	5 (26.3%)	44 (27.8%)
Mixed	10 (17.2%)	8 (25.8%)	9 (18.0%)	4 (21.1%)	31 (19.6%)
Total	58 (100%)	31 (100%)	50 (100%)	19 (100%)	158 (100%)
Final outcome					
Clear winner	38 (65.5%)	26 (83.9%)	29 (58.0%)	15 (78.9%)	108 (68.4%)
Winner—but	2 (3.4%)	0	1 (2.0%)	0	3 (1.9%)
Clear loser	1 (1.7%)	2 (6.5%)	10 (20.0%)	0	13 (8.2%)
Loser—but	6 (10.3%)	1 (3.2%)	3 (6.0%)	0	10 (6.3%)
Mixed	11 (19.0%)	2 (6.5%)	7 (14.0%)	4 (21.1%)	24 (15.2%)
Total	58 (100%)	31 (100%)	50 (100%)	19 (100%)	158 (100%)

Violence is overwhelmingly a male activity. 82.9 percent of participants were male, and a further 8.4 percent were not clearly identified. Only 8.7 percent of participants in violence were female. The largest group of female participants were passive receivers; 18 of the 34 women involved in violence were in this group.

Most participants in violence (58.7 percent) were ordinary citizens who had no particular relationship to the law. This was particularly likely for passive receivers of whom 73.3 percent were ordinary citizens. Law enforcement officers were thinly represented (5.9 percent of the participants); "semilaw enforcement" (private detectives, etc.) were rather more prominent with 9.7 percent of participants. "Semilaw enforcement" participants were over represented 18.9 percent among the reciprocators. Criminals accounted for 24.5 percent of all participants and were most likely to appear as instigators of violence. 34.7 percent of instigators were criminals, compared with 16.9 percent of noninstigators.

Table 10 examines the moral status of participants in violence. (They were classified as "good," "bad," or "neutral, mixed, unclear.") There appears to be no moral opprobrium associated with the use of or involvement in violence. Instigators are less likely to be "good" (33.5 percent) than they are to be "bad" (45.7 percent), but this still means that one in three acts of violence is instigated by a clearly "good" character and that less than half are instigated by a clearly "bad" one. Reciprocators are more likely to be "good" (58.4 percent) than they are to be "bad" (24.5 percent). If we combine these categories and the mixed instigator/reciprocator category to look at all those participants who

Table 12: Outcomes and moral status of "bad" characters

	Instigator	Reciprocator	Receiver	Mixed	All
Immediate outcome					
Winner	39 (49.4%)	2 (15.4%)	0	5 (45.5%)	46 (34.3%)
Loser	32 (40.5%)	11 (84.6%)	26 (83.9%)	5 (45.5%)	74 (55.2%)
Mixed	8 (10.1%)	0	5 (16.1%)	1 (9.1%)	14 (10.4%)
Total	79 (100%)	13 (100%)	31 (100%)	11 (100%)	134 (100%)
Final outcome					
Clear winner	1 (1.3%)	1 (7.7%)	1 (3.2%)	0	3 (2.2%)
Winner—but	1 (1.3%)	0	0	0	1 (0.75%)
Clear loser	73 (92.4%)	11 (84.6%)	28 (90.3%)	10 (90.9%)	122 (91.0%)
Loser—but	0	0	0	0	0
Mixed	4 (5.1%)	1 (7.7%)	2 (6.5%)	1 (9.1%)	8 (6.0%)
Total	79 (100%)	13 (100%)	31 (100%)	11 (100%)	134 (100%)

commit violence, "good" participants (108 or 39.7 percent) slightly out-number "bad" (103 or 37.7 percent). Clearly "good" participants are as well represented as "bad" among those who commit violence, but the "bad" participants' involvement comes disproportionately from insti-gating the violence, while the "good" participants' involvement comes disproportionately from reciprocating it. Passive receivers of violence are more likely to be "good" (41.7 percent), than "bad" (25.8 percent).

Another way of examining the moral context of violence is to look at the attitudes and responses of witnesses to violence (Table 13). In the relatively few situations where there was a clear witness response, more than twice as many cases involved showing approval as involved show-ing disapproval and that more witnesses joined in the violence than at-tempted to restrain or seek alternatives to it. The use of violence does not seem to violate the sensitivities of those among whom it takes place.

Another way of looking at the norms associated with the use of vio-lence on television drama is to consider its outcomes: who wins the vio-lent incident and what is the final outcome of the program for the partici-pants in the incident.

In the short term, violence pays off. 57.2 percent of instigators of vio-lent incidents emerged victorious from the incident, and only 27.7 per-cent clearly lost the incident. When attacked on television, it pays to defend yourself; 45.3 percent of reciprocators won the violent incident and 37.7 percent lost, while only 13.3 percent of nonviolent receivers won the incident and 67.5 percent lost.

When we consider the final outcomes of the programs, the odds are much less in favour of the instigators of violence. Nearly twice as many instigators were clear losers at the end of the program (47.4 percent as were clear winners (24.9 percent) The odds in favor of reciprocators, however, improve considerably, 54.7 percent emerge as clear winners and 30.2 percent as clear losers. Among nonviolent receivers, only 30 percent emerge as clear winners, while 45 percent are clear losers.

These relationships are clarified if we take into account the moral sta-tus of the participants (Tables 11 and 12). "Good" participants of all kinds are more likely to be winners than their "bad" equivalents. Over all incidents, 52.5 percent of "good" participants win and 27.8 percent lose, while 34.2 percent of "bad" participants win and 55.2 percent lose. "Good" instigators are most likely to win (74.1 percent), followed by reciprocators (61.3 percent); "good" receivers are very much less likely to win (22 percent). The same pattern holds for "bad" characters, but the chances of winning are lower in each case. This difference is particu-larly dramatic in the case of "bad" reciprocators, only 15.4 percent of whom are likely to win.

The chances of winning a particular incident are governed by a combi-nation of moral status and type of participation. "Good" characters win more often than "bad," but "bad" instigators win more often than

Table 13: Witness to violence

No witnesses, or no or mixed reactions	139 (70.9%)
Express disapproval	8 (4.1%)
Express approval	19 (9.7%)
Intervene, refrain, see alternatives to violence	13 (6.6%)
Join in violence	17 (8.7%)
Total	196 (100%)

"good" receivers. However, the chances of a successful final outcome depend very heavily on moral status. 68.4 percent of "good" participants are clear winners at the end of the program and only 8.2 percent clear losers. Of "bad" participants, 2.2 percent are clear winners and 91 percent clear losers. Type of participation makes very little difference to the final outcomes for "bad" participants; however, reciprocators are slightly more likely to be winners.

Type of participation has a greater effect on the outcomes for "good" participants. "Good" reciprocators are the most likely to emerge as clear winners (83.9 percent), followed by instigators (65.5 percent) and receivers (58.0 percent). Thus, being actively involved in violence, and in particular meeting violence with violence, is associated with both immediate and final victory for "good" participants.

Table 14: Violence and program outcomes

	No violence	Violence but outcome does not depend on it	Outcome depends on violence	All
Happy	15 (42.9%)	7 (46.7%)	16 (64.0%)	38 (50.7%)
Unhappy	1 (2.9%)	1 (6.7%)	2 (8.0%)	4 (5.3%)
Mixed	19 (54.3%)	7 (46.7%)	7 (28.0%)	33 (44.0%)
Total	35 (100%)	15 (100%)	25 (100%)	75* (100%)

* The four programs which contained only accidental violence were not included.

This acceptance of violent means as a way of securing ends for morally approved characters is also apparent when we look at program outcomes in terms of the means used to achieve them.(Table 14).

Programs whose outcomes depend on violence are more likely to have happy endings than either violent programs whose endings do not depend on violence or nonviolent programs. If we exclude domestic serials with mixed or unclear endings (which include a high number of nonviolent programs), programs with outcomes depending on violence are still just as likely to end happily as are nonviolent programs.

Violence, then, is presented as both acceptable and successful. Instigators of violence usually win that particular incident, and "good" instigators usually win at the end of the program. Instigators are more likely to be "bad" than "good," but there is still a sizable number of "good" instigators. A violent response to violence is more effective than a passive responser in terms both of the immediate incident and of the outcome of the program.

The role of the reciprocator is a particularly interesting one. It is strongly associated with "good" participants and forms a substantial proportion of "good" participation in violence, It is also strongly associated with success, both immediately and in the final outcome. The reciprocator appears to be typically a "hero" role (and interestingly is disproportionately likely to be a "semilaw enforcement" agent, Table 10). The successful hero commits violence, but he often does so only after he has been attacked, while "bad" characters or villains are more likely to initiate the violence.

SUMMARY: VIOLENCE IN TELEVISION DRAMA

Violence is clearly an important part of television drama. It occurred in 55.7 percent of all the programs studied and was usually essential to the plot. Most of the participants in violent incidents were also essential to the plot. Its incidence was routinized and predictable, occurring heavily in certain kinds of programs—in particular crime, western, and action-adventure programs and cartoons.

Most violence was deliberate, and it was usually shown on the screen. A wide range of physical injuries were produced, and more than one in five incidents resulted in death.

Violence tended to occur in exotic or faraway times, places, and settings. Familiar environments were much less likely to be violent. Most violent incidents involved the use of weapons.

Participants in violence usually played roles essential to the plot and were nearly always male. Violence was effective in the short term and was effective for "good" characters in the long term. "Good" participants were just as likely to commit violence as were "bad" participants but were less likely to initiate it.

Violence did not appear to be disapproved of by those among whom it took place, and programs whose outcomes depended on violence were more likely to end happily than those whose outcomes did not.

Clearly violence can serve a range of dramatic or symbolic functions; these can vary according to the type of violence and the type of program. Violence in comedies (mostly occurring in cartoons) is more likely to be accidental, more likely to be shown on the screen, and less likely to be essential to the plot. It seems to occur largely as a component of slapstick humor.

Violence in serious programs, mostly occurring in crime, western, and action-adventure programs, is usually an important plot element and is an important factor in determining the outcome of these programs. Violence is a crucial element of the symbolic conflict between good and bad; it is by responding violently to the villain's use of violence that the hero secures victory.

VIOLENCE IN NEWS, DOCUMENTARY, AND CURRENT AFFAIRS PROGRAMS

During the week we studied 56 news, documentary, and current affairs programs were broadcast on BBC-1 and ATV, taking up 23.9 program hours. These programs wer monitored, and violent incidents in them were coded using the first ten variables of the fictional incident coding sheet.

The results from this analysis are reported in order to give a complete picture of violence on television during the week and also to provide comparisons between the fictional violence in television drama and the real violence reported in news and documentary programs. The amounts of violence in the various kinds of news and documentary programs are shown in Table 15. Program scores are calculated, but these are not really comparable with the scores for fiction. In news programs the incidents are entirely independent, while both in fiction and in documentaries they usually relate in some way to the story or theme of the program. Therefore the occurrence of a violent incident in a news program, which makes it a violent program, has no implications for the content of the rest of the program, while this is not so in fiction or in documentaries.

Table 15: Violence in news, documentary and current affairs programs

	No. of programs	% containing violence	Violent incidents Rate per program	Rate per hour	Program score
National news	28	89.3%	2.00	7.72	108.74
Regional news	10	50.0	0.70	1.18	53.76
Current affairs	8	50.0	0.25	2.03	56.56
Documentaries	10	50.0	2.20	3.57	61.54
All	56	69.6	1.70	3.92	80.84

Of the 56 programs, 39 (or 69.7 percent contained a total of 95 violent incidents. Most of these occurred in news programs. The 38 national and regional news programs contained 63 violent incidents, 66 percent of the total. There were two violent incidents per national news program (very little more than the overall rate) but news programs have a very much higher rate of incidents per hour, mainly because news bulletins are shorter than documentaries or current affairs programs.

Comparing Tables 7 and 8 with Tables 16 and 17, we can see some of the differences between real and fictional violence on television.

The first contrast with fictional violence is in the presentation of incidents. While 88.3 percent of the fictional violence was shown on the screen, only 35.8 percent of real violence was shown. This is not surprising in view of the need for news reports to react to events which they may not have pictures of, and in view of the difference between reporting events as news and creating them for dramatic purposes. But when we look at the differences between news programs and current affairs and documentary programs, it seems that the first factor is very much more important than the second and that wherever possible stories of violence are presented visually. In news programs with their stress on immediacy of reactions, only 23.8 percent of the violent episodes are shown on the screen, while in current affairs and documentaries, where there is more choice of coverage and more time to prepare material, 59.4 percent of the violent incidents are shown on the screen.

Table 16: Violence in news, documentaries, etc. by presentation and type

	News programs	Documentary and current affairs	All
Presentation			
Shown on screen	15 (23.8%)	19 (59.42%)	34 (35.8%)
Implied or described	48 (76.2%)	13 (40.6%)	61 (64.2%)
Type			
Deliberate physical violence	25 (39.7%)	27 (84.4%)	52 (54.7%)
Accidental violence	36 (57.1%)	4 (12.5%)	40 (42.1%)
Serious threats	2 (3.2%)	1 (3.1%)	3 (3.2%)
Total	63 (100%)	32 (100%)	95 (100%)

Much more real than fictional violence on the screen is accidental. Only 11.7 percent of the fictional material was coded as accidental, compared with 42.1 percent of real violence. Once again it is the news programs which largely create this difference; the current affairs and documentary programs are very similar to fictional programs with 12.5 percent of incidents accidental, while the news programs have 57.1 percent accidental incidents.

A much higher proportion of the real incidents occurred in the context of war or civil strife; together these accounted for 69.1 percent, compared with 9.2 percent for fictional programs. Criminal violence, law enforcement, family and other personal contexts were accordingly much lower. Wars occupied a higher proportion of documentary and current affairs programs, and law enforcement and crime occupied a higher proportion of news.[10]

Table 17: Location of types and contexts of violence

	Britain	Location Abroad	All
Accidental violence	39	1	40
	(67.2%)	(2.7%)	(42.1%)
War	2	26	28
	(3.4%)	(70.3%)	(29.5%)
Civil strife, riots	5	5	10
	(8.6%)	(13.5%)	(10.5%)
Criminal and law enforcement	9	2	11
	(15.5%)	(5.4%)	(11.6%)
Family and personal	2	1	3
	(3.4%)	(2.7%)	(3.2%)
Other	1	2	3
	(1.7%)	(5.4%)	(3.2%)
Total	58	37	95

Perhaps the most dramatic difference between real and fictional violence on television is in its location. As has already been noted, fictional violence is disproportionately likely to occur in faraway locations; only 21.2 percent of the incidents occurring in Britain. This pattern is reversed in the coverage of real violence, where 61.1 percent of the incidents occurred in Britain. Obviously events close at hand are more salient in news terms than those in more remote areas, and once again it is the news programs rather than the current affairs and documentary programs that create these differences. 77.8 percent of incidents in the news occurred in Britain, compared with 28.1 percent of those in current affairs and documentaries. These differences are in part explained by the type and context of violence being reported.

As has already been noted, most violence in fiction, current affairs, and documentary programs was deliberate, while more than half of the violence reported in news programs was accidental. Table 17 shows that while almost all the accidental real violence occurred in Britain, over two-thirds of the deliberate real violence occurred abroad. Put another way: 67.2 percent of the violence occurring in Britain was accidental, and the largest category of the deliberate violence was in a criminal or law enforcement context. In contrast, only 2.7 percent of the violent incidents occurring abroad were accidental, while 70 percent were in the context of war.

In general, real violence in news and documentary programs is more home-centered than is fictional violence; partly as a consequence of this, it is much more likely to be accidental. Most deliberate violence reported occurs abroad and consists to a great extent of reports of wars and similar dramatic events. Real violence is much less likely than fictional violence to be shown on the screen, probably more because of the practical problems of news collecting than because of the different functions of television news and television fiction.

The material reported here is inadequate for a systematic study of the different "pictures of the world" offered in television fiction and in television news and documentaries. Such a study would be an important part of any large-scale analysis of the functions and consequences of various kinds of television material, and needs to deal with a wider area of interest than violence.

SEXUAL AND ROMANTIC RELATIONSHIPS IN TELEVISION DRAMA

We felt that to concentrate on sexual incidents in programs, while it might be of interest to those who want to censor such scenes, would be to miss a much more important part of television's presentation of sex. Sexual incidents occur within the context of sexual or romantic relationships. What is of interest is to see how television presents such relationships, how explicitly sex is shown as a part of them, what is presented as the kind of behavior appropriate to different kinds of relationships, and how happily or unhappily various relationships turn out.

The units of analysis for sex are the program, which is coded in terms of whether or not certain relationships and incidents occurred, and the sexual or romantic relationship, which is coded in terms of its type and outcome and the degree of sexual explicitness with which it is presented. Relationships occurring in serials with more than one episode in the week were only coded once.

Just over half the programs included some sort of romantic relationship and most of these were essential to the plot (Table 18). More ATV than BBC programs included love or romance, probably because of the far higher ATV share of domestic serials. Kissing or embracing was shown in 27 programs, 34.2 percent of the total and 67.5 percent of all programs involving sexual or romantic relationships.

The variables relating to sexual relations or sexual intercourse in programs did not reach acceptable reliability, but in no more than seven

Table 18: Sexual relations in fiction programs

	BBC	ATV	Both
Love or romance			
Does not occur	24	15	39
	(61.5%)	(37.5%)	(49.4%)
Incidental to plot	2	2	4
	(5.1%)	(5.0%)	(5.1%)
Essential to plot	13	23	36
	(33.3%)	(57.5%)	(45.6%)
Kissing, embracing			
Shown on screen	11	16	27
	(28.2%)	(40.0%)	(34.2%)
None	28	24	52
	(71.8%)	(60.0%)	(65.8%)
Adultery			
Does not occur	34	38	72
	(87.2%)	(95.0%)	(91.1%)
Incidental to plot	1	1	2
	(2.6%)	(2.5%)	(2.5%)
Essential to plot	4	1	5
	(10.3%)	(2.5%)	(6.3%)
Total	39	40	79
	(100%)	(100%)	(100%)

programs (8.9 percent) did sexual relations occur and in no case was sexual intercourse shown on the screen. Adultery occurred in six programs (7.6 percent), and in five of these it was essential to the plot (defined as needing to be included in a one-page summary of the plot).

In the forty programs which contained sexual or romantic relationships, a total of 60 relationships in fact occurred. Marital relationships accounted for 14 of these; a further 30 were stable and 16 casual relationships.[11] Twenty-five of the relationships (or 41.7 percent) ended happily and 33.3 percent unhappily, with 25.0 percent having a mixed or unclear outcome. None of the happy endings were for casual relationships (almost by definition), and stable relationships were slightly more likely to end happily than marital relationships.

Four of the thirty stable relationships ended in marriage (Table 20).

Just over half of the relationships involved kissing or embracing on the screen, and this was so for a slightly higher proportion of marital than nonmarital relationships.

Sexual intercourse was implied or referred to as part of nine of the sixty relationships (or 15 percent). This was so for 18.8 percent of casual relationships, compared with 13.3 percent of stable and 14.3 percent of marital relationships. In no case was sexual intercourse shown on the screen (Table 20).

One way of looking at the normative context within which sexual relations are presented on the screen is to consider the outcomes of relationships which have varying levels of sexual content. In Table 19, relationships in which sexual intercourse was a part are compared with those
where it was not in terms of how likely they were to have a happy ending.

Table 19: Sexual explicitness and outcomes

	Sexual intercourse implied	No sexual intercourse
Marital relations		
Happy	0	7
Unhappy	1	3
Mixed	1	2
Total	2	12
Nonmarital relations		
Happy	1	17
Unhappy	5	11
Mixed	1	11
Total	7	39
All		
Happy	1	24
Unhappy	6	14
Mixed	2	13
Total	9	51

Relationships in which sexual intercourse was a part are very much
less likely to end happily than those where it is not. Only one of the relationships containing sex ended happily; six (or two-thirds) ended unhappily, while nearly half of the nonsex relationships ended happily and less
than one in three ended unhappily. This is even true for marital relationships: neither of the two of these where sex was a part ended happily.

Love and romance is clearly an important part of television drama. It
occurs in over half the programs and is usually essential to the plot. Relationships may end happily or unhappily, but the largest single group is
that of stable relationships (typically relationships where the partners
meet during the program) ending happily and sometimes explicitly ending in marriage. More than half the relationships involve kissing and
embracing being shown on the screen but sexual relations are rarely
shown as part of a relationship and were never shown on the screen.

The number of relations in which sexual intercourse was a part was
very small, and the figures should be interpreted with care. But it seems
that television displays a moral orthodoxy in which sex is neither seen as

Table 20: Sexual or romantic relationships; outcomes and sexual explicitness.

	Marriage	Stable	Casual	All
Outcome				
Happy	7	18	0	25
	(50.0%)	(60.0%)		(41.7%)
Unhappy	4	7	9	20
	(28.6%)	(23.3%)	(56.3%)	(33.3%)
Mixed	3	5	7	15
	(21.4%)	(16.7%)	(43.8%)	(25.0%)
Ends in marriage				
Yes	-	4	0	4
		(13.3%)		(8.7%)
No	-	26	16	42
		(86.7%)	(100%)	(91.3%)
Kissing, embracing				
Shown on screen	8	15	8	31
	(57.1%)	(50.0%)	(50.0%)	(51.7%)
Implied, referred to	0	0	0	0
None	6	15	8	29
	(42.9%)	(50.0%)	(50.0%)	(48.3%)
Sexual intercourse				
Shown on screen	0	0	0	0
Implied, referred to	2	4	3	9
	(14.3%)	(13.3%)	(18.8%)	(15.0%)
None	12	26	13	51
	(85.7%)	(86.7%)	(81.3%)	(85.0%)
Total	14	30	16	60
	(100%)	(100%)	(100%)	(100%)

an appropriate part of a happy or satisfactory nonmarital relationship nor displayed as part of a happy marriage. In particular, relationships of which sex is shown as a part are extremely unlikely to end happily.

CONCLUDING REMARKS

Let us now see what we have learned from this pilot study that may be of some use to us in planning further research. First let us return to the content/effects problem referred to earlier in this report.

The data which can be generated by content analysis range from, at the most simple level, frequency counts (how often a particular unit of content occurs) to the more complex descriptions of the ways in which units of content occur together to form recurring structures. An example of the generalizations based on this sort of analysis might be: "Villains typically commit violence by instigating the violence while heroes typically respond to someone else's use of violence."

In this way, at first simple and then (hopefully) increasingly complex descriptions of communications content can be constructed. A problem arises, however, when we want to move from these descriptions to statements about what the content implies about its source or how it is perceived by its audience. In particular we have to establish the degree of equivalence between the meanings which we attribute to the content and the meanings attributed by its source and/or audience. This can be a particularly acute problem when we are dealing with programs which may be directed to a large and diverse audience. We already know that different people can perceive and use the same media content in different ways. If, to quote George Gerbner, we are to use the results of content analysis to "... show what system of images and messages network television *as a whole releases into the national consciousness,*"[12] we must establish to what extent there is a shared universe of meanings corresponding to the shared symbolic environment provided by the media. When we are coding sex and age, guns and knives, this may not seem a problem. But when we want to talk about values and relationships, dramatic structures and symbolic functions, it becomes crucial.

One way in which this might be done is to see if the simple generalizations about the frequency and structure of content units have the status of messages—that is, whether they are perceived by various audiences in the same way as they are coded by the content analyst.

A small-scale pilot study in this area was carried out by Guy Cumberbatch at the Centre for Mass Communication Research. In this study a questionnaire was administered to 28 grammar school girls aged 14-15. The girls were asked what typically happened in certain situations in nine television programs, chosen as being crime/adventure programs of a similar type which usually contained violence. The questions were designed to elicit information about the same categories of content and relationships between content units which had been measured for these same programs by the content analysis. The girls were asked whether violence was usually justified in these programs, how witnesses reacted to violence, and so on.

The results suggest that in general the perceptions and recollections of these elements of the programs by the girls were very similar to the generalizations from the content study. This applied to areas like amount of violence, whether it was accidental or deliberate, its relevance to the plot, whether it was justified, and the reaction of witnesses.

While it would be inappropriate to regard the results from such a study as more than very tentative, they at least do not contradict the assumption that units and structures of content may be regarded as "messages," and suggests that a larger scale study of this kind might be a feasible way of testing the universality of "shared perspectives" derived from television.

Another study in this area was conducted by Ursula Dobraszczyc, a graduate student at the Centre. This was a larger scale study covering several groups of viewers. The aim was to study in a more open-ended way the perceptions and definitions of television violence of different social groups, and their relevance to the definitions and assumptions used in the construction of content analysis categories.

Four groups of viewers—two of working-class adolescents, one of trainee teachers, and one of middle-class housewives, 86 persons altogether—were each shown the same two television programs (both of which contained violence) and completed a questionnaire immediately after each program. They were all asked to describe the programs and incidents in the programs, and they were then asked about violence in the program and about specific violent incidents.

The analysis suggests that although the open-ended questions resulted in a considerable range of responses, in general there was agreement between the groups in the selection of violent incidents and in the intensity of violence attributed to them. The groups were also consistent in attributing a greater degree of violence to one program than to the other, and this ordering was the same as would have emerged from a content analysis. However, the notion of a "violent incident" seemed far less central to the perceptions and definitions of violence used by the audience groups than they were to the content analysis categories. Many elements which could not be regarded as violent incidents were included in the descriptions of violence, such as the potential for violence and the threat posed by certain situations. Moreover, more than half of the audience did not mention any specific violent incident in their description of the program's story, regardless of whether they thought the program a violent one or not.

Another feature to emerge was that in describing the program the subjects took over the language of the program and appeared to accept the implicit assumptions of the program. For example, the legitimacy of certain sorts of behavior on the part of heroes—even though this behavior was, in conventional social terms, questionable—appeared to be accepted.

Both these audience studies were concerned with the specific area of violence, and both were relatively simple pilot studies which should be interpreted with caution. They do suggest, though, that the descriptions of content units arising from the content analysis can be seen as corresponding to (or at least as not being contradicted by) audience perceptions. The second study suggests, however, that there may be many varied aspects of content which are perceived by the audience as relevant but which are not catered to by the content categories so far used.

At different places in this report we have argued that program content, with regard both to its creation and reception, should be studied in the appropriate social context. We have also stressed the necessity of examining structures and relationships within which units of content occur rather than the units themselves. However, it will be obvious to readers that the pilot study of sex and violence in television drama reported here hardly meets these criteria. This work was carried out with great constraints on time and resources and must not be regarded as anything other than a pilot study. For example, the main content analysis reported in this paper is very much incident-oriented and deals with structures of units only at the most simple level.

Moreover, as mentioned earlier, the study of the control of television material tends to be top-heavy in that it draws disproportionately on official statements and was not able to benefit from close observation of the day to day process of program-making. As part of the belief system of the institution, such official statements are important and must be studied, but (and this is no reflection on the integrity of the various authors and speakers) they do not in themselves constitute adequate explanations, and they ought not to be seen as an accurate or complete account of what actually takes place. In all institutions there are gaps (researchable gaps) between the official and the real explanation. However, these statements do point to areas that ought to be looked at closely in any future research project.

The studies of audience perceptions are piecemeal in the range of programs, the content area covered, and the selection of viewers. In a pilot study of this type all this is more or less inevitable. The whole study should be regarded as nothing more and nothing less than a necessary preliminary to a large-scale comparative study of television content, its control, and its use.

Nevertheless, despite these reservations (and bearing in mind the fact that the various parts of the study were conducted more or less independently), it is worth mentioning some of the ways in which the three parts of the pilot study are related and have implications for each other, and for future research developments. First of all, it would apear that the areas of greatest sensitivity to content (such as plays) are not the areas where most of the violence on television occurs. Most violence is a routinized and predictable occurrence in adventure and crime programs, usually feature films which are often imported.

As we have seen, the structure of the organization and the nature of the decision-making processes with regard to programs are extremely complex. Decisions are taken for a variety of reasons with several, possibly conflicting, objectives in view. Consequently, many of the decisions which in some way or other influence the amount of violence shown have to do with such things as programming "mix" or balance, purchasing policy, import quotas, and so on. It is worth noting that these decisions are taken on grounds not directly concerned with violence. If one wishes to study the factors governing the portrayal of violence, it is not enough to confine one's attention to the operation of the code.

Explicit policy with regard to violence is concerned with the outside limits of what can be physically shown. It makes no mention of the institutionalized place of violence in certain types of programs, or the sorts of implications for social power and social values which the successful and approved use of violence in many stereotyped situations may have. On the whole, most concern seems to be expressed about specific incidents or scenes rather than about the recurring system of images, messages, and meanings which the media provide.

This brings us back once more to the important question of the choice of content areas and units and levels of analysis. We need to remember that the choice of areas and units of analysis is not assumption-free. To focus, for instance, on sex and violence implies that these areas are felt to be important. To code violent incidents and the weapons of violence or to count nudes and scenes of sexual intercourse implies that these are the most appropriate ways of looking at sex and violence. This might be an appropriate orientation for those wishing to censor these areas or for persons adhering to a simple stimulus-response view of media effects. But it is an inadequate approach for an understanding of the role and functions of sexual and violent material in television drama and its relationship to the audience perception of media material and to sex and violence in the real world. We need to be concerned with the social relationships within which scenes of sex and violence (and many other units of content) occur and their meaning within these relationships. This might mean coding all sexual or emotional relationships, whether or not sex is overtly a part of them. Violence can be taken as an indicator of social power, but it is only one way in which power operates. It may be necessary to consider all conflict or power relations in the material studied, violent and nonviolent and to look at such relations in terms of their outcome and the legitimacy of various types and uses of power.

But, so it could be argued, control of television programs is not directly operated in these terms. This of course is true. It is arguable (granted another value position) that control as at present exercised tends to concentrate on the superficial or even on the irrelevant and that the things that do matter are ignored. This, were it true, would have its own important cultural implications and would be worth studying for this alone.

In operational terms, such a study would mean that in studying program control in media institutions we should not start with our sex and violence blinkers on. We should set out to study all the factors that control all the content. Where, for practical reasons, we have to limit our approach to a more modest objective in making our decisions, we should have in mind social scientific considerations rather than political expediency.

Unfortunately, this is easier said than done, for media institutions and other grant-giving bodies are not likely to support or facilitate research that they do not see having an immediate payoff for them on their own terms. In Great Britain it is unlikely that ITA will ever again write a blank cheque for social research. The BBC never has done this and has made it clear that it has no intention of changing this policy.

It is arguable that public opinion and political pressure had reached a fair pitch before the BBC decided to carry out research in this field; even then it is questionable whether the Corporation made the most intelligent use of its allegedly scarce resources. The recommendations of the Television Research Committee about future research needs and developments were warmly supported by the Social Science Research Council, but not by the media. This whole question suggests that as far as research is concerned, not only are public service responsibilities articulated only when problems arise, but, even when they are finally articulated, they are presented in such a way so as to ensure a maintenance of the statute quo.

The social scientist wishes to study the mass media because he assumes that media institutions are important in society. He assumes that television is important, not just because of its possible social effects (for example, with regard to sex and violence), but also because of its position in the social structure and its relationship to other media and other institutions—because it relays cultural symbols, conveys meanings, structures the social debate, uses human and social resources, and reflects the interrelationship of economic, political, social and professional forces.

The social scientist should not be surprised if the professional broadcaster tries to keep him at bay, for, as we have seen, the broadcaster often seems to give the impression of knowing all the answers. He knows quite well what he is doing. He understands how television operates, what forces are at work, and what the effects of his operation are. Researchers may be necessary to count heads and check audience reactions—i.e., to serve the media—but not to question its policies, practices, basic assumptions, and conventional wisdom. When researchers claim the right to go beyond head counting they frequently encounter evasion, at times even hostility. Broadcasters often argue that the creative and control processes are not susceptible to research: "Vital decisions are taken on the way to the toilet, in the bath, over a glass of sherry."

Of course, we know the broadcaster is not quite knowledgeable or self-aware as he would have us believe. It has also been suggested that there might be good reason why he feels compelled to tell us in no uncertain terms that he understands the communication process, and why he feels the need to convince us of the overall excellence and propriety of his activities and to justify the continued unchanged existence of his institution.

This sort of conviction and certainty is not confined to broadcasters by any means, but it could be that the nature of broadcasting and its position in contemporary society provide at least a partial explanation for these attitudes of television management. When one considers the complexity of the situation and the intermeshing of the various forces in the production process, and takes into account the high social visibility, the political and social salience, and the accompanying vulnerabilities, one thinks it would indeed be strange if we did not have some such manifestations.

We know what is normally said about those who protest too much. We also know that when people overdo their attempts to convince others of their value and their righteousness, suspicions develop, and one begins to wonder what the problem is. In this case we can guess, but we do not really know, and one of the main points of this paper is that this is an area in which we cannot afford to remain ignorant.

It is not unreasonable to hypothesize that the professional television man knows very little about the workings of his institution, about its relationship with society and other institutions, or about the nature of the communication process. However, as we have seen, he is unwilling or unable to admit it. Social scientists, too, know very little about the media but lose little by admitting this. They are, after all, looking for information about somebody else's institution, not their own. We have seen that in one way the media may be held responsible for their lack of knowledge, but it would be a mistake if we didn't say that social scientists themselves are in some way to blame. It might even be argued that the approach adopted in this paper is not likely to improve matters. But diplomacy has too often triumphed at the cost of knowledge in this field. It is at least arguable that a change of tactics is long overdue.

As social scientists, we must press on with our work, but when proposing to carry out research in these relatively unchartered areas in the field of media research, we do need to bear in mind the differences between broadcaster and social scientist as far as social visibility and vulnerability are concerned. We have everything to gain from the research cooperation proposed in these pages. The broadcaster at least feels that he may have something to lose. We should not lose sight of this.

FOOTNOTES

1. National news bulletins for all areas are provided by Independent Television News, a nonprofit making company in which all the companies are shareholders.
2. ITA and BBC use different methods and units of audience measurement. This leads, among other things, to apparently conflicting claims about audience size.
3. M.F. Eleey. Variations in generalizability resulting from sampling characteristics of content analysis data: a case study. Annenberg School of Communications, University of Pennsylvania, 1969.

4. G. Gerbner. Dimensions of violence in television drama. Annenberg School of Communications, University of Pennsylvania, 1969.

5. W.A. Scott, Reliability of content analysis: the case of nominal scale coding. *Public Opinion Quarterly*, 1955, **17**(3), 321-25.

6. The category "play" refers to a "one-off" drama production.

7. G. Gerbner. Violence in television drama: trends and symbolic functions. (Elsewhere in this volume.) While this is a very useful way of combining the extent and frequency of violence in various kinds of programs, it has disadvantages. The percentage of programs containing violence has an upper limit, while the others do not. This means that the formula is less flexible when all of the programs being considered contain violence than when they do not.

8. The distinction between major and minor suffering could not be used, as it had been inadequately defined and did not reach an acceptable level of reliability. This is particularly unfortunate when we consider the differences between the effects of violence in serious and comic programs, where a potentially interesting difference is lost.

9. Of these, only "threats" is an exclusive category; the other incidents were coded for as many types of weapons as were used.

10. These figures refer to the percentage of nonaccidental violence. The percentage of all real violence taking place in the context of war or civil strife was a much lower 40 percent.

11. A marital relationship is one in which the partners are married for the majority of the length of the program. The mere presence of a married couple does not of itself constitute a relationship. Love or sex must occur or the marriage must be a theme of the program. A stable relationship is one that predates the beginning of a program or lasts beyond its end. A casual relationship is one that both begins and ends during the program.

12. This idea might be better interpreted as "made available" than as "released into."

Structure and Content of Television Broadcasting in Israel

Dov Shinar with Pnina Parnes and Dan Caspi and with an
introduction by Elihu Katz

The Hebrew University of Jerusalem
The Communications Institute

INTRODUCTION

Television in Israel is just three years old. It was born in a unique situation—during the year following the Six Days War. Like television in other new nations, high hopes were held out for the role of television in the integration of the society and in the renaissance of its culture. In Israel, there was the additional hope that television might contribute to the promise of a dialogue between Jews and Arabs.

While occasional programs reflect some of these hopes, television in Israel is not really different from television anywhere. Except for the relatively few hours of broadcasting, and the important fact that it

493

broadcasts both in Hebrew and in Arabic, Israel television reflects the same kind of programming mix that has come to be typical of television around the world. Sixty per cent of its programs are bought on the world market, and inevitably—or so it seems—these include the world's most popular programs - *Bonanza, Family Affair, Mission Impossible,* and the like. Children (and their parents) in Jerusalem can watch different episodes of *Bewitched* on successive nights on Jordan Television and Israel Television. Entertainment follows the Italian or French formats— whether produced locally or acquired abroad. The news is the conventional succession of brief, disconnected items complete with fashionable presentation and standardized by the international news services.

Institutionally, broadcasting is based on the British model—with a BBC-like Broadcasting Authority (somewhat more closely tied to government, perhaps). The present report describes the organizational structure, analyzing and exemplifying the ways in which internalized controls, as well as informal and formal pressures, act to influence programming decisions. While the focus of the discussion is in the field of violence and sex, it will be noted that these are not matters of major concern for Israeli broadcasters. Their "scale of sensitive subjects" ranks these subjects for behind politics, security, religion, and other social problems. The views of producers, department heads, and members of the Authority are presented, and an interview with the head of Arabic programs is reproduced verbatim because of the special cultural considerations it brings forward.

The report also indicates how much programming is produced locally, and how much is acquired from local and foreign producers. It is evident from the table that the decision-making process with respect to the acquisition of foreign programs and films must be given careful attention. Nor may one be satisfied with analysis of the "demand" side of the equation. The "supply"situation must be given equal attention. The process by which the call for a renaissance of indigenous culture is answered by *Peyton Place* and *Hawaii Five-O*—in country after country— deserves research attention.

The authors discuss the diffusion of television sets and the patterns of viewing. They indicate the relative popularity of different types of programs. It is important to note that Israeli viewers insist they want more domestic programming (despite its necessarily lower technical standard). The higher education groups (12 years of education or more) say they would be satisfied with less entertainment in exchange for more material for thought.

The content analysis of a week's broadcasting is based on a necessarily small number of programs, but it indicates that the violence in Israel television entertainment is virtually all imported. Whether or not its symbolic *meaning* is the same as in the originating cultures is a high priority question for research.

Elihu Katz

INSTITUTIONAL STRUCTURES AND CONTROL PROCESSES OF TELEVISION IN ISRAEL
Legal structure

Television broadcasting in Israel operates within the framework of the Israel Broadcasting Authority (which includes also radio services), whose legal and operational "charter" is the Broadcasting Authority Law of March 1965 (amended in August 1966 and December 1968).[1] Television was annexed to the Authority in 1969. From its first broadcast in the middle of 1967 until its incorporation into the Authority, it operated as a *Task-Force* belonging to the Prime Minister's Office.

According to the Law, the Authority is a National Service and a corporate entity. Its functions are:

1) to broadcast educational, entertainment and informational programs in the field of politics, social life, economics, culture, science and art, with a view to:
   a) reflecting the life, struggle, creative effort and achievements of the State;
   b) fostering good citizenship;
   c) strengthening the ties with, and deepening the knowledge of the Jewish heritage and its values;
   d) reflecting the life and cultural assets of all sections of the people from the different countries;
   e) broadening education and disseminating knowledge;
   f) reflecting the life of Diaspora Jewry;
   g) furthering the aims of State Education Law, 5713-1953.
2) to promote Hebrew and Israeli creative endeavor;
3) to provide broadcasts in the Arabic language for the requirements of the Arabic speaking population and broadcasts for the promotion of understanding and peace with the neighboring states in accordance with the basic tendencies of the State;

4) to provide broadcasts to Diaspora Jewry;

5) to provide broadcasts to foreign countries.

The responsibility for the execution of the law falls upon a minister of the government, who operates through the following entities of the Authority:

a) *The Plenum* of 31 members, appointed by the President of the State and recommended by the Government after consultation with the representative organizations of writers, teachers and artists, universities, the Hebrew Language Academy, and other public bodies. No more than four members may be State employees. The functions of the Plenum are as follows:

1) to lay down the policies of the Authority;

1a) to discuss the reports and surveys of the committee appointed by the Authority;

2) to issue directions to the Managing Committee as to the discharge of its duties;

3) to approve the seasonal program schedules without, however, derogating from its authority to decide from time to time on specific broadcasts in all their aspects;

3a) to receive from the Managing Committee proposals for the ordinary budget and the development budget prepared by it, to discuss them and to pass its recommendations to the Managing Committee;

4) to receive from the Managing Committee and from the Director, on its demand, reports and surveys of the ongoing work, to consider those reports and surveys and to formulate conclusions;

5) to consider the annual report to be submitted to it by the Managing Committee, and to formulate its conclusions;

6) to discuss any other matter it deems fit, and to formulate its conclusions.

b) *The Managing Committee* of seven members, consisting of members of the Plenum appointed by the Government, and including no more than two State Employees.

The functions of the Managing Committee are as follows:

1) to consider and decide upon matters of the Broadcasting Service;

2) to receive from the general director reports of the ongoing work of the Broadcasting Service;

3) to prepare the ordinary budget and development budget of the Authority for the financial year beginning on April first of every year, and submit them to the government for approval, together with the recommendations of the Plenum according to section 13 (3a); provided that expenditures

not covered by the revenue of the Authority but by allocations from the Treasury shall require approval of the
Knesset;

4)   to supervise the implementation of the approved budget in
accordance with the financial and economical procedure
obtaining in respect of the State Budget;

5)   to submit to the Plenum an annual report of its activities
and any report the Plenum may demand;

6)   to submit to the minister any report he may demand and to
notify the Plenum thereof.

c)   *The director general* of the Authority, appointed by the Government for a period of five years. Candidates for this task may be
either persons proposed by the minister in charge of the execution of the Law, or a person supported by a majority of the
members of the Plenum. The director general is responsible for
the implementation of policies and procedures decided upon by
the higher levels.

Although the Authority has a source of income in the license fees
imposed for the maintenance of receiving sets, the Broadcasting Authority budget is controlled by Parliament through its Finance Committee, and its submission for approval is made according to regulations
issued by the Ministry of Finance. There is no television advertising,
although advertising exists in radio.

In summary, the law gives the Authority the status of a public, non-
governmental organization with partial dependence on government.
Formally, this status is expressed in several ways—in the Plenum,
which reflects the cultural spectrum of the country; or in the provisions
that set a limit on the number of state employees who may be appointed
as members of the various managing bodies. On the other hand, the law
permits different pressure groups to influence directly. Thus the appointment of the members of the Managing Committee reflects, more or
less, the political spectrum, including the left and right wings, religious
parties, coalition-opposition parties, and so on. Obviously, these groups
are in a position which allows them to exert pressure regarding contents,
personnel, and budgets.

On the operational level, the functions of administration and engineering apply to the entire Authority (television and radio). These functions
include administrative services, financial and economic matters, personnel, and engineering services (including studios, laboratories, and equipment).

The television station broadcasts four hours daily—three hours in
"Hebrew" and one hour in "Arabic." [2] The station operates under the
direction of a controller for television and includes five departments:
Hebrew News, Arabic News, Hebrew Programs, Arabic Programs, and
Production Services. Each department has a head and is staffed by edi-
tors (news), producers (programs) and directors. Graphics, Acquired

Films, and Operations units (Production Services) serve the station as a whole. This structure is not yet entirely institutionalized but reflects a rather experimental stage, which permits expectation of substantial changes. Recently, for example, a new intermediate level was created between the head of Hebrew programs and his producers—the level of senior producers.

Lines of organization and authority in determining program policy

On the most general level, television programming can be classified along two main axes:

a) *Type of content:* news and current affairs; programs (Hebrew and Arabic).

b) *Production and/or distribution source: locally produced* by own television staff; *locally* produced by private producers; *films acquired from abroad.*

For news programs, a general production process is followed. A daily meeting of the editorial staff (editor for the day, reports, head of department) is held in the morning. This meeting determines the general structure of the news editions for the same day—content and form of items and events to be covered. The news items typically come from the morning papers, from releases from different sources, and/or from ideas initiated (and sometimes decided upon by consultation with management) by the heads of both (Hebrew and Arabic) news departments. In the afternoon, as soon as news material from abroad arrives, a second meeting is held, in which the edition receives its final shape. It should be noted that the format of the news has undergone various changes during television's short existence: program length has been shortened from 45 to 20 minutes; internal division of items has been instituted; a short edition has been added at the end of the evening.

Current affairs programs produced by the news departments—such as *Moked,* a variation of *Meet the Press* are determined in a way very similar to other local programs, which are detailed in the following paragraphs.

Other types of productions are usually planned on a seasonal, rather than a day-to-day basis, and therefore the decision-making procedure is quite different. Seasonal programming is brought by the director general to various committees of the Authority and then to the Managing Committee for final approval. The following operative stages take place within the station:

a) *Preparation of overall formal and "slots,"* including the type of content (drama, full features, documentaries, children's, etc.), the hour and amount of time allocated to each type and the source (local, acquired). The controller of television, together with the heads of Hebrew and Arabic programs, prepares this preliminary stage.

b) *Determining specific content for each slot*. These are selected in three ways. Suggestions for *local productions* to be produced at the station are brought by producers to occasional departmental meetings or to the head of their department. The final recommendation is made by the heads of departments, and the decision whether to include a program in the draft submitted to the director general is made by the controller of television, together with the heads of the Hebrew and Arabic program departments.

Final decisions about *local productions to be acquired* are made by a special commission, including the heads of program departments, the deputy director general, and the head of the Economics Department in the Authority. However, since the heads of Television Programs (Hebrew and Arabic) and the controller of television are those who contact outside producers and agents and receive synopses and samples, they have the biggest share of influence.

According to the policy and principles set forth by the heads of Programs, the head of the Acquired Films Department orders the *programs to be acquired abroad*. The final decisions are made by the heads of Programs. Usually all types of programs are seen first as pilots—especially programs acquired locally and abroad, but more recently in-house programs too.

Some 60 percent of the total programming are programs acquired abroad. The proportion among Hebrew programs alone is even higher.

Major influences on program policy: violence and sex

Being a relatively young station and a public national service; having in mind the long controversy that accompanied the establishment of television in other countries; and being responsible for only three hours per day in Hebrew and one hour in Arabic, the Authority tends to be sensitive to any deviation from moral, social, and ideological "middle-of-the-road" standards. In regard to violence and sex, this tendency finds its most general expression in the small amount of time spent on broadcasting violent and sexual contents. Series such as *The Avengers* and *Mannix* have not been acquired, on the grounds of "too much violence." Local productions do not present a significant amount of violence. News personnel abstain from showing corpses of killed Arab terrorists or sharp closeups of violence scenes.

It should be noted that other sensitive types of content—security matters, internal politics, or ideological problems—are broadcast in a much larger amount. It is only natural that a majority of the control mechanisms, at least the formal ones, have concentrated on these issues, rather than on violence or sex. These controls include, among others, internal directives and regulations, censorship, various pressure groups such as religious parties and the Histadrut (Trade Unions Confederation), professional critics, the press, and letters from the audience. Some of these mechanisms are also applied where violence and sex are concerned.

Effective as they may be, the administrative and direct control mechanisms seem to be only secondary to the personal attitudes, considerations, and standards held by the professional staff. Even though the Managing Committee is the body which discusses and approves the seasonal programming, the substantive initiative and the majority of decisions are taken at subordinate levels—the controller of television and his department heads. Actually, the gatekeepers of the entire system seem to be the heads of Programming and News, since they start the planning process by bringing plans and suggestions, discussing and preparing them, and (together with the controller) presenting the final draft to the director general and the Managing Committee. This leaves a great deal of freedom to the department heads and to the reporters and producers in charge of filling the general program structure with actual content.

The Managing Committee has some "preventive" control in that its expectations are well known by the professional staff. Its members may express their dissatisfaction with certain series (such as *Bonanza* or *Gunsmoke)* or with programs, but only *post factum.*.

The director general, who is closer to the professional staff and sometimes participates in their periodic meetings, may exert influence in a more direct way. Thus, when the question of whether to broadcast the film *The Servant* was brought to the weekly meeting of the department heads, the director general expressed his opinion that, because of the (moral, mental) cruelty in the film "we should wait a little before broadcasting it." [3]

Prior-to-broadcast consultations or briefings with the director general or the Managing Committee are held very seldom and only in very special cases. The only program not broadcast, although scheduled, was an Israeli version of *Meet the Press* on which the director of the Ports Authority was to have been interviewed live, According to our interviewees, the pressure of the government and the Histadrut on the members of the Managing Committee caused it to decide to cancel the program. However, several programs intentionally remained unscheduled after their production had been completed.

On the other hand, both the Managing Committee and the director general have had a great deal of influence on the selection of staff, especially in senior positions, by means of participation of members of the Managing Committee and of the director general or his representative on the interviewing committees.

These facts emphasize the importance of the personal attitudes, considerations, and standards of the professional staff as effective control mechanisms in regard to different types of sensitive content, including violence and sex. On the basis of the interviews conducted with the different levels, this will be described in the next section (1) to be followed by (2) a description of the formal internal mechanisms and codes and (3) external control mechanisms such as censorship and pressure groups.

Attitudes, considerations, and standards

Sensitive subjects. A high measure of consensus exists among the entire staff in regard to the "hierarchy of sensitive subjects" and its reasons. The head of Hebrew programming, news editors, and producers expressed the almost general view that, as a public station, they are concerned about equilibrium, impartiality, and representativeness, especially in the fields of politics, religion, and social problems. This concern, according to the interviewees, is caused, first, by the relative public saliencey of these subjects; second, by the clearly political structure of the Managing Committee; and finally, by television's central position among the media, which creates special public awareness about television broadcasting. Thus the criteria of sensitiveness are partly exterior to programming *per se*. One expression of this attitude, according to a news editor, is "the wish to reflect equally all the elements in Parliament, while there exists a clear disproportion among the parties." This, comment together with the small amount of violent and sexual contents presented, illustrates the "low" position of violence and sex in the hierarchy of sensitiveness.."

Sensitivity to violence and sex. Staff consensus has formed around the opinion that violence and sex should not be arbitrarily taken off the screen, providing they are integral and/or functional to the entire program/item and are presented in right proportions. This consensus applies also to the view that television's role as a family medium should be taken into consideration in the treatment of violence and sex. Several distinctions were introduced by interviewees. One generally accepted distinction is between violence and horror, though not explained clearly. One news editor said that, in his view, a violent picture is "a policeman shooting a Viet Cong right in his head in downtown Saigon," while the pictures of the corpses of three children killed in a landslide in Israel, or people killed in car accidents, belong to the category of horror. Reason: "In pictures of horror one is impressed by the visual presentation itself rather than by the causes of violence, its background, etc." In his opinion, the first picture in the example should be broadcast, while the second should not. A similar distinction applies to sex.

A second distinction is made between formal or "make-believe" violence and violence in news and current affairs. The deputy chairman of the Authority says that the former case is less dangerous, because the viewer is able to put the violent content into its proper context; the latter is far more dangerous by "giving ideas."

Insofar as news and current affairs are concerned, the Israel Broadcasting Authority (IBA) military reporter and one of the news editors did not entirely agree with the view that content is the primary source of influence on the viewer. They mentioned that the subject's treatment and presentation are more important than the subject *per se*. Example: the military reporter, while covering the Elrom Affair in Turkey (kidnapping and murder of Israel's General Consul in Istanbul, May 1971), instead of describing or showing the Turkish interrogation methods, solved his problem by saying, "Turkey has a long tradition of interrogating prisoners. . ."The same reporter prefers understatement (long shots presentation) to showing blood.

Another news editor answered a question about the horror pictures of the Vietnam war by saying, "Every war has its image. For example, Biafra's image is hungry children, swollen corpses. The image is created by correspondents at the spot, but it may be edited in different ways." In this view, the role of presentation in shaping the images of news events in peopple's heads cannot be ignored.

The coverage of the war in Israel and elsewhere seems to be an illustrative case study. Says one news editor, "In the U.S., the majority of television people are doves. Therefore the share of violence in the coverage is very big." Adds the military reporter, "The basic rule of American television is to show everything, while ours is to show the facts, providing they do not harm morale and security." On the other hand, one producer says, "The glorification of the Army is more dangerous than the presentation of sheer violence." A number of news editors and reporters explain the difference between Israel and the U.S. in terms of social considerations along with security censorship; they mention the fact that Israel is a "state with a message" which has something new to offer and lives in peculiar circumstances. As such, it is expected to live in constant agitation. This agitation is not, however, expressed by internal violence—although there are potential sources, such as the local version of the Black Panthers.

Israel is a "family state," in which, due to its small size and particular composition of the population, "everyone knows everyone." Therefore it would be much too shocking to present on air faces and names of soldiers killed in action before the family is advised. The absence of blood-thirstiness explains the fact that news coverage should not include pictures of corpses or killed men—Jews or Arabs. The military reporter cut out scenes of corpses of dead Arab saboteurs being loaded onto a truck because the cameraman used closeups, despite instructions to the contrary. A scene showing the wounds of an Israeli soldier in closeup was also cut out.

Concerning formal or "make-believe" violence, the deputy chairman of the Authority points out at least one of its dangerous facets; the vulgar attitude towards serious matters. For example, a child views the British thriller *Department S* as a story. On the other hand, *The Saint* is more dangerous, in the opinion of the deputy chairman, because it involves moral values, presented in a false and distorted way.

The head of Hebrew program distinguishes among several degrees of violence from fighting to brutal sequences. In his view, brutality should not be shown and should be looked for very carefully. One of the reasons is connected with scheduling. It is his opinion that "at 2 a.m. we could allow ourselves to be less strict." He mentions one episode of *Arrest and Trial*, in which a boy commits murder, which was not allowed to be broadcast because the episode did not include any "artistic truth" worthwhile to be shown.

The catalytic effect of violence on television. Producers, news editors, and the IBA spokesman we interviewed do not believe that violence on television is necessarily a stimulus to actual use of violence in society. One producer goes so far as to delcare that he believes presentation of violence on television influences towards antiviolence. The general consensus is around the opinion that the translation of television violence into real-life violence depends on the treatment given to the subject and on the context. The spokesman and the producer think that the influence is selective. The spokesman said that the healthy personality will not be influenced, while the unstable personality might be upset by the visual stimulus.

Formal considerations and standards

If formal considerations are defined as actual tools representing attitudes and if personal standards are institutionalized personal considerations, then it seems that, while the Israel Television staff has plenty of considerations (which, necessarily, come up as ways to solve daily problems), these have not yet crystalized into stable personal or group norms. One of the producers said that this is one of the distinctions between television in Israel and abroad, obviously because of the short time Israel Television has been broadcasting and because of the even shorter professional biography of its staff.

Therefore a list was compiled of the most outstanding considerations, as expressed by the staff. In addition, several items and stories which were disqualified or included in programs by the reporters, news editors, and producers themselves were mentioned. These are to be regarded as possible indices to what may or may not become professional standards.

As this section is meant to be a partial summary, the list includes material already mentioned in the course of the description.

a) *List of considerations recommended by the news and programs staffs as useful and desirable.*

　1) *Violence and/or sex should be presented whenever the subject exists significantly and is of public interest.*

2) *Violence and/or sex contents should be presented whenever integral and functional to the item or story or program. Violence and sex are legitimate as long as they express the artistic truth.*

3) *The manner of presentation* or treatment of violence and/or sex is as important as the content *per se.*

4) Professional and ethical standards, including the rational-moral aspects (always opposed to sensationalism) should guide the presentation of violence/sex.

5) The amount of violence and sex should be proportional to the rest of the content in the item/story/program.

6) Violence and sex should be presented in proper perspective. The news editor must be aware of the possible implications resulting from overemphasis of violent items.

7) Distinctions should be made between violence and horror/brutality; between actual (or documentary) and fictional (or feature) violence/sex; and between moral and immoral values. The viewer should be kept informed regarding the factual/non-factual character of the program.

8) The presentation of violence/sex should take into consideration the following facts: a) Television is a public organization, serving the different facets and scales of values in a "state with a message," a "family state," and one with a "Jewish mentality."

   b) Television is an "open medium", especially in the family context.

   c) Television should not harm the morale of the army and the civil population, from the security point of view, but it should also refrain from exaggerated glorification of military aspects.

b) *Cases in which a sequence, an item, or a story was disqualified by reporters, news editors, or producers.* Examples of sequences which were disqualified by news editors are:

1) In Tel Aviv Central Bus Station, after hand grenades were thrown by Arab terrorists. Among the crowd searching for Arabs, a watermelon trader threatens Arab with long knife, without leaving room for any misunderstanding as to his intentions. *Reason for cutting:* too much violence.

2) Executions in Africa. Same reason.

3) Entire item on cosmetics course in woman's prison, for prisoners who are prostitutes, disqualified by news editor because of vulgarity in reporter's treatment of the subject.

4) Sequence of modern theatre item in which girl is seen masturbating was disqualified by news editor on the grounds of being disfunctional to the item and possibly hurting feelings of part of the audience

5) Sequence of "Marat Sade" ommitted, after consultation, from program on theatre because the story could be told by the participants, without showing actual scenes.

6) Entire subject of narcotics was abandoned by producer of *Boom-erang* (panel discussion show), although the head of Hebrew Programs wanted the subject to be included. *Reason:* the producer thought about the suggestive effect of television. In his opinion, since the program was a panel discussion, the producer had to invite one or two participants who support the use of narcotics. The producer was anxious about the possibility that these supporters might convince even ten persons in the audience to use narcotics and that, as a result, even a single viewer could commit some sort of violence against himself or against others.

7) Italian full-feature films, acquired as part of a package deal, were disqualified by the head of Hebrew Programmes because of presentation of sex that was not considered integral and organic to plots. He was anxious about hurting people's feelings.

c) *Cases in which violent or sexual sequences were broadcast*

1) *Boomerang* on sexual behavior included film interviews with two homosexuals who told their stories and with a girl who declared she liked sex for its own sake. *Reason:* the producer declared that, as long as these sequences served as illustrations for the discussion, he was entitled to broadcast them. In a pure documentary he would not have included these sequences.

2) In the same program, on prostitution, a sequence of a man beating a prostitute was included for the same reason.

3) Series like *Bonanza, Gunsmoke, Mission: Impossible, The Prisoner, The Saint, Department S,* etc., were approved by the head of Hebrew Programs.

4) The news editor decided to include a closeup showing a Turkish soldier hitting a demonstrator with a club right on his head. *Reason:* consideration of integrality and "organity" of sequence to entire story. Here the "message" is the relationship between the Army and the Left, in which the use of power is a clear feature. The events of 1968 in France are another example of including violent scenes for their authenticity.

Internal control mechanisms

Formal directives and regulations. This mechanism exists only regarding the most problematic cases (which violence and sex, as mentioned, usually are not). Even in these cases, directives are usually issued only after the producer or reporter asks for them. This fact may be explained by the professional staff's general knowledge of the expectations of them by the audience and the Authority institutions, such as the Managing Committee and the director general. When a producer or reporter has the feeling he is "going too far", he asks for advice. The majority of the interviewees did not remember many such cases, but they did remember cases of consultation with their superiors. One news editor recalled that he disqualified the sequence on the Central Bus Station after consultating the Director of Television. The head of Hebrew Programs said that written directives or regulations are ineffective and meaningless and that there are always ways of avoiding them. The deputy chairman of the Authority said the Managing Committee is unable to issue directives on the grounds that the professional staff's responsibility is indivisible. This points out again the importance of the mechanisms of selection and socialization (or conditioning) of the staff. However, formal directives exist in a more clear shape in at least two areas: the military and the legal.

The military aspect is described below in the discussion of censorship. Regarding legal controls, there are cases in which instructions were issued by the director general to have material examined by the Authority's legal adviser, and then, in the light of his recommendations, to cut out various sequences or scenes. The most illustrative such case was a documentary on juvenile delinquency, broadcast as background for a panel discussion. Since the subject is rather problematic, the producers were instructed to show the film to the legal adviser, who recommended disqualifying scenes where the faces of delinquents appear in such a manner as to permit their identification and scenes showing the use and trade of narcotics—the former in order to avoid "self-incrimination" on the part of the photographed delinquents, and the latter in order to avoid the producer's breaking the law against possession of narcotics which obliges any knowledge or information to be reported to the police. After serious arguments a "compromise" was reached by the director general, the legal adviser, and the producers; faces were blackened in one sequence and parts of the material were omitted.

Internal pressure and criticism. There are two major quasi-informal tools. Insofar as violence and sex are concerned, the general consensus is that preproduction or pretransmission pressures do not exist and have never been employed. Concerning political matters, however, there seems to be some disagreement among the professional staff. It is worthwhile to examine several cases from the "methodological" point of view. One news editor said "Pressure from within does not exist at present and was never used in the past." He remembered a demonstration at the Holy Sepulchre Church concerning the status of Jerusalem, which he decided not to cover. After this decision he received a telephone call on behalf of the minister in charge of the Broadcasting Authority Law, asking the news department not to cover the event. And even then, says the editor, it was not a dictate but only a request. . . .In addition to the support given by this example to the importance of the socialization element, it suggests one of the methods of pressure used by outside factors, in this case the Government.

The opinion of another producer, joined by the Hebrew Programs director, may suggest that the news editor quoted above, is missing the point. The producer's opinion was that pressures *do* exist and are expressed quite clearly concerning matters of high sensitivity such as politics, religion, and so on: "In these matters there is a great deal of dictation and interference on the part of the Managing Committee and the director general and his staff, including the controller of Television. In these cases their considerations are determined by factors alien to the strict artistic or documentary value of the program." This producer said technical methods of pressure are exerted directly, often without passing all the levels down the hierarchy. The Controller may talk directly to a producer, without talking to the intermediate level — the director of Programs. "Actually," the producer says, "it depends on who he meets first." The Controller's sensitivity is in the following direction and order of importance: Managing Committee, Parliament, government, press. These elements will be discussed later.

Post factum criticism applies to violence and sex to a higher degree and serves as a rather effective mechanism. One producer declared categorically that while prior censorship in the station is rather weak, *post factum* criticism may be so powerful that he, personally, prefers to compromise. The same producer described one of his experiences: "I was producing a program about marriage. Yemenite marriage ritual includes the slaughter of a cow, a very shocking scene. The upper levels, and even my production assistant and the film editor exerted strong pressure to omit this scene. I refused, firstly, because it was an organic part of the story, and, secondly, to show that I would not accept any pressure. The scene was broadcast. Very sharp reactions were expressed from 'up there,' though indirectly, including the director general."

An independent account of the same story by the head of Hebrew Programs helps to clarify the matter: "Although the scene included 'documentary truth,' it shocked many viewers. Should we show a cow's slaughter? Certainly not in the way it was represented. However, the main complaint was related to the early hour at which the program was broadcast, so that children could witness this horrible scene."

A news editor included in his last weekly news magazine for 1970 a picture of a hungry child in Biafra accompanied by the following comment: "Apparently, this boy will not see the year 1971." The reaction: he was told that the scene was exaggerated, especially because the magazine was broadcast on Sabbath's eve. The editor's conclusion is that the prevailing approach is to spare the viewers' feelings regarding violence and horror.

Post factum criticism functions also as a tool for the Managing Committee. Actually, it seems to be its major means of control. The deputy chairman of the Authority declared that the Committee prefers to criticize rather than to exercise direct control. Usually criticism is expressed through the work of the various subcommittees (drama, music, entertainment, etc.), on which members of the Managing

Committee function as presidents. The Committee as a whole discusses, especially, local production. Criticism is also expressed in other ways; for example, the Managing Committee expressed its disatisfaction with programs acquired abroad and sent one member to Europe together with the head of Hebrew Programs in order to select better material.

External control mechanisms

Censorship. Television in Israel is connected with two types of censorship. On the security level it is subject (as are the other media) to military censorship and to the Army spokesman's regulations. On the moral and aesthetic level there exists an agreement with the Board of Criticism of Films and Plays. The former concerns itself almost only with news material (with certain exceptions), while the latter concerns itself only with programs and features.

The military reporter said there are no clear regulations as part of the military censorship. All material that seems to be sensitive is shown to the censors, who may approve or disapprove almost arbitrarily, according to their own standards. The same applies to the Army spokesman. However, there exists a wide range of agreement between censorship and television staff. The following exerpts from our interviews illustrate this point.

1) Regarding a scene where a soldier tells how an Arab saboteur was killed, the Army spokesman said that the viewer could conclude that the saboteur was defenseless while being shot at by the soldiers. The scene was not broadcast.

2) Parts of scenes photographed during a raid into Syria were omitted by the Military Censorship on the grounds of exposing military secrets.

3) News editors' and reporters' opinions: "If the Army spokesman does not permit one to show everything, one should show whatever is permitted without hurting authenticity." "There exists a greater amount of agreement with the censors regarding security matters where the rule of not showing anything that may be considered as informing the enemy is rather clear. However, regarding morale, the standards are far more ambiguous." Concerning the occupied territories, a newsman said, "Objectively, our occupation regime is rather liberal and enlightened, thus I have no problems in reporting what happens there."

In one case Security Censorship employed its authority in a rather surprising way. An interview with David Ben-Gurion was prepared on film to illustrate a panel discussion about "Nazi hunters." For the first time since the event, Ben Gurion declared in the interview that the Israeli Security Agency captured Adolph Eichmann in Argentina. The censor did not approve and the scene was omitted from the interview. (Later in the same week the same fact was disclosed both in the press and over the radio.)

As far as aesthetic and moral censorship is involved, television enjoys more freedom. As far as film and plays are concerned, this type of censorship is performed by the Board of Criticism of Film and Plays, according to a Law approved by Parliament and executed under the responsibility of the Ministry of Interior Affairs. Since the establishment of television there have been several attempts to include its broadcasts within the range of the Board. But the Authority has tried to keep its freedom. After discussions at various levels, the present situation is that the Authority is not subject to the Board, but they work in cooperation. This means: a) the Board has informed the Authority of all films limited or forbidden; b) a special Commission was appointed by the Authority to work out these matters; its members are the legal adviser, the controller of Television and the director general or his representative; c) special attention is given to the differences between television broadcasting and the specific field of the Board (theatrical presentations).

For example, the Board does not take into consideration the broadcasting hours. Thus, films approved by the Board are not always approved by the Commission. On the other hand, the Board's disapproval of films in the past does not always apply to the present, due to criteria which have become obsolete. In these cases the Commission may approve. This explains the fact that the Commission, since its appointment six months ago, has met only once and discussed working criteria. It has not yet dealt with any concrete cases.

Pressure groups. Obviously a number of pressure groups and coalitions of interest try to influence programming policy. However, these groups are not greatly concerned about violence and sex, preferring more sensitive targets like political and ideological content. Political parties — including the religious establishment—do have a quite powerful influence through their representatives in the Authority Plenum and Managing Committee. Other types of pressure include letters and telephone calls, lobbying through various channels, and complaints. Following is an attempt to classify groups and types of pressure and several examples, concerning sex and violence:

Type of Group	Complaint	Type of Pressure
Histadrut (Confederation of Trade Unions)	Insufficient and one-sided exposure	Threat of establishing own station; lobbying through political parties and Parliament.

Religious groups and parties	Insufficient and inaccurate exposure	Through representatives in Authority institutions, party newspapers, political parties, government and Parliament, letters from audience.
Big industry and business	One-sided exposure in interviewing "Israeli Ralph Nader."	Telephone calls, letters. (Solution: "Equal Time.")
Smaller elite groups (kibbutzim, intellectuals)	Low program quality.	Through representatives in different institutions, articles and letters in press, personal connections.
Professional critics		Media, particularly press. (Retroactive pressure)
Audience	Quality of programs, technical problems (subtitling, etc.).	Letters, telephone calls, press.

1) *Bonanza* - According to the Authority Spokesman, when this series was broadcast, religious groups wrote letters, called by phone and acted through the religious members of Parliament, Managing Committee, etc. Transmission of the series was completed according to seasonal schedule.

2) *Mission Impossible* - After this series was taken off the air, hundreds (or even thousands) of letters addressed to the Authority directly or through the Press, were sent including petitions, such as that of the electricity workers, to continue broadcasting the series. The series is still off the air. Additional examples of the same type are connected with "The Prisoner", "Gunsmoke", etc.

The interviewees could not remember any example of pressure group activity regarding sex.

THE SPECIAL PROBLEMS OF PROGRAMMING FOR ARABIC-SPEAKING AUDIENCES: INTERVIEW WITH SALIM FATTAL, DIRECTOR OF THE ARAB PROGRAMS DEPARTMENT

Q. "What is your criterion of violence?"

A. "It is difficult to answer this question, as it is to define that violence is. There are different kinds of violence: suicide, murder on romantic grounds or in punishment of immorality, blood-feuds. One can say that the 75 films that were broadcast contained all in all very few violent incidents of the above-mentioned types."

Q. "Violence in purchased Arab films—do you think it is intended to reflect the Arab mentality or to gratify some need in the spectators?"

A. "The Arabs have a great potential for violence. In the fields of morality and sex, for example, a wanton woman, blood-feuds, can be causes for murder. Even in modern times there have been manifestations of barbarity in hangings, in the treatment of war prisoners. There are manifestations of violence in everyday life —the Jordanian Army's harsh and totally inconsiderate treatment of terrorists and civilians suspected of collaboration with the saboteurs. The sense of the value of human life as an end in itself is little developed—at least among the Arab leaders. As far as moral values go, an Arab is capable of priding himself on having murdered his own sister for her wantonness.

This potential for violent outbursts finds actual expression in practice, too. The interesting paradox lies in the fact that even though one expects to find this potential for violence reflected in Arab works of art, evidence of it is scanty. In Egyptian movies, for example, the percentage of violence is low. There is a tendency towards refinement. These films are mostly comedies, dealing with social affairs. There are the villain, the drug gangs, shootings. But my impression is that violence in the arts stands in no proportion to the violence in reality."

Q. "What are the most common expressions of violence in an Arab film?"

A. "There is violence in a nonextreme and mollified form, as in
    quarrels, etc., but this too not to a considerable degree. Most
    plots are built on comedy and romance."

Q. "Why do you refrain from presenting violent films?"

A. "Out of educational considerations. The woman in charge of the
    films is instructed to bring to me for examination every movie
    which contains a murder incident. I tend to let implicit violence
    pass by. The decisive factor lies in the question, "Is there a mor-
    al?" If there is one, then even a violent act within the plot would
    not present such a grave problem and there would be no need to
    censor it. But whenever a murder is presented for its own sake,
    there is no sense in showing it even if it be in the most didactic of
    films. The imported series are nonviolent, perhaps intentionally
    so. There have been two cases of scenes censored out for exces-
    sive violence."

Q. "Can you give us an example of a series rejected as a whole for
    violence in great degrees or quantities?"

A. "Yes, the *Phil Silver's Show*."

Q. "When you reject something, do you weigh the implications re-
    garding the Arab viewer?"

A. "Certainly, because I believe our broadcasts do serve to some
    end."

Q. "What about actual events — for example, bodies of saboteurs
    killed in action?

A. "There is very little of that, generally speaking. We used to show
    terrorists' corpses. But I do not think it is necessary (the news
    department does not come under my jurisdiction). A dead body
    does not scare anybody off; rather, it turns the terrorist into a
    martyr. Perhaps the only thing that could deter a terrorist would
    be a death sentence."

Q. "Do you think one ought to show demonstrations of protest,
    etc., by Jewish groups?"

A. "Yes, certainly. Because that is reality."

Q. "What about the fear of mistaken interpretations?"

A. "The decisive point is authenticity. Likewise, it is important how
    you present the matter. The issue is related to the question of
    majorities and minorities. A minority group which appears on
    television grows objectively much larger, for the whole country
    watches it and learns its opinions. Here too, it is our duty to pre-
    sent reality, but this must be done in a way which would allay
    violence. One does not have to show blood and wounds."

On the subject of sex, Mr. Fattal offered some background information:

"The whole subject is considered almost taboo in the Arab sector,
the reason for this lying in the Arabs' ethnic and traditional background. The guarding of women's chastity is practically a religious

commandment. This attitude prevails among the intelligentsia as well. Once violence does break out in defence of a family's honour — it is extreme.

"This situation bears still another implication: Sexual perversion, where it is manifest, is also extreme, amounting to prostitution in the case of women, and homosexuality in men.

"Lately, however, there has been a change in Arab society born from the contact with the outside world, and which can be discerned in a) the process of westernization, resulting from immigration; b) external factors which penetrate the Arab world, including mixed marriages; c) the intellectual awakening — it is no longer becoming for an intellectual to return to tradition.

"There is a conflict between the old and the new, but on the whole, the progressive intelligentsia has the lead. But despite the change, orthodoxy on the subject of sex still prevails, especially when it comes to what is 'mine, 'in my home.' One example is the case of an educated Arab who asked a television photographer to photograph his wife only from her waist up.

"In this Israeli Arab society, there is a difference between urban and rural centers, whereas in the ouccpied territories there has been no significant change in this field during the last three years, not even in Jerusalem. Here, of course, one must distinguish between the Moslem and Christian Arabs, the latter being much more liberal."

Q. "How does this mentality influence television programs?"

A. "In the Arab long-feature films, 95 per cent of which are produced and directed in Egypt, there is the common occurrence of sexual stimulation through the appearance in most films of a belly-dancer — often very scantily clad and erotic in her movements. But one should keep in mind that for the Arab, the belly-dancer is identified more closely with the whore than with art. The attitude towards the whole subject is one of depreciation (which is why, in my opinion, the arts of women's singing and dancing have not developed among the Arabs).

Regarding the film industry: The themes are rather commonplace: love, longing, all that we call "kitsch." It is difficult to run a film industry feeding upon such hackneyed motifs all the time. Therefore, there is need for occasional "blood transfusions," which take the form of: a) the long songs — a breathing space for stretching out the film; b) the belly-dances. These last also offer a form of relief, since all other forms of daring sexual expression would not be acceptable. It is interesting to note that despite all this, pornographic films intended for men only and shown in clubs and in private parties are extremely welcome."

Q. "What about implicit sex in films?"

A. "Straightforward sex, in the form of kissing, bedroom scenes, etc., is still very modest in the Arab movie. In the Saudi-Arabian television, for example, every scene which includes a kiss is drastically and roughly censored out. Liberalization, to the extent that it does exist, is still extremely 'polite.'

Q. "In summary, do we or do we not have a censorship over sex in films?"

A. "No, there is no need for it, the reasoning being that if these films are allowed in Egypt, we can certainly show them here."

Q. "What about programs produced here?"

A. "All the producers are aware of the problem and familiar with it. Actually, in all our programs there is no place for sex for its own sake. In *For the Family*, questions of sex do not arise directly. Instead, the program deals with subjects that contain criticism of the present state of affairs—For instance, a dramatized version of a song about a girl who rebels against tradition.

Another program, *This Is Your Problem*, has been dealing with topics such as birth control, 'the adjustment of the Arab girl to the new fashions,' and 'mixed marriages.' In every case, the problem is treated by giving expression to a variety of opinions and leaving the conclusions to the audience."

Q. "Have you had responses from the viewers?"

A. "Very few. There are hardly any. It has to do with the distrust of the viewing public, particularly in the occupied territories, for anything connected with the Israeli establishment. In the occupied territories such a response might be taken as a sign of cooperation."

Q. "What about responses to the children's programs?"

A. Here the situation is different. We receive plenty of responses and we encourage them, since they help in forming fruitful internal criticism and since this is our future audience. We have introduced the prize method to measure the extent of our audience, and the method works very well."

Q. "Is there a critical review of these programs in the Arab press?"

A. "In the local Arab press — very little. The reviews are periodical, once a month. But when they do appear, they are often extremely critical and based on incorrect information. On the other hand, there is an informative coverage of the programs to be broadcasted. This goes particularly for "El-Anba." "El-Kuds" boycotts the television completely.

On the other hand, reviews are published in the Jordanian, Egyptian, and Lebanese press. Their criticism is severe, expressing their fear that the Israeli television as an organ of Israeli propaganda penetrates Arab homes and fulfills its function through children's programs, documentaries, information, and entertainment, such as the Friday movie (which is more popular than any other program on Jordanian television that day). The

Jordanians are trying to combat the influence of our broadcast of Arab movies by broadcasting a similar feature-film about two hours before our broadcast, or by offering thrillers or popular sports programs (with little success), and further by forbidding the transfer of 16 mm films to the West Bank and by maintaining strict supervision over the transfer of 35 mm films. The Arab League itself became involved in the struggle to prevent the broadcasting of Arab movies on Israeli television."

Q. "What is the desirable approach in the locally prdouced programs? Is it to advance certain ends or to present both sides of the coin?"

A. "I believe that using the medium for guidance is not the right policy. There is no place for an editorial on television. There is no room for preaching even on series like *For the Family*. There is room for commentary, which should be attributed to an expert or to an authorized commentator."

Q. "Have there been cases of sex scenes which were found to be to daring and were therefore cut out?"

A. "There have been no such cases."

Q. "Are you consulted personally regarding these subjects?"

A. "Yes. For example, in the science program, a dancer was used to demonstrate the color scale. There came a reaction from above calling it too daring, but I did not find the sequence too bold and it was broadcast."

Q. "Have there been features that were presented on the Hebrew television program which would not have shown on the Arab program?"

A. "Yes. For example, verbal sex (as in the film about the Academy Awards, which featured scenes from the winning movies)."

Q. "What are your considerations in selecting the purchased programs (folklore, entertainment series, *Tonight in Person*)?"

A. "The first thing I have to consider is the time at my disposal — its length, the hour of the day. For example, 18.30 is a good hour for programs intended for the whole family. Secondly, the quality of the series. I put special emphasis on programs for children because they constitute the basis of our future audience. In all the imported series, the sex element occupies only a minor place."

Q. "How do you differentiate between daring and nondaring sex? For instance, is a ballet dancer considered to be sex?"

A. "It is very difficult to define the borderline. We have no standing orders to uphold modesty, nor to choose special angles in photographing. But since one must define a borderline, our limit is — nudity."

Q. "Aren't you afraid that in this way you are reinforcing the impression already prevalent in parts of the Arab population to the effect that 'all of Israel is nothing but a big whorehouse'?"

A. "Television has not created this image, nor has it contributed anything to corroborate it. I am not bothered on this account."

Q. "Have you rejected any imported series for containing too much sex?"

A. "In France I was shown documentary series which included sequences in the nude. I made it clear to the distributor that if I ever broadcast the series in Israel, I would leave out the nude scenes. There have been separate programs about a primitive African tribe whose women walk around naked. Out of the total 20 minutes of this feature, there were six or seven shots of this kind, and I felt that they should not be shown here."

PRODUCTION/DISTRIBUTION SOURCES OF PROGRAMS

Table 1 reports on the source of program materials for the winter season 1970/71, in the third year of the existence of Israel Television. It makes clear that more than half of all programming time is purchased abroad and that contracting to local producers outside the station represents about 15 per cent of all local production. It is of some interest to note that the *relative* proportion of home-produced programs in "Arabic" is greater than that in "Hebrew."[4] However, since time allotted to Hebrew broadcasting is three times that allotted to Arabic broadcasting, the *absolute* production figures are not much different.

Table 1: Division of broadcast time by intended audience and source of production—Winter 1970-71.

Type	Minutes per month		Percent per month		Minutes per month	Percent per month
	Hebrew	Arabic	Hebrew	Arabic	Total	
Produced at station	1093	480	22.6	42.8	1573	32.7
Acquired locally	350	-	9.2	-	350	7.2
Acquired abroad	2245	640	68.2	57.2	2885	60.1
Total	3688	1120	100.0	100.0	4805	100.0

Source   Television Programming 1971-72, draft submitted to the IBA Managing Committee and Plenum, January 1971.

AUDIENCE FIGURES

The sharp increase in ownership of receivers began after 1967, when Israeli Television started transmitting. In 1969, about 20 percent of families had receivers; in 1970, about 50 percent. The total number of receivers is estimated at 410,000.

The modal number of daily viewing hours (for about 60 percent of the total number of viewers) is between two and three.

The size of audiences and their attitudes toward different types of programs

When we examine the size of the audience and its attitude toward different programs we must take into account the facts that (1) the station has been broadcasting four hours daily—three hours in Hebrew and one hour in Arabic, and (2) the population of the different surveys conducted in the four biggest cities has usually been Jewish and over 14 years of age. (This limitation has special relevance for considering viewing of Arabic programs and children's programs: the data cover only Arabic-speaking Jews and persons over 14.)

Within these limitations, we can present a summary of findings from recent surveys relating to popularity (frequency of viewing) of different programs. Survey subjects responded to three questions: "Do you usually watch this program?" "How interesting do you find this program?" "Would you like to see more or fewer programs of this type?"

Children's programs (6-6:30 p.m.) cartoons are the most popular programs within this category, followed by *Flipper*. Around half the audience expressed interest in these programs, while some 30 percent expressed interest in locally produced children's magazine programs (*Six, Headlines and Margins*, sports).

Mixed-age programs (7:30-8 p.m.). The most popular programs are *Family Affair* (84.3 percent) and *Bewitched* (75.3 percent). These programs are also considered the most interesting, followed by *The Count of Monte Cristo* (50 percent), the local quiz program, and *Sound and Movement* (around 35 percent). The program considered least interesting is *Shelf of Books*. (19.1 percent).

"Arabic" programs (6:30-7:30 p.m.). The most popular program is *Music and Song* (some 60 percent). Considering that a large number of viewers of this type of program do not understand the language, it is obvious that the *Full Feature Film* (50 percent), *Hollywood and the Stars* (48 percent), and other movies are rather popular. Arabic talk shows are less popular. Exceptions to this are *Sami and Sussu* (with Hebrew subtitles, 50 percent) and *For the Family* (housekeeping magazine program, 38 percent).

"Hebrew" programs (8:20-10 or 11 p.m.). Four programs are most popular: *Israel Entertainment* (87 percent), *Full Feature Films* (86 percent), *The News Magazine* (84 percent), and *Entertainment from Abroad* (81 percent).

News (8-8:20 a.m., 10-10:05 p.m.). The Hebrew major daily edition at 8 a.m. is the most popular program on Israeli Television (93.6 percent of all viewers).

Negative attitudes toward different programs are expressed by criticism, rather than by not viewing the programs. Thus, one-third of the viewers of *The Match of the Week* and *The Prisoner*, and one-fourth of the viewers of *Bewitched*, are not interested in the shows. The highest ratio of "interested" viewers to total viewers is for the weekly *News Magazine*.

It should be noted that traditional programs are rather popular (up to 75 percent). Action programs, such as *Run for Your Life* or *The Storefront Lawyers*, are popular and considered interesting as well.

Table 2 shows the distribution of viewer attitudes according to level of education.

Table 2: Attitudes toward different types of programs, according to education (years in school)

Years at school	Would like				Total
	More progs. of this type	Less progs. of this type	Same amount of progs. of this type	Does not know this type of prog.	
A. "Western" (such as *Bonanza, Gunsmoke* **and Law (such as** *Arrest & Trial***)**					
0	46.0%	20.0%	33.0%	1.0%	100% (76)
1 - 4	65.0%	7.0%	26.0%	1.0%	99% (69)
5 - 8	52.0%	16.0%	31.0%	1.0%	100% (393)
9 - 10	45.0%	17.0%	36.0%	1.0%	99% (248)
11 - 12	38.0%	24.0%	37.0%	1.0%	100% (336)
12 + (no degree)	28.0%	35.0%	35.0%	2.0%	100% (130)
12 + (with degree)	25.0%	39.0%	33.0%	3.0%	100% (61)
All	44.0%	21.0%	34.0%	1.0%	100%(1313)
B. Mission Impossible					
0	52.0%	16.0%	32.0%	0	100% (73)
1 - 4	68.0%	13.0%	18.0%	1.0%	100% (52)
5 - 8	50.0%	21.0%	28.0%	0	99% (402)
9 - 10	40.0%	17.0%	43.0%	0	100% (249)
11 - 12	34.0%	23.0%	42.0%	0	199% (349)
12 + (no degree)	17.0%	35.0%	46.0%	2.0%	100% (125)
12 + (with degree)	18.0%	39.0%	42.0%	2.0%	101% (62)
All	40.0%	22.0%	37.0%	1.0%	100%(1313)
C. Documentaries					
0	33.0%	19.0%	48.0%	0	100% (75)
1 - 4	31.0%	30.0%	39.0%	0	100% (67)
5 - 8	39.0%	21.0%	40.0%	1.0%	101% (396)
9 0 10	41.0%	16.0%	43.0%	0	100% (258)
11 - 12	43.0%	19.0%	38.0%	0	100% (367)
12 + (no degree)	56.0%	11.0%	32.0%	2.0%	101% (133)
12 + (with degree)	64.0%	14.0%	20.0%	2.0%	100% (64)
All	42.0%	18.0%	39.0%	0	99%(1360)

D. Serious talk shows or panel discussions (such as *Boomerang, Focus*)

0	23.0%	34.0%	42.0%	2.0%	101% (65)
1 - 4	28.0%	34.0%	36.0%	2.0%	100% (64)
5 - 8	33.0%	28.0%	37.0%	2.0%	100% (389)
9 - 10	39.0%	20.0%	40.0%	0	99% (247)
11 - 12	48.0%	14.0%	38.0%	0	100% (364)
12 + (no degree)	55.0%	11.0%	33.0%	2.0%	101% (132)
12 + (with degree)	62.0%	9.0%	29.0%	0	100% (65)
All	41.0%	21.0%	37.0%	1.0%	100%(1326)

E. Full feature films

0	48.6%	17.0%	35.0%	0	100% (83)
1 - 4	63.0%	8.0%	29.0%	0	100% (72)
5 - 8	57.0%	13.0%	30.0%	1.0%	101% (423)
9 - 10	48.0%	14.0%	38.0%	0	100% (261)
11 - 12	51.0%	14.0%	34.0%	0	99% (366)
12 + (no degree)	43.0%	17.0%	39.0%	1.0%	100% (127)
12 + (with degree)	58.0%	8.0%	34.0%	0	100% (65)
All	52.0%	14.0%	34.0%	0	100%(1397)

F. Israeli entertainment and personality shows

0	70.0%	55.0%	23.0%	2.0%	100% (83)
1 - 4	62.0%	10.0%	26.0%	1.0%	99% (68)
5 - 8	57.0%	13.0%	30.0%	0	100% (402)
9 - 10	56.0%	10.0%	34.0%	1.0%	101% (252)
11 - 12	51.0%	13.0%	30.0%	0	100% (354)
12 + (no degree)	39.0%	9.0%	50.0%	2.0%	100% (127)
12 + (with degree)	33.0%	21.0%	44.0%	2.0%	100% (57)
All	53.0%	12.0%	34.0%	1.0%	100%(1345)

G. Entertainment from abroad

0	45.0%	18.0%	38.0%	0	101% (85)
0 - 4	60.0%	16.0%	24.0%	0	100% (75)
5 - 8	60.0%	11.0%	29.0%	0	100% (426)
9 - 10	59.0%	13.0%	27.0%	0	99% (262)
11 - 12	53.0%	14.0%	33.0%	0	100% (374)
12 + (no degree)	44.0%	23.0%	33.0%	1.0%	101% (131)
12 + (with degree)	38.0%	22.0%	40.0%	0	100% (65)
All	55.0%	14.0%	31.0%	0	100%(1418)

Source: *The Continuing Survey,* 1969, of the Communication Institute of
the Hebrew University and the Israel Institute of Applied Social Research,
Jerusalem. Trimestral studies of a representative sample (N 1500) of the
adult Jewish population in Jerusalem, Tel Aviv, Haifa, and Beer-Sheva.

In general, the groups of lower education (up to nine or ten years) would like to have more "action" and "thriller" programs, like *Mission: Impossible,* while more educated viewers would like the same amount now offered or less.

Groups of higher education, especially university graduates, would like to see more talk shows, panel discussions, and documentaries, while the other groups are satisfied with the present amounts.

Both groups would like to see more feature films and entertainment from abroad. Still, it should be noted that there is a drop in the popularity of these programs among the better-educated. The majority of secondary school graduates prefer the same amount or less.

Since television in Israel is very new, it is interesting to see how people's expectations of the medium change with increased exposure to it and to the fare it provides. Note (Table 3) the decline in the percentage naming "culture" as their primary expectation of television: though a minority to begin with, the culture-seekers declined from 24 to 12 percent of the population in a little over a year.

Table 3: "What do you especially expect from television: entertainment, culture and education, current information?"

	February 1968	April 1968	October 1969	January 1970
Entertainment	35%	47%	40%	33%
Culture	24%	17%	17%	12%
Information	41%	36%	43%	55%
	100%	100%	100%	100%

Nevertheless, there is still not complete acceptance of the television menu as offered. Although the proportion of imported programs has increased over time, there is still a clear preference—among those viewers who have preferences—for home-produced programs at the expense of programs acquired abroad (see Table 4). This preference is *not* reflected, however, in actual viewing or in expressed interest in domestic *vs.* imported programs.

Table 4: Attitudes toward local and imported programs

Too many imported and not enough local programs	33%
Too many local and not enough imported programs	15%
The present amount of local and imported programs is all right	28%
Don't know	24%
	100%

Source: The Continuing Survey

CONTENT ANALYSIS

Programs broadcast between May 9 and May 15, 1971 were monitored by five persons and coded according to the BBC questionnaires and

codes (P368 TV Study), many of whose categories are broadly comparable to the Gerbner study. A consensus of three of the five coders was
used as a criterion. Accordingly, the data were classified into two categories:

1. *"Technical data"* (for entire programs, including the *target audience* (children, mixed age, adults (Hebrew), and adults (Arabic);
   for the *length* of programs; for the *country of origin of production;* and for the *type of program* (series, serials, etc., and western, crime, modern dramatic).

2. "Content data," including the type of the program and the overall amount of violence, as well as details for violent and sexual
   incidents or episodes and for the parties and characters participating in these episodes.

The total number of these programs was 65; they were divided into
types and languages as follows:

	Fiction, drama	Entertainment	News	Informational	Total
Hebrew	8	4	15	16	43
Arabic	1	4	11	6	22
Total	9	8	26	22	65

Since a very small number of violent and sexual incidents or episodes
were included in these programs (52 violent incidents and 20 sexual incidents in all programs; 38 violent incidents in the fiction drama), the data
were processed according to their possibilities, which, due to the small
number of cases, should be regarded only as very general guidelines.

The definitions guiding the analysis were as follows:

Violent incidents. A violent incident is defined as a continuous action
involving the same set of characters in which any act(s) that may cause
physical and/or psychological injury, hurt or death to persons, animals
and property, whether intentional or accidental, actually shown on the
screen, suggested or verbal, take place.

Sexual incidents. A sexual incident is defined as a continuous action,
involving the same set of characters, which includes sexual elements,
actually shown on the screen, suggested or verbal, in which one or more
persons (men, women) take part.

Instigator. The person or people who intentionally *started* the violent
or sexual action, in any violent or sexual incident.

Receiver/Reciprocator. The person who "received" the violence or
sex (the "object"), whether or not he returned it.

Major characters. Characters who play important central parts in the
program and who are on the screen a good deal of the time.

Summary of the data

Generally, the data show a very low amount of violence and sex, as Table 5 shows.

Table 5: Average number of violent and sexual incidents per program
(number of incidents: number of programs)

1. Audience	Violence		Sex
1. Children's programs (6 − 6:30 p.m.)	0.4		0
2. Mixed children-adults (7:30 − 8 p.m.)	0.8		0.2
3. Adults' programs (Arabic 6:30 − 7:30 p.m.)	0.6		0.1
4. Adults' programs (Hebrew 8 − 10 or 11 p.m.)	0.8		0.3
2. Length of program			
1. 15 minutes or less	0.3		0
2. 16 − 30 minutes	0.7		0.2
3. 31 − 45 minutes	0		0
4. 46 − 60 minutes	2.1		1
5. Over 61 minutes	2.5		1.5
6. Total number of programs	0.8		0.3
3. Country of origin of production			
1. Israel	0.4	(o.1 when news not included)	0.09
2. Unites States	1.2		0.7
3. Britain	1.7		0.6
4. Arabic countries	1.0		1
5. Total number of programs	0.8		0.3
4. Type of program (only for fiction drama)			
a) Series, serials, etc.			
1. Television series	5.0		3.0
2. Television serial	2.0		1.0
3. Television play	*		*
4. "Special"	0		0
5. Feature film	4.0		1.6
6. Total number of programs	3.8		0.3
B) Genre			
1. Western	*		*
2. Crime or detective	4.5		2.5
3. Spy or Secret agent	10.0		4.0
4. War film, story	7.0		3.0
5. Modern drama	1.5		1.7
6. Historical drama	2.0		1.0
7. Children's drama	4.0		0
8. Adventure, horror, mystery, science fiction	*		*
9. Total Number of programs	3.8		0.3

* No programs of this type during week of study.

The "technical data" give the following general picture:

1. The Hebrew adult programs are the most violent, followed by children's programs and adult Arabic programs. Children's programs are least violent. In amount of sex, the order is: Hebrew adult, Arabic adult, and mixed-age programs. It should be noted that the violence in adults' programs seems to appear in the form of isolated incidents; the programs as a whole are considered not violent. The same overall judgment applies to programs in which sexual incidents take place. On the other hand, when violence appears in children's programs, it seems to be a central theme. Children's programs do not include any sexual incidents (see Tables 6 and 7).

Table 6: Violence in programs by audience type

	Total no. of programs	No. of programs including at least 1 violent incident	Total no. of violent incidents
Children's programs	14 (21.4%)	4 (21.1%)	6 (11.5%)
Mixed children's-adults	7 (10.7%)	3 (9.1%)	6 (11.5%)
Adults (Arabic)	19 (29.5%)	10 (30.4%)	13 (24.1%)
Adults (Hebrew)	25 (38.4%)	16 (48.4%)	27 (52.0%)
Total	65 (100.0%)	33 (100.0%)	52 (100.0%)

2. Programs over 46 minutes include the largest amount of violent episodes, while programs of 15 minutes and less are the least violent. Between them come the categories of 16-30 and 31-45 minutes. The same order applies to sexual incidents.

Table 7: Sexual incidents in programs by audience type

	Total no. of programs	Number of progs. including at least 1 sexual incident	All sexual incidents
Children's	14 (21.4%)	0	0
Mixed audience	7 (10.7%)	2 (20.0%)	2 (10.0%)
Adults (arabic)	19 (29.5%)	2 (20.0%)	3 (15.0%)
Adults (hebrew)	25 (38.4%)	6 (60.0%)	15 (75.0%)
Total	65 (100.0%)	10 (100.0%)	20 (100.0%)

3. According to the classification by the country of origin of production, American and British programs are the most violent and the most sexual; they far outdistance Arabic and Israeli programs. (see Tables 8 and 9).

4. Television series—especially those dealing with crime, detective stories and espionage stories—are the most violent programs; sex, at least by our definition, does not seem to concentrate in any category. The least violent type of program is the serial, especially historical drama (see Tables 10 and 11).

Table 8: Violence in programs by country of original production

	Including news			News not included		
	Total no. of progs	No. of progs. including at Least 1 violent incident	Total no. of violent incidents	Total no. of progs.	No. of progs. including at least 1 violent incident	Total no. of violent incidents
Israel	41 (63.0%)	26 (48.4%)	20 (38.4%)	21 (46.6%)	2 (10.5%)	4 (11.1%)
U.S.	14 (21.4%)	12 (36.3%)	17 (32.6%)	14 (31.1%)	12 (63.3%)	17 (47.2%)
Britain	8 (12.0%)	4 (12.1%)	14 (26.9%)	8 (17.7%)	4 (21.0%)	14 (38.8%)
Arabic countries	1	(1.8%)	1 (32.1%)	1 (2.1%)	1 (5.2%)	1 (2.9%)
Other countries	1 (1.8%)	0	0	1 (2.3%)	0	0
Total	65 (100.0%)	33 (100.0%)	52 (100.0%)	45 (100.0%)	19 (100.0%)	36 (100.0%)

Table 9: Sexual incidents in programs by country of origin of production

Origin	Total no. of programs	Number of programs including at least 1 sexual incident	Total no. of sexual incidents
Israel	21 (46.6%)	1 (10.0%)	2 (10.0%)
U.S.	14 (13.1%)	6 (60.0%)	11 (55.0%)
Britain	8 (17.7%)	2 (20.0%)	5 (25.0%)
Arabic countries	1 (2.3%)	1 (10.0%)	2 (10.0%)
Other countries	1 (2.3%)	0	0
Total	45 (100.0%)	10 (100.0%)	20 (100.0%)

Table 10: Violence by type of program

	Total no. of programs	No. of progs. including at least 1 violent incident	Total no. of violent incidents
Television series	4	3	20 (52.6%)
Television serial	3	3	6 (15.7%)
Television play	*	*	*
"Special"	*	*	*
Feature film	3	3	12 (31.4%)
Total	10	9	38 (100.0%)

The majority of violent and sexual incidents are presented in a very (or fairly) realistic style and include more "serious" than humorous contents. In regard to violence, fiction programs are more realistic than others, whereas there are no significant differences concerning the amount of seriousness.

The violent and sexual incidents in fictional drama are summarized in Table 12.

Table 11: Sexual incidents by type of program (fiction drama)

	Total no. of programs	No. of progs. including at least 1 violent incident	Total no. of violent incidents
Television series	4 (33.3%)	3 (33.3%)	12 (60.0%)
Television serial	3 (33.3%)	3 (33.3%)	3 (15.0%)
Television play	*	*	*
"Special"	*	*	*
Feature film	3 (33.3%)	3 (33.3%)	5 (25.0%)
Total	10 (99.9%)	9 (99.9%)	20 (100.0%)

* No programs of this type.

Table 12: Description of violent and sexual incidents

12.1: Presentation of violence/sex

	Violence (n=38)	Sex (n=20)
Closeup	20 (52.7%)	6 (30.0%)
From a distance	3 (8.5%)	4 (20.0%)
Strongly implied	13 (33.3%)	9 (45.0%)
Consensus 1 + 2	2 (6.7%)	1 (5.0%)
All incidents	(100.0%)	(100.0%)

12.2 Type

	Violence (n=38)	Sex (n=20)
Physical, intentional	21 (55.2%)	10 (50.0%)
Accidental	3 (8.3%)	3 (15.0%)
Verbal	8 (21.1%)	5 (25.0%)
Threatened, physical	5 (15.4%)	consensus 2+3 2 (10.0%)
All incidents	(100.0%)	(100.0%)

12.3: Was the violence reciprocated?

	Violence (n=38)	Sex (n=20)
Violence one-sided, not reciprocated	26 (66.6%)	0
Violence on both sides, reciprocated	12 (33.3%)	12 (60%)
Unclear	0	8 (40%)
All violent incidents	38 (99.9%)	20 (100%)

12.4: If the violence was physical and intentional, which methods were used? (n=27)

Body	12 (44.0%)
Objects from daily life	1 (4.0%)
Hand guns, pistols, rifles	1 (4.0%)
Military weapons, machine guns, bombs	0
Knife, sword, other stabbing instrument	0
Club, truncheon, rope, chain, other hitting instrument	1 (4.0%)
Torture, traps, poison, other specialized devices	0

Two weapons	3 (12.0%)
Three weapons	8 (32.0%)
All intentional violent incidents	(100.0%)

12.5: Physical Effects of violence shown on screen (n=38)

a. Pain, suffering

No pain or suffering shown	20 (52.7%)
Minor pain or suffering shown	14 (36.3%)
Major pain or suffering shown	2 (5.5%)
Death, apparent destruction	2 (5.5%)
All violent incidents	(100.0%)

b. Blood, wounds (n=38)

No blood, wounds, etc., shown	32 (83.3%)
Small amount of blood, wounds, etc., shown	3 (8.3%)
Fair amount of blood, wounds, etc., shown	0
Large amount of blood, wounds, etc., shown	2 (5.5%)
Consensus 1+2	1 (2.9%)
All violent incidents	(100.0%)

12.6: Context of violence (n=34)

a) Violence only

War, armed forces action	2 (5.8%)
Civil strife, riots	3 (8.8%)
Criminal act of violence	2 (23.2%)
Carrying out of the law	5 (12.6%)
"Domestic," family	2 (5.8%)
Other "personal" violence	9 (29.2%)
Other	6 (14.6%)
All violent incidents	(100.0%)

b) Violence and sex

	Violence (n=38)	Sex)n=20)
Serious context	36 (94.5%)	14 (70.0%)
As "play"	2 (5.5%)	3 (15.0%)
Humorous context	0	3 (15.0%)
All incidents	(100.0%)	(100.0%)

12.7: Relationship of violent parties (n=32)

Members of same family	3 (8.8%)
Friends, neighbours, colleagues	9 (26.4%)
Known enemies, opponents or competitors	12 (38.8%)
Law enforcement officers and criminals	2 (5.8%)
Police or soldiers and demonstrators	0
Different racial groups	0
A minority group and a dominant group	2 (5.8%)
Other	5 (13.4%)
All violent incidents	(100.0%)

12.8: Relationship of sexual parties (n=20)

Husband and wife	2 (10.0%)
Other family relationship	0
Strangers	10 (50.0%)
Professional context (striptease)	2 (10.0%)
"Accidental" context (dress, behaviour)	6 (30.0%)
All sexual incidents	(100.0%)

Most incidents of violence are presented in closeup or strongly implied, rather than presented in middle and long shots. Sexual incidents are usually presented by implication, rather than photographed directly (see Table 12.1).

The usual type of violence and sex is physical and intentional (see Table 12.2).

The violence is usually one-sided, not reciprocated. Sex is reciprocated (see Table 12.3).

The human body is the most common weapon in violent incidents (see Table 12.4).

Pain, blood, or wounds are very seldom shown, and in minor amounts (see Table 12.5).

The context of violence usually applies to criminal acts or other "personal" violence. Sex is presented most often in a frivolous context (see Table 12.6).

The violent parties are usually enemies or known opponents and competitors; sometimes they are friends, neighbors, and colleagues. The sexual relationship typically involves strangers (see Tables 12.7 and 12.8).

Table 13 describes the role characteristics in violent and sexual incidents.

Table 13: Characteristics and fates of instigators and receivers of violence and sex

13.1	Instigator		Receiver/reciprocator	
	Violence	Sex	Violence	Sex
Male individual or group of males	30 (90.7%)	9 (75.0%)	18 (72.7%)	4 (33.3%)
Female individual or group of females	2 (9.3%)	3 (25.0%)	1 (9.2%)	8 (66.6%)
Mixed	0	0	2 (18.2%)	0
Indeterminate	0	0	0	0
All violent incidents	32 (100.0%)	12 (100.0%)	11 (100.0%)	12 (100.0%)

13.2: Membership of a group

	Instigator		Receiver/reciprocator	
	Violence	Sex	Violence	Sex
Group leader	12 (37.5%)	7 (58.4%)	4 (36.3%)	4 (33.3%)
Group member	16 (50.0%)	4 (33.3%)	3 (27.2%)	6 (50.0%)
Group as a whole	4 (12.5%)	1 (8.3%)	2 (18.1%)	2 (11.7%)
Isolated individual	0	0	2 (18.1%)	0
All incidents	32 (100.0%)	12 (100.0%)	11 (100.0%)	12 (100.0%)

13.3: Good-bad

	Instigator (n=32)	Receiver/reciprocator (n=11)
Good	12 (37.2%)	4 (36.0%)
Bad	17 (53.1%)	3 (27.0%)
Good-bad	2 (6.2%)	2 (19.0%)
Irrelevant	1 (3.5%)	2 (18.0%)
All violent incidents	(100.0%)	(100.0%)

13.4: Relationship to law

	Instigator	Receiver/reciprocator
No special relationship to the law portrayed	12 (40.6%)	7 (62.8%)
Law enforcement officer	2 (6.2%)	1 (9.0%)
Semilaw enforcement	1 (3.1%)	0
Secret service agent (spy) working for a government	4 (12.5%)	0
Criminal, outlaw	12 (37.5%)	3 (28.2%)
All violent incidents	(99.9%	(100.0%)

13.5: Justification of violence

	(n = 31)	(n = 11)
Believed themselves to have been wronged	8 (25.8%)	3 (27.2%)
Believed themselves to have long-standing grievance	7 (22.6%)	2 (18.1%)
Acting under orders or believed so	10 (32.5%)	2 (18.3%)
No just reason for violence	14 (12.9%)	3 (27.2%)
Other	2 (6.2%)	1 (9.2%)
All violent incidents	(100.0%)	(100.0%)

13.6: The violence was used in the hope of benefiting . . .

	Instigator (n=32)	Receiver/reciprocator
Himself/themselves	14 (43.7%)	5 (45.1%)
Family/friends	2 (6.2%)	2 (18.3%)
Some "formal" "legal" organization	4 (12.5%)	0
Some "ideals" organization	7 (21.8%)	2 (18.3%)
Some "ideals", ideology	5 (15.8%)	2 (18.3%)
Society as a whole, humanity	0	0
All violent incidents	(100.0%)	(100.0%)

13.7: Final outcome of this violent incident for the characters involved

	(n=31)	(n=11)
Clear winner))	22 (70.9%)	1 (9.0%)
Winner — but)		
Loser — but))	4 (12.8%)	6 (62.0%)
Clear loser)		
Neither gain nor loss shown, unclear	5 (16.3%)	4 (29.0%)
All violent incidents	(100.0%)	(100.0%)

In the majority of both violent and sexual incidents, one party definitely initiates the violence (90.6 percent) and sex (58.4 percent). However, in the majority of cases, violence is not reciprocated (reciprocation occurring in 12.5 percent of cases), while sex is reciprocated in 75 percent of cases.

Instigators, in both types of incidents, are usually males, group leaders in cases of sex (58.4 percent), and group members in cases of violence (50 percent). Recivers/reciprocators are other males in cases of violence (78 percent) and females in cases of sex (see Table 13.1 and 13.2).

In violent incidents, instigators are usually "bad" (53.1 percent), have no special relationship to the law (40.6 percent), or are criminals (37.5 percent). They act under orders and use violence in hope of benefitting themselves (43.7 percent). Instigators are also winners in most violent incidents in which they take part (70.9 percent). Receivers in violent incidents are predominantly "good" (40.6 percent), but 37.5 percent of them are "bad"; their majority have no special relation to the law (65.6 percent), and they use violence primarily in the hope of benefitting themselves (48.2 percent). Receivers are usually losers in violent incidents (70.0 percent). These data are summarized in Table 13.4-13.7.

Heroes and other "positive" characters are 63 percent of all characters; villains are 30 percent. Their characteristics and their fates are summarized in Table 14.

Table 14: Characteristics and fates of heroes and villains

14.1: <u>Sex</u>

	Heroes	Villains	Total
Male	12 (70.6%)	7 (87.5%)	20 (80.0%)
Female	5 (29.4%)	1 (12.5%)	5 (20.0%)
Total	17 (100.0%)	8 (100.0%)	25 (100.0%)

14.2: <u>Age</u>

	Heroes	Villains	Total
12 or under	1 (5.8%)	1 (12.5%)	2 (7.4%)
13—19	0	0	0
20—39	13 (76.8%)	6 (50.0%)	9 (70.3%)
40—59	2 (11.6%)	13 (37.5%)	5 (18.5%)
60 or over	1 (5.8%)	0	1 (3.8%)
Total	17 (100.0%)	20 (100.0%)	27 (100.0%)

14.3: <u>Major occupation</u>

	Heroes	Villains	Total
Armed forces)			
)			
Official law enforcement officer)	5 (27.4%)	1 (12.5%)	6 (25.0%)
Secret service agent (spy)			
working for a government)			

Illegal	1 (3.9%)	3 (37.5%)	4 (15.0%)
Business, professional	4 (23.5%)	1 (12.5%)	5 (20.0%)
Housewife	0	0	0
Other	7 (45.2%)	3 (37.5%)	10 (40.0%)
Total	17 (100.0%)	8 (100.0%)	25 (100.0%)

14.4: Victim of violence

Not subjected to violence	4 (23.5%)	2 (25.0%)	6 (25.0%)
Subjected to violence, not fatal	13 (76.5%)	4 (50.0%)	17 (67.0%)
Dies violent death	0	2 (25.0%)	2 (8.0%)
Total	17 (100.0%)	8 (100.0%)	25 (100.0%)

14.5: Acts aggressively in violent incidents

	Heroes	Villains	Total
Does not subject another to violence	5 (29.4%)	1 (12.5%)	6 (25.0%)
Subjects another to violence, not fatal	10 (58.8%)	4 (50.0%)	14 (54.0%)
Commits violence which kills someone	0	2 (25.0%)	2 (8.0%)
Indirectly subjects another to violence	2 (11.8%)	1 (12.5%)	3 (13.0%)
Total	17 (100.0%)	8 (100.0%)	25 (100.0%)

14.6: Final outcome for the character

Clearly successful/happy)			
)	9 (52.9%)	0	9 (36.0%)
Mostly successful/happy)			
Mostly failure/unhappy)			
)	1 (5.8%)	6 (75.0%)	7 (28.0%)
Clearly failure/unhappy)			
Mixed, unclear	7 (41.2%)	2 (25.0%)	9 (36.0%)
Total	17 (99.9%)	8 (100.0%)	25 (100.0%)

14.7: Values held by the character

Wellbeing of his/her family, home	10 (29.4%)	1 (6.3%)	11 (22.0%)
Respect for the law	5 (14.7%)	0	5 (10.0%)
Desire for money, material goods	2 (5.9%)	5 (31.2%)	7 (14.0%)
Ambition, will for power	1 (2.9%)	6 (37.5%)	7 (14.0%)
Well being of society, humanity	8 (23.5%)	0	8 (16.0%)
Evil, destructive goals	0	2 (12.5%)	10 (20.0%)
Self-preservation	8 (23.5%)	2 (12.5%)	10 (20.0%)
Religious	0	0	0
Total value	34 (99.9%)	16 (100.0%)	50 (100.0%)

    Both heroes and villains are usually males. The majority are between 20 and 39 years of age, but villains are also represented as older. Heroes are usually businessmen and professionals, while villains are usually of illegal or "other" occupations. Heroes are usually subject to violence, but it is not fatal, and no hero dies a violent death. Twenty-five percent of the villains die violently, and half are subject to violence. Heroes subject others to violence almost as frequently as do villains, but no hero commits violence which kills. Twenty-five percent (two) of the villains kill someone, while half (four) subject others to violence directly and 12.5 percent (one) indirectly. Heroes are usually successful overall (52.9 percent), while villains are losers (75 percent).

The values held by the majority of the heroes are (in descending order): wellbeing of family, wellbeing of society, self-preservation, respect for the law, desire for money or material goods, and ambition. The villains hold the following values: ambition, desire for money, self-preservation, destructive goals, and wellbeing of family.

DISCUSSION

Although the Israeli data refer to a very small number of broadcasting hours and to an even smaller amount of violence and sex (thus serving as a rather weak basis for a significant analysis), it is worthwhile to pay some attention to the questions, problems, and hypotheses that appear in connection with the findings. These could suggest trends for further research, both on the local, actual level as well as on the theoretical, explorative, and analytical level.

The first question suggested by the Israeli material refers to the amount of violence and sex: What are the significance and the functions of "small doses" of violence and sex in the entire schedule, compared to the concentration of these elements in certain specific program types? This applies especially to children's programs, where, in spite of the small number of violent incidents, violence appears to be a central theme. Is there a significant difference between the importance and the functions of violence in programs defined as "nonviolent" (but which include violent incidents) and programs defined as violent "as a whole" (some 37 percent of all programs as compared to 38 percent defined as nonviolent)? This refers especially to programs which are popular, such as *Flipper, Lassie, Bewitched, or even News*, which were labeled nonviolent but do include a number of violent episodes.

A second important question refers to the "degree of personal approval" of the entire program, particularly in light of the finding that the majority of the viewers are exposed to programs they do not like (expressing dissatisfaction by criticism rathern than by turning off the TV set). To what degree is this context significant to the functions and effects of violence and sex?

What is the difference between local and acquired programs insofar as the "symbolic value" of the contents is concerned? Local programs are practically nonviolent, whereas programs acquired abroad make up 68 percent of the schedule in "Hebrew" programming and 57 percent in "Arabic." What are the functions and effects of violence "imported" from other cultures (in this case American and British), especially when the majority of the viewers who prefer programs including violence belong to the lower educational categories? Or, to pose the question in another form, does the universality of violence "neutralize" the cultural context?

FOOTNOTES

1. The information for this section was gathered from the Broadcasting Authority Law and from some 15 interviews with officials and creative staff of the Israeli Broadcasting Authority.
2. The quotation marks are intended to emphasize that *Bonanza* or *Forsyte* with subtitles in Hebrew are classified as "Hebrew" programs.
3. At the time this meeting was held, the decision whether to include television broadcasts within the range of authority of the Board of Criticism of Films and Plays was still pending. In the director general's opinion, the transmission of this film would strengthen those who favored the inclusion.
4. The quotation marks signify they imported and subtitled programs are classified as "Arabic" or "Hebrew" according to the time slot in which they are broadcast. For example, *Mission Impossible* is a "Hebrew" program.

Television in the Socialization Process: Structures and Programming of the Swedish Broadcasting Corporation

Peter Dahlgren
Sveriges Radio

The legal form of Sveriges Radio (the Swedish Broadcasting Corporation) is that of an "aktiebolag," or limited company, and consequently the Corporation is guided in part by the pertinant laws which define and regulate all such enterprises. At the same time, Sveriges Radio has a unique relation to the State, defined by law and the Agreement with the Government (1967), and functions as a nonprofit public corporation.

The State has no financial interests in Sveriges Radio. The shares in the corporation are divided between press organizations (20 percent), industry and commerce (20 percent), and the popular movements (60 percent); the total number of shareholders is 80. Among the press, the

Swedish Central News Agency, the Publishers' Association, and the dailies have the greatest number of shares. Within the industry-commerce holdings, it is the large associations, unions, and authorities, rather than private companies, who own shares. The popular movements include labor organizations and groups representing religious, academic, and athlete interests, among others.

The foundations of Sveriges Radio's special status vis à vis the State are to be found in the Radio Act of 1966 and the Agreement. The Act says in article 5: "A corporation so designated by the King in Council has the sole and exclusive right to determine which radio[1] programs shall be included in broadcast transmissions from transmitters with the Realm." The Agreement with the Government gives Sveriges Radio this "sole and exclusive" right. The Agreement came into effect July 1, 1967 and remains so for 10 years; it is then renewable for five years at a time.

While the Agreement gives Sveriges Radio a monopoly of the airwaves, it at the same time outlines the guiding principles for the broadcasting company; these principles, which serve as the starting point for Sveriges Radio's own program policies, are intended to give the maximum amount of freedom to the broadcasters within the context of a democratic framework. Article 6 states:

> The program services shall be conducted with regard for the central position of radio and television in the national life. It follows from the foregoing that the Corporation is required *inter alia*, to disseminate, in suitable form, information on current events as well as information on important cultural and social issues, and to encourage debate.

Article 7 focuses on program content:

> ...They shall satisfy, to a reasonable extent, different interests within religion, music, drama, art, literature, science, etc. Programs shall provide good diversion and entertainment, with due regard for differences of taste. The special interests of minority audiences shall also be catered for to the extent practical.

> To see that the Corporation exercises its exclusive broadcasting rights with "impartiality and objectivity" and observes "to a reasonable extent ....(a) balance between different opinions and interests" (Art. 8), the State nominates a Radio Council of seven members. In addition to examining the programs sent over the air and making a yearly report to the minister of communication, the Radio Council also considers complaints which may be lodged against specific programs. The Council serves as a review committee and can make recommendations to the State, but it has no authority to issue instructions to Sveriges Radio concerning policies or the form or content of the programming. For that matter, Art. 8 of the Radio Act clearly states: "No authority or other public body may examine in advance or prescribe the advance examination of radio programs or prohibit radio transmissions or wire transmissions on account of content."

> While Sveriges Radio is in charge of the programming, the transmissions facilities are handled by the National Telecommunications Administration, which works in close cooperation with the Engineering Division of SR. The National Telecommunications Administration is "responsible for the distribution of programs, the control of interference with transmissions, and the collection of fees for the possession of receivers..." (Art. 3 of the Agreement). The coordination and division of the technical activity between SR and the NTA is governed by regulations which appear in an appendix to the agreement.

FINANCING

The general broadcasting activities of Sveriges Radio are primarily financed by radio and television set license fees; educational and external broadcasting are paid for through public funds—i.e., taxes. Commerical advertising in return for remuneration is not permitted. However, SR does not receive all the money which is collected from the fees, since the sum is divided by the State between SR, the National Telecommunications Administration (which is in charge of the collection of these fees), and the National Board of Building and Planning, which builds and maintains the premises for SR. According to Art. 14 of the Agreement, "the Corporation is entitled each year to that amount which is deemed necessary to finance its operations." SR, through the Radio Council, submits a "statement of the estimated budget needs for the coming fiscal year"; this request for appropriations is of course based on extensive coordinated planning between all the divisions within SR. Any funds remaining at the end of a fiscal year are then returned to the State. Article 18 states that "allocations to the Corporation's capital reserve shall be discontinued when the reserve amounts to 20 percent of the share capital."

A combined radio-television license fee costs 180: -Swedish kronor per year. Persons with only a sound radio receiver pay only Skr. 50: per year, while those with color television sets pay an additional Skr. 100:- yearly. At present there are about 2,550,000 television-radio licenses, plus about 160,000 color television licenses. This means that about 91 percent of the Swedish population has access to television.

The budget for fiscal year 1969-70 looked like this:

Income

Radio:	License fees; research subsidies, miscellaneous	108,395,129
TV:	License fees, research subsidies, miscellaneous	243,625,342

Allocations from the national budget for
school radio + television programs, external
broadcasting, and the Radio Conservatory
Miscellaneous income from external broad-
casting   25,811,579
Publications
Income from shares
Interest earned

Total	377,832,050
Expenditures	377,702,450
The year's profit	129,600

1969-70 was a rather atypical year in that, three months prior to the start of that fiscal year (April 1969), the old system of separate radio and television licenses was replaced with the present combination license fee, so that radio and television's respective incomes may look a little different in the future. In December 1969, the second television channel began operations. The figure for 1970-71 would no doubt give a more accurate indication of the future, since it is the first full fiscal year where both television channels have been in operations; however, these figures are not available at the present writing. It can be said, though, that the present prognosis sees a need for significant income increases over the next five years. This estimate is based not only on expected annual price rises, but also on the plans for increased television broadcasting time from a present 68 hours per week to over 100 hours per week. Sound radio broadcasting and regional activity are also expected to show sharp increases.

STRUCTURE

In the Government bill 1966:136 (which deals with the continued broadcasting activities of SR), the Parliament put forth a plan for a re-structuring of the Corporation, with the emphasis on extensive decentralization. Previously, the main responsibility for radio and television programs rested with the director general, but after the subsequent reorganization, this responsibility was largely transferred to the heads of the respective program divisions: Sound radio, TV1, TV2, the Joint News Office, educational broadcasting, external broadcasting, and regional broadcasting. The heads of these bodies have far-reaching independence and are responsible for the operations and activities of their divisions.

It is one of the objectives of the new organization that no restrictions in the program divisions' freedom and responsibility should exist other than those which the general management's responsibility unavoidably demands according to the laws and the Agreement; thus, within this established framework, the divisions have some degree of freedom in formulating their own program policy, and are at great liberty to choose staff, utilize the funds alotted them and decide which programs are to be produced and broadcast. The director general is in a sense only the managing director, since his responsibilities regarding programming are limited to ensuring that the legal obligations of the Corporation and those described by the Agreement are fulfilled and that current policy and program regulations are followed.

The director general and the heads of the seven program divisions are appointed by the Board of Governors. It is here that the State's indirect influence enters the picture; the Chairman of the Board and half of the members are appointed by the State, while the other half are elected by the shareholders in proportion to their holdings. With the Chairman, the Board consists of 21 members, ten of whom are alternates.

The members and alternates are to represent cultural and public interests as well as administrative, economic, and technical expertise. The Board of Governors has the ultimate responsibility for the operations, management, and activities of Sveriges Radio; among its most important duties is the allocation of funds to the seven different program divisions. Together with the program management and the technical division, the Board is also responsible for long-term planning, but it does not concern itself with planning or the production of programs. However, program regulations and policies are frequently discussed at the Board's regular meetings; it must see that the principles of broadcasting are adhered to. This may entail issuing directives on special questions. It should be pointed out that no Board member may participate in the consideration of any matter in which he himself holds substantial financial interests.

In addition to fixing the annual budget for each program division, the Board also sets aside funds for a number of common functions. The aim is that all expenses directly caused by the program divisions, and which can be controlled by their heads, shall be included in their expense limits. These expenses include not only salaries, fees, production costs, and purchase of films and programs, but also the expense for using technical facilities and material and the services of other departments. Such services are paid for by those who order them, through a system of internal debiting according to price lists. When this internal debiting system has been entirely carried out, capital, service costs, etc. will also be included in the allocations to program divisions.

The two television divisions receive equivalent allotments based on their ratio of weekly program output; TV2's output is expected to equal that of TV1 in two or three years' time. Each television division is further divided into smaller production groups. The regional offices too are in charge of television production to some extent, but the heads of TV1 and TV2 decide if and when a program produced by one of the 11 regions shall be broadcast. (The regions, however, have full control over their respective local radio programming.) Nevertheless, since the regions defray the costs of these programs, it is financially profitable for the program divisions at the central office to take advantage of the region's offers.

The resulting structure, which is popularly called "internal competition," does not, however, preclude coordination of certain functions. The Television Program Services coordinates purchases of foreign programs, the exchange of programs with Eurovision, Nordvision, and Intervision, and the transmissions in the two television channels. With two competing television organizations, there is a tendency, especially in the evenings, to compete with the same types of programs. In order to increase the public's freedom of choice, the Television Program Services endeavors to coordinate the programming in such a fashion that simultaneous programs have contrasting character and that the channels shift programs at the same time as often as possible during the evening. TVS also coordinates the use of the technical facilities and mediates in any eventual argument over the sharing of the common resources. However, TVS has no authority to give orders to the television divisions, and if a situation should arise where the two channels can not reach agreement through TVS' mediation, the director general will then intervene. The foreign programs which TVS obtains are ordered by and paid for by the respective television divisions.

While a certain amount of coordination of the program schedule can be viewed as a slight deviation from the competitive principle for the purpose of increasing the public's freedom of choice, the establishment of a joint news office is an economically justified exception from the competition and independence that should otherwise prevail.[2] A complete news organization for each of the television divisions and for radio, with their own home and foreign correspondents, would be of prohibitive expense. The joint news office handles the gathering and editing of news and the transmission of the short, "hard" news programs on both radio and television. It is then the responsibility of the radio and television divisions to produce programs on current affairs which contain commentaries, analyses and reportage.

The technical division, too, is a joint service, and it is the responsibility of the management to make sure that it serves all the programming bodies fairly. Sveriges Radio Symphony Orchestra is in a sense also a joint body; it belongs to the radio but may also be used by the television channels.

Though the program divisions and the regions draw up their own organization and necessary instructions, they are nevertheless part of one and the same corporation with responsibility for the work as a whole and with common technical and other resources. Mutual competition still requires certain rules and regulations to define the limits within which each entity can operate freely. These regulations have been worked out with the intention of avoiding constant intervention by the director general, and to allow sufficient flexibility so that the concerned parties can operate as freely as possible and work out the agreements by themselves, as in the case of TVS. The role of management here can be seen as fixing the framework in which activity takes place: to watch that agreements between program divisions facilitate cooperation yet at the same time do not become unduly restrictive of competition. It is a delicate balance, yet it is very central to the functioning of Sveriges Radio.

INFORMATION AND CONSULTATION

To allow the personnel as well as the management to share in information and consultation as much as possible, there are many internal communication channels. The primary ones, briefly, are:

1. Word-of-mouth, both informal and through regular meetings and conferences which are held within all the units of SR. These take many forms and vary from daily meetings to those which are held one or two times a year.
2. The Information Board, where about 80 people from management meet weekly to inform each other of current decisions, policies, and plans.
3. District conferences—held at least yearly within each of the districts usually with representatives from the central office.
4. Weekly internal radio information programs to the personnel.
5. The Corporation Council, with its subcommittees, serves as a channel between management and employees.
6. The twice weekly personnel bulletin.
7. A periodical, issued seven times yearly, with articles and commentaries on various topics.
8. "Sveriges Radio in the Press" comes out daily and weekly, with summaries on articles and comments on SR.
9. The Yearbook—which contains articles, statistics, and other information on SR's activities.
10. Regular information bulletins from the different units.

There has been an increased drive in recent years towards "democratization" within the corporation to allow the personnel to share in the decision-making process to as great extent as is feasible. However, with 3,700 people employed at Sveriges Radio and with a framework for policy, responsibility, and authority already established by law, this democratization can have little or no effect on program content and generally has to do with work conditions, organization and functioning within the units, etc. The existing channels for consultation can be summarized as follows:

1. Meetings with the different divisions. Since no two units have an identical structure, decision-making functions and responsibilities within the units vary. We will be looking at the television divisions in this report.
2. The heads of the different divisions and services meet with the director general each week to discuss how program policy is being carried out and if any adjustment needs to be made. Particular attention is given to news and politics, as well as any complaints which may have been made to the Radio Council.

3. The Corporation Council discuss issues of management-employee affairs. It meets four times a year (twice with district representatives). Half the members represent management; the other half, *via* unions, represent personnel.
4. The Educational Council, consisting of representatives from the units, management, and the personnel, discusses long range planning for internal information, special courses, and job training.
5. Administrative aspects of the Corporation (economy, personnel, facilities and premises, etc.) are discussed and acted upon in weekly meetings of the Board of Directors, with the director general acting as chairman.

TV 1

TV1 interprets the Radio Act and the Agreement to mean that programming should be as comprehensive as possible in respect to subject matter and points of view. Of course, it is realized that this cannot be fulfilled literally, so the policy is to aim for a representative selection of subject matter, covering the essential aspects, and conveying this in a format of high quality. Though "comprehensiveness" is one of the formal instructions for SR, TV1 views it as a stimulating challenge to give the audience new experiences and lead them to discover for themselves new subject areas.

TV1 feels an obligation to partake in a continuous discussion concerning the role of television in society and its relationship to other media; indeed it seeks to educate the public to the advantages and risks involved with television so that the public can independently stimulate the medium and so that common goals may be defined and reached.

It is imperative that television programs foster humanitarian ideals by showing respect for the worth of human life and avoiding needless brutality. While the final, conclusive research findings on the effects of violence are as yet not in, TV1 feels that to use violence as a form of entertainment is too great a risk to take. It is also the purpose of TV1 to try to foster an atmosphere where intolerance and prejudice would have no part.

It is also the policy of TV1 not to hesitate to bring up controversial questions for discussion. Among the many social questions which TV1 wants to put before a public forum is the problem of "culture"; notions that "culture" is created by a few for the many must be challenged, and attention must be given to how each individual's self-realization can be maximized. In addition, the policy states:

> TV can play a significant role in opposing a future class-structured society, which threatens to build upon people's differing capacities to seek out and utilize the relevant information from the entire flood which threatens to drown the man of the future...

The program producing units within TV1 consist of project groups; a project is generally taken to mean either a single program or a series of programs related in form or content. It can also mean specified long-term planning activities or services rendered within a given field to other project groups. Thus, the project groups are basically *ad hoc*. Each group is headed by a project leader, appointed by the TV1 management. In a program production unit, the project leader is generally also the person responsible for the program.

The program director, who heads TV1 and has the final authority and responsibility for the programs, is provided with information and advice (on which to base policy decisions) from an organ called the Program Council. The Program Council is primarily concerned with the content of programs and with production conditions, but its function is purely advisory; it has no power to make decisions. It is made up of a permanent core of members which can be supplemented for various periods by special experts as needed.

The Program Secretariat is the executive organ of the program management in program questions. Its activities can be divided into idea registration, idea planning, research, publicity, and the follow-up of results.

Below the level of the Program Secretariat have arisen seven drafting committees, which are not really a part of the formal organization of TV1. These seven committees have the following areas of competence: theater; music; children's programs; entertainment; culture; politics and social questions; and science/medicine/leisure time. The general pattern is that a suggestion from the Program Secretariat is sent to the appropriate drafting committee, where it is discussed and a position is reached. This information goes back to the secretariat and then the Program Council, where the final position is formulated and then given to the director. Each drafting committee has a chairman and secretary, who generally also are a part of the Program Council. Thus, the drafting committees can be seen as a substructure which attempts to involve the staff as much as possible, to seek their opinions and utilize their expertise.

TV 2

TV2 began broadcasting in December, 1969. Its program policy emphasizes the fact that television does not function in isolation from society; its impact is not to be underestimated. The medium is viewed as a great opportunity to increase the viewer's capacity to be informed and consequently his ability to share in decisions which will shape the future of his society. It is not felt that each and every program should simply strive to get the maximum number of viewers, but rather, to stimulate interest and dialogue, even if this means presenting material which is not

MEDIA CONTENT AND CONTROL

necessarily "popular" in the conventional sense. It is the intention that every program be geared to a specific audience; if the audience is large or small depends on the content of the program.

The policy has crystallized around three key words: comprehension, identification, and diversity. The audience is not homogeneous in regard to education; the present "television generation" (those who have experienced television all their lives) also roughly marks the start of the big education "explosion." These differences must always be considered, especially in the case of information programs, so that the content is comprehensible to the audience for which it is intended.

Identification means that the programs strive to be relevant to people's lives—that the viewer should be able to recognize situations in the programs which pertain to his own daily life. At the same time, this also means that the boundaries of what the audience can relate to should be continuously widened, so that the viewer will be able to identify with situations removed from his own geographic and cultural setting.

Diversity can be discussed in terms of the *types* of programs—news, theatre, music, sport, entertainment, discussions, etc. However, a varied programming can also be attained by considering the different functions which programs can have for the audience—challenge, amusement, information, esthetic experience, and so on. This approach is regarded as more productive in terms of intellectual and artistic freedom for the producers.

Regarding violence, TV2's policy paper states: "Violence exists as a fact of life in our world. The total program offering can not avoid showing violence, since this would distort reality." Those documentaries which do have violence should show it in its "social and human context." And in those cases violence is present in a nondocumentary program, its motives and consequences must be made explicitly clear. Violence is not to be used as diversion or a means to attract a larger audience.

As can be seen on the chart, the primary units within TV2 are the five sections: news commentaries, current affairs and documentaries, children's programs, light entertainment, and theater-ballet-music. These units meet weekly to discuss programming and other topics, and they attempt to maintain TV2's policies on all relevant questions. The proposals which result from these meetings are then forwarded to the Management Committee, which meets every week. The Management Committee is comprised of the director, the heads of these five sections, plus the heads of Program Planning, Special Projects, and Administration. As with TV1, the director has the ultimate authority over programming.

TV2 also has a nonformal substructure in the form of a Policy Group. In a sense, this Policy Group acts as an informal balance to the Steering Committee, although it has no authority as such. The Group makes suggestions to the Committee, discusses the application of TV2's policy to the programming, serves as an information organ within the division, plans the all-division meetings, and also leads the weekly program evaluation sessions, which meet to discuss and criticize the past week's programming. These sessions are open to the whole division. The membership of the Policy Group is elected by the whole division and includes representatives from each of the five sections.

PROGRAMMING

At present, the total weekly transmission time for TV1 is about 40 hours, and for TV2, 28 hours. 'The two channels have the right to decide for themselves to what extent their programming will consist of their own live or film production or programs purchased from the outside (regional productions, relays from abroad, rented film from abroad, or freelance Swedish production). During the first year of TV2, money was allocated for about 20 hours of transmission per week. However, for reasons of economy, it was planned that a proportional reduction of domestic production would take place, so that of the total increase in transmission hours, only six would consist of Swedish production. The rest would be nearly 12 hours of foreign material plus one and one-half hours of repeats. This has been continuously changing to the point that today well over half of TV2 transmissions are domestic productions, which also holds true for TV1. This includes the six hours of weekly programming prepared by the Joint News Office, as well programs by the districts and the educational broadcasting division. There is also a small fraction of freelance productions.

The program content of the two channels according to subject matter is shown below. The figures represent percents of the average number of hours per week devoted to each category (November 29, 1969-June 30, 1970).

Program content	TV1	TV2
General (messages, spot announcements, intermission programming).	8.3	3.8
Culture (religion, literature, art, biography, etc.)	8.1	7.1
Political and social issues	8.3	16.8
Sport and leisure	13.2	10.5
Science and medicine	3.4	1.5
Music and dance	2.8	.8
Children's shows	13.3	11.1
Theatre and film	8.8	21.0
Entertainment (variety, series, quiz shows, etc.)	20.0	12.5
News and commentary	12.4	14.9
Adult education	1.5	0
	100	100

As can be surmised, fiction shows account for only a small minority of the programming. Some may be found in children's shows, though these often tend to be nonfiction. The "entertainment" category contains fiction, but only in the subheading "series," since variety shows, quiz programs, and amusement "documentaries" are excluded. The average weekly percents for "series" are 10.4 for TV1 and 3.4 for TV2. "Theatre and film" too of course will have fictitious programs, but both channels regard television theatre as a dynamic and expanding art form which can readily to be used as a format for portraying contemporary social issues. Though fictitious, they often strive for a psychological and social realism, rather than pure "escapism."

A content analysis of TV programming was made for the week of May 24-30, 1971. The total time of fiction programming was 8 hours 55 minutes in TV1, and 8 hours 30 minutes in TV2. (This includes those children's shows which were basically fictitious, such as those with puppets, cartoons, and clips from old-time silent movies.)

During the course of the analysis, it was soon discovered that there was so little violence and sex that an elaborate schedule became meaningless. Those programs which did contain some violence were the following:

1. *Arsène Lupin* (Mon. TV1; 55 min.). This is a French crime-detective series. The tone is semiserious, though it lacks the studied irony of the *Man from U.N.C.L.E.* genre. There were a number of "violent" incidents, but these can best be described as "mild"— the villains overpowering the hero and tying him up, brief scuffles, etc. There were no killings shown in the story, although one corpse was "discovered." In the end, the villains' plan fails, though not all of them are brought to justice.

2. *Doom Watch* (Tues. TV1, 55 min.). A British series depicting political conflict around the theme of environmental catastrophe. A plane crash, caused by the negligence of scientific researchers, is shown, though no individuals are depicted. Also there are some semiviolent manifestations of tension and panic aboard a second plane which nearly crashes.

3. *Paths of Glory* (Thurs. TV1, 1 hour, 30 minutes). An American movie (1957) set in the trenches of World War 1. The violent scenes consisted of a brief attack across "no man's land" where soldiers are shown falling, though no closeups are shown; a fist fight in a military prison; and the execution of three soldiers. The movie was basically "antiwar" and did in no way glorify the military.

4. *The Empress's Courier* (Thurs. TV1, 25 minutes). An Austrian adventure series set in the 18th century. A civilian is wounded in the arm by a guard who mistook him for a spy. The incident is treated as a regrettable error.

5. *Paul Temple* (Sat. TV1, 50 minutes). A British "crime-adventure" series. The villain knifes one victim and attempts to overpower the hero, resulting in a fist fight. He is killed, off camera, in the end. All the violence occurs very quickly; it is not shown in "detail." The tone is serious and the theme was that of a wartime traitor finally being exposed.

6. *Topper Takes A Trip* (Mon. TV2, 1 hour 20 minutes). An American comedy film from 1938. A punch in the nose and a slap on the cheek are administered by the "ghost."

7. *Anna—the Diary of a Schizophrenic* (Wed. TV2, 1 hour 45 minutes). An Italian television drama which had semiviolent outbursts to display a severe schizophrenic condition (thrashing of arms, etc., not directed at anyone personally).

8. *Le Jour se Lève* (Sat. TV2, 1 hour 30 minutes). A French film from 1939. The main character, in a rage, shoots the man who stands between him and the girl he loves, feeling he was deceived by both of them. The police lay seige to his apartment and shots are exchanged, though nobody is hit. In the end he takes his own life. It seems to be a typical "crime of passion," and the display of violence is minimal. The emphasis is clearly on the intensity of the emotions.

9. *Tittskåpet (The Viewing Closet)* (Sat. TV2, 25 minutes). A children's show with a collection of short excerpts from silent films. These were of the extreme "pie-in-the-face" slapstick style, and included the announcer making commentaries which added to the understanding that such things do not happen in real life. The "violence" included a bullet through the hat, a stagecoach collision, and a dynamite explosion.

It may be of interest to note that two nonfiction programs contained considerable violence. One was called *The Hour of Violence* (Thurs. TV2, 45 minutes). It was an anonymous documentary dealing with strikes and police terror in Argentina during the winter of 1968-69. The program included considerable footage of street riots, both closeups and distance shots. The format was strictly documentary, however. The other program was a discussion panel following "Paths of Glory", where film clips from three war movies were used to illustrate military fanaticism among high ranking officers. The focus of the films and the discussion was on the psychology of leaders rather than the actual violence itself.

"Sex and romance" occurred even less than did violence. To begin with there were no "explicit" love scenes or nudity in the week studied, though they do occur sometimes, primarily in television theatre productions. There is no formal policy pertaining specifically to "sex" at TV1 or TV2, and generally speaking, the management of the two channels do not feel it is an issue of much significance. The tacit policy is that "sex" should not be edited out of a program if it serves a proper and meaningful function in the context of the program's purpose (this would be a distortion of reality). On the other hand, sensationalism in regard to sex is not indulged in; such a program would be incompatible with the goals and responsibilities of television as put forth in the Agreement as well as in TV1's and TV2's stated policies, even though these statements do not make *direct* reference to sex. It is felt that material which sensanalizes sex *should* be available to individuals who want it, but at their own initiative and not on television.

The incidents of "romance" were the following:

1. *Arsène Lupin.* A woman in the criminal gang becomes enamoured with the hero and helps him escape. No physical intimacies are shown and the relationship does not end in marriage.
2. *Det händer i Sålunda* (Sat. TV1, 30 minutes) A television theatre piece dealing with the functioning of local government. An adulterous relationship is implied, but not shown.
3. *Judge Hardy and Son* (Sun. TV1, 1 hour 30 minutes). An American movie from 1939 with the typical Andy Hardy "puppy love" of kissing and hand holding.
4. *Topper Takes a Trip.* Comical treatment of an extramarital romance; it does not develop beyond the kissing stage.
5. *Le Jour se Lève.* The protagonist clearly has two affairs—one with the girl he loves and one with the ex-girl friend of his current rival. However, the camera does not show more than embracing. The story ends with tragedy for all concerned.

In sum, fiction is only a small part of the total television programming of Sveriges Radio. While sex and violence occur in the programming, the incidents are not of high frequency and their absense may be more telling than analyses of cases where they do occur. The little sex and violence in the week which was analyzed did not transgress the guidelines which govern broadcasting; it may be of significance to note that policy positions are firmly and explicitly taken on the questions of violence, whereas sex is not deemed to be a crucial separate issue. If more detailed research is to be carried out in Sweden on the role of television in the socialization process, it may be advised not to limit itself to fiction programs.

FOOTNOTES

1. "Radio" means both sound and picture transmission.
2. An analysis of the news division at Sveriges Radio is currently being conducted by an internal study group. Their report, with any proposals for reorganization, is expected to be finished by the end of 1971.

13-401